THE FIRST AMERICANS
THEN AND NOW

The First Americans

THEN AND NOW

WILLIAM H. HODGE

Holt, Rinehart and Winston
New York   Chicago   San Francisco   Dallas
Montreal   Toronto   London   Sydney

Library of Congress Cataloging in Publication Data
Hodge, William H   1932–
   The First Americans.

   Bibliographies
   1. Indians of North America. I. Title.
E77.H695   970.004'97   80-22310
ISBN 0-03-056721-1

Printed in the United States of America

1 2 3 4 5   144   9 8 7 6 5 4 3 2 1

For Susan, Matthew, and Peter

PREFACE

THE PLAN OF THE BOOK

This book describes the nature of 13 native American groups as they were prior to White domination and as they have become in the last half of the twentieth century. Particular groups were selected because information concerning them was sufficient for the "then-and-now" time perspective of this book. Initially, an essential question is posed: What are these people like? The answer consists of a discussion about who, where, and when are Indians. The meaning of urban residence and the nature of Indian ethnicity are then considered. Following this, New World prehistory is briefly examined to demonstrate that the essential outlines of native American existence developed largely within the confines of the Western Hemisphere. The roots of the native American present most certainly lie buried deep within an American past. This development of modern aboriginal life is briefly outlined, and the possibility of transoceanic contacts influencing that development is discussed. A brief comment is made on native languages, and finally the nature and implications of one central, theoretical concept, the culture area, are presented.

With this general answer as a backdrop, the nature of native American life is considered in a specific sense by describing, within the then-and-now format, the dimensions of existence of 13 individual groups of people, ranging from the Eskimo of the Arctic to the Papago and Eastern Cherokee peoples in the south. Finally, both the general and the specific are pulled together within a contemporary framework, and the first Americans are presented as people who are an integral part of modern American life. Indians are both in and of our times and must be understood as such.

WHY STUDY AMERICAN INDIANS?

The distinguished anthropologist Carleton S. Coon* speaks of "a haunting fear of the imminent end of the world" that now prevades our daily

*Coon, Carleton S. Overview. *Annual Review of Anthropology, vol. 6.* Palo Alto, California: Annual Reviews, 1977, p. 1.

vii

lives and is shared by the majority of the human residents of this planet. John R. Platt*, considering such a fear, has said:

> We have . . . reached a kind of plateau in the area of "over-kill," since both the Russians and the Americans now have enough megatons of nuclear weapons in their arsenals to destroy not only themselves but all life on the planet several times over—with the equivalent of more than 10 tons of explosive for every man, woman, and child alive today, as John F. Kennedy once put it. How can we worry more? The worst is already here.

However, Platt also comments that:

> . . . the present generation is the hinge of history. We see that if we can survive for the next twenty or thirty years, we can move into a high-technology world society reaching across the solar system, with new levels of well-being and hope and fulfillment—a society that might find out how to keep itself alive and evolving for thousands or millions or billions of years. This "step to Man" will be a transition to a new stage in biological and social and intellectual evolution. *But the time for the decision is now.* [Emphasis mine]

The first Americans also had "a haunting fear of the imminent end of the world." All too often their fears were realized. But many American Indian peoples, including the 13 groups presented in this text, did survive. In doing so, they learned many difficult and valuable lessons and techniques with respect to coexisting with forces and peoples much stronger than themselves and over whom they had no control or for whom, at times, they did not have much understanding. If we are willing to benefit from their experience, we can take a significant step now in this time of decision when we, our native American brothers and sisters, and others are "the hinge of history." If we ignore what they have learned at such great cost, we imperil or perhaps are in danger of obviating what could be our own bright future. Hence the following pages are something more than an illustration of what may seem to some of us as a preoccupation with the quaint and curious from-womb-to-tomb account of peoples throughout native North America. The contents of this book must be viewed as a report of several vital and successful experiments in the art of survival under extreme and difficult conditions.

On a less dramatic note, there are other reasons to study the native American experience. For the first three decades of this century, American anthropology was largely the study of American Indians. The ethnography and ethnology of native North American life are still of great

*Platt, John R. Shaping the Evolutionary Future. In H. V. Kraemer, ed., *Youth and Culture: A Human-Development Approach.* Monterey, California: Brooks/Cole, 1974, pp. 10–46; quotations on pp. 18, 19.

consequence for the discipline. Accordingly, to understand anthropology is to know something about our native peoples. On a more general note, New World native peoples form a vital part of the human spectrum and have done so both in the past and now. An understanding of such individuals is a prerequisite to the valid perception of the nature of humanity.

Oshkosh, Wisconsin   W. H. H.

ACKNOWLEDGMENTS

This book could not have been written without the help of many people and organizations. Jim Howard, Robert Manners, David Aberle, Marshall Tome, John Price, Harriet White, Nancy Lurie, Helen Codere, and George and Louise Spindler have devoted much time and effort to further my understanding of native peoples. The authors and editors of other Indian textbooks, including Ruth Underhill; H. E. Driver; E. B. Leacock and N. O. Lurie; R. E. Spencer, Jesse D. Jennings et al.; W. W. Newcomb, Jr.; A. M. Josephy, Jr.; M. S. Garbarino; John A. Price; and W. H. Oswalt, have provided valuable accounts of native American life, which have been carefully studied. Jim Howard, Richard Woodbury, Nancy Lurie, and George and Louise Spindler, plus a host of anonymous reviewers, did much to stimulate my thinking.

Many thoughtful and competent scholars have supplied illustrations: Jim Howard, who allowed me to use his "photoessay" on the Micmac; the Milwaukee Public Museum, who gave me access to their extensive photo collections; Carmelo Guadagno, curator of photography, Museum of the American Indian, Heye Foundation, who helped me use their photographic archives and select appropriate pictures; Jim Hornbuckle, tribal official of the Eastern Band of Cherokees, who arranged for pictures and also allowed me to study and use an unpublished manuscript that he has written with Lawrence French. Ken Kania supplied a number of photographs on modern Cheyenne life. Ellen Horn of the Arizona State Museum gave prompt, conscientious assistance in a number of ways. Ronald Rohner lent me the bulk of his collection of black and white photos on the Kwakiutl. Joel S. Savishinsky supplied pictures of the Hare. Nelson H. H. Graburn went to considerable trouble to furnish photographs of the people of Sugluk. Boyd Gibbs was of considerable help with a number of photographic assignments. Additional sources of photographs were the Lowie Museum of Anthropology, the National Anthropological Archives of the Smithsonian Institution, the Oregon Historical Society, the Halifax Museum of Nova Scotia, and the Oshkosh City Museum.

Others have contributed in special ways to help me understand particular facets of the Indian experience. Jack Campisi, after allowing me to use his Ph.D. dissertation on the Oneida as a principal resource, constructively criticized the resulting chapter. Joel Savishinsky gave me full access to his materials on the Hare and corrected a number of errors in my manuscript. Emory Sekaquaptewa, working on a very short time, was able to add considerable depth of meaning to the Hopi chapter. Seymour Priestly generously give of his time and thought to share his extensive Menominee experiences with me. Ken Kania thought and wrote at great length regarding his encounters with the Northern Cheyenne and other peoples of our northern Plains. Anne S. Straus and Katherine M. Weist were of great help regarding these same people. The attorney Angelo A. Iadarola and his colleagues of the law firm of Wilkinson, Cragun and Barker, Washington, D.C., supplied a large amount of material concerning the current and past legal activities of the Menominee and Klamath. Jack O. Waddell helped me to understand something of the scope and significance of Papago life. Steve Feraca and Bob Pennington of the Bureau of Indian Affairs have taken great trouble through the years to discuss the many involved questions associated with the problems of Indian administration. A number of officials concerned with native affairs in Canada have been equally helpful.

The staff of Polk Library, University of Wisconsin-Oshkosh, and Gerald J. Krueger, in particular, of the Government Documents Section, worked arduously and well to supply a wide range of needed materials. The Oshkosh Public Library has provided considerable support.

I am indeed grateful to the following sources who permitted me to quote from several of their works: the General Publishing Company, Limited, Viking Press, University of Washington Press, University of North Carolina Press, *The Coalition News, The Wall Street Journal*, Griffin House, and University of Arizona Press.

David Boynton of Holt, Rinehart and Winston plus a number of other staff members provided timely, sympathetic, and invaluable support in the final stages of preparation. George and Louise Spindler first suggested that I submit the manuscript to David Boynton. The book would not have been published without their interest and help. My debts to my wife are great for skillful editorial work, typing, and boundless encouragement.

Finally, my most profound thanks must be reserved for the hundreds of native Americans who with intelligent patience and good humor have attempted to teach me something about their lives over a period of two and one half decades. I hope that my work will encourage others to learn more about them because all of them have so enriched my life. All of these friends and many others have fully demonstrated for me the validity of Proverbs XV:31. "Whoever listens to wholesome reproof shall enjoy the society of the wise."

Oshkosh, Wisconsin   W. H. H.

CONTENTS

THE FIRST AMERICANS

THEN AND NOW

CHAPTER *1*

A FRAME OF REFERENCE FOR THE STUDY OF INDIAN BEHAVIOR

> The Indians survived our open intention of wiping them out, and since the tide turned they have even weathered our good intentions toward them, which can be much more deadly.
>
> John Steinbeck, *America and Americans*

This book provides an understanding of Indian behavior by presenting descriptions of Indian life in the past and present. Equal emphasis is given to the then and the now because both are equally important in an appreciation of the Indian experience. Thirteen different groups are described. Specific groups have been selected because they represent the major culture areas or divisions of native North American ethnography.

An effort has been made to show American Indians and American Indian groups as people, not as collections of culture traits and complexes. Each of the 13 groups follows a distinctive way of life that was slowly created in the past; responded to various cultural, historical, and ecological currents through time; persists in the present; and will continue into the future. I hope that the readers of this book will experience vicariously the nature and consequences of distinctive Indian ways of life and by this means come to a better understanding of all human behavior, particularly their own.

THE AMERICAN INDIAN: A DEFINITION

A necessary prelude to any consideration of American Indian life is the conscious, explicit understanding of the ethnic label "Indian." Today, as in the past, the general public maintains a vague but persistent concern with Indians. Various aspects of clothing mirror this influence through the headbands, fringed leather garments, and beaded Indian ornaments often made in Hong Kong or Japan. Devoted fathers and their earnest sons and daughters study "Indian Lore" under the benevolent aegis of the YMCA, the Boy Scouts, and the Girl Scouts. Most non-Indian people, with the possible exception of reservation border town residents, are passively sympathetic toward the Indians' struggle for compensation for past injuries and their search for self-selected opportunities in today's society.

The public and even some anthropologists have a highly distorted image of American Indians. Some anthropologists today see native Americans as people with a culture that existed only in the past. Some Indians used to hunt buffalo, others resided in elaborate pit houses, and still others lived on acorns and fish. Only the archaeologist and the ethnohistorian can now view the remnants of these life-styles. Other anthropologists study the Indian as an individual or a member of a group in the process of acculturating or assimilating into the general, sometimes self-satisfied, and often poorly understood currents of modern American life. People find in museums the articles that Indians used to produce, and they shudder at the Hollywood and television versions of past Indian misdeeds. But the nature of *modern* American Indian life today is as much of a mystery to most people as American

Indian life of the fifteenth and sixteenth centuries was to the Western Europeans of that time. Few school textbooks acknowledge how much we owe to the American aborigines in areas such as speech, clothing, medicine, sports, recreation, music, and literature. Hallowell (1963: 519–531) discusses the concept of transculturalization whereby individuals, in this case Whites, assumed an Indian identity on a temporary or permanent basis. Such cases have been far from isolated and throughout the past three centuries can be numbered in the thousands. The absence of public recognition of the significant, influential nature of Indians in the mainstream of American life is undoubtedly rooted in racism, serving in part as a justification for mistreatment of many Indians by some Whites.

One of the most difficult problems to resolve then when talking to non-Indians about Indians is how to explain to them what an Indian is. What is Indianness? What is Indian ethnicity? Eagle feathers, buckskin, cleverly woven rugs, and beautiful silver and turquoise jewelry are only a small part of the reality. Other aspects include the prevalence of poverty, the appallingly high rates of alcoholism and of adolescent suicide, and the gnawing ache of winter hunger. Federal and private agencies have noted correctly that there is no adequate legal definition of the status "Indian." Anthropologists and other social scientists have tried, with disappointing results, to provide a definition based on general cultural content and behavior. Genetics or blood does not always differentiate the Indian from the non-Indian. For present purposes, the problem will be met by answering the following questions: Who is an Indian? Where is an Indian? When is an Indian?

Who and Where Are Indians?

As a working generic definition, this book relies upon the one developed by Marshall Hanson (1962: 5): *An Indian is a person who regards himself as an Indian, is so regarded by other Indians, and on one basis or another may validly assume the legal status of an Indian.* This last provision usually implies that an individual has at least one grandparent who was a full blood and/or that he himself may be found listed on a tribal roll. The crucial point to realize at this stage, however, is that although this definition will serve well enough for present purposes by setting off from the general population an aggregate of people who are, in fact, Indians, there will be considerable variation within this number.

It is reasonable to assume that there are at least one million Indians and Eskimos in North America. In 1970 U.S. Census figures (Trimble, 1972: 102) gave a total Indian population of 827,091. The largest centers of population were Oklahoma with 97,731; Arizona, 95,812; New Mexico, 72,788; Alaska, 51,528; South Dakota, 32,365; Montana, 27,130; and the state of Washington, 33,386. A total of 284 Indian land units existed, including reservations, colonies, rancherias, and scattered public-domain allotments as well as 147 Indian communities in Alaska. The nature of contemporary Indian life and the limitations of the Census Bureau to monitor the dimensions of that life both suggest that these and other population figures are far from accurate. Indian rural/reservation-urban migration patterns and the standardized approaches used by census takers to count people plus a wide range of more subtle factors ensure errors. Readers, however, cannot go too far wrong if they assume that approximately one million Indians now live in North America and that the states listed above have the largest populations.

In 1969 tribal lands totaled almost 40 million acres plus an additional 12 million in allotted land. Individual reservations varied enormously in size, ranging from the Navajo reservation in New Mexico, Utah, and Arizona with more than 15 million acres down to very small communities such as the Pequots in Connecticut, Shinnecocks on Long Island, and Mattaponys in Virginia, where the people had blended into White society while still retaining their distinctive sense of being Indian. Many people still counted themselves as Indian even though they had no reservation and they lived entirely like other Americans (Josephy, 1969: 359–360).

It is important to keep in mind that most Indians in one way or another regard themselves as members of a tribe, which more often than not is small in number as well as area of land occupied. The reader should recognize here that there is no commonly accepted definition of the term *tribe* among anthropologists and many others. Indians themselves imply a wide range of political complications by its use. A minimum definition of a tribe, however, is an aggregate of people having a name, a dialect, and a territory (Kroeber, 1925: 474), and it is in this sense that the term is used throughout this book. It should also be mentioned that currently in Alaska the term *tribe* is no longer officially used. When the federal government found itself facing 450 separate entities for contracting purposes under the Indian Self-Determination Act and the distribution of other federal funds and services, it remedied the problem by consolidating the 450 individual groups into 12 regional nonprofit corporations (U.S. Congress, 1977: 1).

The situation is also complicated by the fact that the Canadian government does not officially use the term *tribe* but speaks instead of *band*. As the following quotation shows, the band assumes a nebulous meaning because of the convolutions of Canadian law.

> The Indian band, a legally defined grouping is a body of Indians "for whose use and benefit in common" lands have been set aside, and/or "for

whose use and benefit in common, moneys are held by Her Majesty'', or which is declared by the governor-in-council to be a band for the purpose of the Indian Act (2.(1) (a)). The membership of the band is legally defined, as are the methods by which such membership may be gained, given up, or changed. Since to be Indian is to belong to a special legal category, there is no necessary coincidence between Indian status and Indian ancestry. A White woman who marries an Indian band member becomes an Indian band member herself, while persons of Indian ancestry are scattered throughout the non-Indian community as a result of enfranchisement. Only individuals with the legal status of Indians can belong to an Indian band.[1]

The legal definition of a band and band membership is, in addition, clouded by the official Canadian definitions of the terms *Indian* and *reserve* (the Canadian counterpart of the American *reservation*).

The U.S. American Indian Policy Review Commision *Newletter* of April 1976 determined that at present 52.7 percent of American tribes have populations of 200 or less; 75.8 percent, of 500 or less; and 82.9 percent, of 1,000 or less. The importance of the fact that most Indians live as members of small communities occupying restricted land areas surrounded by a sea of Whites living on White-owned and controlled lands cannot be overestimated. One of the prime implications of this situation is the fact that Indian behavior from shortly after the era of significant European contact to the present is White-modified. Further, one can gain only a limited knowledge of modern Indians without knowing a great deal about their White contemporaries. In this book, however, because of limitations of space, I consider this White matrix within which Indian activities are embedded in only a latent and secondary fashion.

When Is an Indian?

The question of ''When is an Indian?'' is much more difficult to answer than the queries: Who and where is an Indian? Whereas the self-conception of Indianness probably remains constant or varies only within narrow limits once emotional maturity has been achieved, community or group consensus is vital. A comprehensive answer to this question (that is, when is an Indian?) hinges around the way in which people view themselves and their surroundings and how these surroundings influence them. A Menominee resident of Milwaukee is an Indian at all times to his family, other local relatives, and Indian friends who also live in the city. The same identification will be used by his relatives and friends in his home community. But to his fellow passengers on a city

[1]H. B. Hawthorn et al., 1966: 270–271.

bus, he is not Indian. Nor do clerks in a store or those who use the same sidewalk with him view him as Indian. To these individuals he is a person or sometimes merely an object with whom they must share an extremely limited amount of urban space. In short, his Indian identity is greatly diminished within the urban situation. The fact that it is limited in this fashion is due to the necessity of an Indian's conforming to the demands of city living. Ultimately, this situation means to the urban Indian that he utilizes his full human potential only a part of the time in stark contrast to the full-time humanness of the Indian as a member of his reservation or home community.

Indians Camp in Cities but They Really Don't Live There

One of the most crucial aspects of Indian life now and in the recent past is the migration between rural places and cities. It is estimated that at least 60 percent of American Indians currently are full- or part-time residents of cities. Obviously then, in studying these people, social scientists find their urban environments very important. At the same time, attention must also be given to Indians who live on reservations or in other kinds of rural communities because, for most Indians, rural and urban living are part of one pattern of life or one system. Both kinds of residence must be considered if either is to be understood.

The examination of past and present Indian life as movement per se should also be stressed. One of the central integrating aspects of all Indian life is travel. Indians perceive travel not only as a necessity to gain that which makes life possible, but also as a great good in itself. To be Indian is to seek constantly new vistas and challenges, but then to return home. This perpetual wandering and camping is a very old endeavor for Indians. It is as old as North American cities themselves. From Jamestown, Virginia, to the concrete wilderness of Los Angeles, Indians have come, looked, briefly lived in cities, and then moved on to be replaced by others of their kind. Throughout this process, most have remained Indians first, last, and always.

This desire for travel, used as a frame of reference and placed in sharper focus, illuminates the interrelationships among three variables as they relate to fluctuation in resources: migration, residence, and behavior. Fluctuation in resources, in turn, is correlated with a variety of social and cultural changes, the instability of resources, and levels and fluctuations of population. These changes cannot always be readily predicted by those most closely influenced by such developments. Hence, Indian life is based upon a variety of subsistence patterns changing through time, and it consequently assumes an effervescent kind of texture characterized earlier as movement, travel, or migration.

The Indian population has been increasing at a significant rate for at least the past 50 years. During this period the resources upon which Indians relied within the confines of their reservations or rural communities either remained constant or decreased in magnitude. The various modes of subsistence, such as pastoralism or limited dry and wet farming supplemented by a modicum of hunting and gathering, have been inadequate to support increasing population numbers. Accordingly, wage labor and some form of welfare support have become more important, both generally being sought outside the home. The utilization of wage labor and welfare implies some form of migration, often to an urban area, on the part of individuals or individuals as members of families. Hence, the growing Indian population is largely urban-centered.

The Meaning of City Living for Indians

City living for most Indians is a way to avoid the disadvantages temporarily imposed by reservation or rural living. It further marks a segment of their life cycle when they are most likely to be in a position to take advantage of aspects of large city life that are considered to be desirable, such as a broad spectrum of commercial entertainment and professional sports activities plus a good standard of material living. Access to both of these is made possible by urban wages. Portions of an Indian's salary can often be used to help create a future residential niche away from a large city once the penalties of urban life begin to outweigh its rewards, usually after the age of 50 is reached and sometimes before.

Large cities can also provide a temporary haven for those who need the specific and selected benefits that a large city can offer on a short-term, nonwage earning basis. Children can usually acquire a better formal education here than elsewhere. Old people who are often in poor health can spend a more comfortable winter with younger relatives in a city than would be afforded them by the low standard housing found on a reservation or in or near a small town located in a rural area. Those few who seek the nearly perpetual intoxication of alcohol or drugs can often find both more easily in a larger city than in other places because a social network consisting of those with similar tastes but highly variable financial resources can be created and utilized.

In sum, a city appears to be a place where it is possible for the majority of Indians to find and selectively use, during limited portions of their lives, particular articles, ways, and means that are regarded for the moment to be advantageous to them. City living is usually a temporary compromise with the demands of a distinctive heritage and the implications of having a specific ethnic identity created and maintained by a subordinate position in a complex, culturally pluralistic society.

The Nature of Indian Ethnicity

Indians differ from other ethnic groups in North America in that they view themselves as being different. In addition, the way they live and their views of the world around them set them apart from other ethnic categories. Most Indians do not want to live, work, and be where the majority of American society is. The much vaunted melting pot of American culture, which integrated the cultural differences of Americans of various but essentially similar European backgrounds, failed to assimilate the Indians of America because their history and cultural mystique did not include the European experience.

Empirically, what distinquishes Indians from non-Indians is their participation in an elaborate exchange system consisting of goods, services, and emotional support. These goods, services, and emotional support differ on occasion in kind and certainly in degree from those used by non-Indians. Such a system, however, connects at various points with non-Indian exchange systems. There is not a single Indian exchange system but a vast number of them, each centering in a particular reservation, rural community, or tribal center with extensions into the larger society, particularly urban areas. The specific form of participation in such an exchange system is influenced by both cultural background and position in the life cycle. In short, American Indians occupy distinctive parts of the larger societal network.

Today, as in much of the past, Indians seek their own world in their own time. This is a world that includes many material items, produced by modern technology but used in an Indian way. Trucks and cars can provide adventure, access to ceremonies, visits to other Indians, and not just efficient transportation from one geographical point to another. Central heating, modern sanitation, and some forms of health care can contribute to physical comfort, but they don't become ends in themselves. In those cases where modern technology cannot be made to serve Indian purposes directly, it is ignored or discounted. Why— when the demands of Indian life keep him or her away from home so much of the time—should an Indian spend a great deal of effort and money building and maintaining a modern house with a well-kept lawn and garden? Why should he or she be concerned with maintaining impressive bank accounts and buying life insurance policies when the most important support that an Indian seeks comes not from the impersonal technological comforts that cash will provide, but from the immediate direct material and emotional aid that Indian relatives and friends will supply?

To exist and function in a satisfactory way, Indians rely upon mutual aid. To be Indian is to be near those Indians who will help and support you because you help and support them, to seek out and possess those things and customs that the larger society and Indian tradition have declared to be Indian. The net result of being Indian is to behave in a way that often puzzles and angers Whites, but a way that, for Indian people, makes the question of routine existence by turns amusing, challenging, and often dangerous. As the Winnebago Reuben Snake, Jr., has said in part (1972):

> Being Indian is paying $15 a piece for eagle feathers today when you don't have enough food for tomorrow's meals. Being Indian is to be *the best you can possibly be* at what you do, but *not* to openly compete with your fellow man to your own aggrandisement and glorification and his shame and humiliation. Being Indian is having at least one alcoholic relative put the touch on you once a day. Being Indian is having at least a dozen missionaries from twelve different faiths trying to save your heathen soul every year. Being Indian is missing work at least two days a month because so many of your friends and relatives are dying. Being Indian is living on borrowed time after your 44th birthday. Being Indian is feeling Grey Wolf, Thunder Chief, and Smoke Walker are more beautiful names than Smith, Jones, Brown or Johnson. Being an Indian is forever!

Finally, being Indian is to be aware of a distinctive history not just in an intellectual sense, but to regard that past as a guide and justification for the present and future. History and prehistory are not a sequential ordering of dates, places, and events for Indians, but the very essence of life itself. But what indeed of the Indian past? How did North American Indians come to be as they are now?

SOME OF THE BEGINNING AND WHAT CAME AFTER

The hallmark of a sound characterization of the birth and growth of New World native cultures is careful generalization based upon intelligent guesswork. The prehistory of the Western Hemisphere is so vast in terms of time and space and so complex in development as to make other approaches impractical. The essential, dramatic climaxes of this cultural evolution, however, can be briefly stated.

A very long time ago, physically modern human beings resembling many of the contemporary peoples of Asia began to occupy the northern reaches of the Western Hemisphere. Their descendants and those of other migrants were eventually to occupy North, Middle, and South America, a total area of more than 16 million square miles comprising about 28 percent of the earth's surface. The distance from the Bering Strait, which lies between Russian Siberia and American Alaska, to Tierra del Fuego at the southern tip of South America is approximately 10,000 miles. In order to acquire an intelligent perspective about the populating of this New World and the cultural development of its native peoples, one must understand the vast reaches not only of space but also of time and the consequent cultural development through time. Dean Snow (1976: 16–19) comments on the difficulty of achieving such a perspective.

> One of the hardest things for a modern student to grasp about prehistory is the immensity of time involved, and the imperceptible steps by which cultures progressed through that dimension. Today, change plunges through foreshortened time, not allowing any of us to grow old and die in the same cultures into which we were born. Added to this is our curious western concept that progress means technological innovation, and that it is measurable in increments called "inventions." The result is that we tend to think of prehistory as a sequence of great events. Inasmuch as archaeologists are forced to deal with material remains, the great events are often identified as events of technological or artistic creation. Worse, our minds tend to collapse the prehistoric time-scale so that events seem to have followed upon one another with the speed to which our modern senses have become accustomed. The genesis of the wheel is a good case in point. Had an observer been on hand, it is unlikely that he would have been able to give either the name of the inventor, or the time of the invention, since the wheel emerged over a very long period. There were probably no shouts of "eureka" or any word of similar meaning. The immediate impact of the innovation, or more probably the long string of small innovations, was not revolutionary. Application of the wheel took centuries to emerge; indeed it is still emerging.

What were these first New World people like? They probably did not view themselves as explorers or pioneers. They undoubtedly did not realize that they were moving across the threshold of two huge continents and traveling into regions that human beings had never seen before. They were skilled hunters following the animals upon which they depended for survival. They were also closely attuned to the demanding cold, temperate climate. The most prominent feature of such a climate was the glaciers or vast sheets of ice that locked up large volumes of water, creating a land bridge stretching between Siberia and Alaska. The ice caps also covered large areas of the northern New World, leaving, for a time only, a narrow corridor along which migration to the south proceeded.

About 10,000 years ago the Ice Age began ending, and an entire continent was open to be occupied to the limits that population pressure, ensuing waves of migration, and the particular patterns of cultural adaptability permitted. These migrants found vast and varied areas of land unoccupied by other human beings. The climate and terrain demanded a series of different responses. Ultimately, such responses resulted in the wide variety of cultural and social differences that have persisted down to the present. With certain qualified possible exceptions to be discussed later, cultural development within the New World has been an internal matter owing little or nothing to cultural development and diffusion elsewhere.

The larger outlines of New World prehistory and history are evident. The arrivals came as hunters who devoted most of their time to obtaining and processing food. Their clothing was sparse but adequate for basic climatic demands. Out of necessity but not necessarily choice, they had an immediate, direct relationship with the surrounding natural environment and lived and died according to its harsh, relentless demands. Because they learned the hard lessons of survival well, populations increased, and slow, irregular waves of migrants and their descendants moved south to occupy all of the Western Hemisphere. As New World people learned more about their environment and about themselves, the quality of their lives changed and, by some standards, improved. Many plants and a few animals were domesticated. Larger and larger numbers of people lived in one place for relatively long periods of time; fewer and fewer people continued to practice a nomadic hunting and gathering way of life. Urban centers appeared in some places, their existence implying a complicated division of labor and a highly successful kind of technology capable of producing dependable surpluses of food and all the other necessities that people require in order to live together in large numbers.

The sixteenth century brought the arrival of significant numbers of Europeans to the New World. With some limited, regional exceptions in South America, within the next three centuries more than 30,000 years of cultural evolution and achievement were destroyed, broken, or remolded to a Western European image. Specifically, business and government, which fostered both superior technology and disease in a formidable and implacable combination, subdued the native peoples of the New World.

For centuries before reaching the New World, Europeans had thought, experimented, and traveled. They had made a number of important discoveries about others and themselves. They had decided that a powerful government and far-flung business enterprises were highly advantageous to those who developed them first. Other peoples, tribes, and nations who were slower to realize the virtues of economic and political advancement could be used to promote both. The native peoples of the Americas were chosen among others to assist selected European governments and individuals in this task. Together, Europeans and Indians plus those from Asia and Africa who came later were to make the New World what it has become today.

Within this setting, the fruits of military and economic conquest were assured. The prime influence of disease in the destruction and radical modification of native American life cannot be ignored. Before 1900, more than 60 serious epidemics ravaged the native North Americans (H. F. Dobyns, 1976: 21–22). Smallpox, bubonic plague, measles, typhoid, and other similar influences were all of significance in the political subjugation of the New World by the Old, since they abruptly and radically reduced populations, weakening their ability to resist the invaders.

But what are some of the more crucial, specific benchmarks of indigenous life throughout the centuries of development unimpeded by foreign influence? The nature of such developments can be supplied through a study of a prehistory that is complex. To date, prehistorians or archaeologists have not been concerned, out of necessity, with specific peoples or societies but with the things that people have produced and the ideas, concepts, and thoughts that are implied by these things. In turn, chance burial and preservation followed by judicious excavation and analysis have produced the subject matter and conclusions of the archaeologist. In the following paragraphs both things and the ideas and techniques that they imply are discussed. In doing so, I owe a great debt to the archaeologists Gordon Willey (1961), Jesse D. Jennings (1974 and 1978), Mark Cohen (1977), James Stoltman (1978), and a large number of other capable students of prehistory.

It is useful to consider the universal themes of human existence as a way of summarizing the ebb and flow of cultural development in the New World. These basic themes are technology, environmental adaptation, subsistence, and settlement. What means did people develop in the Western Hemisphere to use the raw materials that were available to them? How did they provide sufficient food for themselves? How did they gain shelter from the elements? How did they live so as to make effective cooperation with other people possible? In order to provide answers to these and a number of other related questions, we must consider North, Central, and South America as a whole, even though the basic concern of this book centers around North America.

Five central questions can be raised concerning the essential lines of development by which the native peoples of the New World came to be as they are:

1. Who were the earliest inhabitants of the New World? Where did they come from and when did they come? How did they live once they arrived on this continent?
2. What were the origins and relationships of the specialized food-collecting subsistence patterns of post-Pleistocene times?
3. Where and when did food plant domestication first occur in the New World? What was the influence of such domestication on society and culture?
4. At what time and location did sedentary village life based upon farming arise in the New World? How did this way of life spread on this continent?

5. What is known about the evolution of the civilizations of Nuclear America? How did they begin and develop? What were their interrelationships within the Nuclear sphere? How were such civilizations related to non-Nuclear America?

Although all the facts are not in and will not be in for a long time, if ever, it is possible to discuss at least in a general way what is known about these various questions. Before we proceed further, it is necessary to define two critical terms: *food collecting* and *Nuclear America*. Food collecting pertains to the specialization and diversification in the taking of wild plant and animal foods. Nuclear America consists of the southern two-thirds of Mexico, all of Central America, Andean and coastal Colombia, Ecuador, Peru, and adjoining portions of Bolivia. Nuclear America was the center of agriculture and the locus for two pre-Columbian centers of civilization.

Early People in America

Although many archaeologists have been working on the problems recently, there is still a great deal that is not known about when the first people came to North America. Dates as long ago as 30,000 or 40,000 years have been proposed, but these early sites have not been generally accepted as authentic. Indeed, the evidence for such early habitation is so scanty and so questionable that authorities such as Cohen (1977) and Martin (1967) doubt if human beings had arrived this soon because if they had, more evidence should have appeared by this time. Reliable dates for the presence of people in the New World begin about 25,000 years ago, but how long before that human beings arrived here no one can say.

Archaeologists do agree on two central facts: the first arrivals on this continent were *Homo sapiens*—essentially modern man in physical characteristics—and they came here from Siberia over the Bering Strait land bridge at some time when the ice had locked up enough water to expose it. During some periods, the land bridge, Beringia, was about 1,000 miles wide, and there is no reason to suppose that the people who crossed it realized that they were moving onto a new continent. Nor is there any reason to postulate one large mass movement into the New World. In all probability, small bands of hunters crossed over many times in pursuit of the familiar animals that were their prey. Although huge glaciers covered Canada and extended as far south as Illinois and Missouri during the Wisconsin glacial stage, portions of interior Alaska were never ice-covered. Once people had arrived there, they were able to make their way south down an ice-free corridor between the massive Canadian glaciers. This corridor probably opened and closed a number of times during the Pleistocene or Ice Age, but there is no reliable evidence of exactly when human beings first made use of it.

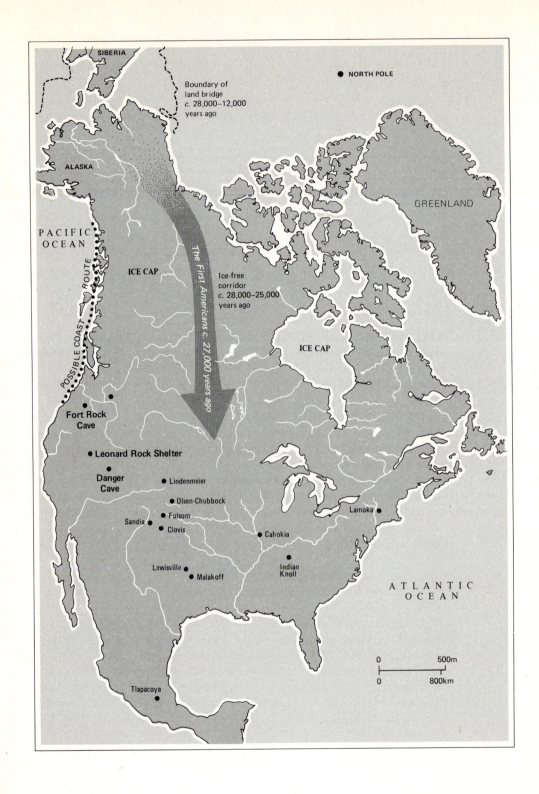

SIBERIA

Boundary of
land bridge
c. 28,000–12,000
years ago

● NORTH POLE

ALASKA

GREENLAND

PACIFIC
OCEAN

ICE CAP

Ice-free
corridor
c. 28,000–25,000
years ago

The First Americans c. 27,000 years ago

POSSIBLE COAST ROUTE

ICE CAP

● Fort Rock
Cave

● Leonard Rock Shelter

● Danger
Cave

● Lindenmeier

● Olsen-Chubbock

● Folsom
Sandia ●
● Clovis

● Lamoka

● Cahokia

Lewisville ●
● Malakoff

Indian
Knoll ●

ATLANTIC
OCEAN

Tlapacoya ●

0   500m
0   800km

A recent publication (Fladmark, 1979) disputes the ice-free corridor theory. Fladmark believes that a midcontinent corridor, even if ice-free, would have been inhospitable to people for reasons of climate and hydrology—large postglacial lakes would have covered much of the area. He feels that the easiest route for early humans would have been along the north Pacific Coast, where people possessing simple water skills could have harvested a relatively abundant living from the sea. No archaeological evidence can be found to support this theory, for areas that were coast then are now under water, but Fladmark's ideas are convincing.

The earliest fully accepted documentation of the human occupation of North America is associated with the *Clovis point,* which was a large lance-shaped projectile fluted at the base and flaked on both sides. Clovis points, although they probably originated on the western plains, have been found scattered throughout the Plains, the Southwest, and the East; and they are usually associated with the killing of big game such as the mammoth, the caribou, and the long-horned bison. These early hunters relied in part on hunting of large animals for their subsistence because neither fishing equipment nor implements for grinding vegetal foods have been found in the earliest Paleo-Indian sites, which are dated before 11,000 years ago. Many of the mammals hunted by the Paleo-Indians are now extinct. The list includes the mammoth, the mastodon, the long-horned bison, the peccary, the camelid (a form of camel), the dire wolf, the giant armadillo, the giant beaver, and the ground sloth. The question of why so many of these large mammals became extinct at the end of the Pleistocene Age has received a great deal of speculation from archaeologists. Did the changes in climate associated with the retreat of the ice destroy these animals, or was it disease, or did people destroy them through efficient techniques of hunting? Cohen (1977: 187) concludes that the reason was probably a combination of factors, but no one really has a satisfactory answer as yet.

The Food Collectors

Whatever the reasons for the extinction of the large mammals, once they were gone, people in the New World were forced to turn to, or perhaps continued to use, other means of subsistence. Richard B. Woodbury (Personal Communication, 1979) makes an interesting observation in this respect.

Food collecting almost certainly accompanied big game hunting, although it doesn't show as easily in the archaeological record. It's even been suggested that there never was a "big-game hunting period" but the early Indians hunted whatever there was, and for 364 days of the year their luck was rabbits and a few deer and on the 365th it was a mammoth. When extinction of these and other large animals came, their way of life didn't have to change all that much.

Beginning about 8,000 years ago, many different patterns, dependent on climate and location, began to appear. Hunting remained important, although the animals who were hunted changed. In the East, for instance, white-tailed deer became the most important source of protein. Throughout the New World, people turned increasingly toward food collecting to supply their dietary needs.

There are several major known food-collecting centers in the New World. A Desert Pattern was represented by a long, stratigraphical sequence at Danger Cave, Utah. Similar situations occurred at Leonard Rock Shelter, Nevada, and Fort Rock Cave in western Oregon. Here the great emphasis placed upon wild seed gathering was reflected by the large numbers of elaborately woven baskets and crude milling stones used in making flour. Examples of this Desert Culture were also found in southern New Mexico and Arizona and at several locations in Mexico.

Another center of food collecting was located in the woodlands of eastern North America. A number of sites such as Graham Cave in Missouri reflected an adaptation to forest and riverine conditions of hunting, the sophisticated use of wild plants, fishing, and the catching of shellfish. A variety of indications suggest that here a transition occurred from big-game hunting to food collecting about 8,000 years ago. During the several thousand years that followed, these eastern woodland collecting or Archaic cultures showed a series of successful adaptations to a variety of regional conditions in that a wide variety of plants, animals, and other edible materials were used by a relatively large number of people living over an extensive area. Stone-working techniques improved and resulted in an elaborate variety of projectile points, vessels, weights for throwing sticks, and a number of different kinds of ceremonial or ornamental objects. Indian Knoll, Kentucky, and Lamoka, New York, illustrate food-collecting patterns. In addition, many of these Archaic sites located along rivers or on the Atlantic Coast also had large shell heaps indicating a persistent use of mussels as a food resource.

Another food-collecting pattern was located along the Pacific Coast of North America. It was similar to that of the Eastern Woodlands. Here semisedentary societies, established by at least 4,000 years ago, were dependent on fishing and acorn gathering. Similar societies based upon fishing were located from southern Alaska to southern California. Groups of people lived in like fashion at about the same time in parts of South America on the coasts of Venezuela, Brazil, and northern Chile.

In the Plains areas of North and South America there were modified retentions of big-game hunting patterns into later times, but these hunters had become part-time seed collectors as well, as evidenced by the presence of food-grinding implements.

Food Plant Domestication

One of the truly great revolutions in history was the domestication of wild forms of plants as a basic food source. This development was comparable in nature to the human control and use of fire. It seems likely that New World people did not consciously and deliberately seek to invent domesticated plants but were gradually inclined to do so because wild plant forms did not supply an adequate food source for the growing population.

The earliest known location for the beginnings of North American agriculture occurred in Mexico, where three locations have been intensively studied: the state of Tamaulipas in the northeast; the Tehuacan Valley in the south central region; and the Valley of Oaxaca in the south (Cohen, 1977: 211–222). In each of these locations well-preserved dry cave refuse yielded evidence of the very slow transition from hunting to farming. Although experimentation in cultivation may have begun 7,000 or 8,000 years ago, it took 3,000 or 4,000 years before domesticated crops became really important in the diet of the people. The three major crops developed in Mexico were maize (possibly derived from a wild grass called teosinte), squash, and beans. Of lesser importance were avocados and chili peppers.

The evolution of agriculture and the growth of the population had a marked effect upon settlement patterns. Small bands were able to congregate into villages, permanent dwellings were constructed, and pottery was invented or introduced. By 1000 B.C., the cultivation of improved maize had spread through Middle America as far south as Peru. By the time the Christian Era had begun, it was known in the southwestern United States, the Mississippi Valley, and South America. The spread of maize had a dynamic effect on all cultures involved.

Lima beans in some coastal areas of Peru, the potato in the Peruvian highlands, and root crops such as manioc in the tropical forest areas of other parts of South America may have been domesticated at least as early as maize was to the north. The effects of such domestication generally paralleled those associated with maize. More people lived in one place for longer periods of time because their primary food sources were located in restricted areas. Maize diffused to the south, but here it entered an already developed horticultural pattern. The effects of its transmittal were consequently different from those in Mexico.

The discussion to this point does not imply that there is a necessary and invariable causal relationship between agriculture and the development of cultural complexity. Speaking of the Andean region of Nuclear America, M. E. Mosely (1975: 115) remarked that civilizations have the potential of rising from any type of subsistence economy that could support a sedentary and dense population in which the people did not have to spend all their time in food procurement. In this region, sea animals, especially mollusks, were so abundant that villages dependent upon them for food could be formed.

Village Farming in Nuclear and Non-Nuclear America—The Rise of Cities

As was mentioned earlier, the development of villages was closely associated with the domestication of plants, particularly maize. In most instances, villages and domesticated plants seemed to have spread or diffused together. In Nuclear America, however, agricultural villages more often than not eventually developed into larger settlements or towns and in a few instances into large urban concentrations or cities. Prominent examples of such urban places are found in the Valley of Mexico and some coastal areas and adjacent valleys of Peru. An important aspect of emerging town life was the existence of the temple and undoubtedly some form of priesthood. The temple in its earliest form was a flat-topped pyramidal mound of earth and rock associated with village farming cultures. Initially, its importance was limited to the small village surrounding it. In some cases, the living areas associated with the temple were scattered throughout the general area. In either case, the activities associated with the temple and its priesthood were a central focus for the settlement, probably because the religious ceremonies that took place there were closely tied to a successful agricultural cycle upon which survival depended. When some of these temple-towns grew in size along with the population that they served, a genuine urban evolution took place.

The temple mound-town pattern appeared in a number of elaborate forms outside of Nuclear America. M. L. Fowler (1975: 93–101) describes a pre-Columbian urban center on the Mississippi River east of St. Louis. This center, whose most prominent site was Cahokia, a complex that included some 120 mounds, appeared about A.D. 1000 and was the most populous settlement north of Mexico. It represented the spread of a North American idea to the Mississippi Valley.

In Nuclear America there was no sharp division between towns and cities in time. Both forms were undoubtedly contemporaneous. A cultural inventory, however, can clearly distinquish one from the other. Cities were larger in area and population. They were marked by large public buildings and the presence of the arts. Formal pantheons of deities were worshiped in temples under the supervision of organized priesthoods. Populations were divided into social classes with clear differences in wealth and style of living. Trade in raw materials and finished luxury items was carried on between cities and their supporting regions. Writing and science existed, particularly mathematics and a kind of astronomy under the patronage of leaders having strong religious and political powers. Not all cities in Nuclear America had all these features, but the majority of them did. Two types existed, those with dispersed settlement patterns and those with concentrated settlement patterns. Dispersed cities were limited to the lowland Maya centers of the classic period such as Tikal or Palenque. The concentrated city adhered in form more to its Western European counterpart. Such places were truly urban conglomerations with a heterogeneous population, a complex division of labor, and an elaborate bureaucratic structure. They were usually the capitals of empires with influence over a large territorial domain. Examples were Chan Chan in Peru, the Aztec's Tenotchtitlan, and the "Toltec" Teotihuacan III with its immense temples of the sun and moon. According to Willey (1961: 570), these cities were able to draw on a common heritage of culture built up over the centuries and kept alive through the bonds of interchange and contact.

An interesting question is why cities appeared in one particular area and not another. Willey (1966, 144–145), citing R. L. Carneiro as a stimulus, speaks of a "compression" or "circumscription" factor that acted to trap small populations in territories of small size but rich agricultural potential. Examples of areas like this are the coastal and upland valleys of Middle America and Peru, where cities did indeed develop. In other areas where the conditions for population compression were lacking and people could more easily move away, development of cities may have been slower.

The relevance for North American Indian cultural evolution of these details—particularly the spread of important ideas and skills such as farming (crops plus techniques) and pottery to the Southwest and Southeast, of stratified society and temple-pyramids to the lower Mississippi Valley, and of a number of religious concepts such as the possible diffusion of the Morning Star sacrifice and the feathered serpent—is enormous, complex, and controversial among anthropologists and others. Further comment cannot be made here besides the acknowledgment of the immense debt owed by North American native cultures to their Central American and, indirectly, to their South American counterparts.

TRANSOCEANIC CONTACTS AND NEW WORLD DEVELOPMENT

At present there is a continuing controversy over the possible effects of transoceanic influences on New World native peoples prior to fifteenth-century European contact. A decisive resolution of this question is complicated by the lack of agreement on standards of evidence for significant diffusion from one region to another. Meggers, Evans, and Estrada (1965) and Ford (1969) argue that sailors or colonizers from southern Japan landed on the coast of Ecuador and introduced Valdivia pottery along with a number of religious practices. Such a contact was a significant stimulus for cultural development in a number of places in South America and Central America. Meggers (1975: 1) states that the Olmec civilization of Mesoamerica may have originated from a transpacific stimulus in the earlier Shang civilization of China. Another archaeologist, David D. Grove (1976: 634–637), strongly disagrees. Still other archaeologists such as Ekholm (1950) and Heine-Geldern (1952) have maintained that there are significant parallels in form and function between particular items in various parts of India and Asia and Mesoamerica; for example, plant design motifs on buildings, games, and religious art. Many anthropologists disagree with these findings. R. L. Rands (1953: 79–153), after making a thorough analysis of the water lily form and its position in Mayan art, concludes that a historical relationship with an alleged water lily form in India is spurious. Some archaeologists take issue with the methods of analysis and the ensuing conclusions of Meggers, Estrada, Evans, and Ford, but accept the sound arguments of Ekholm, David Kelly, and others.

Botanists and others have raised the question of the diffusion of such economically crucial plants as sweet potatoes, coconuts, and gourds in an east-to-west passage across the Pacific, but the several arguments founder on a number of grounds, particularly standards of plant classification and the processes of hybridization.

Possible transatlantic contacts have also been considered. Alice B. Kehoe (1971: 275–292) concludes that given the presence of seagoing skin boats, marine diffusion might easily account for the similarities between northwestern European cultures and northeastern American cultures both in the third millennium B.C. and at the end of the second millennium B.C.

Despite the possible validity of many of the arguments favoring transoceanic diffusion, it seems likely that most of the basic contours of New World culture have been internally generated within its geographical confines. Further specific pertinent archaeological and historical events are considered as particular tribes are described later in the book.

THE NATIVE LANGUAGES: SOME CHARACTERISTICS AND OBSERVATIONS

At the time of significant European contact, about 300 different Indian languages belonging to half a dozen or so families were spoken by more than one million people living north of Mexico. About half these languages are now extinct. Further, about half of those that survive are not spoken by children of the tribes concerned, and their survival beyond the present century is questionable. Those languages that may have the greatest duration of use are Cree, Chippewa, Eskimo, Navajo, Hopi, and Zuni. English has replaced native dialects in many cases and is the lingua franca of today's Indians.

Scholars have long been interested in North American Indian languages for a number of reasons. Like all other languages, each has a system of sounds or *phonology*, a basic structure or grammar or *morphology*, and *a syntax* (the way in which structured units are combined to produce phrases and sentences). Hence, Indian languages provide provocative research materials for the linguist.

Although there is disagreement about whether or not there is any relationship between a type of language and the cultural system that employs it, most anthropologists who have an interest in native North America regard Indian languages as one way of classifying Indian cultures. The use of the interrelated *glottochronology* and *lexicostatistics* may potentially provide a way of ordering cultures with regard to time depth or temporal sequences. Glottochronology is the study of the rate of change of a language, while lexicostatistics concentrates on a statistical study of vocabulary. Both methods are based on the assumption that a language will change at a predictable rate (Hymes, 1960: 4).

Less esoteric and of much wider application is the assumption that the more closely related given languages are, the nearer the relationship of the cultures concerned. Some of the better known and more widely used language classifications are those of J. W. Powell (1891), whose was the first comprehensive classification; of Boas (1911), whose classification contains also a classic discussion of some of the major characteristics of these languages; of Edward Sapir (1929); and of C. F. and M. F. Voegelin (1966), who presented in map form a commonly used ordering currently relied upon.

A crucial point to remember, however, is that whereas language classifications may be helpful for making sense out of the diversity of Indian life during the first half of the nineteenth century or before, they have far less utility in providing an understanding of contemporary American Indian interrelationships. In this endeavor, other means must be relied upon.

THE CONCEPT OF CULTURE AREA

This textbook, along with many others dealing with North American Indians, relies heavily upon the concept of *culture area* as a basic organizing principle. M. Foley (1976: 104–111) defined culture area as a region where the inhabitants share such things as ecological conditions, economic systems, social systems, and ideological systems. Richard B. Woodbury (Personal Communication, 1979) provided added precision to the meaning of the concept, stating:

> A culture area may or may not be the result of a group or a lifeway expanding from a central point. It is an abstraction, a classificatory device convenient for grouping tribes that are similar in terms of many aspects of their culture, but primarily subsistence. Since descriptive convenience and the degree of generalization that is attractive or acceptable will vary from person to person, no single culture area scheme has ever become the "final" or "correct" one. The number may be eight or ten, or twice that. It is a useful device for exposition at a simple and intermediate level, but not much more.

Organization by culture area has some drawbacks. First, the group being described is frozen in time, usually a time just prior to White conquest. Secondly, the concept stresses *material culture*—the things that people have such as canoes, weapons, skin lodges, and pottery— at the expense of other aspects of culture. Within a given area, a number of tribes may be grouped as similar when, in fact, they differ in a number of important respects. Finally, as Woodbury has said, anthropologists disagree about the number of culture areas and the specific tribes that should be assigned to each area. These objections notwithstanding, the tribes considered in this text have been, in part, selected because they generally represent the major divisions of North American ethnography referred to as culture areas. The ecological, economic, social, and ideological parallels that they imply make such an approach valid.

The nine culture areas used in this book are Northeast/Woodlands, Southeast, Plains, Southwest, California, Plateau, Northwest Coast, Subarctic, and Arctic. A tenth area, the Great Basin, is not represented by a tribe in this book. There follows a brief characterization of each area and of the tribe in each selected for discussion.

Northeast/Woodlands

The Northeast/Woodlands area shows considerable cultural variation and is represented in this text by the Micmac, Oneida, and Menominee. It includes the Canadian provinces of Quebec (less the Subarctic), New Brunswick, Nova Scotia, and Ontario, as well as the states of the Midwest and New England. The differences in the subsistence patterns of the three groups selected for discussion mirror the variations to be found in the Woodlands area. The Micmac were nomadic hunters and fishermen, the Oneidas were village dwellers who relied upon hunting and farming, and the Menominees were hunters and fishermen who used agriculture to a limited extent. All groups within this area had as wide a resource base as opportunity permitted, and they used their resources in an ingenious fashion.

In general, Woodland people were at home in the forests; on the lakes, rivers, and streams; and, in some cases, in seacoast waters. They ate a wide variety of foods; wore skin and fur clothing appropriate for the climate; and lived in skin tents, bark houses, or large lodges of bark. They traveled by bark canoe in the summer and by snowshoes or sleds in the winter. They were prepared and eager to fight if necessary, and their weapons included tomahawks, war clubs, and the bow and arrow. Like all other native peoples of North America, they enjoyed games and gambling.

The Southeast

The Southeast area is bounded by Louisiana on the west, Tennessee to the north, the Atlantic Ocean to the east, and Florida to the south. Culturally and socially this area is more homogeneous than the Northeast/Woodlands, and its peoples had more elaborate forms of sociopolitical organization. The peoples of the Southeast appear to have had a far more sophisticated and catholic approach to the demands of life than did their neighbors to the north, possibly owing to the influences stemming ultimately from the Caribbean and Mesoamerican regions to the south. It is not without good reason that the native peoples of the Southeast were referred to as "civilized." The Cherokees, who represent the Southeast in this book, probably had one of the most coherent and well-balanced cultures of this area. Their ability to survive and even prosper under adverse conditions before as well as after White conquest is indicative of this fact.

The Plains

The Plains fill the center of the North American continent, stretching from the southern prairies of Canada to the north central reaches of Texas. Ruth Underhill (1971: 144–185) divided Plains Indians into two categories: nomadic and village. The Cheyenne, the subject of Chapter 6, occupied a kind of intermediate position between the two. They were militarily weak farmers and hunters who were forced out on the Plains and soon took on the appearance of other nomadic buffalo hunters. The impact of their agricultural past remained with them, however, and was melded in the late eighteenth and early nineteenth centuries with a Plains form of life.

Because of its portrayal in an endless series of movies and TV Westerns, Plains culture has become associated with "Indianness" in the minds of many, although they were certainly no more Indian than peoples in other areas. They were, however, exciting and dramatic individuals as the following quotation, written in 1856 about the Crow at Fort Union on the Missouri River, shows.[2]

> The Crows are cunning, active, and very intelligent in everything appertaining to the chase, war, or their own individual bargaining. . . . The warrior class . . . are all tall, straight, well formed, with bold, fierce eyes, and as usual good teeth. These dress elegantly and expensively. . . . [The women have] bad features and worse shapes, filthy habits, dresses and persons smeared with dirt and grease, hair cut short and full of vermin, faces daubed over with their own blood in mourning for dead relations, and fingers cut off so that scarcely a whole hand is to be found among them. . . .
>
> When the camp is on the move in the summer, this tribe presents a gay and lively appearance. On these occasions both men and women dress in their best clothes. Their numerous horses are decked out with highly ornamented saddles and bridles of their own making, scarlet collars and housings with feathers on their horses' heads and tails. . . . They are so expeditious in packing that after their horses are caught, they are saddled, the tents struck, everything put on the horses and on the march in less than twenty minutes. The great number and good quality of their horses make a showy appearance. Both men and women are capital riders.

The Southwest

The Southwest, occupying the states of Arizona, New Mexico, and parts of Colorado and Utah, is a complex area having a long history and an involved series of interactions with Mexico to the south, the California area to the west, the Plains on the east, and the Basin-Plateau to the north. I have included three peoples from the Southwest—the Navajo, Hopi, and Papago—all of whom are very different from each other. Nor do these three groups represent all the possible variations of culture in the area. As is the case with the other groups and areas, a distinctive aggregation of customs and material items set the Southwest off from other places. Any one item or practice alone, of course, will not do this. It is the pattern or system of relationships among items, traits, customs, and practices that produces this culture area distinctiveness here and elsewhere.

Although the various peoples of the Southwest may live in different

[2]Denig, 1856 (1953): 29–36.

types of houses, eat different foods, and organize their societies in different ways, all of them have a strong belief in the importance of harmony with nature. Nowhere is this better exemplified than in the Navajo Blessingway chant:[3]

> Earth I beg of you, Changing Woman I beg of you, White Shell Woman I
>   beg of you,
> Long life I beg of you, happiness I beg of you,
> My mother [Earth], my mother's mother, this day let my children be
>   recovered, let them return to me if you say so, I have made an offering
>   to you. A fine white shell I have made an offering to you,
> A fine white shell I have made an offering to you,
> A fine turquoise I have made an offering to you,
> A fine abalone, I have made an offering to you. . . .
> May I be long life, happiness.
> Before me may it be blessed, behind me may it be blessed!
> It has become blessed again, it has become blessed again!
> By means of Sky's feet may I go through life.

California

For a very long time California has been the home for a great number of small Indian groups scattered throughout its mountains, valleys, and coastlands. Although these groups possessed a diversity of languages and customs, none of them used agriculture except those along the Colorado River. Instead of farming, they relied for food upon excellent hunting and fishing and upon gathering of native fauna, especially acorns, which were leached and converted into flour. Characteristic of the experience of all California native people was the devastation that outsiders, and especially White Americans, inflicted upon them. This was due to both the force of the contact and the nature of the Indian cultures themselves. Perhaps more than any other Indians considered in this book, the native Californians required an abundant, stable food supply and isolation from foreign peoples seeking to dominate them. When one or both conditions were lacking, their survival was often in question. The California people discussed in this book are the Pomo who lived in Central California.

The Plateau

The Plateau area covers what is now western Montana, eastern Washington State, southeastern British Columbia, and parts of northern Oregon and Idaho. Some anthropologists have said that the Plateau

[3]Wyman, 1970: 223–224 (from a prayer said by Rock Crystal Talking God).

lacks a cultural focus in the sense of California, the Northwest Coast, and the Plains. The area reflects a diversity of influences over a period of time. Prior to the eighteenth century, it was influenced by Northwest Coast hunting, fishing, and gathering activities plus the behavior and customs of the Great Basin desert people to the south and southeast. After this time, Plains influences, particularly the horse and all that went along with it, plus White characteristics brought at first by traders and later by settlers were introduced.

The Plateau people as a rule were not farmers, but gatherers of wild plants and seeds. They caught salmon and other kinds of fish and hunted deer, elk, beaver, and mountain sheep. In early times they lived in winter earth lodges and summer gabled arbors. On the whole, they were a relatively peaceful people. The Klamath, discussed in Chapter 11, were quite typical of the other Plateau cultures.

The Great Basin

The boundaries between the Great Basin and the Plateau area are very imprecise, and previously anthropologists considered the two areas as one. The Great Basin is literally a basin or depression covering a huge area. In earlier times it was the site of 68 lakes, but the dry climate of modern times has evaporated all but a few, most prominent of which is the Great Salt Lake. In general, the Great Basin covers the arid deserts of Nevada and Utah and is bordered by mountains—the Sierra Nevadas and the Cascades to the west and the Rockies to the east. Great Basin, Plateau, and California peoples all have much in common. All rely on hunting and gathering rather than farming. Some Great Basin peoples are the Bannock, Shoshone, Paiute, Ute, and Washo. They are the descendants of a variety of poorly known desert inhabitants who have successfully lived in one of the most desolate areas of the world.

The Northwest Coast

The Northwest Coast, the coastal strip of land extending from the mouth of the Columbia River to southeastern Alaska, has sheltered in its heavily wooded bays and inlets an independent and original group of people. The Kwakiutl, discussed in Chapter 12, live about midway along this coastline and combine characteristics of more northern and more southern groups. Northwest Coast peoples are not agriculturists, but they do observe a seasonal round of life dominated by the fish and the wild plants on which they depend for food. They are justly famous for their elaborate social structure, political organization, and economic sharing through the custom of potlatching.

The Subarctic

The peoples of the Subarctic live in a broad belt of boreal or northern coniferous forest extending throughout Canada and into Alaska. They are separated from the Eskimos, who live along the coastal rim of the continent, by the barren grounds or tundra, where both groups occasionally go to hunt caribou. Helm and Leacock (1971: 345) divided the Canadian subarctic forest into three ethnographic zones: the northeastern domain of the Montagnais-Naskapi; the Central zone occupied by the Cree; and a northwest portion where the Athabaskan-speaking tribes live.

For the most part, Whites have avoided and even feared this area. In 1898, J. W. Tyrrell described "the great mysterious region of *terra incognita*" thusly: "Of almost this entire territory less was known than of the remotest districts of Darkest Africa, and, with but few exceptions, its vast and dreary plains had never been trodden by the foot of man, save that of the dusky savage" (1898: 7). Tyrrell may as well have been speaking of the Hare of Coville Lake, discussed in Chapter 13, who live to the northwest of this region of exploration. Like the other Indian groups of the Subarctic, however, the Hare know their environment and themselves well and have adjusted to their implacable country.

The Arctic

Traditional Eskimo territory extends over 5,000 miles across land areas now controlled by the Soviet Union, Alaska (U.S.A.), Canada, and Greenland (Denmark). A total population of about 100,000 live in thinly scattered fashion, for the most part at places along the coast, where food resources are most readily available. A relatively small number, however, occupy inland areas.

Chapter 14 considers three categories of Eskimos: the Netsilik, who at the time they were studied exhibited a pan-Eskimo culture of precontact Canada; the village dwellers of Sugluk in Canada and Kaktovik in Alaska, whose ways of life reflect both past and present; and the people of Eastern Canada, with emphasis on how they have interacted with the many Whites moving into the area.

Culture Areas Now

Of what use is the culture area concept for understanding contemporary Native American existence? This concept has little or no utility for such a purpose because all native peoples have become a part of modern Canadian and American life. Today distinctive aspects of particular forms of native life for the most part consist of *ethnic ideologies*—the integrated assertions, theories, and aims that constitute a sociopolitical program that, in turn, is subject to local definition. Historical, social, and cultural factors can and do play an important part in such a definition as well. These ethnic ideologies and Native Americans in contemporary life form the subject matter of the final chapter of this textbook.

All references listed in the sections following each chapter were not necessarily directly referred to in the chapter. Nevertheless, they constitute important resource material for a thorough consideration of the subject matter.

REFERENCES

Boas, Franz. Handbook of American Indian Languages, Part 1. In *Bulletin 40, Bureau of American Ethnology, Smithsonian Institution.* Washington, D.C.: Government Printing Office, 1911, pp. 1–83.

Burling, Robbins. *Man's Many Voices: Language in Its Cultural Context.* New York: Holt, Rinehart and Winston, 1970.

Cohen, Mark Nathan. *The Food Crisis in Prehistory: Overpopulation and the Origins of Agriculture.* New Haven: Yale University Press, 1977.

Denig, Edwin T. Of the Crow Nation. *Anthropology Papers No. 33. Bureau of American Ethnology, Bulletin 151.* Washington, D.C.: Government Printing Office, 1953.

Dobyns, Henry F. *Native American Historical Demography: A Critical Bibliography.* Bloomington: Indiana University Press, 1976.

Edwards, Clinton R. Aboriginal Watercraft on the Pacific Coast of South America. *Ibero-Americana 47.* Berkeley and Los Angeles: University of California Press, 1965.

———. New World Perspectives on Pre-European Voyaging in the Pacific. *Center Reprint No. 6.* Milwaukee: Center for Latin American Studies, University of Wisconsin-Milwaukee, 1969.

———. Possibilities of Pre-Columbian Maritime Contacts among New World Civilizations. *Pamphlet No. 8.* Latin American Center Pamphlet Series. Milwaukee: Center for Latin American Studies, University of Wisconsin-Milwaukee, 1970.

Ekholm, G. F. Is American Indian Culture Asiatic? *Natural History 59,* 344–351, 382, 1950.

Fladmark, K. R. Routes: Alternate Migration Corridors for Early Man in North America. *American Antiquity 44,* 55–69, January 1979.

Foley, M. Culture Area *and* Culture Areas of the World. In D. E. Hunter and P. Whitten, eds., *Encyclopedia of Anthropology,* New York: Harper & Row, 1976, 104–111.

Ford, James A. A Comparison of Formative Cultures in the Americas: Diffusion or the Psychic Unity of Man. *Smithsonian Contributions to Anthropology 11.* Washington, D.C.: Smithsonian Institution Press, 1969.

Fowler, Melvin L. A Pre-Columbian Urban Center on the Mississippi. *Scientific American 233,* 92–101, August 1975.

Fromkin, Victoria, and Robert Rodman. *An Introduction to Language*. New York: Holt, Rinehart and Winston, 1974.

Grove, David C. Olmec Origins and Transpacific Diffusion: Reply to Meggers. *American Anthropologist 78*, 634–637, September 1976.

Gudschinsky, Sarah C. *How to Learn an Unwritten Language*. New York: Holt, Rinehart and Winston, 1967.

Hadley, J. Nixon. Demography of the American Indians. *The Annals of the American Academy of Political and Social Science 311*, 23–30, May 1957.

Hallowell, A. Irving. The Impact of the American Indian on American Culture. *American Anthropologist 59*, 201–217, April 1957.

———. American Indians, White and Black: The Phenomenon of Transculturatization. *Current Anthropology 4*, 519–531, December 1963.

Hanson, Marshall. Plains Indians and Urbanization. Ph.D. dissertation, Stanford University, 1962.

Harris, Marvin, and G. E. B. Morren. The Limitations of the Principle of Limited Possibilities. *American Anthropologist 68*, 122–127, February 1966.

Hawthorne, H. B., et al. *A Survey of the Contemporary Indians of Canada: Economic, Political, Education Needs and Policies in Two Volumes*. Indian Affairs Branch, Ottawa, 1966.

Heine-Geldern, R. Some Problems of Migration in the Pacific. In W. Koppers, ed., *Kultur und Sprache*. Wiener Beitrage zur Kulturgeschichte und Linguistik, Annual 9, pp. 313–362, 1952.

Helm, June, and Eleanor Leacock. The Hunting Tribes of Subarctic Canada. In E. B. Leacock and N. O. Lurie, eds., *North American Indians in Historical Perspective*. New York: Random House, 1971, 343–374.

Hodge, F. W., ed. Handbook of American Indians North of Mexico. *Bulletin 30, Bureau of American Ethnology, Smithsonian Institution. Parts 1 and 2*. Washington, D.C.: Government Printing Office, 1907–1910.

Hymes, D. H. Lexicostatistics. *Current Anthropology 1*, 3–44, January 1960.

Jennings, Jesse D. *Prehistory of North America* (2d ed.). New York: McGraw-Hill Book Co., 1974.

———, ed. *Ancient Native Americans*. San Francisco: W. H. Freeman and Company, 1978.

Johnston, Denis Foster. An Analysis of Sources of Information on the Population of the Navaho. *Bulletin 197, Bureau of American Ethnology*. Washington, D.C.; Government Printing Office, 1966.

Josephy, Alvin M., Jr. *The Indian Heritage of America*. New York: A. A. Knopf, 1968; rpt. New York: Bantam Books Inc., 1969.

Kehoe, Alice B. Small Boats upon the North Atlantic. In C. D. Riley et al., eds., *Man across the Sea: Problems of Pre-Columbian Contact*. Austin: University of Texas Press, 1971, pp. 275–292.

Leacock, E. B., and N. O. Lurie, eds. *North American Indians in Historical Perspective*. New York: Random House, 1971.

McNickle, D'Arcy. Indian, North American. *Encyclopaedia Britannica*, Vol. 12, (1969), pp. 62–79.

Martin, P. S., and H. E. Wright, Jr., eds. *Pleistocene Extinctions: The Search for a Cause*. New Haven: Yale University Press, 1967.

Meggers, B. J. The Transpacific Origin of Mesoamerican Civilization: A Preliminary Review of the Evidence and Its Theoretical Implications. *American Anthropologist 77*, 1–27, March 1975.

———, C. Evans, and E. Estrada. Early Formative Period of Coastal Ecuador: The Valdivia and Machalilla Phases. *Smithsonian Contributions to Anthropology 1*. Washington, D.C.: Smithsonian Institution, 1965.

Moseley, M. E. *The Maritime Foundations of Andean Civilization*. Menlo Park, California: Cummings Publishing Co., 1975.

Murdock, George P. *Ethnographic Bibliography of North America* (4th ed.). New Haven: Human Relations Area Files, 1976.

Powell, J. W. Indian Linguistic Families of America North of Mexico. In *Seventh Annual Report, Smithsonian Institution, Bureau of American Ethnology*. Washington, D.C.: Government Printing Office, 1891, pp. 7–142.

Quimby, George I. *Indian Life in the Upper Great Lakes, 11,000 B.C. to A.D. 1800*. Chicago: University of Chicago Press, 1960.

Rands, Robert L. The Water Lily in Maya Art: A Complex of Alleged Asiatic Origin. *Smithsonian Institution Bulletin 151. Bureau of American Ethnology*. 1953.

Report of Committee of American Anthropological Association. Phonetic Transcription of Indian Languages. *Smithsonian Miscellaneous Collections 66:6* (Publication 2415). Washington, D.C.: Smithsonian Institution, 1916 (Rpt.).

Riley, C. L., et al. *Man across the Sea: Problems of Pre-Columbia Contacts*. Austin: University of Texas Press, 1971.

Sapir, Edward. Central and North American Languages. *Encyclopaedia Britannica* (14th ed.). London and New York, Encyclopaedia Britannica Co., 1929, vol. 5, pp. 138–141.

Snake, Reuben, Jr. *Being Indian is . . .* Macy, Nebraska: Nebraska Indian Press, 1972.

Snow, Dean. *The Archaeology of North America*. New York: The Viking Press, 1976.

Stoltman, James B. Temporal Models in Prehistory: An Example from Eastern North America. *Current Anthropology 19*, 703–746, December 1978.

Struever, Stuart, ed. *Prehistoric Agriculture: American Museum Sourcebooks in Anthropology*. Garden City, N.Y.: Natural History Press (Doubleday), 1971.

Tax, Sol. The Impact of Urbanization on American Indians. *The Annals of the American Academy of Political and Social Science 436*, 121–136, March 1978.

Tester, K. V. American Indian Linguistics. pp. 411–424 In B. J. Siegel, A. R. Beals, and S. A. Tyler, eds. *Annual Review of Anthropology, vol. I*. Palo Alto, California: Annual Reviews, Inc., 1972.

Trimble, Joseph E. *An Index of the Social Indicators of the American Indian in Oklahoma*. Oklahoma: Office of Community Affairs and Planning, 1972.

Tyrrell, J. W. *Across the Sub-Arctics of Canada: A Journey of 3200 Miles by Canoe and Snowshoe through the Barren Lands*. London: T. Fisher Unwin, 1898.

Underhill, Ruth. *Red Man's America: A History of Indians in the United States* (rev. ed.). Chicago: University of Chicago Press, 1971.

U.S. American Indian Policy Review Commission. *Newsletter*. April 1976.

U.S. Congress. Senate. Select Committee on Indian Affairs. *Pueblo Lands and Alaska Natives Governing Bodies: Hearing before the Committee on S. 1789 and S. 2046.* 95th Cong., 1st sess., 1977.

U.S. Department of Health, Education, and Welfare. Office of Special Concerns. *A Study of Selected Socio-Economic Characteristics of Ethnic Minorities Based on the 1970 Census, Vol. III: American Indians.*

Voeglin, C. F., and F. N. Voeglin. *Map of North American Indian Languages* (rev. ed.). American Ethnological Society. Prepared and Printed by Rand McNally & Co., 1966.

Willey, Gordon R. New World Prehistory. In *The Smithsonian Report for 1960.* (Publication 4455). Washington, D.C.: Smithsonian Institution, 1961, pp. 551–575.

———. *An Introduction to American Archaeology: Vol. One. North and Middle America.* Englewood Cliffs, N.J.: Prentice-Hall, 1966.

———. New World Archaeology in 1965. In "Archaeology: Horizons New and Old." *Preceedings of the American Philosophical Society 110,* April 1966, pp. 140–145.

———, ed. *Archaeological Researches in Retrospect.* Cambridge, Mass.: Winthrop Publishers, 1974.

Woodall, J. Ned. 5. The Decline of the Caddo: An Exercise. In *An Introduction to Modern Archeology.* Cambridge, Mass.: Schenkman Publishing Co., 1972, pp. 81–96.

Woodbury, Richard B. Personal Communications, 1979.

Wyman, Leland C. *Blessingway.* Tucson: The University of Arizona Press, 1970.

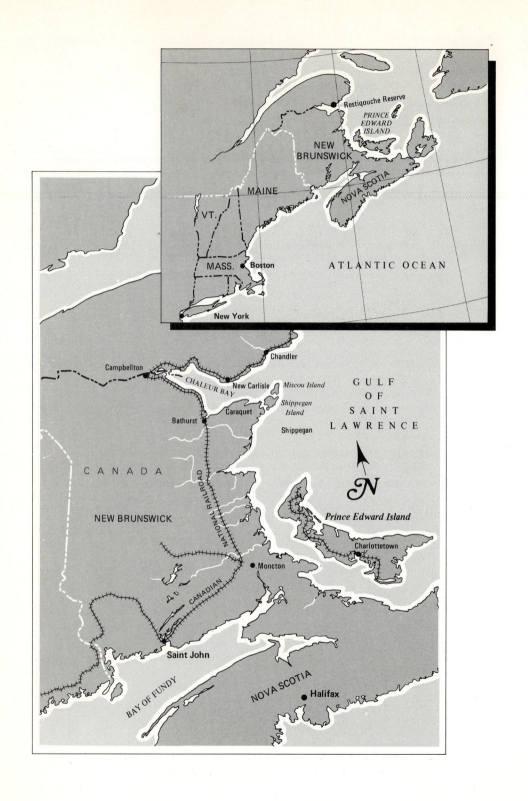

Restiqouche Reserve

*PRINCE
EDWARD
ISLAND*

NEW
BRUNSWICK

MAINE

NOVA SCOTIA

VT.

MASS.   Boston

ATLANTIC OCEAN

New York

Chandler

Campbellton   New Carlisle   *Miscou Island*
CHALEUR BAY
                                               *Shippegan
                      Caraquet   Island*
Bathurst
                                               Shippegan

GULF
OF
SAINT
LAWRENCE

CANADA

N

NEW BRUNSWICK

Prince Edward Island

Charlottetown

Moncton

Saint John

BAY OF FUNDY

NOVA SCOTIA   Halifax

CHAPTER 2

THE MICMAC INDIANS OF CANADA AND NEW ENGLAND
The Resourceful Wanderers

I kinda hate to leave Canada. It's beautiful there in the summer, just like I remember it. It's good for the kids, they're still young. . . . Last summer I made more than three dollars an hour at Sal's, with tips. I always have a good time working there.

A Micmac woman in Jeanne
Guillemin's *Urban Renegades*

THE PAST

The Micmac are Algonquian-speaking Indians who, at the time of their discovery, occupied the entire province of Nova Scotia, including Cape Breton Island, the northeastern portion of New Brunswick, and Prince Edward Island, together forming a region now referred to as the Canadian Maritimes (Jenness, 1955: 267). They have the distinction of being one of the first tribes on the North American continent to be encountered by Europeans. Norse voyagers may have met a few about A.D. 1000. They were possibly seen next by John Cabot in 1497, and from this time forward were constantly visited by explorers and European fishermen from France and England. Acting as middlemen between the Europeans and the Indians farther to the west and south, they lived as subordinate members of the French and British colonial administrations during the seventeenth and the eighteenth centuries. For about 500 years they have constantly been faced with a series of grave problems centering around the fact that they are native peoples dominated by political elements foreign to their heritage. Much of the nature of Micmac life then and now must be understood in this light.

Mooney (1928) estimated that there were 3,500 Micmac in 1600. The seventeenth century probably saw a sharp drop in population, induced by White-carried diseases for which the Indians had no immunity. Their health also deteriorated because new European foods were not as nutritious as their native diet or were spoiled by the time the Indians received them, and European clothing was not as protective as their own (Guillemin, 1975: 29). It is, however, impossible to give exact population figures for any historical time, especially because the Micmac were not a sedentary people. After the seventeenth century their numbers increased slowly but steadily to their current level of around 10,000.

The Land

Micmac country is geographically conditioned by two central factors, its close proximity to the sea, lakes, and rivers and the thick growth of coniferous and deciduous forests. During late spring, throughout the summer, and into the fall, rain is relatively heavy, with an average of more than 30 inches per year. During late fall and winter, periods of heavy snow occur along with strong winds from the northwest and northeast. While much of the surface of the area is sandy, rocky, and hilly from the interior to the sea, there are many areas of rich, red, fertile soil. Temperatures range from below zero (Fahrenheit) to the high eighties of July and August.

Micmac territory was bounded by other Algonquian tribes, such as

Camp at Dartmouth, Nova Scotia. Man and boy outside conical birchbark tipi overlooking a shoreline. 1860.   Smithsonian Institution National Anthropological Archives.

the Penobscot, Passamaquoddy, and Malecite to the south, the Algonquian Beothuk to the east in Newfoundland, the Iroquois to the west, and the Eskimo and Montagnais-Naskapi on the north shore of the Gulf of St. Lawrence. The Micmac fought at one time or another with all these groups. Their worst enemies, however, were natives with a different heritage, such as the Eskimo, in whose territory they occasionally hunted. From the seventeenth through the nineteenth centuries, when Iroquois power was at its height, some northern Algonquian tribes, with the help of the Ottawas as mediators, formed the Wabanaki Confederacy as a defense against the Mohawks, who were raiding their settlements. The Penobscots were the most active group in this movement, which also included the Passamaquoddy, the Malecite, and the Micmac as "younger brothers" with little power (Guillemin, 1975: 46–47). In spite of the continual feuding with outsiders, the Micmac were peaceful, hospitable, and cooperative within their own group.

The Way of Life

DISTRIBUTION.   Much of what is known about the way the Micmac lived in the past comes from the early Catholic missionaries writing in the *Jesuit Relations* (Thwaites, 1896). This account of the Micmac past relies heavily on Wallis and Wallis (1955), who not only researched the historical documents, but also did fieldwork with the Micmac—Wilson Wallis from 1911 to 1912, and both Wilson and Ruth Sawtell Wallis in

1950 and 1953. Although it is impossible to put an exact date on the customs described in the following pages, it seems reasonable to assume that the behavior discussed existed through the eighteenth and into the early nineteenth centuries.

Micmac villages, both now and in the past, are located throughout the Canadian Maritimes, some on river banks, others along the coast, and still others inland near a major water source. Their number and location during the period 1600 to 1850 cannot be determined now with any accuracy. Swanton (1953: 580), quoting Rand, states that the Micmac distinguished seven districts. He then lists 23 villages, giving their known and assumed locations. The dates when these villages existed are not supplied. A Canadian federal publication, *Tawow* (1976), states that the seven divisions of the tribe are Annapolis, Shubenacadie, Eshegawaage, Cape Breton, Pictou, Memramcook, and Restigouche. They appear to be essentially geographical areas where particular bands or extended families lived in the past and remain at present. The interesting question as to what specific groups of aboriginal Micmac resided in what particular reserves cannot be answered. It is likely that current residence patterns are the joint result of well-established residence preferences and the administrative convenience of the Canadian national and provincial governments.

The National Atlas of Canada (Canada, 1973: 119–120) shows 31 "occupied Indian Reserves" as of 1961 but adds that "one symbol may represent a group of reserves." Bock (1978: 120) shows a total of 27 reserves in 1972: four in Quebec, nine in New Brunswick, 12 in Nova Scotia, and two on Prince Edward Island. The total population then was 9,805, but only 70 percent of this number lived on a reserve at any one time. It may well be that villages were formerly only intermittently or partially occupied. The nature and extent of contact between villages is not clear.

Given the available facts, the following reconstruction seems reasonable: the Micmac traditionally lived where food resources were available, and such resources were seasonal, renewable, and to a degree unpredictable, so the Micmac were prepared to move about as necessity dictated. Migration made existence possible; travel was life itself. These conditions have persisted to the present. This pattern of settlement and migration was mirrored and, in fact, facilitated by the artifacts and other associated influences of Western European culture that were to come to the Micmac in halting, uneven fashion in later years. As Calvin Martin (1975: 111) stated:

> What to the seventeenth-century French was little more than a mundane article of commerce became, to the Acadian Micmac, an institution with noteworthy economic, ceremonial, spiritual, and demographic connota-

tions. Utilizing portable kettles, Micmac households became less inclined to camp near their immobile wooden cauldrons which now served a diminishing function as the symbolic locus of settlement. The copper kettle thus afforded these people the opportunity to move about at random as they hunted game for the fur trade.

The automobile, to be introduced more than two centuries later, was to enlarge the scope of migration even more.

A HUNTING PEOPLE.   As far as we know, the Micmac were traditionally a hunting group who practiced no agriculture except some tobacco growing. Living in a country rich in game and fish, they relied on seasonal migration between seacoast and woodland to find food. In 1616, Father Biard, living at Port Royal, recorded the monthly hunting cycle of the Micmac.[1]

TIME	GAME	LOCATION
January	Seal	Sea coast
February to March	Beaver, otter, moose, bear, caribou	Forest
Mid-March	Spawning of smelt	Rivers
End of April	Spawning of herring, sturgeon and salmon. Waterfowl eggs.	Inland waters
May to September	Fish and shellfish. Migratory birds: wild pigeons, partridge. Rabbits, eels.	Coast and rivers
October to November	Elk (moose), beavers	Forest
December	Dog-fish or tom cod	Under river ice

Wallis and Wallis point out that Father Biard's picture was unduly bright because he did not mention the frequent famines that occurred when travel was difficult owing to rain or melting snow. The Jesuit Le Clercq stated that during such periods the Micmac survived by eating "curdled blood, scrapings of skin, old moccasins," and, on extreme occasions, one another (Bock, 1966: 4). The increasing importance of the fur trade exacerbated the cycle of feast or famine. Striving to supply the incessant demands of the European traders, the Indians decimated the game in their own territory, especially after guns were introduced in the mid-seventeenth century. They were, therefore, constantly forced to go farther afield in order to bring back pelts with which to purchase trade goods (Guillemin, 1975: 34–42).

In addition to the animals mentioned in Father Biard's list, the Mic-

[1]Wallis and Wallis, 1955: 25–26.

mac ate porcupine, muskrat, and dog meat at special feasts. Meat was either roasted over the fire or boiled, and every scrap was valued. Intestines were eaten or saved to make sausage, and blood served as a tasty gravy into which pieces of moose were dipped. During the summer the Micmac supplemented their diet with wild berries. Dried cakes of huckleberries, blueberries, and cranberries lasted through part of the winter. The Micmac made tea from twigs of yellow birch, winterberries, or from various roots. They tapped maple trees for sugar and obtained salt by evaporation from seawater. Before the coming of the French, the Micmac grew no grain and ate no bread, a fact that astonished the newcomers.

Before European weapons became available, the Micmac hunted with bows made of fir, spruce, or rock maple, strung with deer or caribou thong, and with fire-hardened, wooden arrows. In warfare they poisoned the arrows with a preparation made from bark, root, and "a bush" (Wallis and Wallis, 1955: 33), but they never hunted game with these arrows. They dug shellfish out of the sand with a stick and caught fish with wooden spears or bone fishhooks, in nets of intertwined branches, or in fish traps made of brush supported by sticks driven into the mud. Skillful seal hunters neared their prey by pretending to be one of them or by using a decoy seal in order to get close enough to use their harpoons.

Bark canoe. Bear River, Nova Scotia. 1916.   Photograph courtesy of Museum of the American Indian, Heye Foundation.

Transportation among the Micmac varied according to the season. Birchbark canoes were used at sea to hunt porpoises or seals and on the rivers for hunting fish or fowl. These flat-bottomed canoes with no keel were sailed into the wind but otherwise were paddled. On land both toboggans and sleds were employed; *taba'gan* is a Micmac word that has been incorporated into English. Square-toed snowshoes made with thongs of moose or caribou hide allowed travel over the snow.

SHELTER AND CRAFTS.   The Micmac were sheltered by small, circular birchbark wigwams, so light and portable that their covers could be carried by the women from one location to the next. Wigwams were also covered with skins, evergreen boughs, woven mats, or, in more recent times, even tar paper (Bock, 1978: 112–113). For warmth, the earth floor was covered with fir twigs topped with animal skins. Wigwams sheltered a single nuclear family, but in the summer several families sometimes shared a long, open structure.

Although conditions in that time were nowhere very sanitary, early priests mentioned a number of drawbacks to living in wigwams. The cooking fire was built in the center, so smoke constantly irritated everyone's eyes, and there was the danger of fire's destroying everything or causing burns. LeClercq stated (Wallis and Wallis, 1955: 230) that the approaches to the wigwam were filthy with excrement, feathers, chips, shreds of skin, entrails of animals and fish; that the Mimac washed their meat only superficially and never cleaned the kettle; and that their clothes were filthy and soaked with oil and grease. Furthermore, they had the habit of hunting for vermin on their bodies and eating them. In spite of its disadvantages, the wigwam remained the standard Micmac dwelling well into the nineteenth century.

For clothing, the Micmac utilized the resources around them. During the summer, a waist girdle was often the only garment for both sexes. If the sun was bright, a light jacket of deerskin served as a sunshade. In the winter, kneelength trousers and jackets or sometimes a robe instead of trousers was cut from the belly skin of a moose and worn by men. Cloaks lined with beaver skins afforded protection from the cold for both sexes. The Micmac early adopted European bed blankets as cloaks, which they decorated with beadwork and polished sea shells. Socks were made from the skin of muskrats, rabbits, or woodchucks; and leggings and moccasins, from the shanks of moose or deer. Skin and bark caps were worn after European contact. During the Wallises' second trip to the Micmac country in 1953, they found that no aboriginal style clothing remained.

The Micmac made utensils, like their clothing, from the resources around them. They fashioned rough wooden kettles for stone-boiling meat from burned-out tree trunks. Birchbark cups and cooking vessels

"Indian of the Mic-Mac Tribe" from a lithograph by Robert Petley, 1837.   Nova Scotia Museum, Halifax.

were sewn with cedar root. Baskets were made of wood splints from cedar, spruce, or juniper. Jenness (1955: 268) mentions finding fragments of clay cooking pots but is not sure whether these were made by the Micmac or some earlier tribe in Nova Scotia. Other early artifacts that have been found include flint knives, stone tomahawks, wooden hoes, bone awls, brooms made of spruce branches, quahog clamshell spoons, and cedar bark thongs. The Micmac showed no desire to continue using these things after the French had appeared and turned eagerly to European copper kettles, knives, and weapons.

Micmac artists dyed porcupine quills for decoration of clothing and jewelry. Although today birchbark boxes decorated with porcupine quills are associated with the Micmac, Wallis and Wallis noted that this craft was not aboriginal but was probably started by the Ursuline nuns in the eighteenth century in an attempt to give the Indians a source of income. Moose hair embroidery was practiced before contact with White people, as was carving in stone and wood and painting on wigwams and robes.

SOCIAL STRUCTURE.   The Micmac lacked an elaborate and formal social structure. Bands of about 200 came together only during summer gatherings, devoted to feasting and originating for any of a number of reasons: ceremonies for curing or leave taking, celebration of a boy's first hunting kill, marriages, funerals, thanksgiving for peace, or planning for war. No overreaching tribal structure existed, although the Micmac acknowledged Cape Breton Island as their "head district" and its chief as their "Grand Chief" (Bock, 1978: 110). During the fall and winter, Micmac formed small groups, usually of related families, each with its own chief or leader, who had limited power. Chiefs received their

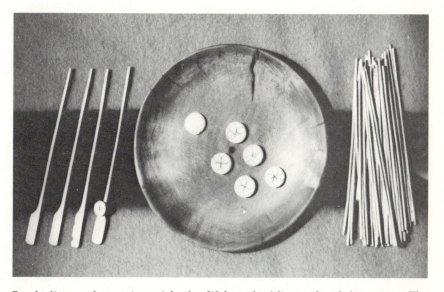

Bowl, dice, and counting sticks for *Waltes*, the Micmac bowl dice game. The game had social, religious, and even war functions (locating enemy spies). Eskasoni Reserve, Cape Breton Island, 1962.   Photographer, Jim Howard.

authority either through inheritance or by being named by the old chief. Charisma, competence, and an equitable temperment were regarded as desirable qualities in a leader. These leaders were responsible for matters such as allotting land for hunting, questioning strangers, advising people in peace, and leading them in war. Assisting the chief was the shaman or medicine man, who could predict the future and acted as an adviser. Under this system, individuals were able to exercise a good deal of independence. Bands were held together by the common need for mutual social support, formal rules of courtesy that governed individual behavior, sharing, and the recurrent summer gatherings. When a band member behaved in an antisocial or criminal manner, group consensus was as important as the chief's desire in deciding what would be done with him or her.

Within this loose structure, there were rather formalized rules for the behavior of individuals. Inside the family wigwam, each person was assigned his or her place and required to remain in it. Most wigwams had a single entrance. There is, however, a suggestion in the literature that a larger ceremonial wigwam may have had two entrances: one for hunters and another for women. Strong taboos existed. Women never stepped over a man's legs, sisters and brothers did not speak to each other, and children were taught to respect their elders and not speak to them unless spoken to first. Children, however, were loved and desired. The group as a whole felt responsibility for orphans, and the chief often placed them in the home of one of the best hunters as a part of his family.

Men were responsible for warfare, hunting, and fishing and for setting up the camp and keeping the fire going during the night. Women had a multitude of duties around the camp such as cooking, sewing, making all bark vessels, putting up and taking down wigwams and carrying them to the next location, raising the children, making the canoes, helping with fishing, and making war magic. They had control of their own possessions and were pictured in tribal legends as capable and inventive.

No distinction was made between maternal and paternal kin with respect to descent, although kin terminology did carry age and marital distinctions. There were no specific joking relationships between designated relatives. Girls were regarded as adults around the age of 16; boys, a little later. Marriages were usually arranged by the family, although seldom without the consent of those directly involved. Boys often worked and hunted for the father of their intended bride for two years before the marriage was allowed. Polygyny was practiced by most chiefs and by all others who could afford it. Although as a rule the aged were treated with great respect, on occasion those who were very ill or decrepit were abandoned in the fall when the tribe moved to the interior from the coast. This pattern appeared all over the north because life was so harsh and the requirements for survival so unyielding that the tribe simply could not include individuals who were not economically and physically self-sufficient, especially after the tribe had become involved in hunting for the fur traders.

RELIGION.   The religion of the Micmac, when it was first described, was a mixture of their aboriginal beliefs and Catholicism. They, like other northern Algonquian groups, acknowledged a supreme creator whom they identified with the sun (Bock, 1978: 117). They also sought help from the moon, wife of the sun and mother to mankind. All of the tribes of the Wabanaki Confederacy possessed a gigantic culture hero named Gluskap, who was their protector and whose behavior accounted for many geographical features of the country. Gluskap strode away when the White men came, but the Indians believed that he would come again in time of danger. Other supernatural races also existed: giants, mermen, miniature Indians, and stone Indians who lived in mountain caves.

Ordinary men and women also could possess special powers. Two separate categories existed: *ginap,* the good power, and *buoin,* which could be evil. Individuals who possessed *ginap* had great physical strength. They were believed to have the ability to drink boiling oil, make themselves invisible, travel under water, predict the future, and have unusual luck in acquiring game or, today, modern goods. *Ginap* could appear at any age in either sex. *Buoin* was equated with witchcraft and associated with vengeance. These people could injure anyone simply by thinking. Shamans were often thought to have *buoin*. Much of this belief became mixed in later years with White ideas of witchcraft, so that today these concepts exist, if at all, in a vague and nebulous form. There was also a belief in ghosts called *Skadegamute,* who could be the spirits of dead people or of people still living but about to die.

THE MICMAC WORLD.   What kind of people were these Micmac, living in a relatively small quarter of northeastern Canada prior to the sixteenth century? They were real people living in a real world, as were their descendants in later years. By modern middle-class American standards, the early Micmac led an extremely unpleasant life, in that existence was brutish, short, and filled with the unexpected. They must have realized that they had little control over much that happened to them, for most of what occurred was ultimately determined by the fact that they lived in a climatically harsh environment. As hunters and fishermen, much of their technology revolved around food production and processing. Food supplies were uncertain in location and in amount. This, in turn, meant that critical decisions had to be made constantly on the basis of insufficient information with respect to where to go and what to do. Time, by our standards, meant relatively little, but timing was everything. Proper timing was based upon an astute knowledge of their surroundings and of themselves. Although these early Micmac did not think or live as we do now, we would have benefited greatly from knowing them. For the most part, they must have been strong, dramatic personalities with an appealing zest for life, even though untimely, unpleasant death was a far closer companion for them than it is for most of us today.

Happiness was a full stomach with realistic prospects for getting more food tomorrow and the next day. The human dimensions of the world were small, with associations being limited for the most part to those in the extended family or hunting band. Great esteem and support were extended to the humanity of others. We would have regarded them generally as people who simply could not afford the neurotic obsessions and abrasive habits that some of us have. Far too much time, thought, and energy had to be expended getting food, not drowning while fishing, and not freezing to death during the long, relentless winters. They did, however, resemble us in at least one sense. Like those of Thoreau's New England, they, too, led lives of quiet desperation. Only the reasons for such desperation or stress were different, and these differences were rooted in a cultural legacy. Finally, a comparison of the early Micmac with us suggests, among other things, that the creation and maintenance of human life at any particular corner of time and space is a difficult and even miraculous process worthy, when achieved, of unlimited respect.

THE BEGINNING OF COLONIZATION.   As stated earlier, the French began colonizing Micmac lands in the 1500s, and their arrival brought many changes. The greatest of these was that they drew the Micmac into the fur trade and instigated a demand for European goods, which grew as the fur trade expanded. They also involved the Micmac in their own wars with the English and their Indian allies, mainly the Iroquois, and this, together with newly introduced diseases, decimated the Indian population. Those who survived were subject to the exhortations of the missionaries to change many of their ways. Social disorganization was the inevitable result of these pressures.

French influence gave way to English after the Treaty of Paris in 1763, but this did not improve the situation for the Micmac. In spite of a Royal Proclamation, which stated that the Indians of Canada possessed occupancy rights to all their land that they had not formally surrendered and that the government itself was responsible for enforcing these rights, the greed of new colonists and the corruption of officials worked together to violate these principles and reduce the size of the Micmac lands (Bock, 1966: 12–13).

THE PRESENT: RESERVATION AND CITY LIVING AS ONE RESIDENCE PATTERN

The following description of modern Micmac life is derived mainly from two sources: Philip Bock, *The Micmac Indians of Restigouche: History and Contemporary Description* (1966); and Jeanne Guillemin, *Urban Renegades: The Cultural Strategy of American Indians* (1975). Bock did fieldwork at the Restigouche Reserve in Canada in the 1960s, and Guillemin worked with the Micmac living in Boston, Massachusetts, and on the reserves between 1969 and 1971. Their two works give a vivid picture of how some Micmac live today and what kind of a people they are. This portrait, however, does not describe all Micmac. Those who live in the Maritimes have a predominantly Scottish-Irish population as neighbors rather than the French-Canadians who surround Restigouche, and customs differ between the two groups.

The roots of the Restigouche Micmac go well back before the eighteenth century and are closely interwoven with the consequences of European contact. As Bock (1966: 13) states:

> . . . contacts began with intermittent trading with Europeans whose main interest was fishing. The demand for European goods, which rapidly displaced many native materials, grew with the expansion of the fur trade. Involvement in imperialistic wars contributed to the depopulation of the Algonkian tribes, and this, together with the effects of disease and the efforts of the missionaries, led to large-scale social disintegration.
>
> The Restigouche Micmac were doubtless affected by all these processes; they survived into the eighteenth century as a smaller, more localized group, reintegrated around a Roman Catholic core, but still following a hunting and trapping life. The presence of great commercial salmon resources in their area may have softened the effects of the devaluation of the beaver pelts. But a new era of intensive contact was dawning, and in many ways the worst was yet to come.

The "worst," in the nineteenth century, consisted of the gradually growing influence of Euro-Canadian industrialized and urbanized existence. The Micmacs lost land to non-Indians and gradually became economically integrated into national life. A number of trends were introduced that had the net effect of severely limiting Micmac social and cultural independence.

The Twentieth Century

Important changes in the political, economic, and educational life of the Restigouche community began at the turn of the century, Bock's "Recent Period." In the political sphere, the method used to select the chief changed. Before 1898, the chief and his helpers had been elected for life through a process the Micmac called "understanding by word," which amounted to a consensus arrived at by all males over the age of 15. After this time, elections were held every three years by the majority vote of all electors over the age of 21. The economic life of the Restigouche community was greatly improved by the construction of a sawmill on Chaleur Bay in 1902. Until it burned in 1931, the sawmill was a reliable source of jobs for anyone who wanted one. The mill owners used some of the land they had leased from the tribe to build houses for White workers on the Flats nearby, and the presence of neighboring Whites may have encouraged the Indians to conform more closely to White standards of behavior.

Indian exposure to formal education began in 1903, when the Sisters of the Order of the Holy Rosary built an Indian Day School on the reserve. Academic standards were not high, and until 1920 the only things taught were the cathechism and Bible history in Micmac, but it was the beginning of a system that today demands that its students, both Indian and French Canadian, pass the national examination in order to be promoted to the next grade.

During the twentieth century, the Micmac very gradually increased their contact with White society. Between 1903 and 1921, a local Catholic priest, Father Pacifique, published *The Micmac Messenger* (Bock, 1966: 23), which ran notices for railroad employment along with church news and sermons. This drew some men outside their community. A few of the men enlisted in World War I, and others around this time worked at various jobs in lumber camps, river log drives, and wheat harvests. Most men, however, remained on the reserve, where the mill was providing steady employment until the Great Depression began and there was no work available anywhere. Families lived a marginal existence on social assistance and annuities and spent their free time playing baseball because there was nothing else to do. By this time, most hunting, fishing, and craft skills had been forgotten, so the people were unable to supplement their diet or incomes in traditional ways. In 1935 labor gangs began to travel to Aroostook County, Maine, for the potato harvest, and this custom has continued every fall to the present. The situation on the reserve began improving in 1936, when a pulpwood peeling drum opened, and ships once again visited the harbor. World War II was a turning point in that adult tribal members accepted

Father Pacifique at left. The others are Micmacs. Shubenacadie, Nova Scotia, ca. 1890–1905.   Nova Scotia Museum, Halifax.

the fact that most opportunities for economic advancement were to be found off the reserve. The horizons of the tribe had expanded permanently.

After the war, a pattern gradually emerged that is followed today. Able-bodied adults live off the reserve, working in various towns and cities in the United States and Canada; but they ideally maintain a home base on the reserve in the form of family members or close friends, who are available as a refuge or as surrogate parents for the children. This pattern has been followed not only at Restigouche, but throughout Micmac country. Wallis and Wallis stated that in 1953 the principal place of employment was the United States. Micmac were working in the factories of Hoboken, New Jersey; Boston, Massachusetts; and Connecticut; in the potato warehouses and fertilizer plants of Maine; and anywhere in New England where unskilled labor was needed. In 1968, according to Guillemin (1975: 62), one-third of the adult population was living and working in the United States at locations ranging from approximately 600 to 1,000 miles to the south of their reserve homes. Being a Micmac today usually means being a migrant for most of one's active life.

RESTIGOUCHE RESERVE. Restigouche Reserve is located in the Province of Quebec on the Bay of Chaleur. To the south is the city of Campbellton in the Province of New Brunswick. For over 100 years, ferry service connected Restigouche with Campbellton. A bridge built in 1961 now serves this purpose. The closest town to Restigouche, Cross Point near the causeway leading to the bridge, is populated mainly by French Canadians.

Within the 30 square miles of Restigouche are 150 Indian homes, some old and delapidated but many relatively new and well maintained. The Indian Affairs Branch has financed much of the new construction. Most homes are built on either side of the single, paved road, which parallels the Matapedia River. Two gravel roads run north, one to the Indian cemetery and the other to connect with a road traversing the wooded section of the reserve. The residential section is bisected by the church lot, 400 yards wide, running from the boundary of the reserve to the shore of Chaleur Bay. On this church land are a Capuchin monastery with gardens, a church building, and a cemetery; a convent of the Sisters of the Holy Rosary; a general store; a post office; and an appliance store. Also on church land on the shore of the bay are the Flats, housing units rented to about two dozen French Canadian families by the parish priest. The Indians have always resented this, as it was done without asking their permission or even considering how they might feel about it. East of the church lot is the Indian Agency area, which includes an office, two residences, a jail, and a nursing office. West of the church lot is the main residential section, as well as a number of shops and small businesses and the reserve baseball field. Also on the reserve are an integrated school serving children between the ages of six and 16 and a two-year normal school, both staffed largely by sisters from the convent.

In 1961 the population of Restigouche was 745, nearly half under the age of 16. Total enrollment at this time according to the Canadian government was around 1,100. These numbers constantly change as people move in and out, but it is safe to estimate that one-third of the nominal population is away at all times. Most of this third are adults working in cities. Enrollment figures also vary because of the Canadian law, which states that Indian women who marry non-Indians lose their band membership, as do their children.

THE MICMAC TODAY. Given the fact of the prevalence of migration, we can logically ask what it is that identifies the modern Micmac, both to themselves and to others. The Micmac no longer follow the seasonal cycle of hunting in the winter and fishing in the summer, they wear no aboriginal clothing even at ceremonies, they do not live in wigwams, they make no canoes, and few artisans weave baskets. Are they, in fact, still Micmac? Guillemin and Bock both say they are. They are Micmac because they see themselves as Micmac. The language survives and is spoken in many homes; in religion they are uniformly Roman Catholic, a religion long familiar to these Indians. But more than these things, each individual is brought up to feel loyalty to the tribe, to his or her kin, to the family. The individual moves within a tribal social network that supports maximum interaction among its members. This takes precedence over issues of freedom of choice or right to privacy. Individuals are further constrained within tribal boundaries by the prejudice of outsiders against Indians, by their own needs for the security of the familiar, and by the very real practical needs that tribal members fulfill such as help with jobs, living arrangements, and raising children. To see more clearly how this works, let us look at the family life and social organization of the Micmac today.

SOCIAL ORGANIZATION. Life for a Micmac probably begins on a reserve, for most women prefer to go home to have their babies even if

Modern Micmacs. Wigwams are of tarpaper and for temporary use. Chapel Island, Nova Scotia, 1962.   Photographer, Jim Howard.

they have been working. Details, of course, vary, but in most cases the reserves resemble in general appearance the surrounding non-Indian settlements. Houses range from tar-paper shacks of one or two rooms to relatively well-built, government-constructed frame dwellings having four or five rooms. These homes often reflect by their furnishings that they are used as centers for many individuals in the extended family. Furniture is functional and inexpensive and usually shows the scars of use. Knickknacks and decorations are minimal and are predominantly souvenirs and family snapshots. When Bock was at Restigouche, although almost all homes had electricity and television sets, only one-third had running water and only one-sixth had indoor toilets. Washing machines and electric kettles were common, but refrigerators, toasters, grills, and irons were not. Heating and cooking were still usually done by woodburning stoves. More modernization has occurred since that time.

Most Micmac children grow up as part of a large, extended family. They may remain in one household throughout their youth or live with various family members and relatives, wherever these might be, as the economic situation dictates. People remember who has given room and board to them or their children and later will reciprocate either to that individual or another member of his family (Guillemin, 1975: 84). The life of the Micmac would be much more difficult if they could not count on finding a place to stay wherever they go. Usually one or more women in a family remain on the reserve and maintain a home base for all, for the reserve is regarded as the best place for a child to grow up. There he or she need not worry about conflicts with hostile White children and can develop the physical strength and assertiveness he or she will require later to move out and earn a living. Girls as well as boys are rewarded for physically aggressive behavior and stoicism in the face of pain or frustration, although female endurance is praised more than is physical aggression.

Among the Micmac, children are loved and wanted, and many people are willing to help in their care. They are taught by example, not exhortation, to be independent, to restrain their emotions, and not to whine and cry. Seen as children, not miniature adults, they make their lives around other children, where their triumphs are real victories, not just play. Close relationships often develop among siblings and continue into adulthood.

Girls tend to remain in school longer than boys and to attend church more often and thus are in a better position to learn White values. They can then articulate these values—the importance of attending school until graduation, of going to church, of being married before having children—to the youngsters in their care. This does not mean that Micmac adolescents will adhere to these values or indeed that the women expect them to because their culture often makes it impossible for them to do so. At least, however, they are forewarned about what White standards are and are aware that they may have to make some changes with respect to comfortable habits to adjust well to city life (Guillemin, 1975: 98–100).

Economic support for a Micmac child on the reserve is variable and comes from many sources. The child's mother may choose to remain at home and care for him or her, but just as often may leave the child with her mother or another relative, return to her job in the city, and send what money she can spare from her expenses to help support the child. His or her father, whether or not he has married the mother, will try to send some money to help out. The illegitimacy rate of the Restigouche Reserve has been very close to 20 percent for 100 years (Bock, 1964: 145), but the women's gossip network almost always sees to it that a baby's father is known, and he is under social pressure to contribute to his child's welfare. The reserve itself may yield very minimal resources. Wood is free for the cutting to band members as legally defined by the Canadian government, and a few crops may be planted, berries picked, or an occasional animal shot for food, but the most important source of income is social assistance, which comes from different sources and for various purposes.

Three major outside institutions operate on the reserve at Restigouche: the church, the Indian Agency, and the school. The church, in all of the reserve communites, is Roman Catholic, although there are a few people at Restigouche who have rejected Catholicism for independent Bible study outside the framework of institutionalized Christianity. The Micmac have been Catholics since the 1600s, when the first priests arrived; there is no trace of their old religion left except a few folktales. In spite of this, the church at Restigouche is still a mission church, and the priests there question the depth of commitment of their flock. They worry about such things as the excessive drinking, the illegitimate births, the lack of financial support for the church, and the absence of real piety. In turn, the Micmac, although they firmly support Catholicism, are quite critical of the priests. They resent authoritarian criticism of their behavior, the constant requests for money, and the church's bland assumption that the large area of land given originally by the tribe is theirs to use as they wish.

The major Catholic holiday for the Micmac is St. Anne's Day on July 26. They have long regarded St. Anne as their patron saint, and the holiday is a holdover from the traditional summer gatherings of the bands. Today, however, the nature of the celebration varies among the reserves. Bock stated that at Restigouche it is mainly a moneymaking occasion for the church with almost no Indian content. On the other hand, James Howard (1965: 5–13) attended the festival on "Chapel

Chapel Island, Nova Scotia. Pan-Indian powwow, 1962.   Photographer, Jim Howard.

Island'' in Nova Scotia in 1962 and there found a number of Indian traditions still being observed. He heard Micmac music sung, and there was a powwow or Indian dance, although much of it was pan-Indian in character.

The second major outside institution on Restigouche reserve, the Indian Agency, has diminished in importance lately because the Canadian government has begun to distribute payments through the Quebec Public Assistance Act rather than through the agent. This has removed his former power to decide who gets what, and Bock reported that the agent at Restigouche mentioned that people were speaking to him who had not done so in years.

The school at Restigouche is run by the Roman Catholic church, which integrated it to serve children from surrounding French Canadian communities without informing the Indians. At present, this integration is more theoretical than real because language differences keep the children in separate classes and no extracurricular activities are provided to make it easy for Indians and French-Canadians to mingle after school hours.

The school is an important influence upon tribal members in a number of ways. Its timetable structures the family's schedule, although it fails to adapt itself to tribal economic reality every fall, when many children are removed from school to accompany their families to Maine for the potato harvest. Most adults on the reserve have only a fourth- or fifth-grade education, so a generation gap is developing between them and their better-educated offspring. The children, however, are ambivalent about the values of advanced schooling and often leave early in rebellion against the authoritarian structure, the real or imagined prejudices of the teachers, and the lack of relevance of their education to the problems of their daily life. A feeling has been developing that White prejudice against Indians combined with the poor state of the economy will undermine their interests no matter how much education they have.

WORK LIFE.   After leaving school, Micmac adolescents, both boys and girls, usually go to a city, often one in the United States, in search of wage labor. The most compelling reason for this migration is that there are very few jobs on the reserve. In addition, the city is where the action is—it is the testing ground, the recreation ground, the mating ground. Imagine a young Micmac arriving in Boston, a very large, busy, and unfamiliar city. He or she has no job, no money, no advanced education or particular job skills and is a member of a minority group against which some people are prejudiced. How does this individual survive? What assests does he or she have to keep him or her alive in the city? What will prevent this individual from running back home at the first opportunity?

The answers to all these questions are to be found in the functioning of the Micmac social network. An individual does not exist in a vacuum. He or she has probably arrived in the city with others of the tribe, for cars traveling between the reserve and the city are commonly filled with friends and relatives of the driver, picked up and dropped off along the way. The individual has a place to go offered ahead of time by his or her relative or friend. Along with bed and board comes the most valuable help of all: information about the job market. Freely shared news about job openings is essential to a Micmac's survival because he or she is willing to work at unskilled or semiskilled low-paying jobs that middle-class workers do not care to fill. Jobs like this are often short term with no union protection in case of a reduction of the labor force. In addition, the job itself may be demoralizing. Pushing a broom, washing dishes, or emptying garbage cans does not demand much personal initiative or sociability, nor does work of this type engender a sense of accomplishment because it will simply have to be done over again the next day. Not too surprisingly, the Micmac will accept this mechanization of themselves only so long before quitting, to take a trip back to the reserve or to visit friends or to look for something else that at least has the virtue of being different. The most important thing is remaining a functioning part of Micmac society, which stretches from the Canadian reserves to the various urban places to the south. This is how each person defines his or her identity and lives out his or her life along the understood confines of conventional Micmac existence. With friends to help, another job can eventually be found.

In addition to helping find jobs, Micmac society facilitates the sharing of many different kinds of goods and services. Sharing is essential to survival because given individuals alone have scant economic resources. Men are expected to be generous with their money, not to hoard it or spend it only on themselves. They may be supporting children or sending money home to a family on the reserve. If any money is left over, it is commonly spent in giving a party. Whereas White society may regard this practice as wasteful and irresponsible, to the Micmacs it is an investment in social solidarity, a way of cementing important tribal and personal ties. Furnishings for apartments are also shared among tribal members. If someone leaves the city or dies, his or her things will be given away to other Micmac. Furniture and clothing are not regarded as very important. Too many material goods tend to tie a person down, and the Micmac must remain mobile enough to change jobs and locations with ease if they are to survive. The women are more stable with respect to residence than the men, but even they must be willing to move if necessary. If a woman has chosen to keep her child with her in the city, child care is shared. She commonly has other adults living with her who will share in the care of the infant. The husband or father may help, but so may a younger sister or cousin who has just moved to the city and does not have a job yet. Mothers must often return to work whether they want to or not, because the family cannot do without the extra income.

Although they encounter difficulties, the Micmac see the city also as a source of adventure and excitement. They do not come with the idea of putting down roots or establishing a home for all their working days. The tribal tradition of constantly wandering in search of the best place to live at that time is still maintained. Traveling is seen to be good in itself. Micmac moving to the South End of Boston will find many people there besides friends and relatives. The area also houses a large population of Blacks and Puerto Ricans; a number of Chinese; small groups of Armenians, Syrians, and Greeks; some gypsies; and a few older Irish-Americans who have remained in their old homes instead of moving out to the suburbs. Among this variety of people, the young

Micmac feel the need to test themselves, to define who they are to themselves and others. The more settled tribal members accept the fact that the young men and women must take risks for the tribe to benefit from the most up-to-date information on the ways of the alien society. The risks are very real. Young men can be badly hurt in bar fights with aggressive Blacks or Puerto Ricans. Girls can become pregnant and lack the support of a male to serve as husband and father. Boys can drink too much and be picked up by the police. In 1970 a 17-year-old Micmac youth was found stabbed to death in the Boston railroad yard. The transportation network poses danger, consisting as it does of old cars driven at high speeds over long distances—perhaps by someone who has been drinking. Taking risks, however, is seen as an integral part of being a Micmac.

Because of their interactions on many levels, the young Micmac coming from the reserves are gradually absorbed into networks of their peers. Group experiences serve to define them and to identify them to others. These peer networks are split along sexual lines. Men drink together, freely share information about jobs, and are extremely mobile when it comes to changing jobs or locations. Women are more conservative. They tend to share job information only with close friends or relatives, and two women will often try to work at the same place as well as share an apartment. More often than do men, they tend to get discouraged with urban life and return to the reserve. Although they take risks through sexual competition, they also share sexual information with their peers throughout life. Married men continue to insist on their right to nights out with other men, and women always remain closest emotionally and socially to other women.

In a society so divided along sexual lines, what significance does formal marriage have? Among young adult Micmac men and women, the role of such a union is often minor. Women in their early twenties relish their freedom and mobility as much as the men do and resist being tied down. If an illegitimate child is born, it is accepted into the tribal network and identified as a part of both the mother's and father's lines. A mother will insist that the unmarried father introduce the baby to his side of the family and continue taking the child to visit as he grows older because the child should become familiar with his or her sources of social support as soon as possible. For the young Micmac, such knowledge means the difference between survival and extinction. This introduction is more important than financial support, which the woman realizes can often be impossible to provide. A child very often will be reared by his or her grandmother or other relatives on the reserve, so that the child's mother may be free to produce cash income to support him or her and help those who are caring for him or her. As a woman moves into her mid-twenties and beyond, however, she feels more pressure to conform to what her people expect of her: a more stable residence and a formal social identification as a wife. Then she may marry the man she is living with who has fathered her youngest child. Neither husband nor wife, however, necessarily sees this relationship as permanent. Men owe loyalty and support to their mother and sisters, so that they often do not have the economic means to support a wife and family indefinitely.

The most important single unit among the Micmac is the tribal network rather than the nuclear or extended family because the tribe can insist on conformity to patterns of behavior to a far greater degree than other units. Today, as in the past, the Micmac want to associate mainly with other Micmac. Pan-Indian activities hold little interest for them. Throughout her life, a woman will probably have a deeper relationship with her sisters, female relatives, and girlfriends then she will with any man, whereas a man will be far more protective of his sisters than of his sexual partner.

Guillemin mentioned two exceptions in the Boston area to this pattern of relationships between the sexes. The first occurs when a Micmac man or woman marries a non-Micmac. The Micmac, in general, frown on these marriages because often the result is to remove an active contributing adult from the tribal network. This is especially true for a woman, who, according to Canadian law, loses her tribal citizenship if she marries outside her tribe. The other discrepancy from the usual pattern is evidenced by those few Micmac families who have moved out of the South End to one of the Boston suburbs such as Dorchester, Chelsea, Charlestown, or Somerville. They, too, tend to ignore their Micmac relatives and friends. With their new responsibilities and expenses, they can no longer afford their former openhanded generosity. The only way a Micmac family can afford this kind of life-style is for the husband to have a more or less permanent job, because the practice of avoiding other Micmac implies the loss of important information concerning employment (Guillemin, 1975: 255–257).

The life led by the Micmac in the city is not easy. Although the tribe has always had high mobility, in the past it was more a matter of seasonal shifting to keep up with the best food resources. Now they, along with other marginal groups, such as Blacks and Puerto Ricans, must be highly mobile in order to be employed. As unskilled jobs are usually of limited duration, the Micmac must attempt to work effectively at one job while keeping their eyes open for another. As they do this, they know that their working careers will consist of lengthy series of abrupt and often unpredictable job changes, with many dislocations often accompanied by residential shifts and emotional distress. For most Micmac, this prospect is not an appealing one.

The greater American society finds economically unskilled people expendable. One individual can always be replaced by another because neither has the skills that require extensive vocational training. Our minorities are excluded both socially and politically from full participation in urban life. When help is needed, they must apply to bureaucrats who see them as problems rather than people and who try to fit them into convenient patient or client roles. Because of this, most Micmac want to avoid the social welfare agencies of Boston, preferring, if possible, to return to the reserve when their money runs out or their health fails. Some of the most unfortunate Micmac seen in Boston are those who are too old or too sick to keep up with the fast-paced network of social interaction and job hunting. Out of necessity, they have surrendered themselves to the support of public welfare, all too often with unfortunate results. This can happen quite easily, because, although the Micmac do feel responsibility for caring for their old people, children are always given higher priority because they represent the future (Guillemin, 1975: 249).

The Micmac, along with Indians from other tribes, are gradually getting some political power in Boston through the Boston Indian Council, formed to give a political voice to the Indians living in the city. This organization suffered originally from too much help by people trying to force middle-class standards upon the Indians, but the Indians now represent themselves in their own way. The Boston Indian Council also exists under a handicap characteristic of many Indian organizations. No one leader can retain an effective following for any length of time. This is so because the Indians are convinced that power corrupts and that a single person cannot represent the ideas of all for long without favoring some at the expense of others. The majority of Indians believe that a leader may also lose touch with the people he is supposed to be serving by trying too hard to get along with the White majority. The difficulties involved in leadership in the United States and the Canadian reserves appear to be similar. On the reserve, the chief must stand for election every three years and almost always finds himself voted out at the end of this time. The Indians view this situation as desirable. The general public, however, interprets this behavior as symptomatic of community factionalism and faulty management. Indians, the Canadians conclude, do not know their own minds nor are they capable of long-term, effective community action. To the Indians, though, real democracy and the chance of every individual to voice his or her own opinions are more important than the approval of outsiders. Being together means more than the results of political manipulation. They accordingly accept the consequences of disapproval, which, in practice, amounts to a comprehensive form of alienation from the major social, economic, and political currents of the larger society (Guillemin, 1975: 262–266).

CONCLUSION

In conclusion, the Micmac are a people whose past has prepared them well for the present and, probably, the future. In the past, their movements were largely confined to a relatively inhospitable area of the country because of surrounding and hostile native peoples stronger than themselves who inhabited the more desirable places. In the present, the Micmac have only a limited ability to benefit from the many advantages of a White-dominated industrial society because they lack the motivation, vocational skills, and access to political power that are necessary if the primary benefits of modern life are to be realized. The role of prejudice in Indian subordination is also prominent. The Micmac maintain a way of life, however, that allows them to remain Micmac and yet exchange unskilled and semiskilled labor for the low intermittent wages that will permit them to survive remote from the major channels of contemporary life. The Micmac travel or migrate, and, consequently, they remain Micmac. Their pattern of migration is an impressive accomplishment by any standard, because it makes possible a consistent, meaningful way of life under difficult conditions. Despite the great distances involved in movement, the Micmac live in a world of kinfolk and Micmac friends. They behave like Micmac because the rewards of conformity to the Indian way of life far outweigh the penalties.

REFERENCES

Bailey, Alfred G. *The Conflict of European and Eastern Algonkian Cultures, 1504–1700.* Toronto: University of Toronto Press, 1969. (First published 1937.)

Bock, Philip K. Patterns of Illegitimacy on a Canadian Indian Reserve: 1860–1960. *Journal of Marriage and the Family 26*, 142–148, May 1964.

———. *Bulletin 213. The Micmac Indians of Restigouche: History and Contemporary Description.* Ottawa: National Museum of Canada, 1966.

———. Micmac. In Bruce O. Trigger, ed., *Handbook of North American Indians. Vol. 15. Northeast.* Washington, D.C.: Smithsonian Institution, 1978, pp. 109–122.

Canada. *The National Atlas of Canada* (4th ed.) Ottawa: Surveys and Mapping Branch, Department of Energy, Mines and Resources, 1973.

Charlevoix, Pierre. *History and General Description of New France,* Vol. 1. London: Frances Edwards, 1902. (First published 1743.)

Guillemin, Jeanne. *Urban Renegades: The Cultural Strategy of American Indians.* New York: Columbia University Press, 1975.

Hoffman, Bernard G. "Historical Ethnography of the Micmac of the Sixteenth and Seventeenth Centuries." Unpublished Ph.D. dissertation, University of California, Berkeley, 1955.

Howard, James. The St. Anne's Day Celebration of the Micmac Indians, 1962. *Museum News 26*, 5-13. March–April 1965. South Dakota Museum.

Jenness, Diamond, Indians of Canada. *Bulletin 65, Anthropological Series No. 15* (3d ed.). Ottawa: National Museum of Canada, 1955.

MacDonald, George F. *Debert—A Palaeo-Indian Site in Central Nova Scotia.* Ottawa: National Museum of Canada, Anthropology Papers No. 16, 1968.

Maillard, Anthony. *An Account of the Customs and Manners of the Micmakis and Maricheets Savage Nations.* London: S. Hooper and A. Morley, 1758.

Martin, Calvin. The Four Lives of a Micmac Copper Pot. *Ethnohistory 22,* 111–133, Spring 1975.

The Micmac News. Nova Scotia Micmac Aboriginal Rights Position Paper. Vol. 5, No. 12A, December 1976. Sydney, Cape Breton, Nova Scotia.

Mooney, James. The Aboriginal Population of America North of Mexico. *Smithsonian Miscellaneous Collection 80, No. 7,* 1928.

Swanton, John R. The Indian Tribes of North America. *Bulletin 145, Bureau of American Ethnology, Smithsonian Institution.* Washington, D.C.: Government Printing Office, 1953.

Tawow 5:2 (1976).

Thwaites, Rueben Gold. ed. *The Jesuit Relations and Allied Documents.* Cleveland: The Burrows Brothers Company, 1896.

Wallis, Wilson D., and Ruth S. Wallis. *The Micmac Indians of Eastern Canada.* Minneapolis: University of Minnesota Press, 1955.

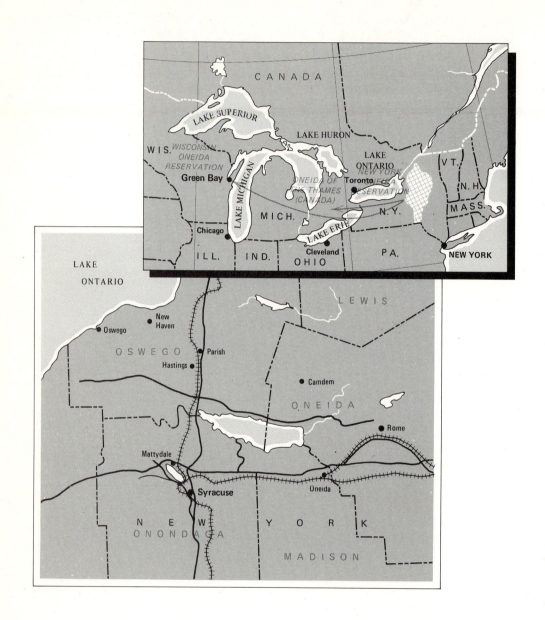

CHAPTER 3

THE ONEIDA
An Iroquois People

Time and its ally, Dark Disarmament,
Have compassed me about,
Have massed their armies, and on battle bent
My forces put to route;
But though I fight alone, and fall and die,
Talk terms of Peace? Not I.

E. Pauline Johnson, Mohawk, *Flint and Feather*

Growing up in a log house without plumbing
hasn't killed anyone yet, nor has joining the Air
Force right after high school. But who needs it?

Loretta Metuxen, Wisconsin Oneida

THE LEAGUE OF THE IROQUOIS

Today the Oneida Indians are divided among three locations: Wisconsin near Green Bay; Ontario, Canada; and New York State. In historic times, however, they were part of the powerful League of the Iroquois in New York State. In spite of their dispersal and the fact that most of their land has been taken from them over the years, the Oneida as a people are growing in population and keenly aware of their identity as Oneida. Their story is a fascinating one.

Like the Micmac, the Iroquois belonged to a part of North America generally known as the Eastern Woodlands. It is, however, difficult to imagine two groups who were more different. Although the Micmac were ready enough to make war, they never became a real power. Living on the northern periphery of the woodlands in a climate unsuitable for agriculture, they were forced to spend so much time and energy on hunting and gathering in order to stay alive that they had little left over for warfare. After contact, the Micmac gave their loyalty to the French, with whom they remained allied throughout the struggle for land with the English. The Iroquois, on the other hand, were warlike, very powerful, and excellent agriculturists who occupied territory more suitable for farming. After contact, the Iroquois formed varied alliances with the Dutch, French, and English. Each tribe within the League acted according to what it conceived to be its best advantage, and at no time did all the members of the League fight as a unit against a common enemy.

According to legend, the League of the Iroquois was formed by the Huron Dekanawidah with the help of Hiawatha, a Mohawk who had originally been an Onondaga and who had become disillusioned with his people and turned to cannabalism. Dekanawidah was distressed because the five nations wasted so much effort fighting among themselves when they were threatened by the Huron, then an aggressive rival. He persuaded Hiawatha to help him create an alliance among the five tribes in order to end intertribal war and promote peace and harmony. The time is variously estimated from A.D. 1390 to A.D. 1600, but most authorities place the event before European contact (Cork, 1962: 31). The League can be pictured as an extended longhouse spreading across New York State. At the Eastern Door on the Hudson River were the Mohawks or the People of the Flint. As they had organized the League, they were known as the Elder Brother. To their west were the Oneidas, or People of the Standing Stone. Then came the Onondagas, or People of the Mountains, who were the Keepers of the Sacred Fire and whose longhouse was the center of League government. West of the Onondagas were the Cayugas, the Great Pipe People, and finally the Senecas, or People of the Great Hill, who were Keepers of the West-

Milwaukee Public Museum.

ern Door. In 1722 these five groups were joined by the Tuscarora, who were driven from their home in the Carolinas by incoming White settlers, and their coming formed the Six Nations.

The League was built on certain moral principles, including the love of peace, the sentiment of human brotherhood, the respect for law, and the reverence for ancestral greatness. Dealing only with intertribal, external matters, it seldom meddled in the internal affairs of its members. It was held together through a formal council composed of 50 chiefs *(sachems)*, nine each from the Mohawks and Oneidas, 14 from the Onondagas, ten from the Cayugas, and eight from the Senecas. As each tribe always voted as a unit, this discrepancy in numbers was unimportant. When the Tuscaroras joined the League, their chiefs were not granted seats on the Council but had to express their wishes through the Oneidas who had sponsored them.

Meetings of the League were open to all Iroquois, both men and women. Those wishing to express an opinion did so through the sachem or chief representing them except for Pine Tree Chiefs, who spoke for themselves. Pine Tree Chiefs were men of special honor derived from Dekanawidah, the first one. Their office was appointive and could not be passed on through inheritance. The central focus of all Iroquois deliberations was the art of debate, which lasted until unanimity had been reached or was clearly seen to be impossible.

It is difficult to describe succinctly the nature of the League in the brief space available here because it was different things at different times to different people. As stated in legend, the League did serve the function of keeping peace between its members because on occasion it could provide common solutions to common problems when such problems centered around satisfactory commercial and political relations with non-Iroquois interests. If common solutions were to be found, internal cooperation or peace must exist. The League was firmly rooted in Iroquois social organization, particularly in its clan and tribal aspects. A rather complex relationship existed between clan, tribe, and League interests that took the form of an elaborate social network of mutual rights and obligations. The era of the League's greatest effectiveness and influence probably ranged from some time prior to White contact to the first quarter of the eighteenth century. The decline of the League coincided with the decline of the fortunes of all Iroquois people, which ultimately stemmed from the fact that many conflicts between European interests were resolved in part in North America. On a more specific and immediate level, the League and the Iroquois people could not for long surmount the military and political might of European governments when both were coupled with the insatiable greed and land hunger of European colonists. The development of reservations and reserves plus a host of other events occurring in the nineteenth century further dissipated the influence of the League. At present the League assumes most tangible form in the Condolence Council or Ceremony. This ceremony is a great convocation for condoling deceased chiefs of the League and raising up their successors. In short, the League has become a burial society with strong implications of the social fabric of life on a number of Iroquois reservations in New York and a number of reserves in Canada. Its significance for those of the Wisconsin Oneida community is far less.

THE IROQUOIS AS A PEOPLE

The Iroquois as a distinct people first came to the attention of Europeans about the middle of the sixteenth century. For some time a number of archaeologists argued that Iroquois life developed in place, in northeastern North America. The prevailing theory now, however, is that the culture is the result of diverse influences diffusing from all points of the compass but particularly from southeastern portions of the United States. A strong support for this theory of southeastern origin is the fact that the Iroquoian language family includes the Cherokee and Tuscarora, tribes of the southeast. Iroquoian also has affinities with Siouan, and some Siouan-speaking groups are known to have moved from the southeast to the Plains. The Huron were also an Iroquoian-speaking group, but most of the Eastern Woodland tribes, including the Micmac, spoke Algonquian. The move of the Iroquois to their present location took place very long ago, for archaeologists have traced their culture back 5,000 years in New York.

From the beginning of contact, the Iroquois were embroiled in European political affairs. Such confrontations usually worked to their disadvantage. The French entered the St. Lawrence River system in 1534, when Jaques Cartier began his explorations. They contacted the Algonquians, Hurons, and Montagnais. Alliances with these groups meant war with the Iroquois. During the next 200 years, the various Iroquois groups were used by the Dutch, French, British, and American colonists as political pawns. The Indians acquired an acquaintance with Christianity, some exposure to formal European education, and an intimate association with intoxicants. Familiarity on all three fronts was to be extended in the coming years, but not at the expense of a strong Iroquois identity.

Population estimates for the early historic periods have varied widely. James Mooney estimated 5,000 people in 1600. Fenton gives an estimate between 4,500 and 15,000 for this time (1971: 135). In 1904 the Six Nations numbered at least 16,000, including thousands of people with mixed blood. Today the total Iroquois population is estimated at 20,000. Population distribution has become both complex and varied. There are Cayugas and Senecas in Oklahoma, Senecas in Pennsylvania, Oneidas in Wisconsin, and representatives of all groups in New York and Canada. It is likely that there are Iroquois residents in most of the major cities of North America.

HISTORICAL BACKGROUND

In the first years of European contact after 1600, the Oneidas were located in central New York State around Lake Oneida. Their land was heavily forested, mostly with hardwoods, and very fertile. The Jesuit priest Bruyas found apple, plum, chestnut, and walnut trees growing in abundance as well as grape vines, mulberries, and strawberries (Campisi, 1974: 29). Fish and game were abundant, and the people cultivated large supplies of corn, beans, and squash, At this time the Oneidas lived in a single village, which was moved about every 30 years when the agricultural fields became exhausted. The first authenticated report of the Oneida village was made in 1634 by a Dutch journalist. He found it situated on a very high hill surrounded by two rows of palisades broken by gates at the east and west sides. Sixty-six houses were located within the palisades, each displaying the clan sign of its owner. The Oneida clans, like the Mohawk, were Bear, Wolf, and Turtle. The other Iroquois tribes had these clans as well as Deer, Eel, Beaver, Ball, Snipe, and Hawk. Kinship was assumed between all members of the same clan regardless of tribe, so these clans provided an important set of bonds within the confederacy.

Residential Life-Style

All Iroquoian speakers lived in a similar fashion. Their homes were rectangular longhouses grouped into villages protected by palisades. Villages varied in size from several hundred people to over 3,000 and were permanently used throughout the year. High, level land near a stream or lake was a popular village location. Longhouses from 30 to 200 feet long and 15 to 25 feet wide were constructed of wood, roofed with a gable framework of poles, and covered with strips of elm bark. The Iroquois lived too far south to use the more suitable birchbark favored by Algonquian groups. Each longhouse was shared by an extended family group related through the female line. Each nuclear family occupied its own compartment, and these compartments were separated by a center aisle down which fireplaces were built. This aisle served also as the social center where children played and adults relaxed on mats of reeds or husks and visited. Sleeping compartments on each side were private territory for the family and curtained with skins at night.

Women were of vital importance in the economic structure of the Iroquois. They held the garden plots and tools in common and were in charge of all horticulture and wild plant gathering. Because all the women in one longhouse were related, the married men were the outsiders. Sons were expected to leave their mother's longhouse upon marriage whereas daughters remained. In cases of conflict, longhouse policies were dominated by the oldest female residents. Women also controlled the distribution of property. Clan mothers were responsible for nominating sachems to represent the tribe at the Onondaga Fireplace, where the Council met; and if the sachem did not perform properly, his clan mother could recommend his removal. Thus although Iroquois women did not have a direct voice in the deliberations of the Council, their influence was very important.

Campisi (1974: 32–34) noted a number of shifts in early Oneida residence. Forty-three years after the visit of the Dutch journalist, the village had been moved to a new location. This settlement was destroyed in 1696 by Vandrevil, a Frenchman under the command of Frontenac. The Oneidas continued to reside in a single village until 1746, when a second one was built. After this time, the towns were not palisaded, and longhouses began to disappear, being replaced by nuclear family cabins. Campisi estimated that the Oneida population never exceeded 1,000 before the nineteenth century and probably varied between 500 and 700 during the 1600s, when both war and disease were taking a severe toll. As the importance of the fur trade grew, war became the most important factor in the lives of all the Iroquois and was responsible for much intermingling among the tribes of the area. The *Jesuit Relations* of 1646 mentioned that the Oneidas were being repopulated by the Mohawks because so many men had been killed in battle with the upper Algonquians, and Bruyas in 1668 said that two-thirds of the Oneida villagers were Algonquians and Hurons who had been adopted by the women to replace slain warriors (*Oneida Indian Reservation*, 1973:4). Adopted captives were undoubtedly eager to fit into their new society because the alternative was death by unspeakably painful torture. The women, therefore, were responsible for much of the cultural continuity of the tribe, for they made the decision either to kill a captive or to adopt him.

Food and Other Needs

Subsistence was a combination of farming, gathering wild plants, and hunting. Although all the Iroquois originally depended, much as the Micmac did, on fishing, gathering wild plants, and hunting for survival, the historic period saw their increasing dependence on the more stable cultivation of maize, beans, and squash. The cultivation of maize was accompanied by a series of ceremonials, the best known of which was the Green Corn Dance celebrating the beginning of the season of plenty. Agricultural ceremonies, usually of four days' duration, were also held for maple syrup, planting of crops, wild strawberries, green beans, and harvest. To supplement the vegetable diet, men netted passenger pigeons and water fowl in the spring and hunted deer in the fall as well as many smaller animals. They used the bow and arrow, spear, snare, and deadfall to take game. Fish were abundant in the New York lakes and streams and were an important part of the diet. Before the coming of the Europeans, food was grilled over flame, boiled in clay pots with rounded bases, or baked in bark containers using hot stones. The Iroquois, however, eagerly adopted kettles of copper, brass, and iron when they were available.

Originally, the Iroquois dressed in furs and cured skins, but these were replaced very early by English and French broadcloth, although buckskin remained in use for hunting and working until the nineteenth century. By the latter part of the eighteenth century, both silk and velvet were used to decorate the broadcloth as well as native materials such as porcupine quills, beads, and fringe. Dramatic clothing styles must have been important to these people.

Trade was crucial to the Iroquois, and the men carried on an active trade cycle first with other tribes and then with the incoming Whites. Principal trade items were furs, corn, articles of adornment, and *wampum,* or strings of trade beads and polished shells manufactured by tribes who lived along the seacoast. Furs, of course, became the major trade commodity, and much of the history of the Iroquois is, in a sense, the history of the fur trade.

In addition to hunting, warfare, and trade, the men had the responsibility for doing the heavy work of clearing the land for planting, cutting firewood, and making weapons, boats, snowshoes, and containers of elm bark for storage. They built and maintained the longhouses and protected the stockades. They often left the village for long periods to roam the forests, but Iroquois society, where women played such an important role, allowed them to do this without suffering any disruption.

Oneida Kinship

An entire volume has been written on the Oneida kinship system (Basehart, 1952), which closely resembled those of other Iroquois groups. Briefly, the basic unit of Oneida society was the matrilineage made up of a matron, her sons and daughters, and all descendants along the female line. These ties to the mother remained strong throughout life for sons as well as daughters, although sons were also influenced by their fathers, maternal uncles, and their peers after adolescence. Both men and women took their clan designation from their mother, and marriage within one's own clan was forbidden. A man's children, therefore, were never members of his clan, and his strongest obligations remained with his mother's rather than his wife's family. This arrangement tended to make Iroquois marriages rather brittle, and divorce was easy to obtain. Maternal uncles were very important, commanding authority over their sisters' children second only to her own. Younger siblings were expected to show respect for older ones who, in turn, were responsible for their care and protection. Grandparents had an intimate and affectionate relationship with their grandchildren. Although the most significant ties were with the mother's line, two important obligations existed toward the father's family. The first was the requirement that upon death the opposite side of the family was responsible for the Condolence Ceremony. The second was that the father's sisters had the right to require their nephews to take to the warpath to avenge the death of a family member or provide a captive for adoption. The paternal aunt could also forbid her nephew to go to war (Campisi, 1974: 40–41).

Ceremonial Life

Iroquois ceremonial life was very complex, dramatic, and colorful. Ritual cleansing for all community members was observed at a New Year's ceremony held in midwinter. Religious belief may have centered around *orenda*, an invisible power that flowed through all nature and could be drawn upon in dreams. The Iroquois also recognized a number of animal spirits and supernatural beings, one of whom was called He Who Holds the Sky. European missionaries were able to transform the idea of this deity to their own God, but to the Iroquois he was one among many. A major concern of the Iroquois was bodily health and well-being. Illness could be caused through natural calamity, witchcraft, or the mind of an individual, all three causes being derived from the machinations of evildoers or the failure to heed the supernatural spirits or the spirits of the dead. Dreams and soothsayers were both important in divining the cause of an illness and in proposing the proper remedy. Indeed, dreams were so important that an individual would go to great lengths to fulfill his dream symbolically lest it become a terrible reality. Some Iroquois even asked their friends to torture them because they had dreamed about being tortured and were convinced that an enemy would do this unless they took steps to prevent it.

One well-known Iroquois organization was the False Face Society, a curing group whose heavy wooden masks can be seen in many museums. A man became a member of the False Face Society by dreaming he had joined. He then went to the Keeper of the False Faces, the single female member, who directed him to carve his own mask from a living tree. Anyone who was ill also went to the Keeper, who then sent out the masked dancers, shaking their turtle shell or elm bark rattles and sprinkling ashes to effect a cure. The False Face Society also performed ceremonies in spring and fall to frighten evil spirits from the village. The Huskface Society, another curing group, made their masks from braided and sewn cornhusks to represent harvest spirits. They danced at the midwinter and green corn festivals and procured success in hunting. Shamans existed among the Iroquois and were appealed to

Some False Face masks, 1874–1910.   Photograph courtesy of Museum of the American Indian, Heye Foundation.

if all else had failed, but these priests with their ability to use magic were less important here than in tribes without organized curing societies.

The preceding section has described, in general, the way in which all Iroquois peoples lived. What follows is a more specific look at what happened to the Oneidas in the seventeenth and eighteenth centuries.

The information in the rest of this chapter is taken from Jack Campisi's 1974 monograph, *Ethnic Identity and Boundary Maintenance in Three Oneida Communities*.

The Fur Trade

Like all the Iroquois, the Oneidas were engaged in the fur trade for the Whites after the beginning of the seventeenth century. By 1640, however, the beaver supply of the eastern Iroquois was becoming insufficient to meet demand, and the Indians, by then heavily dependent on trade goods, faced a crisis. By 1650 two systems existed to supply the European demand for beaver, one composed of the Algonquians, Hurons, and French, and the other of the Iroquois and Dutch-English. In order to gain control of the supply, the Iroquois went to war, and in the next 50 years dispersed or killed off large numbers of the Hurons, Neutrals, Petuns, Potawatomis, Ottawas, Chippewas, and Susquehannahs. In this process, they extended their influence all the way west to the shores of Lake Michigan and south through Pennsylvania. Warfare began to change the political workings of the Iroquois system. Young men under the leadership of Pine Tree Chiefs became more powerful by proving themselves through war. The traditional chiefs or sachems usually attempted to restrain their young men from battle, but they lacked any authority except persuasion to make sure that their wishes were followed. It was because of these hotheaded young men that the League was unable to act as a unit in battle even when their leadership might want to do so.

In 1664 the English defeated the Dutch, taking control of the colony of New Amsterdam and renaming it New York. The Iroquois recognized the transfer of power through the Covenant Chain, which bound them to the British cause until the time of the American Revolution.

Period of Increased Warfare and the Consequences

In the first half of the eighteenth century, a change occurred. The demand for furs decreased and land for settlement became the prime objective of the Whites. This demand was the most intense upon the Mohawks and Oneidas who lived farthest to the east. As the land was gradually cleared, the game supply upon which the Indians depended for food decreased. Throughout this period warfare continued, and the young warriors became increasingly resistant to control. The Oneidas raided as far south as Virginia and Maryland in spite of the opposition of their sachems. Through these power struggles within each tribe, the League itself grew weaker, being replaced by the local village as the center of power. At Oneida, two factions grew up: a chief's faction, deriving power from the clan mothers and tradition, and a warrior faction, holding power through their military accomplishments. Although these warriors had enough power to ignore the wishes of their elders, they lacked a system of beliefs that would validate their taking control over the tribe. In 1766 this lack was supplied from an unexpected source. Samuel Kirkland, a Protestant missionary who adhered to the fundamentalist teachings of Jonathan Edwards, came to exhort the Oneidas to repent and accept Jesus Christ in order to be saved. Kirkland's teachings ran counter to the traditional Iroquois beliefs, but it was no accident that they were eagerly seized by the warrior group. When they accepted baptism and the teachings of Kirkland, they were forced to renounce traditional beliefs, and this meant that the sachems no longer had the moral authority to control them. No other authority had ever existed, and the sachems were forced to yield to the demands of the warriors in order to retain unity within the group.

During the French and Indian Wars of the 1760s, the Oneidas attempted to remain neutral, but both the French and British solicited their services, promising retaliation if they did not enlist. Reluctantly, the Oneidas decided to support the British cause and suffered the consequent social disruption. In a tribe that had engaged in a war not of their own making; was suffering from repeated famines; and was racked by internal dissentions marked by increased alcoholism, factional disputes, and crime, Kirkland had a fertile field. He soon became much more than a preacher. He settled family quarrels, treated illness, and succored the needy from his own small resources. Increasingly, the Oneidas followed him and in doing so became alienated from their Iroquois brothers, most of whom were pro-British and pro-Anglican under the leadership of Sir William Johnson, Indian agent and good friend to the Mohawks. As the American Revolution approached, the League of the Iroquois tried in vain to attain unity through debate , but long discussions failed to produce any consensus. In 1777 the council fires at Onondaga were extinguished, and each tribe was free to support whatever side it wished in the conflict. Johnson had died before the start of the war, but his son, together with Joseph Brandt and his sister Molly, a Mohawk woman who had lived as Johnson's wife and borne him six children, led a large group of Mohawks to Canada to support the British cause. Many of the other tribes struggled to remain neutral, but again were unable to do so. The New York frontier became the scene of raids and counterraids, killings, and burning of villages.

Throughout this time, the Oneidas and their allies the Tuscaroras supported the American cause, repeatedly drawing upon their meager resources to supply Washington's army. They suffered heavily for this support. Oneida villages were burned, their fields destroyed, and the people scattered from Niagara to Schenectady. Their social system was disrupted, they were subject to repeated famines, and the other Iroquois tribes blamed them for the dissolution of the League and turned their backs upon them. Alcoholism, factionalism, murder, and suicide increased as the Oneida tried to adjust to a new era in which their hunting territory was gone for good, and warfare and raiding were over. Farming had always been women's work among them, and the proud Oneida men were reluctant to take up a hoe. When they returned to their old territory at Lake Oneida after the war, these Indians settled in five different villages, each having a council, and these councils could not agree with each other. Life would never be the same for the Oneidas again.

CHANGE AND DISPERSAL

The Handsome Lake religion or Longhouse Movement and the loss of lands had a profound effect on all Iroquois people, including the Oneidas. The Iroquois loss of lands had far less salutary benefits than did the new religion, but both events influenced the lives of nineteenth-century and present-day Iroquois.

The Longhouse Movement

The Longhouse Movement was and is of vital importance both as a religious practice and a nativistic reaction against White domination. Handsome Lake was a Seneca Indian who lived at the community on the Allegheny River from 1735 to 1815. He died at the Onondaga Reservation that same year. This group of Senecas had been strongly influenced by Quaker teachings, which stressed looking within oneself to see what was good and what was bad. Handsome Lake's half brother Cornplanter was very active in this movement, but Handsome Lake himself was rather a wastrel, given to too much drinking and wild living. In June of 1799, he became very ill and fell into a coma at his brother's house. While in this state, he had a series of visions in which the Creator appeared to him giving him some rules whereby the people were supposed to live. When he had recovered, Handsome Lake gave his people the Good Message, which is still recited in the Longhouses every other year. This Handsome Lake Code first of all outlawed liquor because it was ruining the councils of the Iroquois and helping to destroy family life. It then went on to enjoin children to obey their parents and parents to speak kindly to their children and never punish them unjustly. Rules were given to regulate all family relationships. Husbands and wives were to be faithful to each other, but if the man strayed, his wife was encouraged to take him back as if no trouble had occurred. Men were not to boast, and women were to extend hospitality to all visitors and offer them food. Handsome Lake firmly believed that Indians should not live as White men, and he set out some rules to ensure that they did not. He opposed sending the children to White men's schools and told his people that the only White customs they should adopt were growing cattle and building warm, comfortable homes. He also decreed that Iroquois witches should be killed, a practice that White authorities found difficult to understand and impossible to accept (Wilson, 1966: 74–88). The followers of Handsome Lake are not Christians although some Christian teachings such as a belief in heaven and hell have been incorporated. Although only a minority of Iroquois people subscribe to its teachings, it has remained important through the years because it is a repository for Iroquois traditional beliefs and language. Although Longhouse people cannot shun White society to the degree that Handsome Lake suggested— they could not make a living if they did—they do stress the importance of Iroquois ways and beliefs and keep alive the idea of the once great Iroquois Nation, which bowed its head to no man.

The Fate of the Oneida Lands

At first, at the time of the American Revolution, it seemed that both the new United States government and the state of New York recognized the part that the Oneidas had played in the war. Article Two of the federal Treaty of Fort Stanwix negotiated in 1784 read, "The Oneida and Tuscarora Nation shall be secured in the Possession of the Lands on which they are settled" (Hough, 1861: 64 quoted in Campisi, 1974: 88). This guarantee covered nearly six million acres and was reaffirmed in treaties signed in 1789 and 1794. In order to protect the Indian lands, Congress passed the Indian Non-Intercourse Act in 1790, giving to the national government the exclusive right to negotiate with Indian tribes. No state or individual had the right to buy any Indian land without federal approval. In addition, by the treaty of 1794, the government granted the Oneidas $5,000 in compensation for damages they had suffered in the war plus a perpetual annuity of $4,500. It promised to build a gristmill, a church, and a sawmill to help the Oneidas adjust to a new way of life. New York, too, prohibited in its constitution any purchase of Indian lands by individuals without legislative approval and assured the Oneidas that the state had no claim upon their lands. Unfortunately, this same legislature was dominated by the land-hungry aristocracy of the Hudson Valley, and all the promises soon became meaningless. As early as 1785, the Oneidas sold to the state of New York 300,000 acres for $11,500. Three years later nearly five million acres were sold for $15,510, leaving the Oneidas only 245,000 acres in Madison and Oneida counties. Even this was slowly sold in small pieces over the years. By 1846 the Oneida lands in New York were gone. (Those interested in the list of all 31 treaties with the Oneidas should consult Campisi, 1974: 500–503.)

How could this happen to a people apparently so strongly protected by both state and federal law? One important reason was the factionalism within the tribe that allowed the representatives of New York State to bargain with one group against another. After the revolution, Kirkland, who had served as a military chaplain, returned to the Oneidas to find his former power sadly diminished and challenged on one side by Catholic missionaries and on the other by a resurgence of Iroquois beliefs. His warriors still supported him, but their numbers had been reduced by war and their influence had declined. Only through the support of some of the tribes who had moved to Oneida lands—the Tuscaroras, along with the Stockbridge and Brothertown Algonquian-speaking groups—did his influence continue. Kirkland supported the introduction of agriculture among these Indians along with baptism and the renunciation of "pagan" ideas, and because of this he encouraged the sale of surplus lands. Lack of consensus on three central issues gradually emerged to divide the Oneidas: the control of political authority in the tribe, the degree of acceptance of White society, and the policy regarding land sales. Two parties grew up that were divided on these issues: the Pagan or Cornelius party and the Christian or Skenandore party. By 1805 the Pagan party, who favored a return to the old Iroquois beliefs, had become so strong that the reservation was divided along religious lines.

Another reason for the Oneida failure to retain their land was the sheer numbers of settlers who were eager for the fertile farm acreage. The Indians were repeatedly cheated by the state of New York, which bought their land at low cost only to turn around and sell it to speculators, who divided it into farm lots and made fortunes with much of the money involved also lining the pockets of state officials. In Madison County, where the Oneidas lived, the population grew from less than 1,000 White settlers in 1800 to 25,000 by 1810 and 39,000 by 1830. Even more settlers passed through Oneida territory because it provided the only opening between the Adirondacks to the north and a ridge of deep valleys and hills to the south. By the 1820s the Oneidas were surrounded by Whites who coveted even what little the Indians had left. They were an exhausted people who had been at war for 200 years. Now there were strong political and religious divisions among them; they had lost the support of their Iroquois kinsmen, who blamed them for the dissolution of the League and resented their support of the American cause; and the authority base both of their own tribe and the League was gone. In this weakened condition, they were an easy prey to the land-hungry New Yorkers. The federal government, busy with the Indians in the West, made no move to protect the Oneidas as it had promised to do in the treaties with them. In desperation, some Oneidas began to think of moving away to a place where they would be free to live in the way they wished. Prominent factors embedded in the last two centuries of the social history of the United States conspired to change radically the nature of Oneida life and change it in different directions for particular segments of the tribe. Different Oneidas reacted in different ways to military defeat, economic dependence but social and cultural separation, and the introduction of a wide array of foreign elements ranging from technology to various institutionalized forms of Christianity.

White interests felt that their problems with the Oneidas could be resolved in large measure if these Indians could be induced to leave the area by one or a combination of means. This approach resulted in the formation of three new and different kinds of Oneida communities in the nineteenth century—one in Wisconsin, one in southern Ontario, and one in New York. Their similarities can be explained largely by the persistence of a common heritage; and their differences, by varying reactions to different social and geographical environments plus the influence of unique historical events.

THE ONEIDAS OF WISCONSIN—THEN

The Move to Wisconsin

The catalyst for the Oneida's move to Wisconsin was an Episcopalian missionary, Eleazar Williams, who first visited them in 1816. By this time Kirkland had been dead for 11 years, and the Oneidas were supporting themselves largely through the sale of their lands. Even those members of the tribe who opposed the land sales were unable to find an acceptable alternate means of support. The tribe struggled on, each village making its own adjustments to the incoming White settlers. The men were demoralized because their two primary occupations, hunting and fighting, had been eliminated, and only the women managed to provide some basis for a continuing social system and a way to retain Oneida identity. Williams worked so effectively that by 1818 he succeeded in converting not only the Christian party but also many of the Pagan party to his way of thinking. This accomplished, he proposed that the Oneidas move west to an area near Green Bay in Wisconsin Territory.

The Oneidas immediately opposed Williams's idea and requested that he be recalled. Williams, however, remained, strong in his ambition of heading a new Indian nation in Wisconsin made up not only of the Oneidas but of representatives from all Iroquois tribes. He was supported in his endeavor by Congressman Jedidiah Morse, who wanted to protect the Indians from the worst effects of White acculturation, and by the Ogden Land Company, who coveted the remaining Seneca lands to which the company held preemption. By 1820 Williams convinced some Oneidas and Stockbridges to go with him to Green Bay, where they hoped to persuade the Menominee and Winnebago tribes to cede them some territory. The trip ended in Detroit when the group learned that the land they wanted had been ceded to the U.S. government. Returning home, Williams persuaded the two U.S. senators from New York to prevent the ratification of this agreement. The following year he again opened negotiations with the Wisconsin Indians and was successful in working out a compromise whereby the New York group was awarded a strip of land five miles wide extending across the Fox River at Little Chute south of Green Bay. Williams accepted this small tract in the hope of eventually being given much more, but many Oneidas were furious about the arrangement and wanted nothing more to do with him. Again two factions divided the people.

In 1822 a delegation returned to Green Bay and secured an agreement from the Menominees to share all their land in a joint and undivided occupation with the New York contingent. In this agreement the Menominees were probably thinking in Indian terms, visualizing the sharing of their extensive hunting territory. They still did not realize that they themselves would soon be restricted to a small, limited reservation and no longer free to roam as they pleased. For their equal share to four million acres, the Oneidas paid the grand sum of $3,000. President Monroe, however, reduced this vast acreage to the plot they had purchased at Little Chute plus the land between Sturgeon Bay and the Fox River.

In 1823 a small group of Oneidas moved to Wisconsin, but most of the tribe refused to move, and the other Iroquois groups wanted nothing to do with Williams and his ideas concerning them. Meanwhile, arguments continued over whether the sale of land to the New Yorkers was valid. In spite of these questions, several hundred more Oneidas along with some Stockbridges, Brothertowns, and Munsee Indians moved to Green Bay. After much more discussion, the Oneidas negotiated a final treaty at Buffalo Creek, New York, in 1838. This treaty reduced their reserve in Wisconsin to 65,436 acres and ceded some land in New York. By its terms, the tribe also agreed to move to Kansas Territory, a move that never appealed to any tribal faction and was eventually abandoned for a cash settlement.

Life in Wisconsin

The portion of the tribe that settled in Wisconsin quickly increased in number from 654 in 1838 to 1,218 in 1868 and 1,732 in 1887 when the Dawes Act was passed, which allotted tribal land to individuals. At first the Oneidas were able to live in Wisconsin much as they had done before. The men hunted and fished in the ample forests while the women tended the cornfields. Gradually, the men became small farmers, raising cattle, horses, pigs, and sheep. Farming, however, never provided more than a bare subsistence, and the people obtained extra cash through the sale of berries, braided corn husks to be used for bedding, and maple syrup. As time went by, more of the men worked in the growing Wisconsin lumber industry both on and off the reservation. Oneida lands were stripped of their timber, and no attempt was made to manage these resources on a sustained yield basis.

The community was organized around three strong social dimensions: kinship, religion, and neighborhoods. The trend toward the lessening of importance of extended ties with the maternal line continued, and the nuclear family increased in importance. The father was the head of the family, making all the crucial economic decisions and arranging the marriages of his children. Daughters were married early, often at ages 14 or 15, and marriage bonds were stronger than they had been in the past. The most preferred marriage for an Oneida was another Oneida, but even third cousins were considered too close a relation to marry. The church frowned on divorce, which often led to social ostracism. Women were expected to be subservient to their husbands and to avoid contact with the opposite sex. The close relationship between brothers and sisters continued with obligations toward nieces and nephews extending the ties into adult life. Grandparents remained very important to their grandchildren, and they often supplied affection and freedom from the more rigid discipline of the parents. Although families were linked together by kin networks that remained important, the significance of the clans declined except for the role that they played in curing rites.

In the field of religion, the Wisconsin Oneida community split along two lines in the mid-nineteenth century. The first immigrants, who had been Episcopalians, moved to the north end of the reservation. They were followed by a smaller group of Methodists, who settled at the south end. Each group was represented in the tribal council, with the Episcopalians holding approximately two-thirds of the important political positions. The two factions, however, did not socialize to any great extent, and marriage between them was frowned upon.

Eight separate neighborhoods existed on the reservation, and these were the focus of much of the social and economic life. Neighbors were expected to help each other with farm work, construction of homes and outbuildings, and the maintenance of roads. In this pattern, the Oneidas were not alone. All early settlers in rural Wisconsin survived in large measure through the exchange of labor, for no one had spare cash available to pay for essential services, and at that time labor exchange was often more valuable than money. The eight neighborhoods were divided along the geographical and religious lines mentioned above. An individual was either a Southender or a Northender, and the two locations vied with each other in pastimes such as the ball and stick game of lacrosse and the gambling that accompanied it. Each faction believed itself superior to the other.

The hereditary system whereby power was given to sachems who were nominated for their positions by clan mothers gradually declined in Wisconsin. Instead, each Pine Tree Chief gained political power through leadership of one of the factions, through being a good Christian, and through generosity to the needy. Gradually, the emphasis on generosity gave way to the attitudes favoring accumulation so typical of the greater American society. The leadership more and more emphasized the values of the middle class—education, hard work, sobriety, and family responsibility—and the adherence to these became the criteria for determining social position.

In the field of religion, the Wisconsin Oneidas had become staunch Christians, following almost none of the old Iroquois beliefs. What did remain was usually integrated into the Christian frame of reference. Only the fear of witchcraft and the belief in the False Face curing societies remained strong. Dreams were still important in diagnosis of an illness, and herbal medicines were widely used. Funerals were accompanied by elaborate wakes, the original purpose of which had been to ward off witches who may have caused the death.

Political Problems

After they had settled in Wisconsin, the Oneidas were forced to struggle with a number of political problems. The land, which was owned in common, had to be equitably allotted, and questions concerning boundary disputes, permits to cut wood, and the citizenship of individuals had to be resolved. As contacts with surrounding White neighbors grew, the political leadership found it more difficult to enforce their rules. Thefts, murders, alcoholism, and crimes of all kinds increased. By 1880 the hereditary system of government had been replaced by an elective system, which continued until allotment in 1892. The federal government ceased paying the annuity that had been awarded because of the service of the Oneidas during the Revolutionary War, and the tribe was forced to negotiate to get it restored. The Oneidas were under pressure from their missionaries and school teachers to speak English rather than their own tongue. Indian agents assigned to the tribe opposed the hereditary chieftainship and the holding of the land in common and succeeded eventually in destroying both these practices. Once again the Indians found themselves under pressure to sell their land and the timber resources upon it. The Indian agent, supposedly there to protect the interests of the Oneidas, attacked them in the *Green Bay Gazette* in 1868, calling them "uncivilized, thrift-less, reckless, and beastly, the useless consumers of the subsistence of a thousand white men." He suggested that they be moved elsewhere where they could no longer hinder the progress of Green Bay (Campisi, 1974: 146). Cornelius Hill, the Oneida chief, replied to this attack by explaining that the Indians were learning to become drunkards from the White people. It was the agent's business, he said, to protect the Indians from liquor and from people who wanted to steal their land instead of devising plans to strip the tribe of their homes and property.

Matters came to a head with the passage of the General Allotment Act or Dawes Act in 1887. The Dawes Act authorized the President of the United States, at his discretion, to divide an Indian reservation into individual holdings, assigning a parcel of land to each man, woman, and child who was an enrolled member of the tribe. The surplus land could then be sold to homesteaders at $2.50 an acre. Although some proponents of the Dawes Act sincerely felt that the Indians must either change their way of life or be exterminated, others supported it because they were greedy for the land it would free. Both these factions ignored the treaty obligations that the government had toward the Indians and ignored what the Indians themselves wanted. As we shall see, not only the Oneidas but many other tribes were affected by this legislation. Between 1887 and 1930, ninety million acres or almost two-thirds of the Indians' land base was lost to them. To add insult to injury, they not only lost their land, but were also forced to pay the costs of surveying and allotting it (McNickle, 1967: 634–635).

For the Oneidas, the Dawes Act became effective in 1892, and the people had all received their patents in fee simple by 1908. The results were extremely disruptive because land speculators quickly moved in to buy the land from Indians who could not afford the taxes upon it or who had been talked into obtaining mortgages that could then be fore-closed. Some Indian men were simply made drunk and, while they were in that state, offered a paper signing away their land. Under the provisions of the act, each individual had received 40 acres if over 18 and 26 acres if under 18. The allotments given to one family, however, were not necessarily contiguous, and this made farming difficult, to say the least. By 1930 all but a few hundred acres of the 65,000 acre former reservation was owned by Whites. As the land base had disappeared, the only way the Oneida tribe could exist as a legal entity was through the government's continued recognition of the Treaty of 1794, which required payment of the annuity. Although the government made sev-eral attempts to renounce this treaty by paying the Indians a lump sum, the Oneidas managed to hold fast to their right to it. This was all they had left. All former Bureau of Indian Affairs services had been taken over by the town, county, or state, and in 1924 all Indians were automatically made United States citizens.

In spite of the forces trying to push the Oneidas willy-nilly into the mainstream of American life, they continued to hold on to their cultural identification and their own language. Family relationships were still important as were the voluntary associations operating through the churches. In 1934, recognizing some of the hardships that the Dawes Act had caused to most Indians in the country, the United States passed the Indian Reorganization Act. Under its provisions the Oneidas were able to incorporate and secure some federal help. The government purchased 2,106 acres for them, most of it from Oneidas. Again, this acreage was not contiguous but was spread between two counties, Brown and Outagamie, and among four school districts. The tribe wrote a new constitution and chose a tribal council called the Business Committee to act for it.

THE ONEIDAS OF WISCONSIN—NOW

The Oneida reservation today is located 13 miles west of the city of Green Bay but well inside its metropolitan area. The land has long since been cleared of its timber resources and is used mainly for dairy farming. As of 1972 there were approximately 7,200 people enrolled as Oneida tribal members. Campisi attributes the population not only to a high birthrate but also to the fact that Oneidas not previously registered were added to the list in order to share in a one million dollar settlement of land claims made in the early 1960s. In addition, a number of people exercised their right to be enrolled as tribal members in order to benefit from government relocation and help once they had moved to a city to work. Ironically, the practice of relocation, which had been started so that Indians would join the mainstream of society, helped to ensure the awareness of tribal identity instead. Oneida clubs grew up in Milwaukee, Chicago, and Detroit; and urban residents became more aware of, and concerned in, what was going on back on the reservation. Many planned to retire there when their working days were over, and they made every effort to keep in touch with relatives at home. The Oneidas followed a pattern very similar to the Micmac. Young people generally left the reservation to work and seek adventure and returned when they were middle-aged or elderly. For this reason, over half the reservation population was under the age of 18, some 8 percent had retired, and only 39 percent were of working age in 1972.

A Wisconsin Oneida homestead.   Milwaukee Public Museum.

A Poverty Area

The reservation itself can be classified as a poverty area. In 1965 a tribal survey found that over half the population had incomes below $3,000 per year. Housing was substandard with half of the homes being without indoor water or toilet facilities and almost all homes in need of repair. Since that time, some housing projects have been built, but housing remains scarce and dwellings are constantly occupied in spite of their state of disrepair. The Oneidas suffer from chronic unemployment and underemployment principally because of lack of skills and insufficient education. Some people are unable to take advantage of jobs available in Green Bay because of transportation problems, for there is no public transportation between the reservation and the city. Those who do work there are employed in such industries as the paper mills, canning, and packing. A number work as laborers for farmers in the area. Although many Oneidas have gardens, there are none who own and operate their own farms. Following the trends in the larger society, many Oneida women work and no stigma is attached to this fact.

The Oneida Tribe has begun a number of projects to improve the economic situation. Many of these have been funded through the Great Lakes Inter-Tribal Council, which administers programs for all ten Indian tribes and bands in Wisconsin. Included in these programs are Headstart, a Youth Development Program, a Community Health Representative Program, a Home Improvement Program, a Maternal and

Child Health Program, an Employment Program, a Neighborhood Youth Corp Program, and a number of Education Programs. In addition, the tribe has begun the development of their own Industrial Park on tribal land and is investigating the possibility of mining the limestone outcropping found on the reservation (*Oneida Indian Reservation*, 1973). As of 1979, however, no direct action has been taken on this.

Women are important in the Oneida community.   Milwaukee Public Museum.

Social Ties and Religion

In the area of social relationships, the nuclear family continues to be important, but many people no longer know to which clan they should belong. Women have regained much of their traditional importance, and many of them play vital roles in community affairs and the governing of the tribe. In 1972 five out of the nine councillors were women, and some women were also active in the American Indian Movement (AIM). Children are expected to obey their parents and older siblings, although toughness is esteemed and children must learn to stand up for

A Wisconsin Oneida boy.   Milwaukee Public Museum.

A Wisconsin Oneida girl.   Milwaukee Public Museum.

their own rights. Today children are more inclined to rebel against the authority of their parents than they were in the past, and the parents tend to place the blame on the schools and the frequent contact with White children who have been raised more permissively. Ties to the kindred continue to be important, especially the bond between grandparents and their grandchildren. All tribal members must be able to trace their ancestry at least as far back as the 1935 census, so they are aware of exactly who they are and how they fit into the group as a whole. Neighborhoods have declined in importance as people became more mobile, and the mutual help of neighbors was no longer a necessity for survival.

Oneida remains a Christian society with most of the people still divided between the Episcopalians and the Methodists. The only remnants of the old Iroquois beliefs are the fear of witchcraft, some customs associated with death and funerals, and the recognition of curing soci-

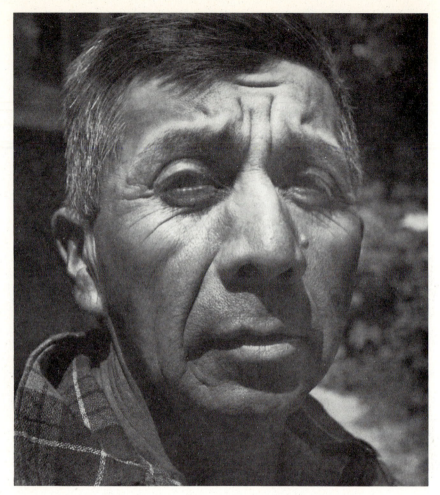

Milwaukee Public Museum.

eties. Even these ideas are now explained in Christian terms. Church organizations such as friendship circles and guilds play important parts in both the social and political life of the community because they provide a forum in which to work out a collective stand on community problems. A number of voluntary mutual aid societies also serve this purpose and bring together people from all ages and social classes in Oneida society. Examples of these are the Oneida Helpers, a burial society that has monthly meetings, and the Senior Citizens.

Although since the time of allotment Whites and Oneidas have shared the former reservation land, the two groups do not mingle socially except in a superficial sense. The Oneida Athletic Association sponsors all-Indian teams, and the Parents' Group has no white members even though the children share the same schools. Campisi believes that the failure of the two groups to interact is due in part to White hostility toward the Indians. Neighbors of different races tend to ignore each other when they meet at stores and public places. In addition to White hostility, the Oneidas have raised boundaries of their own toward more interaction. Oneida groups are linked together by many ties of blood and affinal relationship, religion, and residence, and any White attempting to join them probably feels very much like an outsider (Campisi, 1974: 192–193). In general, Oneida–White relations show the same combination of avoidance, suspicion, and hate often found throughout the western Great Lakes area.

Milwaukee Public Museum.

Future Goals

More and more, the Oneidas of Wisconsin are attempting to recapture the cultural heritage that they have lost. Recently a group of Indian dancers has been formed who have been learning Iroquois songs and dances, a shift from the pan-Indian material they used at first. People from this group have traveled to Canada, where the Oneida people have retained more of the old ways. This search for the Iroquois culture of long ago, however, has in a sense polarized the Wisconsin community. Many older and middle-aged Oneidas there have internalized the White middle-class values about what makes a person successful so that young Oneidas in search of their own heritage must find information not from their elders but from outside the area in Canada or at other Iroquois settlements. The impetus for this regeneration seems to be with the lower socioeconomic strata of Wisconsin Oneidas, who have not acquired enough of the material advantages of the White world and who are looking for more congenial patterns of living. They want to revive the language and the memory of tribal history, to enrich their lives as economically poor rural people, and to feel again a pride in their Iroquois identity.

THE ONEIDAS OF THE THAMES, ONTARIO, CANADA

After a portion of the tribe had moved to Wisconsin, about 600 people remained in New York on 4,500 acres of land. This group found it impossible to remain in New York, beset as they were by pressure from the state and the federal government to move as well as by factionalism within their own ranks. The Treaty of Buffalo Creek, signed in 1838, did more than grant the Wisconsin Oneidas their land. It also provided an opportunity for New York Indians who lived in the state or elsewhere in the United States to move to Kansas Territory to take up land there. No Oneidas wished to move to Kansas, but they were divided as to where to go. In the end, one group of 178 people decided to stay in New York; one group of 158 decided to emigrate, but didn't know where to move; and a third group of 241 people decided to migrate to Canada to seek land there. According to their leader, Moses Schuyler, this was a faction that had called themselves the Peace party during the Revolutionary War. They now affirmed their loyalty to the British crown and their desire to be reunited with their Iroquois brothers who had supported the British cause (Campisi, 1974: 265).

In 1840 this faction of the Oneida tribe was able to purchase 5,200 acres south of the Thames River in Ontario. Each immigrant who desired to live there, male or female, was required to pay $42.00 for his or her section of the land, and it was this payment that determined band membership for years to come. A few people moved without making the payment, asking if they could "sleep there the night." In a few cases, their descendants are still sleeping there today.

By 1845 the initial Canadian party had been joined by 150 more immigrants. Title to the land they had purchased was held in trust by the Crown on the behalf of the Oneida Nation. Individuals could claim the land they had cleared but could sell or will it only to other Oneidas who had made the payment or to their descendants. Three separate settlements gradually evolved, one made up largely of Methodists, one of Episcopalians, and a third having members from a number of religions and families.

The Political Situation

The Canadian Oneidas brought with them more aspects of the traditional Iroquoian culture than had those who settled in Wisconsin. These people on the whole had less desire to assimilate with the White culture and preferred to retain their old ways. They governed themselves through a council made up of three sachems from each of the three clans, Wolf, Bear, and Turtle. The sachems were appointed by their clan mothers and served for life. Men and women who were not members of the council were permitted to attend all its meetings and to request permission to speak.

Soon after the move, the Canadian Oneidas petitioned the chiefs of the Six Nations, asking that they be readmitted to the League of the Iroquois. Their request was granted in 1850. In addition to the League, the Department of Indian Affairs also had an important influence on the political organization of the band. Soon after they had settled in Canada, an attempt was made to tax their lands, but the superintendant of the Department of Indian Affairs succeeded in getting this rule reversed and seeing to it that the Oneidas would share the tax-exempt status of other Canadian Indian groups and be subject to all laws applying to Indians there. The department also acted to settle disputes about land tenure, estate settlement, and band membership that might otherwise have divided the Oneidas. It acted as the final authority over the actions of the Band Council and as trustee of band funds, seeing to it that the Oneidas were absorbed into the structure of Canadian Indian policy. Gradually, the status of the Oneidas in Canada changed from that of independent nation to dependent band, and with this change came a shift in power from the sachems to the agent and the Indian office.

Kinship and Religion

As in Wisconsin, the bonds of kinship remained strong for the Canadian Oneidas. Although the people were forbidden to marry within their clan or espouse any relative closer than a fourth cousin, these restrictions gradually decreased. Marriages were usually arranged by the parents, with great importance being placed on the economic potential and moral reputation of the prospective mate. The Oneidas preferred to marry other Oneidas or other Iroquois. Whites and other Indians were usually considered undesirable as spouses.

In the area of religion, there were important differences between the Oneidas of Wisconsin and those in Canada. At first the Oneidas in Canada identified with three separate religious views: Methodism, Anglicanism, and traditional Iroquois beliefs. The Christian congregations generally had Oneida leaders, and people were able to move easily from one congregation to another if they changed their residence. The Iroquois array of calendrical ceremonials and curing societies fitted well into the culture as a whole and supported the political structure for all. Every sector of the society participated in the curing societies, which helped bind clan loyalties together. As in Wisconsin, the older traditions gradually faded away, only to be abruptly revived in 1904 when a Longhouse of Handsome Lake was established. The Longhouse soon led to factionalism because the leaders of the new movement were strongly opposed to any integration with White society. When the Longhouse leaders insisted that all chiefs should follow the Code of Handsome Lake, the Christian council members expelled them from the council. By 1920 two separate councils existed on the reserve: one Christian and the other Longhouse people. This factionalism has continued to the present time. The groups share the Thames Reserve and have almost nothing to do with each other. The Longhouse people live in a single neighborhood, socialize principally with their peers, and ask nothing more than to be left alone by the other Oneidas.

Economic and Land Problems

When the Oneidas reached Canada, the land they had purchased was covered with virgin timber. They quickly went to work to clear it and establish small farm sites on which they could raise livestock and grow vegetables and grain. Like farm people everywhere, they shared their labor and helped each other so that very little contact with the Whites around them was necessary. By the 1860s, however, the ownership of tillable land had changed to the extent that some people owned enough ground to make commercial agriculture feasible whereas others were reduced to small plots of ten or 15 acres, which could not possibly support them. By 1905 farming supported only one-fourth of the population, and the rest worked as day laborers for the Whites around them who had large farms devoted to growing wheat and flax. A number of people had left Canada to move to Wisconsin, where they believed they could obtain land more easily. Some people were able to survive on part-time occupations such as cutting firewood, trapping, and basket and mat weaving. More and more though, the Oneidas were forced to depend on the dominant White society in order to make a living. This necessity conflicted with the teachings of the Longhouse and led to increased tensions.

During the 1920s the Oneidas in Canada were very involved in pursuing claims to collect damages from both New York State and the United States government for the lands they had lost in New York. Tribal members were asked to support this effort financially, and some of them lost all they had during the negotiations. The efforts to pursue these claims and to settle the claim for the Kansas land that had been successful encouraged more extensive contacts between the Oneidas of Wisconsin, Canada, and New York, reminding them that they were still one people with a common heritage that should not be forgotten. The difficulties over the claims and the problems the Wisconsin Oneidas had with the Dawes Act also had the effect of making all Oneidas more suspicious of White society and more anxious to retain the land they did possess. This suspicion persists today and is virtually universal in Ontario.

HOW THE ONEIDAS OF THE THAMES LIVE TODAY

Although the Oneida Reserve is still farmland, it is only 15 miles away from the large urban center of London, Ontario, with a population of 220,000 people, and from St. Thomas with 35,000. Other large cities and small towns are within easy commuting distance by automobile, bus, or train. The Oneidas have retained the same 5,200 acres that they purchased, but the population had grown to 2,073 members in 1972, 1,200 of whom lived on the reserve.

Although one housing project has been built, most of the homes there are substandard with no central heating, indoor plumbing, or running water. A few wells supply the water for the community. Houses are usually small frame structures with no insulation or storm windows and are heated with wood or kerosene stoves. The Oneidas have been afraid to take out loans to improve their homes because they fear that this will lead to their losing their land. No services of any kind exist on the reserve except for one garage. The people must leave in order to shop or obtain the professional help of physicians, dentists, or attorneys. Fire protection is provided by neighboring communities, but since 1973 the band has employed its own police officer.

Economics and Education

The Oneidas follow the same pattern of working that we have already seen among the Micmac and the Indians in Wisconsin. Men must leave the reserve in order to find work, usually unskilled or semiskilled jobs in the fields of agriculture or construction. Although some work is available in London and other nearby communities, many men have traveled as far as Detroit, Chicago, Syracuse, and Buffalo to find a job. Although some men take their families with them, others return to the reserve every weekend to visit. Only five Oneidas are now farming commercially, and much of the remaining farmland has been leased to Whites by absentee Oneida owners. Women work as well as men, usually as domestics or in the tobacco fields or canning plants around London. Band government provides the few white-collar jobs that are available, positions such as teachers' aids and clerical personnel. It also hires men as janitors, highway crews, and work gangs to clear brush or build houses. Most Oneidas earn very low salaries. Even though an Oneida man has worked off the reserve for his entire adult life, he usually strives to maintain ties and a home base there and plans to return after he has retired.

All neighborhood mutual help practices have fallen by the wayside, and the economy is run on strictly a cash basis. People expect to be paid for giving a ride to their neighbor and even for loaning tools and equipment. People do business with those who they know will give them value for their money, and considerations of kinship and friendship make no difference.

Although education could improve the lot of the Oneidas, very few of them finish high school. After attending a school on the reserve for four years, students are bused to integrated schools in London, and there encounter problems with White hostility that discourage many. Only an occasional Oneida goes on to higher education after high school. Thus they are locked into competition for unskilled jobs, and many men have developed the pattern of transient and unstable work that we have seen among the Micmac.

The Family and Social Control

Over time, the nuclear family has become the most important social unit, although grandparents often play a vital role in raising their grandchildren while the biological parents are off the reserve working.

Contacts with aunts, uncles, and cousins are usually limited to social occasions, and no obligations remain on either side. Children are expected to become independent very early, and often older siblings are responsible for the care of their younger brothers and sisters. Toughness is admired, but this can lead to trouble in the teen years when gangs of boys or girls band together to commit acts of vandalism or arson. Women are no longer expected to be subservient to their husbands and often increase their power and influence in the family as they grow older. Except among some Longhouse people, the clan system has almost been lost to memory, and few people under 40 are able to name their clan.

The Oneidas judge people by conventional White moral standards, although they are willing to allow the young some latitude. Men are expected to be responsible toward their families, to refrain from drunkenness, and to act in a mild and dignified manner without boasting about their accomplishments. Cooperation and willingness to follow directions are valued traits. Oneidas also value being Oneida. Campisi tells of one Chippewa woman who had married an Oneida and had lived among them for years but was never fully accepted. Even her children suffered the stigma of being half Chippewa.

Social control is accomplished through gossip and ridicule to bring an erring band member back into line. People who seem to be moving up the social ladder or earning more money than their neighbors are often castigated for getting above themselves. Another potent method of social control is the threat of being labeled a witch. Such a threat is directed toward those who are miserly, argumentative, violent, unreliable, or dishonest. Although both the Longhouse and the Christian elements of the tribe condemn witchcraft and supposedly no one at Oneida practices it, people still believe on occasion that they have been bewitched. When this happens, the individual afflicted must go to an "Indian Doctor" at Six Nations Reserve in order to be cured and must pay a high fee for this service. If he offends enough people, a man can go broke just paying for his cures.

The Political System

The political system of the Oneida in Canada is quite complex because of the continued split between the Christians and the Longhouse people. There is a Band Council having 12 councillors and one chief elected every two years by all Oneidas aged 21 or over who live at the settlement. This council makes the rules controlling band management and deals with community concerns such as education, welfare, roads, and land transfers. It has a number of standing committees to help it but holds no general meetings. Council meetings are held several times a week, but outsiders are not encouraged to attend, though theoretically they have the right to do so. Councillors are guided by pressures from their supporters, and there is considerable disagreement among them. Decisions are often determined by personal ambitions or jealousy rather than what is best for the band. All decisions of the council are subject to review by the Department of Indian Affairs and the Province of Ontario, so the power they actually wield is limited, especially since the band has no financial resources of its own and must depend on the national or provincial government to finance its projects. Ranged against the official council on almost every issue is a separate Longhouse Council, which offers a structure of government based on traditional Iroquois form. The Longhouse Council consists of nine hereditary chiefs appointed by their clan mothers as well as a few Pine Tree Chiefs chosen for their leadership qualities. It asserts that the elective council lost the right to rule at the beginning of the twentieth century because they accepted the provisions of the Indian Act and followed too many White values and behaviors. The Longhouse Council considers itself a part of the Six Nations Confederacy, which claims that the Iroquois are a sovereign nation still. As a practical matter, the Longhouse Council confines itself to a review of the actions of the elective council and the Canadian government and to participating in intertribal political activities sponsored by the Six Nations Confederacy. It has only two dozen members, and a number of its hereditary positions are vacant. One reason for this is that a requirement for holding office is that the individual live on the reserve or at least near it. Few young people feel they can afford to do this, for most jobs are away from the area. Both the Longhouse Council and the Band Council agree on the very important issues concerning Oneida land. Both believe that all land must be preserved in common ownership with the use of the land being restricted only to those who can legitimately inherit it. The Longhouse Council does not feel that it need take any direct action against the Band Council because Longhouse people believe that sooner or later White society and all who follow its ways will be destroyed. They need only retain the old ways and wait.

THE ONEIDAS OF NEW YORK: PAST AND PRESENT

By 1848, after the bulk of the tribe had moved either to Wisconsin or Ontario, there were fewer than 200 people left in New York. Two settlements existed with little interaction between them because of factional disputes. Each consisted of a core of interrelated families who shared adherence to the Methodist faith. No believers in the Longhouse faith of Handsome Lake existed at either community. Those few Oneidas who did follow it moved to the Onondaga reservation south of Syracuse.

Both communities supported themselves largely through agriculture with the men working for neighboring White farmers as day laborers. Only two Oneidas farmed their own land. Families supplemented their income through gardening and the sale of berries and homecrafts in distant cities and resort areas. The women held their families together economically, being responsible for the gardens and working as domestics to supply cash income. Most men were migrants, taking whatever jobs came along on a temporary basis. The women also owned most of the land, which had been divided among individuals in 1843. Women usually hung on to their portions whereas the men often sold theirs. The two communities remained important to the people who had moved to Wisconsin and Canada. The area was still the sentimental capital of the tribe, and many people visited there.

As the years passed, the women continued to hold the communities together. They determined who could live on the tax-free land and commanded the respect and obedience of their children, especially their daughters. The Oneida language and Iroquois customs gradually faded away as the communities were increasingly exposed to White ways, but the women still remembered that they were Oneida. Even when more and more marriages to Whites occurred, women continued to exercise authority through the influence of the extended family and through the social sanctions of ridicule, gossip, and witchcraft accusations.

After the two migrations had decimated the population in New York, there was little effective political structure left. All the land was owned by individuals, and the two Oneida communities were not really distinguishable from the non-Indian towns around them. Although the oldest women in each village continued to appoint a chief, these chiefs had little real power and few duties. They no longer could control the people because individuals were permitted to sell their land to whomever they pleased. As in Wisconsin after the passage of the Dawes Act, only one thing maintained the Oneidas of New York as a political entity: the Treaty of 1794, which required that the government pay the annuity. To make sure this annuity was fairly distributed, the women of the tribe continued to keep accurate band membership lists. All people having one-quarter Oneida blood were eligible.

At the end of the nineteenth century, the impending settlement of the claim for the Kansas lands, which the tribe had rejected, helped bring the three Oneida settlements closer together. The government had ruled that all Oneidas were eligible to share in the distribution of the judgment of almost two million dollars, even those who had moved to Canada. This decision by the Court of Claims ensured that the Oneidas in New York legally retained their status as a tribal unit with the right to sue the United States.

In the twentieth century, however, other decisions again threw doubt upon their legal status. Today the Oneidas of New York exist in a sort of limbo with neither the United States government nor the state of New York being willing to accept legal responsibility for them. They still reside in two separate communities, each with its own leadership and band list. In addition, several hundred Oneidas live on the Onondaga reservation, and several hundred around Syracuse, New York, making a total of around 700 people who are enrolled members. Kinship continues to be very important, for membership in the tribe is determined through the female line. The two Oneida communities continue to be at odds with each other, neither accepting the legitimacy of the other to represent the New York Oneidas.

Although a few people speak the language, most Iroquois customs have been lost, and these Indians do not even attend ceremonies at other reservations. They still retain, however, a sense of their history, pointing with pride to their part in winning the American Revolution. Children are taught to value their Oneida heritage, which sets them apart from both their White neighbors and other Iroquois.

CONCLUSION

What can we say about the Oneida people as a whole today? Split by migration, by factionalism, by religious differences, these Iroquois still retain their sense of Oneida identity. They still share a language, kinship ties extending to other locations, a set of beliefs in the supernatural, and a common historical tradition. Most important, they care about being Oneidas. Visiting among the communities has always existed, and, if anything, it is increasing today. A number of young Oneidas at Ontario have become interested in the activities of the Longhouse. Membership in militant Indian organizations such as AIM is growing as younger people attempt to realize their ambitions as adult Indians in a turbulent, changing world. A distinct and viable Oneida way of life exists in Wisconsin, Ontario, and New York, and will probably continue to develop.

REFERENCES

Basehart, Harry W. *Historical Changes in the Kinship System of the Oneida Indians.* Ph.D. dissertation, Harvard University, 1952.

Campisi, Jack. *Ethnic Identity and Boundary Maintenance in Three Oneida Communities.* Ph.D. dissertation, Albany State University of New York, 1974.

Cork, Ella. *The Worst of the Bargain.* San Jacinto, California: Foundation for Social Research, 1962.

Curtin, Jeremiah, and J. N. B. Hewitt, collectors. Seneca Fiction, Legends, and Myths. In J. N. B. Hewitt, ed., *Thirty-Second Annual Report, Bureau of American Ethnology, 1910–1911.* Washington, D.C.: Government Printing Office, 1918.

Deardorff, Merle H. The Religion of Handsome Lake: Its Origin and Development. In W. N. Fenton, ed., *Symposium on Local Diversity in Iroquois Culture. Bulletin 146, Bureau of American Ethnology.* Washington, D.C.: 1951, pp. 77–107.

Fenton, William N., ed. Symposium on Local Diversity in Iroquois Culture. *Bureau of American Ethnology Bulletin 149.* Washington, D.C.: Government Printing Office, 1951.

———. The Iroquois Eagle Dance: An Offshoot of the Calumet Dance. *Bulletin 156. Bureau of American Ethnology.* Washington, D.C.: Government Printing Office, 1953.

———. The Iroquois in History. In E. B. Leacock and N. O. Lurie, eds., *North American Indians in Historical Perspective.* New York: Random House, 1971, pp. 129–168.

———. Jesse Cornplanter, Seneca, 1889–1957. In Margot Liberty, ed., *American Indian Intellectuals.* 1976 Proceedings of the American Ethnological Society. St. Paul: West Publishing Co., 1978, pp. 177–195.

———., and John Gulick, eds. Symposium on Cherokee and Iroquois Culture. *Bulletin 180, Bureau of American Ethnology.* Washington, D.C.: Government Printing Office, 1961.

Kurath, Gertrude P. Iroquois Music and Dance: Ceremonial Arts of Two Seneca Longhouses. *Bulletin 187, Bureau of American Ethnology.* Washington, D.C.: Government Printing Office, 1964.

McNickle, Darcy. Indian and European: Indian-White Relations from Discovery to 1887. In Roger Owen, James Deetz, and Anthony Fisher, eds., *The North American Indians: A Sourcebook.* New York: The Macmillan Company, 1967, pp. 622–635.

Morgan, Lewis H. *League of the Ho-De-No Sau-Nee or Iroquois* (2d ed.). Ed. and annotated by H. M. Lloyd. New York: Dodd Mead & Co., 1901.

Oneida Indian Reservation. *701 Comprehensive Planning Program.* Oneida, Wisconsin, 1973.

Ritzenthaler, Robert. Iroquois False-Face Masks. *Milwaukee Public Museum, Publications in Primitive Art 3.* Milwaukee: Milwaukee Public Museum, 1969.

Shimony, Annemarie Anrod. Conservatism among the Iroquois at the Six Nations Reserve. *Yale University Publications in Anthropology Number 65.* New Haven: Department of Anthropology, Yale University, 1961.

Tooker, Elizabeth. *The Iroquois Ceremonial of Midwinter.* Syracuse: Syracuse University Press, 1970.

Wallace, A. F. C. *The Death and Rebirth of the Seneca.* New York: Alfred A. Knopf, Inc., 1970.

Williams, Ted C. *The Reservation.* Syracuse: Syracuse University Press, 1970.

Wilson, Edmund. *Apologies to the Iroquois.* New York: Vintage Books, 1966.

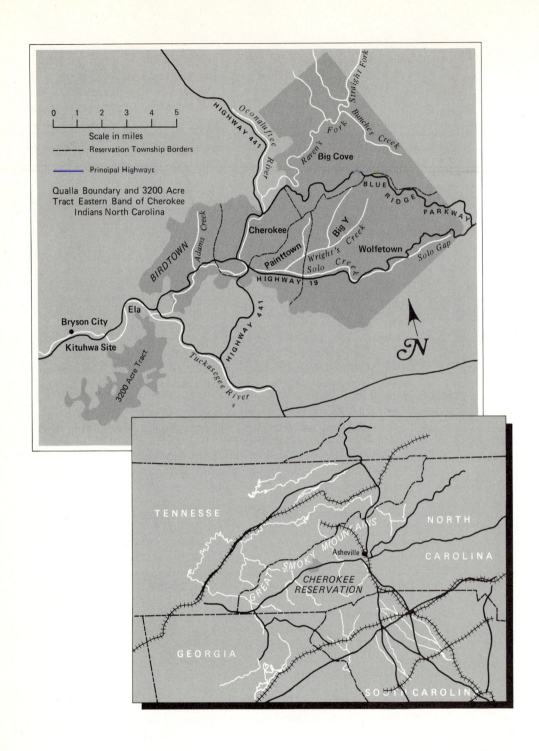

0 1 2 3 4 5

Scale in miles

- - - - - Reservation Township Borders

———— Principal Highways

Qualla Boundary and 3200 Acre Tract Eastern Band of Cherokee Indians North Carolina

HIGHWAY 441

Oconaluftee River

Raven's Fork

Straight Fork

Bunches Creek

Big Cove

BLUE RIDGE PARKWAY

Cherokee

Big Y

Wright's Creek

Wolfetown

Solo *Creek*

Solo Gap

Painttown

HIGHWAY 19

Adams Creek

BIRDTOWN

Ela

Bryson City

Kituhwa Site

3200 Acre Tract

HIGHWAY 441

Tuckasegee River

N

TENNESSE

NORTH

GREAT SMOKY MOUNTAINS

Asheville

CAROLINA

CHEROKEE RESERVATION

GEORGIA

SOUTH CAROLINA

CHAPTER 4

THE EASTERN CHEROKEES
The Real People

We were at Washington at the time that the measure for chasing the last of several tribes of Indians from their forest homes, was canvassed in congress, and finally decided upon by the *fiat* of the President. If the American character may be judged by their conduct in this matter, they are most lamentably deficient in every feeling of honour and integrity.

Mrs. Frances Trollope,
Domestic Manners of the Americans

Every spring the Great Smoky Mountains, home of the Cherokees, become alive with tourists. Approximately five million people visit during the season to see attractions such as Santa's Land, Frontierland, and the Cherokee history play, "Unto These Hills." Another main attraction is the Indians who can be found working as short order cooks or waitresses or dressed in Plains constumes posed before fake teepees. It appears to be the destiny of the Eastern Band of Cherokees to play Indian for the tourists both from America and every other nation in the world. Who are these people? What is their background, history, and culture? This chapter will try to answer these questions.

THE PAST

Although no one is certain about how long the Cherokees have been in the southeastern portion of the United States, recent work (Dickens, 1979: 11–12) places their probable ancestors at their present location by A.D. 600 and traces a long occupation through a cluster of features established archaeologically, such as the building of platform mounds, distinctively stamped ceramics, the cultivation of maize, and a pattern of village development in which large towns had satellite villages clustered around them. Platform mounds are found in many places throughout the southeast, and in the early nineteenth century many people believed that they had not been built by the ancestors of the Indians but by a group of outsiders such as the ancient Romans, Greeks, Egyptians, Hindus, or even the inhabitants of the lost continent of Mu (Hudson, 1976:35). Modern archaeologists, however, have established that the mounds were indeed of Indian origin although it is still a mystery exactly how and why they were used. Linguists have established a relationship between the Cherokees and the Iroquois in the north because Cherokee is an Iroquoian language, but the two peoples might have broken away from each other as long as 3,800 years ago (Lounsbury, 1961: 11).

The Cherokees conceived of three worlds: an Upper World, This World on which they lived, and an Under World. In the beginning there were only two worlds, the Upper World, where everything was perfect and orderly, and the Under World, where chaos reigned. In the Upper World lived deities such as the sun and the moon, whereas the Under World was inhabited by ghosts and monsters. James Mooney (1900: 239–240) recounted the Cherokee myth "How the World Was Made." This World was created because the animals who lived in the Upper World felt they needed more room to relieve the crowding. Water-beetle volunteered to explore the endless waters beneath the Upper World, and in the process he dove beneath the surface and came up with some soft mud, which gradually expanded to become This World, an island floating in a large sea. The island was later fastened to the Upper World by four cords to keep it from sinking, and the Cherokees believed that when the earth grew old, the cords would break and earth would sink beneath the waves forever. The animals of the Upper World sent down the Great Buzzard to prepare the new world for them, and the mountains and valleys of Cherokee country were formed by his wings when fatigue caused him to falter. When the animals came down to earth, they required light, so they set the sun to track overhead. At first the sun was too near, and they were forced to set it back seven times until it traveled in a path just below the vault of the Upper World.

The numbers four and seven are very important in Cherokee mythology. Each of the four cardinal directions had its own associated colors and social values. The number seven stood for the highest level of ritual purity attained by only a few creatures and plants. Those who are interested in further details about the Cherokee belief system can find an excellent description in *The Southeastern Indians* by Charles Hudson (1976: 120–183).

Adequate descriptions of the Cherokees do not exist prior to the mid-eighteenth century, at which time these Indians had already been significantly modified by such influences as White-introduced diseases and disruptions caused by incoming settlers along the southeast coast and elsewhere. The British acted quickly to enlist the Cherokees in the deerskin trade, which made them dependent on European-made goods, especially firearms and ammunition. At this time they occupied eastern Tennessee, western North Carolina, and parts of Kentucky and Georgia, the area of the Great Smoky Mountains. Their population was estimated at 22,000, although Oswalt (1973) believes this was a great exaggeration, perhaps double the true figure. The Eastern Cherokees are the descendants of a remnant of the larger group. When most Cherokees were forcibly moved to Indian Territory (present-day Oklahoma) in the 1830s, about 1,000 remained behind either as citizens of the United States or as fugitives hiding in the mountains.

Geography determined the nature of the early Cherokee settlements. The people usually lived where level land existed for farming and on or near a river or stream, which was important as a source of fish, of game that came to drink there, and for drinking water and daily morning bathing. These villages, noted by Adair in 1775 to number 64, and by Bartram in 1790 to number 43, ranged in population between 350 and 600 people. The villages were connected with the outside world by seven main groups of trails (Gilbert, 1943: 180–181), by means of which the Cherokees could visit the Iroquois, Shawnees, Delawares, Tuscaroras, Catawbas, Eastern Siouans, Yuchi, Cheraws, Creeks, Chickasaws, Chocktaws, and Natchez.

The Nature of the Early Cherokees

What type of people were the early Cherokees? Within their own group they placed strong emphasis on getting along with each other. Anyone was free to express his or her ideas in the town council, and discussion of an issue continued until consensus was reached. An individual who could not compromise his or her views to agree with the majority was allowed to withdraw without penalties. In their relations with other tribes, the Cherokees could be fierce warriors who often attacked neighboring lowland settlements when their mountain farms failed to yield enough food (Gilbert, 1943: 181). Cherokees also went to war in revenge for an attack upon them. In this case, their object was to kill the same number of people that they had lost and to terrorize the enemy. When these things had been accomplished, the war was over and the status quo restored.

PHYSICAL APPEARANCE.   In appearance Cherokees ranged from middle height to tall and had a slender, delicate body build. Their hair was lank and black, and their skin color either light yellow-brown or very dark. Young men wore a scalp lock and later a turban, and women kept their hair long. Facial hair was plucked out. A very distinctive early Cherokee practice was slitting the ears and stretching them to great size, then decorating them with silver pendants and rings hanging from the slits. Clothing was originally very simple, being merely loincloths made of deerskin for the men and skirts of the same material for women. Later on, with pervasive White influence, dress became more elaborate, especially on ceremonial occasions. Children often went naked when the weather was warm. Moccasins and buffalo skin robes supplied protection from cold weather, and feather cloaks were worn in more moderate weather. Young men were often elaborately tattooed in designs of flowers, animals, or geometric forms.

HOUSING.   Early Cherokees resembled other southeastern Indians in that each household group constructed a cluster of dwellings. In warm weather they lived in houses built of poles set vertically into the ground and then interwoven with twigs and covered inside and out with clay mixed with grass. These elaborate houses had rooms, gables, and occasionally even two stories. Some were 60 or 70 feet long and housed a number of families (Hudson, 1976: 216). For the winter a family moved into a circular hot house warmly insulated against the cold. These were heated by a fireplace built in the middle, and Europeans who visited found them unpleasantly smoky in spite of the smoke hole in the roof. A family might also own several small storage huts. In addition, there was a separate house for the women of the family, who retired when visitors arrived as well as when they were menstruating or giving birth (Gilbert, 1943: 341). At the center of the village was the circular council house made of logs with roof of concentric circles of poles. Some were large enough to hold 500 people. One narrow doorway provided entrance, and benches were built inside to accommodate the people who gathered for religious ceremonies, political meetings, and social events.

FOOD AND CRAFTS.   Before their contact with the Europeans, the Cherokees were a farming people, growing squash, maize, beans, pumpkins, and tobacco. Women were in charge of the fields, although the men helped to clear the land and aided occasionally in cultivation. Women, especially the elderly and the young, also gathered a number of wild foods, including starchy roots, berries, grapes, persimmons, plums, and various nuts. If crops failed, villages were abandoned and wild resources became essential for survival. The Cherokees had a very long tradition of collecting wild foods, which predated agriculture, and they were extremely knowledgeable not only about edible plants but also about those having medicinal properties. Men were in charge of hunting and fishing and were skillful with bows and arrows although they shifted to guns when they became available through trade with the Europeans. The principal game animal, the white-tailed deer, was hunted either by men wearing decoy deer heads or by large groups who set fires to drive the animals into a small space, where they could be killed more easily (Hudson, 1976: 175–176). The Cherokees also set fires occasionally to clear out the underbrush, and this practice was beneficial not only for the soil but also for the deer that grazed in the large meadows formed by this practice. Birds and smaller game were taken with nine-foot reed blowguns, which propelled darts. Wild turkeys and passenger pigeons were very plentiful in the southeast, and waterfowl appeared in great numbers during the winter. Cherokee mythology emphasized the idea of natural balance. The spirits of animals became vengeful when they were killed, and it was necessary for a hunter to ask pardon of an animal before he killed it. If this was not done, the spirit of the animal could make the man sick. Plants, however, were friendly to man, and their properties could sometimes cure sickness (Hudson, 1976: 159).

Dogs were the only aboriginal domesticated animals, but soon after the coming of Europeans, horses, hogs, and other varieties of farm animals were introduced, and the Cherokees became accomplished husbandmen. They made a wide variety of good quality cane baskets and pottery as well as elaborately carved stone pipes. The total inventory of material culture reflected the fact that the Cherokees were competent, resourceful craftsmen who understood their environment and used many of its benefits to advantage.

FAMILY RELATIONSHIPS.   Early Cherokee households, which were the basic units of production and consumption, commonly consisted of several families related through the female line. A senior wife and her husband headed the group, which included their daughters with their husbands, unmarried sons, and perhaps the granddaughters of the elderly couple. A father was his son's companion and tutor, but his mother's brother served as the boy's disciplinarian. A man marrying into a family respected his in-laws but had an informal congenial relationship with his wife's brothers and brothers-in-law because they occupied a comparable position in the family. Men maintained close ties with their households of birth after marriage. This practice made Cherokee marriages somewhat fragile, as did the fact that Cherokee men and women had an equal amount of sexual freedom (Hudson, 1976: 201).

Households and families were parts of matrilineages, groups tracing their descent through the female line. Among the Cherokees these matrilineages were grouped into seven clans. Membership in a clan was a basic social necessity because it defined the place of the individual within society. Although clans did not meet as groups, a person visiting a distant village could claim hospitality from members of his clan and would address them by the kin term appropriate to their age and sex. Clans allotted land for agricultural purposes and regulated marriage. A Cherokee could not marry within his clan, even though the individual was not closely related by blood. On the other hand, he could marry a close blood relative who was a member of another clan. If a man had two wives, each from a different clan, their children were free to marry because they obtained their clan identity through their mothers (Hudson, 1976: 193).

Congenial interpersonal relations within the tribe, particularly within villages and families, were rewarded whereas overt conflict was not. Most often aggression was expressed indirectly through gossip and occasionally witchcraft accusation. Each clan was obligated to avenge the killing of one of its members, whether or not the killing was deliberate murder or accidental. If a man loaned his horse to his friend and the friend were thrown and killed, that man was liable for his death. Likewise, a person who killed another in self-defense was liable for the death (Hudson, 1976: 230). A manslayer could expect to be killed by the clan relatives of his victim, and his death ended the matter—the feud did not continue indefinitely. If the manslayer ran away to avoid his fate, one of his clan could be killed in his place, so it was to the advantage of the clan to see that a murderer came forward. If the death had truly been an accident, it was sometimes possible for the killer to pay the bereaved clan for the death instead of sacrificing his life, but that was the decision of the clan and not his (Hudson, 1976: 229– 232).

POLITICAL ACTIVITIES. A general council consisting of priests and seven highly respected elderly men from the various clans was responsible for the affairs of one large community or several smaller ones. The conduct of war or peace, trade relations, and the offenses of the member of one village against another were typical areas of concern. Community consensus was reflected in the ultimate decisions of the council. If dissent existed after a long period of deliberation among a number of village families, family members usually agreed not to stand in the way of the wishes of the majority of the community. Throughout most of the eighteenth century, warfare as a direct and indirect result of White contact was of prime concern for the council. The fact that the Cherokees were able to produce well-organized parties of warriors over a long period of time suggests that political decisions affecting large numbers of people could be made in a relatively effective fashion. The thrusts of conquest and subjugation from various outside non-Cherokee sources were probably responsible for long-standing intervillage alliances. Indeed, the feeling of an individual Cherokee that he was a member of a tribe and owed his allegiance to that tribe rather than just to his own village must have stemmed in part from the need to defend the tribe against outside encroachments that threatened the vested economic and social interests of those associated with the village. This does not mean, however, that Cherokee villages always acted in a united fashion. One of the things that made the British so angry was the continual need to negotiate with each group. The Cherokees came together as a nation only when they all realized the threat of being removed from their territory by the Whites, and then it was too late to resist effectively.

Cherokee political activities were coordinated with the cycle of major religious ceremonies. Officials of the tribe were grouped into two organizations, the White Peace Organization and the Red War Organization. The chief of the tribe was the chief and high priest of the most important village, and each village also had its own chief who was the head of the White Organization. This office was hereditary, being transmitted from a man to his eldest sister's son. The duties of the White chief were varied and included blowing the shell trumpet to summon his counselors and people in case of any emergency or decision to be made. When the people had assembled, the White chief, his right-hand man, and his seven White clan counselors formed the civil and religious tribunal of the town. This court was empowered to pass judgment upon criminals, and the punishment usually followed immediately.

RITUAL IN PEACE AND WAR. A complex round of ceremonialism was in the charge of the White Organization. A monthly purification ritual preceded major ceremonies. As the women were segregated and thought to be unclean during menstruation, purification was necessary to bring the men and women together again. The six great festivals in the Cherokee year were held in the council house of the capital town and attended by everyone in the tribe. They celebrated the planting of corn in spring, the first green corn crop in August, the ripe green corn feast in September, the October feasts of the new moon and of Reconciliation and the making of the new fire ten days later, and finally the Bounding Bush feast in December (Gilbert, 1943: 327). All these major ceremonies were concentrated in the last half of the year. They culminated in a purification ritual in which each individual bathed in the river and allowed his clothes to float away. This ceremony canceled all debts of revenge except murder, so that ideally most individuals started the New Year in harmony with all others. The most important political conferences of the year were held in between these ceremonies.

The White Organization was also in charge of marriage, which was forbidden among members of the same clan. The penalty for breaking this rule was death until the early nineteenth century when whipping was substituted. Divorce was permitted with the possessions of the couple being evenly divided. Children were welcomed into the family and treated with great indulgence. Those destined for the priesthood were given special training for many years beginning about age nine. Boys were also trained in the techniques of hunting and the proper ceremonies to observe.

The Red War Organization was headed by the Great Red War Chief. He was aided by various counselors, surgeons, messengers, and scouts as well as some older, highly respected matrons called Pretty Women, who judged the fate of the captives and had a role in the conduct of the war. The office of War Chief was elective upon nomination by the warriors, a system that must have ensured the best candidate's becoming chief. War was waged in the spring or fall for vengeance upon another tribe, often the Creek, Chickasaw, Choctaw, or Shawnee. A strict body count was kept, and when the proper number of warriors had been captured or killed, the war was over. The War Chief had to have the consent of the tribe to call up his warriors. His signals were the rattle of his gourd, a war whoop, and a mourning song for himself and his men. Messengers repeated these signals in all the villages to gather the tribe. Warriors left for battle provisioned with parched corn cakes made by the women. Weapons were the war club, followed in later times by the tomahawk, the bow and arrow, spear, sling, and knife. Men were protected by wooden or leather shields, buffalo-hide breast pieces, and leather arm bracelets. When the warriors returned from battle, a purification ritual was necessary before a victory dance was held. Important as war was to the Cherokees, the Red Organization was subject to the White in the case of conflict, and the appointment of the Red War Chief had to be approved by the White chief.

During the summer Cherokee people often visited another village to participate in ball contests. The ball game was indigenous to the entire eastern part of North America, and it was related to present-day lacrosse, the national game of Canada. The ball game was an incredibly rough sport played by as many as 50 men on each team. The object was to move a small, tightly wrapped, animal-skin ball from the center of the field to the team's goal line. Ball sticks were used to carry or throw the ball, but it could also be carried anyplace on the body. There were few rules to regulate the conduct of the opposing team, and death was not an uncommon result of a ball game. James Mooney (in Culin, 1907: 586) mentioned seeing a player deliberately crippled by being raised in the air and hurled to the ground so that his collar bone broke. Only the finest young men were allowed to represent their village, and large sums were often waged on the outcome. The ball game was excellent training for war in that it required speed, agility, cunning, and strength.

A TIME OF CHANGE

As was mentioned earlier, White contact with the Cherokees began so early that we have no record of true aboriginal existence. De Soto and his men traveled to the North Carolina highlands in the mid-sixteenth century, and the Cherokees encountered the Spanish in Florida, where they raided for guns and horses. Permanent contact with the English from Virginia Colony was established in the late seventeenth century. The Cherokees signed their first treaty with the Whites in 1684 (French and Hornbuckle, 1976: 62). This was the first of more than two dozen treaties, so that by 1819 they had already conceded 90 percent of their land to White interests, and by the time of removal in 1838, Cherokee holdings were about the size of Massachusetts, a fraction of their original territory.

The Cherokees had an unfortunate history of usually choosing the wrong side in wars waged by the Whites. They fought against the British in the French and Indian War. When the Treaty of Paris in 1763 ceded all land east of the Mississippi to the British, the Cherokees were left in the power of their former enemies. In the Revolutionary War they, along with the Creeks and Chickasaws, fought with the British against the Americans. When this war was over, the Indians became the target of a great deal of hatred, and land-hungry settlers felt justified in grabbing all the Cherokee land they could get.

NEW POLITICAL ORGANIZATIONS.   During this time—the late eighteenth to early nineteenth centuries—a number of important changes occurred in the tribal structure. In 1792, a Grand Cherokee National Council was formed to deal with the issues of national leadership, centralized government, and the development of a strategy to handle Indian White relations, which the Cherokees foresaw would be continuous from that point on. Little Turkey was elected as the first principal chief. Under his leadership, the Cherokees attempted to continue the government by consensus, but were increasingly unable to do so. Formal controls were instituted in 1797, when a police force was created to deal with horse theft. In 1808 the Cherokee Nation was officially formed with written laws and the national election of chiefs and councilmen. In 1810 the National Council weakened clan control by outlawing the practice of clan vengeance. Changes were also occurring in social organization at this time. The Moravian Society of United Brethren began mission work in the late 1700s, and in 1803 the Presbyterians began a mission school. The Cherokees readily accepted formal education for both sexes so that by 1826 they had 18 schools. As farming was increasingly important, Cherokee leaders were afraid with good reason of the White men's treaties, which seemed only to rob them of land. In 1806 it was made a capital offense for any Cherokee to sell land to a non-Cherokee.

The old village organization and government by consensus continued to decline. In 1817 a national legislature with an upper and lower house was established, in 1823 a Supreme Court heard 21 cases, and in 1827 a national constitution was ratified. New Echota, Georgia, was named the national capital. All males 18 years and older were enfranchised, which meant that the Cherokee women lost the very real political power they had had before.

EDUCATION AND THE ECONOMY.   In 1821 a Cherokee alphabet was perfected by a mixed-blood named Sequoya. By this time a number of Scots and Englishmen had interbred with the Cherokees, forming the basis for the strong, vital mixed-blood segment of the tribe. The Cherokees were enthusiastic about their own alphabet and in 1828 began publishing a bilingual newspaper in Cherokee and English. By 1830 approximately half the people (8,000) could read and write in Sequoya's alphabet, and another 200 were literate in English. Tribal members had become successful herdsmen, farmers, and merchants. Cotton, tobacco, wheat, and corn were grown; and large herds of cattle, horses, hogs, and sheep flourished. Cherokee plantation owners even kept slaves, well over a thousand of them at this time. The tribe was economically successful and had become a thriving community to some degree separate from the United States.

Sequoya, also known as George Gist. Smithsonian Institution, National Anthropological Archives.

THE CHEROKEES AND NORTH CAROLINA. All was not perfect, however. The states of North Carolina and Georgia treated the Cherokees within their boundaries very differently. By the treaties of 1791, 1798, and 1819, which moved the boundaries of Cherokee lands ever westward, lands in North Carolina that had once been ceded to the Cherokees became public domain. Under the treaties of 1817 and 1819, Cherokees who owned land in this area could become citizens of the United States and the state of North Carolina by having their names registered with the government agent. A number of Cherokees in North Carolina took advantage of these provisions, buying and selling their own lands in the same manner as did their White neighbors. By 1838 they were described by Congressman Graham, speaking before the House of Representatives, as temperate, orderly, industrious, and peaceable. William Thomas in the same year wrote that each family could read the Scriptures, make their own clothing, and understand farming and the mechanical arts as well as their White neighbors, who helped them and treated them kindly (Bauer, 1970: 11).

THE CHEROKEES AND GEORGIA.   Georgia, on the other hand, when it ceded its western lands to the United States in 1802, entered into an agreement with the government that would extinguish the titles of the Cherokees to all their land within Georgia as soon as it could be done peaceably. The thriving independent Cherokee Nation had its own public roads and flourishing villages as well as extensive holdings in livestock, gardens, and orchards. It had no debt and was contemplating building a national library and museum. To force out these people, Georgia in 1833 declared the Cherokee laws, usages, and customs null and void within its boundaries. It authorized the survey of Cherokee lands in order that they might be divided among its citizens, and Indians were not welcome to apply. Cherokee homes were occupied or burned, lands and livestock were seized, and the Cherokee people were not allowed to testify in court to redress their grievances. This move destroyed the Cherokee Nation as a political entity, and all Indians became subject to the authority of the state in which they lived.

The Cherokees and Federal Pressure

Along with the harsh actions of the state of Georgia, the Cherokees were being subjected to federal pressures as well. In 1830, Congress passed the Indian Removal Act, which required that all southeastern Indians be moved to Indian Territory west of the Mississippi River. The Cherokees fought back through the Supreme Court and won the decision. Indian land was declared sovereign and not subject to state seizure or jurisdiction. Unfortunately for the Cherokees, Andrew Jackson and the citizens of Georgia paid little attention to John Marshall's decision. Confiscation of Indian property such as schools, council houses, and printing plants continued along with raids on villages by local White vigilante groups known as Pony Clubs. In 1835 two delegations from the tribe, led by The Ridge and Chief Ross respectively, appeared in Washington, D.C., to plead their case with the president. Jackson skillfully played one group against the other and managed to convince The Ridge and his friends to sign the Removal Treaty or the Treaty of New Echota. Ross was jailed so that he could not interfere. This treaty, signed by only 20 Cherokees, was approved by Congress with one vote to spare. It provided that all Cherokee land east of the Mississippi River

John Ross (1790–1866). Smithsonian Institution National Anthropological Archives. 1858.

be ceded to the United States in return for approximately seven million acres of land in the Indian Territory (now the state of Oklahoma) and five million dollars to be paid to individual Indians, not representatives of the entire Nation. Removal was to take place voluntarily in two years, or force would be used to get the Cherokees out. This treaty, however, also made the Indians subject to the authority of the state in which they lived. President Jackson thus left the door open so that any Cherokee who wished to remain in the east and purchase his own land could do so, provided he lived in a state that recognized these rights.

The North Carolina Cherokees were quick to take advantage of these provisions. In 1836 they authorized William H. Thomas under a special power of attorney to go to Washington to examine the treaty of New Echota. Thomas discovered that its provisions entitled the North Carolina Cherokees to receive their proportionate share of all sums due, including per capita, to purchase their lands and procure fee simple titles to it. It required that an annual census be taken before payment could be made. Finally, it provided for a Removal Fund of $53.33 for each person to be placed at interest in a safe institution so that those people who desired to migrate to the west would have money with which to do so. Many Indians in North Carolina simply remained on the land that they owned or planned to buy under the treaty provisions with the money the government had promised to pay (Bauer, 1970: 13).

Meanwhile, although about 2,000 Cherokees did move west voluntarily, the majority of the tribe in Georgia managed to convince themselves that the Treaty of New Echota would never be enforced because many other treaties with the government had been ignored. Why should this one be different? The election of Martin Van Buren to the presidency increased their hope that he might overturn Jackson's policies. Chief Ross, as a last hope, petitioned Congress in February of 1838 to nullify the treaty, but Congress voted 36 to 10 against him.

Under the direction of General Winfield Scott and beginning on May 23, 1838, the Cherokees were rounded up and placed in stockades. They were forced to leave behind not only their land, but all property they could not carry with them. In October, led by Chief Ross, close to 13,000 people with 600 wagons headed for Oklahoma. During the time spent in the stockades, on the "Trail of Tears," and getting settled in Indian territory, over 4,000 Cherokees perished, one-fifth of the entire tribe. Many Americans and foreigners were horrified by the inhumanity shown to these people, but President Van Buren, speaking before both houses of Congress, praised the removal as having a happy outcome for all parties.

THE MOONEY MYTH.   In the fall of 1838, there occurred an incident that Fred Bauer, former Vice Chief of the Eastern Band of Cherokees, referred to as the Mooney Myth because it originated in James Mooney's *Myths of the Cherokees*. According to the Mooney Myth, during the removal the wife of Tsali or Charley was killed by the soldiers, and in retaliation Tsali and his sons killed a soldier and fled into the mountains. There they joined many other Cherokees who had also hidden there, and General Scott despaired of ever rounding them all up. He made a deal with the Indians through William Thomas, promising that if Tsali and his sons were surrendered, the other Cherokees could remain until their case could be adjusted by the government. When Tsali heard this, he, along with his brother and two sons, surrendered, and all were executed. About 1,000 Cherokees remained hidden in the mountains as landless aliens until William Thomas persuaded the government to allow them to stay. This small core of survivors became the nucleus for the present-day Eastern Band.

According to Bauer, the Mooney Myth is an entertaining story and is the basis of the Cherokee drama "Unto These Hills," but it is not true. The story told in the original army report submitted to General Scott by Colonel Foster in 1838 is as follows: Tsali and the group with him were captured by Lt. A. J. Smith and his men and taken toward

Fort Scott. Shortly after sunset in October of 1838, the Indians turned upon their captors, killed two, and wounded one. They then fled taking everything they could carry with them. On November 25, the gang was tracked down with the help of Euchella's band, and Tsali was executed. Foster recommended that the 31 individuals in Euchella's band who had helped in the capture be permitted to stay in the Mountains. This story seems to be the basis of Mooney's Myth, but the military records show that the only Cherokees permitted to remain because of the incident were the 31 members of Euchella's band. Those Cherokees who preferred citizenship to tribalism and bought their own lands or planned to buy them were never molested at all. This included some people in Georgia and Tennessee as well as those in North Carolina (Bauer, 1970: 14–15, 24–25).

The New Indian Territory and the Cherokees

As our concern is with the Eastern Cherokees, the fate of those who traveled west is only briefly summarized. Their arrival in the new Indian Territory by no means resolved all their problems. The tribe was split into three factions: one led by Chief Ross, one by The Ridge, and a third group called the old settlers, who had moved west in 1817 to Arkansas. This highly conservative group had been moved into Indian Territory in 1828 and were already present when the majority of the tribe got there. Dissension existed not only among the three Cherokee groups, but also among all the other tribes who had been moved to Indian Territory. The Indians, however, were very successful in establishing themselves in the new land. By 1857 the Cherokees operated 30 public schools serving 1,500 students, published their own newspaper, cultivated 100,000 acres, and owned a quarter of a million head of livestock. More trouble came, however, with the advent of the Civil War. Although the Cherokees at first desired to stay neutral, they were pressured by some of the other tribes and by the Whites to declare for one side or the other. Finally, in August, 1861, they threw their support to the Confederacy. This decision cost them not only five years of destruction and death including 6,000 war casualties, but also terrible punishment under the Reconstruction Treaty of 1866. This treaty superseded the Treaty of New Echota, and gave the federal government the right to establish military posts and railway lines within Cherokee country. In 1887 the Dawes Act allotted all Indian land that had been owned by the various tribes to individuals; and the excess land, now known as Oklahoma Territory, was thrown open to settlers. The Curtis Act of 1898 abolished tribal courts and laws and forced allotment upon everyone not already affected. In 1906 the coup de grace was administered by the United States Congress, which dissolved the government of the Cherokee Nation. The Cherokees fought back with their proposal for an Indian state to encompass all tribal groups living in the old Indian territory, but Congress rejected their ideas to form the state of Oklahoma in 1907. The Cherokee Nation was officially dead, but a Cherokee way of life continued to show a stubborn vitality.

Because Cherokees had been in Oklahoma for a long time and were experienced in government, many were prominent in the formation of the new state. The first United States Senator from Oklahoma, Robert Latham Owen, was a Cherokee. Others served on the Constitutional Convention, were state representatives to Congress, and were active in the judiciary branch.

As of 1951 (Wright: 1951), 47,000 Cherokees were living in Oklahoma. The largest settlements were in the northeastern counties, especially Adair (6,601), Cherokee (6,298), and Delaware (5,066); but there were Cherokees living in nearly all large towns and cities in eastern and central Oklahoma. Engaged in a large variety of jobs and professions, they ran the gamut from rich to extremely poor. Traditional Cherokee cultural values and crafts still existed in the conservative Keetoowah Society, the Sequoyah Weavers' Association, and the Cherokee Basket Association and in the lives and memories of the people themselves. An excellent article by Albert and Jane Wahrhaftig (King, 1979: 223–246) details how present-day traditional Cherokees in Oklahoma have tried through ancient means to reestablish control of their own affairs.

THE EASTERN BAND OF CHEROKEES

While their brothers in the west were being stripped of their lands and rights of nationhood, what was happening to those Cherokees who had remained in North Carolina? William Thomas, adhering to the provisions of the Treaty of New Echota, took a census of the people remaining in North Carolina, South Carolina, and Tennessee in 1840 and 1841. Unfortunately, Congress was not in any hurry to distribute the money it had promised. Thomas was able to obtain some money, which he used to place a down payment upon 38,000 acres for the Indians. When the people had received the money due from the government, they could pay Thomas for the land and receive title to it. The records of the last half of the nineteenth century are extremely difficult to follow because many transactions between Thomas and the Indians were concluded, but the deeds were never properly recorded. The situation was further complicated by the Civil War, during which four companies of Cherokees served the Confederacy, protecting the mountain region from Cumberland Gap southward. After the war they found that their mountains had become infested with bushwackers and criminals who stole their livestock and tools. In addition, Thomas was suffering from ill health, and his financial affairs, including those involving the work he was doing for the Cherokees, were in terrible shape. In 1868 Congress authorized the Commissioner of Indian Affairs to take charge of the Eastern Band of Cherokees. The slaves had gained their freedom, but the Indians had lost theirs.

In 1870, in order to deal with the government, the Eastern Band had formally organized and adopted a constitution. Under this document, no individual surrendered his property rights nor was there any provision made for the Band to own communal property. Gradually, however, through the efforts of Congress and the Indian Bureau, the Eastern Band of Cherokees was transformed into a tribe whose lands were to be held in trust by the government. Although originally the Indians held their land in the same way as their White neighbors and could sell or will it to anyone they pleased, they soon lost the power to sell it to anyone except another Cherokee.

Ready for a ball game, 1907.   Photograph courtesy of Museum of the American Indian, Heye Foundation.

State Incorporation of the Land

On March 11, 1889, North Carolina passed the act for state incorporation of the band. By its provisions, the Cherokees gained legal title to 77,000 acres of land known as the Qualla Indian Boundary, plus 68 scattered tracts. The value of the land was estimated to be one million dollars. At this time, there were 1,514 Cherokees, many of whom were not distinguishable from the Whites because of the high degree of acculturation that had gone on for many years. The people were successful, self-supporting citizens of the state and were not reservation Indians. They lacked, however, the training and experience necessary to manage the corporation lands, which were then held in fee simple, some by individuals and some by the corporation. All Indians who owned their land

Interpreter and policeman, 1907. Photograph courtesy of Museum of the American Indian, Heye Foundation.

Cherokee women in the midst of a busy day. 1907.   Photograph courtesy of Museum of the American Indian, Heye Foundation.

as individuals paid taxes upon it, and the council paid taxes on corporation-owned land. Some people, however, had never received the legal deeds to land for which they had paid because of Thomas's poor records and all the litigation that had gone on since. They paid their taxes to the corporation, which, in turn, paid the state, and everyone recognized that the land really did belong to the individual paying taxes on it (Bauer, 1970: 26).

To resolve this situation, Special Agent Charles L. Davis was sent to Cherokee in 1910 to execute a plan to divide the common lands suitable for homes and farming but hold the timber lands until the timber could be sold. Heirship was to be determined under state laws, and all taxes were to be paid each year by the Indian owners of the land. The council approved Davis's plan, but the greatest stumbling block was the making of yet another membership list so that the money received from the sale of timber could be paid out to all who were entitled to it. The government began the preparation of two different rolls: the Miller Roll for all Eastern Cherokees and the Churchill Roll for the Eastern Band of Cherokees; that is, those who lived in North Carolina, were involved with William Thomas in obtaining legal title to their land, and possessed the right to benefits from the sale of timber. The Miller Roll

Making pottery. 1900. Smithsonian Institution, National Anthropological Archives.

was authorized for the purpose of establishing who was entitled to receive the five million dollars awarded in 1906 by the Court of Claims to the Eastern Cherokees who had chosen to live in any one of several states in the east. Miller received 100,000 applicants for his roll, and enrolled 30,000 of them. Some people who had been included on the Miller Roll demanded that they be placed on the Churchill Roll as well; and when the council objected, Miller argued that the state incorporation was unconstitutional and inoperative. Because of all this dissension, the Davis plan failed to be implemented.

The Merritt Plan and Its Consequences

In 1917 a new plan was proposed by Assistant Commissioner E. B. Merritt to settle the tangled Cherokee land questions. Ignoring the fact that many Cherokees had purchased their own lands and become citizens almost a century earlier, ignoring all deeds recorded in the counties, ignoring the de facto division of land through the years by buying, selling, and inheritance, Merritt proposed that all property should be transferred to the United States in trust so that all assets of the corporation could be disposed of. All persons having one-fourth or less Cherokee blood who did not live at Qualla or on band lands were to receive cash after the disposal instead of land. Merritt thus issued an open invitation for people to claim Cherokee blood in order to benefit from the dispersal of band assets. He proposed, too, that the Indians be

A stained glass window in a Catholic church reflects something of the Cherokee attitude toward the larger society.

given a brief period of immunity from paying taxes on their land in order to "prepare for this responsibility of citizenship" (Bauer, 1970: 29). This was said in spite of the fact that these Indians had been paying taxes for years, and one Jackson County tax collector said that they were always the first to pay. If the Indians agreed to this plan, they would receive in return not the deeds to their land that had been authorized to implement the Davis plan, but first, certificates giving them the right to occupy and use it. These certificates would be followed by trust patents and finally, many years later, patents in fee. Today "many years later" has still not arrived.

Although the council had no authority to place individual Cherokee property under trust, it accepted the promises of the Bureau of Indian Affairs for a speedy settlement. Hearings were held in Congress, and the Merritt plan became law on June 4, 1924. Taxes were immediately suspended on all property, even that of individuals who had always owned their own land, land that the corporation had no right to turn over to the government. Although these people wanted to pay their taxes, they were made to look bad before their neighbors for not doing so. Twelve thousand people applied for a place on the Cherokee rolls, enclosing a fee of five dollars for each adult and coining the name "five dollar Indian," which is still used today. A new roll, the Baker Roll, was made up in 1928 and contained over 3,100 names, 1,200 of which were contested by the Cherokee council. They feared that unless the rolls were changed, the band would lose a third of their land and money to people who were not really Cherokees. In spite of these protests, the Baker Roll was approved by the Bureau of Indian Affairs. The Cherokee council proposed a cash settlement with the 1,200 people who they did not think belonged on the roll in order that valid titles might finally be issued to those people who lived on the Qualla Boundary. Instead, the Bureau suggested that allotment be postponed, a move that proved very advantageous for them because the Great Smoky Mountains National Park was being planned and the Eastern Cherokees were to play an important part in making this park a major tourist attraction. If the land had been allotted as promised, the Bureau would no longer have had any jurisdiction over the Cherokees, nor would they be able to control them to their own advantage. From free people with legal rights to their land, the Cherokees had become tribal Indians. Although the Qualla Boundary had never been a reservation, it was now to be treated as one. In doing so, the federal government erroneously assumed by default that the Cherokees would acquire common interests or common problems with common solutions. This was not to be.

The story of the development of the Great Smoky National Park and the fight of the Cherokees to retain their land in the face of the government's desire to use it for parkland and access roads is a long and complex one. Anyone interested in the details should consult Bauer's *Land of the North Carolina Cherokees* (1970).

The Eastern Cherokee Reservation Today

Today the Eastern Cherokee Reservation or Qualla Boundary is located in western North Carolina, 50 miles west of Asheville. The largest town, Cherokee, stands at the junction of U.S. Highways 441 and 19. The 43,554 acres of the Qualla Boundary consist of about 80 percent of forested mountain slopes, the rest being bottom land and river valleys. The five main centers of population in the Qualla Boundary are each centered around a section of bottom land. They are Big Cove, Wolfstown, Painttown, Cherokee Village, and Birdtown.

Included in the Cherokee Reservation but located outside of the Qualla Boundary are three other areas. The 3,200 Acre Tract, a mountainous ridge located south of the junction of the Tuckasegge and Oconaluftee rivers, is the home of about 15 families. Snowbird township, located about 50 miles west of Cherokee Village, is a group of 23 tracts of land totaling 2,249 acres. Finally, there are 5,571 acres divided among 26 scattered tracts about 80 miles west of Cherokee Village in Cherokee County in extreme western North Carolina. The entire reservation totals 46,574 acres, all but 7,820 of which are in either the Qualla Boundary or the 3,200 Acre Tract. As the available data concentrate on the main reservation, the people living in Snowbird and Cherokee County will be ignored. They would, however, repay further study because they are reputed to be more conservative and have certainly been less affected by tourism.

French and Hornbuckle (1976: 118 ff.) list the seven Cherokee communities and briefly characterize them as follows:

CHEROKEE VILLAGE.   Cherokee Village is located at the eastern entrance of the Great Smoky Mountain National Park and is the home of 723 people. Highly commercialized, it teems with gift shops and tourist attractions, especially along the quarter mile Cherokee Strip where Highways 441 and 19 share the same roadway. Just north of town on 441 are the federal buildings, including housing for federal employees, an elementary school, the B.I.A. Agency, and an Indian Health Service hospital, pharmacy, and outpatient clinic. North of the federal area are tribal offices and beyond these is the Cherokee Historical Association, which runs the Indian museum, the reconstructed historical Indian village, and the outdoor drama "Unto These Hills." At the park entrance are more gift shops, motels, restaurants, and service stations. Paralleling Highway 441 is Acquoni Road, upon which are located two of the three industries on the reservation, the Cherokee Boys' Club, the new Cherokee high school, the housing office, the community building, several homes, and another cluster of gift shops.

PAINTTOWN COMMUNITY.   Painttown Community, with 709 residents, is also highly commercialized. Here are more motels, campgrounds, crafts shops, and restaurants, as well as a major attraction, Frontierland, which includes a replica of an old Indian fort, a Plains Indian village, and an amusement park. As is true for all the communities, most Indian homes are to be found on side roads away from the main traffic pattern. Churches and a community club are centers of the Indian community.

The voting township of Wolftown is divided into two separate communities: Soco and Big Y.

SOCO COMMUNITY.   Located four miles from Cherokee on Highway 19, Soco Community has 746 people scattered over a wide area. The main tourist attraction is Soco is Santa's Land, containing an amusement park and zoo. It also has its share of campgrounds, motels, and gift shope. A number of churches (including Baptist, Church of Christ, and Methodist denominations) are important in the social life. None of these communities can be defined by the degree of Indian blood possessed by the inhabitants. People ranging from full bloods to five-dollar Indians seem scattered equally among the villages.

BIG Y.   Big Y is the smallest community with 357 residents. Located in rugged mountain terrain, it has no industries or tourist attractions. It does contain the tribal timber reserve, on which no cutting is permitted. Homes are scattered, and churches, especially Baptist, are important.

BIG COVE TOWNSHIP.   Big Cove Township, population 672, is the largest in area and is unique in that it cannot be reached on a through highway. It has a reputation of being a bad area with more criminal activity and also of being the home of the "real Indians." French and Hornbuckle, however, claim that these are merely labels and that Big Cove people differ not at all from those in other communities. Although it has a few campgrounds and stores, it is not a tourist area, probably because of the difficulties in getting there. Houses are often so well hidden up side roads that the tourist would see only mail boxes. The terrain is extremely rugged.

BIRDTOWN.   Owing to the fact that it has much land suitable for building houses, Birdtown is the most heavily populated, having as many people as Big Cove and Painttown combined. Adjacent to Cherokee, it is developing along commercial lines with the usual quota of shops along the main roads. Also in Birdtown are a day school, several small general stores, and a number of Baptist churches.

THE 3,200 ACRE TRACT.   Isolated from the main reservation by deeded land, the 3,200 Acre Tract is linked to Birdtown for voting purposes. One hundred and thirty-five residents live in scattered houses along the ridges. Small stores can be found in nearby villages, and churches again play an important role in community life.

SNOWBIRD COMMUNITY.   Snowbird Community, the isolated area mentioned previously, contains 418 residents. Although the children attend the public schools of Graham County, the people seem to retain more of an Indian identity than those on the main reservation. More Cherokee is spoken at home, and family ties remain strong. Adults are employed in various industries in Graham County, and tourism, though present, plays a minor role in the economy.

The Way of Life on the Reservation

POLITICAL ORGANIZATION.   The people inhabiting all these scattered villages and townships are linked by membership in the political entity known as the Eastern Band of Cherokee Indians. Properly enrolled voters, 18 years and older, representing each of the six voting precincts, elect two representatives to the tribal council every two years. The chief and vice-chief of the tribe are elected by voters from all townships every four years. This tribal council is responsible for passing all resolutions pertaining to the everyday running of the tribe. Their decisions, however, are subject to the approval of the B.I.A. Superintendent and the Secretary of the Interior.

HOUSING.   The casual visitor traveling on the reservation has no way of knowing that the houses he sees are owned by Indians. Cherokees no longer live in their aboriginal structures made of wattle and daub. Gulick (1973: 48–50) describes four types of dwellings today. A few very conservative families still live in log or pole houses introduced by early European settlers. Insulation is provided by clay or concrete chinking or by boards nailed to the inside surface of the logs. These houses always have a large field stone chimney, a front porch supported by posts, and a shake roof. Much more common is a simple rectangular frame house built with boards and lacking attic, basement, and sometimes even front porch. Many of these homes have never been painted, and some have been covered with tar paper or asphalt siding. Houses

Top: The Council House, where plans for the Cherokee people are made. *Bottom:* Here the plans are approved or disapproved.

like this are generally heated by the woodburning stove used for cooking, and most lack plumbing except for a hand pump in the kitchen. Windows and doors are seldom screened, and furniture is crude.

A large, two-story frame house, having two or more brick chimneys, a porch, and unpainted clapboard siding, is sometimes found.

A log house 1908.   Photograph courtesy of Museum of the American Indian, Heye Foundation.

This style was introduced in the late nineteenth century and appears in other parts of rural North Carolina. Much more common are bungalow-type houses with one main story and a half a story above for bedrooms or attic. These homes may have a front porch and are often heated with kerosene room furnaces. Exteriors are finished with painted clapboard or composition siding.

In addition to these four basic styles, ranch houses and concrete block structures are beginning to be built with B.I.A. funds, which are also available for remodeling older structures. Electricity is present throughout the reservation and is normally used for lighting, if for nothing else. Sanitation facilities are being improved (Witthoft, 1979: 219).

TYPES OF FAMILIES.   What types of families live in this variety of houses? French and Hornbuckle (1976: 168) divide them into three models: conservative, middle-class, and marginal. Although the nuclear family is the most common pattern found, among conservative people the extended family household is often present. Gulick (1973: 63), using data from Big Cove and Painttown, believes that this three-generation, extended family pattern is not necessarily a reflection of a traditional orientation. Although conservative Cherokees do have a firm commitment to generosity and hospitality, at least in theory, most three-generation households that he found were made necessary by either poverty or the need to care for illegitimate children, a pattern found also among poor North Carolina non-Indian families. The conservatives can be further identified by their adherence to traditional Cherokee values. They are more likely to speak Cherokee in the home. They follow traditional modes of diet, habit, dress, and behavior. Children are indulged and given personal autonomy very early. They and

The women of a conservative household. Using a wooden mortar and pestle probably to make a hickory nut drink (Kunutchi). ca. 1930s. Smithsonian Institution, National Anthropological Archives.

their parents follow the "Harmony Ethic," which stresses the subordination of selfish interests for the sake of group cohesion.

The middle-class families conform to prevalent local American standards. Children are encouraged to be achievers, English is spoken in the home, friends are other middle-class Cherokees or Whites, and houses are expensive and modern.

Marginal families are midway between these two forms and suffer the disadvantages of both. They cannot afford to buy middle-class amenities, and yet they lack the close social network of the conservatives, who find their security in following traditional values. Because their family circumstances are determined by chance and not design, these people often grow up with a very weak self-image, which they pass on to their children to perpetuate the unhappy cycle. French and Hornbuckle assign most Cherokees to this marginal class with about one-third being conservatives and only a few mixed bloods being middle class. They also state that all Cherokees share ambiguous feelings about just who they are and how they are supposed to behave. These feelings are exacerbated by the Indian image presented to the tourists on the Qualla Boundary and the many conflicting social expectations that other people have of the Indians.

Gulick (1973: 63 ff.) makes a number of other statements about Cherokee families. Common law marriage is typical, and illegitimate children are accepted in a matter-of-fact fashion. Although some elderly people remember the old clan system based on descent from the mother, by and large it has been forgotten, and kin ties are determined by conventional American standards. A barrier is no longer placed upon marriage to a person of one's own clan, if indeed this clan is known. As the penalty for in-clan marriage was being stoned to death, this represents a major change in thinking and custom. Kinship alliances between households in a community are frequent, and close contacts are maintained with blood relatives.

EARNING A LIVING.   The ways in which the Cherokees support themselves and their families vary. Because the mountainous regions of the south are generally classified as economically depressed areas, tourism has been of major importance since the opening of Great Smoky Mountain National Park and the development of the varied attractions on the reservation itself. The Cherokees, however, pay a price for tourist dollars. Most of the profit goes not to them but to the Cherokee Historical Association, run by non-Indians, and to individual non-Indian businessmen. For instance, the major parts in the play "Unto These Hills" are taken by students from the University of North Carolina, and the Cherokees must content themselves with bit parts and stagehand roles at minimum wages. In addition, the drama may well have deleterious

A Cherokee "chief" ready to entertain tourists.

effects upon the Indian self-image. According to Bauer (1970: 55), the myth portrayed in the drama cannot help but arouse Cherokee resentment, consisting as it does of the repetition of the many injustices done to the tribe over the years. The historical details are not always accurate, but to the Cherokees the play has become history—they no longer remember any other.

The tourist industry began for the Cherokees during the Great Depression years when the government was engaged in building the access roads for the park. Cherokees were hired under the auspices of work relief programs to build these roads, and the Great Depression was a relatively prosperous time for the tribe. The opening of the park and the development of the various tourist attractions, however, resulted in the development of a cyclical economy. The six months when the tourists appeared were relatively prosperous, but the six winter months did not provide any opportunities for regular income. Because traditional conservative Cherokee values emphasized living for today rather than saving for tomorrow, this cyclical economy forced many people to go on welfare to survive the winter. This situation also has had an unfortunate effect on the emotional stability of many Cherokees. Six months of frantic activity with exposure to American standards of affluence followed by six months of isolation and dependency do not constitute a wholesome life.

Most Cherokees whose jobs depend on tourists work in low-paid capacities as cooks, maids, or shop assistants. About 25 or 30 males are self-employed in the colorful business of "chiefing." These men dress in pan-Indian garb and post themselves in front of the tourist shops as an attraction. They specialize in having their pictures taken with all comers, and the best ones can earn a substantial income through tips. Businessmen are happy to have the "chiefs" there, for they attract customers. Although the B.I.A. and the Cherokee Historical Association publicly discredit chiefing as a humiliating job, they, too , benefit from the increased tourist trade that the chiefs produce. Tourists seem willing to accept the vulgar Indian stereotype the chiefs present, for it fits in with their own preconceived ideas of what an Indian is. Along with the chiefs, Indian dancers and princesses play similar roles in attracting the tourists to the shops before which they perform. These people make most of their money from tips, although they may receive a small salary from the storekeeper.

Full-time, higher-status jobs on the reservation are few and include tribal government positions and middle-class managerial or proprietorial roles. Conservative Indians can be found in the tribal government, but most small business owners or those who work for the federal agencies or the Cherokee Historical Association are "white" Indians who have been groomed for their positions by the Whites. The more prosperous people often combine jobs. One man works for an agency and also runs a farm or a motel, which obviously gives him a distinct advantage over a wage earner.

The Cherokees can no longer rely on farming for subsistence because most of the good bottom land is now owned by non-Indians. Most families do, however, plant a garden that supplies an important part of their diet. This is in contrast to earlier times when cooperative farming by organizations called *gadugi* was extremely important to the

Cherokee economy. Excessive state taxation of the *gadugi* helped force them out of existence. Their present-day offshoots are the Free Labor Companies. Gulick found seven Free Labor Companies in the Qualla Boundary in the 1950s. These organizations supplied mutual aid, including physical labor, to members. Although they did not give continuous help as did Public Assistance, they were invaluable in times of sickness, death, or other emergency. When Williams visited the Cherokees in 1973, however, she found that the Free Labor Companies were almost gone.

Light industry appeared on the reservation in the late 1950s, but it did not help the economy a great deal because it employed mostly women at minimum wages. When unionization was proposed, the industries threatened to move off the Qualla Boundary rather than submit to it. In their prohibition of elections for labor unions, they had the support of the B.I.A. and the tribal government even though such support violated the National Labor Relations Act (French & Hornbuckle, 1976: 159–160).

Gulick (1973: 80–81) lists a number of ways in which people earn extra money. These include logging, novelty production, basket weaving for the tourist trade, selling honey, selling rattlesnakes, splitting and selling cordwood, making beadwork for tourists, quilt-making, wood carving, making aprons, collecting ginseng root, making blowguns, and collecting building stone. Basketmaking is especially popular, particularly with women and girls.

Although one possible solution for Cherokee economic difficulties would be migration to the cities and other areas, this alternative is seldom followed. Seasonal, intermittent opportunities such as harvest in Florida, war production, and special construction jobs are sometimes pursued. A few individuals have moved away permanently, but these are the exceptions. This is true for the middle-class and marginal people as well as for the conservatives.

THE EASTERN CHEROKEE RESERVATION CULTURE: THE COST OF LIVING IN A WHITE WORLD

The Eastern Cherokees have established crucial economic, social, and religious ties with the greater American society. The creation and maintenance of such a linkage have been slow and painful processes. The net result of such ties has been fully satisfactory to neither Indians nor non-Indians.

Wage labor and various forms of part-time relief supply a marginal kind of financial support. Formal education, though providing the essentials of learning, prepares most Cherokees for little more than unskilled and semiskilled labor. Enrolled Indian students do come to realize that most Whites would prefer that they abandon their heritage and conform, for the most part, to middle-class expectations. Available facilities, however, constitute neither the means nor the motivation for such a transition.

Most contemporary Cherokees take a serious interest in institutionalized Christianity. Their churches are Baptist or Methodist with a fundamentalist orientation. Many of the clergymen are lay Cherokees who work at a second job to support themselves. Churches are an important focus of social life, and the doctrines preached there endorse many traditional Cherokee beliefs. The fundamentalist, literal interpretation of Scripture, however, often provides inappropriate answers to the complex problems of Indian survival in a White world.

The physical and mental health of a significant portion of the Cherokees is poor. Alcohol abuse is frequent and often leads to criminal behavior. There are high incidences of respiratory diseases and diabetes as well as many hypertensive, endocrine, nutritional, and metabolic disorders. The accident rate is high.

Reservation life, particularly those crucial activities associated with the family and household, is turbulent and often chaotic. The behavior of children and adults frequently reflects this instability. Listlessness, apathy, and lack of initiative are evident at both the individual and community levels. Violent acts are frequent. Although a Cherokee may be given a number of options with regard to behavioral models such as part-time professional or tourist Indian, the traditional Cherokee conservative backwoodsman, or the successful, middle-class Indian, he is never allowed to forget the fact that by the standards of the world outside the reservation he remains an Indian and hence a subordinate, powerless member of a larger complex society that has little place for him.

The Eastern Cherokees have finally become the kind of Indians that their White contemporaries will allow them to be. More than 250 years of White contact have resulted in their assumption of a subordinate, underclass status for the vast majority of people. Logistical insufficiency produced a series of military defeats by more powerful forces. The resulting political impotence during the first half of the nineteenth century made it impossible for the Cherokees to achieve an economic and social equality with the larger society that surrounded them. The amount and kind of cultural change that accompanied these developments have been extensive. Although much of the Cherokee language and syllabary, the ideas and practices associated with traditional medicine, and a mature adaptable sense of ethnicity have persisted, early eighteenth-century political, economic, and social institutions have long ceased to exist.

Dan McCoy, current (1980) tribal chairman.

THE FUTURE. The people called Cherokee, however, have shown a remarkable vitality in the face of formidable odds, largely because they have been able to survive on resources that the dominant society has not cared enough about to take away from them, particularly areas of land that had little or no obvious commercial use. Even these places, to a great extent, are shared with non-Indians who are successful and prominent entrepreneurs in the tourist industry. The Eastern Cherokees appear to accept exclusive use and ownership of only a very few places, which serve as residential or dormitory communities. An ethnicity that centers around an erratic submission to American influences will probably persist for the foreseeable future as long as a number of supporting circumstances continue. The tourist industry firmly rooted in the existence of the Great Smoky Mountain National Park should provide various segments of the Cherokee population with a marginal kind of income sufficient for survival and yet inadequate to produce healthy economic growth. Limited welfare programs stemming from federal and local sources will also continue to perpetuate their existence. Economic resources to a large extent will be changed to social resources, which nourish a supporting network of kinsmen, friends, and neighbors. The factors of common occupational positions, residential stability and concentration, plus a dependence on common institutions and services will function in turn to maintain a Cherokee people in North Carolina.

REFERENCES

Bauer, Fred B. *Land of the North Carolina Cherokees*. Brevard, North Carolina: Buchanan Press, 1970.

The Constitution and Laws of the Cherokee Nation: Passed at Tahlequah, Cherokee Nation, 1839–51. Tahlequah, Cherokee Nation: 1852.

Culin, Stewart. Games of the North American Indians. *24th Annual Report, Bureau of American Ethnology, Smithsonian Institution*. Washington, D.C.: Government Printing Office, 1907.

Dickens, Roy S., Jr. The Origins and Development of Cherokee Culture. In Duane H. King, ed., *The Cherokee Indian Nation*. Knoxville: University of Tennessee Press, 1979, pp. 3–32.

Fogelson, Raymond D. *The Cherokees: A Critical Bibliography*. Bloomington: Indiana University Press, 1978.

French, Laurence and Jim Hornbuckle. "The Contemporary Cherokees: The Dilemma of Accommodation." Manuscript, 1976.

———. An Analysis of Indian Violence: The Cherokee Example. *American Indian Quarterly 3*. 335–356, Winter 1977–78.

Gilbert, William Harlen, Jr. The Eastern Cherokees. In *Bulletin 133, Bureau of American Ethnology, Smithsonian Institution*. Washington, D.C.: Government Printing Office, 1943, pp. 169–413.

Gulick, John. *Cherokees at the Crossroads* (rev. ed.). Chapel Hill: Institute for Research in Social Science, University of North Carolina, 1973.

Holmes, Ruth Bradley, and Betty Sharp Smith. *Beginning Cherokee*. Norman: University of Oklahoma Press, 1976.

Hudson, Charles M., ed. *Four Centuries of Southern Indians*. Athens: University of Georgia Press, 1975.

———. *The Southeastern Indians*. Knoxville: University of Tennessee Press, 1976.

King, Duane H., ed. *The Cherokee Indian Nation*. Knoxville: University of Tennessee Press, 1979.

Lounsbury, Floyd. Iroquois–Cherokee Linguistic Relations. In W. N. Fenton and J. Gulick, eds., *Symposium on Cherokee and Iroquois Culture, Bulletin 180, Bureau of American Ethnology, Smithsonian Institution*. Washington, D.C.: Government Printing Office, 1961, pp. 11–17.

Mooney, James. Myths of the Cherokee. *19th Annual Report, Part 1. Bureau of American Ethnology, Smithsonian Institution*. Washington, D.C.: Government Printing Office, 1900.

———, and Frans M. Olbrechts. The Swimmer Manuscript: Cherokee Sacred Formulas and Medicinal Prescriptions. *Bulletin 99, Bureau of American Ethnology, Smithsonian Institution*. Washington, D.C.: Government Printing Office, 1932.

Oswalt, Wendell H. The Eastern Cherokees: Farmers of the Southeast. In *This Land Was Theirs* (2d ed.). New York: John Wiley & Sons, 1973, pp. 502–527.

Perdue, Theda. Rising from the Ashes: *The Cherokee Phoenix* as an Ethnohistorical Source. *Ethnohistory 24* (Summer 1977): 207–218.

Royce, Charles C. *The Cherokee Nation of Indians*. Chicago: Aldine Publishing Co., 1975.

Swanton, John R. Indian Tribes of the Lower Mississippi Valley and the Adjacent Coast of the Gulf of Mexico. *Bulletin 43, Bureau of American Ethnology, Smithsonian Institution*. Washington, D.C.: Government Printing Office, 1911.

———. Early History of the Creek Indians and Their Neighbors. *Bulletin 73, Bureau of American Ethnology, Smithsonian Institution*. Washington, D.C.: Government Printing Office, 1922.

———. Aboriginal Culture of the Southeast. In *42nd Annual Report, Bureau of American Ethnology, Smithsonian Institution*. Washington, D.C.: Government Printing Office, 1928, pp. 673–726.

———. Social Organization and Social Usages of the Indians of the Creek Confederacy. *42nd Annual Report, Bureau of American Ethnology, Smithsonian Institution*. Washington, D.C.: Government Printing Office, 1928.

———. The Indians of the Southeastern United States. *Bulletin 137, Bureau of American Ethnology, Smithsonian Institution*. Washington, D.C.: Government Printing Office, 1946.

Wahrhaftig, Albert, and Jane Wahrhaftig. New Militants or Resurrected State? The Five County Northeastern Oklahoma Cherokee Organization. In Duane H. King, *The Cherokee Indian Nation*. Knoxville: University of Tennessee Press, 1979, pp. 223–246.

Williams, Sharlotte Neely. Epilogue: Cherokees at the Crossroads, 1973. In John Gulick, ed. *Cherokees at the Crossroads* (rev.ed.). Chapel Hill: Institute for Research in Social Science, University of North Carolina, 1973, pp. 177–194.

Witthoft, John. Observations on Social Change among the Eastern Cherokees. In Duane H. King, ed., *The Cherokee Indian Nation*. Knoxville: University of Tennessee Press, 1979, pp. 202–222.

Wright, Muriel H. *A Guide to the Indian Tribes of Oklahoma*. Norman: University of Oklahoma Press, 1951.

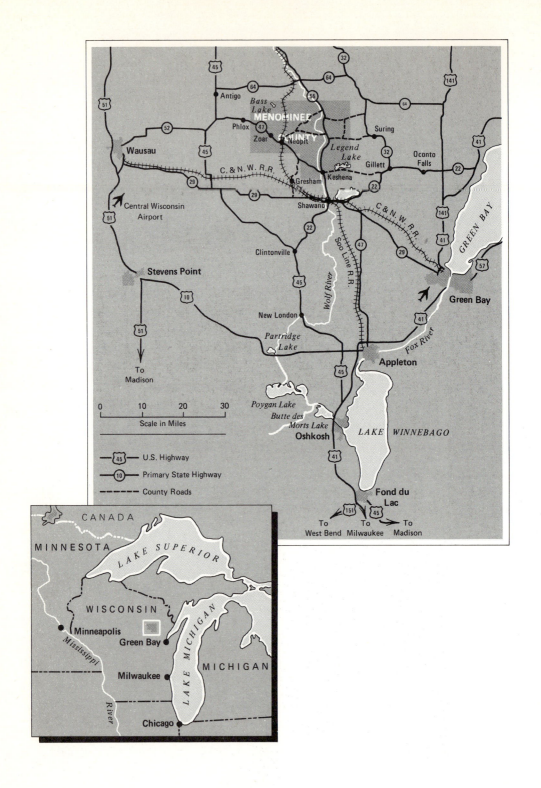

CHAPTER 5

THE MENOMINEES
Woodland Individualists

Beneath the earth there is, in the lowest tier, the great white bear with a long copper tail who, in addition to being the chief and patron of all earthly bears and the traditional ancestor of the Menomini tribe, is the principal power for evil.

Alanson Skinner,
"Material Culture of the Menomini"

The Menominees, like some of the Oneidas, live in Wisconsin, but the Menominees have been there a lot longer. Like the Micmac, Menominees are Algonquian speakers, and they share many facets of the Eastern Woodland type of culture with both the Micmac and the Iroquois. To examine their culture in detail, we will look at three different periods: prereservation times ending in 1854; the Reservation Period, 1854 to 1954; and Reservation Termination and Restoration, 1954 to the present.

Oshkosh, prominent Menominee of the mid-nineteenth century. Taken ca. 1845 and believed to be the first photograph ever taken of an Indian. Oshkosh Public Museum.

MENOMINEE LIFE BEFORE 1854

Scattered, inconclusive evidence suggests that some time after A.D 1000 those people who were to be called Menominee were pushed south and west from an area just northeast of the Great Lakes. They ranged over much of what would become the eastern half of Wisconsin until significant, permanent contacts with Europeans were established during the latter part of the seventeenth century. Prior to that time the culture of the Menominees must have been very different from that of more recent years (Skinner, 1921: 371). Wild rice and fish made up much of their diet. They spent most of their time in lake and riverside villages except for periods in fall and winter, when parties of hunters ranged inland.

A specific mode of prehistoric life attributed to the Menominees is the *Keshena culture* (Willey, 1966: 281; Bennett, 1952: 108–123), described below. In addition to the Menominee, the Sac, Fox, and Chippewa also followed this way of life. Digging at the small campsites of the Keshena culture, archaeologists have found pottery with rounded bases and wide necks, chipped stone points, drills, scrapers, knives, grooved axes, and a considerable variety of pipes. Near the campsite were burials with the bodies either bundled, laid to rest in a flexed position, or cremated. Although small round burial mounds may have been constructed originally, most bodies were found in shallow pits in cemetery groups. Looked at in broad perspective, this Keshena culture represented a kind of northern fringe segment of the widespread Woodland cultural tradition that can be defined by its characteristic cord-marked and fabric-marked ceramics plus the construction of burial mounds and other earthworks. Some form of agriculture may have influenced the peripheral region where Keshena culture was located. The relationship of Kehsena culture to contemporary Woodland developments in the Central Mississippi Valley, the Ohio Valley, and the Northeast cannot be stated with any precision. It is clear, however, that the period of Keshena Culture was a time of considerable unrest and change for the Menominees because the appearance of several Indian groups not indigenous to the area forced them to adjust to new arrivals.

Keesing (1939), using a wide variety of historical sources pertaining to the seventeenth century, has attempted to reconstruct what was happening in Wisconsin when the French arrived there. In the early 1600s, northeastern Wisconsin was peopled only by the Winnebagos, who were Siouan speakers; by the Menominees, who were their allies; and by a small group called the Noquat, now absorbed into the Chippewa. This Winnebago-Menominee alliance was hostile to other Central Algonquian- and Iroquoian-speaking tribes who were located east of Lake Michigan. Indeed, one of the first journeys made by a Frenchman into the area, that of Father Nicollet in 1634, was to arrange peace between the Winnebagos and the Hurons.

In 1635 the Iroquois, who had obtained guns from Dutch traders, went to war. For 20 years they made repeated raids all the way to the eastern shores of Lake Michigan, driving out the tribes who lived there. The Potawatomis, Ottawas, and Sauks fled around the lake to the north whereas the Illinois, Fox, Kickapoos, and Mascoutens went south and west. Although some of these tribes traveled as far west as the Mississippi River, by 1664 when peace was established with the Iroquois, most of them were gathered in Wisconsin in order to take advantage of the new trade opportunities with the French. Their presence there spelled disaster to the Winnebagos and Menominees, who had warred against them for years. Both tribes were reduced to remnants by the combination of the newcomers, who were seeking revenge, and the effects of White-introduced diseases. In 1669, Father Allouez recorded that he found only one Menominee village located at the mouth of the Menominee River, the present-day site of Marinette, Wisconsin, and Menominee, Michigan. This village had a population of 40 warriors plus no more than 200 women and children. Undoubtedly, this violent disruption of Menominee life coming at a time when White contact brought so many changes caused them to lose some ethnic distinctiveness. It also makes reconstruction of aboriginal Menominee life extremely difficult, for by the time the first ethnographers reached the area, even the oldest people remembered only what life had been like during the French period.

FOOD AND CLOTHING.   Given these qualifications, what can be said about early Menominee life? No one knows the original extent of Menominee territory, although it covered a large part of eastern Wisconsin. The Menominees depended largely upon hunting, gathering, and fishing for food. Wisconsin has cold, snowy winters, but warm summers suitable for the growth of many native plants. These plus the abundant fish and game in the streams, lakes, and forests probably meant that the Menominees seldom suffered serious food shortages. Important wild plant foods included wild rice, a variety of berries and nuts, "potatoes" such as Indian spikenard, grapes when available, and tree lichens, wild onions, and large-tooth cress for seasoning. Keesing (1939) questioned whether maple sugar was used much before the French taught the Indians the art of tapping trees and boiling down the sap. He believed that although the Menominees may have cultivated some Indian corn, wild rice was far more important to their diet. Tobacco may or may not have been grown for ceremonial use; smoking additives of "red willow" (an osier, *Cornus stalinifera*) and sumac could have been used.

Wild animals and fish were also an important part of their economy, although hunting probably became more important during the French period when the Menominees spent much time in the woods trapping for furs. Deer supplied not only food but clothing as well. Menominee dress for both men and women was similar, consisting of breechcloth, leggings, and moccasins made of deer hide with a fur cloak thrown over the shoulders for protection in winter. Early French sources commented on the lack of modesty these Indians had; neither men or women went covered above the waist in warm weather. Oiling or greasing their hair and the use of colors for ceremonial occasions were the only decorative techniques employed. Buffalo, moose, and elk all inhabited Wisconsin during earlier times and may have been a part of the Menominee diet, but there are only vague suggestions of this in the literature. Many smaller animals lived there including the lynx, muskrat, beaver, squirrel, and rabbit. Ducks, partridges, and pigeons formed part of the diet. Fishing was done all year round, fish being netted or speared through the ice in winter. Sturgeon were a very important food source, and other fish caught included trout, whitefish, perch, and pike.

HOUSING.   It is easier to speak with certainty about Menominee houses, for they did not change until more recent times. Two types were in use: the quadrangular house of bark for summer and the dome-roofed round lodge for winter (Skinner, 1921: 84–88). The winter lodge was about 15 feet wide with a door facing south to catch the sun and protect the interior from wind and rain. The exterior was covered with cattail mats or birch or elm bark except for a two-foot square smoke hole in the ceiling. Couches or benches covered with mats or boughs lined the inside walls. Temporary ceremonial or religious structures were also erected, including sweat lodges, women's menstrual huts, places for dreaming and fasting, and a juggler's or magician's hut. Summer houses were 15 to 25 feet long and 10 to 12 feet wide with ridged roofs about 10 to 15 feet high. They were unsuitable for winter occupation, being too open and airy for comfort. Both types of houses were built, if possible, on dry sandy soil, which afforded good drainage for moisture in summer and retained heat well in winter.

OTHER FEATURES OF MATERIAL CULTURE.   Much of the Menominee tool inventory and other routinely manufactured products had to do with food production and processing. The art of curing or dressing hides was highly developed. Vegetal-fiber twined string bags were found in all households and used to store a wide variety of possessions (Skinner, 1921: 231). Reed and bark mats served as floor coverings and for hanging on the inner walls of the lodge. As aids for travel, in addition to canoes, the Menominees made snowshoes and various types of burden straps, baskets, and bags. The incoming Europeans also found these items useful and learned to employ them from the Indians. Although a wide variety of wooden objects such as bowls, spoons, troughs, and birchbark buckets and baskets have long been associated with the Menominees, it is questionable whether they were in use before the seventeenth century. In 1669 the visiting Father Allouez mentioned that the savages of the region were usually barbarous in that they did not even know how to make a bark dish or a ladle; they commonly used shells instead (Keesing, 1939: 29). The art of woodworking might have been introduced to the Menominee by the Algonquian tribes displaced by the Iroquois. Weapons of war were bows and arrows, clubs, knives, and axes. No shields have been found in association with the Menominees, although they were used by the Illinois to the south.

At the time in question, the Menominees may have worked copper for ornaments, but all copper artifacts found in the region are of comparatively recent origin (Fox and Younger quoted in Keesing, 1939: 30). The only arts known to be genuinely old are simple geometric forms found on pottery fragments or medicine bags and pouches. The elaborate floral patterns found on many museum items must be a more recent development.

SOCIAL AND POLITICAL ORGANIZATION.   Moving away from material culture, what is known about Menominee social and political organization? The Menominees had a hereditary clan system with two divisions, called *moieties* by anthropologists. These moieties were based on the Menominee myth dealing with their origins. Keesing, quoting Hoffman, gives this version (1939: 36): The bear came out of the ground and was made an Indian. Being lonely, he called the Golden Eagle (also called the Thunderer or Thunderbird) to be his brother. The Eagle, too, took human form. The Beaver and the Elk were then adopted as younger brothers of the Eagle, and the Sturgeon, Crane, and Wolf as the younger brothers of the Bear. The Good Mystery made the Thunderers the laborers, giving them corn and the ability to make fire. Wild rice was the property of the Bear group. One day the Thunderers decided to visit the Bear village at the Menominee River in order to ask the Bear group to join them and live together. They promised to share their knowledge of corn and fire in return for being allowed to share in the wild rice. Ever since that time, the two families have lived together. Other traditions add that the Bear group were responsible for civil leadership whereas the Thunderers provided leadership in war. Although this was all the old people of Hoffman's time (1896) knew about the clan system, it is interesting to note that, on the reservation today, those Menominees who follow the *Midewiwin* or traditional religious practices are firmly divided into Bear and Thunder settlements. Within each moiety, each individual inherited from his father a specific tribal totem such as the White Beaver, the Wolf, the Turtle, the Crane, or the Bear; but specific information on the exact number of totems and how they were related is lacking. When a traditional Menominee dies, his totem is painted, usually upside down, on a stick placed upon his grave (Keesing, 1939: 39).

WARFARE.   Early Jesuit writings mentioned also a Council of Elders and special leaders of war and religious matters among the Menominees. Keesing believed that the Menominee Council did not observe the elaborate ceremonialism so characteristic of the Iroquois, who made a fine art of speeches and gift giving. Nicholas Perrot, however, one of the first French visitors to the Menominees in 1667, recorded that they used tobacco ceremonially within council meetings. The war chiefs were responsible for a number of important tasks. They acted as keepers of the tribal war medicine and as masters of ceremonies or public spokesmen for hereditary leaders. They also policed the wild rice harvest. Warfare among the Menominees was usually a matter of small parties going out on raids. The entire tribe did not go to war. Although the Menominees were said to be brave warriors, they probably did not fight often after the realignment of tribes in the 1600s had reduced their numbers because they were surrounded by larger and more powerful groups.

FAMILY LIFE.   Menominee family life differed from the Iroquois in that it was organized around the father of the family, not the mother. In anthropological terms, it was patrilineal rather than matrilineal. Polygyny was practiced, but we do not know how many wives each male usually had. Children were welcomed into the family and carried about on cradleboards during their infancy. At puberty, boys and at least some girls fasted with blackened faces to induce dreams that would indicate to them something of the nature of their adult lives. Girls were secluded during menstruation. The division of labor was on the basis of sex and age. Boys and girls were expected to emulate their fathers and mothers at the rate that physical and emotional development permitted. Men hunted and fished, conducted warfare, performed ceremonials, prepared sacred artifacts, provided wood for fuel, and made canoes, weapons, tools, nets, snares, and other items connected with food production. Women cooked, took care of the children, did the small amount of cultivation necessary to grow some corn, gathered wild foods, hauled firewood, carried water, packed and moved household goods when necessary, processed hides, made clothing, wove mats and bags, and made household utensils. As individuals grew into old age and their capacities for physical labor diminished, they devoted much of their time to instructing young people with respect to the traditional ways of life. The nature and significance of mythology and ritual were given primary emphasis.

RELIGION.   Much of Menominee religion was based on the origin myth already recorded. The Bear was very important to them, and special ceremonies were performed when one was killed. The Menominees shared a culture hero with other Central Algonquian peoples. He was called Michabous and gave the Indians certain herbs and roots for curing. Other important facets of early Menominee religion were the puberty dream fast, the use of a sweat lodge for purification, a dread of ghosts and witchcraft (which persists today), and the employment of a number of games and dances as part of their ceremonial life. Although the Midewiwin or Medicine Lodge Society probably originated during postcontact times, many of its elements are very old (Spindler, 1979: 715) and are a part of the fundamental religious beliefs of all Central Algonquian groups. The Medicine Lodge was and is an organization dedicated to prolonging life and curing illness as well as providing protection against witchcraft. Membership was restricted through invitation or inheritance of a medicine bag, a small-animal skin such as otter or mink filled with healing herbs and a magical cowrie shell shooter.

The Period of French Influence

What happened to this Menominee culture when the French entered Wisconsin? The primary French reason for being there was to harvest furs, and they proposed to do so by using the Indians. The Indians were very willing to cooperate in this venture because they wanted the European trade goods they could earn, but many changes were inevitable under the new system. My primary source for the French period of Wisconsin history is Keesing (1939: 53–126).

The presence of French fur traders brought back to Wisconsin many of the tribes who had fled westward before the Iroquois. In 1677, 20,000 Indians populated the Fox Valley. Even with prosperity, though, the area could not support so many, and some of the groups soon moved south. Along with the fur traders came the Jesuits, who used Chippewa as a lingua franca to preach to the Indians. They did not, however, remain in Wisconsin long enough to make any major changes.

In 1680 the Iroquois went to war again, and they were joined by the British in 1689, when France and Great Britain were at war. As in earlier times, the Menominees were protected from direct attack by Lake Michigan, but the fur trade was disrupted until peace came in 1696. At this time the Iroquois took advantage of the French confusion by becoming middlemen for British fur interests, and their activities brought a number of eastern culture traits into the Menominee area.

In 1716 the French built a fort at La Baye, site of present-day Green Bay, thus making the Menominee region more important. During much of the early 1700s, French forces were involved in a war against the Fox, which culminated in 1728, when not only the Fox but their allies the Sauk and the Winnebagos fled, leaving the Menominees alone allied to the French and in sole possession of the Green Bay area. About 1740 the Menominees established a second village on the Fox River south of Green Bay. The tribe had grown to a warrior strength of 160. The Menominees continued to aid the French in military expeditions, being involved in the attack of British forces under Braddock in the Ohio Valley and the attack on Fort Henry in 1757, which resulted in their bringing home smallpox. In 1759 a Menominee force fought for the French at the fall of Quebec, but another force attacked the French post at Green Bay to protest fur trade abuses. After Quebec, the French in Wisconsin retreated to Louisiana by way of the Fox-Wisconsin portage, and official French influence was over. By the Treaty of Paris in 1763, New France became British Canada, and British control would dominate Wisconsin until after the War of 1812. Green Bay, however, remained a settlement of Frenchmen, most of whom were married to Menominee women, and they and their mixed-blood children continued to exert an important influence on the region in spite of official British control.

The Coming of the American Presence

The Menominees continued their policy of allying themselves to the Whites in charge rather than to the other tribes. They fought for the British in Pontiac's Rebellion, the American Revolution, and the War of 1812, even though they had technically been under American control since 1784. Because the fur trade was so important to them, the British had remained in Wisconsin after the Revolutionary War, and the Americans were not represented at all until 1815, when the first United States force reached Green Bay.

With the American presence established, an era had ended. The fur trade had reached its height about 1777, and after this period the Indians had to travel farther and farther afield to trap beaver. Under the Americans, a new use was to be found for the extensive Wisconsin forest—lumbering—and the Menominees would play an important part in it. Settlers, many of them immigrants from Europe, began to move into Wisconsin, although they concentrated at first on the lead mining regions of the southwest and the rich, more open farmland of the south. It would not be long, though, before the area where the Menominees

These Menominees have been asked to help celebrate the American victory of Perry over the British in 1813. 1913. Oshkosh Public Museum.

were accustomed to roaming freely would be demanded by others. Catholic missions were started at Green Bay and were followed by Protestant missions and schools. In 1821 a very important change was made, although the Menominees undoubtedly did not recognize its significance at the time. As described in Chapter 3, the Oneidas along with their allies the Stockbridge-Munsee and Brothertown Indians asked for and were given joint ownership of all Menominee land. Although the Menominees almost immediately regretted their agreement and disputed it for the next ten years, the eastern Indians retained their claims and, of course, still live in Wisconsin today.

Menominee tribal population reached a high point around 1820, when one source listed it as 3,900 (Commissioner Morse quoted in Keesing, 1939: 102). By this time, thanks to the fact that all tribes moved around very freely during the fur trade period, there had been a great intermingling of both blood and culture with the Ottawa, Chippewa, Potawatomi, Sac, Fox, and, certainly not least, with Whites. This mingling and culture leveling slowed down considerably after the various tribes had been placed on reservations. In 1834 with a smallpox epidemic, population started a downhill slide. A cholera epidemic followed in 1849, and numbers did not begin to rise again until the beginning of this century.

From Hoffman (1896: 34–35) who quoted a number of early observers of the Menominees, it is possible to establish what they looked like. Zebulon Pike saw a hunting party in 1810 and characterized the males as straight and well made, though not tall, with generally fair complexions, good teeth, and large "languishing" eyes. He considered them handsome men. In 1832, Charles Whittlesey called them thickset men of middle height who were in better condition than most Indians. These and other observations suggest that the Menominees have always been viewed by Whites as attractive but somewhat introverted people who tended to stand aside from most of the conflicts that Whites had with neighboring Indians.

The coming of the French had brought a number of changes to the Menominees. First in importance was a change from a subsistence economy based on hunting, fishing, and gathering with a small amount of cultivation to a fur trade economy based on intensive fall and winter hunting, which took the Menominee men far from home. Because of this basic change in the economy, the entire social organization of the Menominee had to change. The two villages, at the mouth of the Menominee River and on the Fox, became little more than summer headquarters. In the winter the group separated into bands—nine were identified as of 1830—and each band moved out to hunt in its own territory. These bands were loosely based on clan affiliation and friendship. Polygyny gave way to monogamy. As more and more modern

Some descendants of Oshkosh, ca. 1915. Oshkosh Public Museum.

trade goods came into the tribe, standards of living rose to be more like those of the Whites. Fur cloaks gave way to blankets, and deer skins were replaced by shirts and trousers for the men or blouses and long skirts for the women. Indian food was supplemented by wheat products, salt pork, and coffee. Axes, knives, kettles, and twine made the Indians' lives easier because they no longer had to spend so much time making their equivalents. Unfortunately, along with all the good things the White man had brought, the Menominees, like so many other tribes, also adopted the use of liquor but found it a mixed blessing. New leaders grew up, young men who had the ability to deal with Whites and understand what benefited the tribe economically. In 1827 a presidential commission appointed Oshkosh chief of the Menominees with Josette as his second chief.

Events Leading to the Reservation

Between 1830 and 1850 the White population of Wisconsin grew from 4,000 to over 300,000. Time had run out for the old Menominee way of life. In all they signed eight treaties with the United States government, the most important of which are mentioned on the Wisconsin Historical Marker at Poygan Paygrounds on Lake Poygan as follows: "In 1836 the Menominee Indians ceded all their lands between the Wolf and the Fox Rivers to the U.S. Government. Payment was made every October in 20 annual payments on these grounds. All the remaining lands were ceded in 1848 and they were offered a reservation in Minnesota which was refused. In 1852 they moved up the Wolf River where, in 1854, they were granted 8 townships, the present Keshena Reservation."

Charles H. Velte, who grew up on Lake Poygan, gives an interesting account of the story behind this state marker in his book *Historic Lake Poygan*. According to Velte, the Treaty of the Cedars, signed on September 3, 1836, was a compromise forced on the Indians. By its terms they ceded four million acres including the present sites of the cities of Marinette, Oconto, Appleton, Neenah, Menasha, Oshkosh, Wausau, Wisconsin Rapids, and Stevens Point. In return they were to receive $700,000 to be paid in installments for 20 years. In addition to the money, they got some trade goods including tobacco, pork, salt, and blankets. These figures work out at about 17 cents per acre, quite a buy for the Americans. At the time of this treaty, many of the Menominees moved to the paygrounds on Lake Poygan, although scattered bands still roamed freely as they had always done. Velte, using old newspaper stories, paints a vivid picture of what the Menominee encampment was like on payday. Scores of temporary eating houses and boarding places sprang up all over the grounds. On the periphery the liquor dealers waited with their watered down whiskey. An Indian would be escorted to the pay table and protected by a double line of soldiers as he left it, but the protection ran out all too soon. Before he knew what was happening, he would be surrounded by bill collectors snatching at his clothing to find the money they believed was owed to them. If they left him any money, he still had to run the gauntlet of peddlars with their flashy jewelry and trinkets, gamblers, and liquor-dealers. Before long, the payground became the site of a drunken orgy, and far too many of the Indians woke up the next morning with sore heads and no money.

By 1848 the pressures for land had increased so much that government agents forced the Menominees to sign another treaty. In this one they agreed to move to Minnesota within two years and relinquish all lands in Wisconsin. Mixed bloods were paid $40,000 each upon their agreement to give up future tribal benefits. The Menominees, however, objected to Minnesota so much that Oshkosh and some other chiefs went to Washington to protest personally to President Fillmore. The tribe delayed moving from Lake Poygan and the government was forced to compromise. They agreed to give the Menominees ten townships on the upper Wolf River and ordered the Menominees to move there in October 1852. Two thousand of them embarked by canoe on the Wolf River at the beginning of November, and it must have been a cold, miserable, tragic journey. Many Indians perished in the severe winter weather, and others were left along the way to get to the reservation when and how they could. Two years later, in May of 1854, the government gave up all thought of Minnesota and gave the Menominees official title to these Keshena townships as their new reservation, although two townships went to the Stockbridges in 1856, leaving the Menominees with eight. This remains the Menominee Reservation today.

THE RESERVATION PERIOD: 1854 TO 1954

Murray Wax (1971: 65) characterized an Indian reservation as a region reserved by treaty for Indians in order to eliminate their presence from areas that Whites were beginning to exploit. Reservation Indians were to be controlled through an agent having military and judicial powers plus control of rations. Although theoretically the agent might be benevolent, he was more often a self-serving petty tyrant. With the passage of time, the powers the agent possessed were gradually controlled and limited by statute and through the courts. This description of a reservation fits the Menominee situation remarkably well. During the period 1854 to 1954, these Indians ceased to be only hunters, gatherers, and trappers, and became reservation Indians. A relationship of hostile dependency upon a government that was by turns indifferent, ineffective, and protecting was established. The trading bands, consisting of a number of extended families, disappeared, leaving aggregates of nuclear families and family groupings that were subject to phases of fission and fusion as circumstances dictated. The description of how this happened, unless otherwise noted, will rely upon Keesing (1939: 148–243).

The reservation in 1852 was a heavily wooded wilderness already familiar to the Menominees because it had been part of their hunting territory. Shawano, the nearest settlement, had been established as a sawmill town in 1843 and had a small population. There was still some game in the forest, plenty of fish in the numerous lakes and rivers, and extensive wild rice beds on Lake Shawano, but these resources were not enough to support over 2,000 people. For the first two years, the Menominees were forced to live wretchedly on government handouts of pork and flour. Those Menominees who had come up from Lake Poygan were soon joined by members of small bands who had lived on the coast at the mouths of rivers such as the Menominee, Peshtigo, and Oconto and by some mixed bloods. These mixed bloods represented a category of Menominees who persist to the present. Although they are part of the reservation community and full participants in reservation life, by the treaty of 1848 they were paid a fixed amount of money upon their agreement to relinquish all financial benefits given to tribal members through the sale of their lands.

The settlement at Keshena was established as the new payground for Menominees. Various band leaders chose locations that appealed to them because of readily available supplies of wood, water, and food resources. Although some former bands lived together, others broke up as individuals within them chose different places to live (Keesing, 1939: 150). The original bands, however, continued to meet together when the time came for annuities and rations to be given out, so the band organization did not disappear entirely. Bands now consisted of newly formed cooperative work groups, sometimes united on the basis of kinship, but usually based upon convenience and intermittent need. Divisions between those espousing a nominal form of Christianity, usually Catholicism, and those having no interest in Christianity appeared. Christians tended to stay closer to the payground, whereas the followers of the old religion had separate settlements based on the traditional division of Bear and Thunder. Bear people headed by Oshkosh settled along the west bank of the Wolf River, and the Thunder people settled further up the Wolf at a place called Wayka Creek.

In 1855 some government agency buildings were located at the Keshena settlement. A number of corrupt and inefficient agents clearly demonstrated to the Menominees the perils and highly uncertain nature of rewards involved in being under the protection of the federal government. The state of Wisconsin asked that large areas be ceded to them for school and swamp reserves. Timber interests coveted Menominee pine and began a pressure for land and lumber that would not be resolved for 50 years. Although they could not cut Menominee timber legally, they were not above doing so illegally, especially in northern areas where settlement had not reached. White traders and lawyers put in huge claims for money both from annual annuities and from money held in trust by the federal government.

ATTEMPTS AT FARMING. In spite of these difficulties, the Menominees settled down on their new reservation and, encouraged by the government, began to farm. Sawmills were built to process lumber for frame houses; and grist mills, to grind the anticipated wheat crop. With government-supplied tools, implements, seed, and stock, the Indians planted corn, potatoes, wheat, oats, peas, and many vegetables. Unfortunately, the climate and the soil of the reservation were not really suitable for growing crops, and farming through the years became a series of enthusiastic starts followed by disastrous setbacks. Crops were destroyed by frosts that came too late in spring and too early in fall, wheat was attacked by smut and rust, and the light sandy soil near Keshena became depleted, leaving the Menominees with the alternative of clearing heavy forests to get at better soil. It is a tribute to their industry and enthusiasm that some families did this. In spite of all the difficulties, the Menominees seemed determined to make a go of farming. In 1859 the tribe requested that land be allotted to families in 40- and 80-acre units and that they be given more farming implements and stock. Allotment, however, never took place and was later repudiated. Even with the passage of the Dawes Act of 1887, which forced allotment of lands upon so many tribes, including the Oneidas and the Western Cherokees, the Menominees managed to hang on to all their land and to continue owning it in common as a tribe, not as individuals.

By 1861, 400 acres were under cultivation and mostly fenced, and the grist mill ground 3,650 bushels of grain. New mills were built, more barns and fences went up, and a bridge was built across the Wolf River. Much effort went into harvesting the wild marsh hay, which grew profusely in low-lying areas of the reservation. The hay was used to feed increasing numbers of stock. All the effort was a losing battle. In 1863 the Commissioner of Indian Affairs characterized the reservation as "thousands of acres of wet and worthless marsh, and of the remainder a very large proportion is nothing but sand . . ." (Keesing, 1939: 159). An enthusiastic agent recorded that the Menominees "would soon become good farmers if they had any good farming land to till; but the entire reservation is almost utterly worthless" (Keesing, 1939: 159).

Achieving Survival as a People

Difficult though the early reservation days might have been, they taught the Menominees what was required to survive as a subordinate part of an indifferent and implacable White society. The government officially wanted the Menominees to become an integral part of the rural economy of the state, but conditions would not allow them to do so. Out of necessity, much of their subsistence base still came from hunting and gathering plus government rations. Salable fur-bearing animals were no longer available in commercial quantities. The Menominees were now dependent upon the uncertain patronage of a poorly informed, indifferent government and the charity of a sometimes hostile public. Menominee life did not flourish under these conditions.

EDUCATION.   Slowly and gradually, useful channels of integration with the non-Menominee world were established and maintained along political, economic, and educational lines. These channels functioned poorly much of the time, but the Menominee people began to cope successfully with the world surrounding them to the extent that the maintenance and perpetuation of a distinct ethnic identity occurred. Menominee schooling was handled at first by the Dousman family, a mother and her two daughters who had run a small Catholic school at Lake Poygan and had traveled to the reservation with the Indians to teach the girls and women practical skills such as sewing. Schools for both sexes were established in 1862, and although the Menominees were enthusiastic about sending their children, their pattern of making maple syrup in the spring and collecting wild rice in the fall meant that attendance was intermittent. Children were also deterred from school by recurrent epidemics and bad health, poverty, and lack of suitable clothing. Probably the greatest burden these early teachers labored under was the fact that so few Menominees spoke English, and many did not even see that they needed to learn the language. Another problem was that as the tribe continued to disperse from the Keshena area, only boarding schools became practical. Two were eventually built at Keshena: the state school in 1875 and the Catholic school in 1883. They educated the children only through fourth grade. Those wishing to continue went off the reservation to the large Indian boarding schools such as Carlisle in Pennsylvania or Haskell in Kansas. This experience immeasurably broadened the viewpoint of the few children who attended. Before that time, they hardly knew that other Indians existed outside of Wisconsin.

OTHER DEVELOPMENTS.   By the 1870s many Menominees were living in log cabins or frame houses and wearing American-style clothing. A military road had been built across the reservation from Green Bay to Lake

Superior, and this brought more contact with the outside society. Log drives down the Wolf River every spring did the same thing. One hundred and twenty-five Menominees proved their loyalty to the United States by fighting in the Civil War, and one-third of these were killed. The Franciscans established a permanent mission in Keshena in 1880. Along with these positive developments, however, came many troubles and social disruptions. Some Menominees drank too much. Alcohol abuse from this period to the present has both contributed to unrest throughout the community and reflected it. The ready supply of whiskey was due to the unflagging efforts of enterprising bootleggers. The mixed-blood population was a source of conflict because their payment from the treaty of 1848 had long ago run out, and they were not entitled to the government support given to the rest of the tribe. A series of incompetent and even criminal federal agents came and went. These men often disagreed with the Catholic priests who functioned as cultural brokers in attempting to promote changes that they felt would be best for the Indians, but that did not conform to ideas in Washington.

THE ROLE OF LUMBERING.   A major source of conflict as well as the economic hope and future mainstay of the tribe was lumbering. As early as 1863, the tribal council began to realize the importance of their woodlands and requested permission from the Indian Office (later the Bureau of Indian Affairs) to cut "dead and down" timber and sell it. By 1868 the tribe was in conflict with the Pine Ring, a group of powerful White lumber barons who wanted to profit from Menominee timber. In that year a number of fires were purportedly started intentionally to enable these lumber barons to harvest more timber, and the heads of eight Menominee bands officially protested their activities. These Indian leaders alleged that two band chiefs who were supporting the Pine Ring had been bought with bribes and that their opinions should be disregarded. In 1871 this internal dissension was healed when the tribe faced a crisis. Acting at the instigation of the White lumber interests, Congress passed an act enabling the Menominees to sell some of their reservation providing that they had the consent of the council. The council voted unanimously not to sell.

In 1872, acting under the supervision of the Indian agent, the Menominees started a tribal lumber camp using Indian labor. For the first time they were able to profit directly from their own resources. This was an ideal occupation for Menominee men, who had been accustomed to working during the winter at the fur trade, and soon many were accomplished lumberjacks. For five years money flowed to individual workers and to the tribal funds. In 1878 the Pine Ring struck again when the Indian Department ordered logging to cease. For two years the Menominees suffered greatly. Flooding in 1878 ruined their crops, the annual annuities from land sales ran out so that they no longer received the government money and goods they had come to count upon, and they were thrown back on their old economy of hunting and gathering in order to live. An investigation in 1880 found that the only money the tribe had was $153,039 held in trust by the United States Treasury. From this amount the Menominees had the use of only 5 percent interest per year for their needs.

In 1882 a special act of Congress again gave the Menominees permission to harvest their own dead and down timber for a period of six years. In spite of artifically low prices (the Pine Ring was still at work) and the machinations of an agent who would not allow the Indians to work at lumbering in winter if they did not also farm during the summer, revenues and morale once more increased. In 1888, when the six years had run out, the Attorney General ordered the Menominees to stop lumbering once again. He ruled that the Menominees possessed only the right of occupancy on their land; the timber belonged to the government. The Indian Department, however, pushed through a special act of Congress allowing the Menominees to continue. At this, the lumber barons complained that the Indians were refusing to pay their debts to merchants, were spending their money foolishly, and were setting fires to increase the amount of timber they could legally harvest. In 1890 this dispute was resolved by another congressional act. Under its terms, the Menominees were allowed to cut standing timber in certain areas under the supervision of outside, non-Indian contractors. Although the Menominees were not happy at this, it was that or nothing, and in the event, it worked out very profitably for them. By 1905 the Menominee log fund in the U.S. Treasury amounted to two million dollars, and the tribe had become one of the wealthiest in the country.

Some New Developments

During this time while they were struggling to find a secure economic base, other facets of Menominee life were not standing still. As mentioned previously, two boarding schools were started in Keshena. A doctor took up residence there in 1876, and the White man's law became more important. The government acted wisely in this respect by setting up an Indian police organization in 1880 and also a Court of Indian Offenses having three Menominee chiefs as judges. More American settlements were established around the reservation, most of them very small, to serve as lumbering or postal centers, and a number of Menominees moved to these centers to work. In 1881 the *Dream Dance* or Drum Dance or Powwow reached the reservation, brought by Chippewa Indians. The Dream Dance originated in the Plains and appears to have been based on the Omaha Grass Dance. The myth telling the

Man with "war bundle," ca. 1920s. "There was also a system of complex sacred bundles. Each bundle contained 'medicines' such as 'thunder eggs' (rounded stones), miniature war and lacrosse sticks, roots, powders, and so forth, which were invested with powers evoked by ritual, song, and reverence, and that could do great good or harm. There were also pictographs done on birchbark or hides." L. S. Spindler. "Menominee." Vol. 15, Northeast. *Handbook of North American Indians.* Washington: Smithsonian Institution, 1978. p. 712. Photograph, Oshkosh Public Museum.

origin of this rite centers around the experiences of a Sioux girl who, while in the course of escaping White soldiers, was instructed by the Great Spirit with respect to a series of rituals that would ultimately bring good living and great satisfaction to believers. The ceremony itself consists of the use of drums, singing, and the distribution of food and other gifts to those who are active in the procedure. Not only does participation help one to live gracefully with peers, but the faithful also are ideally enabled to obtain the spiritual power necessary for a successful life. Specifically, followers should respect the rights of others, not arouse antagonism, be modest, even-tempered, and guard against undue pride. Some Menominees readily accepted the Dream Dance, but the more committed Christians rejected it. The final result was a deep split between the Christians and those Indians who followed both the Dream Dance and the Midewiwin religion. The Midewiwin group was not united either; some followed the Dream Dance and some did not. One conservative group who believed in the Dream Dance moved away from the conflict entirely and settled at Zoar, a densely forested part of the reservation to the northwest. Here they associated more with wandering bands of Chippewas, Winnebagos, and Potawatomis than with their own tribesmen; and here they remain today, still a conservative group attempting to follow some of the old ways.

It appears that with the close of the nineteenth century, the Menominees were bombarded with a number of ambiguous influences to which they could not respond decisively. The federal government frowned upon all traditional practices, wanting the Indians to become docile wards. White lumber interests cared little what the Menominees did as long as they could profit from the Indians' timber with a minimum of capital investment and responsibility. Other Whites living in the area presented a wide variety of responses to the Indians ranging from intermarriage through passive contempt to the comfortable illusion that because the Indians were vanishing Americans, it really did not matter what did or did not happen to them. Because outsiders gave no uniform responses to the Menominees, each person was forced to respond to situations on an individual basis. Hence, Menominee life at

Some Menominees follow the Medicine Lodge or Midewiwen, ca. 1920s. Note man covering his face with his hat.   Oshkosh Public Museum.

A woman member of the Medicine Lodge with an otter skin Medicine Bag, ca. 1920s.   Oshkosh Public Museum.

the end of the nineteenth century assumed the outward appearance of a kind of anarchy that continues to the present. Although there are rules or codes of conduct, they are always subject to individual interpretation. The accuracy and appropriateness of such interpretations vary widely.

VIOLENCE IN THE COMMUNITY.   Certainly, at the turn of the century, violence was a part of the very fabric of life, but probably no more so than that which was found in the surrounding lumber camps. John V. Satterlee, a Menominee with a White father and a Menominee mother, kept a diary that records many dramatic incidents. Here are a few examples.

> Keshena Wis. Feb 25th 1904. John Harris[1] is being so treacherous on account of drinking liquor on this Date he tried to stab his Father at his House. This is the second time he Did this. the first time several years ago he cut his Father's Hand. he is pretty bad. he will yet stab his father unless he quits drinking Liquor.

[1] All names from the diary are fictitious.

Keshena Wis on this Dates Feb 26″–27″–28″ 1904 A.D. on these three Day in the Evenings Drinking Liquor is Kept up in the House of Jack Hall, his Brothers and Relatives Myron Wilson & Bob Allen ugly & Notorious when he is Drunk. Mary Royce a Bad Case in Running at Nights. there is Liquor Evil & Fornicators in Lenten Season is *So Bad*. A Severer Punishment may be at hand pretty soon as there is already Smallpox Diseases of which pneumonia already had befell some of our Catholic Indians to which *they have died of*.

Gabriel Brunette's Story

The way people lived undoubtedly varied widely during this time. No one was just a farmer or just a lumberman or hunter; everyone worked at whatever came along as a matter of survival. This shows clearly in the life story of Gabriel Brunette, age 82, who gives a fascinating account of what it was like to be a Menominee in the last half of the nineteenth century. Brunette's story was recorded by Felix M. Keesing in 1929 and given to me through the courtesy of George Spindler, who inherited Keesing's unpublished notes. Brunette's story follows.

You want to hear my story? Well I will have to begin a long time back, for my father was part French and my mother was a grandchild of Chief Obeysa the old leader of the Oconto Band. I cannot come to myself till I explain about them. When Chief Obeysa died, my grandmother with her brother Isanapaneny became the leaders of the Oconto people, for in those days a man and a woman led a band, and they were the two. My grand-

Typical Menominee dwelling, ca. 1920.   Oshkosh Public Museum.

mother married a son of Cornwallis, half-white man. He told my mother always "never marry an Indian."

In 1834 came the great smallpox and my grandmother died. Everyone of the Band was sick and starving. My mother with her uncle became the leaders, but before long they quarrelled. Mother wanted to give things to people who were starving and uncle said no. So my mother and her husband and family left to journey to Prairie du Chien, where she had a sister married to a Frenchman. On the way Iometah Cline at Cedar Point, Little Chute, near Appleton invited them to stay. They would not at first but when they found her sister had moved, they went back to Little Chute. After my mother was widowed, she met my father. It was when she went on a visit to the English at Mackinac. Father Van der Brock had a mission then at Little Chute. He said to my grandfather, mother's father, "that man would be a good husband for your daughter." So my grandfather told it to my mother. My father and mother were married by Father Van der Brock on February 14, 1841, and the whole family were baptized into the Catholic Church. My father was born at Shantytown, Green Bay, the son of a French half-breed.

I was born at Lake Poygan in 1847 on the night of the first snow. Father had to cut the fence rails to make a fire to keep me from freezing. It so happened that a priest went by to Prairie du Chien, and stopped at our place so I was baptized when I was eleven days old. I was not the eldest. Both my father and my mother had had children by this other marriage so there were half brothers and sisters. I was the third child of this marriage. Mother and father were both better to their step-children even than they were to us "so as to make up to them" they said. I, like the older children, was strapped on the cradle board. That's why I'm such a straight-backed old man now. But the children born after me—there were three more— were nursed the white way.

I can remember quite a lot of my boyhood, mostly after we went to live at Shantytown on the Fort Howard side of the river opposite Green Bay. There was a mission and a store at Shantytown, and my father worked in the store for seven years. Of course, the country around was all very poor then. No railroads and just a few vessels coming up the river now and then to Green Bay. There was no bridge; only two docks on the Fox. A man called Hoogaty had a skiff and used to cross one or two people for five cents between Fort Howard and Green Bay. Mother used to paddle across with him to Green Bay sometimes when she went to buy seeds. I was too small then to paddle. It was about 1854. Mother would make me a little *mokok* [package] of sugar made of birch bark. A Frenchman, De Pere, with a grocer's store at Fort Howard bought it. There used to be three cent silver pieces then. Mother gave me that when we used to go to Green Bay. When I got to De Pere's store, I bought something but wanted my money back too. He laughed and gave it to me but said I'd better not spend it any more. Those are about the first things I remember.

I'll tell you something mysterious. There was an old lady near our home who could work in metal. She could patch any kind of kettle. For instance, when I was a boy I took a sugar kettle across to her with tobacco. She had common trade scissors that she used to be able to cut the copper with as you or I would cut buckskin. She would make holes in it and fix a patch. I went next day, and the kettle was fixed. Now there was something in that. She used a secret by which she could work the metal. Now these modern silver-workers just file the metal—that is different; anyone could do it.

Always I liked to go around with Mother while she worked and listen to her stories. That way I learned all about our people in the past, and tales of the old Menominee beliefs and of the English and French wars, the trips up and down the St. Lawrence to Quebec and Montreal where they got everything they wanted for a man's winter work and a woman's things like scissors, and to Fort Mackinac. The English at Fort Mackinac gave my grandmother an English flag and my grandfather a medal. Mother did wonderful fine work in buckskin. She made beautiful moccasins and satchels of bark, baskets and mats. My father wasn't much good at woodwork so mother made wood spoons and bowls for maple sugar too. Father was a hunter. I never saw him use those charms though. He used salt for the salt licks to catch deer. Shall I tell you what I know of the way the Indians of our Oconto Band got their food? In the spring they worked making sugar. During the middle of May sturgeon came up to Oconto Falls, so they got great amounts of these big fish. They dried it and smoked it like bacon for the summer supply. Then they picked all sorts of berries—some as big as plums, but they're gone now. They were made into a kind of sauce with maple sugar. I've seen Mother do it, and put into *mokoks* and sealed up with pitch—the fruit all firm and sealed. In the fall, the eighth day of September about, we started wild rice thrashing and collected thousands of bushels at Peak's Point. We used to dry and thresh it and put it in bags or sometimes *mokoks*. I remember threshing it at about twelve years old. I sat in the canoe while Father poled and Mother threshed down the wild rice. When the canoe was full, we went home. To dry it we just put it over a fire and roasted it. About the '50's, the buffalo were up around Fond du Lac, also moose and elk, and I heard about parties going to hunt them. Traders wouldn't buy summer fur so the hunt was in the winter. There were lots of furs those days. Every winter we would leave the shore and go to the headwaters of the rivers to hunt and trap. The cabins were made in the thickets. To fish in the winter the men cut a hole in the ice, then made a hoop the size of the hole and put a blanket over it so they could see the bottom of the river. They watched the fish and speared them as they went past.

I only went to school for three days. I learned to speak French and Menominee at home and then just picked up English. I learned how to read and write from a stoker at a mill where I worked—a white man. As a boy I remember meeting Eleazer Williams, a preacher married to a French Ottawa woman.

The most terrible thing I've ever been in was the Peshtigo fire in 1871. I've seen a great many very strange things in my time too. For instance, when we lived at Duck Creek there was a place not far away that would never freeze unless it was very cold indeed. Above that lived my mother's brother. One day they say something come out of there; it had a head like a dog but it was very big. It dived back in again, for it had a hole. Years later a man started a brickyard there. A loaded scow tipped over at this point, and all the bricks were blown right back from the hole! We were always afraid of it; Mother would never let us go near the place.

My mother died in 1886, and before she went she told me to throw in my lot with the Indians, not the whites. "Stay and help the Menominees," she said. That was why I came to live on the Reservation in 1884. Of course, I had been here often before and gone back and forth, but then I decided to throw in my lot with these people here and came for good. I made a big farm and worked hard to be an example. When I came here to live with the Indians, they had changed. People changed clothes when they got baptized into the Catholic faith. I remember the old way they played La Cross— mixed all the clubs and blindfolded people to pick sides. You followed your club, and there was a feast—soup mainly. They did that for the soul of a dead person or for someone sick. But all that soon changed. They used to cook outside with just a pot and hook, but soon they started to get stoves. The first ones came about 1852, I think, but some still cook outside today.

When I grew up, I did a great many things. I worked in a store and farming and working in lumber camps. I even worked on a boat on the lakes. Shall I tell you about putting in dams on the river for the logging drives? You see we used to cut the pine into saw logs near the bank of the river. Then we built a dam below the logs to flood them out and carry them down stream. I helped with the building of Schultz dam (Schultz was fore- man). After that big Jim's dam had to be repaired; then we went to the Norway dam (now Neopit). It was an old wreck. We fixed it and got it to hold, and then made Hemlock dam and Peavey falls. The logs go tumbling along you know, like matches when they get a start! Devil's Skittle was the nastiest place to get them over.

You know they made me a judge here once. That isn't right. How can I be a judge when I have never been to school or learned to understand law? I tried to do my best and say what was right always, but I made a terrible lot of enemies. People wanted to make me let them off all the time, and I wouldn't if they looked to be in the wrong, so I got out of that when I could.

You know I was married twice but I haven't had any children. I always wanted to have them. My wife that has just died was a very clever worker. She made so many beautiful things, rugs and crochet work and shawls and baskets. She made a beautiful mat once with a church in the middle of it, and when the priest came he liked it so much he asked for it for the church. Most of her other things are gone too now for her aunts came and took them all away when she died. It is an old custom.

Now it is your turn to talk. Tell me again about those things you were talking about last night about your country [New Zealand]. Is the world really round? That's so strange! How do they stay on down there? You say when it is summer here, it is winter there! What is the reason for that? On the other side of the world do you walk upright? Is sounds so funny! Tell me again all the reasons because I want to understand.

There is another thing I want to ask you. What do you know about dreams? What is the cause of them? When my brother comes to see me, always the night before I dream of my father. What is the reason for that?

Success in the Early Twentieth Century

The twentieth century began for the Menominees with a crisis. On July 16, 1905, a severe wind storm blew down forty million board feet of timber, mostly hardwoods. These logs had to be sent to mills as soon as possible to avoid decay, but no sawmills existed on the reservation, and hardwood does not float well enough to use water transportation. The windstorm precipitated a crisis with the United States government, which was managing the Menominee forest under the Act of 1890. The way the government acted during the aftermath of the storm and how they mismanaged the forest subsequently led to a lawsuit 40 years later, the details of which are given in Stephen J. Herzberg's excellent article on the Menominees in the *Wisconsin Magazine of History* (1977). Briefly, on the Wolf River at Neopit the government constructed a sawmill, which was not finished until the end of 1909. This mill was managed by Whites but had a philosophy of full employment for Menominees. Gradually, Neopit became the largest settlement on the reservation, Keshena being reserved for administrative and educational functions. A railroad linked Neopit with the outside world and a state highway

Neopit, 1909.   Milwaukee Public Museum.

was built through it in 1926. In 1925 the mill burned down, but it was quickly replaced by a more modern plant and work continued.

As an economic unit, the tribe did well. For individuals, however, it was often a different story. The mill itself became a focus of Menominee complaints and dissension, turning one segment of the tribe against another and almost all segments against the Whites, whom they accused of having too much power and authority. One continuing problem was what to do about descendants of the mixed bloods who had been paid off in the treaty of 1848. Sensing how valuable Menominee tribal membership was becoming economically, many of them applied for it, and 202 were admitted between 1902 and 1929, when the tribal council called a halt. Because of this and an increased birthrate, tribal population rose to almost 2,000 in 1929. Ill health, however, continued to plague individuals, particularly tuberculosis and diseases connected with excessive alcohol consumption. Under Catholic sponsorship, a hospital was built in Keshena in 1926. The Menominees had to fight off outside business interests who wanted to build a series of dams on the Wolf River to supply hydroelectric power. This move would have ruined the scenic value of the reservation, a value that tourists were beginning to appreciate.

In 1934 the Menominee tribe sued the federal government for maladministration of their affairs and the illegal cutting of timber. In 1951, after 17 years of litigation, the Menominees won over seven and a half million dollars in damages, this sum being put in trust for the tribe in an account in the United States Treasury. This, plus other interest-bearing funds built up over the years, increased tribal funds to almost ten million dollars. Other Menominee tribal assets then were ownership of the 235,000-acre reservation still held in common and unallotted, the forest that was being managed on a sustained yield basis, the sawmill with its policy of employing all Menominee who wanted to work there, two hydroelectric plants, one steam plant, water and sewer systems in Keshena and Neopit, and the 45-bed hospital at Keshena, which served all Menominee people at a cost per family of $38 per year (Herzberg, 1977: 296). Although the Menominee tribe was certainly not wealthy and individual Menominees were most often very poor, it was still doing better than most of the tribes in the country, especially those whose lands had been allotted and who had no industry to support them. Unlike these, the Menominee tribe was able to pay its own way. Tribal funds ran the hospital and the hydroelectric system. Tribal funds supported needy people with welfare and loaned money to the ambitious. Tribal funds even paid the salaries of the federal Indian agents who worked there. The Menominees were a success, and the roof was about to fall in.

RESERVATION TERMINATION AND RESTORATION: 1954 TO THE PRESENT

Termination: 1954 to 1973

The termination of reservation status, or defederalization, stemming ultimately from the national government's desire to be free of unwanted responsibility, posed what is probably the greatest single threat to Menominee survival during the past 300 years. In 1852 they had been forced to accept a small portion of a far larger area that they regarded as their own territory. They were Menominees because they owned this land and fought diligently to retain all of it in the face of hostile lumbering interests and government allotment acts. In 1954 the federal government began the process of removing its protection, protection that was vital to Menominee prosperity because the fact that as Indians they paid no taxes on their sawmill was what enabled it to make money. The Menominee sawmill had always been run to be labor-intensive—to employ all Menominees who wished to work there—and this policy was more costly in the long run than modernizing the mill and using machines instead of people would have been. The mill was getting old by 1954 and having increasing difficulty keeping up with the output of more modern plants. A tax burden on top of these problems was to prove disastrous.

SENATOR ARTHUR WATKINS'S ROLE.   The move to defederalize began innocently enough when the Menominee Tribal Council voted that part of the money they had won in the lawsuit against the government be distributed to individuals. As this could not be done without the approval of Congress, Melvin Laird introduced a bill in the House of Representatives that would allot $1,500 to each enrolled Menominee. It passed the House with no difficulty, but when it went to the Senate, the bill ran head on into the opposition of Senator Arthur Watkins of Utah, the chairman of the Senate Subcommittee on Indian Affairs. Watkins turned the hearings on the bill into a forum for the enactment of Menominee termination legislation. Anyone interested in learning all the details of the legal maneuverings and the very unfair ways the Menominees were treated is urged to read Herzberg's account or the works of Gary Orfield, a political scientist (1966), and Verne F. Ray (1971), an anthropologist, both of whom testified before the United States Court of Claims. Briefly, Watkins led the Menominees to believe that the only way they would receive their money was to vote for termination. At a sparsely attended tribal council meeting in June of 1953, 169 Menominees did so. Five dissented. Although the Menominees did not consider their vote binding and indeed voted soon afterward to give up their own money if they had to accept termination, Watkins continued to regard this initial vote as binding on the entire tribe of 1,400 enfranchised Menominees. After a great many legal maneuverings and delays, termination was signed into law in 1961. It proved to be economically disastrous.

SOME RESULTS OF TERMINATION.   Termination had been based on the assumption that the Menominee forest operations were profitable. By 1960 the actual operating deficit was about $250,000 per year, and the loss of regular federal aids available to Indian tribes made the situation much worse. In addition, the tribe's liquid assets had been diminished first by about five million dollars through the per capita distribution of $1,500 to each individual; second by another $2 million of dividends on forestry operation profits, which the B.I.A. had failed to distribute; and third by expenses incurred in planning for termination, which the government had forced the Menominees to pay. Thus Menominee Enterprises, Inc., which had been formed in 1961 to succeed the B.I.A. as manager of forestry operation, started its life not only with an operating deficit, but with an obligation to pay local property taxes on forest lands. Disruptive as the Dawes Act had been for other tribes in 1887, they at least were given 25 years before they had to pay property taxes. The Menominees were given no time at all.

Menominee Enterprises, Inc. (M.E.I.) was owned by the Menominee people. Each enrolled individual was given a voting trust certificate representing 100 shares of stock plus a 4 percent bond maturing at $3,000 in the year 2000. Many people used these bonds to buy their homes, but others were forced to sell them for ready cash.

Under termination legislation, the government of Wisconsin organized the former reservation as Menominee County. For several years the county was without medical or dental facilities when the old hospital was closed because it failed to meet state health and safety standards. Ironically, the hospital had just been remodeled by the B.I.A. at a cost to the tribe of between $250,000 and $350,000, but the B.I.A. had made no effort to meet the state standards because the Menominees at that time were still wards of the government (U.S. Court of Claims, 1978: 35). The former reservation land, owned communally by the tribe for more than 100 years, was placed under M.E.I. management to continue sustained-yield forestry; but in the villages of Keshena, Neopit, Zoar, and South Branch some of it was sold in individual parcels to Menominee homeowners. Both the M.E.I. and the individual Menominee property owners became responsible for paying property taxes. Flexible work and leisure patterns of the Menominee culture were soon diminished by the necessity of assuming financial responsibility for the support of self-government within the established patterns of White society. Some additional lands were subsequently sold to non-Menominee owners in the vain attempt to shift the tax burden.

The Menominees had always been individualistic. Now the tribe was torn by factionalism. Some Menominees were convinced that the tribe had no real control over its lands. They believed that M.E.I. leadership consisted of other Menominees who served largely their own personal interest. Further, the First Wisconsin Trust Company of Milwaukee, under the provisions of termination, controlled the shares and hence the votes of minors and incompetents. As of 1971, more than 20 percent of the shares were controlled by this firm.

From the standpoint of general Menominee welfare, the worst aspect of termination was the fact that M.E.I. encouraged land developers to sell tracts of land to non-Menominees. Pressures for land sales stemmed largely from the belief that expanding the property tax base through private development would help to meet the expenses of running the county. In an attempt to correct this and other alleged injustices and to improve the operation of the M.E.I, one faction of the tribe in late 1969 formed an organization call DRUMS (standing for Determination of Rights and Unity of Menominee Stockholders). Chapters were formed in Chicago, Milwaukee, and Menominee County. Although this land development was confined to a 14-section area east of Keshena, in which privately owned parcels remained intermixed with lands owned by the tribal corporation, the emotional impact of the land sales cannot be overestimated. This impact was perhaps greatest among the urban Menominees in Milwaukee and Chicago, who tended to regard any alienation of ancestral lands as a threat to their tribal identity. In addition, development of a tax base through private land sales failed to have the desired economic effect, as M.E.I., still the county's major property owner, remained the county's main property taxpayer.

Restoration: 1973 to the Present

Termination ended with restoration of the Menominee people as a federally recognized Indian tribe on December 22, 1973. Statistics for the period 1961 to 1971 indicate that the failure of termination occurred in spite of substantial federal and Wisconsin state government subsidies: the two governments in combination paid over $19 million. During this same period, many of the features described below as characterizing contemporary Menominee life reached fruition. The threat to their very existence had been averted, but the echoes of these 19 years will reverberate for generations. In short, although the many influences impinging upon the Menominee community today are of a different nature from what they have experienced over the past 300 years, these influences have worked to promote a continuation of Menominee life that resembles in many respects that of the past. The Menominees have always been a people who have not met the outside on its own terms and have suffered accordingly. To be Menominee is to live an unbalanced, precarious kind of existence.

A contemporary Menominee reflected, in part, on his early life and times:[2]

> You know, the powwows when I was a kid were about the happiest times of my life. They were always on Sunday. I wanted to be out there dancing because I knew that I belonged there. Yet there was this inner fear, and all the others my age had it too, that we were violating the sacred laws or the rules of our church. We were all taught that, see. But the other times the Indian in us would just break out. Nothing could stop it. Like we'd be playing basketball or baseball and this would come up. A guy would start drumming or something, just with a stick on a board, and all at once we're all whooping and dancing and hollering. Something would get ahold of us. We knew that we were where we had to be. But then we'd think of what the nuns taught us. Maybe being mixed up like this wouldn't have been so hard on me if I had known more about the old ways.

The prominent themes of pride, paradox, conflict, and frustration contained within this statement are among the basic organizing principles of Menominee life today. Others such as tradition, distrust, often hatred of outsiders, and the vivid determination to remain Menominee also function to influence contemporary Menominee life. A crucial assumption is that the ecological position of Menominee territory, especially its manifold ties to non-Indian situations, is a prize determinant of the behavior of the Menominee people. Menominee behavior now and throughout the past must be understood primarily as a response to actual and threatened White encroachment. One important implication of this assumption is that the critical differences between Menominees and others lie not so much in culture content but in their form of cultural integration. The essence of being a Menominee centers around not what possessions are owned, but how they are used. Patterns of interpersonal relations and the ideas and sentiments activating those patterns form the core of a distinctive Menominee ethnicity. Menominees are different from their neighbors in that they are a part of a distinct social system consisting of mutual, complementary relations of obligation, privilege, and conflict, which articulate with, but do not include in a strict sense, noncommunity members.

TRIBAL MEMBERSHIP.   According to a 1976 newspaper report in the *Milwaukee Journal*, there are now more than 5,000 persons enrolled as members of the Menominee tribe. An estimated 2,700 of these live on

[2]Hodge, 1975: 167.

the reservation. It is important to remember that membership on the tribal rolls is a matter of controversy extending from the payment to the mixed bloods in 1849, and for other reasons. Therefore, official tribal membership may or may not correspond with social reality. One implication of the controversy over the tribal roll is that it is a chronic source of resentment for many Menominees much of the time. There is often no valid consensus as to who is and is not a Menominee. Tribal officials assume that about 50 percent of the tribe are living away from the reservation at any given time because sufficient employment opportunities do not exist at home. Of the 50 percent who live on the reservation, half are younger than 18 and many others are elderly. Probably a relatively large number in this group are dependent upon a small number of middle-aged wage workers for survival. This condition coupled with the great emphasis placed on individualism produces a general reaction of hostile dependency. Accordingly, it is probably no accident that many Menominees suffer from what is sometimes called a passive-aggressive personality syndrome. They demonstrate this through obstructionism, procrastination, intentional inefficiency, or stubbornness. These characteristics may well rise from their resentment at failing to find gratification in a relationship with an individual or institution upon which they are overdependent. This overdependence is directed toward Whites as well as Menominees.

The Reservation Social-Political System

To a significant extent, my description of the reservation social-political system that follows crosscuts or overlaps with the Spindlers' (1971) acculturative categories of native-oriented, peyote cult, transitional, lower-status acculturated, and elite acculturated. Their characterization, however, is not used here because I believe that it would best apply to the Menominees during the decades 1940 to 1960. Those seeking a definitive understanding of the Menominees will read their writings with great profit (1955, 1962, 1971).

POVERTY.   The single most important aspect to be considered when describing the central social and political dimensions of modern Menominee life after 1961 is that the Menominees are economically poor people. Many of them also suffer from poor physical and mental health. Significant economic development in the conventional sense of the term is a remote possibility because outside industries with jobs and payrolls have not been interested in extending their operations to the Menominee area. Factors limiting this interest, according to the Planning Support Group Report (U.S. Department of the Interior, 1975: 10), include a high rate of tuberculosis, limited sewer and water facilities, lack of skilled laborers, and the impression that non-Menominees are not welcome. Given these and other conditions, economic poverty will occupy a prominent place in Menominee life for a long time to come.

One implication of poverty is that most Menominees with salable skills are forced to spend much time away from the reservation working for wages. Although they live in a city, most try to ensure the presence of an acceptable niche on the reservation should urban employment fail or opportunities for wage labor appear there. The lumber mill in Neopit is still the chief reservation employer, but work here is often intermittent and uncertain. As a result, the Menominees must often depend on the outside world to survive. The effects of this dependence are mirrored in the uncoordinated, erratic texture of Menominee life. The implacable demands of survival in a non-Menominee world cannot be reconciled easily with the social necessities of a reservation-based life.

SOCIAL AND ECONOMIC UNITS.   The units having social and economic functions are the individual, the nuclear family and household, family groupings or clusters, the "'49ers," the "outsiders," the community, and the tribe. (Much of my interpretation of modern Menominee life is derived from discussion with Seymour Priestly, who lived on the reservation in 1974 and 1975.) The individual is the primary unit of production and consumption. He or she may operate within the context of the nuclear family or well outside of it as the occasion demands. There can be strong dislikes within families between children and parents and among siblings, but strong ties of affection and loyalty are often seen as well. Perceived individual need is usually the basis for cooperation and support. People, however, also have a strong desire to think for themselves and to avoid blind, uncritical loyalty to any person or collection of individuals because such loyalty can often bring more penalties than rewards.

Next in order of abstraction is the nuclear family and household, which consists of those living under the same roof at the same time. Households are large—probably 6 to 12 people—because the Menominees have a high birthrate, and there is a critical housing shortage in the area. Long-term household guests are frequent. In general, the form of marriage is monogamous, but a number of covertly sanctioned variations occur. The compostion of a Menominee daily diet is often a direct reflection of relative economic affluence or its absence. The less cash that is available, the more emphasis is placed on the products of hunting and fishing. It is estimated, however, that no matter how poverty-stricken a family may be, not more than 50 percent of the diet takes the form of game and fish. Quality and type of house construction vary widely. Many of the residentially occupied buildings in Neopit and Keshena were originally built several decades ago for White government personnel. Recent federal efforts have produced a number of small wooden frame houses that are heated either with bottled gas or by wood fires. Some older log buildings are also used as homes, and a number of families are forced to live in tents, especially during the summer, for lack of anything else.

Family groupings or clusters consist of two or more families related by kinship and common goals or interest of a financial/political nature. These family groups do not share cash but do cooperate in obtaining jobs with the tribe or with private employers off the reservation. Sisters who have established large families often cooperate in situations of perceived mutual advantage. Nonfamily members recognize the commonality of interests within such groupings and respond accordingly. If one assaults a member of a family cluster, he can expect harsh retribution from other members of that family. On rare occasions, a shooting feud between family clusters is established that may continue sporadically for years without being resolved. However, conflict between individual members of two clusters does not invariably lead to prolonged hostilities involving everyone in both families. Such quarrels and family cluster responses to them function, in part, to define and maintain the awareness of unity within families. It should be stressed, however, that allegiance to a family group does not override the respect and autonomy accorded to the individual as long as his actions do not prejudice the rights and security of the other family members. If a family cluster tries to make an adult member do something that he does not want to do, that adult may drop out of the situation by moving off the reservation for a time or simply by not responding to the pressure. Family clusters are scattered and not localized. In general, it appears that such relatives live far enough from each other to preclude constant firsthand interaction that could lead to quarrels, but close enough to come together if a particular situation requires it.

ELIGIBILITY FOR THE TRIBAL ROLE. The '49ers are the descendants of those involved in the mixed-blood settlement payment of 1849, when they signed away forever the rights of their descendants to tribal affiliation in return for a cash settlement. In 1939 an enrollment regulation made the previous arrangement invalid, and a number of people became Menominees officially. Many other Menominees, however, continued to regard these descendants as non-Menominees and often referred to them as White. The chronic disputes associated with the right to be placed on the tribal roll ensure the continuation of the distinctiveness of this category of individuals. The roll will probably always be a matter of contention because those listed on it potentially or actually share in financial and other benefits.

The largest reservation communities are Keshena, Neopit, and

Zoar. Keshena has an elementary school, tribal offices, a small post office, and the fairgrounds and Legion Hall, both used for social gatherings. To some extent, it is also a dormitory community for commuters to surrounding towns. In September of 1977, after the Menominees had gone 16 years without a hospital, a new medical clinic worth $1.4 million was dedicated in Keshena. It contains outpatient, dental, mental health, community health, and nutritional services and fills a long-neglected need. Neopit, of course, still has the tribal sawmill, and the town houses many people who work there. The mill has undergone some remodeling, and in June of 1978 the tribe held a ceremony to dedicate the new $7.1 million refurbishment and renovation made possible by a grant from the Economic Development Administration. The grant not only enabled the tribe to add equipment, but also to comply with the requirements of the Occupational Safety and Health Act (OSHA), so that the mill is now a cleaner and safer place for all those who work there. Zoar continues to be populated by those with a conservative orientation. Important traditional ceremonies such as the Dream Dance and Medicine Lodge rituals are most likely to be performed here. Indeed, Zoar has been revitalized with a new building designed for Dream Dance ceremonies. Menominees living elsewhere with a genuine interest in traditional religion are welcome to attend ceremonies there, but outsiders are discouraged.

THE OUTSIDERS.   Crosscutting the levels of organization of the individual, nuclear family, family cluster, and community is the designation *outsider*. An outsider is a non-Menominee who lives on the reservation or a Menominee who lives and works off the reservation but has more or less regular contacts with relatives and friends there. If one is a non-Menominee outsider, he is used to advantage but systematically excluded from all activities where he might be a disruptive or threatening force. Examples of outsiders are clergymen of various denominations and the owners of recreational property who are part-time residents but who pay state taxes on their property. The status of Menominee outsiders depends on the degree to which they support local reservation interests.

THE TRIBE AS A UNIT.   Finally, the tribe is a unit that seldom makes itself evident. It has a corporate nature in that it consists of an aggregation of individuals claiming distinctive rights in land use and sometimes legal ownership of land. This use/ownership is validated by the fact that these people acknowledge Menominee ethnicity by right of descent plus the discernible content and structure of their behavior. Menominee people argue that they are Menominees because they live on tribal land and act like Menominees. All individuals are distinctive because they share the common experiences of the past, have a common land base and social routine in the present, and fully intend to maintain both in the future. Some observers of the Menominee situation have referred to the tribe as the sleeping giant. A deep, pervasive awareness of Menominee tribal identity exists but becomes readily apparent only when a large majority of Menominees agree that their welfare is threatened. Such occasions are rare, but they do happen. The most recent example occurred in the summer of 1978, when a trial judge in the United States Court of Claims granted the Menominees the right to sue the United States government over a number of issues, including mill and forest mismanagement, termination expenses, and the mismanagement of tribal funds. The government intends to appeal the decision, and the case is still pending (Iadarola, 1978).

In sum, Menominee life today is a social and cultural collage with a very loose, disordered sort of internal cohesion. Life has meaning and order only if it can proceed on the basis of individual choice. Menominee communities and the tribe itself articulate with the larger society in oblique and haphazard fashions. To be Menominee is to live with many loose ends. On a bright October day in 1974, two Menominees stood on a hill watching a scattered number of geese circle in the air over Menominee country. One asked the other, "I wonder what kind of geese those are?" The other replied, "Those gotta be Menominee geese. See how each one goes its own way!"

REFERENCES

Bennett, John W. The Prehistory of the Northern Mississippi Valley. In J. B. Griffin, ed., *Archeology of Eastern United States*. Chicago: University of Chicago Press, 1952, pp. 108–123.

Bloomfield, Leonard. *The Menomini Language*. New Haven: Yale University Press, 1962.

Callender, Charles. Social Organization of the Central Algonkian Indians. *Milwaukee Public Museum Publications in Anthropology No. 7*, 1962.

Herzberg, Stephen J. The Menominee Indians: From Treaty to Termination. *Wisconsin Magazine of History 60* , 267–329, Summer 1977.

Hodge, C. Stuart et al. *Art of the Great Lakes Indians*. Flint, Michigan: Flint Institute of Arts, 1973.

Hodge, William H. The Indians of Wisconsin: Highlights of Their History and Culture Illustrated by Selected Life Stories, with Recommended Additional Reading. *The State of Wisconsin 1975 Blue Book*. Compiled by Wisconsin Legislative Reference Bureau, Madison, Wisconsin, pp. 95–192.

Hoffman, Walter James. The Menomini Indians. *14th Annual Report of the Bureau of Ethnology, 1892–1893, part 1*. Washington, D.C.: Government Printing Office, 1896.

Iadarola, Angelo A., lawyer for the Menominee Tribe, Personal communication, August 15, 1978.

Keesing, Felix H. Leaders of the Menomini Tribe: A Sketch from the Contemporary Records and from the Memories of Old Indians of Today. 1930. On file at the Wisconsin State Historical Society, Madison.

———. *The Menomini Indians of Wisconsin*. New York: Johnson Reprint Corporation, 1971. (First published 1939.)

———. Unpublished notes.

Lurie, Nancy O. Menominee Termination: From Reservation to Colony. *Human Organization 21*, 257–270, Fall 1972.

Orfield, Gary. *A Study of the Termination Policy*. Denver, Colorado: National Congress of American Indians, 1966.

Priestly, Seymour. Personal Communication, 1975.

Ray, Verne F. *The Menominee Tribe of Indians: 1940–1970*. United State Court of Claims Docket No. 134-67. Washington, D.C., 1971.

Ritzenthaler, R. E., and P. Ritzenthaler. *The Woodland Indians*. Garden City, N.Y.: The Natural History Press, 1970.

Skinner, Alanson. Medicine Ceremony of the Menomini, Iowa, and Wahpeton Dakota, with Notes on the Ceremony Among the Ponca, Bungi, Ojibwa, and Potawatomi. *Indian Notes and Menographs, Vol 4*. New York: Museum of the American Indian, Heye Foundation, 1920.

———. Material Culture of the Menomini. *Indian Notes and Monographs, vol. 20*. New York: Museum of the American Indian, Heye Foundation, 1921.

Slotkin, J. S. Menomini Peyotism: A Study of Individual Variation in a Primary Group with a Homogeneous Culture. *Transactions of the American Philosophical Society*, New Series, Vol. 42, Part 4, 1952, pp. 565–700.

Spindler, George D. Sociocultural and Psychological Processes in Menomini Indian Acculturation. *University of California Publications in Culture and Society, vol. 5*. Berkeley: University of California Press, 1955.

———, and Louise Spindler. *Dreamers Without Power. The Menomini Indians*. New York: Holt, Rinehart and Winston, 1971.

Spindler, Louise. Menomini Women and Culture Change. *American Anthropological Association Memoir 91*. Menasha, Wisconsin: Banta and Sons, 1962.

———. Menomini Witchcraft. In D. Walker, ed., *Systems of North American Witchcraft and Sorcery*. Moscow, Idaho: University of Idaho, 1971.

———. Menomini. In Bruce C. Trigger, ed., *Handbook of North American Indians, vol. 15*. Washington, D.C., Smithsonian Institution, 1979, pp. 708–724.

U.S. Court of Claims, Trial Division. Docket No. 134-67 (Basic). Filed July 19, 1978. The Menominee Tribe of Indians v. The United States.

U.S. Department of the Interior, Bureau of Indian Affairs. *Report No. 230. Menominee Indian Tribe of Wisconsin, Part I: Inventory of Resources; Part II: Annotated Bibliography*. Billings, Montana: The Planning Support Group, 1975.

Velte, Charles H. *Historic Lake Poygan*. Copyright by Charles H. Velte, 838 Louise Road, Neenah, Wisconsin, 54956. 1977.

Wax, Murray. *American Indians, Unity and Diversity*. Englewood Cliffs, New Jersey: Prentice-Hall, Inc., 1971.

Willey, Gordon R. *An Introduction to American Archaeology. vol. 1. North and Middle America*. Englewood Cliffs, New Jersey: Prentice-Hall, Inc., 1966.

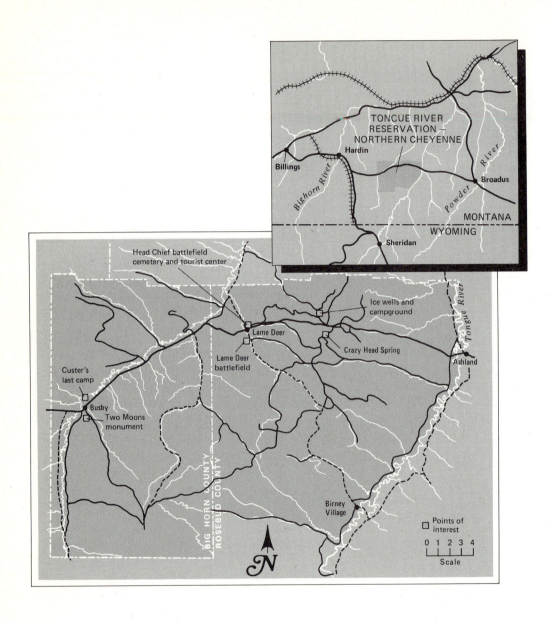

TONGUE RIVER
RESERVATION—
NORTHERN CHEYENNE

Billings

Hardin

Broadus

Bighorn River

Powder River

MONTANA

WYOMING

Sheridan

Head Chief battlefield
cemetery and tourist center

Ice wells and
campground

Lame Deer

Crazy Head Spring

Lame Deer
battlefield

Ashland

Custer's
last camp

Busby

Two Moons
monument

Tongue River

Birney
Village

BIG HORN COUNTY

ROSEBUD COUNTY

Points of
interest

0 1 2 3 4
Scale

N

CHAPTER 6

THE NORTHERN CHEYENNE
Those Who Suffered Much

"Good-by, you are going on a very hard road."

"The stones are all that last long."

From two Cheyenne war songs

To the casual observer, no two groups look more dissimilar than the Cheyenne, riders on the Plains and hunters of buffalo, and the Menominee, those gatherers of wild rice and trappers of fur who have remained in Wisconsin throughout their known history. It is surprising, therefore, to discover that the Cheyenne, too, are Central Algonquian speakers with a background of fishing and farming. Cheyenne tradition states that they originally lived near the Great Lakes area,

Poison, a Cheyenne woman almost 100 years old when this photograph was taken in 1888. Note that a portion of the little finger, left hand, is missing. This has been cut off in mourning for a dead relative.   National Archives and Records Service, G.S.A.

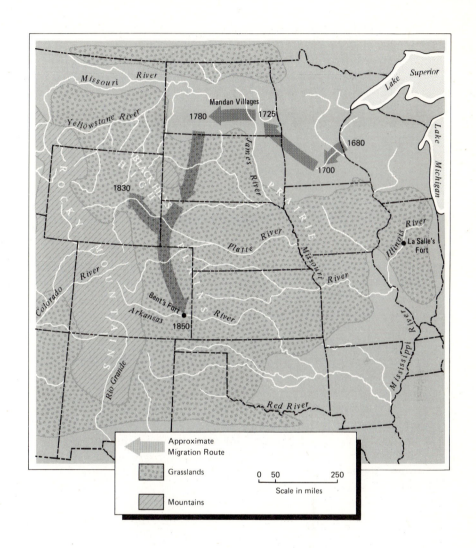

Missouri River

Yellowstone River

Mandan Villages
1780 ← 1725

1680

1700

ROCKY

BLACK HILLS

1830

Lake Superior

Lake Michigan

James River

PRAIRIE

Illinois River

La Salle's Fort

Platte River

Missouri River

Colorado River

M O U N T A I N S

Bent's Fort
Arkansas River
1850

Rio Grande

Red River

Mississippi River

Approximate
Migration Route

Grasslands

Mountains

0   50   250
      Scale in miles

where they subsisted on fish and wild rice. Wood (1971: 52–54), quoting a variety of sources, places the tribe first in or near Minnesota and Wisconsin. Very early they were a small group cut off from their Algonquian-speaking relatives, and Cheyenne language reflects this separation. A French map, dated around 1700, shows the Cheyenne with seven other groups along the east side of the Mississippi River above the mouth of the Wisconsin River. Sioux tradition places them in southwestern Minnesota as farmers living in earth lodge villages. These varied locations probably reflect the fact that the Cheyenne moved in small bands and not as a single tribe, but their movement was continually westward.

Military pressures from the east and north forced some Cheyennes to an area around the Sheyenne River in North Dakota. Their migration to this region probably marked the beginning of their transition from village farmers to nomadic hunters and gatherers with a special interest in buffalo. Agriculture, however, continued to be important for a time. Gardens were planted with corn, beans, and squash. Enough vegetables were produced so that a surplus was often traded to the Chippewa to the east.

Why did the Cheyenne keep moving while the Menominee stayed put? The Menominee had powerful allies: first, the Winnebagos and then French, British, and (finally) American colonizers. These allies offered not only protection, but also trade and prosperity. The Menominees also had the advantage of being tucked away in the northeastern part of Wisconsin, where they were protected by Lake Michigan from the powerful Iroquois attacking from the east. The Cheyenne, on the other hand, moving always in small bands to new territory, had no such protection. They were always inferior to their new neighbors in numbers and weapons, and they suffered also from the disadvantages of moving into someone else's territory. Between 1650 and 1800, an overarching principle of their existence consisted of a dreary cycle, repeated every 20 to 30 years, of partial and temporary adjustment to superior forces followed by flight and temporary accommodation once more. The Cheyennes, as Mooney has noted, were "brave to desperation" because they had to be.

Once they had reached the Plains, the Cheyennes needed one further acquisition, the horse, to complete their transformation from farmers and fishermen to buffalo hunters and mounted warriors. Whereas the Cheyennes began to be aware of the horse perhaps as early as 1760, it took them until about 1830 to accumulate enough horses and guns through trade with southern and northeastern Indian groups to give up farming and become nomadic buffalo hunters. They had finally reached a location that was isolated enough from other tribes so that they could remain there. It was not, unfortunately, isolated so much that they could avoid conflict. Indeed, the history of the 1800s is one long series of wars and skirmishes, not only with Indians, but more and more with Whites as the population expanded and the demand for land grew greater. Before considering a few of these conflicts, however, we will look at what life was like for a Cheyenne living on the High Plains in the 1800s.

CHEYENNE LIFE IN THE 1800s

APPEARANCE.   What did the Cheyenne people look like? Perhaps the earliest description we have is provided by Lewis and Clark, who met the Cheyenne in 1804 and 1806 in the Dakotas. The *Journals* (1905) describe Cheyenne men as large and portly with high cheeks, straight limbs, and high noses. They were dressed in the summer in light buffalo skins covering a breech clout. Some wore leggings and moccasins made of deer or antelope hide. It was evident to Lewis and Clark that the Cheyennes had trade relationships with other Indians because they wore as ornaments items such as blue beads, shell, red paint, rings of brass, and brooches. They also used objects such as bear claw or otter skin necklaces. Their hair was cut in bangs in front and either braided or flowing loose behind. The two explorers did not find Cheyenne women so impressive. They characterized them as homely with coarse features and wide mouths. Women wore simple leather dresses ornamented with beads, shells, and elk tusks. Their hair was loose and flowing, and their ears often were decorated with blue beads. Lest we take Lewis and Clark too literally, it should be noted that Henry (1897) found the Cheyenne to be far more attractive people in manners, appearance, and dress than other Indians he had known. A modern observer (Kania, 1972–1977) states that Cheyenne men today are regarded as handsome and the women as very attractive.

The Role of the Buffalo in the Cheyenne Life-Style

During this period, the most important task for the Cheyenne men was to provide food for their families. By 1830 the Cheyennes were dependent upon the buffalo for food. The reliance on buffalo meant staying near the migratory herds, and it was this necessity that made gardening and a sedentary life impossible, although the Corn Dance continued to be held until 1876. The Cheyennes regarded the hunting of buffalo as a hard, dangerous business. Although buffalo were basically timid animals, when they were overtaken and wounded they were quite capable of turning upon their attackers. George Catlin (1973) noted that horses were often destroyed by buffalo charges, but the Indian riders usually managed to escape.

Buffalo hunts were governed by rules that were carefully enforced by camp soldiers and public opinion. If many buffalo were grouped together, a communal hunt took place. Before the Cheyennes had enough horses, they surrounded the herd and gradually closed in from all sides. Ideally, such an approach would cause the animals to mill about in a circle without running away from the hunters. With the buffalo thus locked into a compact mass, all of the animals could be killed in a relatively short time. Before guns became available, bows and arrows were used effectively. Usually, the buffalo were shot at a distance of no more than two to three yards by mounted hunters, although these weapons could be used successfully up to about 150 yards. A skilled hunter using a well-made bow could kill a large buffalo with a single arrow. Also at times buffalo were driven into pens or corrals. Since they were afraid to jump over or break out of the enclosures, they could be killed easily. On occasion, buffalo were killed with lances, but this was a more dangerous and awkward form of slaughter.

If there were only small numbers of buffalo around and other food sources were available, men were allowed to hunt individually or in small groups. One of the easiest methods of taking buffalo was for the hunters to drive them into snow drifts blocking the bottoms of ravines. Once trapped there, they could be killed with a minimum of effort. But winter hunting had its shortcomings because it required small parties of hunters to be away from camp for long periods of time. Not as much meat could be secured from a single kill as was the case during the warmer months. Sudden severe storms could result in frozen hands and feet or even death. All agreed that buffalo hunting was a dangerous business, and it was not unusual for a few hunters to be killed every year.

Women had the chief responsibility for processing the buffalo carcass into food, utensils, and tools. Berthrong (1963: 32–33) comments on the way every bit of the animal was used except for the hoofs. Hides were carefully tanned and used for teepee covers, robes, and, in the case of older animals, moccasin soles, carrying packs, and shields. Every bit of the flesh was eaten. The tongue and nose were considered delicacies. Intestines were filled with chopped meat and roasted or boiled. The lungs were dried and roasted; the bone marrow eaten; and even the blood was cooked in the buffalo stomach until it turned to jelly. Meat that could not be eaten immediately was sliced and dried on racks or made into *pemmican* by pulverizing the roasted flesh and adding melted fat, bone marrow, and powdered, dried wild cherries. Among the Cheyenne, pemmican was not stored as an emergency food for times of privation, but was eaten fairly soon.

Household utensils came from the raw materials supplied by the buffalo and other animals. Spoons and ladles were made from horns of buffalo or mountain sheep. Water was carried in the paunch of the buffalo or in the bladder. Rawhide, made from buffalo hide that had been bleached in the sun for several days, was used for binding together the

wood and stone parts of implements and for making various recepta-
cles. Before they got metal tools, the Cheyennes used animal bones to
make various implements, such as hoes, scrapers, and wedges.

Elk, deer, wild sheep, and an occasional black bear were also used
for food, but to a much lesser extent than the buffalo. The obvious
importance of the buffalo to these Indians can be demonstrated by sub-
tracting buffalo meat and its products from the cultural inventory of the
mid-nineteenth-century Cheyennes. Life clearly would not have been
the same.

OTHER FOODS.   To supplement their meat diet, Cheyenne women collected a wide variety of plants for food. Mint was used for tea, acorns
were made into a mush, many kinds of nuts were collected, boiled box
elder sap was used as sweetening, and berries were dried and stored
for winter. In spite of this variety of food sources, the Cheyennes, like
most tribes of the buffalo Plains, often faced want (Grinnell, 1923: 258).

A Typical Day in a Cheyenne Village

Grinnell (1923: 63–72) described a Cheyenne village on a lovely summer's day. The Indians had pitched camp in a broad flat area of land
near water but somewhat sheltered between low, rolling hills. They
arranged their skin lodges in a large circle about half a mile in diameter.
Women awoke before dawn to kindle cooking fires. As columns of gray
smoke issued from the open teepee flaps, the women drew fresh water
from the stream. Some men and boys awoke and bathed in the icy clear
water, but they were not joined by females. Teen-aged boys mounted
horses tethered to the lodges overnight and rode to the nearby meadows to bring in the horse herds that had grazed there during the night.
When they returned, the morning meal of boiled meat was ready to eat.
This completed, several of the men mounted their horses to begin a
hunt. Before they left, they listened to the crier shout out the orders of
the chiefs and items of personal news. Such announcements may have
been that buffalo were not to be disturbed that day or that camp would
be moved to another spot or merely that someone had lost a piece of
riding gear and would like it returned if found.

After the men had ridden out of camp, women formed work groups
on the basis of kinship and friendship to perform tasks that could not
be done alone, such as sewing skins together to make a new lodge.
Children no longer physically dependent upon their mothers formed
play groups. Young men practiced archery and sometimes gambled.
Some women, laughing and joking, addressed themselves to the perpetual tasks of gathering fresh wood for the fire and collecting wild
plants. Others sewed clothing or pounded wild berries into cakes.

A number of men were always left in camp. The older ones devoted themselves to smoking, gossiping, and talking about their younger days before an eager audience of young boys. Young men often spent much time on their personal appearance, plucking hairs from their eyebrows, lips, and cheeks; combing and braiding their hair; and painting their faces. After this had been done, they dressed in their finest clothing and rode around camp so that people could admire them.

As the day became warmer, the sides of the teepees were partially rolled up to allow the breeze to circulate. For an hour or two there was stillness in the camp and on the vast plains stretching in all directions. This cohesive relationship with an occasionally beneficent nature was one of the rewards of being Cheyenne. There were also many penalties.

In the late afternoon, the hunters returned laden with meat, and the groups of women came in from gathering wild roots and berries. There was much laughter and joking, sounds of people enjoying each other's company after a day of hard work. Dusk arrived, cooking fires were built up, and an evening meal was prepared. Guests were often invited and were treated with relaxed courtesy. After the meal, gambling games began in some lodges. These games had considerable social and ceremonial significance in that gambling provided one means of signifying social alliances and distributing wealth. The act of gambling was also a way of communing with the supernatural because it was felt that spiritual forces often played some role in determining the outcome. Evening was also a time of courtship between young people, of music, dancing, and drumming. At last, one by one, the fires burned down and the camp became silent.

Cheyenne Behavior

All observers of the Cheyennes during the mid-1800s have been impressed by these Indians' voiced desire for order structured by custom and reinforced through a mythology that had immediate daily implications for all. They actively sought the peace and decorum within their ranks that was vehemently denied them by the harsh outside world. They seemed to believe that if feelings and actions could be controlled at the individual level, they would be better able to resist the insidious forces from without that perpetually sought their destruction. When in doubt or danger, the Cheyennes tried to conform to the group interest. Far too often, however, the rewards of conformity and order were either minimal or unsatisfactory. Being good in the Cheyenne way could be a frustrating, tedious affair. Being bad could mean the loss of group support. Most Cheyennes lived out their lives uneasily suspended between these two extremes.

A most abrasive feature in Cheyenne culture was a contradiction with respect to proper adult behavior. Men were expected to be aggressive, successful hunters and warriors while at the same time being

Teepee where the Sacred Buffalo Hat is kept. Along with the Medicine Arrows, the Hat is the essence of the spirit of the Cheyenne people. The acting Hat Bundle Keeper stands in front of the tent. 1971.   W. H. Hodge.

reserved, cooperative individuals in their relations with other Cheyennes. Women were docile, industrious drudges who processed hides and meat, reared children, and were responsibile for moving camp. Unlike the Iroquois, whose women could play important political roles, among the Cheyenne all governmental posts were held by men, and the husband was the head of his household. These roles caused a good deal of volatile behavior and conflict between the sexes.

Social and Political Organization

Cheyenne social and political organization was extremely complex. They shared with other Plains groups features such as military societies for men, the Sun Dance, and band divisions. They differed, however, in having a centralized political organization and sacred tribal objects, the Medicine Arrows and the Sacred Buffalo Hat. Although the basic social group was the nuclear family, consisting of husband, wife, children, and dependent relatives, the primary economic unit was the extended family or camp. Husbands at marriage moved in with their wife's relatives, forming a camp containing several hunters and enough women to prepare the meat and hides on the occasion of a large kill. If disruption or death broke up a marriage, this household would care for the children. The Cheyennes also practiced sororal polygyny; that is, a man could marry real or classificatory sisters.

THE BAND. A Cheyenne band consisted of 25 to 30 extended families acting as a political unit and guided by a band leader selected on the basis of charisma and a reputation for common sense. Local extended family groups were satisfactory units for hunting and gathering, but they were vulnerable to attack by hostile war parties. There were ten bands within the Cheyenne tribe. A man kept his band affiliation after marriage and could return to it or, if necessary, join another band. Each band had a fixed place within the great tribal camp circle. Such a circle was formed during the summer for the tribal ceremonials and hunts.

When they were village-dwelling gardeners, the Cheyennes had had clans. During the 1800s the clans still served to prohibit marriage to any clan member who was considered a relative.

THE TRIBE. The tribe was the largest social group of significance. It had a common language, political and social organization, and culture. There was a keen sense of internal cohesion and ethnic distinctiveness. The tribe came together only during a part of the summer when enough food was available for everyone. Then at least one of the great ceremonies signifying tribal unity was held—the Renewal of the Medicine Arrows, the Sun Dance, or the Animal Dance. The Medicine Arrows were the great symbolic integrator of the tribe because they symbolized its prosperity and welfare and guaranteed the authority of the tribal chiefs and medicine men (Hoebel, 1960: 10–11). The Sun Dance helped to renew the vital resources of the universe upon which the Cheyenne depended. In addition, during the course of a Sun Dance ceremony, individuals could perform acts of self-sacrifice as a fulfillment of a vow, to cure a sick relative, or to acquire personal power to triumph over danger in time of war. The Animal Dance was done to help perpetuate the supply of game, especially buffalo. One of the most dramatic parts of this ceremony was a symbolic killing of animals by clowns, called Contraries because during this time they did everything backwards. All of these ceremonies reaffirmed tribal unity, customs, beliefs, and welfare and, in addition, gave each individual an avenue for acquisition of prestige and activity above the band level of organization (Weist, 1971: 34).

OTHER POLITICAL AND SOCIAL GROUPS. During the summer months, the Council of Forty-four, a group of peace chiefs, and the military societies were most influential. The council decided such matters of common interest as the moving of camp, warfare, and alliances with other tribes.

The last living Clown or Contrary is standing on the right. His is the first generation of reservation Indians. 1971.   W. H. Hodge.

The council, in addition, determined the time and place of the communal hunt and named a military society to police the event. Finally, they ruled on the punishment for intratribal homicide and attempted to settle serious quarrels that arose between important people within the tribe. Council members were highly respected because each man embodied all that was valued by the tribe—success in war and a charitable, cooperative attitude toward other Cheyennes. Each of the ten bands selected four chiefs, and the heads of such vital societies as the Medicine Lodge and the Animal Society made up the balance of the membership. The military societies included members of all bands. Each had its distinctive paraphernalia, rituals, dances, and songs (Anderson, 1951: 122). These societies acted as police during tribal encampments, marches, hunts, wars, and ceremonies. Each was led by two military chiefs, who functioned also as tribal war leaders. Although the Council of Forty-four ultimately decided matters of tribal war and peace, they had to take into account the interests of the military societies. There were usually mutual deference and careful politics between tribal chiefs and military chiefs. The position of tribal chief was more honorable, but military chiefs also had a strong position by virtue of the fact that they were men of direct action who commanded the loyalty of most of the fighters (Llewellyn & Hoebel, 1941: 91).

CHEYENNE CHARACTERISTICS.   One of the most important generaliza-
tions that can be made concerning Cheyenne life during the mid-1800s
is the fact that, despite the massive external threats to survival, life for
a Cheyenne was meaningful and consistent. People knew what was
expected of them and could usually come to terms with such demands.
The difficulties and insecurities of the nomadic Plains existence meant
that individuals were allowed a great deal of flexibility. Men had control of their own property and could shift from one band to another at
will. They were aided in obtaining power by a vision quest performed
at any time they wanted according to a prescribed ritual. Leadership in
the band and tribe was granted to the bravest in warfare and the
wealthiest, but along with bravery, a good Cheyenne was even-tempered, good-natured, energetic, wise, kindly, and concerned for others.

Historical Events before 1880

Now that we have examined the way the Cheyennes lived, we can take
a look at some of the historical events that affected their lives once they
had settled on the Plains. By the time they got there, very few full-
blooded Cheyennes were left. Their long association with the village
tribes of the Missouri, such as the Arikara, Mandan, and Hidatsa, had
resulted in a great deal of intermarriage. Their practice of taking captives in warfare and then raising them as Cheyennes who married into
the tribe further added to their mixed genetic heritage. Grinnell (1911)
lists 28 tribes from which captives had been taken by the Cheyenne.

The enemies of the Cheyenne were many and powerful, the most
prominent being the Crow, Ute, Pawnee, Assiniboin, Shoshone, and
Kiowa. The Crows resented the Cheyennes because they invaded territory that the Crows regarded as their own to the west of the Missouri
River. Cheyenne battles with the Crow continued for more than 70
years. When Cheyennes and Crows met in combat, no quarter was
asked or given. The Crows were by any standard dramatic people.
Denig (1953: 29) characterized them as cunning, active, and very intelligent in matters pertaining to hunting, war, or their own individual
bargaining, but ignorant in all else. In addition to the tribes mentioned
above, the Cheyennes had occasional conflicts with the Blackfeet, who
lived well north of them. Denig (1930: 470) called these people the most
numerous and bloodthirsty on the upper Missouri. To the south, the
Pawnee sometimes offered warfare and in 1830 or 1833 captured the
four sacred arrows, the most treasured Cheyenne possession, which
had been given to them by Sweet Medicine, their culture hero. Two of
the arrows were eventually regained, and two more created. Hyde
(1974: 184–187) tells a grim story of a Cheyenne woman's being sacri-
ficed to Morning Star by the Pawnees in 1833 despite the efforts of an
Indian agent to save her. On that occasion the whole prairie was covered with Pawnees galloping their horses in madly swirling groups,

Buffalo robe painted in 1871 by Red Cloud, a Cheyenne leader. The painting represents a fight that he had several years earlier with a party of Shosoni. Photograph courtesy of Museum of the American Indian, Heye Foundation.

each group led by a warrior who swung above his head a leather thong with a piece of the woman's bloody flesh attached.

To help them combat these enemies, the Cheyennes allied themselves to the Sioux and the Arapaho. The Arapaho were another Algonquian-speaking group who had come from the east and entered the Plains before the Cheyenne. Together the Cheyennes and the Arapaho controlled eastern Colorado and southeastern Wyoming but ranged widely over the Plains (Eggan, 1937: 36). The Arapaho tribe was probably about the same size as the Cheyenne, estimated at 3,460 in 1822 (Morse quoted in Mooney, 1907b: 402). Mooney believed that the Cheyennes reached their greatest strength of about 4,000 by 1863. Thereafter they were decimated by increasing warfare with the Whites, as well as by disease, starvation, and exposure. By 1875, when they had been brought under effective government supervision and the tribe had been divided into Northern and Southern branches, there were 1,727 Northern Cheyennes and 2,055 Southern Cheyennes, or a total of 3,782 for the whole tribe. By 1906 total population had dropped further to 3,334.

This division between the Northern and Southern branches of the

A painted buffalo hide representing a Cheyenne horse-stealing raid. Their enemies are not identified. The taking of a scalp is shown in the left hand corner.
1850–1875.   Photograph courtesy of Museum of the American Indian, Heye
Foundation.

tribe occurred in 1834, when Bent's Fort was established on the Arkansas River in southeastern Colorado. The group calling themselves the
Southern Cheyenne began to trade directly with the people at the fort
for European goods. The Northern Cheyenne preferred to trade with
other Indians.

AFTER 1850.   After 1850 Cheyenne history is the story of ever-intensi-
fying battles with encroaching Whites. In 1841 the first emigrant train
moved up the Platt River on its way to Oregon. The swarm of emigrants
began to disrupt the natural resources, particularly the herds of buffalo.
The presence of small numbers of inexperienced, poorly led federal
troops on the Plains led to unfortunate incidents where camps of Indians near trading posts were attacked because of the depredations of
those living well away from American settlements. Innocent Cheyennes, among others, were killed in these encounters. Many Plains
Indians became convinced that most Whites wanted only to fight and

responded accordingly. Pressures intensified in 1858, when gold was discovered in Colorado. By 1859 stage coach lines were established through the center of Cheyenne and Arapaho country. Cheyennes, in general, did not respond with violence but often cared for lost, starving miners, many of whom had gone mad after learning the true nature of the vast, harsh country and sensing their inability to meet its challenges.

In 1861 regular troops were removed from the area to fight in the Civil War. Whereas the Kiowas and Comanches staged minor raids, the Cheyennes and Arapahos maintained a generally favorable attitude toward the non-Indian population. That year the Arapahos and Cheyennes signed a treaty at Fort Wise, Kansas Territory, giving up their claims on most of their hunting grounds in return for a reservation where they could, after appropriate instruction, farm. They further agreed to the quiet and peaceful possession of their future home and pledged their good behavior. Unfortunately, this was not to be, largely because the interests of the general public and those of the Indians were irreconcilable. Non-Indians wanted full access to land as opportunity and inclination directed. The Cheyennes and other Plains Indians insisted on the right to follow their old way of life or be given the means to develop a new but equally satisfactory kind of existence. The controlling economic interests in the United States vetoed both alternatives. Tragedy for the Indians was inevitable and began in 1864 with the Sand Creek Massacre.

THE SAND CREEK MASSACRE.   The Sand Creek Massacre occurred during a period when the civilian approach to the most mundane Indian behavior often verged on hysteria. Indians were slaughtered for little or no reason in an arbitrary fashion. When the Indians responded in kind or stole the ranchers' livestock to substitute for the decreasing buffalo meat available, fear and antagonism increased against them. Not surprisingly, the Indians came to believe that most Whites were insane or hopelessly undependable and were obsessed with the idea of destroying all Indians. One who fitted this description was Colonel J. M. Chivington, who had ambitions to be the governor of Colorado. In November of 1864, he led a troop of militia who attacked a camp of more than 500 Cheyennes and Arapahos who had gathered at Sand Creek, hoping to make peace. Several hundred may have been killed, perhaps two-thirds of the dead being women and children. Chivington disgraced himself by allowing his soldiers to scalp the dead, cut up and mutilate the bodies, and take over a hundred scalps back to Denver, where they were exhibited between the acts of a theatrical performance (Grinnell, 1956: 173–174). Several prominent Cheyenne leaders who had favored peace were among those murdered. A congressional committee later condemned the action of Chivington and his friends, but many Cheyennes were now convinced that they should die fighting rather than be

Dull Knife (seated) with Little Wolf. Taken prior to 1877. Smithsonian Institution, National Anthropological Archives.

conveniently grouped in camps waiting for the fatal attentions of the nearest armed body. One group, who decided to fight, went north and allied themselves with the Sioux and Northern Arapahos. A second group, who desired peace, followed Black Kettle to the south, but many were killed by Custer's troops at the Battle of the Washita.

CUSTER'S DEFEAT AND THE CONSEQUENCES.   During the next 12 years, if the conditions were at all favorable to them, Cheyennes and their allies fought well against a variety of military units assisted by White and Indian scouts, usually Crow. Their bravery could not change what had to happen. The territory they controlled and their numbers steadily dwindled. Perhaps the best remembered but most needless episode of the Indian battles on the Northern Plains was Custer's defeat at the Little Big Horn on June 25, 1876. Custer was ordered by his superior, General A. H. Terry, to locate a number of Indians who had left their reservations in response to illegal harassment. Terry hoped that once the Indians had been found, they could be persuaded to return peacefully to their assigned areas. Custer, however, had keen political ambitions and was aware of what a decisive victory over Indian forces could mean for him in a national election. He therefore attacked an Indian encampment on the Little Big Horn River. Too late, he and several companies of the Seventh Cavalry learned that they had challenged an aggregate of more than 4,000 Sioux, Cheyenne, and Arapaho. In less than an hour, Custer and 265 men were dead. The Indians then scattered, some going to Canada for a time, for they knew that their victory would bring swift reprisals.

Dull Knife's village was captured in November 1876. Those Cheyennes who had survived the attack and escaped surrendered the next year. Two Moon's camp was destroyed in 1878. From this point on, the Cheyennes were incapable of opposing the larger society through armed conflict. Some Cheyennes made a final gallant attempt to prevail in spite of the overwhelming military superiority of their enemies. The Northern Cheyennes had been herded south and confined in Indian Territory, now Oklahoma, with the Southern Cheyennes. Decimated by disease and malnutrition in the unfamiliar climate, 300 of them, under the leadership of Dull Knife, defied the Indian agent in the summer of 1878 and began the long march home. Opposed along the way by 13,000 troops, they fought and marched until they reached their homeland, where they laid down their arms. Government officials, in an effort to force them to march back to Oklahoma in the dead of winter, confined the group in unheated barracks at Fort Robinson without food or water. On the night of January 9, 1879, the remnant left the fort to meet death. Sixty-four were killed by the troops and 78 were recaptured. Thirty or so escaped. Shortly thereafter, the survivors at last got their way. Separate reservations for the Cheyennes were established, one on the Tongue River in Montana, and the other in southwestern Oklahoma (Hoebel, 1960: 203). Thus the Cheyennes ended more than 200 years of conflict. Had the essential relationship among food resources, the means to exploit those resources, and the various Indian populations been left undisturbed, the Plains groups would probably have continued for generations. By 1880, however, the Cheyennes had been decisively defeated in combat. Tribal life on the open Plains in

Yellow Bear, a Southern Cheyenne, Cantonment, Oklahoma, 1909. Smithsonian Institution, National Anthropological Archives, Bureau of American Ethnology Collection.

pursuit of the buffalo was gone forever. The time of the reservation had come. The Cheyennes were now forced to find another satisfactory way to exist, one that would have only tenuous linkages with the past. Their search has continued for almost a century and has not yet been resolved.

THE SAD FATE OF THE CHEYENNE.   Few people in the history of the world have been forced to make so many difficult adjustments to such

brought prestige and community approval, which could no longer be gained in warfare.

THE 1920s.   The decade of the 1920s is now regarded by many older Cheyennes as a pleasant time when many people were small-scale farmers with gardens, chickens, and cattle. During this good time, their grandparents who had experienced the period of prereservation independence of the mid-nineteenth century were alive to advise their younger kinsmen and supply a feeling of continuity. The fact that the 1920s were also marked by widespread disease and poverty is not remembered. This decade is used as a kind of measure to determine the good and the bad with respect to the present.

THE 1930s.   After this good time came the ever-increasing theme of alcohol abuse and the radical change in family and household life. Correlated also with these changes is the improper care of the Sacred Buffalo Hat. In the 1930s came the Great Depression and the partial allotment of land. Civilian Conservation Corps camps were set up to provide employment for the Cheyennes, but, in order to participate, they had to live in the various villages where trucks could pick them up and transport them to the camps. Former administrative centers such as Lame Deer, Busby, and Muddy grew into towns. When the Great Depression was over and the camps were closed, the Indians were unable to move back to their former rural homes because these had been leased to American ranchers. Thus began the tendency to move into towns, which is still continuing.

The Indian Reorganization Act of 1934, subscribed to by the Northern Cheyennes, ended future allotments of land. It also helped create a tribal council consisting of ten representatives elected from each district

The Northern Cheyenne Reservation near Lame Deer, Montana. 1971.   W. H. Hodge.

and a tribally elected president. The council made decisions for the tribe, but all its ordinances and resolutions had to be approved by the secretary of the interior. The tribal council appointed a court system and police force with Indian personnel. By 1940 the Cheyennes were being given more choices of action along social, political, and religious lines. Adequate guidelines with respect to choice, however, were often lacking. Quite often individuals had to make choices on the basis of immediate gain rather than the consideration of long-term goals, and, to make things more difficult, the situation was continually changing. As the old Cheyenne institutions continued to break down, people were often forced to make choices on the basis of perceived individual need rather than group consensus. The ten members of the tribal council formed various alliances that pitted the mixed-bloods against the full-bloods and the Catholics against the peyote people. Many mixed-bloods had become relatively successful ranchers by the 1950s. As they controlled a large portion of reservation land, the others resented them.

FROM 1940 TO 1955. World War II and the Korean War introduced about 86 Cheyennes to the experience of military service. Other adults left the reservation to work in war industries, but most returned after the war. The period 1945 to 1950 was one of isolation, poverty, and little discernible change. Some tribal members were actually starving, and the old men wanted to open the Sacred Buffalo Hat bundle to see if this would bring relief to the tribe (Dusenberry, 1956: 138). Nothing, however, was done. A study of 334 Northern Cheyenne families made by the Bureau of Indian Affairs (B.I.A.) in 1950 (U.S. Department of the Interior, 1951) gave the average family income as $1,421. Twenty-four percent of this was obtained from welfare, and other major sources were the sale of crops and livestock and casual labor. The population was then about 1,800 on the reservation, with approximately one-eighth of the people living outside. This small number of people working outside was thought to have been caused by isolation and very few contacts with non-Indians, so that the Cheyenne rate of assimilation and acculturation were both low. The B.I.A. found the Cheyennes more Indian in culture and behavior than any other similar group in the Missouri River basin. Cheyenne was the primary language, and about one-third of the people knew no English. It was difficult to leave the reservation because transportation facilities were poor, being limited to a few graveled roads. Some contacts continued with the Southern Cheyennes in Oklahoma, and some ceremonial events were attended off the reservation, such as the Crow Fair and fairs and rodeos in Wyoming and the Dakotas.

Why did so many Cheyennes find the American mainstream repugnant? Dusenberry (1956b; 158) suggested that it was a combination of all they had suffered over the years, including troubles over land, the

Northern Cheyenne Tribal Office, Lame Deer, Montana, 1971.   W. H. Hodge.

monotonous diet supplied by government rations, the restrictions on their religious and educational practices, the Great Depression and its associated created work, and the disruption of family life caused by the war. Over the years neither the policies of the B.I.A. nor the exhortations of the churches and schools nor the resources of American technology had convinced the Northern Cheyennes that they would gain from closer association with the White world. Rather than move to a city where they would risk losing the close ties with Indian relatives, friends, and customs, they preferred to put up with all the hardships that went along with reservation living.

TWENTY YEARS OF CONTEMPORARY RESERVATION LIFE: 1955–1975

In 1973 four Indian high school students at St. Labre Mission wrote and illustrated a compelling soliloquy entitled "life on the reservation." Its contents provide a vivid interpretation of reservation life in the 1970s from the standpoint of young people.

> . . . life on the res . . . is to enjoy yourself at a pow-wow with your friends; riding bareback on a horse; having the tribal council compete with one another and not care about the young on the reservation; having a forty-nine on Saturday night;

is having your own gas can and hose;

having a wife at fifteen; being eaten up by mosquitoes; working at the mission factory; having the B.I.A push you around; having a rodeo for your own tribe; having the Tribal Council Jealous of Students who go off to college; having your own Super Bowl, right in the middle of Main Street; having buffalo berries and Kellogg's Corn Flakes for breakfast; eating buffalo meat; riding horses and going hunting; having the tribal police beat up teenagers and shoot them with tear gas for nothing; playing basketball for your school; having your own air-conditioned toilets;

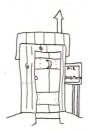

living on government rations; to show all your Indian Crafts at the Tribal Fair; having your own fair grounds; playing fussball at the rec hall; bootlegging white port to Indians; having the Tribal Council keep the Tribal money in a bank and tell the people there is no money; going to peyote meetings and having a big dinner the next day; waiting for your annuity money; having the Tribal police put you in jail; helping Indian relations do their work; having a big drinking party off the reservation so you won't go to jail for drinking on the reservation; having lots of jerky to eat; being able to drive the old one-eyed Ford pick up; to enjoy all the Tribal Indian games; having the B.I.A. tell you what to buy with your own money; to go to your Tribal ceremonies and to believe in them; watching your reservation from the new overpass; slaughtering your own cows; life on the res is BEAUTIFUL.

It can readily be seen from these remarks that much of contemporary Cheyenne life stems from the past half century. Far more continuity than change is evident with respect to culture content, its structure, and the marked persistence of a Cheyenne ethnic identity. The year 1976, in many respects, appears to be 1950 and before written a little larger.

A young Cheyenne girl on the reservation near Ashland, Montana. 1971.   W. H. Hodge.

Attempts to Make the Cheyennes Conform

The federal government was still determined to make the Cheyennes conform to American life. In the 1950s they attempted to accomplish this by the voluntary relocation of some Cheyennes to urban centers with the aid of partial financial support and, if necessary, vocational training. In addition, as many services as possible were to be transferred from the B.I.A. to state agencies. Finally, reservation status would be terminated. Some Cheyennes did go on relocation, but many of these returned to attempt to use their urban-acquired skills on the reservation. Some movement off the reservation also occurred on a self-sponsored basis. State support has not supplanted, but only supplemented, federal assistance of various kinds. Reservation termination has not occurred, nor is it likely to within the present generation.

201

A greater knowledge of the outside world has been facilitated by the addition of paved roads to the reservation and by the installation of electricity, which has made possible the widespread use of radio and television sets. A number of families receive the Billings daily newspaper. Although there are a few Cheyennes who do not speak some English, for many children English is now a first language.

An increase in employment opportunities through a mission-sponsored jewelry factory, various federal agencies, and very few small local businesses brought the average annual family income to $3,000 in 1967. Other sources of income were ranching and welfare. In 1963, aided by a federal loan, the tribe bought all land owned by Whites on the reservation and canceled all White-held grazing permits.

The Cheyenne land claims case against the federal government was settled in the tribe's favor. A federal court ruled that Cheyennes had been inadequately compensated for lands lost for various reasons in the past, and hence the Cheyenne people were entitled to additional funds over and above those provided by treaty. The tribe received $3.8 million. Every Cheyenne on the tribal roll received amounts not exceeding $1,000, which could be spent under a loose kind of federal supervision. The remainder of the land claims payment has been used for economic development and education programs. A balance of approximately $250,000 remains in a United States Treasury account for the tribe.

Other religious denominations have joined the Catholics and Mennonites on the reservation. The traditional religious beliefs associated with the Sacred Arrows, the Sun Dance, and the Sacred Buffalo Hat persist. Most Cheyennes are now familiar with a number of religious denominations. Commitment to one denomination or another often has political overtones.

Pan-Indianism

Although many Cheyennes are interested in one or more aspects of Pan-Indianism because they believe that it is possible for different Indian groups to have common problems, they do not really want to get involved. The tribe still finds it rewarding to hold powwows at Tongue River, which are attended not only by Cheyennes but by members of other Indian communities in Wyoming, North and South Dakota, Nebraska, Oklahoma, and other reservations in Montana. In turn, Northern Cheyennes frequently travel to these places for the dances there. The dance-feast-giveaway complex appears to have expanded under the influence of Pan-Indian stimuli.

The American Indian Movement (AIM) is not popular on the reservation because, although most Cheyennes approve of the stated goals of that organization, few will accept their methods. The fact that AIM comes from without and is not Cheyenne also makes it unacceptable in

High school students. A Crow is seated in the last desk, second row. The others are Cheyenne. 1979.   Ken Kania.

most cases. A few Cheyenne young people took part in the Trail-of-Broken-Treaties affair, which resulted in the temporary occupation and partial destruction of B.I.A. headquarters in Washington, D.C., in 1972. These individuals now regard that experience as an unfortunate one.

In 1967 there were 250 Whites living on the reservation in service (largely missionary and teaching) and administrative capacities (Weist, 1971: 73). Although there is no permanent White community, there has been a marked increase in daily Indian-White interaction.

Problems Facing the Cheyennes Today

These and other developments that have taken place during the period between 1955 and 1975 have resulted in there being a number of ways of living for the Cheyennes that, given the situation, can be contradictory, unfulfilling, or even insidious in effect at both the individual and community levels. There is a lack of broad integrating principles or behavioral guidelines that are acceptable to all Cheyennes at Tongue River. John Woodenlegs, a former tribal council chairman and a universally respected elderly Cheyenne, spoke to an audience of teachers at the beginning of the school year in September 1973. He described his conception of the contemporary Cheyenne good life, and also reflected upon what actually was and what might be. In part, he said:

Reservation meeting hall. Hand games and give-aways are sometimes held here. 1980.   Ken Kania.

So we are not using those good Cheyenne Ways that made us proud of ourselves in the past. We're using just any old Way and it's really hurting us. Some of our Young People trying to be leaders seem to want personal power and recognition instead of wanting to really help all the People. The attitude is more "What can I get for myself?"

I believe many of those same good Ways could be used today to make our lives have meaning and be useful:
—to be close to spirit our Creator
—to respect one another as people
—to help one another, cooperate together
—to be good to one another, use no harsh words
—to be honest
—to do what is right
—to keep ourselves healthy and strong, in body and mind because Spirit created us. Not to misuse our bodies and minds with alcohol, drugs or other harmful things.
—to have reverence for the earth and all of life
—to know how to take care of ourselves in the best way: not to have to depend on others. Teach our children to become responsible people each day as they are growing up. Learn how to do our share of the responsibilities of living. Make our own decisions.
—to work for the good of all, not just ourselves.

Woodenlegs was concerned over the ominous fact that although in the past the Cheyennes had workable guidelines for group conduct, these same directives are not being accepted now. Given the poverty and social conditions existing on the reservation, conduct regarded as proper within a traditional frame of reference is not sufficiently rewarding to contemporary Cheyennes. Instead self-interest promotes survival. This is not to deny that altruism is present, but when a Cheyenne strives to be good and do good, whose directives should he follow?

B.I.A. administrators, missionaries, kinsmen, and school teachers all give different advice. Cheyennes must deal with many behavioral codes or models that are often inconsistent to the point of frustration for an individual. Each person must interpret his or her own situation according to individually perceived needs and respond accordingly. These responses may be rewarded on one occasion and punished on another. The fabric of life itself then becomes contradictory. To be Cheyenne is to be inconsistent and erratic both in relations with others and in self-conception. The normal, uneasy tempo of reservation life is aggravated by the many demands made by non-Cheyennes such as federal and state governments, private industrial interests, and nearby communities. These demands require group consensus to answer, but given the frequent necessity of individually oriented behavior, consensus seldom appears.

Drugs and alcohol are two ways to gain relief from the tensions and penalties of socially determined conflict. When intoxicated by either, the individual finds temporary relief from the conflicts that he or she experienced while sober. Drunks and drug users can enjoy the rewards of being consistently inconsistent. Reservation public opinion grants this privilege on a selective and temporary basis. Suicide, or more accurately attempted suicide, can be another way provided that friends and relatives respond to the behavior by decreasing conflict for the intended victim. The same person often uses both attempted suicide and abuse of alcohol and drugs.

Because the reservation is both a part of the larger society and at the same time a semidetached community experiencing a variety of foreign stimuli, the code of conduct is inconsistent. As a result, modern Cheyennes must make radical adjustments in behavior and its supporting ideology faster than Cheyennes were ever required to do. Contemporary Cheyenne life implies a chronic identity crisis for too many people. By this, I mean a loss of the sense of the sameness and historical continuity of the self. People are unable to accept or adopt the role expected of them by others. Both denial and failure are frequently expressed by isolation, withdrawal, extremism, rebelliousness, and negativity.

Description of the Tongue River Reservation

Stresses are greater in some phases of the life cycle than they are in others. Childhood and old age for the Cheyennes are times of relative tranquility and ease. Adolescence and young adulthood are periods of great upheaval and threat. During the years between 12 and 35, Cheyennes learn or do not learn how to live with the social and emotional ambiguity that forms an intrinsic part of the foundation of reservation existence. The following description of the contemporary (1970s) reservation should be viewed within this frame of reference.

The Tongue River Reservation today consists of 433,000 acres, or a little more than 675 square miles. About 262,000 acres are tribally owned, with more than 171,000 acres being allotted to individuals. The tribe's mineral resources provide a tribal income of $300,000 per year, and farming provides the rest, according to a U.S. Department of Commerce report of 1974 (282–284). With this money, the Cheyennes are able to employ over 20 people and to sponsor organizations designed to strengthen reservation resources. Among these are the Land Acquisition Enterprise, the Steer Enterprise, the Cheyenne Livestock Association, and the Northern Cheyenne Arts and Crafts Association. In addition, the tribe belongs to the Big Horn Economic Development Corporation, which includes the Crow Indian Reservation.

Reservation services have still not reached the standards of most American communities. A good highway, U.S. 212, runs through the reservation from east to west and provides transportation to Billings, the nearest large city, 98 miles to the northwest. Truck and air service is available in Billings; and truck, bus, and rail service at Crow Agency, 18 miles west of the Northern Cheyenne reservation. The tribe operates water and partial sewer systems in Lame Deer and Busby, but only bottled gas is available for heating and cooking. The Montana Power Company supplies electricity, although service tends to be sporadic. The U.S. Public Health Service provides modern medical facilities, which suffer from overcrowding and underfinancing. These services are provided for the 2,926 Cheyennes living on the reservation. In 1973,

A traditional home west of Ashland, 1971.   W. H. Hodge.

according to a State of Montana and Northern Cheyenne Tribal Council document (45), 718 people lived away from Tongue River.

CHARACTERISTICS OF FULL-BLOOD CHEYENNES TODAY.   Individuals living on the reservation can be divided into four social categories, using the criteria of blood, religion, political affiliation, and residence. Traditional full bloods are characterized by being members of either the Native American or the Catholic church, by their being conservative in politics, and by living in conservative reservation towns such as Birney. Traditional Cheyennes attempt to follow the tribal code of behavior. They are never loud, especially at home. They never interrupt another person, seek attention, or attempt to be better than somebody else. They place strong emphasis on the virtue of generosity. Many traditional families still speak Cheyenne and enjoy social outlets such as dances and hand games, the traditional Cheyenne method of gambling. Traditional people see life as a cycle consisting of childhood, adolescence, adulthood, and old age. The cycle is circular with no real beginning and no end. Children, up to the age of 13 or 14, are pampered by adults and rarely disciplined. Adolescents are also treated permissively and allowed to experiment. Behaviors such as getting drunk, driving too fast, and promiscuity are all forgiven because the adolescent is presumed not to know any better. When adulthood arrives between the ages of 25 and 35, however, the male individual is expected to settle down and make a good life by providing for a wife and family. He should show a concern for tribal welfare and take part in traditional Cheyenne ceremonies. Those who do not settle down by 35 are labeled by the community as alcoholics or untrustworthy, as people who do "crazy" things. Reform is not possible after this age, for trust, once lost, cannot be regained. Old people are those who have started to slow down physically. Their job is to pass on wisdom to the younger generation and to safeguard the tribe ceremonially. Old people often have medicine power, and all good Cheyennes should listen to what they say. Traditionals believe that upon death they go up to the Milky Way to the camp of the dead. It is right that people die and do not return to life because if they did, they would be too brave and there would be too much fighting. Those who do return are evil ghosts.

THE HALF-BREEDS.   The second category within the tribe is the "half-breeds." Half-breeds are sometimes Catholic, but more often Pentecostal or Protestant. Many of them live in Busby or in and around Ashland. These people are still the most powerful politically because they control most of the land. Most of the successful cattlemen are half-breeds, holding long-term leases on land with exclusive grazing rights. Perhaps 75 percent of all the Cheyennes on the reservation, however, live in the towns.

A house in Rabbit Town, a suburb of Ashland, 1979.   Ken Kania.

THE WHITES.   The third category is that of Whites, although you can be a registered Cheyenne and still be considered a White. Whites have no predominating religious affiliation, but could belong to any denomination. They tend to get very involved in politics, but are not as powerful as the half-breeds. They do not participate in traditional ceremonies such as the Sun Dance and the Arrow Renewal, as the full bloods do. Surprisingly, the very American pastimes of football and basketball crosscut all social categories on the reservation, being universally popular.

THE ISOLATES.   The final category is the isolates, who are Whites with a difference. The isolates are ignored by the rest of the Cheyennes and by people who are genetically white, but they don't seem to mind it. Although they associate with some close relatives on the reservation, they never get involved with traditional things such as powwows, the Sun Dance, or peyote meetings. Most of the isolates are nominal Catholics, but they attend church only when a child marries or there is a funeral. They are never persecuted, but are simply ignored except for some perfunctory attention on rare occasions. Many isolates have children married to Crows, the traditional enemies of the Cheyennes, and perhaps this is why others dislike them. (I am obligated to Ken Kania, a teacher on the Cheyenne reservation, for defining these categories for me.)

INDIVIDUALS AND THE FAMILY.   Within each category, there are two levels of organization: the individual and the family. Adults are free to act in their own interests provided that they have first satisfied the needs of other family members. Men are expected to provide adequate food, clothing, and shelter either through holding a job or the various forms of welfare. Isolates and Whites are seldom forced to resort to welfare. Most families live in frame houses and trailers of varying degrees of size, quality, and repair, but few still occupy log cabins.

Individuals who are unsuccessful or bad are regarded as "crazy." Many Cheyennes believe that if someone leads a drunken life, violates the strict traditional sexual mores, or resorts to drug abuse, he or she does so because his or her crazy souls control his or her behavior (Straus: Personal Communication. The writings of Dr. Straus, unfortunately not published at this time, contain many valuable observations regarding Cheyenne personality and closely related matters.). According to this belief, each Cheyenne has four souls, two good and two crazy, and each soul struggles for domination. Souls do not inhabit the

A successful Cheyenne rancher. 1979.   Ken Kania.

body but walk in front, behind, and on either side. At times these souls are visible to other people, especially at the moment of death. This concept of souls serves to mitigate personal guilt and community hostility, for once the good souls regain control from the bad ones, the person is forgiven the deeds his or her crazy souls caused him or her to commit. Entire families can also be labeled as crazy. The parents could be alcoholics and the children loud, boisterous, and difficult to control. This type of behavior is the antithesis of traditional Cheyenne morality.

All the social categories listed above share a belief in the importance of relatives and relationships with relatives. Survival is not possible without their help. There are, however, variations among the categories with respect to how well they get along with relatives.

The behavior of all people on the reservation is structured by a seasonal cycle conditioned by tradition and by weather. Winter is a time for basketball games and the hand game. With good weather in spring come the powwows, followed by the major ceremonies of summer: the Sun Dance, the Arrow Renewal, and the worship of the Sacred Buffalo Hat. Fall means football and perhaps a few more powwows. School attendance of the children affects the entire family, for all must adjust to the schedule. Imposed on this schedule, too, is the necessity for the wage earners of the family to find jobs, a task that is often easier off the reservation than on it.

A more concrete idea of the nature of life on the reservation can be gained through the conversation of an elderly Cheyenne man as he describes and reflects upon the events of a single day:

> I woke up before light. Old lady wife, she tells me to come and eat. So I put my clothes on, washed and eat. Then I prayed. Then I watched Oral Roberts on TV. When that's finished, I made a wooden box for my tools. Then my cousin comes to my house and he wants to borrow my pickup. His youngest son was taken to the Crow Agency hospital early in the morning so fast that nobody remembered to bring his clothes along. So now his father will bring him his clothes. I say o.k. but come back before 12 o'clock noon becae one of my sons wants to use the pickup. So he brings it back, my son took it, and then my daughter wants to use it but it's too late. Her brother has it.
>
> About 2:00 in the afternoon a friend of mine and a chief comes to my house to go with me to a meeting. We want to ask the Tribal Council for money to help us with organizing a powwow and some medicine things. But at the same time, I tell them about my cousin's son being sick and we pray pretty long time for him to get well. Then I go home and watch TV. Young boys who live around me play football until almost dark. Then wife comes and says we should eat again so I do.
>
> After supper I read something that these Bahai Christians send me. All about their way. Then I watch TV and fall asleep. Pretty soon young nephew comes to my house and asks me if I have key to get in tribal office.

I tell him I only got one key but it will open any door and I point to big red crow bar hanging on wall. My nephew goes away. Then I lie down in one bed and the wife in the other. But soon a grandson comes to the door and asks me for a quarter. I give it to him and then he tells me that a bunch of drunk Cheyennes pretty close around, so I better keep lights off and be asleep. Old lady and I do this. Most days like that.

THE NATURE OF THE CHEYENNE COMMUNITY.   Moving beyond the individual and family levels, what is the essential nature of the Cheyenne community? It consists of a relatively small number of people united by a common tradition and culture and by the bonds of kinship, friendship, and reservation residence, but divided with respect to the social categories discussed above. Life is structured by the seasonal round, the recognized phases of the life cycle, and the relentless demands of adjusting to an indifferent, sometimes hostile, White world. The engineering of this system is far from perfect, but there are certain recognized, if not approved, methods of responding to stress. Individuals indulge in alcohol or drugs, commit suicide, practice or are terrified by witchcraft, or gossip. Gossip is by far the most effective tension reliever because there is a consensus on what is proper Cheyenne behavior. Those who follow it are rewarded with public approval, which is vital to their welfare.

THE COAL CONTROVERSY.   Community consciousness becomes apparent when the interests of the reservation as a whole are threatened by outside forces. At no time has this been more apparent than in the controversy that occurred over the coal resources on the reservation. Those wishing a detailed description are urged to read K. Ross Toole's *The Rape of the Great Plains,* but I will briefly summarize what happened. Between 1966 and 1973, the B.I.A. authorized the granting of permits for both exploration and actual strip mining of coal over 214,000 acres of the Cheyenne reservation, half of the total area. As the Northern Cheyenne, along with other Indian tribes, believe that their very identity is bound up in their land, this move threatened their existence. This fact overrode the desperate financial condition of most of the Indians, with their unemployment rate ranging between 26 and 40 percent.

Working under the direction of a young Indian lawyer, George Grossland, the tribe discovered that all coal leases had been granted by the B.I.A. in direct violation of the *Code of Federal Regulations,* Regulation 25, Part 177, known as 25 CFR. This code required that before any leases could legally be granted, a technical examination of the land must be made, which would include a study of the protection of other resources; the control of erosion, flooding, and water pollution; isolation of toxic materials; prevention of air pollution; reclamation of land;

prevention of slides; protection of fish and wildlife; and prevention of hazards to public health and safety. Such studies were never made.

The bidder for all the Cheyenne coal was the Peabody Coal Company. The royalty they offered was 17.5 cents per ton, with a reduction of 2.5 cents per ton for any coal used on the reservation plus a bonus of 12 cents per acre foot of water. These figures compared poorly to those the B.I.A. had obtained at Black Mesa on the Navajo and Hopi reservations. There Peabody paid a royalty of 25 cents per ton and $6.67 per acre foot for water pumped from deep wells. The event that made it clear to the Cheyenne tribe that they were not being given proper protection by the federal agencies whose job it was to look after their interests was an offer in July 1972 from Consolidation Coal Company. Consolidation, acting directly and not through the B.I.A., offered the Cheyennes $25 per acre foot as a bonus and a royalty of 25 cents per ton with no reduction for coal consumed on the reservation. By this time the Cheyennes had learned that Peabody's plan was to build huge mine-mouth-generating and coal-gasification plants on the reservation, where most of the coal would be burned at the lower royalty rate. As part of its offer, Consolidation would donate $1.5 million toward the cost of a new health center.

On June 4, 1974, Rogers C. B. Morton, secretary of the interior, issued a document invalidating Peabody's leases until such time that an environmental impact study could be done by sources outside the Department of the Interior. His statement made it clear that the tribe was free to sue the coal company and that the Department of Interior would pay for legal fees if they did so. The tribe, acting together, had won an important victory.

It is impossible to know now what the final disposition of the Cheyenne coal resources will be. The tribe has called in many outside experts and is engaged in a study of what would be the best ways to exploit their coal without destroying their homeland. One possibility would be to form their own petrochemical project on the reservation to convert the coal into by-products rather than burn it. It will be interesting to see what happens in the future. For anything to occur, the Cheyenne tribe must form a consensus and act as a unit, and this has always been difficult for them to do.

THE CHEYENNES AND OTHER AMERICANS.   The Northern Cheyenne tribe and the individuals within it are very much a part of the larger American society. Periods of growth and decline in the national economy are quickly felt on the reservation. The economic dimension, however, along with the social and political dimensions of United States culture, impinges upon the Northern Cheyennes for the most part as mediated through local citizens and institutions. Cheyenne relationships with other American citizens on the Northern Plains are far too complicated a subject for a comprehensive treatment here. It must be sufficient to say that these Indians occupy a passive, subordinate position with respect to the interests of other Montana citizens. For the most part, the Indians have only the option of responding to, rather than initiating, significant political and social directions. They are given freedom to exist along their own lines only as long as such freedom does not interfere with these interests. One of the central problems facing both Indians and other Montana residents is the fact that satisfactory guidelines for mutual interaction across ethnic borders do not exist. The incorporation of the Northern Cheyenne people into the larger society has an incomplete and immature flavor about it. The only thing one can say with certainty now is that an ethnically distinct group called Northern Cheyenne will probably exist far into the future.

Everyone who looks at Cheyenne history must agree with the Acting U.S. Indian agent Captain George W. H. Stouch when he wrote in 1896: "They have been among the bravest of the brave, as is well known, and when they laid down their arms and surrendered their old life for the new they did it in good faith, and have kept their word" (U.S. Congress, 1897: 195). May this new life at last be filled with the justice, prosperity, and abundance that the past 350 years have denied them!

REFERENCES

Anderson, John A. *The Sioux of the Rosebud: A History in Pictures.* Text by H. V. Hamilton and J. T. Hamilton. Norman: University of Oklahoma Press, 1971.

———, Eugene Buechel, S. J., and Don Doll, S. J. *Crying for a Vision: A Rosebud Sioux Trilogy, 1886–1976.* Dobbs Ferry, New York: Morgan and Morgan, 1976.

Anderson, Robert. A Study of Cheyenne Culture History, with Special Reference to the Northern Cheyenne. Ph.D. dissertation, Department of Anthropology, University of Michigan, 1951.

Berthrong, Donald J. *The Southern Cheyennes.* Norman: University of Oklahoma Press, 1963.

Brown, Joseph Epes, ed. *The Sacred Pipe: Black Elk's Account of the Seven Rites of the Oglala Sioux.* Baltimore: Penquin Books, 1971.

Catlin, George. *Letters and Notes on the Manners, Customs, and Conditions of North American Indians. Vols. I and II.* New York: Dover Publications, Inc., 1973.

Denig, Edwin T. Indian Tribes of the Upper Missouri. *46th Annual Report 1928–1929, Bureau of American Ethnology* J. N. B. Hewitt, ed. Washington, D.C.: Government Printing Office, 1930.

———. Of the Crow Nation. Anthropological Papers No. 33. *Bulletin 151, Bureau of American Ethnology.* Washington, D.C.: Government Printing Office, 1953.

Dusenberry, Verne. The Varying Culture of the Northern Cheyenne. Master's thesis, Montana State University, 1956.

Eggan, Fred. The Cheyenne and Arapaho Kinship System. In Fred Eggan, ed., *Social Anthropology of North American Indian Tribes.* Chicago: University of Chicago Press, 1937, pp. 33–95.

Grinnell, George Bird. *The Indians of To-Day* (rev. ed.). New York: Duffield & Co., 1911.

——. *The Cheyenne Indians, Their History and Ways of Life.* 2 vols. New Haven: Yale University Press, 1923.

——. *The Fighting Cheyennes.* Norman: University of Oklahoma Press, 1956.

Hoebel, E. A. *The Cheyennes: Indians of the Great Plains.* New York: Holt, Rinehart and Winston, 1960.

Hyde, George E. *The Pawnee Indians* (new ed.). Norman: University of Oklahoma Press, 1974.

Jablow, Joseph. The Cheyenne in Plains Indian Trade Relations 1795–1840. *Monographs of the American Ethnological Society 19.* New York: J. J. Augustin, 1951.

Kania, Kenneth. Personal Communications, 1972–1977.

Kappler, Charles J., comp. and ed. *Indian Treaties 1778–1883.* New York: Interland Publishing Inc., 1972.

Lewis, Meriwether, and William Clark. *Original Journals of the Lewis and Clark Expedition, 1804–1806.* Printed from the original manuscripts. . .together with Manuscript Material of Lewis and Clark from other sources . . . now for the first time published in full and exactly as written. Ed. (with introduction, notes, and index) Reuben Gold Thwaites, L.D.D. 8 vols. New York: Dodd, Mead & Co., 1904–1905.

Llewellyn, Karl N., and E. Adamson Hoebel. *The Cheyenne Way: Conflict and Case Law in Primitive Jurisprudence.* Norman: University of Oklahoma Press, 1941.

Lowie, Robert H. *Indians of the Plains.* Garden City, N.Y: The Natural History Press, 1963.

——. *The Crow Indians.* New York: Holt, Rinehart and Winston, 1935.

Mooney, James, "The Ghost-Dance Religion and the Sioux Outbreak of 1890." *Fourteenth Annual Report of the Bureau of Ethnology 1892–1893. Part 2.* Washington, D.C.: Government Printing Office, 1896.

——. Cheyenne. In F. W. Hodge, ed., *Handbook of American Indians North of Mexico. Bulletin 30, Part 1. Bureau of American Ethnology.* Washington, D.C.: Government Printing Office, 1907a, pp. 250–257.

——. The Cheyenne Indians. In *Memoirs of the American Anthropological Association 1:6,* 1907b, pp. 357–495.

Powell, Peter. *Sweet Medicine: The Continuing Role of the Sacred Arrows, the Sun Dance, and the Sacred Buffalo Hat in Northern Cheyenne History.* Vol 1. Norman: University of Oklahoma Press, 1969.

Powers, William K. *Oglala Religion.* Lincoln: University of Nebraska Press, 1977.

Roe, Frank G. *The Indian and the Horse.* Norman: University of Oklahoma Press, 1955.

——. *The North American Buffalo: A Critical Study of the Species in Its Wild State* (2d ed.). Toronto: University of Toronto Press, 1970.

Schlesier, Karl H. Action Anthropology and the Southern Cheyenne. *Current Anthropology 15*, 277–283, September 1974.

Schusky, Ernest L. *The Forgotton Sioux: An Ethnohistory of the Lower Brule Reservation*. Chicago: Nelson Hall, 1975.

Stands in Timber, John, and Margot Liberty, with the assistance of Robert M. Utley. *Cheyenne Memories*. New Haven: Yale University Press, 1967.

State of Montana and Northern Cheyenne Tribal Council. *Northern Cheyenne Planning Study: Socio-economic Analysis of Potential Coal Development*. Prepared by Wirth Associates, Billings, Montana, 1973.

Straus, Anne S. Personal Communications, 1978.

Toole, J. Ross. *The Rape of the Great Plains: Northwest America Cattle and Coal*. Boston: Atlantic Monthly Press Book, Little Brown & Co., 1976.

U.S. Congress. Report of Tongue River Agency, Geo. W. H. Stouch, Captain, Third Infantry, Acting United States Indian Agent. Report of the Secretary of the Interior, Being Part of the Message and Documents Communicated to the two Houses of Congress, Document No. 5, vol. 13. 54th Cong., 2nd sess., 1897.

U.S. Department of Commerce. *Federal and State Indian Reservations and Indian Trust Areas*. Washington, D.C.: Government Printing Office, 1974.

U.S. Department of the Interior. Bureau of Indian Affairs. Social and Economic Study of the Northern Cheyenne Reservation, Montana. *Missouri River Basin Investigations. Report No. 116*. Billings: Billings Area Office, 1951, Mimeo.

Weist, Katherine M. The Northern Cheyennes: Diversity in a Loosely Structured Society. Ph.D. dissertation, University of California, Berkeley, 1971.

Welch, James. *Winter in the Blood*. New York: Bantam Books, 1975.

———. *Riding the Earthboy 40*. New York: Harper & Row, 1976.

———. *The Death of Jim Loney*. New York: Harper & Row, 1979.

Wood, W. Raymond. Biesterfeldt: A Post-Contact Coalescent Site on the Northeastern Plains. *Smithsonian Contributions to Anthropology No. 15*. Washington, D.C.: Smithsonian Institution Press, 1971.

Woodenlegs, John. Cheyenne Ways—Past and Present. Position Paper written for the Fifth Annual Teachers' Workshop, Lame Deer Public School, Northern Cheyenne Reservation, September 9, 1973.

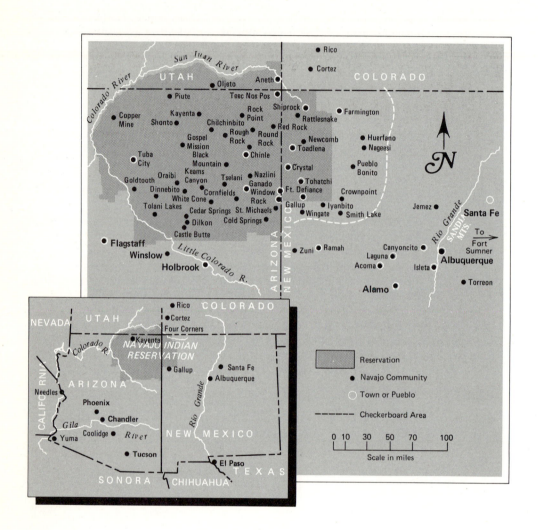

CHAPTER 7

THE NAVAJOS
Three Individuals

For long years I have kept this beauty within me,
It has been my life.
It is sacred.
I give it now that coming generations may know
    the truth
About my people.
I give it as the dew falls,
I give it as sacred pollen,
That there may increase a better understanding
    among men.

Old Man Buffalo Grass

Because I spent two years in Albuquerque, New Mexico, doing field work among the Navajos living there, I will discuss Navajo life as seen through the eyes of three very different individuals. I feel that this personalized view, although it may omit some ethnographic detail that my discussions of the other tribes include, provides a dynamic picture of what it is like to be a Navajo today. Before moving to the lives of these

Cayatanita, a brother of Manuelito. Member of a Navajo delegation to Washington, D.C., 1874. Smithsonian Institution National Anthropological Archives, Bureau of American Ethnology Collection.

three people, however, I will briefly summarize the history of the tribe, using Vogt's (1961) characterization of the general patterns of Navajo existence. Those who are interested in knowing more about Navajo ethnography are urged to read *The Navaho* and *Children of the People* by Kluckhohn and Leighton (1948, 1951).

HISTORY OF NAVAJO CULTURE

Beyond the fact that they are all Indians, there are no connections between the Navajos and the groups we have discussed. The ancestors of those who were to become Navajos first came to this country from Siberia over the Bering Strait about 2,000 years ago. At this time they were part of an undifferentiated group of Nadene speakers, a linguistic family that soon began to separate into distinct parts as the migrants dispersed. Athapaskan speakers, who appeared on the Pacific coast between 1,300 and 1,600 years ago, were one of these elements. About 1,000 to 1,300 years ago, the Athapaskan migration moved toward the Southwest. At least as early as 400 to 500 years ago, the Apacheans, speaking a variety of Athapaskan tongues, appeared in the Southwest and marked the beginnings of some contemporary tribes, including the Navajo and Apache groups.

These Apacheans were seminomadic hunters and gatherers with a limited material culture inventory. The women probably collected various forms of wild plants, while the men, using a sinew-backed bow, hunted deer, antelope, bison, and small game, including rabbits, porcupines, and turkeys. They lived in small encampments scattered throughout a wide range of territory and moved as plant-gathering and hunting seasons dictated.

The most important social units were the small number of extended families who made up a particular camp. A great deal of freedom of choice was available to the individual with regard to where he lived and what relatives he paid attention to outside of his immediate blood kin. The people lived in shelters made of a pole framework covered with a variety of materials, including hides, earth, and evergreen boughs. Sweathouses, built in the same fashion but smaller, were located nearby. As hunters and gatherers, the Apacheans had to remain mobile, so their possessions were few. In addition to the sinew-backed hunting bow already mentioned, they used fire drills; conical-based, undecorated pottery; and baskets. Clothing consisted of moccasins and skins.

If we assume that these early proto-Navajos resembled other hunters and gatherers having a similar development at other times and places in the world, political influence was limited to the advice offered by respected older men with regard to hunting and camping areas.

Social control consisted of informal sanctions supplied by the group as a whole. Outstanding warriors probably organized occasional raids for a variety of reasons.

Relations with the supernatural were coordinated by a shaman, an individual gifted with special powers for manipulating the spirit world on his own behalf and that of others. Girls' puberty rites were important ceremonially (Vogt, 1961: 289). These people feared ghosts and the dead and regarded lightning and certain animals such as the bear as having the power to cause illness.

By A.D. 1630, these newly arrived Athapaskan-speaking proto-Navajos had adopted from their long-established Pueblo neighbors a number of traits, practices, and ideas that were to serve them well in the coming centuries. They had acquired agriculture and become good enough farmers to produce surpluses that required a sophisticated means of storage. They had developed effective ways of dealing with the Pueblos and other non-Navajo groups around them through a combination of war, trade, and a tranquil kind of social symbiosis. Accompanying these acquisitions were efficient communication skills such as multilingualism and a strongly felt sense of possessing and defending a particular territory. These Athapaskans also may have begun to acquire forms of Pueblo ritual and certain matrilineal institutions, but available sources suggest that at this time they were little more than modified hunters and gatherers.

Spanish and Mexican Influences

Spain and Mexico between 1630 and 1846 introduced influences of a different kind and contributed to the continuing maturation of ideas and articles that had been introduced earlier. The Navajo acquired sheep and horses from the Spanish settlers living in the northern Rio Grande Valley. Abrasive Spanish contact with many Pueblo communities forced greater Navajo–Pueblo interaction, which stimulated the qualified Navajo–Pueblo cultural transmission that had begun earlier. It was probably during this time that the Navajos learned more about agriculture and animal husbandry from their neighbors and adopted some of their techniques in weaving and pottery making. In addition to these material things, the Navajos also absorbed into their own culture many Pueblo religious and social concepts. These included the use of ceremonial masks, altars, prayer sticks, corn meal, and sand paintings. New Navajo clans were formed from groups of Pueblo refugees who moved in with them, including the Jemez clan, the Zia clan, and the Black Sheep People, who came from San Felipe.

By the time the Americans took over control of the Southwest in 1846, the essential outlines of modern Navajo life had been established.

Navajos were using animal husbandry and Pueblo pottery and weaving techniques and were growing such Spanish-originated crops as wheat, melons, and peaches. In addition, Navajos were living in hogan clusters as matrilocal extended families. Sweathouses, sheep corrals, and summer shades of poles and brush formed an additional part of this residential complex. Clothing styles had shifted from the use of animal hides to textile garments reminiscent of Pueblo and Spanish wear. Men

Peshlakai, or Slender Silver-maker, a famous Navajo smith. He holds a concho belt, a bridle is to his right, while bracelets and tools are to his left. ca. 1885.   Smithsonian Institution National Anthropological Archives, Bureau of American Ethnology Collection.

owned and cared for horses, hunted, did heavy agricultural work, and, when necessary, fought and raided enemy settlements. Women herded and owned most of the sheep, wove fabrics of wool, and helped with the lighter agricultural tasks. Exogamous, matrilineal clans, unified by an origin myth, were present. Such clans, which may have been localized, formed a corporate group for the ownership or use of land and ceremonial property and set the limits of socially acceptable behavior for their members.

Political organization had matured to the stage where there was a local band headman or peace chief and one or more war leaders selected on the basis of physical prowess and ritual attainment. Raiding with horses on the Rio Grande Pueblo settlements was widespread, gaining for the Navajos sheep, horses, agricultural commodities, and slaves. Pueblo ideas continued to influence the development of religious concepts, mythology, and ceremonial activities.

The American Period

The American Period includes a series of specific events that have made Navajo country and Navajos what they are today. United States military forces conquered these Indians and forced about 8,000, a large portion of their numbers, into captivity at Fort Sumner, New Mexico, between 1864 and 1868. In 1868 they were returned to their traditional location and a reservation was formed. American influences came to the Navajos with substantial force via a transcontinental railroad in 1880. Following this development was a significant growth in the White population, the encroachment on Indian lands, the livestock reduction program of the 1930s under the aegis of John Collier, commissioner of Indian affairs, and the introduction of the peyote cult, particularly in the northeastern portion of the reservation. Some Navajos served in World War II, and many more were involved in off-reservation wage work. With the discovery of commercially exploitable natural resources, particularly oil, in the 1920s, Whites began to take a serious interest in Navajo reservation affairs. A Navajo Tribal Council was formed, largely as a convenience for federal and industrial interests. By the end of World War II, the Navajo people were closely tied to the larger society in an economic sense, but remained estranged socially and culturally from it. This condition has persisted to the present time.

A careful study of the life histories presented in this chapter shows, among other things, that the direct influence of Navajo tribal government on these three individuals appears to be slight or even covert. The role of tribal government, however, especially today, on the Navajo population and the people and places in the areas surrounding the res-

Landscape near Ganado, Arizona, Navajo Reservation. 1904. Photograph courtesy of Museum of the American Indian, Heye Foundation.

ervation is significant. Tribal politicians with their supporting staffs and tribal politics must always be considered if a wide variety of events occurring in the Southwest is to be understood. The sheer size of Navajo government with its 5,000 or more employees and the ambitions of those who run it are most impressive. One anthropologist, L. R. Stucki (1971), has concluded that the Navajo Reservation may well become the fifty-first state in the Union.

Arroyo with horses in background, Chaco Canyon, New Mexico, Navajo Reservation, 1898. Photograph courtesy of Museum of the American Indian, Heye Foundation.

NAVAJO COUNTRY DEFINED.   Navajo country is a vast arid desert and mountainous region that today occupies much of the northeastern quadrant of Arizona, a small portion of southeastern Utah, and western New Mexico. This main reservation consists of an area of about 24,000 square miles and is about the size of West Virginia. Out of a tribal population of around 150,000, approximately 100,000 Navajos live here today. The Navajo Tribe is the largest in the country: one out of every five Indians is a Navajo. There are three smaller communities, Alamo or Puertocito, Ramah, and Canyoncito, all in New Mexico, each having an area of less than 100 square miles and an enrolled tribal population of fewer than 1,000 people. At present, much of Navajo country consists of barren, overgrazed, unproductive agricultural lands that cannot support a growing population. Off-reservation wage work and a variety of forms of relief have been prominent sources of support for the past several generations. This country is beautiful, rugged, and a source of both inspiration and despair for those who live within its confines. Its geography and history do not lend themselves to easy characterization.

NAVAJOS REMAIN NAVAJOS.   Federal policy toward the Navajos has been, by default and design, to encourage the Navajo people to become economically independent through a maximum development of reservation resources tied to reservation industrialization. Navajos have also been encouraged in a number of ways to participate in off-reservation life. However, there continues to be, as has been the case for the past two or more centuries, a strong tendency for Navajos to remain Navajo in spite of the changes due to specific additions to, or subtractions from, culture content. A number of anthropologists have referred to the *incorporative nature* of Navajo culture, by which is meant this ability to ingest non-Navajo traits, ideas, or practices and to use or mold them with the basic patterns of traditional Navajo culture.

In a more specific fashion, there is a "resistant institutional core" (Vogt, 1961: 326–327), which accounts for much of the continuity of Navajo life. This core consists of a number of social relationships and ecological adjustments that have formed the distinctive Navajo pattern of life since 1700. Among them are the scattered settlement pattern of the reservation, the inheritance of clan and residence through the mother, the continuing use of the hogan as a residence, with its accompanying sweathouse and sheep corral all facing east, and political leadership based on a local headman. Navajo ceremonialism has always been focused on individual curing ceremonies, and people believe they are sick when they feel out of harmony with nature and those around them as well as when they experience symptoms that all of us associate with illness. Ghosts and witchcraft are very much feared, and anyone wishing to acquire information about the subject is urged to read

Navajo Witchcraft by Clyde Kluckhohn (1963). To support themselves, the Navajos have long followed a combination of farming and sheep husbandry supplemented by weaving and silversmithing. The Navajo language is still widely spoken on the reservation.

This resistant core constitutes the baseline with which to compare the three life histories to be presented. Those interested in the life histories of Navajos of an earlier time should read Dyk's books about Left Handed and Old Mexican, who lived in the late nineteenth and early twentieth centuries (1938, 1947).

Within the last 20 years, wage work off and especially on the reservation has come to be regarded by a significant number of Navajos as a desirable way of making a living. The B.I.A. and other economic planners, however, have always taken it for granted that Navajos educated in the White man's way would desire to put their new economic values above social values, leave the reservation, and work at jobs in cities (Adams & Ruffing, 1977: 80). As we will see in the life histories, this is far from being universally true. Fortunately for the Navajo, jobs on the reservation are increasing, especially in the fields of strip mining of coal, uranium extraction, and the construction and operation of power plants. There is, however, a darker side to some of these jobs. The Mesa uranium mine near Shiprock, New Mexico, had to be closed in 1969 because too many of its Navajo employees were dying of cancer (Spake, 1974). The full impact of this and other mining and energy projects may not be realized for another generation. However, given the Navajos' reaction to direct and indirect attempts by a number of sources to change them in the past, it seems likely that Navajo life in the future will reflect the essential continuity that it has always done.

THE ALBUQUERQUE NAVAJOS

In another publication (Hodge, 1969), I was concerned with migration patterns between the larger Navajo reservation and the city of Albuquerque, New Mexico. Albuquerque in 1960 was a city of 200,000 located in a valley just west of the Sandia Mountains. Most of the wage earners of the community depended directly or indirectly upon the federal and state governments for salaries. For the past 260 years this area has been regarded as a way station, transportation center, and general meeting place for travelers. The Spanish, the Mexicans, the Americans, and especially the Indians have always viewed it as important to them.

Between 1959 and 1961, I tried to learn something about the 275 Navajos who lived in Albuquerque. Thanks to their natural courtesy and great patience, I was able to share and observe many aspects of their urban and reservation lives. The Albuquerque Navajos worked at a variety of jobs, usually in the unskilled and semiskilled categories.

They have been doing so here for the past 65 years. They lived scattered through the 56 square miles the city then encompassed. Some were traditional Navajos in the strictest meaning of the term. A few had rejected their Navajo heritage and regarded themselves as Indian only in a genetic sense. Most Navajos fell somewhere in between these extremes and had no conscious awareness of the extent of their emotional and cultural commitment to a Navajo way of life. The traditionals and those in between regarded their urban residence as temporary and hoped to return to the reservation to live. The traditionals wanted to live as their ancestors always had; the others desired to secure jobs, usually with the tribal or federal government. This later group still regarded itself as Navajo but wanted selected aspects of Western technology such as housing, sanitation, and health care. Both categories seemed to regard urban residence as a means to live until a desirable niche appeared on the reservation. The Albuquerque Navajos' desire to stay in the city or return to the reservation was not determined by such seemingly obvious factors as prejudice, the ability to survive financially in the city, or a variety of related variables. Both residence and migration are processes that must be understood at a more sophisticated level of analysis. In my earlier book I discussed specific push and pull factors toward and away from the reservation and toward and away from the city. These forces affect what an individual does as much as kin groups, alliances, and patterns of resource use. Other dimensions such as personality and idiosyncratic variables also play a part in a Navajo's decision about where to live.

Using pseudonyms, I will examine three life histories, each showing a different kind of adaptation to the demands of contemporary existence within an urban situation but against a vivid background of reservation life. These adaptations are labeled "successful," "ambivalent," and "failure." These life histories closely follow Hodge (1969: 53–65).

John Powell—A Successful Navajo Who Left the Reservation

Powell, a relaxed and confident individual, was congenial and willing to discuss most aspects of his life with me. He lived at Isleta Pueblo because he had married an Isleta woman. Although he had little interest in the traditional aspects of Pueblo life, he was reluctant to discuss his place in the Pueblo and the activities of his affinal relatives there.

EARLY YEARS.   John was born in 1933 at Rattlesnake, Arizona. His parents had no formal education, but his father could speak enough English to work at various menial jobs. The effects of the stock reduction program, instituted by John Collier, commissioner of the Bureau of Indian Affairs, to slow the erosion of reservation lands, reached the

Powell family about 1937. They were forced to give up most of their small livestock holdings. All their horses had to be sold, and there were only a few sheep left, just enough to fill one corral. The family had a small farm that could have been irrigated, but they had no implements for cultivation. Their few remaining sheep were moved to his father's mother's herd, and his father went to work for the B.I.A. on a nearby experimental farm and then took a job near Fort Wingate. During these preschool years, Powell led a pleasant life, spending most of his time playing with his younger brother and a cousin. As his family had no livestock around, he had no herding responsibilities. At age six he was sent to the Methodist Mission School at Farmington, New Mexico, which at that time probably offered the best academic training in the area. Discipline was harsh but did not approach the excesses of the Albuquerque Indian School in the 1887 to 1929 period. His brother was soon enrolled there also. Powell enjoyed the studying but resented the discipline. When his brother was being whipped for some offense, he attempted to "clobber" the disciplinarian. As a result, both boys were beaten. Powell also "had all the Christian religion pounded out of me." When he was ten, the family moved to Rico, Colorado, because his father had gotten a job in the mine there. Powell adjusted well to the elementary school and was delighted with participating in sports such as baseball and basketball. He and his brother were immediately accepted by the Anglo school children and their parents, and they were included in most community activities. His parents, however, had no friends in Rico because they lacked education and English language skills.

During this period the family went back to Rattlesnake three or four times in the summer to visit relatives and take part in squaw dances. The parents enjoyed these, but John didn't "because I just couldn't sing right." He suffered from severe headaches about this time and was cured by a sing. "A hand trembler told my mother that when she was pregnant with me, my father had seen some human bones and this caused it all." The entire procedure amused Powell.

HIGH SCHOOL YEARS.   The years passed pleasantly for John, and he completed eight years of schooling in Rico. His family decided to send him to Albuquerque Indian School for high school training because he wanted to go there. While at the Intertribal Ceremonial in Gallup one year, he had seen some Navajo boys wearing the school's athletic letter sweaters, and he wanted to have one, too. In 1947, at age 14, he came to Albuquerque.

The city seemed large and forbidding at first, but by the end of his freshman year John had come to enjoy the urban environment. He did well in athletics and maintained a *B* average in his classroom work.

John also met his future wife, Ann. The summer of his freshman year he returned to Rico but was very lonesome for Albuquerque. During his sophomore year his father became seriously ill and had to quit mine work. His parents then worked harvesting vegetables in southern Arizona until his father died. John wanted to leave school to help his mother, but she insisted that he fulfill his father's wishes and continue his education. Encouraged by one of the male teachers, Powell thought about going to college to study mining engineering. Because of his precarious financial position, he later realized that he would never have the means to go to college, so he decided to become an electrician because he enjoyed the training in this area that Albuquerque Indian School offered. During the summers until his graduation, he worked at skilled jobs in construction at Shiprock, New Mexico, and in Colorado and Utah.

AFTER SCHOOL.   When he graduated, he was accepted by the electrician's union to enter an apprentice program, but it was about six months before he could begin work. He worked at various odd jobs in Albuquerque and Phoenix and then was hired on a permanent basis by Western Electric as an assembler and installer of complex equipment for telephone switchboard centers. About this time, he narrowly escaped being jailed for drunken and disorderly conduct at a dance at the Indian school. A note in his school record dated October 2, 1951, reads as follows:

> Letter from C. W. Franklin to Mr. Fred Williams, Principal: Please write a letter to John in no uncertain terms that we can do without his presence hereafter on the campus as he came out to the school last Saturday night in an intoxicated condition and engaged in a fight with a person by the name of Zuni from Isleta. After the fight I immediately collared him and told Mr. Dave Coleman to take the advisor's car and get him off campus immediately or take him to jail. Dave reported he jumped out of the window of the car and made a get-away. I would have had the Police come out and pick him up but I had to get rid of him write away as he was creating a disturbance.

Powell tried to enlist in the navy and the air force but was rejected because of a football injury. When he started work at Western Electric, he married Ann Naranjo of Isleta. When I met him, he had worked for Western Electric for eight years and hoped to continue until he retired. He seemed to derive a great deal of satisfaction from his job. He said:

> It's really interesting. It's everything that we do. No routine, not like the maintenance of a telephone office. We start with a brand new telephone office; there's nothing in the telephone office to begin with except the building. We install superstructure made of iron and we solder and put

them together from drawings. Then we run our cables and then we connect them up to the equipment according to drawings. Then we test them to see if it works. Then when we find that it does work, we turn it over to the telephone company. And it's theirs from there. Like I say, there's some routine all right, like putting it together, but after you get in the testing stage it's really interesting. You get all lost in there. Have quite a time. We work anything that's in communication. And that's to me just interesting.

In 1962, Isleta had a population of about 1,900. John and his family lived in a small area on the east side of the Rio Grande River. Parsons (1932: 208) described this section as a small group of Earth Yellow People who were said to be mean in behavior. Their speech had a slight dialectical difference from those in the larger section of Isleta. When I interviewed Powell, only one house remained here. His wife's parents lived in one-half with their own separate entrance. The halves were separated inside by a thick adobe wall.

Powell cooperated fully with the Pueblo authorities and with his wife's parents. His son and two daughters spoke English and Tiwa but not Navajo. His wife and children were active in the appropriate societies and participated in public dancing. John commented nervously, "I don't agree with them or disagree with them or anything else. I'm neutral. My father-in-law who is a war captain said he would like to get them initiated, so I go along with it to keep peace in the family anyway."

Powell was one of the two Navajos resident in the Pueblo. I know of three others who had lived there in the past. John said that he had many friends at Isleta whom he had first met at Albuquerque Indian School. A few middle-aged people in the Pueblo didn't like Navajos, but he didn't know why. He had been in the kiva once to attend a ceremony in which his wife's father took an active part. "They had a dance down there and so forth. I could have gone down before, but I'm just not interested. My wife wanted me to go because of her father so I went."

POWELL'S STYLE OF LIVING.   John's style of living was quite different from that of others at Isleta. His house had seven rooms: a large living room, dining room, kitchen, bath, and three bedrooms. The walls were of thick adobe covered with a layer of stucco. All floors were wooden. He had his own septic tank and a private well, which supplied more than enough water. With the exception of the kitchen and bathroom, all rooms had wall-to-wall carpeting and modern furnishings. The family owned a stereo phonograph and a large TV set. The house was heated by butane gas, and Powell was in the process of installing air conditioning. He was an excellent craftsman and had improved his home considerably. When he and his wife had first moved in, the place was in poor condition and probably resembled most of the other dwellings in the Pueblo. John drove a new Chevrolet station wagon. His wife's kitchen was well supplied with electric appliances, including an electric frying pan, deep fryer, toaster, and a large deep freeze stocked with meat. The yard surrounding the house was not planted in grass, and there was no garage. Powell and his family dressed well. Most of their affluence was due to his salary, but his wife also worked full-time as a receptionist in a dentist's office in Albuquerque.

Powell seemed to be leading a pleasant life. He described his daily routine:

> Well, any normal day for me is getting up probably about 6:30 or a quarter to seven. With the wife working, I don't know when she gets up. I have to fix my own breakfast, a cup of coffee and a doughnut or something. Then I normally have a ride going into town if I work in town. I get to work around 8:00 o'clock, start off wherever I left off the previous day, depending on what I was doing. Then I have a coffee break about 10:00 o'clock or so, take about twenty minutes. Then go back to whatever we're doing and normally the days go pretty fast. Like I say, it depends on what type of work I'm involved in at the time. I don't take my lunch, so I normally experiment with all the restaurants or places to eat. We normally have another coffee break at 3:00 o'clock to kind of break up the day and get off at 5:00. I usually catch a bus to where my wife works, and I wait until she gets off. Our baby sitter usually has supper ready for us about the time we get home. The baby sitter is just a neighbor. She's a single woman. She stays and feeds the kids and leaves the supper on the table or in the stove for us. We're usually home by six or so, so we eat or read the paper and watch TV for a little while and then that's about the end of the day. We're in bed by 9:00 o'clock and try to get the children in bed before that.

The whole family went to a drive-in movie at least once a week and had taken short trips to the Mescalero Reservation, Carlsbad Caverns, and other scenic attractions on vacations. Powell occasionally read men's magazines, *Life,* and the *Reader's Digest.* He and his wife visited ten or twelve of his co-workers and their families occasionally.

"It's mostly conversation, whatever might happen, dance or something and have something to eat, snacks and stuff. Take something some time and some beer or what you want to drink. They sit around and gossip."

Some associations were maintained by more indirect means: "We had to write about 200 Christmas cards last year and we receive just about that amount too. You know once those things get started, you almost gotta continue them because a guy will get mad at you if you don't send him one."

Powell hunted a great deal with his father-in-law and his brother, who worked in Utah. They traveled over most of New Mexico and Arizona after deer. The marshes and fields around his house were full of ducks and partridge.

His wife and children regularly attended the Catholic church at the Pueblo, but Powell went no more than once or twice a year. His mother had remarried a traditional Navajo and had had two daughters since Powell's father died. She lived at Rattlesnake. Visiting her in 1956, Powell and his wife attended a squaw dance for about an hour "but my wife didn't like it at all, so we left." His mother called him collect about once a month from a nearby trading post, but he made no effort to contact her or any other relative on the reservation.

His children attended Albuquerque public schools. They were officially registered with the Navajo Tribe, but only so that they might be eligible for the available benefits. Navajos with a high school diploma were then eligible to apply for a tribal college scholarship of $4,800. Albuquerque Navajo school children received two complete outfits of clothing a year as did their counterparts on the reservation. Powell said that he had no interest in the reservation because "nothing that goes on out there could affect me." He never voted in local, tribal, state, or national elections; but he did vote in the annual Pueblo election for governor and lieutenant governor.

When I asked Powell what his central goals in life were, he replied: "Me, I gotta be financially situated and have a happy family and be satisfied with whatever I'm doing." He appeared to have what he wanted, and this situation will probably persist.

EVALUATION OF POWELL'S "SUCCESS."   A number of questions can be raised with regard to assessing John Powell's adjustment. In what sense is his life successful? How was this success achieved? To what extent has he been able to make his own life, and to what extent is his comfortable position due to appropriate responses to circumstances beyond his control? John Powell acknowledged that he had achieved success. He was financially solvent, and he and his family found their immediate round of activities satisfying. Powell had been able to develop his satisfying life because he had always been oriented far more toward off-reservation living than a traditional or traditionally modified niche on the reservation. Because they could not follow traditional reservation subsistence practices, John's mother and father were forced to live away from the reservation and became dependent upon wage work for survival. Consequently, Powell acquired an understanding and inclination for life in the larger society. Yet at the same time, because of his brief attendance at schools on the reservation and then at Indian schools in Farmington and Albuquerque, he associated with other Indians to the extent that he could be comfortable around them. He learned to move between Indian and non-Indian worlds with a minimum of stress or discomfort. The probability of success was further buttressed by his realistic assessment of his motivation and abilities in dealing with the demands that a non-Indian world would make upon him and his ability to behave appropriately. To the extent that anyone can do so in these times, he has charted his own destiny. It would take an unforeseen and unusually virulent combination of misfortunes for him to fail.

The Ambivalent World of Joseph Barnes

Joseph Barnes was a short and rather nervous person. He was very willing to work with me, and I recorded more data from him than from any other Navajo in Albuquerque. Unlike Powell, however, he failed to discuss the painful events of his life in any detail. Much of the data he supplied concerned his association with the traditional aspects of Navajo life. He spoke of these things with an obvious relish and satisfaction.

EARLY YEARS.   Barnes was born in 1933 near Tohatchi, the youngest son of the family. His preschool years were spent in the winter "down in the flat country below Chuskai Mountain." During the warmer months he stayed in a summer camp near the crest of Chuskai Peak established at a place called "the arrow was uprooted by water" because "there was always enough water and grass there for all the sheep we

Navajo family in Canyon de Chelley, New Mexico Territory, 1873. Woman is weaving at a vertical loom.   National Archives and Records Service, G.S.A.

Navajo sheepherder near Chinle, Arizona. September, 1970. Arizona State Museum. Photographer, Helga Teiwes.

had then." Joseph's mother and an infant sister died when he was two. His father showed little interest in his family and was mainly concerned with a pickup truck and the consumption of wine and whiskey. Accordingly, Barnes stayed with his mother's family most of the time. His mother's sister, Aunt Charlotte; his mother's parents, Many Horses Begay and Old Charlotte; and Old Charlotte's sister, Mrs. Smith, were the most important adults during his childhood. His mother's younger brothers, Willie, Harry, Deswood, and Nealwood; two of his future wife's brothers, Everett and Johnny; and his own brother Eddie were his principal companions. All of these people were traditional and spoke no English. Barnes did not meet a non-Navajo until he entered the government boarding school at Tohatchi when he was about six.

These young years were generally satisfying ones for him. "My Aunt Charlotte, she sing me songs I never hear any more." During the periods when the adults had little to do, they told him of the events of their early years between 1864 and 1910. A Ute raiding party once attacked the sheep camp around 1910, but was driven off with the loss of two of its members. "Old Charlotte, she caught one and choked him to death by stuffing sand in his mouth." About this time two renegade Anglos had stolen some horses from another sheep camp nearby. "Many Horses Begay and his father Many Horses, they and lots of others found them and beat them to death with big rocks. They was awful glad about that." Barnes also heard in great detail of the Long Walk to Fort Sumner and how some of his elders had escaped from federal troops and hidden alone in the mountains in small groups for the four years 1864 to 1868.

When he was about five, he began to herd sheep. "The way I took care of them was in the morning take them out of corral there—this would be in summer camp. We start to look for good pasture land for the day. Take them out there and just try to keep them all together. Not have any strays. Have to keep coyotes away. I move around the circle of the whole herd every ten to fifteen minutes anyway. Maybe sing to them. Then at the end of the day keep track, count up, make sure none gone. It was monotonous. I was out there all by myself most of the time anyway."

When Joseph was six, Aunt Charlotte and Mrs. Smith took him and his brother to school at Tohatchi. He had one of the first baths in his life, was given some overalls, and placed in a large room with many toys. Like John Powell, he enjoyed the classroom work but hated the discipline. All children were forced to go to church. Every Sunday morning all the boys were marched to a storeroom where they put on "their" suits. Immediately after church they were marched back and exchanged the suits for overalls. The meals at the school must have been inadequate because Barnes mentioned how on several different occa-

Elementary school session, Window Rock, Arizona, September, 1972.   Arizona State Museum. Photographer, Helga Teiwes.

sions he and other students had broken into food storage cellars "and then we really ate good." During his first school year Barnes's class was taken to see a circus in Gallup. They enjoyed the circus but found Gallup frightening.

Barnes's interest in traditional Navajo life persisted, and he often ran away from school "but only on weekends" to watch Many Horses Begay work as a singer. He attended at least two dozen sings. His interest was heightened when his mother's brothers became assistants. He was usually barred from most of this activity because "they kept telling me little kids shouldn't get too close to something like that." Because he was away at school during the winter, he missed learning many details of ceremonial lore, for traditionals feel that these can be discussed safely only after the crops have been harvested and before spring planting has begun. One of his favorite pastimes at school was playing "Black Jacks" with his friends. When he went back to the sheep camp that summer, 1940, he again herded sheep and began going to squaw dances and playing the shoe game.

The effects of the stock reduction program were experienced later by his family than by Navajos living in other areas of the reservation. This may have been due to the fact that his family lived in a relatively isolated area, and Navajos living in the northeastern portion of the reservation resisted stock reduction more successfully than those living elsewhere. About this time the federal government took the majority of the livestock owned by Many Horses Begay and fined his relatives, but did not treat them as sternly as the families of many of my other informants. In some cases, flocks were driven into deep trenches, saturated with gasoline, and burned alive.

During this summer Aunt Charlotte died of tuberculosis. Several of the family had the disease, but she was the first to die. Barnes's father appeared at the funeral and succeeded in getting his son half drunk on cheap wine. For the next five years of his life Barnes fell into the routine of attending school in the winter and working around the sheep camp in summer. He continued to enjoy school and found working in the carpentry shop especially satisfying. When he was about nine or ten, his grandfather started to teach him the medicinal and ceremonial uses of many wild plants and herbs. He became convinced that "these things really work and there is something to these old ways."

In 1944, Many Horses Begay took his sons, Willie, Harry, Deswood, and Nealwood, and they went to California to work as laborers. Willie, however, got into trouble "and it took all of their money to get him out of jail, so they just came right back." Barnes thought that this incident was very funny.

In 1945, when he was 12, Joseph started going to the Catholic Mission School at St. Michaels. By this time he played poker quite well and found the game to be exceptionally lucrative when he cheated. With the ten dollars he had won from his inept but honest companions at the sheep camp, he was able to purchase most of his school supplies. "But it really turned out all right, because the next time me and them boys went into Gallup on a Saturday, I paid their way to this show and got some candy too. They just couldn't figure out why I was so nice to them."

Barnes soon became a Catholic and must have impressed the good fathers as being unusually pious because he was made an altar boy. He found this role rather irksome until one day before Mass he drank a bottle of wine intended for Communion. "That was about the funniest thing I ever done. And they never did find out that I done it."

His classroom study continued to go well, and he was allowed to skip two grades although he spent some time in a hospital at Fort Defiance because he was suspected of having heart trouble and trachoma. When Barnes came back to the sheep camp in 1946, he found the area very depressing. "Everything was real bad. People weren't friendly no more. There wasn't no food much. Before you could just go around to where anybody was living and they'd be eating and give you all you wanted, but then they just ate at meal times and wouldn't eat at all if you was there. Nobody had much sheep, not much money either." This condition could have been the result of the loss of wartime wage work, which was a hardship to many areas of the reservation.

HIGH SCHOOL YEARS. In 1947, when he was 14, he was sent to the Indian School in Albuquerque. He learned to get around the city within a month and apparently had no unpleasant experiences doing so. He enjoyed the classes and soon told one of his teachers that he wanted to go to college. After the first year's work at Albuquerque, he returned home to the sheep camp, which was now located in the southern part of the Lukachukai Mountains. He got "awful drunk" from drinking a bottle of wine and some "Four Rose" whiskey supplied by Deswood. His grandparents were amused by this but insisted that he continue herding sheep. He returned to Albuquerque in the fall and spent most of the next summer picking peaches in southwestern Colorado because his family had no livestock left and there were few crops to cultivate.

Barnes also worked 11 days as a laborer for a railroad in Colorado, but he soon had to quit because one of the railroad unions went on strike. He was then 17 and showed a great deal of self-reliance and endurance. He had traveled alone by bus from Gallup to Colorado and then walked several miles at night to the railroad siding where many other Navajos lived in converted boxcars. After going without sleep for 36 hours, he put in a full day's work laying new track ties.

Shortly after he returned to Albuquerque Indian School in the fall, his grandfather, Many Horses Begay, was critically injured in a car accident. Joseph and his brother returned briefly to the reservation just before he died.

The summer before his senior year in high school, Barnes worked for a florist in Albuquerque doing menial tasks and making flower arrangements. During his senior year he applied to a small liberal arts college for a scholarship and to the tribal council for an educational loan. (Tribal college scholarships were not offered until 1954.) Although neither was granted, the faculty of the school thought highly of him. References in his file, in part, are as follows: "Pleasant to work with and applies himself to his work. Absolutely dependable, hard working, cooperative and capable of independent work. If he has any failing, it would be that of acting too impulsively without thinking before hand. Good powers of organization, absolutely honest. Pronounced stammer when excited. Despite his mildness of manner and slightness of figure, he has guts." He was valedictorian of his class.

ADULT LIFE.   Barnes returned to the reservation but came back to Albuquerque in a few days because "there was nothing there, just nothing." I pressed for his reasons for staying around Albuquerque. He replied, "Maybe I just wanted to get away from herding sheep. I never did know what kept me here except maybe it was that summer working for the florist. I liked the job and being here in town."

When he got back to town, he tried to enlist in the air force, but he was rejected because of ingrown toenails. He had this condition remedied but decided not to enlist. He saw an opening advertised in the paper for a delivery boy at a local paint and glass company and applied for the job. He was accepted but then realized that he had no driver's license and didn't know how to drive. By spending a week observing the college boy he was replacing, he learned how to handle the delivery truck and acquired a driver's license about a year later.

In 1954, Barnes married a classmate who had grown up near his grandparents' sheep camp. They were married by a justice of the peace. By 1958 they had two sons and two daughters. Joseph had been promoted to bookkeeper with the paint company. In the spring of that year he contracted tuberculosis and spent about eight months in a sanatorium. Shortly thereafter his wife was also sent there, and their children were placed in foster homes in Gallup. When he was discharged from the hospital, Barnes returned to the paint company and acted as an assistant manager of the store. After his wife recovered, their children were returned. In 1960 they bought a new five-room house, and life settled into a regular pattern.

He described his daily routine: "Well, during the winter months, I would get up around seven and then I would rush to get to leave home about seven thirty. Sometime I have breakfast, sometime I don't. Then pick up mail and go to work and take care of sales at the store all day, have lunch at the store, and then get back home at five thirty. Then have supper and then we be around here or go down to shop or run errands, and have the kids in bed around nine and then stay up until ten or ten thirty."

Barnes probably didn't make more than $6,000 to $6,500 a year, but he had most of the desirable things that urban living could provide. His new five room, stucco frame house was located in a pleasant suburban neighborhood. It was centrally heated and had a combination bath and shower. His wife cooked on a new electric stove and used modern electric kitchen utensils. The furnishings were new, and he had a new car. The family's reading was confined to mysteries, the daily paper, and a few popular magazines. For entertainment Barnes frequently attended local minor league baseball games and an occasional wrestling match. In the winter he did some league bowling. He had no interest in local, state, or federal politics and seldom voted in a national election, although he and his wife voted in tribal elections.

The family seemed to have few contacts with others. One or two of his Spanish-American co-workers visited him about once a year, and he returned their visits as often. Their closest contacts were with his wife's sister and her Navajo husband, who was an office manager for a large furniture store. Both families helped each other by baby-sitting and fending off relatives from the reservation. Barnes belonged to the Navajo Club and a smaller Indian organization. His wife and children went to the Catholic Church, but he did not. The Barnes family visited his relatives on the reservation three or four times a year during the summer and visited hers once a year. Relatives called collect about once a month asking for money. Joseph did not say whether or not they gave them any. He had no contacts with his classmates from Albuquerque Indian School who were still living in town.

The family dressed well. Joseph and his wife spoke Navajo in their home only when they wanted to keep secrets from their children, who were not learning the language.

Joseph hoped to have a small paint and glass store of his own, but he was afraid it would not make enough money. As he had mastered all the tasks involved in the business, it no longer seemed desirable.

> Now [after seven years of experience] I mix paint, cut glass, wait on people, keep books, just as well as anybody. Nothing more to learn. I'm an old hand now. But I don't know. The way it's going there's nothing more to learn. It was interesting to me. I never did keep track of time before until just lately anyways where it seems like now everything is slowing down. I don't see any more promotion at least nothing more unless we set up some more dealers here in town or around the state.

Manuelito. War leader, 1855–1872. Died 1893. Taken while he was visiting Washington, D.C., with a Navajo delegation in 1874.   Smithsonian Institution National Anthropological Archives, Bureau of American Ethnology Collection.

Soon after we had finished work, Barnes was passed over for a new dealership, and the position was given to an Anglo man. This action may or may not have been justified. He had also developed a skin allergy to paint fumes. Joseph said that he would go back to the reservation if he could work for the tribe and live right, but there were very few jobs, and the few that existed were filled. He thought that the reservation might be abolished in 15 or 20 years, so perhaps such a job, even if it were available, might not have much future. He also said that when he did see his relatives, they told him that he was no longer a Navajo because "he lived like an Anglo." Just before I left Albuquerque, he asked me if I thought it would be possible for him to open a bowling alley on the reservation, preferably at Window Rock. I could not answer this question.

As I finished the last session, he commented: "You know, if I hadn't gone to school, I wouldn't know about all this [urban life with its rewards, disappointments and annoyances]. I'd probably be still living out there with all my relatives." I seriously doubt if he could decide whether his current status was a blessing or a curse.

Joseph's great-grandfather was Manuelito, one of the last Navajo war chiefs and a prominent figure after the return from Fort Sumner. Shortly before he died, he made the following statement to an interpreter, Chee Dodge, who later became chairman of the tribal council: "My grandchild, the whites have many things which we Navajos need. But we cannot get them. It is as though the whites were in a grassy canyon and there they have wagons, plows, and plenty of food. We Navajos are up on the dry mesa. We can hear them talking but we cannot get to them. My grandchild, education is the ladder. Tell our people to take it" (Underhill, 1953: 4). I wonder if Manuelito would say the same thing today if he could know the fate of one of his descendants.

EVALUATION OF JOSEPH BARNES'S ACHIEVEMENTS.   A number of questions can be raised to underline the salient dimensions of ambiguity in the life of Joseph Barnes. Why can it be said that Barnes has failed to live comfortably in either the Navajo or White worlds and that he has had to seek an uneasy niche somewhere in between? What are the significant differences between Powell and Barnes with regard to abilities, aspirations, and achievement? How is Barnes different from a hypothetical but nonetheless real traditional Navajo of today?

Barnes has failed to live comfortably in either the Navajo or White worlds for a number of complex reasons. His reservation situation was sufficient to provide him with the means to enjoy a relatively pleasant childhood as a junior member of a traditionally oriented aggregate of kinsmen. Available resources, particularly federal and mission boarding schools on and off the reservation, supplemented what his family could provide. Barnes, however, grew up. The most important Navajo relatives in his life either died or were incapable of providing a reservation niche for him as an adult. Hampered by a limited kind of formal education and at times plagued with poor physical health, Barnes could find only a vaguely acceptable place in the urban American world.

Barnes differs from John Powell essentially in that he was not prepared or did not adequately prepare himself for the opportunities that were available. Much of the lack of preparation centered around the fact that too many of his formative years were spent leading a traditional life on the reservation. Powell was forced to learn to survive in a White world on White terms at a much earlier period of his life. The absence of a reservation niche made continuing residence in the White world a necessity for him. Barnes could return to the reservation periodically and both benefited from, and was penalized by, this opportunity. The intangible factor of luck also helps to explain the differences between Barnes and Powell. Why was it that Powell during his later high school years was encouraged to follow a lucrative trade that would require the kind of vocational preparation that was available to him? Why was Barnes encouraged to graduate from college when his chances of obtaining the necessary financial means were virtually nonexistent?

In some ways the life of a traditional Navajo on the reservation today resembles that of Barnes. They are similar in that there is a common interest in, and reverence for, traditional ceremonial practice. The familiarity with the Navajo language would also be a common bond. Beyond this, significant differences do appear. A traditionally oriented Navajo attempts to spend as much time on the reservation as possible, living in accordance with standards or customs of his grandparents. Barnes regarded the reservation only as a place to visit some relatives on rare occasions. He desired his modern urban conveniences. In particular, the world of the traditional Navajo is a world of kinsmen. Although cash is important, its principal value lies in the ways that it can be used to maintain and extend an elaborate series of direct and indirect ties, obligations, and rights. For Barnes, at least at this particular phase in his life cycle, relatives were a potential or actual liability, especially when they lived on the reservation. This threat existed because he was far better off economically than they could ever be. Grazing rights and social and emotional support from relatives no longer mattered as they had done when he was a child or as they would if he should ever choose to retire to the reservation.

Barnes's life had a socially isolated or estranged nature that was supported in somewhat ironic fashion by the accoutrements of physical comfort. His traditional Navajo contemporaries were supported by the interaction of kinsmen and friends amidst the squalor of a modern rural slum that is the reservation. Both Barnes's behavior and that of his traditional counterparts stemmed from these critical differences.

Joe Sandoval: Failure in the Navajo and White Worlds

Joe Sandoval was a thin, wan individual with a personal intensity that penetrated the language barrier between us. He readily agreed to be an informant because of a remote kin tie with my interpreter, which both recognized and honored. As is discussed below, he resented most Anglos and many Navajos. This resentment may have been positively correlated with his witch troubles, for witchcraft often provides a socially recognized channel for the culturally disallowed to express some of their aberrant impulses (Kluckhohn, 1963: 85).

Sandoval, like other traditionals that I have known, gave relatively few details when asked to tell about his past life. Most of these were

Modern Navajo hogan. Traditional winter dwelling.   Arizona State Museum.
Photographer, Helga Teiwes.

mentioned when we talked about traditional ceremonial practice, agriculture, and technology. Thus the order in this case history is mine, not his, but it is not a distortion of the facts.

In 1960, Joe was 40 or 42; he was not sure which. His father, a very conservative individual, had married two sisters. Joe's mother was the younger sister, who had three other sons and two daughters. Sandoval was the youngest boy in the family. Five of his siblings had died when they were infants. His mother's father was an Anglo soldier who had left the area before she was born. Joe's father, who occasionally served as a tribal councilman, had a Mexican grandparent.

EARLY YEARS.   Most of Joe's past life is related in his own words. The prose, of course, is that of my interpreter.

> I was born around 1920 in a kind of hogan near Red Rock that had the floor dug into the ground about five or six feet. I was born on a sheep skin. When I was born, we did all our singing ceremonials and had happiness and sadness as well in this hogan. It don't look like much but the people inside were very much alive. When I was three years old, I had to behave according to what my father told me. I guess that's the reason why I never went to school in those days. When I was five, I started herding the little

rams. I guess every Navajo knows about taking care of the rams. The rams have to be kept separate until breeding time in the fall. And then they are turned over with the rest of the flock. I herded the sheep all winter long. My job when I wasn't doing these things was to take care of the horses until I became fifteen years old. It was a very dull life. I didn't have toys like some of the children today. We made our own toys, me and my brother. Then when I became fifteen, I was promoted to bigger jobs such as breaking horses and taking care of wagons. Now and then I would herd the sheep. I felt that herding sheep was for the women, so I broke quite a few horses.

Sandoval was frail and sickly as a child. He had a number of sings and a great deal of exposure to traditional ceremonial practices. Such exposure was pleasant and comforting. As he stated:

They take the bull roarer outside and the first time in the east, then south, west, and then north. When this is making all this noise in full tune, it can be heard by *cheendi* [roughly translated as "a disharmonious spiritual state"], by coyotes, and by all evil people. Even some of the witches prob-

A "shade," traditional Navajo summer dwelling, usually built on a mountain side near the sheep grazing areas. September, 1903.   National Archives and Records Service, G.S.A.

Lorenzo Hubbell Trading Post near Ganado, Arizona. Still open, it is the longest continuously operating trading post on the reservation. It is now a National Monument.   Arizona State Museum. Photographer, Helga Teiwes.

ably hear that and know to stay away. I remember vividly years ago when I was very small, I was told to go outside and take this bull roarer, and I was scared until this bull roarer made this roaring, and I felt much better after that. It seemed to have a psychological effect on me. When I got this bull roarer at that time and I made this roar and I went all the way around the hogan, the corral, and out to the horses, but I never did hit any [evil things] with it, not that I know of anyway.

Then when I was about twenty years of age, I started going to the squaw dances and all the Navajo ceremonials and seeing the Navajo singers. And I guess you might say that I raised Cain, and there was nothing that I didn't do. Stealing horses, cars, all this I have done under the influence of liquor.

SANDOVAL'S YOUTH.   My interpreter, who had known Joe about this time, said that he used to be very wild; he used too much whiskey and peyote. He would tell everybody that he was just going to the trading post for a couple of hours, and then no one would see him again for a month. He used to run around in the winter without a coat on, and he came back from those little trips half dead. This wild behavior may have stemmed from the fact that Sandoval's family lost most of their livestock about this time, supposedly because of the machinations of a witch. My interpreter described the situation as follows:

Sandoval's family has had a lot of trouble with witches, especially his oldest brother, Lee Crane. Crane was rather successful financially for a while and had over 1,000 head of sheep. Every spring and fall he had lots of cash [from the sale of wool in spring and lambs in fall], and he always paid cash for a new pickup. All the men in the family would drive to Durango, Col-

244

orado, just to get beer. The brother started bragging a lot about his wealth, and people in the neighborhood got jealous. His sheep started dying in bunches of 20 or 30. They'd come down to the water hole and refused to move off, and then they died very soon. Lee started feeling funny and called in my father to ask for his advice. My father immediately realized that the loss of sheep was the work of a witch. He told Lee to keep his mouth shut about being wealthy and maybe the witch would stop bothering him. By the next spring Lee was down to fewer than 100 sheep, and he never was wealthy again. Joe was about sixteen or seventeen at the time. One day about then he was riding a horse down a twisting, rocky mountain trail. All at once he looked up and saw a witch sitting on a flat rock looking down at the area where Sandoval's family lived. The horse then fell and nearly killed him. Ever since then, Joe has believed in witches. The witch was finally driven off by some kind of anti-witch ceremony.

Sandoval's family tried to divert him away from these erring ways. "My folks tried to make a farmer out of me, and they told me to plant corn, melons, and a lot of other things like the Anglo people do. They told me that the time was going to come where I was going to have to do these things."

Apparently their efforts along these lines were unsuccessful. Sandoval wanted to become a singer, but his drunken behavior made this impossible. "I really wanted to be a singer. I liked the easy-come, easy-go money, but after a while nobody would take me as an apprentice because my hands shook too much from drinking all that whiskey and wine. I couldn't make straight lines with the colors" [on sand paintings]. In spite of this, he associated as closely as he could with such activities. "I had this *chongo* [long hair worn in a knot on the back of the head], and wore beads around my neck on occasions like squaw dances, and went to different sings. When you are singing or at a ceremonial, all Navajos including the patient are dressed with a sweat band and beads around the neck. You wear red moccasins and have a mark on both sides of your cheek. This signifies that you are taking part in a sing. That's when I was really a Navajo, when I wore that *chongo* on my head and wore the red moccasins."

Several times during my sessions with him, Sandoval stated that traditional life had not provided the material wealth that he desired. "I always wanted lots of sheep, goats, and plenty of hard goods [silver and turquoise jewelry], but I never did get them. I guess I am a failure that way."

His family was too poor to afford the proper traditional wedding ceremony for him. He still resented this at the time I knew him. "We were married the Navajo way, yet we didn't have the full ceremony like old times. Sorta like elope to get away from all the ceremony. To go through the regular ceremonial for Navajo marriage, you have to take

Crafts are an important part of traditional Navajo life. Navajo basket weaver splitting sumac. She is dressed in traditional fashion. September, 1972.   Arizona State Museum, Photograher, Helga Teiwes.

your finger in this huge dish of mush. You take some with your finger and lick some off the south side first, and then west, north, and east. Maybe that's why I have been sick all my life, because of that. The old time Navajos do that. When I got married, it was the short cut. My relatives wanted this elopement that does away with all property exchange.''

ADULT YEARS.   Living in a hogan near Red Rock at a place called Cougar-Eats-the-Sheep, Joe and Carolyn had three sons and a daughter. Only the eldest son survived. Sandoval said nothing more about his wife except that she had divorced him and was living in Boulder, Colorado, with their son. I know few of the details and the sequence of events of this part of his life. His health continued to be poor, and he used peyote for a short time in a fruitless effort to obtain relief. He continued:

> With all this wrong doing that I've done plus breaking horses, and I been spilled by a lot of plow horses and wild horses, somewhere I was injured.

So I entered the hospital at Shiprock for an examination in 1947. They didn't say what I was sick from, but I was laid up in bed for two months. While I was in bed, I wondered about the things that I had done such as breaking horses, bull-dogging steers, roping and branding cattle. Somewhere I must have strained my lungs or liver. Something must have happened to me. It got me thinking all the way back. When you are young, you don't hesitate to jump on a bronco like I did. When I had been laid up for about five months, the doctors diagnosed TB. I was taken to the TB sanitorium in Albuquerque in 1947 when I was about 26 years old. I stayed there nine years.

After four years of complete bed rest, Sandoval was well enough to attend the sanatorium's school. He had five years of studying but learned very little, developing no facility for English. A successful operation removed a diseased portion of one lung, and in 1956 he was discharged. His physician told me that Sandoval had an arrested case of tuberculosis but would probably be able to lead a normal life if he got

Navajo weaver. Her rug when finished will sell for more than $1,000. February, 1970.   Arizona State Museum. Photographer, Helga Teiwes.

enough rest and could have an adequate diet. As his family around Red Rock could not provide him with either, he remained in Albuquerque working at menial jobs. He drifted to Skid Row and was soon drinking heavily. His renewed use of alcohol may have been due to his extreme difficulties in adjusting to urban life. Another traditional Albuquerque Navajo, George Hawkins, described his reaction to the city. His feelings probably mirrored those of Sandoval.

> If you never went to school, it's pretty hard to know anyone. You know a person by how he dresses and, if he has a mustache, that's what you call him. You don't actually know his name. So it's pretty difficult for a person like myself to get around the city, much less speak English to people on the street. When a person is mad at you, even if you don't understand him, you can tell he is mad. That's one thing that don't change. There are several things that you just learn from observation. In a town the size of Albuquerque, it's pretty hard for me to get around. You have to learn to read and speak English, and that way you get to read these signs along the road. I always wish I could read and speak the language. They just have all kinds of writing all over the place, and I can't read it. I can't even argue with a person because they tell me to get out, and I know what they mean.

While Joe was hospitalized, he realized—possibly with the help of a conscientious hospital chaplain—that he was going to die because he had led such a wicked life. He vowed that if he recovered, he would become a Christian. I know nothing of his activities during the first few months after his release from the hospital except for his consumption of liquor. Apparently he soon came under the influence of the Christian missionaries working around the Skid Row area and was persuaded to stop drinking. He became a Catholic and then a Baptist. Tiring of his difficult life in Albuquerque, he attended the Indian Bible School at Cortez, Colorado. While he was there, he learned how to read Navajo orthography and was given a Bible written in Navajo. Armed with this, he felt prepared to "preach the Gospel" to other traditional Navajos. As I have suggested elsewhere (1964: 73–93), Joe and other Navajo pentecostals like him were not true converts to Christianity. Their interest in the Faith, as I interpret it, represented a mutual accommodation of two different systems: traditional ceremonial practice and Christianity. Sandoval ran away from the Bible School and returned to Albuquerque, where he worked as a silversmith at two different shops. He cheerfully admitted that he was fired at both places because he didn't work hard enough. In addition, the jobs were rather dull, and he didn't feel well. He then found work running a dishwashing machine at a plush motel. The pay wasn't much, but the work was easy and there was always plenty of food around to eat. While I knew him, he was still at work in this capacity.

A modern smith, Chinle, Arizona, March, 1974 How much does he have in common with Peshlakai (p. 221)? Arizona State Museum. Photographer, Helga Teiwes.

SANDOVAL'S LIFE-STYLE.   When I first met him, he was living in an unheated tool shed behind the house of another pentecostal, Henry Chavez. They had first become friends when they were both patrons of the Skid Row taverns. Sandoval took two of his meals with Chavez, but he did not live in the house simply because there was no room. The floor of the shed was covered with linoleum. An iron pipe clothes rack held approximately two dozen good quality sports shirts and slacks. Three religious calendars were on one wall. I noticed two radios. On top of a small chest of drawers a Navajo Bible and a prayer book were prominently displayed. A basketball hoop was nailed to the wall over the bed. The place was very drafty, and daylight showed through several cracks in one wall. At the other end of the narrow room were several coffee cans full of nails and bolts. The narrow single bed was made with new, good-quality blankets. A shaded light bulb hung from the ceiling. A battered rocking chair was drawn up close to the bed. During my first winter in town, Sandoval developed a serious chest cold from sleeping in the tool shed. He then moved into a shabby but warm room near the center of town.

Sandoval dressed well in new Levi's and shirts, well-polished Wellington boots, and a good quality Stetson hat. He had a large silver Navajo belt buckle with an arrow point fastened to the back. The Franciscan fathers (1910: 411) mentioned that arrow points were secured to a patient's hair in the course of some ceremonies and were worn by some even after the ceremony if the charm represented a holy rite.

Joe's daily routine would have been demanding for a healthy person. He must have regarded it as a burden.

> I work at night, start work at four o'clock in the afternoon. One of the things about this job, I can get up any time in the morning I feel like—six, sometimes nine. It depends on the people who bang on my door in the morning [who were his traditional Navajo friends]. I get to work at 4:00 and run the dishwashing machine all the four hours until 8:00. Then we eat lunch. Then from 8:00 to 2:00, sometimes I stay there as long as 2:00 a.m. It depends how long it takes to wash the dishes. I generally get off at 12:30. Then I go home and go to bed. I don't get a chance to watch TV or anything like that because when I get off they're all closed and everybody's asleep. If I wander around at that hour, I might get put in jail. I get up most of the time around eight o'clock. After I get up, I eat breakfast which takes one hour by the time I walk down to the cafe next to the waiting place of the long dog [the Greyhound Bus Station]. Then I see those people over at the Baptist Church. I go to school there from eleven to one to learn how to read and write English. Afterwards I visit some of my friends and eat dinner there. At 2:00 I go to work because I have to catch a bus so I need to walk only five miles. Sometimes when I get off work, I catch a ride back here but mostly I walk back approximately fifteen miles. I generally am in the house about two or three in the morning.

His contacts with others seemed to be limited.

> If I have to walk home all the way from the motel, I have no energy left to go around visiting everybody. I stay in and rest most of the day. My friends come around here about twice a week to visit me, and Henry comes to see me about once a week. I go over there about once a week. But I see most of these people every Sunday at church [an all-Navajo pentecostal church located just north of Isleta Pueblo]. But some of these people [traditional Navajos living in town], they never come around to visit me. They know where I live, but they just don't want to be bothered. The only time a lot of

these people visit me is when they want to borrow something. The other people around here, the neighbors [who are Anglo], they just speak to me, but I never visit them.

Sandoval tried to visit the reservation at least once a month, but this was difficult to do in the winter because of the poor reservation roads. When he could get a ride to Red Rock with a friend, he visited as many relatives as he could and spent lots of time talking with the old people "because they know the right way how to live and to do things right." He had no contact with his former wife and son.

SANDOVAL'S PROBLEMS.   The necessity of trying to live simultaneously in a traditional and an urban world had been a harsh experience for him. His perception of some Anglos and Navajos reflected this bitter struggle.

> From the beginning the wine and whiskey were brought into this country by the Anglos which seems wrong to me, just like giving dope to teenagers. My friends on the reservation ask me how we live in the city with all this hurry-hurry. Have to be at a certain place a certain time, which to my people is fantastic. You can't afford to make mistakes in this place.
>
> A lot of Navajos neglect their family. They're supposed to be looking for a job off the reservation, and then you hear about them in the state pen at Santa Fe. And here's another bad Navajo. He makes a lot of money off the reservation, he gets paid several hundred dollars in ready cash, he has a few drinks, and he sounds worse than the Texans. Finally another Navajo tells him to shut up. By doing this he gets in a fight with this character, and they both go to jail by the time the day is over, and it takes all their money to pay the fines to get out which is downright stupid I agree. The next morning he has a hangover and he says, "What happen?" Then he hears, "Your fine was this much." Then he brags about how much he paid. But worst of all kinds of Navajo are the witches.

Sandoval's fear of witches was well founded. In May of 1960, while sleeping in a car at Canyoncito after an evening of Gospel preaching, he was attacked. "I been asleep about two hours. Suddenly a tapping on the car and a cold wind [the car windows were closed] woke me up. The car started to shake. My mind felt small, and it was being dragged away. I hollered out, 'Jesus and God' as loud as I could for several times. Finally everything stopped, and the witch went away. I still feel sick. I'm going to have to go the the reservation for a sing."

Sandoval's average annual earnings of $1,800 provided him with the essentials of life in an urban setting, but allowed few luxuries. He attempted to buy a secondhand car on the installment plan but lost it after a few months because of his failure to make the payments. His chief pleasure seemed to be taking part in pentecostal church services and discussing the Gospel with his Navajo associates. I believe that he also gained a certain measure of solace from this. He also enjoyed "going to the great big sweat house" [steam room] at Vic Taney's Gym.

"This sweat house is much better than the kind that they have on the reservation. In this one you could even dance around while you are inside. I really think that the tribal council should build a lot of these for people out on the reservation."

After 15 months of contact with Sandoval, I had the strong impression that he regarded urban residence as nothing more than a painful necessity. The only aspects of the Anglo world that he valued were medical practices, "but only for the Anglo kind of diseases," and a few technological developments such as cars and TV. His orientation was toward the traditional reservation, although he was interested in the tribal council politics at Window Rock. He felt that his doctor at the sanatorium really didn't understand his illness as well as a singer would have. This was why he was still sick. As soon as he felt better, he wanted to return permanently to the reservation and have "lots of horses and sheep and a big irrigated farm." He realized, however, that he would probably never have these things. "The Navajo way is the best. All a Navajo wants out of life is living. He should live on his land in pride and dignity, as tall as a pine tree. But I will never have land. In about twenty years I can see myself back around Red Rock just chopping wood and things like that." Sandoval frequently commented that "you can't live the White way and the Navajo way at the same time." His life was an eloquent testimonial to the validity of his belief.

Incidentally, Joe proved to be a remarkably good prophet. As of 1979 he was living near Red Rock in a modest and inconspicuous fashion.

EVALUATION OF JOE SANDOVAL.   From the material presented above, you might get the impression that Joe was a cynical, embittered individual, but this was only partially true. Despite his difficulties, he seemed to have an admirable zest for living. He was an excellent teller of myths, and he could make such figures as Coyote, Changing Woman, and Big Monster assume a vividness that is impossible for me to describe. Although he mistrusted and feared many Anglos and Navajos, he recognized that both races also had desirable people. Subjectively, I would say that most of the time he was a Navajo who "walked in Beauty."

In considering the life of Joe Sandoval, a couple of questions concerning his failure to live successfully in either the Navajo or White world come to mind. What is the definition of failure in both situations? Why did Sandoval fail in each instance? Sandoval failed to conform to the behavioral expectations of traditional Navajo life because he failed to live up to the expectations of his family. He failed to acquire the rewards of traditional reservation living because of his family's poverty and his own poor physical health. His central response to the stresses of poverty and illness was an adherence to the *culture of excitement*. The

The heirs of Manuelito and Cayatanita. Fort Defiance, Arizona, March, 1974.   Arizona State Museum. Photographer, Helga Teiwes.

culture of excitement has been defined as explosive bursts of excitement that relieve a monotonous existence. Although these bursts may involve unpleasant activities such as physical violence or trouble with the police, they are welcomed because they distract an individual from preoccupation with his own failure and provide a subject for future talk and laughter (White, 1970: 175–197). Participation in the culture of excitement for Sandoval did amount to failure. Yet, out of necessity, he regarded the traditional world of the reservation as the only one that might eventually provide a secure place for him. He had entered the urban world as a patient in a tuberculosis sanatorium. Neither his reservation years nor his hospital experiences prepared him to benefit from urban life. He was able to survive physically but little more than this. Given his abilities, lack of vocational skills, and the precarious state of his health, his future seemed ominous. Yet his past also illustrated the breadth of the human spirit and the ingenuity of a handicapped Navajo under prolonged duress.

CONCLUSION

It seems evident that all three individuals, Powell, Barnes, and Sandoval, have retained Navajo identity, but each has a different identity, which has been determined by his own background. The content and structure of each individual's identity will continue to vary as each is influenced by his residence and migration patterns.

REFERENCES

Adams, William Y. Shonto: A Study of the Role of the Trader in a Modern Navaho Community. *Bulletin 188, Bureau of American Ethnology, Smithsonian Institution.* Washington, D.C.: Government Printing Office, 1963.

———, and Lorraine T. Ruffing. Shonto Revisited: Measures of Social and Economic Change in a Navajo Community, 1955–1971. *American Anthropologist 79,* 58–83, March 1977.

Brugge, David M., et al., comps. *Navajo Bibliography. Navajoland Publications Series B.* Window Rock, Arizona: The Navajo Tribe, 1967.

Counselor, Jim, and Ann Counselor. *Wild, Woolly and Wonderful.* New York: Vantage Press, 1954.

Dyk, Walter. A Navaho Autobiography. *Viking Fund Publications in Anthropology Number Eight.* New York: The Viking Fund Inc., 1947.

Dyk, Walter. *Son of Old Man Hat: A Navaho Autobiography.* New York: Harcourt, Brace, and Co., 1938.

Franciscan Fathers. *An Ethnologic Dictionary of the Navaho Language.* St. Michaels, Arizona, 1910.

Hodge, William H. Navaho Pentecostalism. *Anthropological Quarterly 37,* 73–93, 1964.

———. The Albuquerque Navajos. *Anthropological Papers No. 11.* Tucson: University of Arizona Press, 1969.

Johnston, Denis F. An Analysis of Sources of Information on the Population of the Navaho. *Bureau of American Ethnology, Bulletin 197.* 1966.

Kluckhohn, Clyde. *Navaho Witchcraft.* Boston: Beacon Press, 1963.

———. The Ramah Navaho. *Anthropological Papers, No. 79, Bulletin 196, Bureau of American Ethnology, Smithsonian Institution.* Washington, D.C.: Government Printing Office, 1966.

———, W. W. Hill, and Lucy W. Kluckhohn. *Navaho Material Culture.* Cambridge, Mass.: The Belknap Press of Harvard University Press, 1971.

———, and Dorothea Leighton. *The Navaho.* Cambridge, Mass.: Harvard University Press, 1951.

———, and Katherine Spencer. *A Bibliography of the Navaho Indians.* New York: J. J. Augustin, 1940.

Ladd, John. *The Structure of a Moral Code: A Philosophical Analysis of Ethical Discourse Applied to the Ethics of the Navaho Indians.* Cambridge, Mass.: Harvard University Press, 1957.

Leighton, Dorothea, and Clyde Kluckhohn. *Children of the People: The Navajo Individual and His Development.* Cambridge, Mass.: Harvard University Press, 1948.

Matthews, Washington. The Night Chant: A Navaho Ceremony. *Memoirs of the American Museum of Natural History, Vol. 6.* New York: American Museum of Natural History, 1902.

Parsons, Elsie Clews. Isleta, New Mexico. *47th Annual Report, Bureau of American Ethnology.* Washington, D.C.: Government Printing Office, 1932.

Reichard, Gladys A. *Navaho Religion: A Study of Symbolism.* Vols. 1 and 2. New York: Bollingen Foundation Inc., 1950.

Spake, Amanda. Plight of Dying Indians Causes Little Stir. *The Milwaukee Journal,* part II, June 10, 1974, p. 9.

Stucki, Larry R. The Case Against Population Control: The Probable Creation of the First American Indian State. *Human Organization 30,* 393–400, Winter 1971.

Underhill, Ruth. *Here Come the Navaho!* Haskell: U.S. Indian Service, 1953.

U.S. Commission on Civil Rights. *The Farmington Report: A Conflict of Cultures.* New Mexico Advisory Committee to the U.S. Commission on Civil Rights, July, 1975.

U.S. Department of the Interior, Office of Indian Affairs. *Dine Bikéyah* by Richard F. Van Valkenburgh. Ed. L. W. Adams and John McPhee. Window Rock, Arizona: Navajo Service, 1941.

Vogt, E. Z. Navaho. In E. H. Spicer, ed., *Perspectives in American Indian Culture Change.* Chicago: University of Chicago Press, 1961, pp. 278–336.

White, Robert A., S. J. The Lower-Class "Culture of Excitement" among the Contemporary Sioux. In Ethel Nurge, ed., *The Modern Sioux Social Systems and Reservation Culture.* Lincoln: The University of Nebraska Press, 1970, pp. 175–197.

Witherspoon, Gary. *Navajo Kinship and Marriage.* Chicago: University of Chicago Press, 1975.

Wyman, Leland C. *Blessingway: With Three Versions of the Myth Recorded and Translated from the Navajo by Father Berard Haile, O.F.M.* Tucson: University of Arizona Press, 1970.

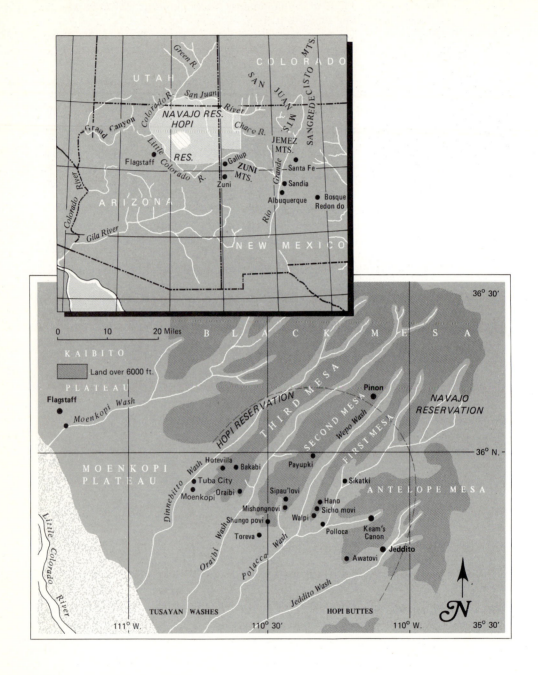

CHAPTER 8

THE HOPI
The People of Quiet Strength

From the edge of the great cliff one looked down on the immense stretches of the desert. Grazed-out long ago by flocks that were held too close to the pueblo, the land had become barren, a sea of drifting sand that stirred and lifted in the winds. But in this sand were the cornfields and bean patches of the stubborn race. The Hopi, whatever else he may be, is the greatest dry-farmer on earth.

Leo Crane. *Indians of the Enchanted Desert*

This chapter has benefited from a careful critical reading by Dr. Emory Sekaquaptewa, a professional anthropologist, the coordinator of Indian programs at the University of Arizona, and a Hopi who is dedicated to serving the best interests of his people. Neither Dr. Sekaquaptewa nor I in this chapter attempts to resolve a number of contemporary and controversial issues associated with Hopi life. Nor does Dr. Sekaquaptewa intend to speak for all Hopis. What he does do is to present an informed opinion concerning certain complex issues where mutually satisfactory solutions are difficult to obtain and as yet have not been found. In a number of places, Dr. Sekaquaptewa's comments are inserted without editorial revision to indicate something of the nature of this complexity. These comments are set in brackets and prefaced by the notation *ES-PC '80* which stands for "Emory Sekaquaptewa, Personal Communication, 1980."

The Hopi, like all other native Americans, are a part and parcel of modern American life. This close integration makes living for them at times a difficult and challenging business. The response to difficulty and challenge along culturally sanctioned lines is the real essence of Hopi existence today. In many respects, the current Hopi situation is a reflection of one basic, essential question that all people throughout the world are attempting to answer: How shall we live within the difficult matrix of contemporary life, given our past experiences, our present desires and needs, and our future encounters?

BACKGROUND AND HISTORY

Black Mesa in Arizona is the home of the Hopi Indians, the "peaceful ones." The mesa, underlain by resistant sandstone, is about 60 miles in diameter and has an elevation ranging between 2,000 and 7,000 feet above sea level. The villages are built on three projecting fingers of Black Mesa, named, by visitors from the east, First Mesa, Second Mesa, and Third Mesa. The three towns on First Mesa are Walpi, Sichimovi, and Hano or Tewa Village. Walpi, which was built on the mesa top soon after 1680, is a village occupying a narrow strip of land only 150 feet wide at the most. It has slowly been losing population for a long time, going from 232 people in 1890 to 80 in 1968 (James, 1974: 16). To the naked eye, Sichimovi and Hano are indistinguishable, as there is no space between them. There are, however, great differences because Hano was founded by Tewa Indians who were fleeing from their Rio Grande villages after the Spaniards had reconquered the Pueblo Indians who had rebelled against their rule in 1680. Through the years the people of Hano have retained their Tewa language and some of their ceremonies, while at the same time living in close proximity to the Hopi and, more and more, intermarrying with them. Edward P. Dozier's case

Hopi country. Storm coming up between First and Second Mesas. October, 1973. Arizona State Museum. Photographer, Helga Teiwes.

study, *Hano, a Tewa Indian Community in Arizona* (1966), is an excellent work describing how they have retained their cultural identity and how much they have contributed to the people of First Mesa and the Hopi tribe in general. The populations of Sichimovi and Hano have both grown, Sichimovi from 103 in 1890 to 364 in 1968, and Hano from 161 in 1890 to 241 in 1968 (James, 1974: 16). Below First Mesa to the east is the village of Polacca, which grew up around a day school during the 1890s. Most residents of Polacca, however, still owe political and religious allegiance to their village of origin on the top of the mesa, and many people maintain homes in both places.

To the west is Second Mesa, containing the Pueblos of Mishongnovi, Shipolovi, and Shongopovi. All were founded at their present locations between 1680 and 1700, and their populations have been growing or remaining stable during this century. In 1968 there were 530 people at Mishongnovi, 142 at Shipolovi, and 475 at Shongopovi (James, 1974: 16).

Third Mesa is the location of Old Oraibi. Founded about A.D. 1150,

Shiplovi, Second Mesa. June, 1973.   Arizona State Museum. Photographer, Helga Teiwes.

it is probably the oldest continuously inhabited village in the United States. Although today parts of it are falling to ruin, 167 people still lived there in 1968. Old Oraibi, once the largest of the Hopi villages, was split by dissension in the early 1900s, when a group of people moved away to found the village of Hotevilla and later Bacobi, both on Third Mesa about eight miles to the northwest of Oraibi. At about the same time, some Hopis began moving to the bottom of Third Mesa, where they founded the community of New Oraibi, which is now one of the larger Hopi villages and the headquarters for the Hopi Tribal Council.

Forty miles to the west of Third Mesa is Moencopi on the Navajo Reservation. Built at a site where permanent springs make irrigation possible, Moencopi began as a summer farming settlement for the people of Oraibi in the late 1800s. It gradually became a permanent settlement as people were attracted to it not only by the irrigation but also by the possibilities of wage work in Tuba City and Flagstaff. Although it looks like one community, there are really two Moencopis, one conservative and one more modern in political and cultural orientation. Upper Moencopi, the more modern section, had 432 people in 1968 whereas Lower Moencopi had 278 (James, 1974: 16).

The Anasazi Peoples

All the Pueblo peoples of the Southwest are thought to have descended from the Anasazi who, along with the Hohokam to the south and the Mogollon in the Mogollon Highlands, evolved around the time of Christ from even earlier groups. Although not all traits appeared at the same time or in all areas, the Anasazi generally were characterized by their gray and black coiled pottery, their use of full grooved stone axes, their practice of burying the dead in flexed positions, and their building of stone apartment houses called *pueblos* and underground ceremonial chambers called *kivas* (Lipe, 1978: 366). In addition, although they gathered many wild foods and probably depended quite heavily upon them, they were committed to the cultivation of maize, beans, and squash by about A.D. 500. These crops were grown through the use of dry farming or floodwater farming. Unlike the Hohokam, the Anasazi did not construct elaborate irrigation systems. In the Hopi area in particular, these early inhabitants developed the system of overplanting in many small plots with the hope that at least some of them would produce crops. This system, coupled with the extensive storage of surpluses, is still in use today (Cordell & Plog, 1979: 419).

By about A.D. 1000, or shortly thereafter, the Anasazi peoples had reached the height of their geographical spread and were near the maximum in population. The edifices they built around this period, though

Old Oraibi, Third Mesa. June, 1973.   Arizona State Museum. Photographer, Helga Teiwes.

partially fallen into ruin, still attract thousands of visitors each year to places such as Chaco Canyon and Mesa Verde. No one can say exactly why the Anasazi florescence ended, but probably a combination of factors including drought, arroyo cutting, and the pressures of increased population encouraged most Pueblo peoples to move to the east, where rainfall was heavier and soils were better for agriculture. Although many Pueblo peoples established new homes along the Rio Grande in New Mexico, some remained in the west at places such as Acoma, Laguna, Zuni, and the Hopi villages.

Although the Hopis share a common ancestry with other Pueblo peoples, there are differences between them. The Hopis are one of the few groups who do not live together in a single village. Not only do they inhabit several villages, but the Hopis also do not think or act in unison when faced with pressures from the outside. Their history, from the earliest Spanish contact to the present, has been a series of conflicts among people who wished to accept the ideas of the newcomers and those who did not. Another difference is language: the Hopis alone among the Pueblos speak a Shoshonean tongue belonging to the Uto-Aztecan linguistic stock. Linguistically, the Hopis are related to the Comanche, Ute, and Paiute peoples, and remotely to the Aztecs of ancient Mexico (Simpson, 1953: 7). Physically, the Hopis are smaller than most other Pueblo people. They are, however, strong and graceful with straight black hair, high cheekbones, reddish-brown skin, and pleasant expressions. Perhaps the most significant difference between the Hopi and the other Pueblos has been the fact that the Hopis live at such a distance from the centers of civilization established first by the Spaniards and then the Americans. They were so far away and so hard to contact that they were protected in large measure from the forced conversion to Christianity and White men's ways, which other groups had to accept in order to survive at all. Because an understanding of their history is so essential to further the knowledge of what the Hopi are like, this chapter will be divided into three sections, History, Traditional Culture, and Modern Life among the Hopi.

The following section about Hopi history is taken largely from Spicer's *Cycles of Conquest* (1962). Those readers desiring more detail are urged to consult either Spicer or Harry James's *Pages from Hopi History* (1974). Spicer has characterized Hopi history as unique among the Pueblos because the Hopi were the only people who were able to reassert their own beliefs and values after they had received substantial exposure to the Christian religion taught by the Spaniards (1962: 188). Given this response and the number of Hopi villages with their varied forms of Hopi life, Hopi culture today can be said to be vital and enduring.

The Spanish Presence

Recorded history began for the Hopis in 1540 when Coronado, during his first visit to many southwestern groups, sent a detachment of about 20 men to the west from Zuni, where he was staying. These men attacked Kawaiokuh, a village to the east of First Mesa in the Jeddito Valley. The Spanish force defeated the villagers so decisively that the Hopis concluded that nonaggression was to their advantage. Several years later the Hopis guided another Spanish party to the Grand Canyon. About this time, they abandoned Kawaiokuh in the Jeddito Valley and Sikyatki in Polacca Valley, but the falling water table probably had more to do with their flight than did the Spaniards.

Other Spanish parties visited the Hopis in 1583 and 1598, but no one remained there and no attempt was made to convert the Indians until 1629, when three Franciscan missionaries were assigned to the area. Three missions were built: at Awatovi on the Jeddito Plateau; at Shungopovi, then located below Second Mesa; and at Oraibi. We know little about the success of the missionaries in converting the Indians to Christianity, but, judging by an incident in 1655, they were largely failures. At that time the Hopis sent a delegation to the Spanish authorities to protest the behavior of a priest, Father Salvador de Guerra, who had discovered an Indian in an act of idolatry, which could have been something as innocuous as making a *kachina doll,* a wooden figure that represents a Hopi supernatural being. The Hopi was beaten in the plaza until he was "bathed in blood," then taken to the church and beaten again. After this he was doused with turpentine and set on fire, of which treatment he died (James, 1974: 48). For this behavior, Father de Guerra was removed from Oraibi, but he was permitted to serve in New Mexico. In another hearing before the Inquisition in Mexico City in 1663, priests at Hopi were accused of forcing penitent Indians to dress as hermits in haircloth shirts and beads, parade about carrying large crosses, and subsist only on pots of herbs to the point of starvation. For this behavior, the priests were removed (James, 1974: 49).

In 1680, perhaps convinced by such events and obvious signs of Spanish weakness, Indians in the majority of pueblos revolted, led by Popé, the religious leader of the San Juan community. The Hopis, far from the center of activity, killed the four missionaries assigned to them, but they sent no men to help drive the Spanish from Santa Fe, the seat of government. Over the next 12 years, the Spanish attempted to regain power and finally succeeded, and during this time the Hopis provided refuge for many Eastern Pueblo peoples who sought their protection. They also concluded that caution was in order, and the villages of Walpi, Shungopovi, and Michongnovi all were moved to the tops of

First and Second Mesas respectively. In addition, Tewa peoples from the Rio Grande founded the village of Hano on First Mesa, being granted the land for a promise to protect the Hopi from their enemies. On Second Mesa, Eastern Pueblo peoples founded Payupki, and some Hopis from Shungopovi founded Shipaulovi in order to have a place to hide sacred ceremonial objects. When the Spaniard De Vargas led an expedition to the Hopis in 1692, they swore allegiance to Spain in order to avoid a fight, but they felt secure enough in their newly fortified and relocated villages that in 1700 they sent a delegation to Santa Fe proposing religious freedom for themselves as a condition to signing a peace treaty. The authorities in New Mexico indignantly refused this bargain. At about this same time, a nucleus of Christian Hopis at Awatovi on the Jeddito Plateau offered to rebuild their mission. This stand so alarmed the non-Christian Hopi majority that they attacked Awatovi, killing the men and distributing the surviving women and children among the other villages. Land claimed by Awatovi went to people from First and Second Mesas.

The early 1700s saw a series of small skirmishes between the Spanish and Hopis, but none had decisive results. One aim of the Spaniards was to force the Eastern Pueblo peoples resident at Hopi to move back to their homes where they would again fall under nearby Spanish authority. These attempts failed at Hano when the people from Walpi said that they would let the Tewas go back only if the Spanish came to the mesa top and got them. At Payupki on Second Mesa, though, the Spanish eventually succeeded. Four hundred and forty-one people returned to Isleta in 1742, and another 350 to Sandia in 1748. At that time the Hopi population of about 8,000 allowed various Spanish priests to come and preach to them, but they remained unwilling to embrace Catholic doctrine.

By 1779 the Hopis were suffering drought and famine, always a danger for them in their homeland of low rainfall. In order to survive, many people moved temporarily to Havasupai, Zuni, Sandia, and other Rio Grande villages. Population dropped to 798 people, and in 1781 those who remained were struck by a smallpox epidemic. In that year, however, the rains came again, and by 1782 the Hopi were reported to be better off than any Rio Grande pueblo.

By the early 1880s the Hopis began to be subject to harassment by the Navajos, who raided their farms and flocks. Finally seeing some use for the Spanish, the Hopis petitioned them for help; but the Spanish, headquartered in distant Santa Fe, had no resources to spare even though they must have longed to take advantage of the opportunity to influence a people who had resisted them for so long. Their day was over, and by mid-century, Americans were in control of the entire Southwest.

The American Presence

Because of the Hopis's remote location, the change in government meant little to them at first. In 1850 they protested to the new government about Navajo raids, but the Americans were no more able to help them than the Spanish had been. For the next decade the Hopis got along well with the few Americans they saw, mostly those making government surveys of the new territory plus some Mormons from Utah who became interested in the Hopis as potential converts and founded a colony near Moencopi in 1875. In 1864 the Americans responded to all the complaints about Navajo raiding by sending Kit Carson to round up the Navajos by force and march them to Bosque Redondo in New Mexico. There they remained for four years, but in 1868 they were allowed to return to their traditional homeland. Squeezed by population pressures, many of them began settling on land that the Hopi considered their own.

In 1882 the Americans officially recognized the Hopis when they created the Hopi Reservation, a rectangle extending about 50 miles north and south of the Hopi villages. The reservation did not include all the land that the Hopi considered their own by custom, tradition, and occupation. The reservation, in addition, was established for the Hopi " . . . and such other Indians as the Secretary of the Interior may see fit to settle thereon" (U.S. Executive Document, 1882). This wording was to give both the Hopis and the Navajos much difficulty in the future. In the spring of 1887 the first representative of the United States government to the Hopi, James Gallaher, moved into the newly created Indian Agency at Keams Canyon, the site of a trading post near First Mesa. By that fall Gallaher had opened a boarding school for 52 Hopi pupils, and he was being kept very busy making long trips to various Navajo hogans in a futile attempt to stop their raiding of Hopi fields and animals (James, 1974: 106–107). From the school's inception, most people at Oraibi refused to send their children there, and during the next ten years a split formed at that village. This split was eventually radically to change Oraibi, the largest of the Hopi towns. [ES-PC '80: The factional division was over the differences in the interpretation of the teachings of prophecy and how this gave rise to the opportunity for the usurpation of power (in a political sense) by opposition leaders. On the surface it seemed that the question was only a matter over acceptance or rejection of the White men's ways, when in fact it was not.]

On one government project, that of land allotment, all the Hopis agreed: they wanted nothing to do with it. The Hopi practice of farming many small fields in varied locations would not have been possible under land allotment, and the Hopis' correct decision to oppose it prevailed when they convinced the government not to allot their land.

Nampayo seated with examples of her work, ca. 1900.   National Archives and Record Service, G.S.A.

HOPI REACTION TO THE AMERICANS.   Gradually, under a series of Indian agents who were virtual dictators and did not exercise their authority wisely, American control and influence grew stronger. [ES-PC '80: American influence on Hopi is also due, in part, to Hopi acceptance based on interpretation of prophecy.] A Baptist mission and a day school were built at the foot of First Mesa, where they formed the nucleus for the new town of Polacca. Day schools were constructed at Toreva below Second Mesa and at Oraibi. Smallpox, introduced to a people with no natural immunity, killed hundreds, and the government practice of innoculating the Indians against it with no adequate explanation of what they were doing made the Hopis even more hostile. The Hopis began to learn the art of silversmithing, making beautiful jewelry to sell to the tourists who were beginning to find their way to the distant mesas to watch dramatic Hopi dances and ceremonies. On First Mesa a woman named Nampeyo, a Tewa from Hano, obtained some fragments of ancient Hopi pottery from her husband who was helping archaeologists at the ruins of Sikyatki. Using the old design motifs and her own inventiveness, she began making beautiful, striking pottery,

and she taught the other women to make it too. Traditional Hopi baskets and plaques also found a market with tourists. Men from Hano,
who had always been bilingual in Tewa and Hopi, began to learn
English so that they could interpret for the Whites, and the people at
First Mesa seemed willing to accept some White ways. The people at
Second Mesa only endured the newcomers, and at Oraibi, in 1906, open
animosity broke out between the "friendlies," who were willing to go
along with the Americans and send their children to school, and the
"hostiles," who were not. (These names, needless to say, were coined
by the Americans, not the Hopis.) [ES-PC '80: Differences in the interpretation of prophecy and its teachings concerning the environmental
depletion of Oraibi were beneath the open factional hostility—the governmental intervention simply gave dramatic impetus to the division
necessary for survival, according to Hopi historians.]

Matters came to a head at Oraibi when Youkeoma, the leader of the
"hostile" faction, invited some people from Shongopovi to live at
Oraibi and support him. Tewaquaptewa, the opposing leader, objected
to the invitation because drought threatened and food supplies were
scarce. The allies of the hostiles came despite the opposition, and just
before the Snake Dance was held in 1906, it looked as if fighting would
break out in the village. Men were sharpening knives and oiling guns.
The Hopi distaste for physical violence prevailed when Youkeoma
scratched a line on the ground and announced that if the other side
could push him over that line, he would take his people and leave
Oraibi. Men fanned out behind him and the great push began. Youkeoma was tossed about, being forced up into the air on several occasions; but when it was over, he had been fairly pushed over the line.
He and his followers collected what belongings they could carry and
treked northwest on Third Mesa to the site of several permanent
springs, where they founded Hotevilla. The next day they were permitted to return to Oraibi for the rest of their possessions. The United
States government, which had not interfered directly in the schism up
to this time, stepped in after all had been settled to make a bad situation
worse. Many of the men of Hotevilla, struggling in the fall of the year
to build homes and find food to make their families secure, were carted
off to jail, leaving the women and children to face the winter alone. At
the same time, the government deprived Tewaquaptewa, the village
chief of Oraibi, of his office and sent him, along with his wife and
children and an ally from Moencopi, to Sherman Institute in Riverside,
California, where for four years he was made to learn English and
Christianity. This experience so embittered him that he hated all White
customs and especially Christianity when he returned. He was particularly enraged over an incident that occurred while he was away. A
group of people from Hotevilla decided they really wanted to return to

Oraibi, and they settled there in spite of the opposition of the acting chief, Tewaquaptewa's brother. Back in California, government officials persuaded Tewaquaptewa to sign a statement in English urging the people of Oraibi to do everything the Americans told them to do and to allow the Hotevilla contingent to remain at Oraibi. Tewaquaptewa's brother, however, did not believe this statement, and indeed Tewaquaptewa sent oral messages repudiating it. The migrants from Hotevilla were forced to leave Oraibi. In October of 1907, they founded the village of Bacabi about a mile southeast of Hotevilla (James, 1974: 142).

The Hopi, and especially Tewaquaptewa, were capable of arousing strong passions in outsiders, as this somewhat biased statement by Leo Crane (1926: 86–87) suggests:

> Tewaquaptewa's portrait appears in that fine book of Indian chants, edited by Miss Natalie Curtis and published by the Harpers; and his singing countenance presents a rapt ecstatic expression as he yodels the Butterfly Song. The translation of his name is there given as "Sun-down-shining," and is imperfect as most translations, but just as good as any other, providing you do not have to consider him on a Governmental basis. I never dealt with him on a musical scale, and his undoubted genius in this respect made no appeal to me. As his Indian Agent, however, I tried for eight long years to make a sensible human being of him, and failed, for lack of material. After having tried him as an Indian judge, and then as an Indian policeman, in the hope of preserving his dignity and authority as hereditary chief, he was found to be the most negatively contentious savage and unreconstructed rebel remaining in the Oraibi community, so filled with malicious mischief-making to his benefit that a group of his own people petitioned me to exile him from the mesa settlement, in the hope that they might then exist in peace. Of course, this had little to do with his "Sun-down-shining" or his Butterfly chanting; but when the folks at home cannot get along with father, there is something wrong.

Once Tewaquaptewa had returned to Oraibi, many of his people did not agree with his anti-American attitude, and the exodus to New Oraibi at the foot of the mesa began about 1910. Here were a trading post and the government day school, and here the government helped the people build more modern houses and construct a reliable water supply. On his mesa top, Tewaquaptewa lived until 1960, always hoping that Old Oraibi would not die until he did. In fact, it still survives today, although it is filled with crumbling ruins haunted by unsettling memories; and although many people may visit there for ceremonies, very few remain for long.

THE EARLY TWENTIETH CENTURY.   During the first part of the twentieth century, the Hopi continued to be plagued by disease, which spread rapidly among the children who were forced to attend the unsanitary, overcrowded government schools. Trachoma caused blindness among many, and others died of tuberculosis, measles, dysentery, or smallpox when their undernourished bodies could not fight off the germs. The fact that many children were dying did not stop the government agents from continuing to force them to attend school, and they went so far as to hold roundups on the mesa tops during which children were chased and forcibly removed from their homes, sometimes with inadequate clothing in bitter weather. Some were forced to remain at the Keams Canyon boarding school for as long as four years without a vacation or a chance to go home with their families. Not all the actions of the Indian agents, however, were this harsh or destructive. They also made efforts to introduce new crops to the Hopi area, to improve the livestock breeding, to drill new wells, and to curb the inroads of the Navajos.

THE TRIBAL COUNCIL.   In the 1930s and 1940s, the national government brought still more changes to the Hopis. As a result of the Indian Reorganization Act of 1934, the Hopis established a tribal council. Although they had never had a centralized form of government, but rather a system of councils in each village that were integrated with the clan and religious affiliations of the members, the Hopis were persuaded in 1936 to adopt a constitution and set up a Tribal Court. [ES-PC '80: By this time, education for Hopis was an established fact and enough adults had an understanding of the democratic process to exercise a decision resulting in the adoption of the Constitution.] The first Tribal Council meeting was held in 1937. Not surprisingly, the Tribal Council was supported by people from First Mesa who had a history of adapting to the modern world. The people of Second and Third Mesas repudiated it, and at one point the Tribal Council was disbanded completely, only to be reformed in 1951. Although some Hopis still do not acknowledge it, it is functioning now. Its role in leasing Hopi land to the Peabody Coal Company for mining is explored in the last part of this chapter. [ES-PC '80: A very large majority of Hopis acknowledge the Tribal Council today, which they compartmentalize as strictly a new political system of control. These same people are as active and supportive of the traditional institutions as those few who are outspoken against the Council.]

THE STOCK REDUCTION PROGRAM.   The second major change of this period had to do with the stock reduction program, which the government forced on both the Hopis and the Navajos in order to preserve what grazing land was left for their herds of animals. Although the program was necessary to preserve what remained of range lands, it was not always carried out in the most diplomatic fashion so that the Indians thoroughly understood the reasons behind it. One major problem among the Hopis was that the people of Third Mesa were required to reduce their stock by 44 percent in contrast to those of First and Second Mesas, who reduced stock by 20 and 22 percent respectively (James,

1974: 206). Although the government assured the Indians that the reason for this inequity was that the land around Oraibi was the most badly eroded, the Indians could not help but suspect that they were being singled out because they had so consistently opposed "Washington" on so many issues. Stock reduction was a serious threat to a people living on an income of less than $500 per family in the 1940s; every sheep counted.

A LAND DISPUTE.   Along with the stock reduction came another governmental action that the Hopis saw as a deliberate theft of their traditional lands. Back in 1882 their reservation had been established as 2,499,558 acres, but they were not given exclusive use of this territory. Now, in 1943, along with the stock reduction program, the government set up Land Management Districts for the entire Navajo-Hopi territory. It arbitrarily assigned to the Hopis Land Management District Six, which was only 631,194 acres, a reduction to one-fourth of the old reservation. As even the original reservation had been smaller than the areas that the Hopis through long tradition considered their own, they eventually, in 1958, filed suit in federal court to regain the land that the Navajos and the federal government had taken from them. The Navajos immediately filed a quit-title action, and the struggle for the land has been litigated. This question is explored further at the end of this chapter.

SOME IMPROVEMENTS.   Today the Hopis are no longer as isolated as in the past by distance and poor roads from modern society. Good roads pass the mesas, and the Hopis have learned to welcome most tourists who buy their arts and crafts and enjoy the public parts of their ceremonies. The tribal economy has been supplemented by light industry in the area. Electricity and modern water systems are slowly being built as well as more housing, community centers, a tribal administration headquarters, and The Hopi Cultural Center on Second Mesa, which has a museum, motel, and restaurant (James, 1974: 221–222). There remain many ways to live as a Hopi: on the mesa top in a traditional stone house or at its bottom in a modern one; in Los Angeles or Phoenix or Tucson or Winslow; in Moencopi or Keams Canyon. The ties of the Hopi religion and of the clan system are still strong and valid, and the Hopis will somehow endure in the future as they have in the past.

TRADITIONAL CULTURE

Following the organization of Ruth Simpson in *The Hopi Indians* (1953), I will divide this discussion of Hopi traditional culture into two sections: the spiritual and the material. Because the spiritual realm is so important and permeates all other areas of life, I will begin with that. No attempt can be made to date the customs referred to here, but most are of long standing and only gradually faded away or were modified as more and more contact took place with outsiders.

The Spiritual Culture

ORIGIN MYTH.   The Hopis have as many origin myths as they have clans, for each clan wandered through a number of places before settling finally on the mesa. Most Hopis, however, share a common belief about how life began in this world for them. The version given here is taken from James (1974: 2–8), and it deals with the emergence of the people from the Underworld.

Originally the people and the animals lived in an Underworld in great contentment, growing corn, beans, squash, and beautiful flowers. Eventually, though, this world grew too crowded, and people began to quarrel and fight with each other. All the wisest councillors were called together by the chief of all the people, and they met in solemn conclave for four days. Their final decision was to leave that world for one either above or beneath it where they could live in peace. In order to do this, they called Mockingbird to help them, and he, in turn, suggested that they summon Yellow Bird, who, he said, was the wisest of all. The two birds then changed themselves into tall, handsome men and returned to the council for a long discussion of the problem. The final decision was to seek an opening to another world where men could once more live in peace. The council enlisted the support of a number of birds to help find an opening: Golden Eagle, Sparrow Hawk, Cliff Swallow, and Mourning Dove. Although Golden Eagle saw an opening high above him, no bird had the strength to reach it until the council called upon Shrike, who managed to fly into the Upper World. Here he met Maasau, a Spirit Being. The bird beseeched Maasau on behalf of the people that they might live with him here in this world. Maasau said, "It is up to them, if they are willing to live by the law that I live, which is hard by the planting stick" (ES-PC '80).

The people in the Underworld were willing to accept these conditions, but now the problem was to find a way for them to reach the entrance to the Upper World. They were helped by one of the grandsons of Spider Woman, who suggested that they ask Chipmunk for aid because he had the ability to make plants grow rapidly. Chipmunk was summoned to the council and agreed to try his skill. His first efforts, a spruce tree, several pine trees, and a giant sunflower, failed to grow tall enough to reach the opening, but finally he planted the root cutting from a tall reed, and this grew right through the opening. Chipmunk gnawed a hole through the reed so that the people could climb up its hollow interior, and the next morning the Chief led the way for all the good people who wished to enter the Upper World. Two horned priests were appointed to stand guard to make sure that no evil people joined them. For as long as it took Shrike to sing songs of thanksgiving and Mockingbird to assign everyone places in the Upper World and teach them new languages, people continued to climb the reed. Once the songs were finished, those left inside were forbidden to climb further, and their bodies formed the joints you can see on the reed today. The opening to the Upper World is called Sipaapu by the Hopis, and it is still a sacred place symbolized in all their rituals today.

RELIGION.   For the Hopis, religion is at the center of life and structures everything they do. The Hopi religion is based on four principles: spiritual power is in all things; the universe and nature are unchanging and reliable; the universe is dominated by two opposing principles, one good and one evil (duality); and finally there is a spirit being in every object, rocks and mountains as well as persons, plants, and animals (Simpson, 1953: 16). Two major concerns of the Hopi religion are curing and the bringing of rain. So important is this latter interest that it might be one of the reasons the Hopis have never embraced Christianity in large numbers. Christianity has no ceremony to call down the rain, and the Hopis must have it if their crops are to thrive.

The Hopis recognize many gods to whom they can appeal through animistic spirits or *kachinas*, who come to the Hopi villages every year in December and remain there until July when they return to their homes in the San Francisco Mountains, carrying messages from the Hopis to the gods. Five major ceremonies are held during the half year when the kachinas are present: Winter Solstice, at which they arrive; Pamuya, associated with the January moon; the Bean Ceremony; the Water Serpent ceremony; and finally Niman, or the Home-going ceremony. To say this, however, gives a very inadequate idea of the scope and variety of Hopi ceremonial life. Each clan has its associated kachinas, which commemorate some legend that is a part of the rich Hopi history. Nor does the ceremonial life of the Hopis end when the kachinas have returned to the San Francisco Mountains in July. Two very ancient and very important rites, Snake and Antelope Dances asking for rain, are held in August. In November comes the Wuwuchim or Grown Man ceremony, at which boys are initiated into full adult status. Also in the fall are the women's ceremonies giving thanks for the harvest. Those who are interested in the kachinas and Hopi mythology and cermonialism are advised to consult one of the many excellent sources on these subjects because space does not permit going into detail here. Examples are Colton (1950); Fewkes (1897); Fewkes (1903); Voth (1903); Voth (1905); and Voth (1912).

CLANS AND RELIGIOUS SOCIETIES.   The Hopi Kachina Cult was, until the creation of the Hopi Tribal Council, the only tribalwide organization among the Hopi, and the Kachina Cult is dependent upon clans that transcend the village organization. Each Hopi is born into his or her mother's clan, a *clan* being a group of people who trace their ancestry to a common migrating group to Hopi country. Such descent is stipulated or assumed but not demonstrated. Clans are numerous among the Hopi, they vary from village to village, and they are in flux because it is possible for two clans to combine or for a single clan to split into two parts. Some clans among the Hopi are antelope, bear, and reed, but there are many more. To the Hopi, clan rather than family is the primary kinship unit. Each clan is composed of one or more *matrilineal lineages,* or lines of descent traced through the female side. A family household, then, would consist of a woman with her husband, her daughters, married or unmarried, and her unmarried sons. Very close by, that woman's sisters would have their homes. The husband of this woman would continue to owe allegiance to his own clan and would return to his mother's home, perhaps in another village, for ceremonies there. Sons of the couple would also return to their mother's home for ceremonies after thay had married and moved in elsewhere with their wives' families. Daughters, after marriage, would theoretically either remain under their mother's roof with their new husbands or build a new home nearby. Not all people followed this pattern, but the literature states it was a common form of residence. Sekaquaptewa, however, disagrees. [ES-PC '80: To the best of my knowledge and early childhood recollections, there is no traditional practice of family households in some close proximity to each other. "Nawipti," meaning to go independent in housekeeping, also was understood to mean that the

Kachinas of the Powámû or "Bean-Planting" ceremony. Walpi, First Mesa, 1893.   Smithsonian Institution, National Anthropological Archives.

Hopi women's dance, Old Oraibi, 1877.   National Archives and Records Service, G.S.A.

new couple would build where it was convenient for them to build without regard to closeness or proximity to the family group.]

Clans rather than individuals or families controlled the use of all springs, garden plots, and farmlands. Husbands worked the land belonging to their wife's clan, but in addition they could own as individuals their livestock and fruit trees. If the couple should divorce, the woman and her children were still economically secure because her brothers could help her work her land.

Each Hopi clan recognizes a permanent, traditional ancestral home. In this home lives the *clan mother,* whose duty it is to care for the clan fetishes and ceremonial paraphernalia and to feed them. Her brother, not her husband, is the "ceremonial" clan head, whose duty it is to conduct the ceremonies that belong to the clan. He does this with the help of other clan members and with the help of a religious society. Twelve of these societies exist among all the Hopi villages, not every society being found in every village. Nine of them are exclusively male, and the other three are exclusively female. Initiation of any person is sponsored by a member. The initiate must be of the right age and sex and must be willing to accept the responsibilities of carrying out the ceremonies (Thompson, 1950: 69–70). The male societies ritually control all the major ceremonies, and even those minor ceremonies controlled by the women's societies usually require some male ritual participation. The religious life of the Hopis is therefore as firmly in charge of the men as the clan life is in charge of the women. This leads to a balanced social order in which both the men and the women are vital for the proper functioning of the society (Thompson, 1950: 70).

The leadership of each village is also determined through these religious societies. The "ceremonial" clan chief who is head of the most important religious society is also the village chief. In most cases, this would be the head of the Soyal Society, which conducts the Winter Solstice ceremony at which the kachinas arrive. He is the most important because this ceremony is so vital for the welfare of all people. [ES-PC '80: In general terms, prayers are made for all people, and not just for Hopis or for the village.] Traditionally in all villages except Walpi, Sichimovi, Hotevilla, and Bacabi, this man would be the head of the Bear clan, as this clan originally owned all the Hopi lands and parceled them out to each of the other clans as it arrived at the village. This chief governs with the aid of other ceremonial clan chiefs, who together form the town council. The chief is responsible for regulating land disputes; for leading the ceremonial council, who control the annual ceremonial cycle; and for concentrating all his forces on the physical, mental, and spiritual welfare of the village and of all mankind (Thompson, 1950: 72). In order to free him for these tasks, the people of the village will cultivate his land for him and protect him from mundane, routine worries and concerns so that he might better serve them. [ES-PC '80: Many Hopi historians say this practice was borrowed from the Spanish priests in their tyrannical rule. They say chiefs were like all other people, and expected to live by the same rules. Humbleness was the most important attribute of a chief.] The village chief will select his own successor from among the sons of his sisters, and he will train this successor from childhood on. The position is, therefore, never something to strive for, but something that is associated with greater responsibility and moral worth. Ideally, other ceremonial leaders follow this same pattern in selecting and training their successors.

Although Thompson makes the point that this system is strong because it equally divides function and authority between the women who control the clans and the men who control the religious societies and hence the ceremonies, it also has some built-in weaknesses that have not served the Hopis well. In the first place, no provision has been made for leadership beyond the village level. In any crisis affecting the tribe as a whole, the Hopis have no overall organization that will automatically set itself to deal with the situation; they must first create lines of communication and authority among all the villages. Although they were able to do this in some cases when facing the Spanish threat, the history of Oraibi points out quite clearly how badly they have failed when dealing with the Americans. Not only did the leadership of Oraibi fail to coalesce with the leadership of any other Hopi villages, but they also could not even agree with each other, so that Oraibi splintered into factions. Well before the final physical split of the village, the religious societies had divided into two, and each half was holding its own cycle of ceremonies.

A second serious drawback of this system of authority lies in the way in which power is transferred. Each leader is responsible for replacing himself by training a youngster to learn the proper rituals so that he can eventually take the place of the elder and the Hopi sacred ceremonies can continue. If this continuity is interrupted for any reason—early death, conversion to Christianity, movement away to take an outside job—the entire village is in danger of losing one of its essential ceremonies. [ES-PC '80: On the premise that unity was the most effective way of dealing with the White man's pressure, this paragraph makes sense. On the other hand, the term "tiingavi" implies that the "split" of Oraibi was a fulfillment of prophecy which taught that people in their worldly ambitions and aspirations would bring about a society corrupted by "man-made" institutions under the guise of religion, and this would soon result in moral and physical corruption to the environment. It was necessary to find an issue on the surface, but which was emotionally charged enough, to cause people to be willing to sever their roots at Oraibi and re-establish them elsewhere. Thus, with smaller groups in a new environment, people could begin with the basics. Among the admonitions to the factional groups was one which said that they should not "transplant" certain rituals in their new settlements.]

It is no wonder that the Hopi Tribal Council has had a difficult time getting established. There is no historical precedent for it, and its existence in many ways threatens traditional life, as, of course, all inevitable change threatens traditional life. [ES-PC '80: The new tribal council *per se* does not threaten "traditional life." It would if it were organized to replace it. Fact is, many Hopis in the council also hold ceremonial priesthood offices. On the other hand, many so-called traditional activists hold no ceremonial priesthoods. The tribal constitution mandates the council to preserve and protect the Hopi way of life.]

LIFE CYCLE.   This discussion of the Hopi life cycle is placed under the spiritual side of life because Hopi religious beliefs and actions condition all that they do from birth to old age and death. Through precept and example, through gossip and teasing and punishment if necessary, all Hopi children are taught the Hopi Way in which they must travel to obtain peace, prosperity, and happiness not only for themselves but for

Mother with child on cradle board. n.d. but probably ca. 1900.   Smithsonian Institution, National Anthropological Archives.

the pueblo as a whole. This Hopi Way lies in the acceptance of the idea that each individual is simply one unit in the social whole, and the whole can function only if its members assume the responsibility of being an active, vital member of that society and not just a passive individual living within it (Thompson, 1950: 126). To be Hopi is to assume now and forever a devoutly religious communal posture.

Hopi children were traditionally born at home, where they were cared for by their mother and their paternal aunts, who were responsible for making sure that the room was darkened for several days after the birth and that the baby was bathed in yucca suds and rubbed with ashes as a talcum. The mother was allowed to eat no salt or meat for this time. On the twentieth day after birth, a naming ceremony was held at which the child was presented to the sun with names that were bestowed on it. For the first year of their lives, Hopi babies enjoyed a pleasant life, always near their mothers, nursed on demand, and rarely treated roughly or tossed into the air. They were kept on a cradle board constantly at first, and the time was gradually reduced until the cradle board was discontinued entirely when the child reached one year old or started walking. Toddlers, too, were treated permissively. They ate when, what, and where they wished; were gradually and patiently encouraged to go outside the house for elimination; and were often carried about by their older siblings, who looked after them during the day. The terrain in which they grew up, however, ensured that they also learned discipline during this time. The mesa tops were dangerous places for children, who had to be taught the dangers of heights, of fire, and of innocently violating ceremonial taboos.

At about the age of six, Hopi children of both sexes began giving up their life of full-time play. Boys developed their bodies by running to the spring and bathing there before dawn. They were given responsibilities such as guarding their fathers' fields, chopping wood, hunting, and doing simple farming tasks. Girls assumed responsibility for the care of their younger siblings, carried water, ran errands, swept, cooked, tended the garden, and generally helped their mothers. Hopi children were made to feel that they were a very important part of their society in this way. Their responsibilities were vital contributions to the welfare of all, and thus they were educated in the Hopi Way.

For most Hopi children, guidance in the proper behavior by being scolded, teased, or ridiculed was sufficient. Approval and praise were also used so that children felt good about behaving properly. In a few cases, however, more strenuous measures were necessary. If a child was really bad, his mother's brother could be called upon. This uncle might whip him or hold him by the heels over a smoky fire so that he quickly realized the error of his ways. One special case of misbehavior, that of bed wetting beyond the age of six or so, was treated ceremonially. The boy was carried at dawn on his uncle's back to a house of the Water clan. There he and the other boys who had accompanied him were ritually doused with cold water, which was supposed to effect a cure. Another way that Hopi children were kept in line was through the use of the kachinas. Between the ages of six and ten, both boys and girls were initiated into the kachina cult and, as a part of this ceremony, were sometimes ceremonially whipped by selected cult members. [ES-PC '80: Not every initiate was whipped. There are two Orders, one in which no whipping was done. The choice is the parent's, for the child. Very few went into the Order which included ceremonial whipping.] This whipping, when it was done, was so painful and traumatic that simply the threat of being whipped in the future helped to ensure good behavior.

Between the ages of 15 and 20, boys went through a second initiation into one of the religious societies. After this, they were considered men with men's privileges and responsibilities. Adulthood for girls was traditionally marked by a four-day corn grinding ceremony around the time of their first menses. They indicated that they were ready for courtship by putting up their hair in the squash blossom or butterfly hairdress. Young Hopi girls were closely supervised and kept at home during the day, but young men were allowed to visit with them through a window or a door during the evening. Once a couple had decided to marry, both their families entered enthusiastically into all the necessary wedding preparations. It was the duty of the boy's male relatives to weave a set of cotton wedding robes and bridal sash for the girl, whereas her female relatives had to help her grind the hundreds of pounds of corn required to feed all the wedding guests for several days. After the ceremony, the young couple generally moved in with the girl's family, and the new husband began cultivating his wife's clan-controlled lands.

The strongest bond in Hopi society was between siblings, not marriage partners, and separation was made easy for those who did not get along. If she wished a divorce, all a wife had to do was place her husband's belongings outside the closed house door, and he would accept her decision, pick up his things, and return to his mother's home. If he became dissatisfied with her, he could simply pick up and leave. As the life of a Hopi household revolved around a central core of women who had been there since birth and would expect to remain till death, it was usually up to the husband to make the major behavioral adjustments. Once children had been born, the marriage was more likely to endure.

No Hopi of either sex was lazy or indolent—the society and the harsh requirements of the land did not allow them to be so. Women were responsible for tending the children, cooking, gardening, grinding corn, carrying water, and collecting some of the firewood. They also repaired their houses and had control over their building, although men helped with the heavier work. They made baskets or pottery for use at home or, later, for sale to tourists. Men did the strenuous work of planting, cultivating, and harvesting the small scattered fields. They tended their flocks and orchards and were responsible for providing meat for the table either from their domestic animals or from hunting. Men were the weavers and later the jewelry makers. They made trips to bring back wood, coal, and salt. A good share of their time was spent

Weaving a ring basket, Third Mesa, New Oraibi. October, 1973.   Arizona State Museum. Photographer, Helga Teiwes.

in the ceremonial chamber called the kiva, from which women were excluded except for certain ceremonies. There the men wove, carved kachinas, practiced for dances, and told stories, relaxing in the presence of other men. One reason the first initiation for boys was so important was that it admitted them to this exclusively male organization.

At death Hopi ceremonies were simple and dignified. The body of the deceased, dressed in wedding robes if a woman or a special blanket if a man, was buried in the ground. Infants who had died before the 20-day period of life were placed in rock clefts along with food offerings and a stick ladder to guide them to the spirit world. On the fourth day after death, the spirit departed to spend a happy eternity in the underworld from which the Hopis had emerged so long ago. Once the funeral rites had been observed, people preferred to speak seldom or never about the deceased.

Material Culture

FOOD QUEST.   Throughout their history the Hopis have been sedentary farmers who had to battle both nomadic raiders and the weather in order to get enough food to survive. Hopi country is plagued by incredibly difficult growing conditions. High altitude and scant rainfall, only about ten to 12 inches in an average year, combine to ensure a very short growing season. The spring, when crops are planted, is a season of almost no rainfall, so that plants must rely on seepage of groundwater in order to germinate. Once up, they are battered by strong spring winds and sandstorms capable of burying entire houses, to say nothing of tender young plants. Those plants that survive until late July and August might be watered by the summer rains, but they might just as easily be uprooted and carried away by a cloudburst. Finally, they must be harvested quickly before fall frosts come to destroy them. Through the centuries the Hopis have developed their own species of maize and cotton, which germinate and grow to maturity very quickly. The crops are also aided by the topography of Black Mesa itself. The mesa is drained by ephemeral streams that carry not only rain water but also sand and silt off the top of the plateau. Most of this sand is blown back against the mesa by the prevailing southwesterly winds. There it helps to reduce the runoff after rainstorms and to create permanent springs upon which the Hopis depend for drinking water and irrigation of their garden plots (Hack, 1942: xix). Even with the help of the topography, however, not enough rain falls for the Hopi to grow crops without depending upon four different techniques: floodwater farming, sand dune fields, seepage fields, and the few irrigated garden plots. The wise Hopis plant a number of fields in various locations so that if one method does not work in a particular year, another one might be more successful.

Using these techniques, the Hopis grew maize, beans, squash, sunflowers, and cotton as their staple crops. The corn was planted very deep, three to 12 kernels per hole, and was protected by windbreaks until the stalks were strong enough to survive. It was harvested in September and stored for future use. The Spaniards introduced more variety into the Hopi diet. They taught the Indians to grow such things as melons, onions, peppers, tomatoes, lettuce, carrots, turnips, beets, and wheat. In addition, they brought with them cuttings and seeds of fruit trees; and from that day to this, orchards of peaches, almonds, and other fruits have flourished in the Hopi sand dunes.

The Hopis supplemented their diet with some wild plants, although long trips were often necessary to gather what there was. They ate piñon nuts, juniper berries, mesquite beans, and the fruit of the prickly pear cactus as well as a number of other wild seeds, roots, leaves, and fruits (Simmons, 1942: 11). Although their diet was primarily vegetarian, the Hopis enjoyed meat when they could get it. Originally, the men formed hunting parties to pursue native fauna such as bear, deer, antelope, wildcat, and fox, but as the larger animals were driven away by increased populations, they trapped or snared smaller creatures such as prairie dogs and rabbits. The Hopis never ate grubs, insects, or reptiles, and they seldom ate birds. They relied most often on livestock after the Spanish had introduced this dependable meat source. The prehistoric Hopis kept both turkeys and dogs, but there is little evidence they they ate either one.

ARCHITECTURE AND CLOTHING.   Originally, the Hopis lived in very small villages, often containing only one clan. There they arranged their dwellings around a central court, which was used for public religious ceremonies. As the people came together in the mesa-top villages where a number of clans mingled, they retained this pattern, as far as possible, of building the clan houses around a central court or a *kiva*. It was, however, often not possible because kivas could not be dug in the rocky surface but had to be constructed instead in clefts on the mesa sides. First Mesa was so narrow that the clans were forced to place their houses in lines as there was no room to expand sideways. Because of these restrictions, the patterns of houses on the mesa tops were far from neat or orderly. The problem was compounded by the Hopi custom of using the stones of deserted dwellings to build new houses. Old Oraibi has been heavily cannibalized in this way, and several attempts have been made to make it a national monument in order to stop its destruction.

Unlike the Rio Grande pueblos, where houses were constructed of adobe brick, the Hopis used the native sandstone as building blocks, which were then plastered with adobe both inside and out. Because it gets very cold on the high mesa and the wind can be a vicious enemy, houses were built to have the maximum possible exposure to the morning sun. Their thick walls provided excellent insulation. Flat roofs were constructed of beams, small poles, interwoven reeds, willows, and twigs—all topped with earth. If the family wished to expand, they could easily build second- and third-story rooms, using the original roof as a floor. Corner fireplaces supplied heat for winter, but most cooking was done outside in fire pits. The first-floor Hopi dwellings had no windows or doors; access was by a hole cut into the roof. This was an excellent system for defense, but it did not provide the most comfortable living, and the Hopi abandoned the custom for more conventional doors and windows as soon as they felt secure enough to do so.

Hopi furniture was minimal, blankets being used for beds, chairs, and covers at night. Weaving was a major craft practiced by the men, who made not only the blankets, but also cotton shirts, pants, and dresses. After the Spanish had introduced sheep, wool was often substituted for the cotton. Aboriginally, Hopis wore very little clothing. Children, indeed, most often ran about naked, a custom that profoundly irritated the moralistic Americans when they arrived on the

Artist painting seated Kachina, Hopi Cultural Center, Second Mesa, October, 1973. Arizona State Museum. Photographer, Helga Teiwes.

scene. Men dressed in a breechcloth, yucca-fiber sandals, and perhaps rabbit skin robes for warmth. Women had simple, woven-cotton dresses.

ARTS AND CRAFTS. Traditionally, pottery was made in all villages. Today, there is still a little in each village, although for the tourist trade, First Mesa has monopolized this craft (ES-PC '80). The pottery of First Mesa is justly famous for its beauty and value. The women of Second

Mesa are noted for their fine baskets. Silversmithing and jewelry making are becoming more important as modern markets make these skills more valuable. Hopi kachina dolls, originally carved as play toys for children, have become very popular with tourists and other collectors. Some Hopis also do other types of wood carving as well as stone carving, sandpainting, and watercolor painting. Hopi arts and crafts today are an important tribal industry and contribute a great deal to their economic base.

Hopi silversmith solders overlay jewelry. Hopi Cultural Center, Second Mesa. June, 1973.   Arizona State Museum. Photographer, Helga Teiwes.

Silversmith thinning solder wire. Hopi Cultural Center, Second Mesa. June, 1973. Arizona State Museum. Photographer, Helga Teiwes.

MODERN LIFE

For good or ill, many Hopis have moved into the modern age simply because their reservation can no longer support its population through the traditional methods of farming and stock raising. They have been aided in their adjustment to modern life by two important changes in Hopi society: available tribal government is now able to mediate for outside services between the Hopis and the many federal, state, and private organizations who are willing to help them; and social services in fields such as public health, welfare, and schooling have increased to meet the new demands of this time (Nagata, 1971: 116–117). In spite of differing in many ways from the other Hopi villages, Moencopi is an

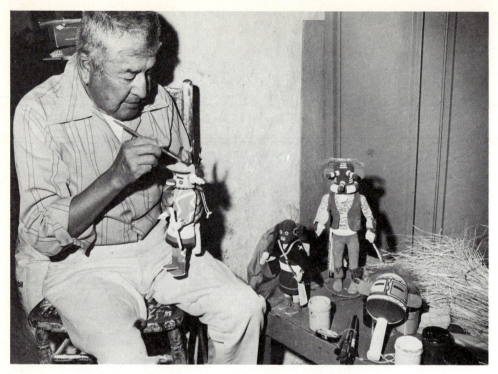

Hopi artist painting antelope Katchina. Shungopovi, Second Mesa. October, 1973. Arizona State Museum. Photographer, Helga Teiwes.

informative place to examine with respect to understanding how the Hopis are adjusting to modern life because Moencopi is essentially a community of wage workers. All of the material concerning Moencopi is derived from the work of a Japanese anthropologist, Shuichi Nagata, who worked there in the 1960s.

Moencopi: Background and History

As was mentioned earlier, Moencopi began its life in the late 1800s as a farming colony of Oraibi. Located 40 miles west of Oraibi, it has a climate that is warmer and drier than that on the mesa top. To compensate for the scanty rainfall, however, Moencopi has permanent water sources that make irrigation farming possible. Judging by the number of prehistoric ruins around, this fact was recognized very early. In historical times the Mormons exploited the possibilities of the site when they colonized Moencopi about 1875. After that Hopis who came there had the benefit of Mormon-built irrigation systems. When the Hopi Reservation was created, Moencopi was outside of its boundaries, and it was eventually made a part of the surrounding Navajo Reservation. There are, however, some individual Hopi land allotments within Moencopi, which account for much of the village area.

UNIQUE FEATURES OF MOENCOPI.   Why is Moencopi so different from the other Hopi villages? First, the fact that it began as a colony has many implications for its ceremonial life. The original settlers of Moencopi belonged to clans that were based at Oraibi, and they naturally returned to their clan houses there for all major ceremonies. Although kivas and dance grounds were eventually constructed at Moencopi, the only initiation held there is for the Kachina Society. Those individuals who wish to join one of the religious societies when they come of age and thus gain entry into the real power structure of the tribe must return to Oraibi or another Hopi village to do so. Second, because of its location and its history, Moencopi finds itself politically dependent much of the time. Because it began as a colony of Oraibi, Moencopi was originally governed by the Town Council there; and although the people of Moencopi had a voice in the council meetings, they were expected to accept the decisions of that body. At the same time, because they were so far away, they had little or no voice in decisions governing Oraibi itself. When Oraibi was divided by factionalism in 1906, there were Moencopi people who favored each side of the conflict; but they managed to live together reasonably well until the 1930s, when the double impact of stock reduction and the creation of the Hopi Tribal Council caused Moencopi, too, to split into two sections: Upper and Lower Moencopi. Upper Moencopi people were willing to cooperate with the Navajos and the B.I.A. personnel in nearby Tuba City in order to reduce their livestock; Lower Moencopi people were not. Upper Moencopi supported the creation of the Hopi Tribal Council and sent delegates to its meetings; Lower Moencopi retained its village chief and did not accept the decisions of the Tribal Council. Physically, the village split in two, although then and now some residents have been uncommitted, and some have lived on the side of town where their sympathies did not lie. By the 1960s the split in Moencopi was nearly complete. Each segment had its own separate land, kivas, dancing grounds, and political organization. Upper Moencopi had paved streets, a modern water supply system, and a modern sewer system; Lower Moencopi had none of these things. Those facilities that the two communities had to share were hedged about with strict usage rules so that the residents of one side could conveniently avoid those of the other side. Even the school shower room was strictly scheduled so that the people of Upper Moencopi could use it one day and the people of Lower Moencopi the next.

CURRENT PROBLEMS AT MOENCOPI AND ATTEMPTED SOLUTIONS. Today Moencopi, as is the case with every other Hopi village, finds itself in an awkward and unique political position because it owes allegiance to so many different jurisdictions. For both Moencopis, federal law controls the handling of major crimes, income tax, the draft laws, and voting rights. The state of Arizona oversees state income tax and voting, welfare benefits, and the public schools. The Hopi Tribal Police patrol the village and have jurisdiction over minor offenses against the public order. [ES-PC '80: Moencopi lies outside of the Hopi Reservation of 1882 and inside the Navajo Reservation of 1934. Police jurisdiction was originally a B.I.A. matter which later was assumed by tribes. As a B.I.A. matter, it did not unduly inconvenience Moencopi. Under the Navajo, it became impractical, so today Hopi police jurisdiction extends to Moencopi.] The Navajo Tribal Land Board controls land assignments for farming, and the Navajo Grazing Committee controls land for grazing. Upper Moencopi has had its own constitution since 1958, and it sends representatives to the Hopi Tribal Council. Lower Moencopi governs itself through the village chief (Nagata, 1970: 68). [ES-PC '80: This is as much self-government as occurs in Lower Moencopi because the governor exercises as much power as the chief.] Hopi-Navajo relations have always been rather strained, and it is to the credit of the people of Moencopi that they are able to make their system work in the face of these difficulties.

The factionalism and split jurisdictions at Moencopi have both advantages and disadvantages for the people there (Nagata, 1970: 69). On the negative side, factionalism has led to the deterioration of cooperative labor necessary in such tasks as keeping the irrigation system in good repair. When the people of Upper Moencopi work one day and the people of Lower Moencopi must work the next so that they do not meet each other, it is difficult to get the job done efficiently. Social control, usually effected through gossip and public pressure, has likewise been diminished, and the function of keeping order has by default been turned over to the Hopi Tribal Police. On the positive side, however, although the community of Moencopi suffers through factionalism, individuals and households may gain a great deal. Individuals are free to participate in the wage economy of the greater society, and households may use the wages gained thereby to buy modern appliances and household goods, which may be frowned upon in more conservative villages. Individuals are also freer to make their own social arrangements and to work out a pleasant life for themselves no matter what the rest of the population are doing.

Contemporary Moencopi

To understand how the people of Moencopi make a living, one must look at the village in relation to the communities around it, for very few individuals now support themselves solely through farming and grazing. These agricultural activities do, indeed, still take place, but they are supplementary rather than main sources of income. The necessary labor in the fields is generally done by men too old to work any longer or by young men who are temporarily unemployed and have the time to devote to agriculture.

ECONOMIC ACTIVITY.   Tuba City, an unincorporated village of approximately 1,500 people located two miles west of Moencopi, is a primary source for jobs. The various government agencies and bureaus located in Tuba City feel that Hopis are dependable, intelligent workers, and they are eager to hire them. So many Hopis work in Tuba City that a minor traffic jam occurs twice a day as the cars head in or out of the village. In addition to office jobs, many Hopis are also entering trade unions, which control jobs in construction and various other trades. Thus young Hopis with good vocational training are able to put that training to work close to home and need not move to a large city to find employment. An interesting fact about the Tuba City B.I.A. Agency is that, although it employs a number of Hopis, it has jurisdiction over the Navajos in the area but not over the Hopis. The Keams Canyon Agency controls Moencopi as it does all the other Hopi villages.

Another city important to the people of Moencopi is Flagstaff, 70 miles to the south. In addition to offering some employment, Flagstaff serves as the major shopping center for Moencopi. Even though groceries are available in Tuba City, many Hopis prefer to make the trip to Flagstaff, where they have a larger choice of produce and where prices are somewhat lower. The expenses of the trip, however, can easily wipe out any savings.

Wage work has become so important to the Moencopi Hopis that those who find themselves unemployed now waste no time hunting for another job even if it means leaving the village. Unemployment benefits are freely used, and if the unemployment goes on too long, welfare services can be obtained through Keans Canyon Agency. Any empty dwellings in the village, even small shacks, attract Hopis from the other villages, who move in and rent while they work in Tuba City. Such people, however, seldom become permanent residents. A job opportunity network often operates among related households so that one person employed at an agency can often see to it that a number of his or her relatives end up working there, too.

Little economic activity goes on in or around the village itself. No tourist attractions have been built, perhaps because much of the land is owned by the Navajos, and they alone would benefit from any rents collected. Four small Hopi-run businesses exist at Moencopi: two stores, a shoe repair shop, and a garage. Even these few establishments may be open only on nights and weekends because their owners work in Tuba City during the day.

THE FAMILY.   In all of the Hopi villages, the nuclear family is becoming the prevalent pattern of residence rather than the extended family, but nowhere is this truer than at Moencopi. With wage work rather than agriculture the basis for most of the family income, the nuclear family forms a foundation from which individual family members are free to leave if they find wage work elsewhere. Today most newlyweds spend little or no time living with the wife's parents; they are too eager to establish homes of their own, and wage work provides the means with which to do so. If a family needs help for some larger task such as farming, they call upon relatives from both sides, not just from the female side of the family.

THE TRANSFORMATION OF MOENCOPI.   In Moencopi many of the community functions that other Hopi villages supply have been surrendered. As so many activities take place outside of the village, Moencopi is becoming more and more of a bedroom town, with the result that the town leaders have difficulty getting people to do the necessary work on communal projects such as the maintenance of the irrigation system. The majority of babies are born at Tuba City Hospital rather than at home, the sick are cared for there, and those who do not recover are buried in the Tuba City cemetery. Children attend school there, after completing the first four grades at Moencopi Day School. Although a Kachina Society initiation is held at Moencopi every second year, boys wishing to join one of the religious societies must go to one of the Third Mesa villages. Many Moencopi families don't bother at all with this step, so that the first kachina initiation has come to stand for membership in the tribe. Few social dances are now held at Moencopi, and life in the village has become rather dull. On weekends most of the population departs either for shopping at Flagstaff or to visit friends or relatives at one of the mesa villages. It is then that the Mennonite church at Moencopi plays hymn tunes—to an almost empty pueblo. There is a Mormon church there as well, but the Hopis treat both as sources for recreation and welfare rather than for religion. Christianity is doing no better among them today than it did in the past. [ES-PC '80: This paragraph takes a very negative attitude toward the change and its effects on the life of Moencopi. I get the feeling that traditional life is viewed as a static thing whose value is preserved as though a museum piece. I feel there is much support for tradition and its teachings by people of both Upper and Lower Moencopi—their differences are in interpretation and applications toward what is the good life in modern times.]

At the conclusion of his book, Nagata (1970: 314–315) speaks of the "suburbanization" of Moencopi, which has transformed it into the most modern of the Hopi villages. He goes on to discuss how this has happened. Some of the more important developments include the following:

1. The replacement of a subsistence economy by a cash economy.
2. The absence of economic classes because of unstable employment conditions, scarce supply of skilled laborers, lack of investment capital, and governmental control of land.
3. The transformation of Moencopi from a farming colony to a wage labor reservoir for Tuba City.
4. The control of village secular functions by outside federal and tribal agencies in Tuba City, Flagstaff, and beyond.
5. The surrender of traditional religious functions to the villages of Third Mesa. [ES-PC '80: There is no surrender when, as a colony, they never had an independent system. Today, with Upper Moencopi, there is a developing autonomy in Kachina and social institutions that at one time may have depended on Old Oraibi for approval.]

On the whole, the surrender of vital community functions to outside agencies has led individuals to participate more in the larger society and less in voluntary organizations within their own village. Hence, Moencopi has become a part of the larger whole that is the greater Southwest in the last quarter of the twentieth century. Although some modernization has occurred at the other Hopi villages, nowhere has it advanced as far as it has at Moencopi.

Two Contemporary Problems

LAND DISPUTE WITH THE NAVAJOS. It is impossible to end this discussion of the Hopi without briefly discussing two problems with which the Hopis have been struggling for some time and for which solutions have still not been found. The first has to do with the continuing dispute with the Navajos over the land of the original reservation—land that by congressional decree was given to the Hopis "and such other Indians as the Secretary of the Interior may see fit to settle there on." [ES-PC '80: On the issues over land between the Hopi and Navajo Tribes, there are presently highly sophisticated political groups that have intervened, each interested in its own goals that have wider, and even national implications. Any general treatment of this issue runs the risk of conflict with one or more positions on the issues.] For a very long time, the Navajos, whose birthrate and population are both far greater than that of the Hopis, have been encroaching on land that the Hopis have considered theirs by right of long tradition and custom. Both tribes filed suit to quit-title in the land in federal court in 1962, and the court decreed that about 1.9 million acres should be used jointly by the two tribes. By 1974 some individuals had decided that the two tribes could not live together on joint use land, and the court ordered that one last attempt at compromise would be made. If this did not work, the court itself would divide the land between the Hopis and the Navajos. This is exactly what has happened, and the division of land by the court was completed in 1979. This division of land means that those Navajos living on what has been designated Hopi land and those Hopis on Navajo land must relocate. [ES-PC '80: Relocation is a legal reality and the Relocation Commission of the Federal Court has gone ahead with relocating of people in pursuance of law. There is constant political opposition to the relocation program, and each year there are new bills in Congress to change conditions of relocation, such as life estates, etc.] The problem is a huge one. As an example of some of the complications, I quote here the last paragraph of a letter sent to the United States Senate by Timothy Begay, the chapter president of the Navajo Hardrock Chapter; Percy Deal, the chapter vice-president; Etta Yazzie, the chapter secretary; and Phillip Bedoni, the council delegate.

> The current Relocation Commission estimate of the number who will have to be relocated is 4,800 people. The most recent study . . . found that a more accurate figure is 6,000 people at an estimated cost of over $200,000,000. . . . An unworkable monster of death and destruction has been created by Public Law 93-531. Past history has shown that the Relocation plan is not workable and future horrors are probably beyond comprehension at this point in time. [U.S. Senate, 1979: 106]

On the other hand, Abbott Sekaquaptewa, chairman of the Hopi Tribal Council, testified for the Hopi point of view during the Hearing on S. 1714 in 1978. If enacted, Senate Bill S. 1714 "would amend Public Law 93-531 by allowing the heads of households who would otherwise have to relocate to elect to remain where they are with their families for a fixed term not to exceed 35 years or until their death." Part of Sekaquaptewa's testimony follows.

It is with a deep sense of frustration and disillusionment that I find myself once again having to come before this Committee to listen to testimony that has been put into the records of the Congress and the Courts of the United States over and over again for the past fifteen years. I am frustrated because to me it appears obvious that Senate Bill 1714 seeks to overrule the decision of the U.S. Supreme Court, which considered all of the equities in this case before giving half of the disputed land to the Navajo Tribe and half to the Hopi Tribe. Enactment of Senate Bill 1714 would be a travesty on justice because it was the Congress that authorized the Courts to have the rights of the tribes judicially determined in the first place.

I am disillusioned because the Navajo Tribe has proven itself equally incapable, along with the whiteman's government, of honoring its treaty obligations. The Navajo Treaty of June 1, 1868, provides in part that the Navajo Tribe "will not as a tribe make any permanent settlement elsewhere", and that "if any Navajo Indian or Indians shall leave the reservation herein described to settle elsewhere, he or they shall forfeit all the rights, privileges, and annuities conferred by the terms of this treaty . . ."

Judging by the conduct of the Navajo Tribe since 1868, that treaty is not worth the paper it is written on as far as the promises of the Navajo Tribe are concerned. . . .

Studies are still being made and new ones proposed. Hopi people continue to be bounced back and forth between government agencies and officials unwilling and afraid to carry out lawful orders of the Courts designed to restore the rights of the Hopi people, and now I see this Committee itself vacillating by entertaining a bill which can result in nothing more than complicating and making more difficult the final resolution to this problem. This continued vacillation and delay is not only unfair, but if the bill is enacted into law, will continue a breach of faith and would amount to the Congress reneging on its commitment. We have been down this same road numerous times over the past several years listening to the same exaggerated claims of hardship. For example, when the 1974 Act was under consideration by Congress, the Navajos claimed at various times that 8,500, 9,000, and even 15,000 Navajos would have to move. The truth is that less than 3,500 will actually be relocated under the Act. . . .

In twenty-five years the situation will be greatly complicated by the large increase in Navajo population in the Hopi area. The practical effect is that the Hopi people will never have their lands restored because of the massive problems that will be created in another twenty-five years. In all candor, we must say that we fear that this is the true intent of this bill.

The Navajos will attempt to tell you today that the Hopi view this problem as only a land matter and that we don't care about people. Let me assure you that the Hopis do care about people. I am disappointed that in this hearing you will receive statements only from those people who are currently residing in the Joint Use Area. I ask you not to forget about those Hopi people who are not testifying but who have been forced off the land. You will hear the Navajos say that they did not force the Hopi off the Joint Use Area and that any depredations that occurred were committed generations ago. I ask you to remember the words of the Hopis who have given you their statements today that these harassments continue to this very day. Just last week, one and one-quarter miles of fence constructed around the partition line were torn down. Portions of fence have also been tied up so that the Navajo sheep can go into the Hopi partitioned area.

The people issue has been weighed by both the courts and Congress time and time again, and it has been found that the equities lie with the Hopi. . . . (U.S. Senate, 1978: 20–22).

Congressional hearings have already provided life estates for those Indians who are older or are so sick or disabled that moving would be an unmanageable hardship. The Navajos, however, are trying to lower the age for eligibility. [ES-PC '80: Another important consideration is that the land is overburdened with use. Relocation, among other things, is to alleviate this burden. Land is now 700 percent overgrazed, a condition which will take decades to recover if there was no burden on it and if appropriate conservation work is done.] In a situation with this many ramifications, any solution will undoubtedly be unfair to some people.

COAL MINING ON THE BLACK MESA.   The second problem for the Hopis concerns the mining of coal on Black Mesa. Both the Hopi and the Navajo tribes own some of the land involved, and the fact that they are feuding over the joint use area does not make it any easier for them to get together to fight the strip mining that the traditionalists of both tribes deplore. Very briefly, the Peabody Coal Company, a subsidiary of Kennecott Copper Company, made agreements with the two tribal councils in the mid-60s to strip-mine the coal on Black Mesa. They planned to build six coal-burning plants to produce electricity, which would be contracted for by 23 power companies called WEST (Western Energy Supply and Transmission). These power companies would supply the electricity not to the Indians but to cities such as Los Angeles, San Diego, Phoenix, Tucson, and Las Vegas. California especially would benefit from this arrangement because by California law no polluting, coal-burning plants could be built near its large cities. Not only do these power plants produce fly ash and sulfur dioxide, which darken the landscape of the entire Southwest, but they also use the water of Black Mesa at a frightening rate in order to transport the coal by slurry line. The Indians fear that if the water table is lowered too much, the springs upon which they depend for drinking water will dry up, and the agricultural reserve will be depleted. [ES-PC '80: The ecological arguments are mostly attributable to non-Indian environmental groups—although greater awareness and understanding of environmental impact today certainly strengthens the argument and the potential impact as claimed. All Hopi people, regardless of political leanings, are concerned about this.]

Among the Hopi, the controversy about the Black Mesa coal has widened the split between the Hopi Tribal Council, which signed the original leases, and the Hopi traditionals, who have always opposed the coal mining and who do not recognize the authority of the council to act for them. [ES-PC '80: The so-called traditional motive is to be the recognized political authority for Hopi—their efforts and appeals to Congress and to the UN are to accomplish this purpose. As with the Council, there is no precedent for a single traditional authority for all the Hopi people.] First of all, the traditionals feel that the tribe is not being paid enough for its coal. Peabody has contracted for 337 million tons of coal, 220 million from the Navajo Tribal Council and 117 million from the Hopi Tribal Council. For this coal they have agreed to pay the Hopis $14.5 million and the Navajos $58.5 million. They can, however, turn around and sell that same coal for $750 million ("Four Corners Battleground," *Akwasasne Notes,* December, 1971: 9). Secondly, the traditionals deplore the desecration of their land—and Black Mesa contains many sites that are sacred to the Hopis as well as being a sort of oasis in the desert with forests and grazing areas for livestock. On this beautiful plateau the coal company is producing huge, ugly trenches; piles of overburden, which they have removed to reach the coal seams; pools of black, dirty water caused by blocked drainage; and roads built all over the mesa top and sides without regard for sacred sites, the people who are living there, or the dangers of erosion. Although Peabody Coal Company promised to restore the land to its original condition except for normal wear and tear, it seems unlikely that they can do so with the best will in the world. On one small experimental plot, they found that seeding accomplished nothing when they simply seeded the overburden plowed back into the trenches, and they have announced no plans to bring in topsoil. The Hopis are also worried about the effect of air pollution upon their growing season, and as more and more of the proposed coal-fired plants are built, the pollution is increasing all over the Southwest. They also fear that the runoff from the spoil banks of the mine will wash down upon their cornfields below the mesa top and ruin the soil there for generations to come (Josephy, 1972: 841).

Because of these factors and others among the Navajos, the Indians are gradually succeeding through congressional hearings and actions at law in curbing the power of WEST and making the Peabody Coal Company more responsible for its actions. The profound feelings of the Hopis toward their land were expressed in a letter that the traditional chiefs of four villages wrote to President Nixon in 1971 (U.S. Senate, 1972: 79):

The white man, through his insensitivity to the way of nature, has desecrated the face of Mother Earth. The white man's advanced technological capacity has occurred as the result of his lack of regard for the spiritual path and for the way of all living things. The white man's desire for material possessions and power has blinded him to the pain he has caused Mother Earth by his quest for what he calls natural resources. All over the country, Living creatures die from poisons left because of industry. And the path of the Great Spirit has become difficult to see by all men, even by many Indians who have chosen instead to follow the path of the white man.

[ES-PC '80: The above is a very racist statement. All Hopi, without exception, have in many ways followed the path of the White Man, because he too possesses certain truths. If we believed for a moment that the White Man or his way were evil, then we cannot be Hopi.]

Hopi means "peaceful people." But these gentle people who have never fought except to protect themselves and their property have had a government foisted upon them by the United States, a much stronger power with whom they have never signed a treaty. [ES-PC '80: A treaty has never been an insurance against the onslaught of change and influence from a dominating culture.] Now their ancestral land, the very center of their existence as a people, is being desecrated because White industrial interests have declared that the riches of the earth are of greater value than the riches of the human spirit. At the moment, the Hopis suffer because of this decision. Who will be next?

A MORE POSITIVE NOTE.   But it would not be in keeping with the traditional Hopi view of life to end this account on a negative note. Perhaps the words of Don Telayesva or *Sun Chief* (Simmons, 1942: 381) can bring this chapter to a more appropriate conclusion as he contemplates his declining years:

> It is a pleasant future to look forward to; but until then, I want to stay in Oraibi and have plenty to eat—especially flour, sugar, coffee, and the good old Hopi foods. When I am too old and feeble to follow my sheep or cultivate my corn, I plan to sit in the house, carve Katcina dolls, and tell my nephews and nieces the story of my life. And I would like to keep on writing my diary as long as my mind holds out. Finally, when I have reached the helpless stage, I hope to die in my sleep and without any pain. Then I want to be buried in the Hopi way. Perhaps my boy will dress me in the costume of a Special Officer, place a few beads around my neck, put a paho (prayer stick) and some sacred corn meal in my hand, and fasten inlaid turquoise to my ears. If he wishes to put me in a a coffin, he may do even that, but he must leave the lid unlocked, place food near by, and set up a grave ladder so that I can climb out. I shall hasten to my dear ones, but I will return with good rains and dance as a Katcina in the plaza with my ancestors—even if Oraibi is in ruins.

REFERENCES

Aberle, David F. The Psychosocial Analysis of a Hopi Life History. *Comparative Psychology Monographs 21, No. 1 serial No. 107,* December 1951.

Beaglehole, Ernest. Notes on Hopi Economic Life. *Yale University Publications in Anthopology No. 15.* New Haven: Yale University Press, 1937.

Colton, Harold S. *Hopi Kachina Dolls with a Key to Their Identification.* (rev. ed.) Albuquerque: University of New Mexico Press, 1950.

Cordell, Linda S., and Fred Plog. Escaping the Confines of Normative Thought: A Reevaluation of Puebloan Prehistory. *American Antiquity 44,* 405–429, July 1979.

Cox, Bruce A. What Is Hopi Gossip About? Information Management and Hopi Factions. *Man 5,* 88–98, March 1970.

Crane, Leo. *Indians of the Enchanted Desert.* London: Leonard Parsons, 1926.

Dozier, Edward P. *Hano: A Tewa Indian Community in Arizona.* New York: Holt, Rinehart and Winston, 1966.

————. *The Pueblo Indians of North America.* New York: Holt, Rinehart and Winston, 1970.

Fewkes, Jesse Walter. Hopi Katcinas Drawn by Native Artists. *Bureau of American Ethnology Annual Report 21.* Washington, D.C.: Government Printing Office, 1903.

————. Tusayan Katcinas. *Bureau of American Ethnology Annual Report 15.* Washington, D.C.: Government Printing Office, 1897.

Fontana, Bernard L. The Hopi-Navajo Colony on the Lower Colorado River: A Problem in Ethnohistorical Interpretation. *Ethnohistory 10,* 162–182, Spring 1963.

Four Corners Battleground: Power versus People. *Akwesasne Notes,* December 1971, p. 9.

Hack, John T. *The Changing Physical Environment of the Hopi Indians of Arizona.* Cambridge, Mass.: Peabody Museum, Harvard University Report No. 1, 1942.

James, Harry C. *Pages from Hopi History.* Tuscon: University of Arizona Press, 1974.

Josephy, Alvin M., Jr. The Murder of the Southwest. In *Federal Protection of Indian Resources.* Hearings before the Subcommittee on Administrative Practice and Procedure of the Committee of the Judiciary. U.S. Senate. 92nd Cong., 1st sess., Part 3. January 3, 1972, pp. 831–843. (Reprinted from *Audubon Magazine,* July 1971.)

Kunitz, Stephen J. Demographic Change among the Hopi and Navajo Indians. *Lake Powell Research Bulletin No. 2.* Rochester: National Science Foundation, 1973.

Lipe, William P. The Southwest. In Jesse D. Jennings, ed., *Ancient Native Americans.* San Francisco: W. H. Freeman & Co., 1978, pp. 327–401.

Lummis, Charles F. *Bullying the Moqui.* ed. Robert Easton and Mackenzie Brown. Prescott: Prescott College Press, 1968.

Montgomery, Ross G., Watson Smith, and J. O. Brew. Franciscan Awatovi: The Excavation and Conjectural Reconstruction of a 17th-Century Spanish Mission Establishment at a Hopi Indian Town in Northeastern Arizona. *Papers of the Peabody Museum of American Archaeology and Ethnology, Harvard University Vol. 36*. Cambridge, Mass., 1949.

Nagata, Shuichi. *Modern Transformations of Moenkopi Pueblo*. Urbana: University of Illinois Press, 1970.

———. The Reservation Community and the Urban Community: Hopi Indians of Moenkopi. In J. O. Waddell and O. M. Watson, eds., *The American Indian in Urban Society*. Boston: Little, Brown & Co., 1971, pp. 115–159.

Sekaquaptewa, Emory. Personal Communication, 1980.

Simmons, Leo W., ed. *Sun Chief: The Autobiography of a Hopi Indian*. New Haven: Yale University Press, 1942.

Simpson, Ruth DeEtte. *The Hopi Indians*. Southwest Museum Leaflets No. 25. Los Angeles: Southwest Museum, 1953.

Smith, Watson, Kiva Mural Decorations at Awatovi and Kawaika-a with a Survey of Other Wall Paintings in the Pueblo Southwest. *Papers of American Archeology and Ethnology. Harvard University Vol. 37*. Cambridge, Mass., 1952.

Spicer, Edward H. *Cycles of Conquest*. Tucson: University of Arizona Press, 1962.

Stephen, Alexander. Hopi Journal. Ed. E. C. Parsons. *Columbia University Contributions to Anthropology, No. 23, Vols. 1 and 2*. New York, 1936.

Thompson, Laura. *Culture in Crisis*. New York: Harper & Row, 1950.

Titiev, Mischa. *The Hopi Indians of Old Oraibi. Change and Continuity*. Ann Arbor: University of Michigan Press, 1942.

———. Old Oraibi: A Study of the Hopi Indians of Third Mesa. *Papers of the Peabody Museum of American Archaeology and Ethnology. Harvard University Vol. 22:1*. Cambridge, Mass., 1944.

U.S. Executive Document. President Chester A. Arthur, Dec. 16, 1882.

U.S. Senate. Committee on Indian Affairs. Relocation of Certain Hopi and Navajo Indians. Hearing on S. 1714. 95th Cong., 2nd sess., February 10, 1978.

———. Relocation of Certain Hopi and Navajo Indians. Hearing on S. 751 and S. 1977. 96th Cong., 1st sess., May 15, 1979.

U.S. Senate. Committee on the Judiciary. Fact Summary of the Southwest Powerplants: Ecological and Cultural Effects; Recommended Action. Prepared by Native American Rights Fund. In *Federal Protection of Indian Resources*. Hearings before the subcommittee on Administrative Practice and Procedure. 92nd Cong., 1st sess., Part 3. January 3, 1972, pp. 791–804.

Voth, H. R. The Oraibi Summer Snake Ceremony. *Anthropology Series Publication No. 83. Field Columbian Museum 3:4*. Chicago, 1903.

———. The Traditions of the Hopi. *Anthropology Series Publication No. 96. Field Columbian Museum 8*. Chicago, 1905.

———. Brief Miscellaneous Hopi Papers. *Anthropology Series Publication No. 157. Field Museum of Natural History 9:2*. Chicago, 1912.

Wright, Barton, *Kachinas: A Hopi Artist's Documentary*. Flagstaff: The Northland Press with the Heard Museum, 1973.

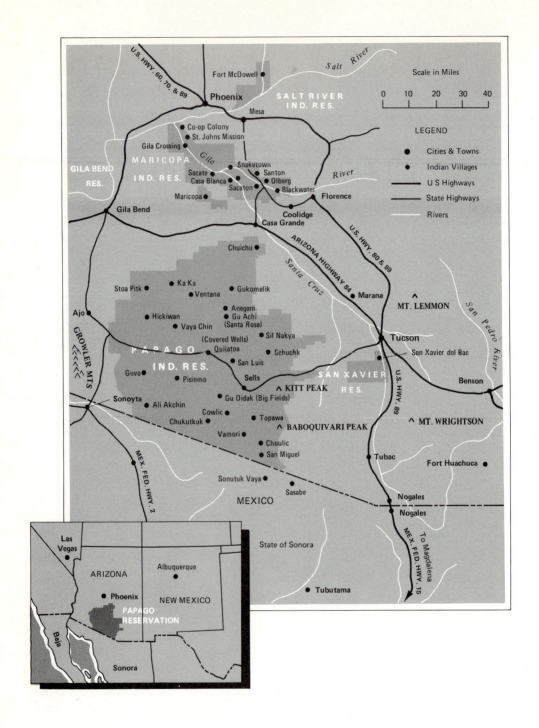

Scale in Miles

0   10   20   30   40

LEGEND

● Cities & Towns

• Indian Villages

— U S Highways

— State Highways

— Rivers

Salt River

SALT RIVER IND. RES.

Fort McDowell

U.S. HWY. 60, 70, & 89

Phoenix

Mesa

Co-op Colony

St. Johns Mission

Gila Crossing

MARICOPA IND. RES.

Gila

GILA BEND RES.

Snaketown

Sacate

Casa Blanca

Santon

Olberg

Sacaton

Blackwater

River

Florence

Maricopa

Gila Bend

Coolidge

Casa Grande

Chuichu

ARIZONA HIGHWAY 84

U.S. HWY. 80 & 89

Santa Cruz

Ka Ka

Stoa Pitk

Ventana

Gukomelik

Marana

MT. LEMMON

San Pedro River

Ajo

Hickiwan

Anegam

Gu Achi (Santa Rosa)

Vaya Chin

(Covered Wells)

Sil Nakya

PAPAGO

Quijotoa

Schuchk

Tucson

San Xavior dol Bac

IND. RES.

San Luis

SAN XAVIER

U.S. HWY. 89

Guvo

Pisinmo

Sells

RES.

Benson

GROWLER MTS

Sonoyta

Ali Akchin

Gu Oidak (Big Fields)

KITT PEAK

MT. WRIGHTSON

Chukutkuk

Cowlic

Topawa

BABOQUIVARI PEAK

Vamori

Choulic

San Miguel

Tubac

Fort Huachuca

MEX. FED. HWY. 2

Sonutuk Vaya

MEXICO

Sasabe

Nogales

Nogales

State of Sonora

To Magdalena

MEX. FED. HWY. 15

Tubutama

Las Vegas

ARIZONA

Albuquerque

Phoenix

NEW MEXICO

PAPAGO RESERVATION

Baja

Sonora

CHAPTER 9

THE PAPAGO
Those Who Live with the Desert

Oh! I have seen many things in this world and I
have been in this world a long time.

How shall I begin my song
In the blue night that is settling?
I will sit here and begin my song.

Two Papago songs collected
by Frances Densmore

Long before the Navajos reached the Southwest, the ancestors of the Papago Indians were living there. The southwestern cultural tradition had its origins more than 9,000 years ago in the desert food-collecting pattern of western North America located in the Great Basin country of Utah and Nevada (Willey, 1966: 181 ff). This tradition spread south and southwest to be combined with influences moving north from many places in Mexico and Central America. One of the most significant ideas to come from the south was the domestication of plants, specifically varieties of corn, beans, and squash. During the period 100 B.C. to A.D. 400, successful village agriculture was established. The Hohokam sub-area, occupying much of southern Arizona, assumed a distinct form at the end of this time, as suggested by the stratigraphy of Ventana Cave, 100 miles west of Tucson. The Hohokam located their towns in desert valleys where farming depended upon intensive irrigation. They were

"Oh! I have seen many things in this world and I have been in this world a long time." ca. 1919.   Courtesy of the Museum of the American Indian, Heye Foundation

"How shall I begin my song
In the blue night that is settling?
I will sit here and begin my song." October, 1966.   Arizona State Museum.
Photographer, Helga Teiwes.

skillful builders of canals, which either led river or arroyo water to their fields or, in areas where streams were not available such as the modern Papago reservation, accumulated and directed surface runoff to fertile ground. As the rainfall in this area is very unpredictable, the latter must have been a risky method, but it worked much of the time.

Because of their investment of labor in fields and canals, the Hoho-kam formed permanent villages, but these were not notable for architectural ingenuity as were the large towns built by the Anasazi in northern Arizona, New Mexico, and Colorado. Hohokam houses were simple roofed-over pits that looked like earthen mounds from the outside. They built no kivas, the round ceremonial structures so plentiful at both Anasazi and Mogollon ruins. In 1958, however, archaeologists excavated a pyramidal temple base near Gila Bend dating from about A.D. 1100 (Haury, 1974: 14). As we know of many flat-topped pyramids in the Valley of Mexico, this one shows that some culture traits must have been moving up from the south. Another striking feature of Hohokam sites was the large ball court, also borrowed from Mexico and Central America. An old ball of native rubber was found in a pottery jar near Casa Grande, but we know little about the rules of the game or how it was played.

Archaeologists have traced at least 1,500 years of Hohokam pottery, a rather simple buff-colored ware painted with red-brown iron oxide pigment. These people also grew cotton and made many fine textiles, few of which have survived because the Hohokam cremated their dead. They sculptured small objects out of stone and etched designs on seashells, using an acid probably made of the fermented juice of the saguaro cactus fruit.

About A.D. 1400, this thriving, long-lived Hohokam culture declined, and no one knows exactly why. The reasons most often suggested are changes in climate that lessened the water available and pressures from incoming peoples. Most anthropologists assume that the modern Papago and Pima are descendants of the Hohokam.

The Spaniards and the Papago

The first historical record we have of the Papago was made in 1687 by a Spanish Jesuit, Father Eusebio Kino, who met them at Altar Valley in Sonora, Mexico. Kino, a missionary-priest, soon extended his work to the north, where the Upper Piman people lived. He and his Jesuit colleagues were most successful in establishing missions in the area and converting the population to Catholicism. These missionaries succeeded not only because they posed no threat to Indian land, but also because they taught their converts how to grow new crops such as wheat, chick-peas, onions, and melons and, in addition, introduced horses and cattle to the economy. The Indians asked for more missionaries than the Jesuit order could provide, and some Papagos occasionally traveled to Mexico for baptism and instruction in Catholic doctrine. Kino died in 1711, and the Jesuit order was expelled from Mexico in 1767. The Franciscans carried on some work with the people, but for the most part native-modified forms of Catholicism perpetuated themselves. One of the better known and more tangible results of this time is the Church of San Xavier del Bac, located near Tucson.

In 1821 Mexico became a republic independent of Spain, and missionaries were no longer sent to the Papago. Twenty-seven years later, the United States fought and won a war with Mexico acquiring thereby a parcel of land north of the Gila River, where the Pima lived. Most of the Papago territory came to the United States in the Gadsden Purchase of 1854, leaving only a very small portion of it in northern Sonora.

The Coming of the Americans

Once the Americans had gained control of Papago territory, they exerted a largely beneficial influence on the Indians. No Americans were interested in acquiring permanent possession or even regular use of the Papagos' arid desert tracts. Instead they settled in areas adjacent to reliable water supplies and convenient transportation routes. The Papagos, who had long ago derived a highly efficient means for survival in their harsh, arid environment, were thus able to retain their land and at the same time ally themselves to American interests as circumstances dictated. All settlers in the area had a common enemy in the Apache bands located to the east and north. Raiding White and Papago settlements for cattle and horses, the Apaches occasionally took women and children captives as well, especially from about 1850 through 1875. After this time, combined Papago and American efforts succeeded in keeping the Apaches restricted to the areas north of the Gila River and in the Chiricahua Mountains.

Also during this period, the Americans made a sharp distinction between the Pima, who had a more or less constant supply of water and lived in the northeastern part of the area, and the Papago, found in the drier, southwestern parts of the region. This division reflected an ethnic division made by the Pima and Papago themselves. In addition, the Papagos acknowledged dialect and regional differences within their own group.

In 1874 an executive order created a reservation of about 69,000 acres surrounding the mission of San Xavier. In 1884 the federal government formed the small Gila Bend Reservation on the Gila River to the north. As the majority of the Papagos had fought on the side of the Americans against the Apaches, the government had never found reason to make a treaty with them to establish peaceful relations. This oversight eventually denied to the Papagos legal protection from later White encroachment. At the same time these two reservations were established, only 400 to 500 Papagos out of a total population of about 5,000 actually lived on them (Spicer, 1962: 136–137). The remainder were scattered over three million acres from the Santa Cruz River to the Gulf of California. Whites were interested in this land area because some of it was good for ranching, provided an adequate water supply could be secured by digging wells. Other places in Papago country had extensive ore deposits of copper, silver, and lead. Small mining towns appeared briefly, lasting only as long as mines could be worked for profit. Papagos living in the mining areas got along well with Whites and must have gained some knowledge of their ways, but they did not suffer the loss of critical resources like land and water.

By contrast, in the eastern part of Papago territory, conflicts grew from the appropriation of both water and grazing lands by the American ranchers. Nevertheless, many Papago men worked as cowboys and learned something about the cattle industry, with several Papago families becoming successful ranchers. Throughout this time, the majority of Papagos remained free of alien supervision and influences. Many who had lived in Sonora moved north to the United States because of disputes with Mexican ranchers over water use, political instability under Porfirio Diaz, and the possibility of a better standard of living through greater opportunities for wage labor in agricultural areas and the developing urban centers. By 1900 the Papagos had been exposed to the essentials of American culture in a gradual and palatable fashion. They had given up little of their vital natural resources or their patterns of traditional culture, but gained much that helped them exploit their environment in useful new ways. On the whole, they were very well prepared for the more pervasive American influences of the twentieth century.

PAPAGO LIFE BETWEEN 1750 AND 1850

APPEARANCE.   What did the Papago look like? Underhill (1938: 2) described them as "a gentle, poetic branch of the race which produced the Aztec conquerors." Many were tall and broad-shouldered, whereas others were of medium height or short and slender. All had a delicate bone structure with small hands and feet. Hair and eyes were normally dark brown. A quiet, self-contained, and reserved people, they disliked personal questions from strangers. Among themselves, however, they enjoyed laughing, joking, and singing (Joseph, Spicer, & Chesky, 1949: 7–10).

PHYSICAL GEOGRAPHY OF THE PAPAGO HABITAT.   The Papagos lived in a hot, dry desert where life could exist only along very narrow lines. The Lower Sonoran Desert extends north to the Mogollon Rim in Arizona,

The Papago name for themselves is "Tóno-oōhtom" signifying "people of the desert." ca. 1919.   Photographs courtesy of Museum of the American Indian, Heye Foundation.

west to southeastern California and into Baja California, and south along the west coast of Sonora and Sinaloa in Mexico. The area is subject to long-lasting drought and occasional torrential rains with considerable changes in daily and seasonal temperatures. Running roughly northwest to southeast are a series of small mountain ranges having wide alluvial valleys crossed by networks of *arroyos,* stream channels carrying water briefly only after rains. The mountains in the area are low in elevation, the highest being the Baboquivari Range on the east, with a crest of more than 8,000 feet.

Rainfall is scarce and unpredictable. In winter there can be periods of steady, light rain lasting several days, but summer rainfall comes suddenly and runs off quickly. In the mountains of eastern Papagueria, annual rainfall can be as high as 18 inches, but in the west totals decrease to 13 inches in the mountain valleys and five inches or less in and around the Growler Mountains. There are many years when there is little or no rainfall over the entire area. Temperatures vary widely, dropping as low as 15° F. on winter nights and going up to 120° F. on hot summer days.

FLORA AND FAUNA.   A wide variety of vegetation grows in this hot and dry land. Cholla cactus and creosote bush grow on valley floors; mesquite, in the arroyos; saltbush, wherever there are alkaline soils. In the foothills are paloverde, ironwood, and the giant saguaro cactus, which requires more than 50 years to mature. In the lower reaches of the mountains, shrub growth consists of false mesquite, yucca, bear grass, and gramma grass. Some oak and scrub pine grow in the high mountains. Thousands of other plants grow here, but those listed above have the most economic significance.

Reptiles and insects abound in this desert, and a surprising number of large animals live there, too, including the deer, peccary, mountain lion, coatimundi, coyote, jackrabbit, gopher, pack rat, and many birds. Bear, mountain sheep, and wolves roam in the mountains.

INDIAN NEIGHBORS.   The closest Indian neighbors of the Papago, both culturally and linguistically, were the Pima, who lived in the valleys of the Gila and Salt Rivers in south central Arizona. The Pima farmed near rivers, which gave them a dependable water supply. Their fixed location, however, also made them more vulnerable to formative non-Indian influences than were the Papago. The Pima differed from the Papago during the period between 1750 and 1850 in that they had a more concentrated settlement pattern with intervillage cooperation in water management (Hackenberg, 1962: 193). There was tribalwide political leadership among the Pima, functioning in war and mobilization for defense. The Pima were able to produce a surplus of farm products, which they offered for sale and trade, thus escaping from the need for wild foods except in years of poor water supply. Finally, the money they earned through the sale of their farm produce accelerated the process of social differentiation among them. Some individuals became rich, and others obtained jobs as farm laborers. Like the Papagos, the Pimas lived peaceably with all their neighbors except the Apaches, with whom they skirmished off and on until 1875, when the Apaches were defeated once and for all by American troops.

Three different groups of Apaches, the Chiricahua, Mimbreño, and Gila, lived to the east and northeast of Papago country. Of Denean or Athapaskan linguistic stock, they were closely related to the Navajo. These mountain-dwelling hunters and gatherers regarded all non-Apache people as fair game and subjected them to raids for agricultural produce and captives. The Papagos, aided by their desert terrain, successfully repelled most of these forays, but they never failed to take the Apache threat seriously.

The Papagos were usually left alone by other Indians and the incoming Spanish and American peoples. This meant that they were in a position to select what they wanted or could use from many sources. Much Papago behavior must be seen in this light.

FOOD RESOURCES.   During the period under discussion, 1750 to 1850, the Papago lived through a combination of hunting and gathering plus growing crops to the extent that fresh water resources would permit. The amount of water was the critical variable that determined whether cultivated or wild foods formed the central part of their diet for any given season. Papago families grew corn, beans, squash, and some European-derived crops such as wheat, pumpkins, and melons in tiny garden patches located at the mouths of arroyos where water flowed out of the wash channels onto flat ground. The men planted seeds in damp earth with *digging sticks,* long pieces of wood with one end sharpened and fire-hardened. Soil depletion was not a problem because the sudden torrential rains that filled the arroyos carried fresh soil from upstream. Cultivation, however, called for time-consuming diligence. If the ground surface was caked, seedlings had to be cultivated within a few days of planting, or the shoots could not break through the surface. Religious activities, particularly singing, were regarded as a necessary part of gardening. Women were responsible for harvesting and processing the crops. Some Papagos, even in the drier western portions of their country, irrigated their fields through a series of ditches and dikes to direct the flow of water. In the east, an occasional spring or well could be tapped through this system. Irrigation, however, never approached the extent that it did among the Pima, who could rely upon river water. The minor advantage of a slightly better water supply in the east was offset by the greater likelihood of Apache raids. There was no genuine advantage to be gained in growing more food if it was likely to be lost, along with the farmers' lives, to implacable enemies.

In years when insufficient rain fell to mature their crops, many Papago families traveled north to Pima country or south to the Altar Valley in Sonora. Here they worked in the fields in exchange for enough food to keep them going for a while. Thus the modern Papago practice of migrating from the reservation to look for seasonal farm work has very old roots.

Wild foods and animals probably constituted a much larger and more dependable fraction of the total Papago food resources than did cultivated plants. Almost every variety of cactus in Papagueria produced edible fruit. Prickly pear was eaten raw after the thorns had been removed; cholla buds were baked on a bed of coals for 36 hours. The fruit of the saguaro was made into a mildly alcoholic drink and a sweet jam. Wild plant seeds were ground into a tasty flour, many roots were eaten like potatoes, and the stalks of the century and yucca plants were roasted. When the women were able to gather more cactus fruit than they needed, the excess was sometimes dried and buried in family storage pits to be saved for winter, when the food supply was lower. Poor

Woman cooking corn cakes inside a cornhusk shelter; young girl scraping corn into a basket. 1916. Smithsonian Institution, National Anthropological Archives.

as Papago country was, no Indian hoarded property or quarreled about land boundaries. Generosity was the norm, and food surpluses were usually given away rather than stored. As all gifts of food were eventually returned, an essential theme of Papago social life was the interaction of individuals as members of groups having gift-exchange relations.

Papago men supplied a significant part of the diet through hunting with bows and arrows. Jackrabbits made up the largest portion of the meat supply, for they were large and plentiful, but ground squirrels and desert rats were also dug out of their burrows. Each village or group of villages laid informal claim to a hunting ground for deer. Deer were either tracked down on foot by deer runners who could keep up with them for days, or they were hunted by means of a special deerhead disguise aided with songs and dreams. Men who wore this disguise were called headbearers and were a specialist group who hunted all year around except in January and February. Because a headbearer had no time to grow crops to feed his family, a close relative often did this for him in return for venison. Deer were not plentiful; a headbearer was lucky to kill 12 deer in a year (Underhill, 1946: 86). Another system for taking game was the community drive, in which beaters drove deer or rabbits into a canyon that they had partially blocked with a brush fence. Once the animals had been trapped there, they were easy to kill. Hereditary hunt chiefs directed these drives after the appropriate cleansing ceremony had been held.

Although the Papago had owned cattle and horses since the time of Father Kino, it is not clear how important cattle were to the general economy during this period. Horses were traded to tribes in central and northern Arizona. Men were responsible for livestock management.

In general, it can be said that obtaining a predictable and adequate food supply was the greatest single challenge the Papagos faced. Remaining in their desert, they were seriously menaced only by the Apaches, but to survive there they had to use virtually all available food sources. This fact has pervasive consequences for social structure, their system of economics, and their relationship with the supernatural.

WATER SOURCES.   Water was also a critical factor in determining where the Papagos could live. Unfortunately, reliable sources of water and land suitable for farming were seldom found close together. The Papago compromised through migration between two villages. A reserve village, located at the foot of mountains or foothills where there was a dependable water supply, was occupied during the winter. During the summer, the people moved to their farming village near the floodwater fields described above. In the last century, deep wells have been dug in the farming villages so the intervillage migration is no longer necessary.

PAPAGO VILLAGES.   During the time that the Apaches were actively
raiding among them, the Papagos consolidated their small villages into
11 large defense centers, each representing one or more distinct descent
groups. From these centers, additional villages were gradually formed,
each sheltering between 50 and 100 persons. Occasionally, older, larger
villages were abandoned for various reasons, including the dictates of
cattle raising and the fluctuations in water supply and level of
population.

Papago dwellings were dome-shaped brush huts covered with
earth and scattered about the landscape haphazardly. The huts were
windowless and were entered by crawling through a small door. Each
village usually contained several extended families, but separate dwellings were maintained for each household. Residence was usually patrilocal, with married sons bringing their wives to their father's village.
Cooking was done outside over a simple fireplace with a fence of brush
arranged to keep out some of the blowing sand and dust. Usually three
or four houses shared one fire. Other units in the community were
small storehouses, open-sided arbors roofed with brush and dirt for the
hottest part of the year, and menstrual huts for the women to retire to.
Menstrual taboos were so strong that one secluded woman, seeing a
group of Apache raiders, could not bring herself to leave her hut and

Woman making baskets outside stick and wattle dwelling, 1916.   Smithsonian
Institution, National Anthropological Archives.

warn the other villagers (Joseph, Spicer, & Chesky, 1949: 53). According to Papago tradition, she would have brought supernatural punishment to the entire village by doing so. Larger villages had round ceremonial houses big enough to accommodate all the men. At least 25 feet in diameter, they were built of brush and dirt upon a log framework. Most villages had a racetrack nearby for footraces.

PAPAGO CLOTHING.   Papago dress was not elaborate. Women wore a skirt made of buckskin or cotton cloth; men, a breechclout of buckskin or cotton. Children went naked except in very cold weather. Both sexes went barefoot except when making long journeys over rough terrain. Then they wore sandals made of hide or the fibers of various plants twisted into string. Hair was worn long, and men enjoyed decorating themselves with jewelry. In extremely cold weather, individuals rubbed grease on the upper parts of their bodies for warmth. On special ceremonial occasions, the Papago painted their bodies red, yellow, and white. If a man killed an enemy in war, he blackened his face and remained outside the community for a prescribed cleansing period, after which a ceremony was held to honor him. Women, after puberty, were tattooed with blue lines from the mouth to the chin.

HANDICRAFTS.   A variety of fiber provided twine, which was woven, usually by men, into carrying nets and bags used by women to carry food. Basketry was a highly developed women's skill. Papago baskets have great esthetic appeal besides their practical value as food containers, sleeping mats, and eating trays. They also figured in a variety of ceremonies. Commonly employed materials were willow, yucca, devil's claw, and bear grass. Coiling was the principal basketry technique. Prominent design elements were dog tracks, saguaro, turtle, devil's claw, and juice-falling-from-saguaro-fruit. Women also produced pottery, but it did not reach the levels of development of basketry. Men made various weapons and ceremonial objects as well as the stone tools used in processing various food stuffs such as grinding stones for flour.

SOCIAL ORGANIZATION.   Papago social organization was conditioned by ties of blood and marriage and by the factor of residence. The group was divided into two halves or *moieties* called Coyote and Buzzard. Children inherited membership in the moiety of their father. Moiety membership had important ceremonial functions, being responsible for special rituals during harvest ceremonies and corn dances. Four or perhaps five *sibs* or clans existed, membership being exclusive and determined by patrilineal descent. The sibs may have been localized; that is, all members of a particular sib occupied the same general territory. An

Papago pottery making, Topawa, Arizona, December, 1972. Arizona State Museum. Photographer, Helga Teiwes.

individual belonged to both a moiety and a sib, but the relationship between them is not clear.

The most important relatives to a Papago were the members of his extended family, especially those who lived close to him. The difficulties of the terrain and lack of water made it difficult to keep in close touch with relatives who had moved to distant villages. Members of one extended family living in the same village were known as a geographic group, and this group was the basic unit of production, distribution, and consumption. Being a Papago meant being born into, living, and dying as a member of this geographic group, which also functioned to guide relationships with outsiders.

Important supporting social ties were marked by a number of mutual rights and obligations between certain classes of relatives. Brothers and sisters had close ties with each other, but, as they grew older, social convention encouraged them to spend their time with peer groups of their own sex. Boys learned proper behavior by imitating their fathers; girls, their mothers. After they had grown up, brothers cultivated land together, shared various obligations in ceremonies, and, if necessary, assumed responsibility for the members of each other's household. If a man died, his younger unmarried brother could marry his widow, although she also had the option of returning to her own village to be supported there by her brothers or remarried elsewhere. A widow usually followed her brothers' wishes in this matter. If a wife died, one of her younger sisters could marry her husband. Cousins were often regarded as siblings, although the factor of spatial closeness was important in determining whether or not a cousin was considered a sibling or just another relative. Older siblings had authority over younger ones and were responsible to a degree in protecting their interests. Sisters deferred to brothers, provided that such behavior did not conflict with the wishes of their husbands.

The father was the economic head of the household, and his sons supported him as he directed. As long as he was physically active, a father was held responsible for the behavior of his sons and their wives. The father bequeathed his land and water resources to all his sons and chose his successor as family leader from among them. If he had only daughters, his sons-in-law would inherit. Mothers bore the chief responsibility for the girls in the family. A mother, her unmarried daughters, and her sons' wives made up the women's work group that was responsible for gathering wild foods and for preparing all meals. When a woman was widowed, she normally lived with her oldest son or the one chosen by the father to succeed him. In cases of remarriage, stepparents assumed the positions of their predecessors and were treated as such. The Papagos placed a strong emphasis on maintaining a continuity of relationships within the family.

William Nelson, Papago near Blackwater, Arizona, 1919.   Photograph courtesy of Museum of the American Indian, Heye Foundation.

The oldest uncle on the father's, and at times the mother's, side of the family was expected to take a protective interest in the welfare of his nephews and nieces. Most of the time, he acted as a surrogate father. Relationships between him and his brothers' children were maintained by the exchange of food gifts. Aunts were important, too, if they lived near enough to the village. In some instances, a man would take his wife's sister as a second wife, and she would become very important to the younger members of the family.

Grandparents in the male line were the most influential leaders and teachers of the family and village. As parents were often away from home, seeking food, grandparents played an important role in child

Woman with burden net outside her house of tules and grass. Papago near Blackwater, Arizona, 1919.   Photograph courtesy of Museum of the American Indian, Heye Foundation.

rearing. Strong demarcation by sex, however, was observed. Grand-
mothers helped, advised, and were supported by granddaughters, and
grandfathers by grandsons. Once grandparents became enfeebled by
age, they assumed a dependent noninfluential status, and the others in
the family began to refer to them as younger siblings because they now
required the constant care given to children.

Husbands and wives supported and respected each other, although
wives were expected to defer to their husbands in matters of interfamily
relations and ceremonial activities. Wealthier men could have two
wives, but a woman had only one husband. Divorce could occur for
reasons of incompatibility, laziness, sexual indiscretion, or dissatisfac-
tion upon any grounds. It is interesting to note that available literature
on Papago divorce implies that wives far more than husbands were
responsible for the failure of a marriage, perhaps because they were
outsiders in their husbands' villages and thus had to make more of an
adjustment to married life than men who remained in familiar surroundings. Divorced individuals in good health usually remarried
soon.

POLITICAL ORGANIZATION.   As stated above, there were eleven village
units in Papago territory. A village unit consisted of a mother village
with its field site during the growing season and its reserve site for
winter, plus any number of offshoot daughter villages that had grown
up around it as the population expanded. A Papago individual gave his
highest loyalty to his village and its offshoots rather than to other village units. There were dialectical differences between village groups
and differences in customs, so that people preferred to marry within
their own village group if they could do so. As the Papagos lacked a
central government, each village unit was autonomous, although two
or more units could join together for work, gambling, or dancing.

Each village had its ceremonial leader, the Keeper of the Meeting,
who was responsible for the sacred objects, the village talismans, supposedly acquired from supernatural sources. Often these were found
relics left by the Hohokam, such as carved green stone frogs, slate pal-
ettes, and pendants. When not in use, these articles were stored by the
Keeper in a special basket and hidden in the nearby hills. Such a man
also knew the Wise Speeches or orations, which, along with the sacred
objects, could bring rain if given properly. The Keeper acted as adviser
to the village and chose his own successor, usually his eldest son or
younger brother. Other village offices included a crier, a war leader, a
hunt leader, a game leader, and a song leader.

The real governing body of the village was the council, which consisted of the male heads of each resident family. Customarily, it met
every night, and sometimes meetings lasted until dawn. The council

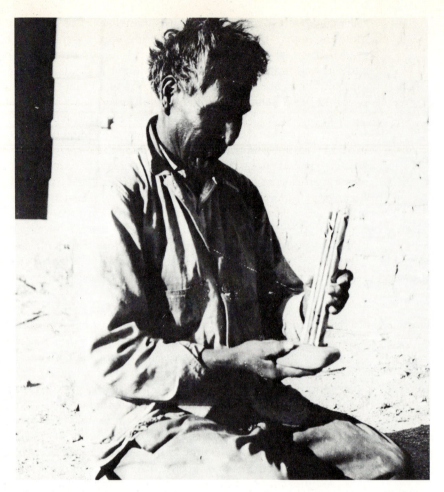

Edward Wesley, bouncing gambling sticks on flatstone. Papago near Blackwater, Arizona, 1919.   Photograph courtesy of Museum of the American Indian, Heye Foundation.

was empowered to decide upon such communal activities as agricultural work, hunting, war, and the dates of ceremonies and games with other villages. If there were no pressing matters requiring immediate consideration, the meeting became a male social occasion. The council was informally but clearly divided into two segments, the wise men and the listeners. Wise men were older and more experienced and were tacitly considered by village members to be more intelligent than the listeners. In many villages a wise man had to be one who had been through the lengthy purification associated with salt gathering or enemy killing. During a council meeting all wise men were expected to speak thoughtfully and well about particular topics being considered. Unanimity or near accord was required for decisive village action. Early in the seventeenth century, the Spanish created the positions of governor and his assistants in the southern and eastern areas that they influenced. The council remained, but its manner of articulation with this new position varied from village to village.

MISBEHAVIOR.   Although direct verbal aggression or open hostility within a village did occur, it could sometimes be successfully ignored by those offended. Because Papago existence was confined to the limits of a small group, an individual who gave offense to his associates threatened the support that was vital to his own survival. No one could survive for long in the desert on his own, and Papagos who did not usually conform to the expectations of those around them were serious threats to themselves and others. Two kinds of offenses were recognized: those directed toward individuals and those against society. Common offenses against individuals were selfishness, dishonesty, treachery, and sexual looseness. Gossip was an important sanction against such behavior. An erring Papago was never reprimanded directly, but he could be sure that his imperfections would be discussed at length by others when he was not around. As he would not know exactly what was being said, his imagination could be more brutal than hidden public opinion. Covert gossip was usually coupled with other forms of control such as the withholding of gifts of food and the withdrawal of cooperation in crucial tasks requiring group effort, especially those connected with food production. As far as the village was concerned, the individual and his family were inseparable. One was held responsible for the actions of the other. Hence, if a man was consistently guilty of any of the sins mentioned above, women would be unwilling to marry into his family. Because this attitude could have serious consequences for his closest relatives, they often called his misbehavior to his attention immediately. A person who was a chronic offender might be labeled a witch. Successful shamans were in constant danger of being labeled witches because supernatural power could be used for either good or evil. Shamans who performed witchcraft and other wrongdoers were also subject to supernatural sanctions. The form and timing of such retribution could be known to the victim only after the fact; hence this kind of negative sanction was a very effective form of social control, for it was difficult to determine whether an unfortunate event had supernatural origins. The only certainty for everyone was that misbehavior was punished sooner or later by human or non-human forces.

Major offenses against society were incest, defined as sexual relations with a relative; a woman's failure to segregate herself at menstruation or childbirth; and the practice of witchcraft. All of these offenses were believed to bring negative sanctions against the entire community. The village, for example, could be flooded or struck by lightning. Sins against society were first censured by immediate relatives, but if this did not stop the behavior, the Keeper of the Meeting or the governor expressed his disapproval. If this also failed, the offender could be rejected by his family, which in practice usually meant that he had to leave the village. The punishment for witchcraft could be execution. Other crimes against society were murder (usually rare among the peace-loving Papagos), adultery, which was punished by whipping (probably a Spanish innovation), and crimes against possessions such as the theft of food, food hoarding, and the moving of land boundaries. For these latter offenses, the Keeper asked the family of the offender to make restitution. A persistent offender was banned from the village for life. Homosexuality has been recorded as present among men only, but it was not regarded as a breach of public or private order.

Available literature gives the impression that most Papagos usually behaved, and misbehavior for the most part was confined to quarrels within the family. The rewards of conformity apparently were sufficient to ensure harmony. For most Papagos, indeed, virtue was its own reward, for the people placed great value on human life and the sanctity of the individual. The loss of a single person was a genuine tragedy for the rest of the group, because the labor and social support he had provided were gone. Group survival required personal interdependence, and most Papagos never forgot this fact.

RELATIONS WITH OTHERS.   Although the Papagos generally lived peacefully with each other, they sometimes fought outsiders, especially the Apaches. Papagos generally raided Apache settlements at least once each winter in retaliation for Apache raids upon them. These raids were considered successful by the Papagos if they killed one or more Apache adults, burned dwellings, destroyed food supplies, and captured children, who could be sold to the Mexicans as slaves. The scalps and possessions of a slain Apache bestowed great supernatural power on the successful Papago warrior, who had to be depowered before he could return to his normal village existence. During this ceremony, the power of the enemy scalp was transferred to the community well-being in the form of rain, magic, and increased fertility. War, however, did not hold the same fascination for Papagos as it did for Plains peoples like the Cheyenne. The good life was not to be found in the glories of war, but in living and eating well in the desert.

The Papagos maintained trade relationships within their village group, with the residents of other villages, and with other peoples such as the Pima, the Yuma, and the non-Indian residents of northern Mexico. Hunters exchanged venison for beans, corn, saguaro syrup, or melons. A dresser of hides could be paid in bushels of corn or beans. Cotton, originally obtained from the Pima, was exchanged for salt, buckskins, hair rope from horses, or baskets of beans and corn. Trade with other tribes often took place in winter, when some Papago individuals wandered about trading their goods or labor instead of settling down in their reserve village. They often traded with the same friends or relatives in distant areas year after year.

Labor exchange associated with food production, particularly harvesting, was an important means of binding various groups of people together within Papago country. Payment was usually made in food. Those invited to help were often relatives, particularly those who had had a poor crop for that season. If enough relatives were not available, neighbors were enlisted.

The Dance of Greeting and Blessing, which preceded intervillage games, was an important ceremony that tied certain villages together through the mutual exchange of large payments. A number of elaborately costumed people from one village traveled to another to dance and sing for them. The dancing and singing were believed to bring rain and other blessings through magic. Accordingly, the dancers were paid

Papago Rain Dancers, February, 1974.   Arizona State Museum. Photographer, Helga Teiwes.

Papago Rain Dancers, n.d.   Arizona State Museum. Photographer, Helga Teiwes.

for their services by the host village in food. These trips were typically made in fall after the harvest and were reciprocated by the host village the following year. Individuals from both villages often exchanged gifts at the same time.

The Papago have always enjoyed games, which served to maintain and promote social cohesion within and between villages. All games involved gambling. More goods were exchanged in the betting on games than during any other occasion in Papago life, not excluding marriage. The two main types of games were sedentary games of chance and athletic contests. Men gambled with the hidden ball game, the hand game, and the dice game; women played stick dice. Each village had its famous gamblers, who challenged those in other villages. Male athletes competed in kickball and foot racing. Women also raced, but over a shorter course than the men. Even children wagered small amounts on their games of ring and pin, cat's cradle, and foot racing. The stakes in all these contests were usually manufactured items such as mats, pots, and baskets.

Other intervillage games were long-distance racing over a course of 20 to 35 miles, and relay racing. These contests occurred yearly, usually in November after the harvest had been completed. Challenges were offered within a village, between village units, or with the Pima. Food, personal possessions, and occasionally horses were wagered. All forms of games had to have supernatural support to be successful. Villages matched their best runners, and their shamans attempted to work their magic powers against the opposition's runners. The contestants with the most able shaman always won.

PAPAGO RELIGION AND MYTHOLOGY.   Papago religion and mythology were rich and complex, as the following summary of their creation myth demonstrates. In the beginning, there was only darkness. Earthmaker and Turkey Vulture floated in a void. Earthmaker decided to make a world, forming it from a part of his heart. He placed mountains on his world, and in the mountains placed shamans. Earth and sky joined together and produced I'toi, a small man with a beard and golden hair. From the northwest came Coyote, a foolish but powerful being, who became the messenger for the supernaturals. Two spider people sewed the earth and sky together. Earthmaker created the sun, moon, and stars, and from his body made people. These people were evil, and the

Papago Indian girls playing "Toka." Santa Rosa village, Indian Day Activities. Papago Indian Reservation, September 21, 1979.   Arizona State Museum. Photographer, Helga Teiwes.

supernaturals destroyed them in a flood. I'toi, Earthmaker, and Coyote then each made a new population of clay, but only those made by I'toi were normal. Earthmaker and I'toi quarreled, and Earthmaker sank into the earth spreading disease as he went. The clay people of I'toi gradually came to life and became the Pima, the Papago, the Apache, and the Maricopa. I'toi claimed the Papago for his own, teaching them to make bows and arrows and houses. He taught them to perform the drinking ceremony to bring rain, the eagle ceremony, and the prayer-stick festival. After his work was done, I'toi retired to a cave on Mount Baboquiviri, but he still helped the Papago when they asked him to. The Papago became angry with I'toi because he raped their virgin girls at the puberty ceremony, so Turkey Vulture shot him with a gun. I'toi was dead for four years, but revived himself using the four winds. He went to the far west to ask help from the people who were to become the Pima and the Papago. In return for their help, I'toi created the deer, who came to the surface of the earth and drove away the Hohokam, "those who have gone." After fighting wars with other people far away, the Pima and Papago settled in their present country, and I'toi went underground again to reappear occasionally when his help was needed. When the railroad first came through Papagueria, he appeared in order to drive the game away to safety. Because of his help, the Papago believe they are conquerers of their land and people favored by the central powers of the universe (Underhill, 1946: 8–12).

THE PAPAGO LIFE CYCLE. What sort of life cycle did traditional Papagos have? Women gave birth in the segregation hut with the aid of other women. The mother, her husband, and other close relatives had to observe a number of restrictions before and after birth for their own protection and that of the baby. Children were nursed until they were two or three years old. If this primitive method of birth control failed and another pregnancy started too soon, the older child was in jeopardy, since there was no other source of milk for him. Childhood was prolonged until the onset of menstruation for girls and physical maturation for boys. During this time children were treated permissively and encouraged to get along with everyone. Good Papagos were those who blended in with their society and gave help to friends and relatives when asked. Good Papagos did not excel or stand out in any way from the majority. To be enduring of hunger, thirst, cold, and heat was the greatest Papago virtue.

After he married, a male was still considered a boy until he performed some action that stamped him as an adult, such as marked success in war, dealings with the supernatural, or achievement in trading, hunting, gambling, or racing. If a man dreamed properly, he became a shaman or lay curer, but it was not proper to seek dreams or special favors from the supernatural. These either came of their own volition, or they did not. Shamans were expected to be aggressive in their dealings with supernatural forces, but if such conduct influenced their relations with other people, they were suspected of being witches and dealt with accordingly.

All adults except the male *berdache* or transvestite and the very old were expected to be married. Marriage was regarded not only as a binding union between two adults, but also as the joining of two groups of kinsmen. A lasting marriage increased the chances of useful social and economic cooperation significantly. Divorce destroyed this cooperation and lessened the economic and social health of relatives on both sides. Marriages, therefore, were carefully planned and cultivated with continual exchanges of food between relatives. Divorce was infrequent.

One highlight of the summer season not mentioned before was the rain-making festival, which involved sexual and verbal excesses to bring the rain. During this festival, it was proper behavior to get drunk on *nawait* made from fermented saguaro fruit.

Warriors who were killed in war were cremated. In *Autobiography of a Papago Woman* (1936), Underhill mentioned another interesting requirement of war. When a Papago man had killed his enemy, he was required to withdraw immediately from the skirmish so that he would not contaminate his fellow Papagos. He blackened his face and remained secluded for a number of days until a purification ceremony could be held. Imagine the implications today if soldiers everywhere were made to do this.

Papagos who died a natural death were buried with their personal belongings in the hope that they would be happy in the afterlife and not wish to come back to haunt their kinsmen. The dead were feared, and after the mourning period was completed, the name of the dead person was not spoken again.

PAPAGO LIFE IN THE PRESENT

Since the period discussed above, the Papagos have been exposed to more than a century of non-Indian influences in ranching, mining, and religion. How has this affected them? Compared to many other tribes, the Papagos have been very lucky in that they have been able to take what they wanted from the cultures around them when they wanted it. Living in their vast, hot, dry country, they were never pushed aside by others who wanted their land and were not willing to wait for the Indians to adjust or change their ways. The physical survival of the Papagos and their right to live on their own territory have never been in doubt.

In 1917 the Papagos finally were granted legal rights to the land they had considered theirs for centuries. By executive order, the Sells Reservation of almost three million acres was established, the second largest reservation in the United States. With the establishment of intertribal peace under the Americans, Papago population zoomed, increasing to about 11,000 in 1960 (Spicer, 1962: 145–146). Tribal villages at first increased over the old territory until they totaled around 60. In the 1950s, however, many Papagos began to move outside the limits of their old territory in order to work as agricultural laborers or, as the schooling level increased, at city jobs. As Papago population grew, it embraced wide variations in patterns of settlement, subsistence, and family and political organization (Hackenberg, 1967: 481). Indian values, motives, nutrition, health, and environment were penetrated by non-Indian ways of life. In spite of this, however, the Papagos retained their ethnic identity, intermarrying and speaking their own language.

Papago country has seen many changes since 1850. Within three decades after the Civil War, the reservation had been depleted of game, stripped of its precious metals, and deprived of much grassland owing to mesquite invasion and severe soil erosion caused by overgrazing and drought. By the dry 1890s, many cattle had died and subsistence farming had declined. This economic base was partially replaced by new labor opportunities and imported food supplies. Improved health conditions, better housing, and safe water supplies contributed to population growth. During the First World War, the Goodyear Company began experimental cotton farming in the Salt River Valley and hired many Papagos as laborers. At the same time, a new open-pit copper mine at Ajo and the industrial growth of Tucson provided employment for many more families. Some Papagos who remained on the reservation supported themselves by cattle ranching whereas others found wage work for the B.I.A. and the Public Health Service. Many became agricultural migrants, dividing their time between the reservation and the fields of their employers.

In 1936, for the first time, the Papagos reorganized and created a true tribal government. It now has a chairman elected by all members of the tribe and 11 representatives, each elected by his own district. Tribal offices, along with health, education, and welfare services, are in the town of Sells, Arizona (Hackenberg, 1967: 480–481).

A strong trend toward the social, economic, and political institutions of the larger society has affected Papago country and its environs. More and more Papagos commute between urban and reservation spheres in a quest for adequate financial, social, and political support. At the same time, reservation communities have been holding their own and even increasing because of the gradual but significant increase in Papago population during the last 100 years. The Papago tribe is a viable political and social entity, but its achievements must be regarded as a qualified success because the quality of the Indians' lives, by their own standards, leaves much to be desired. It is their way of life in cities and on the reservation that is examined next.

Life off the Reservation

The people of Arizona make their living for the most part by working in various phases of manufacturing, mining, and farming. Arizona produces a number of metals, including about 55 percent of the nation's supply of copper. Many Papagos have jobs that are associated with these industries. In 1959, Jack Waddell studied 1,106 Papago men of employable age who lived off the reservation, and he charted their residence patterns (Waddell, 1969). Of this number, 767 had come from the reservation originally, 73 were from northern Mexico, and 266 had been born and reared off the reservation in southern Arizona. Waddell identified six major off-reservation areas where most of these Papagos lived and worked. The copper mining area around Ajo gave employment to 282 Indians. Papagos have been living in this area for several generations beginning in the first decade of this century. By 1959 about 32 percent of the total working force there were second-generation residents. The commercial farming area around Coolidge, spatially and numerically the largest, supported 285 Papago men, who depended mostly on wage labor from cotton farming. Tucson, the third area, employed 240 Papago men, many of whom had lived there continuously throughout their working lives. Occupations in Tucson covered a wide range of skilled and unskilled jobs. A significant number of Papagos living there suffered from unemployment or underemployment much of the time and vacillated from temporary jobs to seasonal farm work in the surrounding agricultural area. Gila Bend, which includes the Gila Bend Papago Reservation, was the fourth major concentration of Papago workers, employing 78 men. Like Coolidge, it is a commercial farming area. Papagos who work here have very strong ties to their reservation communities. The Marana area, the last major farming location in southern Arizona employing a sizable number of Papagos, extends from the vicinity of Marana through the Avra Valley west of Tucson to the Santa Cruz Valley. Sixty-six Papago men worked there. The sixth area, Phoenix and its environs, has had a small but stable Papago population for at least the past 50 years. Sixty-five Papago men were working there in 1959. The 90 individuals remaining in Waddell's sample of 1,106 lived mainly at the extremities of the areas of greatest concentration. Most were wage workers in the commercial farm system.

COMMUNITY ORGANIZATION OFF THE RESERVATION. Waddell (1969: 26–33) also presented a typology of communities, settlements, or residences that these Papago men and their families assumed. He identified six general patterns: rural family cluster, rural family isolate, planned settlement, off-reservation Indian village, urban family cluster, and urban isolate. In following these residence patterns, Papagos resembled many other Indians in the state.

The most prevalent type of residence, the *rural family cluster*, refers to a number of buildings attached to a particular commercial farming enterprise. These buildings were occupied rent-free by a permanent nucleus of one or more nuclear or extended families who lived there all year around. As long as some members of an extended family were working, all could live there. Other families came and went as the agricultural work available dictated. White farmers owned the land on which the buildings were located and were responsible for providing a necessary minimum of sanitary facilities. Camps were served by public health nurses, public school buses, clergymen, salesmen, and peddlars. Some camps had their own chapel.

The *rural family isolate* was a small category in which a single dwelling stood alone either attached to a small farm or separated from other houses of a camp. As long as one family member was permanently employed at the farm, the family could remain in the house.

Planned settlements were those designed and operated by some form of housing authority or agency. Rents were either free or very low. As in Ajo, these places often became segregated Indian settlements by default when only Indians desired to settle in houses theoretically open to all. These communities had planned streets and convenient access to nearby stores, churches, schools, and other services. The Pinal County Housing Authority Farm Labor Camp in the Coolidge Occupational Area was an example of a planned settlement. For the most part, planned settlements consisted of nuclear families occupying a single housing unit. Occasionally, an extended family lived in a house designed for much smaller numbers, but such behavior was discouraged by housing authorities.

Off-reservation Indian villages were Papago enclaves that had existed long before many Anglos lived in the area. As the White population increased and Whites moved in around them, the Papagos already there simply continued to squat on the land or lease the land from the new owners. Papagos in these settlements have continued to build their own adobe houses, ramadas (sheds made of branches), corrals, feast houses, dance pavilions, and chapels. In addition, they still use traditional village organization with an elected chief and councilmen. Off-reservation Indian villages generally maintain kinship and sociopolitical ties with certain on-reservation villages and districts. Examples of this type of residence are Gila Bend and Florence, where most of the men are farm workers, and Bates Well and Darby Well in the Ajo Area, where most work in the mines.

Urban family clusters were permanent settlements located within larger urban communities such as Tucson and Phoenix. Papagos living in these cities have a long history of dwelling in the same neighborhoods in order to enhance and maintain their family stability. These clusters often included housing occupied by other ethnic groups. Although the nuclear family was the principal social unit, relatives and friends from the reservation often came and went as they explored the possibilities of temporary work or adventure in the city. The quality of this type of housing varied considerably, with most people renting, but some owning, their own homes.

The *urban isolate* was a stable form of residence consisting of a single nuclear family or a single individual living in a non-Papago neighborhood. Papagos living in this fashion might or might not maintain ties with other Papagos and a home community back on the reservation. The adjustment of urban isolates to the urban situation varied from the commendable to the atrocious, from solid, hardworking citizens to skid row drunks.

One point cannot be overemphasized. The Papagos today constitute a highly mobile, widely dispersed population whose nature is not fully understood. It is impossible to generalize about "a Papago" because so many ways of living as a Papago exist. Despite the multiple outside influences that have affected the Papago in the last century, a vital part of the Papago experience is still Papagueria. Joseph, Spicer, and Chesky (1949) have described villages and village life in the eastern and western portions of the Sells reservation as they were in 1942 and 1943. Their description is generally valid for the present despite the significant changes that have occurred as a result of a variety of programs aimed at improving the economic climate and the health of tribal members (Waddell, 1975).

The Sells Reservation

What does the reservation look like? The old forms of housing, round structures with thatched grass roofs, went out of use about 1890. Today home to a Papago is often a low, earth-colored, one-room house, although large families may have several rooms or several small houses. Nearby is a ramada roofed with grass and protected by a paling of saguaro ribs or ocotillo branches from wind and sand. Hanging from pegs in its ceiling beams are various household paraphernalia such as bridles, the family washtub, and pots and pans. A forked pole holds a large pottery jar containing fresh water for the entire family. Water is still a precious commodity as it must be hauled to the house from deep wells that may be several miles off. Nearby are one or more tiny huts in which to store tools and grain. Often a chicken yard and a corral complete the encampment. Papagos are accustomed to spending most of their lives outdoors, eating, working, visiting, and sleeping there in good weather. In spite of this, each family has a high degree of privacy because the brush and the distance between house clusters shield them from their neighbors. House interiors reflect the degree of acculturation and financial status of their occupants. Catholic families usually display holy pictures or small altars adorned with candles. In many areas of the reservation this pattern is changing as more modern houses built by HUD or Community Development programs increase.

Coffee, tortillas, beans, and locally grown vegetables are dietary staples. Most diets are deficient in vitamin C, and many children show signs of malnutrition.

Papago house and ramada, February 10, 1969.   Papago Indian Reservation. Arizona State Museum. Photographer, Helga Teiwes.

Papago Indian Reservation, Sycamore Canyon, home of ocotillo and adobe, December, 1976.   Arizona State Museum. Photographer, Helga Teiwes.

Papago Indian Reservation, Sycamore Canyon, home of adobe bricks, December, 1976.   Arizona State Museum. Photographer, Helga Teiwes.

FAMILY LIFE.   Most households shelter extended families, three generations being common. Upon marriage, sons still tend to live with their
family whereas daughters move away, although the reverse also happens. The general prestige, status, or wealth of the parents, when coupled with the needs of the newlyweds, determines residence patterns
more often than not. Additional relatives may be present, for kinsmen
are welcome provided that they are willing to assume their share of
responsibilities. The most important people to a Papago are his or her
relatives. The mutual obligations described for the Papago in the past
still exist and show considerable vitality. Marriage is still regarded as
proper for all physically normal adults, although in recent years more
single individuals can be found than formerly. With few exceptions,
these single adults live off the reservation and work for wages. Polygyny is no longer practiced. Ideally, a marriage partner should be
selected from another village because the different residence implies
that the couple will not be too closely related. In practice, this usually
means that marriage between first cousins is forbidden, and marriage
with a second cousin is infrequent. Sexual relations occur outside marriage and often produce children who customarily live in the household
of one of their biological parents with no stigma being attached to
them.

Divorce can occur, especially if the bride or groom cannot adjust
well enough to the spouse and other affinal relatives. Poor adjustment
is defined as the failure to cooperate effectively in crucial social and
economic affairs so that the cohesive functioning of the extended family
is threatened. Family leadership is provided by the genealogically
senior couple. If the newly married individuals cannot gain and keep
the support of this couple, the marriage is bound to be of short duration. Clergymen may condemn divorce, but Papago public opinion
does not.

The birth of children, more than any other single act, solemnizes a
marriage, and a childless couple is rare. Child-rearing practices have
not changed much from the past. In a relaxed permissive fashion at an
early age, children are encouraged to emulate the adults of the appropriate sex who are spatially and genealogically closest to them. Mild
public and private censure is usually sufficient to curb the instances of
misbehavior when they appear. Almost all Papago children now spend
much of their time in school once a degree of physical and emotional
independence has been achieved. They remain in school until they
reach adulthood. A child now becomes an adult when he or she has
achieved an adequate measure of economic independence and marries.
This normally occurs sometime between the ages of 15 and 25. Despite
the fact that the modern school experience differs in many respects from
the Papago round of life, its influence does not undermine the results

of Papago socialization. For a number of reasons, most Papagos today have been adequately prepared to cope with the challenges of the White world. Their early years as Papagos also condition them to accept and often enjoy the implications of a Papago identity.

The family is the principal unit of production and consumption. Women defer to men, and the young to the old. Few, if any, decisions are reached and courses of action taken without the unanimous consent of the family. Children learn to conform to the expectations of other Papagos, especially close relatives, because the rewards of such conduct are so immediate and so generally satisfying that misbehavior is obviously self-defeating. The primary unit of social control is the family. Formal litigation in White or tribal courts usually is resorted to only if a very distant relative or a nonrelative is involved. As in the past, misbehavior is rare. Most prominent cases of deviance are associated with alcohol abuse, and even here wide latitude is granted before the abuse is recognized.

The sib–moiety structure that existed in the past is less important today, although it is still recognized in ceremonial contexts. Village and dialect groups still have more importance for the Papagos than tribal allegiance does. Communities are now more stabilized, and the movement between the field and reserve villages is no longer practiced. The home village is important to a Papago because it is his or her most immediate source of emotional, social, and financial support.

THE VILLAGES.   Papago villages are dispersed over a wide area much as Cherokee villages are, and few houses are visible from the highway. Although some dwellings may cluster around the school or church, many are in the middle of fields or located up small wagon trails. There are no streets or other spatial regularities. Often related families have houses clustered fairly close together. Life in these villages proceeds at a slow, measured pace. People work continuously but calmly, their days punctuated by occasional fiestas, roundups, weddings, or funerals.

Although reservation land belongs to the tribe, the land in and around the village is thought of as belonging to that community. Land used by a given family or household is apportioned by the village leadership, sometimes with the support of the district council. Villages are organized for cooperative undertakings such as livestock production, the maintenance of irrigation and other water facilities, and fence repair. There can be other community enterprises such as a blacksmith shop or a village well.

Village leadership is assumed by a chief and his two assistants, who are elected officials. A chief serves as a judge, mayor, and sheriff. He may, if requested, arbitrate personal disputes over family problems, division of lands, disagreements over water, damages done by straying cattle, and other mundane sources of discord. He is also the head of the village council, which assigns farmlands, resolves problems associated with livestock, and can serve as a point of contact with the B.I.A. In the past, unanimity was necessary for action. In the present, there are so many decisions for this body to make that there is no time for the sort of discussion that was formerly required for complete accord. Discussion, however, proceeds apace, often without resolution. Hence the effectiveness of this body is limited. The responsibility for decisive action frequently has been shifted to various tribal facilities, often with unsatisfactory results.

At present, there are far more intervillage political activities on the eastern side of the reservation than on the west. Some ties of an economic nature exist also. For example, if a village is without a general store, residents may patronize one in a nearby village. Feelings of unity still exist between parent and offshoot daughter villages to the extent that intermarriage between them is frequent.

After the family and village, the dialect group is of prime importance as a social entity. Its significance centers around the fact that the dialect group consists of both near and distant relatives plus those who share common mannerisms, traditions, and pronunciation. There are about six central dialect groups now on the reservation plus several mixed groups in areas where central dialect groups adjoin. The various dialect groups in some cases may well represent the different origins of those now calling themselves Papago.

As mentioned earlier, in 1936 the Papagos ratified a constitution that divides the main reservation into nine districts, the small reservations at San Xavier and Gila Bend constituting two additional districts for a total of 11. Each district was empowered to elect a council to provide local self-government and to send two delegates to the tribal council to serve for two years or until recalled and replaced by the district council. It is important to keep in mind that this tribal structure came into existence largely because some internal reservation facility was necessary to attempt to implement a wide variety of economic and social development programs imposed by the federal government to improve the welfare of the Papago people. The Papagos themselves agreed that the quality of their lives could be improved in many respects, especially in the areas of economics and personal and public health. The tribal council today is not an effective decision-making body, not only because the many programs that it was expected to foster have not lived up to either Papago or federal expectations, but also because it is so difficult for the council members to reach a consensus. The reasons for this failure include the great diversity of the Indian communities that renders any uniform improvement program impotent, the difficulties that the residents of Papago communities have in keeping pace with the rapid and multiple changes outside the reservations, and the unsatisfactory form of articulation that the Papagos by law must maintain with the federal government. The specifics of this situation for the Papagos and other tribes are discussed in a report by the John Hay Whitney Foundation (*Indian Tribes as Governments*, 1975).

THE PAPAGOS AND THE DOMINANT SOCIETY. Given these and other limitations, the majority of Papagos now find themselves out of step with the ever-encroaching dominant society. Although most Papagos appear to be well adjusted as individuals, they are unable to cooperate as part of a tribal political unit. Unfortunately, the modern situation increasingly calls for this sort of collective response. Papagos often lack the necessary levels of formal education and health to exploit the few genuine opportunities for betterment that do appear. As a result, they will continue to exist on those products of reservation life and the American world that their limited means can provide. A prognosis of the situation is not favorable. The future of the Papagos as a tribe seems grim largely because at present they are a tribe in name only. The chances of developing this greater political maturity necessary to meet the demands of the twentieth century appear to be slight because there are so many barriers in the way of the massive economic development required to support such a policy. Hackenberg (1962: 193) argued that the Papago could not become industrial agriculturalists until they were capable of coming to terms with a new set of agricultural variables, including credit, land preparation, fertilization, equipment rental, seed selection, strict water measurement, and systematic irrigation. He implied that their chances of soon gaining the sophistication necessary to understand these variables was slight. A former commissioner of Indian Affairs, Robert L. Bennett (1968: 670), was even more pessimistic when he called the Papago the most economically depressed of all American groups. Although he felt that the possibility of mineral development offered some hope, he felt that the tribe had little chance of prosperity as long as they retained their scattered and loosely related small villages and failed to develop any system of community cooperation.

The Papagos continue to believe that it is necessary to come to terms not only with the secular but the sacred as well. It is difficult to generalize about Papago religious beliefs, for both on and off the reservation people adhere to aboriginal beliefs as well as to the Sonoran Catholic, Roman Catholic, Presbyterian, and Baptist faiths. Belief in these religions varies according to district and age. Catholicism is the most common religion, and fiestas are held in most villages to observe a saint's day, All-Souls' Day, Christmas, and Easter. A mass, dancing, and eating structure these celebrations. Some Papago Catholics make pilgrimages to the church of San Francisco Xavier at Magdalena in Sonora, Mexico, each year. Such an activity is not only of a religious nature, but has many elements of secular recreation as well. Men can drink heavily in the bars while women shop and gossip, but the acquiring of supernatural support for the entire spectrum of life is the central concern. The native religion is still important to almost all Papagos except for the strictest Presbyterians, and many people combine elements of it with Christianity. Even the Presbyterians still visit the old medicine men. In ceremonies for rain and good health, villagers continue to circle-dance and use their fetishes. The village games and races, however, have been abandoned because their preparation and staging are now impractical.

The Papagos have grave health problems, and it is probably not unusual for a Papago to be unable to work for several weeks or even months out of the year because of poor health. They still believe that misfortune and illness come to a person because supernatural forces have been offended intentionally or otherwise. Ghosts can bring sickness as can the spirits of animals. Evil thoughts produce illness. When a Papago is sick on the reservation, he will consult a medicine man who determines the origin of his illness. Treatment is then administered by singing. A medicine man can also predict weather. In general, he has the obligation of keeping evil away from his village and working to ensure the general welfare of its inhabitants. Nearly every village today has a medicine man, and a few are probably regarded by some as being bad medicine men or witches.

Papagos appear to be eclectic in their approach to the supernatural. The source of supernatural support is far less important than its results. The Papagos believe that to be successful in this life, the individual must obtain the spiritual sponsorship of all those forces capable of giving it. Thus a strict adherence to one creed is to ignore too much that could be of potential help.

In conclusion, I quote a letter written to the *Tucson Daily Citizen* by a Papago Indian on February 26, 1971. Nothing could show better how difficult it is for the calm, easygoing Papagos to adjust to modern civilization.

> I am a Papago Indian very proud to be one, and what I want to say I hope you'll understand for I don't know much about the so-called English grammar.
>
> The main problem I'm concerned with is unemployment for Papago Indians. Some of the problems I have in keeping a job I will discuss. I have worked with white people, but couldn't get along with them or maybe they didn't get along with me.
>
> The people I worked with were all non-Indians. They talked behind my back (luckily I had a nosey friend to tell me all this.) They criticized the

way I dressed. A great many Papagos disapprove of the white shirt and necktie bit. This is one reason why the Papago turns away clerical jobs, or vice versa. The Papago tries to be neat in every way—if he can afford it.

They criticized how quiet I was. They wished they hired someone else who'd be a little bit more lively. Well, this Indian isn't concerned about how much he should open his mouth, but rather how he should get his work done.

They criticized how rude I was not to say: good morning, good afternoon, hi, goodbye, etc., to every one of them. To the Papago it is silly to greet each other with the same word day after day, because it will only become meaningless.

The Papago, when greeting on a morning or anytime, will say what he wants to, but it is no greeting like "good morning." At times he will ask "Are you feeling fine," which I think has a little more meaning than the word, "Hi."

They criticized how rude it was not to introduce myself to a new person on the job. If a Papago wants to know who somebody is, he will ask someone else or he'll hear his name mentioned. You know, to the Papago it's quite funny to see people shake hands when introduced. Shaking hands is done only for religious purposes. When meeting a new person a smile shows the person is already accepted as a friend.

36th Annual Papago Rodeo and Fair, Junior Rodeo Contestants. Papago Indian Reservation, November 17, 1972.   Arizona State Museum Photo. Photographer, Helga Teiwes.

They criticized how rude I was not to say thank you when done a favor. To the Papago there is no such word. When a favor is done or a gift is given, he shows appreciation by returning something of equal value to the giver. (Those people never saw the favors I returned which meant thank you.)

These are some of the reasons I was told to quit my job. So now I'm looking for another, knowing I'll face the same problems in the white society. [Quoted in Weaver and Cartell, 1974: 85–86]

Even a superficial glance at Papago life today suggests that they face as many threats to their survival now as their early nineteenth-century ancestors did as hunters, gatherers, and farmers living in the desert. The reasons for their perilous state center around the fact that the Papagos, perhaps more than ever before, are competing for limited resources with limited means and with a larger number and variety of people. The continuing Papago emphasis on resourceful endurance in the face of hardship, however, serves them well, given the abrasive dimensions of their present existence.

REFERENCES

Baylor, Byrd, *Yes Is Better Than No.* New York: Charles Scribner's Sons, 1977.

Bennett, Robert L. Problems and Prospects in Developing Indian Communities. *Arizona Law Review 10*, 649–660, Winter 1968.

Castetter, Edward F., and Willis H. Bell. *Pima and Papago Indian Agriculture.* Albuquerque: University of New Mexico Press, 1942.

Densmore, Frances. Papago Music. *Bulletin 90. Bureau of American Ethnology, Smithsonian Institution.* Washington, D.C.: Government Printing Office, 1929.

Fontana, Bernard L. Contemporary Indians. In Thomas Weaver, ed., *Indians of Arizona: A Contemporary Perspective.* Tucson: University of Arizona Press, 1974, pp. 54–71.

———, ed. Jose Lewis Brennan's Account of Papago "Customs and Other References." *Ethnohistory 6*, 226–237, 1959.

———, et al. "Papago Indian Pottery." *American Ethnological Society Monograph No. 38.* Seattle: University of Washington Press, 1962.

Hackenberg, Robert A. Economic Alternatives in Arid Lands: A Case Study of the Pima and Papago Indians. *Ethnology 1*, 186–196, April 1962.

———. The Parameters of an Ethnic Group: A Method for Studying the Total Tribe. *American Anthropologist 69*, 478–492, October 1967.

Haury, Emil W. Before History. In Thomas Weaver, ed., *Indians of Arizona: A Contemporary Perspective.* Tucson: University of Arizona Press, 1974.

Indian Tribes as Governments. New York: John Hay Whitney Foundation, 1975. Mimeographed.

Joseph, Alice, Rosamond B. Spicer, and Jane Chesky. *The Desert People: A Study of the Papago Indians.* Chicago: University of Chicago Press, 1949.

Lumholtz, Carl. *New Trails in Mexico: An Account of One Year's Exploration in North-Western Sonora, Mexico, and South-Western Arizona, 1909–1910*. New York: Charles Scribner's Sons, 1912.

Spicer, Edward H. *Cycles of Conquest: The Impact of Spain, Mexico, and the United States on the Indians of the Southwest, 1533–1960*. Tucson: University of Arizona Press, 1962.

Underhill, Ruth. The Autobiography of a Papago Woman. *Memoirs of the American Anthropological Association No. 46*. American Anthropological Association, 1936.

———. *Singing for Power: The Song Magic of the Papago Indians of Southern Arizona*. Berkeley: University of California Press, 1938.

———. Social Organization of the Papago Indians. *Columbia University Contributions to Anthropology 30*. New York: Columbia University Press, 1939.

———. Papago Indian Religion. *Columbia University Contributions to Anthropology 33*. New York: Columbia University Press, 1946.

Waddell, Jack O. Papago Indians at Work. *Anthropological Papers of the University of Arizona, No. 12*. Tucson: University of Arizona Press, 1969.

———. Personal communication, August 18, 1975.

Weaver, Thomas, and Ruth Hughes Gartell. The Urban Indian: Man of Two Worlds. In Thomas Weaver, ed., *Indians of Arizona. A Contemporary Perspective*. Tucson: University of Arizona Press, 1974, pp. 72–96.

Willey, Gordon. *An Introduction to American Archaeology*. Vol. 1, *North and Middle America*. Englewood Cliffs, New Jersey: Prentice-Hall, Inc., 1966.

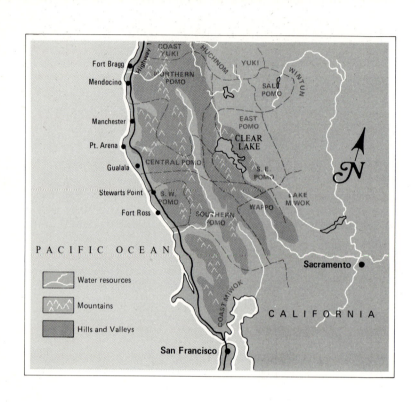

Fort Bragg

Mendocino

Manchester

Pt. Arena

Gualala

Stewarts Point

Fort Ross

Highway 1

COAST YUKI

NORTHERN POMO

HUCHNOM

YUKI

WINTUN

SALT POMO

EAST POMO

CLEAR LAKE

CENTRAL POMO

S. E. POMO

S. W. POMO

LAKE MIWOK

WAPPO

SOUTHERN POMO

PACIFIC OCEAN

N

Water resources

Mountains

Hills and Valleys

COAST MIWOK

Sacramento

CALIFORNIA

San Francisco

CHAPTER *10*

THE POMO INDIANS OF CALIFORNIA
The Survivors

[Coyote] treated us Indians in the woods and gave us very healthy food to eat so our people never got sick but grew old and just died. They didn't have the sweet food the white men brought that makes us sick.

A Pomo myth from *Kashaya Texts* by Robert Oswalt

Like the Iroquois Indians in New York, the Pomo of California are not really a tribe. Seven different languages were spoken by the people that anthropologists have called the Pomo, and these languages were not mutually intelligible. These groups were the Southwestern Pomo or Kashaya, the Southern Pomo, the Central Pomo, the Northern Pomo, the Northeastern Pomo, the Eastern Pomo, and the Southeastern Pomo. The seven languages were all part of a widespread linguistic stock called Hokan. Within these seven groups, the Pomo were divided into smaller tribelets or villages, and each of these divisions spoke its own distinctive dialect of one of the seven languages. It is difficult to generalize about Pomo culture, for there was not one culture but a number of closely related types. Keep in mind, therefore, that the description of Pomo life given here may not have been true for all Pomo groups at a given time or through time.

The Pomo lived in an area immediately north of San Francisco Bay, extending about 130 miles north and south and about 100 miles east and west. Crucial geographic features of this region include the sea-

Pomo woman grinding acorns. n.d.   Photograph courtesy of Museum of the American Indian, Heye Foundation.

coast, the coastal mountains, and the hills and valleys of the central and eastern area. The Pacific coast was lined with rocky cliffs alternating with sandy beaches and some grasslands. Many small streams and rivers flowed into the ocean. The coastal mountains rose from coastal foot hills to elevations ranging between 3,000 and 6,000 feet. This mountainous area was divided by many waterways and covered with a thick growth of redwood forest. The central area consisted of rolling hills and flat valleys on both banks of the Russian River, which flowed from north to south and then west into the ocean. Land elevation in the Russian River area was about 600 feet. Oak forests predominated but were supplemented by tracts of chaparral and belts of grassland. Vegetation in the eastern portion of Pomo country resembled that in the Russian River area. Here the major water source and predominant geographical feature was Clear Lake, 25 miles long and more than seven miles wide in places. Snow fell only on the higher hills around Clear Lake in the winter months and was not a dominant feature of the weather. The climate was Mediterranean, with an annual rainfall between 20 and 30 inches in the south and as much as 40 inches in the north. Rainfall was largely seasonal, occurring for the most part during winter and early spring. Inland temperatures ranged from a low of 45° F. to a high of 100° F. in the summer and between 26° F. and 70° F. in the winter. Along the coast, winter and summer temperatures were slightly cooler. Prevailing winds and rains came from the west, and the Pacific Ocean was the dominant influence on various weather patterns.

The Pomo were surrounded by a number of interesting and culturally varied Indian groups. The Coast Yuki and Yuki proper to the north were similar to the Pomo in that they were hunters and gatherers. They were rude and hardy mountaineers, much given to gambling and resentment (Kroeber, 1925: 169). Yuki population peaked in the late eighteenth century at about 2,000. Between the two Yuki branches lived a small group called the Huchnom, whose culture also seemed like a loose reworking of Pomo life. To the east of the Pomo were more than 12,000 Wintun, who had an elaborate culture that included secret societies. They traded widely with other peoples in the area. South and southwest of the Pomo lived over 11,000 Lake Miwok and Coast Miwok who, like the Wintun, were Penutian speakers. The Coast Miwok were the first native people to be seen by the English adventurer Sir Francis Drake in 1579. The Indians probably regarded Drake and those with him as their own returned dead, for they greeted them with great veneration and wailing, lacerating themselves and sacrificially burning feathers. In the mountains and mountain valleys lived the Wappo, a small remnant of about 1,000 in 1770, who probably were remnants of a much bigger group. Their culture gradually became similar to their politically dominant neighbors, the Pomo.

With the possible exception of the Wintun, the Pomo stood well above their neighbors in size of territory occupied, population numbers, and probably a more efficient kind of exploitation of their natural and social environment. At the beginning of the nineteenth century, the total Pomo population was approximately 14,410 individuals, occupying a territory of 2,454 square miles (Baumhoff, 1963: 231). In general, the Pomo were an insular, largely independent people who were content to live out their lives along well-defined lines dictated by utility and tradition. This was made possible by a good ecological balance and isolation from politically and economically expanding groups.

Although the Pomo area is rich in archaeological sites, little work has been done, so it is impossible to say exactly when they reached California or what their cultural background was before they got there. Clamshell disk beads manufactured and traded by the Pomo entered the exchange system of northern California about A.D. 1500, so their residence there must extend at least this far back (Bean & Theodoratus, 1978: 298). California was a marginal area, difficult of access, and many small groups made their way there over a long period of time (Heizer, 1964, 131). Harrington (1942) and Beardsley (1948) were convinced that the Pomo were the first settlers in the region.

The following description of Pomo life focuses on the late eighteenth century, a time just prior to the domination of incoming European-derived peoples. Although I give a general ethnographic description for the Pomo as a whole, remember that there was considerable regional diversity among the seven subgroups. Unless otherwise noted, the information has been taken from the three chapters on the Pomo in the *Handbook of American Indians,* Volume 8, on California (Bean & Theodoratus, 1978; McLendon & Lowy, 1978; McLendon & Oswalt, 1978).

THE POMO IN THE LATE 1700s

One of the most impressive aspects of early Pomo life was the thorough, comprehensive use of plant and animal resources. The Pomo were hunters and gatherers who relied upon acorns as the mainstay of their diet. All members of a Pomo family cooperated in the fall to gather nuts from the seven species of oaks that grew in the area. The nuts were stored in granaries until needed and were prepared by a process that separated the bitter tannin from the meat. The remaining sticky mass was either cooked into mush by stone-boiling in baskets or baked directly on hot ashes as unleavened cakes. In addition to acorns, the Pomo gathered berries, buckeye nuts, wild greens, and seeds from a variety of grasses. They dug roots and bulbs from the earth and collected kelp and seaweed from the ocean. These, when dried, were con-

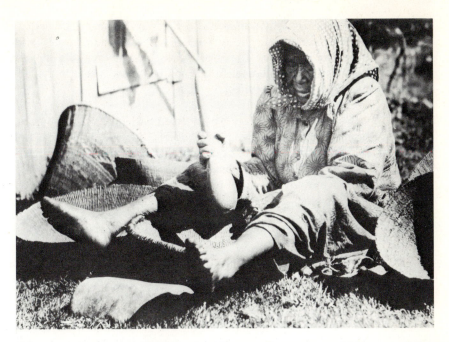

Woman making acorn flour. n.d. Photograph courtesy of Museum of the American Indian, Heye Foundation.

sidered delicacies. Grasshoppers, caterpillars, and larvae were eaten. The most important hunted animals were the mule deer, two kinds of elk, and the pronghorn antelope. To a far lesser extent, the Indians ate sea lions, bear, raccoons, rabbits, and squirrels. Ducks, quail, and grouse were trapped or netted. A variety of freshwater and saltwater fish such as salmon, trout, suckers, codfish, and smelt supplied part of the diet. Plant foods were preferred over game animals and fish.

Like the Papagos, the Pomo had individuals who wore deerhead masks and disguises. In their hunt, they were aided by drivers and packers. At other times several families who lived close together participated in a drive during which the deer were herded into a brush enclosure that had been prepared in advance. Cooperative drives were also used to hunt rabbits. Weapons used included bows and arrows, heavy spears or clubs for bear, and spears for sea animals. Smaller game and birds were taken by bolas, low brush fences, nets, snares, and basket traps. Fish were either trapped or caught on hooks and lines. Although some Pomo fished during all seasons, those living around Clear Lake concentrated their efforts on the spring spawning season, when the fish moved into shallow water and were easy to catch in large numbers.

Although food supplies were usually ample and dependable, the

Pomo occasionally suffered shortages. When acorns were in short supply, less-preferred foods were used, and additional food could be obtained by trade. The ready and constant availability of food in all Pomo areas enabled these Indians to follow a relatively sedentary and parochial pattern of life.

POMO DWELLINGS.   Living in fixed villages, the Pomo built several types of dwellings. Coastal peoples constructed conical huts made of sections of redwood bark or a variety of wood slabs arranged in a circle around a large center post. Although these dwellings were only six to eight feet high and eight to 15 feet in diameter, they housed as many as 12 people, usually members of a nuclear family. In the interior, along the Russian River and at Clear Lake, several families shared a large house that could be circular, elliptical, or L-shaped. These were built either with bundles of coarse-textured grass, or, at Clear Lake, with bunches of tule, a species of large bulrush that the Pomo also used to make boats, skirts, moccasins, and leggings. Relatives often built their houses near one another. During the summer and fall, when the Pomo left their villages to gather plant foods, they separated into nuclear family units and constructed crude brush shelters to provide shade from the burning summer sun. The last type of house built by the Pomo was

Pomo house and arbor, Ukiah, California. n.d. Photograph courtesy of Museum of the American Indian, Heye Foundation.

Man drilling beads, Ukiah, California, ca. 1890s. Smithsonian Office of Anthropology.

a semisubterranean structure, which served two specialized purposes. Small ones built in spring were used by the men of the village as sweathouses and social clubs; larger houses up to 70 feet in diameter were used for dances and ceremonials.

POMO CLOTHING.   Given the generally mild climate, men ordinarily did not wear clothing except on ceremonial occasions. Dress at such times was elaborate. Clamshell beads and cylinders, magnesite cylinders, brilliantly colored abalone shells, and many types of feathers were all used to decorate ceremonial dress. During cold or rainy weather, men protected themselves with capes made from tule or bark or, for the wealthier, from rabbit skins. Women always wore long skirts made of vegetable fiber or skins. Mantles tied around their shoulders covered the upper parts of their bodies. Both sexes generally went barefoot, but men sometimes wore hide coverings on their feet when traveling in rough country. Hair was worn long. Some tattooing was used for body ornamentation, and the ears of both sexes were pierced for the insertion of elaborate ceremonial decorations. Boys had their nasal septums punctured for decorative wooden rods or bone tubes.

TECHNOLOGY.   The Pomo are perhaps best known today by museum visitors and collectors for the wide variety and excellent quality of their baskets. These containers were used for cooking, storage, gift-giving, and ceremonies. Design elements such as goose-excrement, grasshopper elbow, killdeer eyebrow, bat's wing, acorn, arrowhead, fish vertebrae, and stars were prominent (Barrett, 1908). Baskets also served as containers for shell beads and magnesite cylinders, which functioned as money. The use of this money was limited largely to funerary offerings and the settlement of disputes between individuals and communities.

Other aspects of Pomo technology were known for their mediocrity and general lack of development. The Pomo were indifferent woodworkers, producing bows and arrows, fire drills, tubular pipes, digging sticks, mortars, trays, and staffs. They did not practice loom weaving or pottery making. They had no domesticated animals and did not keep dogs. The Pomo traveled on foot, and their women usually carried the

Pomo baskets can be large. Storage basket, diameter at the rim, three feet. n.d. Photograph courtesy of Museum of the American Indian, Heye Foundation.

Man, Tom, in reed (tule) boat. 1908.   Photograph courtesy of Museum of the American Indian, Heye Foundation.

heavier burdens, using a pack and tumpline arrangement. For water transportation, crude tule canoe-shaped rafts were used on small lakes and in swampy areas. Limited use was made of poorly constructed log rafts. The capability of these vessels was limited to the point where Pomo hunters preferred to swim to offshore clumps of rocks to hunt seals and sea lions rather than rely on their rafts or tule boats.

Social Organization

The Pomo did nothing as a tribe, being bound together only by proximity plus some cultural and linguistic unity. Their social organization was, by conventional anthropological standards, not elaborate. The population of more than 14,000 was divided into 50 to 75 local self-governing aggregates. Usually, each one of these units consisted of a central village with one or two subsidiary groups attached. Each local group, together with its smaller units, had a name derived from its geographical location and spoke a distinctive subdialect. These local groups, averaging 150 to 200 people each, owned a distinctive territory for 100 to 150 miles around, to which they had strong sentimental ties. Although this area was owned communally and its boundaries were recognized by other groups and marked by girdles of leaves tied around trees, within it were some resources such as oak trees that belonged to individuals or families. The resources of one village could be used by another if permission had been granted. This local group, village, or settlement had a far greater unity in name than in fact, for it did not produce, distribute, or consume anything as a whole. Individuals within the community collected acorns, hunted, fished, and went on trading expeditions together, but the results of their labors were consumed by the individuals and their families and not shared with the community.

349

Pomo villages had no characteristic form, although it seems reasonable to assume that the people of a village were tied together by bonds of kinship and friendship. Each extended family within a tribelet or village had its own headman or chief, and the chiefs of all extended families composed the ruling elite, which functioned as a tribal council. Occasionally, several villages would join together to control special resources. War chiefs held in common also bound some groups together and ensured that they would be more effective in battle. The chief's or headman's authority depended largely on charisma, which, in turn, consisted of equal parts of wisdom, tact, effective oratory, and successful adherence to the central dictates of Pomo life. His public duties were chiefly the entertainment of visitors from other Pomo villages and nominal supervision of proper religious ceremonies held at appropriate times. He had an important role as a peacemaker between quarreling individuals and with other villages when they were at odds with his own. In practice, the effectiveness of a chief depended upon his ability to sense the direction of public opinion and to respond appropriately.

In the larger villages a chief usually had assistants called *boy chiefs* or *surrounding chiefs,* who occasionally acted in his absence but more often assisted him in distributing food during ceremonies staged by the community as a whole. Boy chiefs could be sons or nephews of the chief or the sons of friends. If these young chiefs served satisfactorily, they could become chiefs in their turn by either election or hereditary right, depending on the practice of the Pomo group involved. Occasionally, the Pomo had female chiefs, who were usually sisters or daughters of male chiefs. Female chiefs were responsible for preparing and serving food at large ceremonies.

THE FAMILY. The social core of Pomo life was the family. The ideal marriage partner was a person who was not closely related. Marriages outside the village were often advantageous because they provided ties with other Pomo groups, which were valuable for keeping peace or forming economic alliances. Monogamy was customary, but polygyny was possible. Marriages were usually arranged by the families involved, but no Pomo was forced to marry against his or her will, and young people often made informal arrangements before their families got involved. For the first month of the marriage, the boy was expected to move into the girl's home. After this period, the couple was free to move to the boy's village, where a feast was held and gifts were exchanged. Their final residence was variable and depended on the couple's wishes.

Because they had a high population density and were aware that hunger was a possibility, the Pomo employed several methods to control the size of their families, including sexual restrictions, abortion, infanticide, contraceptive devices, and magic. Women also employed magic to become pregnant, for they were uncertain that sexual relations alone were enough. They were careful to follow the prescribed restrictions during pregnancy and gave birth in an isolated hut, where they and the baby remained for about six weeks. Children were weaned after about a year and named at this time for some deceased kinsman whom they were expected to resemble. This name was considered private property and was used only by the child's parents. Others employed relationship terms or nicknames. Childhood extended until about 12 for boys and until the first menses for girls. Ceremonies were held at this time in which boys were presented with their first hair net and bow and arrows. Girls were secluded in a menstrual hut, where they were instructed by older women in the duties of adulthood. Their first release from this confinement was celebrated with gift-giving.

Divorce was easily accomplished, although it was infrequent. Children of a broken marriage usually remained in the household in which they had been living. Often alliances with friends were as important as the ties stemming from descent and marriage. Such unions were based upon personal compatibility and the bonds of mutual interest.

DIVISION OF LABOR.   The division of labor for adults was carried out on the basis of age and sex. Men obtained most of the food resources through hunting, fishing, trapping, and some gathering. Women also did some gathering, especially of staples such as acorns, but their prin-

Woman pounding acorns with stone pestle and basket-mortar, Ukiah, California, ca. 1890s.   Smithsonian Institution, National Archives.

cipal concerns were with the processing of food. This responsibility called for more or less continuous organized effort within and between households. This vital role of women in routine Pomo life may account for their relatively high prestige in comparison to the position of women in other California Indian groups. Women also cared for the young children and made their excellent baskets. Men made their own tools and weapons and built the houses. Most sources on the Pomo give the impression that much time was spent in the obtaining and processing of food and that these activities were a major conditioning factor of the texture and pace of Pomo life.

Some men had the special status of hunter, fisherman, or manufacturer of shell money. No particular authority seems to have been attached to these positions, and various people became known for such skills because aptitude and inclination took them in these directions. Other men became doctors because their dream life indicated that curing was appropriate for them. Women could also become doctors, but did so with less frequency.

RECREATION.   Although food production was a regular and demanding part of Pomo life, there was much time for other activities. Visiting within and between settlements, often accompanied by gambling, regularly occurred. Men were fond of the grass game, in which they tried to guess the location of two short sticks, one plain and the other marked, hidden in clumps of grass held in the hand. Women played stick dice, using six flat sticks with designs burned into one side. Gambling was accompanied by betting, and supernatural forces were believed to have a significant role in the outcome. More active games included shinny, a form of field hockey using crooked sticks and a wooden ball, and foot racing. Gossip, although not a sport, was also an important part of getting together with other people.

Religious Beliefs

Although Pomo life was reasonably full and satisfying, with adequate food, shelter, and interpersonal relationships, one event seems to have been a chronic source of anxiety. This was death, regarded as a most unnatural occurrence and usually blamed on the conscious malice of the living. The anguish associated with cremation rites mirrors a combination of resentment, fear, and sorrow. Relatives of a dying person openly expressed their grief and kept close watch over their loved one to make sure that no poisoner could hasten the end. After death had occurred, the body was kept in the house and mourned for four days, then taken out and cremated. The house and personal possessions of the deceased were burned as well so that no ghost sickness could infect the relatives. All people who had had contact with the body had to undergo a ritual purification to protect them. At the cremation, the mourners openly expressed their grief, chanting and dancing about the pyre and working themselves into wild states in which they tore their clothes, flung their dearest possessions onto the flames, howled, leaped, and tore at their hair and flesh. For important people and the young, a second burning took place at the end of a year at which more gifts were offered to the deceased.

The religious beliefs, ceremonial practices, and supporting body of mythology functioned to compensate, after a fashion, for death and other unresolved ambiguities in Pomo life and to maintain a sense of distinctive ethnic identity. The Pomo believed that a host of unseen spirits occupied the world where they lived. There were creator beings, who were largely remote from human activity, and other spirits, who could bring misfortune either by indifference or intent. Pomo religion actively attempted to engage the support of these spirits in activities such as hunting, fishing, trading, and gambling. Secondarily, religion provided an explanation to the Pomo for those events they considered unexpected and unjust. The Pomo asked of their sacred beings not the spiritual fellowship that the devout Christian seeks with God, but something that comes close to a secular conception of luck. They believed that the absence of luck could result in misfortune and even physical illness, although bad health could also stem from violation of taboos or sorcery. Good health and prosperity for the Pomo were a combination of luck, the proper use of charms, and effective participation in ceremonial life.

BELIEF IN GHOSTS.   Pomo beliefs concerning the supernatural were neither comprehensive nor consistent, and varied, of course, among the seven groups. Ghosts or spirits of the dead could remain on earth, or they could travel to the extreme southern end of the universe. The land of ghosts was a place of perpetual bliss filled with an abundance of food and social harmony. Nevertheless, ghosts often returned to trouble the living. To ensure the absence of trouble from the dead, the Pomo held a four-day Ghost Ceremony, probably their most dramatic and involved ritual. It included elaborate forms of dancing, fire-eating, manipulation of hot coals, and the handling of live rattlesnakes. The Ghost Ceremony was held to atone for offenses against the dead, and it also stressed the initiation of boys into the Ghost Society, thus signifying that they had become adults. The Ghost Ceremony was part of a larger religious complex called the Kuksu, which stressed curing rituals and rites of well-being for the entire group. Among the Southern Pomo the Kuksu was also closely associated with fertility and firstfruit rites. Only males who possessed sacred knowledge could be initiated into the Kuksu cult, whereas all men joined the Ghost Society.

MEDICINE MEN. The Pomo lacked an organized priesthood, but accorded great respect to their part-time doctors or medicine men. The sucking doctor, who received his power directly from a spirit, removed harmful objects or disease from a patient's body by cutting and sucking the afflicted areas. The singing doctor, possessed of clairvoyant powers, learned his art as an apprentice to an experienced older man. In treating an illness, he relied heavily upon a medicine bundle containing a wide assortment of objects. Bear doctors were men who acquired evil powers by wearing a bear costume and receiving the support of supernatural beings. Bear doctors could be either men or women, and they purchased their positions from a previous bear doctor, becoming qualified only after special training and many ritual restrictions. Although bear doctors had special powers of movement and curing, they were feared because they could also be poisoners. Several bear doctors could informally associate and act in concert, and they inspired anxiety and respect in their communities. Their existence may have been the ultimate form of social control.

CONCERN WITH POISONING. It is impossible to leave this discussion of health and curing without mentioning the special fear the Pomo had about being poisoned. Many sources mentioned that they were obsessed with fear of it and routinely warned all children to beware of being poisoned. This fear of poisoning may have acted to isolate the Pomo from their neighbors and to ensure that all people followed strict rules of hospitality and etiquette.

Trade

In spite of their fears, the Pomo routinely traded with the neighboring tribes. Items such as shell beads, clam disk beads, dentalia or tooth shells, moccasins, seashells, mussels, seaweed, salt, and magnesite beads were given to the Yuki in return for furs, beads, baskets, and hides. From other neighbors the Pomo received items including sinew-backed bows of yew, obsidian, woodpecker scalp belts, and cordage for making deer nets. Unfortunately, the frequency and extent of trading activities are not known. It seems reasonable to guess that the existence of the Pomo was not dependent upon continuous trade with their neighbors. It is quite possible that the various Pomo regional groups traded with each other far more than with other Indians outside their territory in order to balance seasonal variations in critical resources. The travel and adventure associated with trading often must have been as important as the goods received, but no data are available to confirm this.

Warfare and Other Expressions of Hostility

There is little evidence to show the Pomo fought very much either among themselves or with non-Pomo groups. What conflicts occurred could be defined more as skirmishes than as warfare. For instance, Loeb (1926: 202–203) described an incident in which 30 warriors from one village killed 8 women and children from another while they were gathering roots. In retaliation the attackers were raided at their own village and 17 of their people died. Those responding to the initial assault later conferred with their enemies, and the conflict ended with discussion and a formal exchange of gifts. Significant destruction of life and property and the political subjugation of the survivors were not often the concerns of the combatants. Men sometimes died, but never in large numbers. Rather than engaging in overt warfare, the Pomo tended more toward an endemic covert anxiety and hostility, which were openly manifested as conflicts between a very small number of individuals. A common cause of this conflict was the desire to avenge poisoning. When a Pomo died, his friends and relatives often assumed he had been poisoned and believed they had to avenge his death. A curing doctor was summoned to determine whether poison had been used and who had done it. Once he had been identified, the poisoner became a target for being poisoned himself, and the feud could continue indefinitely. If a person in a distant village was accused, both villages could become enmeshed in a long-term feud.

The role of poisoner or witch seems to have been a part-time vocation for a select number of highly motivated people. The role was a difficult one, and few people knew enough about it to practice it. Poisoners were taught the arts of their trade as well as the proper songs and rituals, usually by a relative who had the skills. Poisoners had to spend a whole season, from spring to fall, gathering all sorts of plants as they ripened. In addition, they collected spider and snake venom, bee stings, and ant poison. When everything had been stored in small bags, the poisoner performed his rituals with the help of four men. The poison was never given directly to the victim, but indirectly by magical means. Because of the difficulty involved, it is probable that few people were actually selected as the targets of poisoners. The Pomo, however, believed that killing was easy and that they must always be on their guard.

Until the coming of the Mexicans in 1822, the Pomo and the tribes around them were lucky in that they did not have to worry about maintaining their political and geographical boundaries in the face of outside encroachment. For these peoples, population levels, technology, and their resources were in durable balance. They were able to live out their orderly existence without conflict. Unfortunately, this happy state of affairs was soon to change.

EARLY CONTACTS

The earliest contacts the Pomo had with incoming peoples were not particularly disruptive for them. In 1811 the Russians established an agricultural settlement at Fort Ross, on land that they had obtained permission to use from the Kashaya or Southwestern Pomo. The Russians followed a system of cooperation and nonintervention with the natives, and a number of Pomo found work with them as agricultural laborers. Some Russian words made their way into the language, and a few Pomo intermarried with the Russians and adopted some aspects of their culture and religion. The Russians abandoned Fort Ross in 1825.

At about the same time, Spanish missionaries were moving into Pomo country from the south. Although about 600 Pomos were baptized by these early priests, the tribe was generally considered to be savage and difficult to control or convert. In 1822, California was made a part of the new Mexican Republic. Mexicans were given land grants in Pomo territory, and the Indians found themselves in deep trouble. Villages were constantly raided for slaves or simply wiped out. Disease also played a part in decimating the Pomo. They suffered a cholera or maleria epidemic in 1833 and a smallpox epidemic in 1838 and 1839. In spite of their problems, some Pomo managed to maintain their culture in isolated areas under the Mexicans. When the Americans took over California in 1850, things got even worse. Pomos were rounded up and placed on reserves so that their land could be given to Whites. By 1870 the Pomo found themselves drastically reduced in numbers and forced into a system of peonage in order to survive at all. Many Pomos established settlements on land belonging to American ranchers where they were allowed to live and work for low wages. During the summer they followed the harvests and worked as field hands. In the winter, in order to survive, they relied on hunting, fishing, and trapping and managed to hang on to a few of their aboriginal ceremonies. In this way, the Pomo managed to retain their ethnic identity and their culture. It is possible that the hostility of the Whites around them ensured their survival, for they had no crucial social resources but themselves.

POMO LIFE IN THE TWENTIETH CENTURY—THE MANCHESTER BAND

In describing the Pomo as they reacted to modern life, I will rely upon the data furnished by Theodoratus in her description of the Manchester Band (1971; 1974). The people of the Manchester Band are descendants of Pomos who once lived in three main villages, one of which (Icheche) is near the present rancheria of Manchester. These villages and the subsidiary villages attached to them were located in the Coast Central region of Pomo territory. The social and political specifics about these people are impossible to isolate prior to the coming of the Whites. They probably conformed in most ways, however, to the dimensions of Pomo culture given in the first section of this chapter. The description of the Manchester Band begins in the mid-1800s, when these Indians were first placed on a federal reservation, and closes in 1969. Descriptive emphasis is placed on the topics that have been presented for the earlier era.

The Gold Rush of 1849 greatly increased the number of Americans coming into Pomo territory and accelerated the pressures against them. Pomo population and the extent of land they occupied declined at a much faster rate than they had done several decades before. Small bands of armed White civilians roamed the area, killing and looting. No mechanism existed for absorbing Indians readily into the White system, and the Pomos lacked the means to defend their own interests adequately. Following the miners to California came lumbermen interested in exploiting the redwood forests, farmers, and stock raiders. White towns sprang up complete with schools, churches, and businesses. The Americans required exclusive land ownership to maintain and extend their mercantile and social interests and had no compunction about stealing the land from the Pomos by force. They justified the transfer of ownership by portraying Indians as unworthy, subhuman savages who lived an inferior existence. As these Indians would remain inferior or become extinct no matter what they did, the Americans felt they were perfectly correct in putting the land to higher uses.

Something had to be done with the Indians, however, and in 1856 the Mendocino Reserve was created. Into this area, comprising 33 square miles or about 25,000 acres, the army forced 2,000 Indians from a number of tribes, including Coast Central Pomo, Yuki, Wintun, and Coast Miwok. Traditional enemies were forced to become neighbors. Some efforts were made to teach the Indians on the reservation small-scale farming methods and to give them the rudiments of a formal education. In 1867, however, because of the problems of logistics, corrupt and ignorant officials, and the gross indifference of the general population, the Mendocino Reserve was closed. Most of the Indians attempted to return to their former homes, but found them now in the possession of non-Indian farmers and ranchers. If the Indians were lucky, they were permitted to live as squatters on their former lands in return for labor performed for little or no wages. As farm workers, the Pomos not only learned something about modern farming techniques, but also began to develop techniques for their physical and cultural survival. Within a few years, most Pomos had learned a smattering of English, whereas few Whites had any knowledge of the Indians' language.

The former village of Icheche was partially inhabited for a time. More than 20 Pomos lived in the sweathouse until they were driven elsewhere. Because of a marked increase in the non-Indian farming population, the supply of traditional wild food resources dwindled to a level where they would not support the surviving Pomos. To obtain money for food, the Pomos cut ties, picked fruit and hops, and worked as general farm laborers. Nuclear and extended families settled on American farms and ranches, often assuming the name of their employer. Although Theodoratus believed that the assumption of these names meant a corresponding loss of Pomo identity, I do not agree. In Indian groups all over the country the combination of becoming a part of the larger economic picture together with being denied the rights to full participation in all aspects of American life has resulted in the perpetuation or even extension of many aspects of traditional culture. Evidence that this was the case for the Coast Central Pomo is the vitality of their religious life.

TWO CULTS. During the latter part of the nineteenth century, the Pomos participated in two religious revitalization movements. The first was the Ghost Dance, which, in 1870, spread from the Northern Paiute to neighbors of the Pomo, where it was transmuted into the Earth Lodge Cult stressing the coming of the end of the world. The Pomos, who by this time had lost 99 percent of their land, accepted this doctrine and built Earth Lodge houses in locations throughout their territory. The Coast Central Pomos learned of the Earth Lodge Cult by visiting two of the lodges. They were more interested, however, in the second revitilization movement, the Bole Maru cult, which was a derivative of the Earth Lodge Cult developed in central California. The Bole Maru also promised that the Whites would disappear and Indian ways would return. It transferred ceremonial information through Dreamers, who replaced the traditional Pomo techniques of passing on ceremonial ritual that had been dying out anyway. Women as well as men could become Dreamers, and traditional curing rituals were incorporated into the new movement. This new cult, therefore, not only gave the Pomos a focus for their failing culture, but it also gave them a base of political integration in the face of hostile outsiders. The Americans, in the mean-time, often believed that the Pomos were indeed vanishing because it seemed there were fewer Indians around every year. This indifference contributed unintentionally to Indian survival, for the Pomos either maintained a low profile in their work or lived in remote areas away from American settlements, where they could avoid many of the abrasive aspects of White encroachment.

The Manchester or Garcia River Rancheria

By 1900 the Coast Central Pomos had experienced approximately 75 years of non-Indian domination. They remained Pomos in spite of marked decreases in numbers through aggression and disease, the permanent loss of most of their lands, and the hostility and indifference of most of their neighbors. The Pomo tacitly decided not to oppose the Whites openly by force of arms; thus Indian violence was limited in scope and occurred only under the most provocative circumstances. A formerly self-sufficient collection of hunters and gatherers sharing a common culture and homeland had been forced into the lower ranks of a rural underclass, which was part of an expanding American economy.

In 1902 the Coast Central Pomos again were granted a land base. The Northern California Indian Association gave them 40 acres of land near the old village of Icheche. This new village was known as the Manchester or Garcia River Rancheria. It had 15 houses and a population of around 60 people, who had gravitated there from several Central Pomo villages. Within ten years, the property grew to about 106 acres, all held in common by the people living there. Some gardens were planted, but the rancheria was used mainly as a residence for those Indians who were not away doing unskilled farm labor in the nearby valley. A roundhouse was built and used for ceremonies, and a school operated at least part of the time. A small Methodist-Episcopal congregation used one building as a church. The rancheria population was constantly in flux because necessary wage work could be obtained only away from home.

For a number of reasons, decisive community leadership was absent. The Pomos were now under the jurisdiction of the Bureau of Indian Affairs, and guidelines for leaders acceptable to the federal government were vague and contradictory. Those who had had qualifications for leadership a century before were now either dead or unsuitable for the needs of the present. The shifting patterns of residence blurred the sense of community consciousness. Most Pomos who lived there could remember better days in the past and regarded their present residence as a barely adequate refuge rather than a real home. The small number of men who did aspire to leadership were not able to muster the necessary community and government support, and genuine community consensus about vital common interests did not form.

During this time, institutions of Pomo culture were in a state of flux. Marriage was vaguely defined in either aboriginal or conventional American terms. A few people at the rancheria were married in the local Methodist church, whereas others regarded a shared residence with mutual sexual rights as proof of marriage, no matter how often residence and choice of partner might change. Polygyny no longer occurred. There was a slight preference for Pomo spouses, but some Spanish-speakers and Italian-Americans took Pomo wives. In-marrying Whites generally lived harmoniously with their relatives, but they were always subject to community disapproval.

Incomplete information suggests that a necessary level of cooperation existed within families, but there was discernible conflict between Indian families if one had more cash and material goods than another. Other quarrels took the form of Pomo objections to the alleged misbehavior of a non-Pomo husband. The social networks or patterns of social alliance must have been limited in comparison to precontact times. There is a record of some boundary disputes with non-Indian farmers, but the Pomos found these to be little more than a source of chronic irritation and lost no land because of them.

By 1910 the outside world had exerted a comprehensive influence on Pomo life so that their culture must be viewed largely as a hybrid of traditional customs strongly modified by selected White influences. Pomo ethnic identity, however, still existed as defined by an awareness of valid social distinction, differences in physical appearance, residence, and way of life and especially a shared consensus as to who was a Pomo and who was not. White contact per se was the essential factor promoting distinctiveness, for such contact always carried with it a measure of discrimination.

IDEALS OF PHYSICAL BEAUTY.   The Pomos had firm ideas of what constituted physical beauty. They believed a man should not be too dark or plump of face. He should have square shoulders, eyes set wide apart, heavy eyebrows growing in a straight line, heavy black hair, a straight nose, and a flat wide chest. Women should be of square build, about five feet, four inches in height and 120 pounds in weight. Desirable features were plump hands and feet, flat breasts, heavy hair done up at the top of the head, thin lips, small ears, and white teeth (Loeb, 1926: 278–279).

POMO BEHAVIOR.   The Pomos patronized local merchants and usually paid for their purchases with cash. An American physician did what he could to improve standards of public and personal health at the Manchester Rancheria, but the Indians came to believe that there were White diseases and Pomo diseases. Indians and Americans began to meet socially, square dancing together or watching parts of Indian ceremonials, although the outsiders did not always understand everything they saw. Many Indians from the Manchester Rancheria began to resent Indians living on other rancherias, an attitude that may have represented a new form of community consciousness fostered by a shared residence pattern. Some non-Indians enjoyed this new conflict and attempted to promote it. They regarded all Indians who accepted their subordinate positions without expressing hostility as good Indians. Most of the Manchester Band fell into this category.

LIVING CONDITIONS. Living conditions on the rancheria were well below middle-class standards in housing, diet, clothing, and health care. The intermittent support of federal and private agencies was inadequate to improve these conditions significantly. The Americans, however, did change one traditional Pomo practice. Cremation gave way to burial, but traditional artifacts were still often buried with the dead. Excessive alcohol consumption sometimes occurred, and some Pomos believed that they could substitute liquor for more traditional poisons in order to get rid of an undesirable individual. Drunken Pomos were often a danger to themselves and other Indians, but non-Pomos were seldom, if ever, the targets of direct aggression. The fear of poisoning or witchcraft continued, but all deaths were no longer attributed to it. Some suspected poisoners were forced out of the community. Most Pomos continued to believe that if they behaved properly and did not offend others, they would escape being poisoned. Pomo doctors were called in to cure attempts at poisoning and also to treat other ailments that proved resistant to conventional American medicine.

EDUCATION AND RELIGION. Most Indian children attended school for varying lengths of time. They were given not only academic training, but also introduced to American standards of living, which they were expected to emulate. Some Pomos attended Carlisle Indian School in Pennsylvania. Many people assumed a nominal commitment to Christianity, but support of the Bole Maru Cult continued as well. At least two Dreamers were present at the Manchester Rancheria, and the community maintained a roundhouse or dance house.

ECONOMIC CONDITIONS. The Indians still supplied part of their food by hunting and gathering, to the extent that their own resources and the permission of non-Indian landowners would permit. All adults in reasonably good health, however, were forced to seek wage work in order to survive. Because, even when employed, they could not make enough

Roundhouse, Point Arena, Coast Pomo. ca. 1955. Lowie Museum of Anthropology, University of California, Berkeley.

money to buy all their food and necessities, some people raised vegetables on the rancheria, and some farm laborers were given food as part of their salaries. Many people worked away from the rancheria most of the time in lumbering, fire fighting, or other part-time jobs. Migration was forced upon them because there was never enough work available for Indians locally. One Pomo was employed at a midwinter fair in San Francisco, where he was hired to represent "the wild man of Borneo" (Theodoratus, 1971: 167). Despite such resourcefulness, however, many Pomos were underemployed well before the Great Depression of the 1930s, which made their situation worse. By 1936 most Pomos in California were struggling to survive on an average income of $700 per year for a family of five. In order to do so, they turned toward their traditional methods of sharing all resources. Many people stopped working for outsiders and went back to hunting and gathering in order to survive. This shift, plus some federal programs like the Works Progress Administration and the Civilian Conservation Corps, enabled the Pomos to come out of the Great Depression in relatively prosperous shape. During this period also those people who continued to work as laborers gleaned many modern ideas from their fellow workers, ideas that altered their behavior in such areas as food, family relations, credit, religion, habits of speech, and levels of aspiration.

The Point Arena Ranch

World War II accelerated the changes that the Great Depression had begun. Many Pomos entered the armed services or moved to cities to work. They became more aware of the benefits of material possessions and wanted more education so they could achieve success too. Federal programs in California were decreasing, however, and the state did not pick up the slack, so the Pomos found themselves as poor as ever.

In 1936 the federal government had attempted to extend the material benefits of modern living to as many Manchester Band Pomos as possible by purchasing a 254-acre tract called the Point Arena Ranch, to be used as a dairy farm. Profits from the farm were to pay for housing improvements and other programs that ranch residents were given. This enterprise failed because of poor management due to the fact that the rewards and responsibilities associated with ranch operation were poorly distributed. The result was a lack of cooperation within the band and ineffectual contacts with those outside the settlement, particularly the ranch manager and the Bureau of Indian Affairs. The operation of the ranch was intended to lessen band reliance on the B.I.A. and its control over these Indians, but instead it increased it because by law B.I.A. supervision had to be extended. The band was split between those who lived at the old rancheria and those who had moved to the grounds of the new ranch about four miles away. Here eight modern houses were built by the government. By 1960 the ranch operation was discontinued, but the divided residence pattern remained. Those who had stayed at the old rancheria did not receive the improved housing that the others had, but they hoped to have modern housing built once federal money was available. Sufficient funds never did materialize.

Those who remained at the rancheria may have done so by choice. There was some movement back and forth through the years as people moved to houses previously occupied by relatives. Some time after 1955, five more houses were built at the new ranch and more people moved over. Although the data are not clear on this point, choice of residence probably had critical implications with respect to attitudes toward the established pattern of rancheria life, particularly those about economic differentials and attitudes toward the non-Indian society. Those people who had remained behind maintained an active interest in both Pomo and, to a minor degree, Christian religions. Those who had moved away did not.

It may well be that the failure to operate the ranch according to the dictates of American business efficiency was caused by too much dependence on the old social structure associated with hunting and gathering. These activities had continued into the modern period, and cooperation for hunting and gathering did not extend beyond the limits of the family. Individuals often acted independently according to their own perceived needs so that the Manchester Band was essentially a community in name only. *Factionalism,* or the division of major social segments of the group on the basis of variable goals owing to internally and externally derived stresses, also probably had much to do with the absence of band cooperation.

After the new ranch had been settled, the Manchester Rancheria still retained 20 households consisting of 35 adults and 59 children, a total population of 94 living on 105 acres. More than 75 percent of these people had three-quarters or better Indian blood, and about the same proportion were under 50 years of age. A B.I.A. report of 1938 listed 18 biological families and 12 consumption family groups, defined as two or more related nuclear families having a common residence. Only three of these families had shown any interest in the ranch operation before it was established. Family cash incomes were low, and most credit ratings were unsatisfactory. Many Pomos continued to work at part-time jobs away from the rancheria out of necessity. The constant migration must have affected patterns of interpersonal behavior there, but precise effects are impossible to discern. Quite possibly patterns of long-term cooperation could not be established under these conditions.

Pomos and Non-Pomos

During this time, a greater formal concern was shown about band membership, and the question of whether a non-Pomo spouse automatically became a band member was explored. The group did not achieve a satisfactory community consensus about the criteria for band membership. The B.I.A. made an attempt to impose a democratic or representative kind of council leadership in the community but failed because mechanisms for cooperation above the levels of the individual, family, or family consumption group could not be established.

Many situations occurred that suggest that these Pomos had a limited understanding and pervasive distrust of the outside world. They were reluctant to send their children to public schools in nearby towns even though the physical plants and quality of instruction were acknowledged to be better than those on the reservation. Few Indian children graduated from high school, and those who did were reluctant to move to cities and establish a non-Indian way of life. The Pomos were also hesitant about accepting other services available to non-Indians. The Whites in the area ultimately interpreted this reluctance as being symptomatic of a general racial inferiority. Local residents continued to find it difficult to accept social and cultural differences on the part of others. The fact that many Pomos suffered from alcohol abuse did not help the situation. In addition, there were some boundary disputes. Indians charged a small fee to sportsmen for hunting on their land, and tradesmen who came to the rancheria were required to have written permission from the Indians. The rejection of the Indians by the larger society continued to play a role in the maintenance of Pomo identity. Having little else, they clung to certain aspects of their culture such as religion, the ideas associated with poisoning, and the limited use of Pomo language in many situations, especially those having to do with religion. Their spiritual life still included Bole Maru activities, although a few Pomos were attracted to Pentecostalism. Both the Pen-

"Big head" ceremonial headdresses on dance house wall. Kashia Pomo, 1959. Lowie Museum of Anthropology, University of California, Berkeley.

tecostals and the Mormons were more active on the new ranch than at the rancheria, perhaps because they told their converts that they could no longer participate in Maru activities as these were associated with Satan.

When the Point Arena Ranch failed in 1960, its grazing land was leased to a White farmer as the Pomo showed no serious interest in trying to continue an enterprise that had been at best a doubtful financial success. Although the ranch had caused much trouble between many band members, it also played a major part in supporting a distinctive way of life because the B.I.A. had always held band lands, both the rancheria and the ranch, in trust for the Indians. To be a Pomo meant living on Pomo land or at least having the option of living there. The federally imposed form of political organization, however, lacked a genuine vitality and could never really influence community affairs. The Pomos usually felt that all plans or opportunities coming from the outside were unsuitable for their way of life. Community organization never extended beyond the family level and still does not. Most families and individuals continue to pursue their own interests, and the result is often conflict between both individuals and various alliances of family groups. Band membership continues to be a chronic source of discontent in the modern period, especially with respect to individuals who marry into the band and those who have lived away from the community for a while and then returned.

Available evidence makes it difficult to determine the extent to

Pomo Strawberry Festival preparation, 1959.   Lowie Museum of Anthropology, University of California, Berkeley.

which the residents on the rancheria and the ranch regard themselves as separate from each other. Mistrust and jealousy do exist and must often have a residential basis. One band still exists officially, but there may be a trend toward the formation of two separate communities. To date, however, differential access to basic food resources is absent, and Americans in the area still appear to regard the local Pomos as belonging to a single community. Although in most respects there is no direct correlation between residence and specific forms of behavior, those living at the ranch do have a higher cash income on the average.

Both Indians and non-Indians frequently remark on the absence of genuine community leadership. Certainly no system has evolved to replace the positions of chief and his assistants, which existed at least until the middle of the nineteenth century. As these Indians continue to occupy an economically subordinate part of the larger economy, it seems doubtful that a dynamic, responsive kind of leadership can emerge. The Pomos have only the option of reacting to various developments that influence their status as Indians. Their reactions, usually couched in terms of aboriginal culture and ideas, often produce still greater social distance between them and the people around them.

Pomos today continue to show little interest in local public schools and seldom send their children there. They participate in the life of the two nearby towns, Manchester and Point Arena, only to a minimal extent. American merchants regard the local Pomos as being far worse credit risks than their grandparents had been. Business is conducted solely on a cash-and-carry basis, and many Pomos do their shopping at more distant towns where they say the prices are lower. Neither Whites nor Indians know much about each other, but the Pomos by choice avoid Whites most of the time. Because of this attitude and their own indifference, most local people still know little of Indian life. Band res-

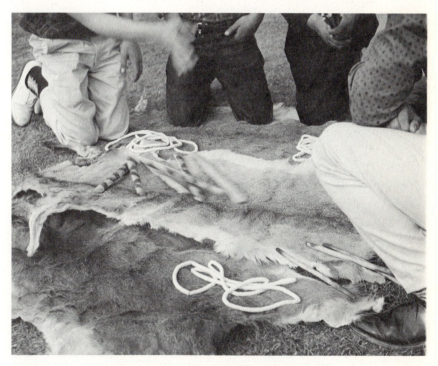

The gambling stick dice are thrown. Kashia Pomo, ca. 1959. Lowie Museum of Anthropology, University of California, Berkeley.

idents, however, continue to work as unskilled members of the area's labor force, with more men than women participating. A few Pomos sometimes find more exciting jobs. Several were hired as extras for the making of the movie *The Blue Dolphin*.

RELIGION TODAY. Noticeable interest is still shown by many band members in their own branch of the Methodist church. A few are Pentecostals, but most refuse to reject their Indian religion. The Bole Maru cult still survives, with ceremonies held on July 4th and Christmas and often attended by Pomos from other communities. Women continue to be Dreamers, and Pomo doctors are still found at both the rancheria and the ranch. Six individuals are referred to as singing doctors, and they are necessary to counteract the poisoners who are still active and

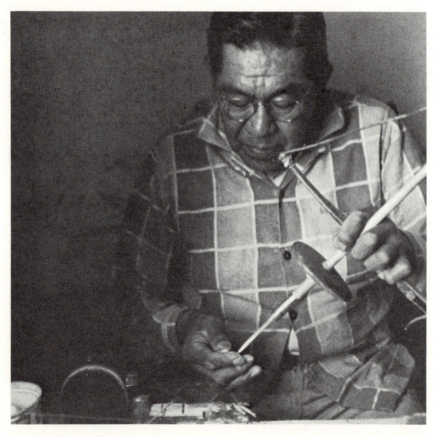

Bead making, Lakeport, Pomo, ca. 1957. Lowie Museum of Anthropology, University of California, Berkeley.

Pomo young men, ca. 1960. Lowie Museum of Anthropology, University of California, Berkeley.

considered to be a source of illness and death. These poisoners, though not often clearly identified, are always thought to be Pomos, either members of the Manchester Band or living elsewhere.

Future Predictions

The state and federal governments and the B.I.A. in particular are at best regarded only as sources of insignificant and unpredictable aid. As long as the B.I.A. continues to safeguard Pomo landholdings from White encroachment, the Indians will probably not show open hostility towards it. Some Pomos, however, believe that the federal government has mismanaged funds held for them by the U.S. Treasury. A recent B.I.A. publication (U.S. Department of the Interior, 1975) gives an estimated membership of 85 for the Manchester Band with 30 people in residence on the 364 acres held in trust. It can be safely assumed that if the government continues to protect Indian land and if the Manchester Band Pomos can maintain their present multiple resource base, the band will continue to exist as it is now for a long time to come.

The same B.I.A. publication gives population figures for the entire Pomo tribe. Four hundred and ninety-six Pomos are registered on six rancherias and two communities that contain Indians of several tribes.

Of this total, 261 people live on tribal land and 235 do not. The implications of these figures are intriguing although only speculation is possible. Baumhoff (1963) estimated that at the beginning of the nineteenth century, there were more than 14,000 Pomos. Even if the B.I.A. total is too conservative, the current Pomo population must be well under 1,000 people. Must one assume that this is the maximum number of people who can exist as Pomos without being assimilated into the larger society and losing their identity completely? Did the Indian population have to decrease to this extent in order for Whites and Indians to coexist?

For the Pomos as a whole, there are several groups, the Sonoma County Coalition for Indian Opportunity and the Mendo-Lake Pomo Council, which are attempting to unite all Pomo people into a tribe that will receive federal and state recognition. If such an amalgamation takes place, there may well be other changes in the broad spectrum that is Pomo life.

REFERENCES

Barrett, S. A. Pomo Indian Basketry, *University of California Publications in American Archaeology and Ethnology 3,* Berkeley: University of California Press, 1908.

———. Pomo Myths. *Bulletin, Public Museum of the City of Milwaukee 15,* 93–94, November 1933.

———. Material Aspects of Pomo Culture. *Bulletin, Public Museum of the City of Milwaukee, Vol. 20, Parts 1 and 2, 1952.*

Baumhoff, Martin A. Ecological Determinants of Aboriginal California Populations. *University of California Publications in American Archaeology and Ethnology 49:2.* Berkeley: University of California Press, 1963.

Bean, Lowell, and Dorothea Theodoratus. Western Pomo and Northeastern Pomo. In Robert F. Heizer, ed., *Handbook of North American Indians. Vol. 8. California.* Washington, D.C.: Smithsonian Institution, 1978, pp. 289–305.

Beardsley, R. K. Culture Sequences in Central California Archeology. *American Antiquity 14:1,* 1–28, 1948.

Davis, James. Trade Routes and Economic Exchange among the Indians of California. *Ballena Press Publications in Archaeology, Ethnology and History No. 3.* Ed. Robert F. Heizer. Ramona, California: Ballena Press, 1974.

Freeland, L. S. Pomo Doctors and Poisoners. *University of California Publications in American Archaeology and Ethnology 20:4.* Berkeley: University of California Press, 1923.

Harrington, M. R. A Glimpse of Pomo Archeology. *Masterkey 14,* 9–12, 1942.

Heizer, Robert F. The Western Coast of North America. In J. D. Jennings and E. Norbeck, eds., *Prehistoric Man in the New World.* Chicago: University of Chicago Press, 1964, pp. 117–148.

Kroeber, A. L. Handbook of the Indians of California. *Bulletin 78, Bureau of American Ethnology.* Washington, D.C.: Smithsonian Institution, 1925.

Loeb, E. M. Pomo Folkways. *University of California Publications in American Archaeology and Ethnology 19:2,* 149–404, 1926.

McLendon, Sally, and Michael J. Lowy. Eastern Pomo and Southeastern Pomo. In Robert F. Heizer, ed., *Handbook of North American Indians, Vol. 8. California.* Washington, D.C.: Smithsonian Institution, 1978. pp. 306–323.

————— and Robert L. Oswalt. Pomo: Introduction. In Robert F. Heizer, ed., *Handbook of North American Indians, Vol. 8. California.* Washington, D.C.: Smithsonian Institution, 1978, pp. 274–288.

Powers, Stephen. *Tribes of California: Contributions to North American Ethnology,* Vol. 3. Washington, D.C.: Government Printing Office, 1877.

Theodoratus, Dorothea J. Identity Crises: Changes in Life Style of the Manchester Band of Pomo Indians. Ph.D. dissertation, Syracuse University, 1971.

—————. Cultural and Social Change among the Coast Central Pomo. *The Journal of California Anthropology 1:2,* 206–219, 1974.

U.S. Department of the Interior. Bureau of Indian Affairs. Tribal Information and Directory. Sacramento Area Office, Sacramento, California, February, 1975. Mimeographed.

Wallace, W. J. The Pomo Indians of Central California. In R. F. Spencer et al., eds., *The Native Americans.* New York: Harper & Row, 1965, pp. 243–253.

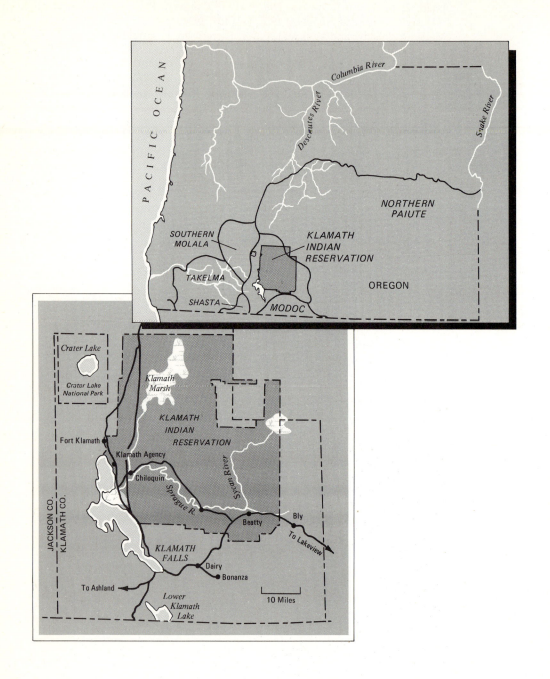

PACIFIC OCEAN

Columbia River

Deschutes River

Snake River

NORTHERN
PAIUTE

SOUTHERN
MOLALA

KLAMATH
INDIAN
RESERVATION

TAKELMA

OREGON

SHASTA

MODOC

Crater Lake

Crater Lake
National Park

Klamath
Marsh

KLAMATH
INDIAN
RESERVATION

Fort Klamath

Klamath Agency

Chiloquin

Sprague R.

Sycan River

Bly

Beatty

To Lakeview

KLAMATH
FALLS

Dairy

Bonanza

JACKSON CO.
KLAMATH CO.

To Ashland

Lower
Klamath
Lake

10 Miles

CHAPTER *11*

THE KLAMATH OF OREGON
The People of the Plateau

The design of the government is to segregate the Indians upon lands set apart for them, separate them from the pernicious influences which association with whites entails upon them, and to cultivate the good, moral, and intellectual qualities they may possess.

Letter of J. W. Perit Huntington to
Lindsay Applegate (Stern, 1966: xv)

The Klamath and their close relatives the Modoc have lived in what is now south central Oregon for a long time. Archaeologists believe that this area has been inhabited by Indians for about 10,000 years, but they cannot demonstrate an unbroken continuity between the modern Klamath and the earlier occupants of the region. I will, therefore, begin by describing what Klamath life was like at the beginning of the nineteenth century before their territory had been invaded by settlers.

THE KLAMATH BEFORE WHITE CONTACT

Like the Pomo, the Klamath were more a collection of individuals who lived near each other and shared a common language than they were an actual tribe with far-ranging social linkages and common leadership. They lived at the conjunction of several culture areas and borrowed traits from all of them: Great Basin, California, and, later in their history, the Northwest Coast. Both the Klamath and the Modocs spoke languages of the Penutian stock, and each believed that it had been closely related to the other at one time. The two tribes were reunited when the Klamath Reservation was formed.

Population estimates for the Klamath vary, but they were never a large tribe. Stern (1966: 5) estimated between 1,200 and 2,000 as the aboriginal population of both Klamath and Modoc, with twice as many Klamath as there were Modoc. Swanton, quoting a number of other people, listed 800 to 1,200 Klamath in 1780 and 755 in 1905, including former slaves and members of other tribes (1953: 461). These people inhabited a marshy region crosscut with streams, lakes, and rolling hills. As the altitude of the Klamath Basin is over 4,000 feet, winters were quite severe. Six to eight feet of snow were common, and the winter of 1890–1891 saw an accumulation of 30-foot drifts in places. Many summers were very dry.

The outer limits of Klamath territory were not wide. They felt close to the Modoc, who spoke their language, and maintained friendly relationships with the Molala, who lived to the west and northwest of Klamath Lake. They alternated between friendship and hostility toward the Paiute and the Sahaptin tribes of the Columbia River, who sometimes raided them. Peoples living west of the Cascade Mountains were their enemies. Finally, the Klamath exploited the Pit River and Shasta Indians to the south, often raiding their territory for slaves and loot.

FOOD SOURCES.   The Klamath had a number of food sources to draw upon, but their territory was not so richly endowed as that of the Pomo, and in late winter and early spring they were apt to be hungry enough to eat boiled or roasted hides. Their year began in August, when the women and children gathered *wokas,* or pond-lily seeds, in the marshes. At this same time of the year, men hunted game, netted waterfowl, and trapped beaver, otter, and rabbits. Klamath women collected a few other types of seeds after the wokas had been gathered, but to the Modoc further south, seeds and berries were much more important. Both tribes wintered in the Cascade Mountains, where they hunted deer and elk. Throughout the winter, the Klamath were able to catch some fish, but otherwise relied upon stored dried fish and meat, roots, seeds, and berries. With the coming of spring, fishing improved, and the suckers began their runs up the rivers. Salmon and trout were also abundant, and families left their winter homes to congregate at good fishing stations. While the men fished, the women harvested edible roots and gathered wild celery and mosses. Waterfowl eggs became available. Once again there was plenty to eat and life was good (Stern, 1966: 13–14).

CLOTHING.   Early Klamath dress was very simple, being limited to fringed fiber skirts and basketry caps for both men and women. In colder weather tule leggings and sandals ensured warm feet, and animal skins or fibers made comfortable cloaks. By the nineteenth century, as the trade routes from the Plains moved more often across the Rockies, buckskin clothing grew popular. Both sexes decorated themselves with shell or stone necklaces, ear pendants, and dentalium shells thrust through the septums of their noses. Their hair was braided. A number of people had flattened brows, an item of beauty attained through the proper strapping upon their cradleboards while infants. Some were tattooed on face, limbs, and body (Stern, 1966: 8).

HOUSING.   During the winter the Klamath lived in earth lodges, semi-subterranean circular pits dug from one to four feet deep. The roof was supported by four central posts, which held horizontal plates covered with rough planks. A hole was left in the top for smoke to exit. The whole lodge was chinked with sticks and bark and covered with rough matting, grass, and finally dirt. Although they were allowed to air while their residents were out digging roots or fishing, lodges often had to be torn down in spring and rebuilt because they quickly became vermin-ridden, smelly, and soggy with melted snow. Summer lodges were much the same but had no earthen cover. Both types usually faced east and were entered via a stairway on the outside and a ladder within. Their floors were covered with mats, and along the walls were beds made of mats over dry grass, covered occasionally by blankets of woven tule, cattail, or animal skin. Dried fish and roots hung from the rafters. Some of these houses were large enough to hold two families, whereas others had only one. Elderly people unable to negotiate the ladder entrance had to try to survive the winter in small huts made of mats.

These winter settlements of the Klamath were relatively small, ranging from only one or two to perhaps a hundred house pits, all of which may not have been occupied at the same time. Villages also included communal storage pits and some mat-covered lodges for cooking, sewing tule mats, and secluding menstruating women or those about to give birth. Most surplus food was commonly stored away from the village in concealed caches because the Klamath had no desire to be hospitable when their food stocks were low (Stern, 1966: 708).

Social Organization

The main social unit for the Klamath tribe was the nuclear family, although the extended family could also be important especially if they lived together in one lodge. Kinship was traced through both the male and the female lines, with the male line holding a slight edge. Beyond the family loyalty in Klamath society, it was each man for himself. People who worked hard and accumulated property were highly respected and often made leaders of the village with the responsibilities of mediating feuds and exhorting their neighbors to maintain harmony and behave well. Robert Spencer (1956) has written an interesting paper, "Exhortation and the Klamath Ethos," describing how this haranguing worked. Not only did the village chief give moral lectures to all the people each morning and evening, but any adult felt free to lecture a child at any time. The advice most often given amounted to exhortations to be good, kind to people, and industrious; never to quarrel; to stay out of trouble and heed one's elders. If all this were done, good things would happen to one. Spencer interpreted the harangue as the device the Klamath used to instill their main value in life, the work ethic.

Klamath were highly individualistic and often self-seeking. The tribelet, consisting of several villages, was a hazy concept to most Klamath; and the tribe, for all practical purposes, did not exist. Even war, that great solidifier of interests, was waged only by men who respected the war leader and had an individual penchant for fighting. Work was what mattered. If you were observed striving and if you accumulated a surplus of goods, you were a good Klamath. There was a basic difference between the way this wealth-accumulation system worked for the Klamath and for the tribes on the Northwest Coast such as the Kwakiutl, at whom we will look next. For the Kwakiutl, the accumulation and distribution of wealth was a formalized system that governed all of society. For the Klamath, it was not. The work was the important thing, not the material goods that resulted, and they had no standardized articles that constituted wealth.

The lack of a distribution system made the lot of those Klamath who were poor unenviable. If they were unskillful hunters and fishermen, they were forced to beg food from others, who then exploited their labor. Klamath society made no provision for sharing, even among members of an extended family, and to beg for help was shameful. The result of this system was that the Klamath individual was isolated and lonely much of the time. Those relatively unsuccessful people sometimes turned to war or feuding to relieve their feelings. Warfare was also the path of some of the ambitious because those who were winners returned home with as much booty as they could carry.

How then did the Klamath cope with the aggression engendered by being constantly judged as producers while being given no real help by formal procedures? They seldom used witchcraft, for shamans, who had the power to do so, were closely watched to make sure that they did not turn their powers upon their fellow villagers. The Klamath handled their hostility in the only way they could—by stealth. In extreme cases, an enemy was murdered, perhaps being ambushed and clubbed down from behind. More commonly the property of an enemy was destroyed: his nets ripped, his canoe holed, his pelts cut, his fish racks kicked over. When these things happened, no formal mechanism existed for bringing the criminal to justice even when people knew who he was. An honest man was expected to suffer in silence, even when he knew one of his own relatives had been responsible. Naturally, a lot of people, while pretending to be stoical, revenged themselves upon their attacker by secretly destroying his property so that the feud continued. Spencer (1956) has traced this same pattern of attacks against property to the Klamath of today and has noted that it is aggravated by the abuse of alcohol. The pattern of exhortation continues also, but it does not really work in curbing hostility.

The only specialists in Klamath society were the shamans, who were allowed to build an earth lodge for themselves. Shamans acted as both curers and entertainers, holding five-day and five-night midwinter performances, which must have been a welcome break in the routine. Spirits were summoned by the shaman and his assistants; there were dancing, singing, tricks such as swallowing fire, and feasting. The shaman's spiritual competence and connection with the supernatural world were demonstrated, and a good time was had by all. In keeping with their spirit of individualism, the Klamath could also seek personal visions through fasting, sweating, or going alone into the mountains. Both men and women engaged in this behavior.

TIME OF TRANSITION

Beginning in the 1840s, White settlers became increasingly interested in Oregon land, and these new contacts brought about a heightened rate of intertribal warfare and intertribal trading. Some Klamath fought against the Whites in an attempt to drive them away, and others sought to find a satisfactory social and political accommodation with them. The first contacts the Klamath had with the newcomers were with representatives of the Hudson's Bay Company, who were not particularly interested in them as there were few beaver in Klamath territory. In 1843 and again in 1846, John C. Fremont, with a government exploratory party, passed through the area. On the second trip he was attacked by a party of warriors and retaliated against an innocent village, including the women and children. This action did not make Whites popular with the Indians. By this time also, the Klamath were suffering from White-introduced diseases against which they had no resistance.

As more and more settlers moved into the area, they simply took over the land they wanted with no consideration for Indians already living there. Their livestock destroyed native food supplies. Much as they wanted to fight, most Klamath found the Whites too powerful to be withstood. New leaders grew up who favored accommodation. They did not have an easy time, however, for many lawless men passed through Klamath territory on their way to the California goldfields. These people were always ready to fight with the Indians, and many of the Klamath were eager to retaliate. Skirmishes were frequent (Stern, 1966: 25–26).

A further change came to Klamath society when they were intro-

Native residents of Klamath country, ca. 1850s.   Lorain Album, Oregon Historical Society.

Klamath Indians signing the Declaration of Allegiance to the United States. Dr. Dixon on left securing signatures, and Captain Applegate of the Modoc War and pioneer of Oregon on extreme right. n.d. Photograph courtesy of Museum of the American Indian, Heye Foundation.

duced to the Dalles, an important center of trade for all tribes in the area, by some French-Canadian trappers about 1835. At the Dalles, the Klamath were able to trade slaves that they had taken from some California tribes for horses. The growing importance of trade decreased the power of the shamans, who had no trading skills, and increased the power of the young adventurous men who were willing to learn the new ways. Trade enhanced their wealth, bringing them not only horses, but modern weapons and Plains clothing. These were the men whom the Whites called chief.

In 1858 an abortive attempt was made to make a treaty with the Klamath and Modoc. Perhaps the Civil War interfered, but the tribes were never called together. In 1864 the acting superintendent of Indian affairs in northern California made an unauthorized treaty with the Modoc, giving them their homeland around Tule Lake, but this treaty was never accepted by the United States government. In spite of this, the Modoc felt their land base was secure. The same year authorized government representatives conferred with the Klamath, Modoc, Yahooskin Snakes, and Walpape Snakes or Paviotso. A treaty was signed with the first three groups that dissolved the Indians' title to all of southeastern Oregon, established a reservation for their exclusive use, and made provisions for eventual allotment of land to individuals (Nash, 1955: 387). The Paviotso signed the treaty the following year, although both they and the Modoc signed it reluctantly. Lindsay Applegate was made subagent in 1865, and he immediately visited the Indians and issued rations to them, an act that was bound to make him popular. In 1866 he began the construction of the new agency in the Lower End, the heart of Klamath territory, where most permanent settlements had formerly been located. A military garrison, Fort Klamath, was established nearby. In 1868 a second community center was established at Yainax in the Upper End section of the reservation. This settlement was isolated from the fort and from White settlements, and it remains relatively so today. Here most of the Modoc and Paviotso eventually settled, whereas most Klamath remained at the Lower End.

EARLY LIFE ON THE RESERVATION

The Modoc War

It did not take long for trouble to break out on the new reservation, though it centered not around the Klamath but around the Modoc, who had been promised they could remain on their tribal lands on Tule Lake in northern California. The leader of the Tule Lake Modoc band was a young man named Captain Jack by the Americans. In 1869, Captain Jack was persuaded against his will to bring his band to the new reservation. Their life there, however, was unhappy because the Klamath persisted in reminding the Modocs that it was Klamath land and streams they were using. Resentful of this attitude, in 1870 almost the entire Modoc tribe, numbering 371, followed Captain Jack off the reservation. The following spring, part of the tribe, under the leadership of Sconchin, returned to the Upper End to settle permanently. Captain Jack and his group, which contained all the more hotheaded elements, remained at Tule Lake, where they made the American settlers increasingly uneasy by their presence. They hoped to persuade the government, in the end, to honor the earlier informal agreement and award them a reservation there. Unfortunately, the government decided to use the army troop stationed at Fort Klamath to force the Modoc back to the Klamath Reservation. Captain Jack's group broke away from their attackers and, in April of 1872, murdered 14 settlers. They then retreated to a natural fort in the lava beds south of Tule Lake, from which they were eventually dislodged by a thousand-man force including both regular troops and Indian scouts. Before this happened, the Indians had shot and killed two members of a peace commission and wounded others. When the Modocs were finally captured, the leaders were executed and the remainder of the band removed to Indian Territory as prisoners of war, thus ending what is called the Modoc War. It had been an unfortunate incident in which Indian aggression was undoubtedly provoked by White encroachment (Nash, 1955: 389–398).

U.S. Government Policy toward the Indians

Meanwhile, on the reservation the Klamath and some Modocs had settled down at the Lower End while Sconchin and his group were firmly entrenched at the Upper End by 1871. The government policy concerning the Indians was fourfold: to provide food and clothing to supplement native provisions, to introduce democratic political institutions, to incorporate the Indians into the White world by making them farmers, and to eliminate shamanism (Nash, 1955: 398–399). The first of these objectives was no problem because there were still relatively few settlers, and the Indians could continue to get a large measure of their subsistence in ways they had always used. A small amount of beef and wheat sufficed to supplement native foods. The second objective was put in motion when O. C. Applegate, the Indian agent, established the election of chiefs by popular vote. A head chief and eight subchiefs were chosen in 1869, along with a sheriff to serve the entire tribe and a constable for each chief.

The third objective, making the Indians into farmers, proved much more difficult. The Klamath, with their tradition of hard work, were certainly willing to try. By 1869 a number of them had begun to fence and plow their own land. A sawmill was built in 1870 and was used first to cut logs for agency buildings and then to supply wood for some frame houses for the Indians. A gristmill was begun in 1871 and completed in 1873, the work being interrupted by the Modoc War. All this industry, however, ran into one insurmountable barrier. The Klamath reservation was at an altitude of 4,000 feet. Year after year, the crops were destroyed by spring or fall frosts. When the frost did not ruin the crops, the summer droughts did. Early agents, sensing they were fighting a losing battle, urged the Indians to turn to stock raising instead. Policies continually changed as Indian agents came and went, and as late as 1897, the Indians were still being encouraged to farm. Stock raising, however, gradually won out, although it too suffered a setback in 1880, when 75 percent of the cattle and 40 percent of the horses did not survive the winter. Farmland was planted more and more in hay and grain for winter feeding. By 1886 there were 1,485 cattle, 3,640 horses, 340 mules, and 195 hogs on the reservation (Stern, 1966: 61).

Besides grazing lands, the Klamath possessed a second important economic asset, their tribal forest. By 1873 the Indians were not only using logs for their own buildings, but also selling them at Fort Klamath and elsewhere. Two years later, however, they ran afoul of the same governmental policy as did the Menominees. The government ruled that the timber should be held in trust status, and the Indians were forbidden to profit from cutting and selling their own wood. Only dead and down trees and those cut incidental to clearing the land could be legally harvested and sold. Many of the more enterprising Klamath ignored the law and sold their timber illegally, trading it to the Whites in return for supplies. By 1896 the sale of lumber to the Whites exceeded a quarter of a million board feet, three-fourths of which had been cut from green timber (Stern, 1966: 62).

The fourth objective of the Klamath Agency, the campaign against shamanism, did not abolish shamans, but it did succeed in reducing their power and influence. Shamans were shackled, imprisoned, and fined. The Klamath observed the impotence of one shaman who had vowed to kill the agent through supernatural power. This policy of destroying shamanism paved the way for three religious revivalistic movements: the Ghost Dance, the Earth Lodge Cult, and the Dream Dance. All three movements can really be considered as parts of a whole that Nash has called "Dream Dancing" (Nash, 1955: 414).

Three Religious Movements

The Ghost Dance began in 1871, brought to the Paviotso on the Upper End by a kinsman from Nevada. Almost every night, men, women, and children moved clockwise around their circle, dancing to bring back the dead. Before long the Klamath and Modoc had joined the movement, and dances were held lasting five nights. The promises given to the Tule Lake Modoc, Captain Jack's group, were very specific. When the grass was eight inches high, the white people would burn up and disappear, leaving no ashes behind. Deer and other animals would return as well as relatives of the dancers. These returned dead would live eternally. Any Indian who did not accept these promises would be turned to rock. When the Ghost Dance did not live up to these promises, the Modocs turned instead to fighting, with the results that we have seen. The Klamath at the Lower End approached the Ghost Dance much more skeptically than the Tule Lake Modoc had done. No threats or promises were made, and they sang only about the message that all people on earth would live together. After about a year, the movement died out throughout the reservation.

In 1874 a new message was brought from northern California by two Pit-River Indians who had been Klamath and Modoc slaves. The Earth Lodge Cult, which I have mentioned in connection with the Pomos, required the construction of dance houses. It, too, taught that the dead would return and that an earthquake would destroy all Whites and unbelievers. Dreaming and fainting during the dance would cause these things to happen sooner (Nash, 1955: 421). Four earth lodges were built, one on the Upper End and three on the Lower End. As dreaming was encouraged, more and more of it occurred, not only during dances but also while the Indians were at home. Imperceptibly, the Earth Lodge Cult merged into the third facet of the movement, the Dream Dance, which focused more on personal visions than group actions. This increasing emphasis on the self was very much in keeping with the individualism that the Klamath had always practiced, and it also reflected the fact that many people had begun to live on their own farms instead of in communal villages. There was an important difference in the way the Upper and Lower End groups reacted to these movements (Nash, 1955, 440–441). Throughout all three, the Upper End people resisted the Whites, felt hostile to them, and were very apprehensive about their own future. The Lower End group, on the other hand, accepted much of White culture, were desirous of trading with them, and felt optimistic about the future. They never accepted the prophecies of the coming death of all Whites with the intensity felt by the others. All aspects of Dream Dancing were unpopular with the Indian agents, who attempted to stop it, but they were unsuccessful until 1878, when a Methodist church was built on the reservation and most Indians became Christians.

FROM ALLOTMENT TO TERMINATION

By 1878 the Klamath were exploiting a number of activities in order to make a living. According to taste, need, and season, they were engaged in lumbering and logging during the fall, winter, and spring; as hired laborers for the fort and surrounding White settlers during the spring and summer; as farmers on their own plots of land; as stockmen; and as hunters and gatherers of aboriginal foods. Many Klamath were also employed in the freighting industry, packing various goods in wagons, each drawn by four horses. Fully half to two-thirds of the men left the reservation on passes after the harvest was in to work for Whites during the winter. They often took their families with them, and everyone became more conversant with White customs and standards. By 1880, when the government annuities ceased, most Indians were able to support themselves.

Unfortunately, along with economic adaptation came a number of social changes and problems. Some Klamath women acted as prostitutes for the troops at Fort Klamath, and others lived with Whites without formal marriage bonds and had children by them. Whiskey was sold freely on the borders of the reservation and added to the social

Klamath Indians. n.d.; possibly late nineteenth century.   Oregon Historical Society.

unrest. Some stable marriages grew from unions between so-called squaw men and Indian women, but the more successful couples almost always moved away from the reservation because the husbands did not want to submit to rule by the Indian agent. Thus, the lessons these women learned about living in the White way could not be passed on to the rest of the Klamath until allotment, when they sometimes rejoined the group (Stern, 1965: 97–98). Children of the less successful mixed unions usually remained on the reservation to be brought up by their relatives and were often resentful of their White blood. In spite of the drawbacks, however, interracial unions continued. White women were scarce, and the Klamath had a surplus.

Education, especially boarding school, also brought changes with it. Boys and girls were no longer available for vision quests or puberty ceremonies, and these practices were dropped. Instead adulthood was reached when a child returned home from school. Education, however, often supplemented rather than replaced Klamath culture, so that the new generation knew something of both worlds. By 1883 two manual training boarding schools were operating on the reservation, one at the agency on the Lower End and one at Yainax. Although reading levels were low, being confined to first-grade material for half of the students, boys were taught the practical skills of farming, stock raising, dairying, lumbering, carpentry, and blacksmithing. Girls learned about housekeeping and making clothes. An apprenticeship system had been established, so that each Indian was assigned to an artisan who instructed him in his particular skill. Conditions were often harsh at the schools, although some teachers tried to be kind. Students were not allowed to speak Klamath. They were punished for infringements of rules by being whipped and deprived of food. School farms had to be kept going all summer by students laboring there on two-week shifts. Other agency programs also were supported by students, for many ablebodied men spent much of their time working away from the reservation (Stern, 1966: 105–108).

Allotment

Beginning early in the reservation period, another change took place in the realm of political authority that was to have long-term effects upon Klamath life. The policy of the Indian agency was to replace Indian leaders with their own administrators because they feared that Klamath leaders would become too independent. This move had the undesired result of making the Klamath unresponsive to all political control by those they regarded as alien. Individualism grew, and when the agency tried to stop it, they were no longer heeded. On top of the decline of effective political power came the dissolution of other social restraints that had in the past been supplied by village chiefs and public opinion. As people became more mobile and family ties weakened, there was little left to hold the tribe together. The influence of the General Allot-

Indian Camp near Klamath Agency. n.d.; possibly late nineteenth century. Oregon Historical Society.

Klamath Agency, 1886.   Oregon Historical Society.

ment Act of 1887 (the Dawes Act) was to aggravate conditions for all concerned (Stern, 1966: 120–121).

Kickingbird and Ducheneaux (1973: 166–178) have summarized the central events of allotment. The government wanted all Indians who resided on reservation lands to participate in allotment. They believed that if an Indian owned a portion of land on an individual basis, he would automatically be freed of the restraints of tribal allegiance and have a far better chance of becoming economically independent. This program presupposed, among other things, that small plots of land could be farmed to support individual families. As we have seen, however, this was certainly not the case with Klamath land because of the difficult climate and the poor soil, composed largely of volcanic ash. In addition, by the 1880s Washington had come to regard Indian governments as unsatisfactory because they were difficult for a central authority to deal with. The government found it convenient to believe that the reservation nominally governed by local Indian leadership backed by Indian agents was responsible for most of the serious problems that Indians were having. If the reservation and all that was associated with it could be eliminated, the problems would also vanish. The allocation of small tracts of land to individuals was one way to destroy a reservation.

Although they were not enthusiastic, 800 out of 933 enrolled tribesmen consented to allotment, which granted each one 80 acres of farmland or 160 acres of grazing land. By 1897 the bulk of the reservation had been allotted, but a dispute over its boundaries with a land company brought delays. Allotment was completed in 1910, when those Modocs who had been sent to Oklahoma for punishment for participating in the rebellion led by Captain Jack returned and claimed lands. The 160-acre parcels of land were too small to be economically profitable for stock raising. Accordingly, most Klamath leased these parcels to Whites, who consolidated lots into larger and more profitable grazing areas.

Termination

When allotment ended, the Klamath Tribe had retained 860,000 acres of land, most of which consisted of rich ponderosa pine cover. By 1929 most allotments had been sold to Whites, for the majority of Klamath could support themselves upon the financial returns from the tribal forest, which was being managed by the federal government. The quarter century of conflict between tribal factions that followed did not promote the welfare of the Klamath people as a whole. In 1950 a constitution was

Money for land. Representatives of various tribes on the Klamath Reservation during deliberations that resulted in a vote to prorate the $5,000,000 recently awarded them by the Supreme Court in a land case judgment. 5/22/38.   Oregon Historical Society.

Some Klamaths can keep their land forever but the whites are still interested.
Klamath burial mound. 5/28/39.   Oregon Historical Society.

adopted that had as one of its central features the voluntary withdrawal
of individual Klamath from legal tribal status.

In 1954, Congress passed Public Law 587, which provided that land
and timber would be sold at reasonable market prices to pay off those
Klamath who wished to withdraw from the tribe. Senator Watkins of
Utah and the B.I.A. both had prominent roles in its creation. Watkins,
as the Menominee chapter mentions, was infatuated with the idea of
reservation termination for all tribes because this would free them from
the allegedly cumbersome restraints of federal guardianship. The B.I.A.
continued to be faced with the problem of administering laws and
directives known to be imperfect and welcomed the prospect of losing
a series of chronic problems long associated with the Klamath people.
One important reason for the passage of termination was that the Klamath were tired of 27 years—1927 to 1954—of dispute about whether
or not there should be a Klamath reservation. Many wanted to be free
of federal governance, and the controversy had divided areas of the
reservation and families and had proved to be a source of torment for
too many individuals for too long a time. It was no longer worthwhile
to have a Klamath reservation.

The actual steps that the termination process entailed proved to be
awkward for all concerned. Amendments were made to the original
law, which provided that the federal government buy the Klamath
marsh for the Fish and Wildlife Service and the balance of the timber-

lands for the Winema National Forest. Those Klamath who decided to remain as tribal members became wards of the United States National Bank of Portland, Oregon. About 78 percent of the Klamath withdrew from tribal status, taking with them their portions of the tribal estate, which amounted to approximately $43,500 per person. The remaining lands were placed in a trust managed by the bank. By law, the trust could be abolished by a majority vote of the remaining members taken every five years after termination became final.

Those Klamath who voted for termination were giving up an annual payment of $800 per person derived from harvesting timber (Kickingbird & Ducheneaux, 1973: 173). As Klamath families averaged five people, this money had often been enough to support them when added to the management of their small farms and ranches. Parents were allowed to vote for 800 minors, who had no say about whether or not they wished to retain their heritage as Klamath. Klamath termination, in a relatively short time, placed on relief many Indians who had

More land is lost. "Newspaper for Klamath Indians is published monthly as part of an education and information program conducted for the tribe during termination. The editors are William Norel (left) and Hiroto Zakoji (right) who heads the program at Chiloquin on the reservation. The paper helps keep Indians informed on termination." 8/25/59.   Oregon Historical Society.

depended upon per capita payments on a regular basis. The lack of experience in money management plus other factors soon reduced the large payment from the tribal estate to little or nothing.

The remaining 474 tribal members agreed to continue the trust in 1964, but in 1969 they voted to abolish it by a slight majority. Many Klamath were convinced that they had voted to manage their own property free of the legal but callous supervision of the Portland bank. The bank, however, informed them that they had formally agreed to liquidate their holdings. The actual inheritance of money from land belonging to the tribe was complicated by the tax problems that it engendered. The value of the timber land has quadrupled since termination, but these lands, when sold, would be subject to state taxes and federal capital gains taxes since that time. No one could agree on how much money this would subtract from the per capita payment. A small group of Klamath petitioned the bank to let them take their shares in land rather than money, an action that caused the bank to turn around and sue the tribe. Those Klamath not involved in the action were concerned that these tactics would cause a delay in their receipt of the money.

A Committee to Save the Remaining Klamath Lands was formed, and it petitioned the government to purchase 135,000 acres for approximately $52 million. In 1972 federal hearings were held on the subject. Senator Mark Hatfield, Senator Bob Packwood, and Representative John Dellenback of Oregon strongly supported the purchase of the remaining lands so they could be added to the Winema National Forest, the original Klamath reservation that the government now owned. The entire tract could then be harvested on a sustained yield basis and at the same time provide the people with recreational land. The government option to purchase the forest would run out on June 30, 1972, and its backers feared that the bank would then sell the land to private interests who would clear-cut it to get a good return on their investment. Once this had been done, it would have adverse effects upon the economy of that part of Oregon that depended on timber and ranching to support all its people, both Whites and Indians.

The Nixon administration and the Department of Agriculture opposed the purchase because they thought the cost would be too high. They suggested instead that the state of Oregon apply its powers of land-use control to protect the forest from abuse by private interests. Senator Hatfield questioned whether Oregon laws could do this and also wondered if any private interests would buy the land if they could not recoup their money through clear-cutting (U.S. Senate, 1972).

The issue was finally resolved when Congress authorized the secretary of agriculture to purchase (condemn) the forest by statute, passed on August 16, 1973. At that time timber prices were at a peak. Therefore, the United States Forest Service waited for the timber market values to go down before formally condemning the property. The formal condemnation took place on November 15, 1974, when timber stumpage prices were low, thus paying the Indians $49,000,000 for the forest condemned. The Klamath Tribe has sued in the U.S. District Court for fair compensation. That lawsuit is still pending.

KLAMATH LIFE IN MODERN TIMES

During the reservation period, which ended with termination in 1954, the Klamath retained a sense of distinct identity. They recognized a single tribal government and shared the proceeds of their tribal estate. It was also a time when the Klamath came to realize that they had little control over tribal assets and were a small ethnic minority within a large, highly complex, and indifferent society. Those who could obtain jobs away from the reservation did so. By 1958 over 50 percent had moved away (Stern, 1966: 185). Many lived in towns near the reservation, but others were scattered throughout the rest of Oregon, large urban centers on the West Coast, and the remainder of the country. Those who had remained on the reservation lived for the most part in small communities such as Chiloquin at the Lower End and Beatty at the Upper End. Forty-seven percent of the population were under 20 years of age (Stern, 1966: 187), and a great deal of intermarriage had occurred with non-Indians. The children of these unions often had little interest in tribal affairs.

TWO KLAMATH COMMUNITIES.   Marilyn Gerber Livingston (1959) studied the Klamath in two communities: Klamath Falls, close to the former reservation, and Eugene-Springfield, 175 miles away. She found Klamath in both locations anxious to leave their Indian identities behind and to join the White community as equal participants in all ways. Those living in Eugene-Springfield had been more successful at doing this for a number of reasons. They had often lived in cities among White people longer, they were free from the worry of frequent visits from Klamath relatives or friends because of the greater distance, and they were in almost all cases able to pass as Whites and participate as equals in community life. In Klamath Falls it was harder to do this because too many people knew about Indian blood and identified as Indian a person who genetically was largely White. Most individuals in both communities took little interest in tribal affairs and made no effort to seek out and socialize with other Klamath unless they were relatives.

TUMBLEWEED.   Brian M. du Toit (1964) studied a small Klamath town, which he named Tumbleweed, located on the former reservation. The people of Tumbleweed were in direct contrast to those successful Klamath whom Livingston found disappearing into the White population of Eugene-Springfield. During the 1920s and 1930s, Tumbleweed had been a satisfying place to live. Its people were served by an active Methodist Mission, a local school, and a young Indian agent willing to organize activities for the children. The Great Depression did not seriously bother the people because those who lost their jobs still had the annual income from the tribal forest. In the 1940s, however, Tumbleweed lost its school, its minister, and its Indian agent. All the activities that had brought the people together as Klamath gradually disappeared. Begin ning even before termination, Whites moved into the town and Indian law enforcement officers were replaced by Whites. The Klamath felt more and more like second-class citizens who were somehow inferior just because they were Indians. Deprived of their former church suppers and youth meetings, the young people began to congregate in local taverns, especially after the 1953 law making liquor legal for Indians. When taverns closed for the evening, the entire group picked up more beer and wine and moved to private homes for drinking parties lasting two or three days. These parties led to many undesirable events: fights, sexual involvements, inability of the young men to hold jobs for very long, increased crime, and neglect of children. But because they also provided a place for the Klamath to come together as a group and confirm their social solidarity, Du Toit saw little hope that this behavior would end soon. Drunkenness had become normal.

In the former reservation area, most of the significant economic activity, ranching and lumbering, was carried on by Whites who had bought or leased the necessary lands. Few Klamath were successful ranchers. In contrast to the Menominees, Klamath men never had been employed in any significant numbers in the sawmill industry. The Klamath had difficulty using wisely, by middle-class American standards, the money they had received from the leasing or sale of land, from salaries, and from their annual payments for lumber. They were not sophisticated in making investments and tended to spend the lump sums they received all at once. The governmental policy of paying the per capita income of $800 in semiannual installments rather than spreading it out during the year was an invitation to squander the money. Before termination, however, many Klamath families had managed to live quite successfully on these payments. That, plus some reliance upon native foods and sharing, was all they had needed. In the end, though, this had a bad effect on some individuals in the tribe because it decreased the interest that people had traditionally shown in hard work. Why work when the money flowed in anyway? For those who decided to terminate their tribal membership, the $800 annual payment ended abruptly. Each person received $43,500 at termination and a further sum of $12,000 in December of 1972 as settlement of litigation involving the original selling price of the land (U.S. Federal Policy Review Commission, 1976, 22–25). If they squandered this money rather than saving it, they were in trouble. For almost 50 percent of the tribe, either minors or those judged incompetent, that final payment was held in trust.

Dissatisfied with their final settlement, the Klamath tribe sued the United States before the Indian Claims Commission in 1971 on five distinct and separate grounds: (1) the overall management of sales of tribal timber over the period 1913 through 1960 was not conducted in the tribe's best interests and resulted in the loss of substantial money by the tribe; (2) the government's harvest of the Klamath Forest between 1952 and 1960 was unreasonably low; (3) the government failed to establish an adequate commercial tribal sawmill on the Klamath Reservation, thus depriving the Indians of the real fruits of their asset; (4) the government failed to respond adequately to the insect infestation (pine beetles) upon the Klamath Reservation between 1914 and 1941; and (5) the government failed to protect the Klamath Forest from fire destruction, specifically from the major fires of 1918. In satisfaction of these claims, the Klamath are seeking damages of $90,555,978. The details of this suit can be found in *Docket No. 100-B-2 before the Indian Claims Commission.* It has not been settled at this time.

MENOMINEE AND KLAMATH TRIBAL POLITICS: SOME DIFFERENCES AND SIMILARITIES

It is interesting to compare the Menominee with the Klamath tribe because they had much in common. Both benefited from the valuable timber land that they owned, and both were terminated at the same time through the machinations of Senator Watkins, who believed that they were rich enough to support themselves. Since termination, however, events have taken a very different course for them. The Menominees have once again been granted tribal status and are succeeding in managing their forest on a sustained yield basis. In June of 1978, they dedicated their newly remodeled sawmill. The Klamath, on the other hand, have lost almost all of their land along with their status as reservation Indians and the benefits that accompany this status. There is no hope that they will ever regain these things. What made the difference?

In the first place, in spite of their factional disputes, the Menominees have always regarded themselves as one people who have shared the same territory for a very long time. When the Pine Ring attempted to acquire their timber, the Menominees worked together to prevent this. In 1887 they held off allotment so their land was not sold piecemeal out from under them. The Klamath, on the other hand, were not one people but a mixture of Klamath, Modoc, and Paviotso, with a sprinkling of Pit River or other California Indians who had been slaves. From the very beginning of the reservation period, they were split by deep divisions, and these divisions continued through the years, with the Lower End Klamath often pitted against the Upper End Modoc and Paviotso. These divisions, in the end, produced so much dissension and conflict that most Klamath were ready to say or do anything to have some peace.

Second, there were many differences in the ways both tribes managed their timber resources. Perhaps it was luck that caused the government to build the sawmill at Neopit. If the windstorm had not blown down all those trees, the mill might not have been built when it was. At any rate, once the Menominees got the mill, they always used it as a source of employment for their men. The Klamath, on the other hand, even though they had sawmills on the reservation, never worked in them and eventually they died out. Klamath timber was then sold to White-operated mills in cities such as Klamath Falls. The Klamath benefited without effort from their $800 per annum payments, but they had no tradition of working with their own timber as the Menominees did. Thus, for a large payment, they were willing to give up their land. The Menominees were not.

It is interesting to speculate about what will happen to the Klamath now. Their future seems uncertain and fraught with peril.

REFERENCES

Barrett, S. A. The Material Culture of the Klamath Lake and Modoc Indians of Northeastern California and Southern Oregon. *University of California Publications in American Archaeology and Ethnology,* Vol. 5, 1910, pp. 239–292.

Clifton, James A. Explorations in Klamath Personality. Ph.D. dissertation, Department of Anthropology, University of Oregon, 1960.

Docket No. 100-B-2 before the Indian Claims Commission. Klamath and Modoc Tribes and Yahooskin Band of Snake Indians v. *The United States of America.* Defendant's Brief and Defendant's Objections to Plaintiff's Introductory Findings. Vol. 1, pp. 7–8.

Du Toit, Brian M. Substitution, a Process in Culture Change. *Human Organization 23,* 16–23, Spring 1964.

Gatschet, Albert S. The Klamath Indians of Southwestern Oregon. *Contributions to North American Ethnology,* Vol. 2. U.S. Geographical and Geological Survey of the Rocky Mountain Region. Washington, D.C.: Government Printing Office, 1890.

Kickingbird, Kirke, and Karen Ducheneaux. *One Hundred Million Acres.* New York: Macmillan, 1973.

Livingston, Marilyn Gerber. Klamath Indians in Two Non-Indian Communities: Klamath Falls and Eugene-Springfield. M.A. Thesis, Department of Anthropology, University of Oregon, 1959.

Nash, Philleo. The Place of Religious Revivalism in the Formation of the Inter-cultural Community on Klamath Reservation. In Fred Eggan, ed., *Social Anthropology of North American Tribes*. 2nd ed. Chicago: University of Chicago Press, 1955, pp. 377–442.

Ray, Verne F. *Primitive Pragmatists: The Modoc Indians of Northern California*. Seattle: University of Washington Press, 1963.

Spencer, Robert F. Exhortation and the Klamath Ethos. *Proceedings of the American Philosophical Society*, 100:1, 77–86, February 1956.

Spier, Leslie. Klamath Ethnography. *University of California Publications in American Archaeology and Ethnology*. Vol. 30. 1930.

Stern, Theodore. *The Klamath Tribe: A People and Their Reservation*. Seattle: University of Washington Press, 1966.

Swanton, John. The Indian Tribes of North America. *Bulletin 145, Bureau of American Ethnology, Smithsonian Institution*. Washington, D.C.: Government Printing Office, 1953.

U.S. American Indian Policy Review Commission. *Report on Terminated and Nonfederally Recognized Indians*. Washington, D.C.: Government Printing Office, 1976.

U.S. Department of the Interior. Office of the Solicitor. *Federal Indian Law*. Washington, D.C.: Government Printing Office, 1958.

U.S. Senate. Committee on Interior and Insular Affairs. Klamath Indian Forest. *Hearing before the committee on S. 3594*. June 16, 1972.

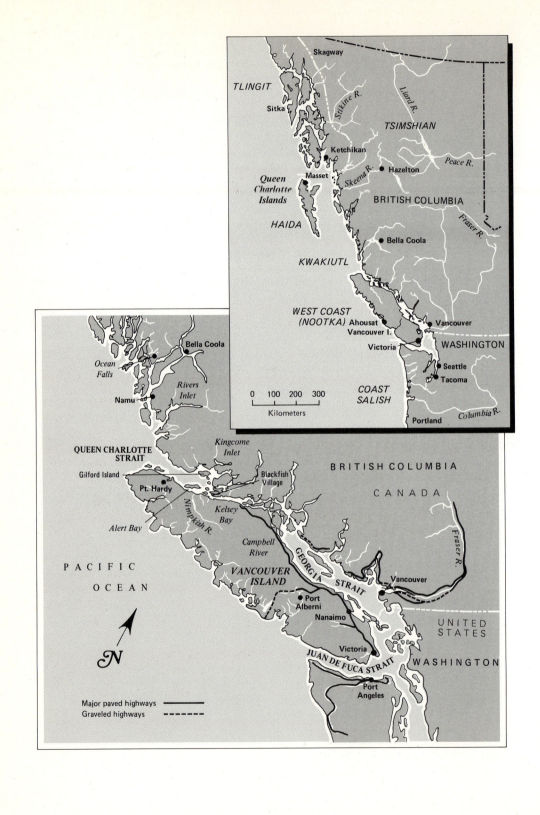

Skagway

TLINGIT

Sitka

Ketchikan

Queen
Charlotte
Islands

Masset

Skeena R.

Stikine R.

Liard R.

TSIMSHIAN

Hazelton

Peace R.

BRITISH COLUMBIA

HAIDA

Fraser R.

KWAKIUTL

Bella Coola

WEST COAST
(NOOTKA) Ahousat

Vancouver I.

Vancouver

Victoria

WASHINGTON

0   100   200   300

Kilometers

COAST
SALISH

Seattle

Tacoma

Portland

Columbia R.

Ocean
Falls

Bella Coola

Namu

Rivers
Inlet

QUEEN CHARLOTTE
STRAIT

Gilford Island

Pt. Hardy

Alert Bay

Kingcome
Inlet

Blackfish
Village

BRITISH COLUMBIA

CANADA

Nimpkish R.

Kelsey
Bay

Campbell
River

PACIFIC

OCEAN

VANCOUVER
ISLAND

GEORGIA STRAIT

Vancouver

Fraser R.

UNITED
STATES

Port
Alberni

Nanaimo

Victoria

JUAN DE FUCA STRAIT

WASHINGTON

Port
Angeles

N

Major paved highways

Graveled highways

CHAPTER 12

THE KWAKIUTL OF THE NORTHWEST COAST
Those of the Smoke of the World

Welcome . . . Welcome . . . Welcome . . . Welcome . . . Welcome . . . Welcome (Chiefs). Come now to your seats, to the seats of your late fathers and just sit down in your seats, chiefs, which are prepared for you. Now sit down well, chiefs, and your people. You do not come here, chiefs, to feel badly in this house of my chief. Now, sing feasting-songs to tell our world, chiefs.

From a welcoming speech to rival chiefs at the beginning of a potlatch. Recorded by Franz Boas in "Ethnology of the Kwakiutl" (1925)

Along the northwest coast of North America from Alaska to Puget Sound are found a number of peoples who share the distinctive Northwest Coast culture, one of the most vital and exciting in all of North America. The Northwest Coast peoples owed little to cultural influences stemming indirectly from Mexico or the continental United States. They were an entity to themselves and had an effect, in turn, upon the west-

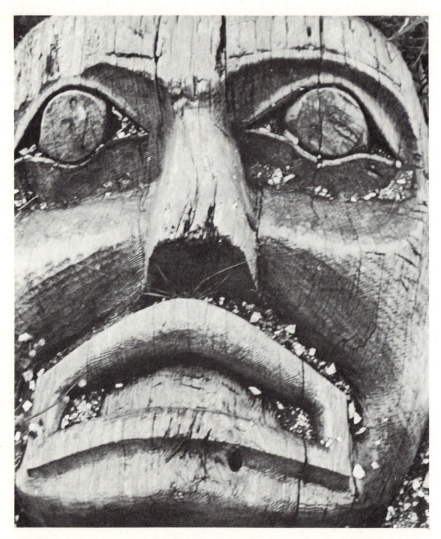

Face on a fallen totem pole. While the change in this carving from its original state is unmistakable, its continuing character and power are impressive. Gilford Island, 1962.   Courtesy of Ronald P. Rohner.

Main street in village. Cape Mudge, Vancouver Island. n.d. but probably late nineteenth century. Photograph courtesy of Museum of the American Indian, Heye Foundation.

ern Eskimos, Alaskan and Canadian Athapaskan speakers, and California natives who came in contact with them.

Definitive archaeological roots for the Kwakiutl have yet to be established, but Willey (1966: 384) postulated two origins for their culture. Some traits may have been imported from peoples to the north, such as the Arctic Eskimos or immigrants from Asia. Others accompanied peoples from the Interior Plateau who moved to the coast. Traits from both these areas probably blended and changed as the people adapted to living on the coast, but no one knows exactly how, when, or where this happened.

It is not accurate to characterize these peoples as members of tribes because the basis of organization among them was the village. Villages that shared the same language and dialect were allied by common participation on social and ceremonial occasions. None of the groups had any overriding tribal government. Northwest Coast peoples spoke a variety of languages because they migrated from Asia at different times and from different places. They differed, too, in physical type, being taller in the north and stockier in the south. Some among them had more facial hair and lighter hair and eyes than most other North American groups.

The Kwakiutl lived in the middle of the Northwest Coast region. Although their culture was a strong one, it differed in a number of ways from the peoples to the north, and little said about the Kwakiutl can be uncritically assumed for any other group. There were about 25 different villages whose people spoke a dialect of Kwakiutl, which, together with

Village and totem pole. Vancouver Island. n.d., but probably late nineteenth century. Photograph courtesy of Museum of the American Indian, Heye Foundation.

Nootka, is classified as a Wakashan language. These villages occupied scattered locations on the shores of the northern part of Vancouver Island, Canada, and the nearby mainland. The land is mountainous and covered by heavy growths of conifer forests and vegetation. Rainfall is abundant, averaging 100 inches a year. Temperatures during the winter months hover around the freezing point, whereas summer readings average 70° F. Traditionally, Kwakiutl subsistence activities closely followed the weather. The wet season, October to March, was reserved for winter ceremonies, religious feasting, and dancing, whereas the remainder of the year was devoted to harvesting and storing fish, game, and wild berries and plants.

For my discussion of Kwakiutl history and culture, I am indebted to Helen Codere's chapter in *Perspectives in American Indian Culture Change* (1961: 431–516). I will follow her division of their history into three periods: the Prepotlatch (1792–1849); the Potlatch (1849–1921); and the Postpotlatch (1930 to the present).[1] The period between 1921 and 1930 is regarded as transitional. Most information about early Kwakiutl life is derived from the fieldwork done by Franz Boas in the last part of the nineteenth century with elderly informants. Boas worked with the Southern Kwakiutl, who occupied the shores of waterways on Vancouver Island and the mainland between Cape Mudge to the south and Rivers Inlet to the north.

THE PREPOTLATCH PERIOD: 1792 to 1849

The year 1792 marks the first known European contact with the Kwakiutl. The Nimpkish village on Cornwan's Island, whose people were a division of the southern Kwakiutl, was visited in this year by Vancouver, Menzies, and an unidentified journalist, all of whom recorded their impressions. They found the Kwakiutl not at all awed by the presence of strangers. The Indians already possessed some European trade goods, including many muskets, but these could have come from the Nootka over the old eulachon or grease trade route to the interior. *Eulachon*, or candlefish, were prized for their oil content, high enough so that the body of the fish would burn if a wick were inserted. As eulachon did not swim up rivers, the Kwakiutl had established an early trade in this valuable commodity. The Nimpkish village was a large one, having about 500 people living in 34 great houses arranged in streetlike rows on the shore of a river. The population might have been higher than usual because the date was July 20, and people could have been attracted to the village by the salmon run. Summer months were typically a time of movement from one food resource area to another, for no one place had all the resources the Indians needed for daily subsistence and storage.

Vancouver's party reported that the Kwakiutl were excellent traders, being able to obtain double the going price of sea otter skins and being very particular about which European goods they found desirable. Although iron was prized by other Indian groups, these people

---

[1] A definition and discussion of the Potlatch ceremony will be found on page 418.

wanted sheet copper and blue broadcloth. The Kwakiutl were to continue their sharp trading practices. In 1836 an impasse developed with the Hudson's Bay Company. Coal was discovered at Beaver Harbour, the later site of Fort Rupert. As the company had been importing coal from Wales to run its steamers and shops and as the needs of new American settlements to the south were growing, this new coal promised profits and cheaper costs. Although the Kwakiutl had never used the coal except as a source of pigment, they quickly realized its value, and when they were approached for mining permission, replied that they preferred to mine the coal themselves and sell it to the Hudson's Bay Company. The impasse lasted for ten years until Fort Rupert was established in 1849, and some Scottish miners were imported to take out a few veins of coal. The Kwakiutl were also skillful in exploiting the competition between the Hudson's Bay Company and several American trading ships, saving the animal skins they had collected for long periods to get the best possible price. In 1838 an official of the Hudson's Bay Company complained that the Indians were obtaining guns and ammunition elsewhere and underselling company prices. Codere (1950: 23) mentioned an incident in which a visiting Englishman asked the officer in charge of Fort Rupert why his cannon were in such rusty, unusable shape. The man replied that the only time it had been fired, to impress the natives, they had run after the spent ball, returned it to the Fort, and asked to trade it back so that it could be used again.

In 1835 there were between 7,500 and 8,000 Southern Kwakiutl, including 1,700 Lekwiltok, and 2,700 Northern Kwakiutl (Duff quoted in Codere, 1961: 456). The Lekwiltok were the southernmost group of Kwakiutl and by far the most warlike. Establishing themselves in historic times at Cape Mudge on the Campbell River, they were able to control and prey upon river traffic that had to pass their location.

WARFARE AND WARRIORS.   By and large the Kwakiutl were a peaceful people who would rather trade with their neighbors than fight. Warfare was more a matter of small raids undertaken to gain ceremonial rights or to alleviate sorrow for a death. In raiding, stealth and trickery were valued attributes. For example, a raid took place in 1835 against the Bella Bella where the extremely important *hamatsa* or Cannibal Dance was acquired for the Kwakiutl. They had been raided by the Bella Coola, who had killed many people, so a large war party of 32 canoes set out to revenge the village. On the way, one of the war leaders suggested that the party attack the Awikeno, a Northern Kwakiutl group, instead of proceeding to their destination. He was overruled, but the war party then encountered a group of Bella Bella chiefs carrying important ceremonial equipment. Assuring the Bella Bella that they would not harm them, the Kwakiutl entered into friendly conversation. When the war leader drew up in his canoe, however, he began killing the

Bella Bella, and all the Kwakiutl joined in and agreed that they "had done a great thing" (Boas, 1897: 427).

Raids undertaken for the purpose of alleviating sorrow caused by a death were carried out in an illogical, arbitrary fashion. The death could have been from natural causes, but the Kwakiutl thought that some other group should be made to feel sorrow as well, so they attacked an innocent village or group of people. Raids of this sort were very limited in extent, and often the war party was satisfied with the taking of one head.

Kwakiutl war leaders were a special class, raised from childhood to be unpleasant to all. These boys were treated roughly and instructed to insult their companions and to seduce girls. They received rigorous physical training in running, swimming, diving, and the use of weapons. An adult warrior must have been an unpleasant sight as he walked by with stiff, jerky motions, perhaps clutching a stone in his hand and ready to attack anyone at the slightest provocation. He wore a heavy beard obtained by rubbing grizzly bear blood on his face, and around his neck hung a necklace made from the toenails of the dead. Because they devoted all their energies to fighting, warriors never accumulated material goods except by plunder and could seldom maintain a family or even marry. They were capable of attacking their own people as well as the enemy and could not have been very popular with anyone. Warfare ceased almost entirely after 1849, in part because maturing outside political control made the former intermittent patterns of raids an impossibility. In addition, the nature of the potlatch changed so that the Kwakiutl said of themselves that they fought with property rather than weapons.

Economic and Social Organization

FOOD SOURCES AND QUEST.   The economic system of the Kwakiutl has always attracted the interest of anthropologists. Not only did they have an abundance of food; they also used a method of distribution to ensure that everyone received his or her share. Sea life included shellfish, crabs, mussels, and clams; saltwater fish such as halibut, cod, eulachon, herring, and salmon; and the larger sea animals such as seals, sea lions, sea otters, and porpoises. Salmon were the most important fish and the staple of Kwakiutl diet. Fish roe, especially that of herring, was collected in large quantities and eaten with oil. The larger sea mammals, whales and seals, were not an important part of Kwakiutl diet, although the dog seal was sometimes killed for the bounty placed upon its head. Before its population became extinct in this region, the sea otter was hunted for furs to trade to the Whites for European goods as well as to make robes for nobles of the tribe.

In the surrounding forest the Indians harvested roots and berries, which grew in abundance at certain times of the year and could be preserved for winter. Women and children, equipped with burden baskets and digging sticks, gathered wild food such as tiger lily, rice root, Easter lily, and wild onions, as well as berries, including viburnum, huckleberries, rowanberries, blueberries, gooseberries, and currants. These were made into cakes flavored with salmon spawn or skunk cabbage leaves or reduced to a thick jam and dried in the sun. Soft fruits such as strawberries and salmon berries were eaten fresh. Hunting played a secondary role to fishing, but land animals available were the deer, mountain goat, wolf, raccoon, squirrel, beaver, mink, otter, bear, lynx, and elk. The southern Kwakiutl hunted deer for their hides but not their flesh because they believed that deer meat caused forgetfulness and confusion of thought. Birds in the area were the grouse, drum partridge, Mexican woodpecker, duck, bullfinch, raven, crow, sea gull, and eagle. These were sought for both food and feathers for decoration, although the sea gull was thought unfit for human consumption.

All members of the society, even the children, were involved in collecting and processing food. Men were responsible for hunting and fishing; women and children, for harvesting of roots and berries and such sedentary sea creatures as clams and mussels. Even such specialists as carvers and canoe makers took part in the daily subsistence tasks. Certain locations for food gathering, such as hunting and gathering grounds and fishing stations, belonged to individuals, who could pass them on to their children.

INHERITANCE.   The social organization of the Kwakiutl differed from the peoples both to the north and the south. In the north the tribes used a system of matrilineal inheritance; in the south, patrilineal. The Kwakiutl used both; that is, a child could inherit rank and privileges through either the father or the mother. In practice this meant that a child inherited the highest rank available to him or her from either side of the family and could join the lineage of either parent. The next child in age would inherit the second-best rank, and thus brothers and sisters could be assigned to different lineages. If both parents were of equal rank, the male line was favored. Lineages were associated with particular villages, and both lineage and village exogamy were practiced, thus ensuring a wider distribution of privileges and ranks.

SOCIAL SYSTEM.   Social organization, proceeding from the smallest unit to the largest, can be summarized as follows (Codere, 1961: 442–443):

1. *The nuclear family*—husband, wife, and children—living together with two or three closely related families in a great

house. Husband and wife were likely to be from different villages and different lineages.

2. *The household,* headed by the senior male member of the lineage to which the house belonged. The household usually consisted of brothers, their wives, and children. However, the possibility existed of a female member of the lineage living there with her husband or of a brother living with his wife's family.

3. *The lineage or numaym,* which was usually restricted to one village but which could have one or more great houses.

4. *The village,* consisting of one or more *numayms.* Villages in this early period were not ranked according to status, but later this was definitely the case through the potlatch system.

5. *The confederacy,* consisting of the uniting of two or more villages. In 1849, Fort Rupert was founded through the amalgamation of four villages. There is some question, however, whether a confederacy existed before this time.

The fundamental unit of this system was the *numaym.* Each *numaym* had its own story dealing with its origin in mythology and its own particular geographical location. The *numaym* has been likened to a landholding corporation consisting of a president-and-chief-stock-

Kwakiutl at Quatsino village, Vancouver Island, 1878.   Photograph courtesy of Museum of the American Indian, Heye Foundation.

Kwakiutl women and babies. n.d. Probably late nineteenth century. Photograph courtesy of Museum of the American Indian, Heye Foundation.

holder, the chief, and a group of other stockholders, who are ranked in order much as a first vice-president, second vice-president, and so forth (Suttles, 1970: 630). Associated with each rank is a "seat" to be taken during ceremonies, and the entire group can be placed in rank and seat order. The duties of the president are to direct the exploitation of real propery owned by the corporation, carry on financial transactions in his own name, and sanction those of other corporation members. Other members are obligated to contribute to the enterprises of their fellows through repaying loans with interest. All share in what is received by the *numaym*. The chief of the *numaym* must bequeath his position to his eldest son. Other members may give their positions to sons, sons-in-law, brothers-in-law, or other relatives. Because of this system of inheritance, the *numaym* is not a kin group. A man can hold positions in more than one *numaym,* he may have close blood relatives in other *numayms,* and he may share any one *numaym* with very distant relatives.

The Potlatch

CRESTS.   Before 1849 the potlatch was not the specialized institution that it later became. Gifts were given and feasts were held to mark special occasions such as marriages, puberty rites, and meetings with outsiders, but societies all over the world do this. The one distinctive Kwakiutl element was the practice of distributing real property to mark the transfer of intangible property such as names or crests. *Crests* were hereditary privileges, which Boas believed the Kwakiutl obtained orig-

406

inally through intermarriage with the peoples north of them. The word *crest* implied many things: guardian spirits, special names, initiation into certain secret societies with the right to perform dances or other ceremonies, and family histories leading back to the supernatural ancestor. In the north, crests were always inherited in the matrilineal line; that is, a father bequeathed his crests to his daughter's husband, who would in turn pass them to his son. Crests were also obtained through warfare by killing the person possessing the name or ceremony, but it is not clear how the details of ceremonics wcrc thus transferred to the victor.

The ceremony for the transfer of a name or crest involved the entire *numaym* in the receiving or distribution of property. Examples of property given at early potlatches were surplus food, copper shields, blankets of fur and mountain goat hair, cedar bark mats, canoes, and slaves. The most common and important item distributed was the blanket; the least important was the slave, who had little or no economic value. No European trade goods were exchanged, although the Kwakiutl had them. Copper shields, or *coppers,* were large thin sheets of beaten copper cut into the form of a shield with a T-shaped ridge running down the middle bottom half. They were painted with black lead and incised with designs. Their use goes back a long time. In reconstructing potlatch history, Codere (1950: 90) noted that two coppers named Moon

House. Kwakiutl Indians, Alert Bay, British Columbia, ca. 1890. Photograph courtesy of Museum of the American Indian, Heye Foundation.

and Sea Lion were given away in 1729. When the potlatch as it developed after 1849 is discussed, we will see the vital role of the copper in keeping an economic balance in the potlatch system.

DISTRIBUTION OF FOOD THROUGH THE POTLATCH. Several authors have recently speculated that the aboriginal potlatch of precontact times played a vital role in distributing equitably all available food resources. Piddocke (1965), Donald and Mitchell (1975), and Suttles (1970) all take exception to the idea that the Kwakiutl had such an abundance of food resources that they never suffered want and thus were able to devote large amounts of time to nonproductive activities such as winter ceremonials and potlatching. In the potlatch period, surpluses for the group as a whole undoubtedly did exist, owing to the decline in population and opportunities for outside income through fur trapping, trading, and outside jobs. Even then, however, and especially earlier, there were local variations in food supplies.

Piddocke (1965: 23) has constructed a convincing theory of the function of aboriginal potlatches. He believes that the potlatch served a subsistence function in that it countered the effects of varying resource productivity between villages by promoting exchanges of food from groups that had a temporary surplus to groups that had a temporary deficit. To support this theory, he presented four hypotheses:

1. The fantastic surpluses spoken of by many sources were not true for individual groups, although they may have been true for the area as a whole.
2. Participants in aboriginal potlatches were chiefs of *numayms.* Therefore, a series of potlatches between two chiefs were really exchanges of food and wealth between villages or *numayms.* Through these exchanges, disparate levels of productivity were minimized and subsistence was maintained for all.
3. Food could be exchanged for wealth such as blankets, slaves, and canoes, and this wealth could in turn be exchanged for prestige when it was given away.
4. Potlatching was motivated by the desire for prestige and status of a chief, and it was encouraged by the status rivalry between chiefs. All the people gained because all were given enough food to survive. Thus the potlatch system was encouraged to continue.

Piddocke supports this thesis with some facts concerning the food supply. Fish runs, although they might have been huge, were seasonal and localized. If bad weather prevented boats from going out when the fish were running, the chance to get enough to store might be lost to a group for that year. Or the fish might not come to an area at all in a particular year. Roots and berries, similarly, could be found only in specific places and at certain times of the year. Trespass on collecting grounds and hunting preserves was a common and seriously regarded crime that often led to armed conflict between groups. This trespass would not have occurred had there been so much available that there was no question of everyone's getting enough. Indeed, starvation and hunger happened to the Kwakiutl. Stories were told of the necessity of eating fern and lupine roots, and recipes were given for salmon tails and roasted salmon backbone (Boas, 1921: 329).

For all the importance of the potlatch in validating status and titles, it is logical to see it first as an essential food distribution system.

Ceremonialism and Supernaturalism

It is difficult to generalize about what the Kwakiutl believed about the supernatural, for each *numaym* had its own origin story, and none related to the tribe as a whole. In general, the Kwakiutl religion was an acknowledgment of supernatural powers. The people prayed to the sun for general blessings, to the weather for help in their own individual concerns, to animals they had killed for some desirable trait. These prayers, however, seemed more a recognition of other powers than supplications for help. The Kwakiutl believed in the power of evil people to cause harm through witchcraft, and shamans were assigned powers of curing, although the belief in the power of shamans was always tentative.

Boas implied that the Kwakiutl were very concerned with warfare, and much of their early ceremonialism was related to war. He cited several family histories that showed cannibal ceremonies performed around 1769 (Codere, 1961: 448). Crests and the elaborately staged dances of the winter ceremonials were an extremely important part of Kwakiutl life. Originally, a small isolated Kwakiutl village might have gained the right to perform some particular dance by making war upon the village that had that right. As time passed, however, crests and dances were transmitted more and more through the pattern of matrilineal inheritance that originated with the peoples to the north. Following this pattern, a man would bequeath his right to a dance to his daughter upon her marriage. The son-in-law would then be able to perform this ceremony, but he was expected to pass it in turn to his own son.

Eventually, the idea of crests and elaborate dances and ceremonies came to be valued for the sake of pageantry and excitement rather than for any true religious significance. Kwakiutl beliefs probably became more secular with the increasing importance of the potlatch after 1849 (Codere, 1961: 450), when ceremonies were enjoyed for their own sake, not for their underlying supernatural powers.

Curing and Material Culture

The Kwakiutl had an expert knowledge of the plant and animal life of their region, and they made good use of plant remedies for sickness. One ingenious remedy for burns was to encase the body of the victim within the blubbery hide of a seal. They also understood how to live successfully in their environment. Through their understanding of seasonal rhythms, they knew when the salmon would run or what was the proper time to harvest plants. They had an excellent knowledge of the physical nature of their country, although they visualized themselves as living on the shores of a great tidal river. As their navigation problems were similar to what they would have been on such a river—strong currents, eddies, and tidal overfalls—perhaps this notion was not so farfetched.

Kwakiutl technology indicated expert knowledge of the materials they dealt with. They used a variety of methods to store food, and one species of fish could be stored in several different ways, depending on the amount of fat it contained when caught, the cut being preserved, the way it was destined to taste and be cooked, and the length of time it would be kept (Codere, 1961: 452). Storage boxes could be manufactured from wood or from kelp for storing euchalon oil. Wood from the extensive forests was used in the manufacture of many items. Canoes were made from a hollowed log, which was then filled with water and human urine to soften it. Red hot stones were placed in the interior to shape and spread it, after which the inside of the canoe was covered with thin pieces of cedarwood. Houses were made from planks mounted on a framework of massive posts and roofed with poles and overlapping cedar planks. These houses were extemely large dwellings, ranging from 40 to 60 feet per side and designed to house four separate nuclear families. They had one front door and no windows. Ventilation was secured by shifting roof boards with long poles to let out the smoke. Fronts of the houses were decorated with the stylized art common to all Northwest Coast peoples. It is regrettable that so few traditional dwellings still stand today. The damp climate is slowly destroying those still in existence, and the Kwakiutl no longer build them. An exception is the community house constructed in Alert Bay in the mid-1960s.

Cedar bark was employed in the making of clothing, blankets, and rope. Aboriginal clothing was scanty, being limited to aprons and blankets of bark or of deer hide, fur robes for the nobles in cold weather, and rain capes and blankets woven of yellow cedar bark incorporated with goat wool, feathers, or dog hair. Hats woven of cedar bark or spruce root were a highly prized decorative item. Moccasins or leggings were not worn. Belts of sealskin held the blankets in place, and men wore bands of fur around their heads to hold back their long hair.

The Kwakiutl manufactured many items for use in obtaining food. Cod and halibut were caught on lines made of kelp with hooks designed of bent fir with a barb made of a splint of long bone. Weirs, nets, and a long rake were employed to catch herring and eulachon, and harpoons were used for larger sea creatures. Hunting was done with bows made from yellow cedar root that had been heated, bent, and rubbed with mountain goat or deer tallow and strung with deerskin or bear guts. Arrows were of red cedar sometimes feathered with two cormorant feathers. Traps, deadfalls, snares, lassos, and nets were also employed in catching land animals and birds.

Although I do not give a comprehensive inventory of all items used, they included wooden tongs for handling firewood and lifting hot stones, baskets, cedar bark mats, rope, mussel-shell tweezers, spoons and knives of clamshell, abalone nose rings and ear pendants, wooden spoons, dishes, masks, chests, boat-shaped cradles, and strainers made of rib bones of the seal tied together along three sticks. Distinctive artwork made many common, ordinary items beautiful.

The Arts

The earliest known Kwakiutl form of design was geometric forms. *Crest art*, the use of animal designs to symbolize social standing, was present when Vancouver visited the group in 1792. Crest art, inherited from the tribes to the north, was a vital part of Kwakiutl life. It is difficult to describe in words the striking impact of boldly painted housefronts and totem poles lining the shores of a bay with a backdrop of pines and mountains. Because the art represented the social status of its owner, it meant much more than pure decoration alone would have done.

The crest idea was also present in the Kwakiutl literary arts before 1849, but here it worked to limit rather than enhance imagination and variety. Too much attention became focused on the retelling of the history of crest privilege, so that imagination and variety in the stories suffered (Codere, 1961: 453).

In short, the Kwakiutl during the Prepotlatch Period were a vital, successful people living in an area of abundant natural resources. They were excellent traders and businessmen and were thus able to take advantage of all the new people and material goods moving into their area. Theirs was a culture in flux. The idea of crests, which came from the north, was changing their ideas of social distinctiveness. Status was becoming vested in an individual, not an entire family, and brothers could differ in rank depending upon what each of them had inherited from which parent. Difference in status was symbolized through art and stories and in ceremonies, architecture, and rhetoric. Religion and the secret societies were also changing as they incorporated the idea of rank.

THE POTLATCH PERIOD: 1849 to 1921

In 1849 a change occurred that had far-reaching implications for the Kwakiutl. The Hudson's Bay Company, interested in mining the coal deposits there, founded the village of Fort Rupert, which was to be the most important Indian village in the area for the next 30 years. People from four different villages moved to Fort Rupert, thus creating a center of power and prestige where none had existed before. In 1881 this center of power shifted to Alert Bay, where the Kwakiutl agency and mission station were established and where they still exist today.

Change continued to come at an accelerated rate. More and more strangers were entering the area, not only traders but also permanent settlers who were employed at local schools, canneries, sawmills, and government jobs. As the White population increased, that of the Indians declined. Of the 7,500 to 8,000 Southern Kwakiutl estimated in 1835, 2,264 remained in 1882, when the first agency census was taken, and by 1924, only a little over a thousand were left. The primary cause of this drastic loss of population was disease. The Kwakiutl were extremely susceptible to all the endemic European diseases: smallpox, measles, influenza, tuberculosis, and veneral disease. Throughout this time of population decline, however, the economy remained healthy, and the Kwakiutl were able to take advantage of their natural abundance to trade with the many people coming into the area. Potlatching grew in importance and size and became the major cultural institution by about the middle of the nineteenth century.

After the founding of Alert Bay in 1881, the Indians came increasingly under Canadian law and law enforcement. Winter dancing and potlatching were forbidden by law, although the Kwakiutl managed to evade these laws and to hold large ceremonies. This period ended in the early 1920s, when the economy of the entire region declined, and the Kwakiutl were caught short by the increased use of motor-powered boats, which they could not afford to buy. As the abundance necessary for the huge giveaways had disappeared, the potlatch could no longer exist.

Contributing to the demise of the potlatch was the effective enforcement of the laws against it. James Sewid, a Kwakiutl Indian who wrote his life story in *Guests Never Leave Hungry* (Spradley, 1969), gives a poignant description of what he observed as a boy of eight in 1922. The government had sent out word that all the people had to give up their masks, coppers, and other ceremonial regalia. Those who did not comply were brought to Alert Bay; jailed in the schoolhouse, where they had to sleep on the floor; and eventually brought to trial. They received sentences as long as six months when convicted.

Community Organization and External Relations

For the majority of Kwakiutl, living in their remote and isolated villages, life went on much as before. In the new community of Fort Rupert, however, the Indians reaped great economic advantages, with the Hudson's Bay Company personnel's providing opportunities for both employment and trade. Fort Rupert citizens had the chance to act as interpreters, as middlemen, and as entrepreneurs with Whites as well as with visiting Indians of their own and other tribes. Their relationship with everyone during this period was for the most part amiable. Although minor disagreements sprang up from time to time, warfare ended completely by 1865. As the people of Fort Rupert increased their wealth, they also attempted to increase their power and status through holding bigger potlatches, and the growth of the potlatch dates from the founding of the town.

Although the Kwakiutl remained the dominant population in their own area, people of all nationalities were flocking to the west. The transcontinental railroad, completed in 1880, encouraged and accelerated this movement. The city of Victoria, on the southern tip of Vancouver Island, went from a population of 500 in 1856 to over 25,000 in 1858 because of the Fraser River gold rush. Victoria became an early center for Indian employment and recreation. Men worked as temporary laborers, and women served as laundresses and prostitutes. Although the Indians living temporarily in Victoria had quarters that were often squalid and filthy, they found the experience worthwhile because urban wages could provide liquor and prestige to be enjoyed back home.

In 1881 the Kwawkewlth Agency at Alert Bay was founded for the purpose of assimilating Indians into the general Canadian population. Official reserves were established on the principle of giving to the Indians all the land they had been using. There was more attempt to enforce laws already on the books—the Indian Liquor Ordinance of 1867 and the Indian Act of 1876, which prohibited potlatching and winter dancing. A post of the Royal Canadian Mounted Police was established at

Alert Bay as well as a mission and mission school, government agencies, and Canadian industries.

There were increased chances for employment on the Indians' own terms. A number of small fish canneries appeared locally, and the Indians could move from one to the next depending on the economic advantage to them. Men worked as fishermen on contract to the cannery, women packed the fish into cans, and even the children contributed with light work. There was some competition from Chinese and Japanese arrivals, but they posed no great threat as their numbers remained fairly small where the Kwakiutl lived. Japanese fishermen were to become much more of an economic threat after the First World War.

The two official contacts with the Indians during this period were those of the agent and the missionary. Although individual agents differed and some were benevolent (one gave a tow to three boatloads of Indians who he knew were on their way to a potlatch), most agents fought a continuous losing battle to stop potlatching and winter dancing. Many felt the whole business was immoral because their charges were enjoying themselves rather than out working and making money. It seems obvious that these agents did not understand the Indians, because one of their main preoccupations was to stop completely the most valued and important social institution that the Kwakiutl had. They also disapproved of the occupation of great houses and of Indians traveling to Victoria.

The missionaries, on the whole, had more personal relationships with individual Indians and were not so much concerned with changing the culture. The first mission school opened in a single room in Alert Bay in 1881. Ten years later vocational training and a girls' residence had been added. As the Kwakiutl valued literacy, which enabled them to keep better potlatch records and trading accounts, school attendance was good. When the mission attempted to teach moral or vocational lessons through housekeeping or industrial tasks, however, the Kwakiutl resented it and left. Thus, many children passed through the school system, but their stay was often brief and interrupted.

In general, the Whites in the area viewed Indians as people who must be westernized. If young, the Kwakiutl belonged in school; if older, on the job. There was little tolerance of Indian social and cultural institutions that did not fit in with Canadian practices. The Indians, on the other hand, found the outsiders useful as a source of trade goods and technical knowledge, but the acknowledgment of their proficiency in technical fields did not extend to social areas. The Kwakiutl did not like being treated as inferiors with strange, immoral habits. The groundwork was being laid for the suspicion and mistrust that flourish today.

Economic and Social Organization

In spite of their declining population, the Kwakiutl maintained and even increased their collective wealth because some traditional cultural habits lent themselves well to new conditions. Not only were they industrious, but they also had a tradition of migratory and seasonal occupations that fitted well into the new conditions. Traditionally, they were independent operators, so each individual could maximize his own opportunities without obtaining group consensus or approval.

In many ways the old economic system persisted. The Kwakiutl were self-sufficient in that they normally provided their food and other necessities of life. The drop in population meant that large surpluses of food were available to support the potlatch system. The seasonal migration pattern of nine months of work from early spring to late fall and three months of winter vacation devoted to ceremonies and feasting did not change, although it was modified to include the activities associated with wage labor. In the modern sense, the Kwakiutl were good businessmen, and outside employment opportunities increased as time went on. The most important source of cash income was always commercial fishing. Trapping animals for furs brought some income, although trapping probably peaked before 1836. As the lumbering industry moved into the area, some Kwakiutl men worked at logging camps and sawmills, but this was never very popular, perhaps because the Kwakiutl traditionally felt much more at home on the water and the shores than in the woods. Smaller numbers of people worked at jobs like hop picking, mining, ethnological work such as being an informant or making articles for sale to museums or tourists, prostitution, guiding, laundering, making canoes, building roads, and building and operating motorboats (Codere, 1950: 31–32).

As the power to buy them increased, new goods entered the economy. One of the most important was the cheap gray-white wool blanket, which became the measure of value in the potlatch system, driving out the older and more beautiful cedar-bark blankets. After 1849, European clothing replaced aboriginal garments, and a variety of consumer goods from Canada and America replaced many formerly handcrafted items. The Kwakiutl diet began to include tea, coffee, liquor, biscuits, and molasses. Theirs was an increasingly wealthy society, and much of this wealth was used to buy manufactured goods. The making of native craft items decreased.

FAMILY AND MARRIAGE. Social organization remained basically the same as that related in the preceding section. The independent nuclear family did not exist as a separate social unit because the common pattern was for four separate families, ideally those of brothers, to live together in a great house. More and more, the social system was built on the idea of individual rank order. People within villages were nobles or commoners, and the villages themselves had a rank order among all other villages. The idea emerged that Fort Rupert people were superior to other people simply by virtue of living there. Gradually, all Kwakiutl villages were ranked from numbers 1 to 13—or 19 if the Lekwiltok were included.

The Kwakiutl were required to marry someone outside their *numaym,* but during this period they often married within their village to ensure that crests and religious prerogatives remained there. Contrary to secular rank, which could be inherited directly, religious privileges were given by a father to his daughter as part of her dowry. They were held but not used by the son-in-law, who was expected to pass them to his son at the appropriate time for initiation into one of the secret societies at a winter ceremonial. Because of the importance of rank, marriages, at least among nobles, were most often arranged by the parents. The same people held both secular and religious rank and arranged the marriages of their children so that more power was added to the family. A boy was expected to marry someone of his own social status. Children from wealthy families usually married early, for they were desirable mates; those with less status were sometimes obliged to wait. The courtship, such as it was, was carried out by the boy's parents; often the boy and girl did not meet before the terms of a marriage contract had been decided. The boy's parents sought to impress those of the girl with such details as genealogy, the important ancestors he had, his wealth, how many coppers he possessed, the potlatches he would give, and what position in a secret society he would inherit through his mother. The parents of the girl, trying to make the best possible bargain, were reluctant to give her up. They would mention how busy she was at weaving beautiful baskets or blankets, how she hated to leave her mother yet, or how absorbed she was in arts and crafts. If conditions were satisfactory, however, a bride price was finally agreed upon.

The wedding itself was a time of rejoicing. The groom, dressed in new wedding garments, went to the bride's house accompanied by all his nearest relatives in newly painted canoes. There was much singing, laughing, and playing of pranks. Upon reaching their destination, the groom's party marched around the home of the bride four times, beating on the outside house walls with batons, but no one appeared to let them in. After the fourth circuit, the door was flung open, and the party was welcomed. The bride and groom were taken to the rear of the house, seated upon a raised platform near the fire, and proclaimed man and wife.

Marriage among the Kwakiutl was monogamous, but it did not necessarily last for life. Divorce, however, was more readily granted if
there were no children involved. A groom was obligated to return his
wife's dowry through giving a potlatch for her relatives. If he did not
do this, she might leave him in disgust for dishonoring her. Although
once he had paid for her, she could be considered to belong again to
her family and given to someone else, this was seldom done if the couple had children.

CHILD CARE.   Children were welcomed and guarded with strict taboos
even in the prenatal period. Pregnant women avoided certain foods
such as salmon eggs or gum, which might impart their stickiness to her
womb and cause a difficult delivery. If either husband or wife saw anything unpleasant, its curse could be removed by waving a piece of cedar
bark over the object four times and then passing the cedar bark four
times down the back of the person (Kwakiutl, 1953: 38).

A baby was given his or her first name at the age of four days, and
this was a signal for a potlatch, dancing, and feasting. The baby's parents gave blankets and other goods to those friends and relatives
attending the feast, and the guests were expected to return the value of
the goods to the child at 100 percent interest within a year, thus giving
the child a foundation of wealth on which to build. The baby was kept
swaddled on a rigid cradleboard made of cedar until able to walk, being
removed only once a day for bathing. The baby's mother carried him or
her around with her all day, perhaps hanging the cradleboard on a
nearby tree to free her for her tasks. When the child was a year old, his
or her cradleboard was ceremoniously placed in a box, never to be
touched again, and the child was given a new name belonging to the
family.

Children were reared in a relaxed manner, learning what they
needed to know mainly by imitating their elders. Boys pretended to be
adult hunters and fishermen and played many games to toughen themselves. In *Smoke from Their Fires,* Charles Nowell (1941) recounted how
he and his friends whipped each other with spruce twigs until they
bled, or played a game in which they threw huge roots at each other. A
test of manhood was the placing of burning hemlock twigs on their
forearms to see how long each boy could bear the pain without throwing off the twig.

Although aggression was encouraged in play, children were punished when they tried to turn the same aggression upon their parents
or guardians. Nowell also told of the severe beatings he got from his
brother for disobeying him. Through these techniques, children were
encouraged to be aggressive and demanding within formal limits, to

compete and win against their peers, but at the same time to obey the rules set by society (Ford, 1941: 77).

Girls were secluded at puberty in small huts, where they were served food by a female shaman and allowed to drink only through a bone tube made from the wing of an eagle in order to avoid the evil consequences of polluting the water. Menstrual seclusion was practiced thereafter. A potlatch would be given to signal a girl's return to the community as an adult eligible for marriage.

A family might give a number of potlatches for a son as he grew up to mark important skills he had learned or to signal a new name which, along with its inherited privileges, was bestowed upon him. The most important potlatch for a boy of noble birth was given when he was initiated into one of the secret societies and received crests and privileges of his own. This ceremony also signaled that he was ready for marriage.

The Potlatch

Rohner and Rohner (1970: 95) define the potlatch in two different ways, depending upon point of view. From the viewpoint of the giver, a *potlatch* is a public display and distribution of property during which one individual or group claims certain hereditary rights or privileges from another group. From the viewpoint of the recipients, a *potlatch* is the people who are invited to witness and validate a host's claims to, or transmission of, hereditary privileges and who receive in return, each according to his or her rank, differential amounts of wealth. Although these definitions would be true before 1849 as well as after, the focus of interest changed after the founding of Fort Rupert. Crests in themselves became less important than the property that was distributed to validate them. As the interest in social status and financial worth increased, the potlatches grew larger and a greater variety of goods, including European goods, were given away. At his final potlatch in 1921, Daniel Cranmer distributed items such as gasboats, Hudson's Bay blankets, pool tables, musical instruments, jewelry, clothing, kitchenware, furniture, and sacks of flour (Codere, 1961: 470).

Throughout the potlatch period, European blankets were used as the baseline of currency. Other objects, especially coppers, were valued in terms of blankets. Coppers usually doubled in value every time they changed hands, and one obtained from the Tsimshian in 1864 rose from a worth of 100 blankets to that of 16,000 blankets when it priced itself out of the market because no one could afford the cost (Codere, 1961: 471–472). Coppers also performed a vital function in the society. It was a mark of the highest status if a chief, rather than giving away a copper, destroyed it, usually by breaking it into pieces and throwing them into the sea. This action brought an end to the constantly increasing debt owed for that copper and thus was a method of destroying credit. If the chief being potlatched could not emulate this feat by destroying in his turn a copper of equal worth, he was in deep disgrace with his *numaym* even though he still retained much wealth.

Piddocke (1965: 254–255) discussed two different interpretations of how the potlatch worked. Codere, in *Fighting with Property* (1950), postulated that the recipient of a potlatch was obligated to give a return potlatch in about a year, when twice as much was given away. This meant that one man would alternately be giver and receiver of a geometrically increasing amount of wealth. In interpreting the potlatch in this way, Codere linked it with the borrowing and lending at interest, which was the method used by chiefs to increase their wealth or to help others who were giving potlatches. Piddocke noted that Curtis (1915: 143–144) did not make this interpretation. Curtis stated that any Kwakiutl complaining that he had not received as much as he had given would be ridiculed for being so greedy. Men seldom received as much at potlatches as they had distributed because some people had died in the interim or were too poor to give a return potlatch. A man could demand that interest be returned on a loan, but he could not demand that someone give a potlatch to pay back freely given gifts. Codere's account of the aboriginal potlatch, however, seems to agree with Curtis because she noted that during this early time there was no increase in value of goods given away.

Ford, in *Smoke from Their Fires* (1941: 18–19) stated that it was the interest rate that increased, not the potlatch gift. If a man received 100 blankets at one potlatch, he would expect to give the same number back. He could, however, loan these same blankets at a rate of 25 percent for a few months, 50 percent for half a year, and 100 percent for a full year. These loans could come due at any time the creditor wished to give a potlatch. If the debtor could not afford to pay them, he would borrow from someone else, or he could borrow from the creditor and relinquish the blankets he would normally receive at the potlatch.

Potlatches were given for many reasons. Some celebrated critical life events such as birth, puberty, marriage, or death. Others functioned to save face for disasters such as the capsizing of a canoe, a bodily injury, or the birth of a deformed child or to wipe out a breech of a ceremonial taboo like laughing, stumbling, or coughing at winter dances (Rohner & Rohner, 1970: 95). Potlatches could be an investment of wealth, so that when a man reached old age he had so many people obligated to him that he did not have to worry about not being able to work. They were given to compete with other ranking chiefs or to take vengeance upon them, perhaps by destroying a copper or by pouring so much euchalon oil upon the fire that the visiting chiefs were forced to move away. Etiquette required them to stay put if possible, and there are records of entire houses burning down during this ordeal by fire. Although this rivalry had its abrasive aspects when the chiefs became too bombastic and tried too hard to surpass a rival, on the whole the system greatly benefited the Kwakiutl people through the exchange of food and wealth.

Rivalry in potlatching substituted for rivalry in war. After about 1865, warfare and raiding disappeared completely, and people no longer had to worry about surprise attacks launched for no apparent reason. In addition to peace, the potlatch system gave each person and each village a social ranking in respect to all other Kwakiutl, not only their own close neighbors and friends. Finally, all the people benefited because in order to make the system work at all, they had to share. In spite of the chief's ferocious reputation as depicted by Ruth Benedict in *Patterns of Culture* (1934), Codere (1956) called the Kwakiutl an amiable people, for regular day-to-day life was usually based on generosity and sharing.

Ceremonialism and Supernaturalism

During the potlatch period, the Kwakiutl maintained their traditional division of the year. The time between March and November was devoted to secular concerns such as food gathering or other economic pursuits. From November to March the people moved to their winter villages to observe the season with ceremonials including dances, potlatches, and feasting. No work was done except that necessary to maintain good health and to produce the ceremonies. A four-day transition period between the two seasons was devoted to commemorating those who had died since the last winter.

The entire social organization changed during this ceremonial time. New names were used, new songs were sung, and serious prohibitions were placed upon the use of secular names. The theme of the season was a youth's encounter with a spirit who kidnapped him, gave him supernatural power, and then returned him to his village. The purpose of the dance was to exorcise the spirit from the youth, who then returned to the village in a state of ecstacy, and to remove his madness (Rohner & Rohner, 1970: 106). As previously stated, the right to participate in these winter ceremonials was inherited, and normally the same people who held secular power had ceremonial power. This divided the Kwakiutl into those who performed and those who served as the audience.

A major shift took place in ceremonialism during this time. Originally, the dances had been connected with symbols of war. The *hamatsa,* or cannibal dancers, actually ate parts of a corpse, usually a slave. After 1849, however, the symbolism used turned to potlatching. Between dances the chiefs boasted about how much they had given away or insulted people who owed repayment for loans. The dances themselves became elaborately staged theatrical performances, during which supernatural birds flew through the air to capture people, men danced on the water, and *hatsamas* disappeared in the midst of crowds. The illusions probably fooled few people, but they must have been entertaining. The Kwakiutl carefully planned these performances, some people even remaining home from summer berrying and fishing in order to dig tunnels under the floor of the dance house. Other devices used to ensure successful illusion were kelp speaking tubes, hidden rooms where dancers could hide until their performance, false-bottomed chests to conceal dancers, and various tricks involving wooden masks, wooden figures let down from the roof on strings, and the use of leather and wooden gloves and slippers when handling fire.

Along with the loss of belief in the real powers of dancers and supernatural figures went a corresponding loss of belief in the powers of shamans. They were generally recognized to be the users of tricks, lies, and deceits to achieve their cures, and they were sometimes attacked with ridicule when their tricks were exposed. The Kwakiutl believed in the power of sorcery and black magic, but made every effort to control it for the good of the society. For instance, a sorcerer at Fort Rupert was declared "not fit to be alive" in a secret meeting of assembled chiefs. The chiefs gathered the necessary blankets for the sorcerer's fee, had some young men get some of his excreta, and told him that they wished the death of another chief because of potlatching rivalry. The sorcerer performed the appropriate ceremony, using his own excreta unknowingly, and killed himself (Codere, 1961: 477-478). This incident implies that the Kwakiutl understood that human hatred and ill will were behind evil sorcery, not the power of the supernatural (Codere, 1961: 478).

Curing and Knowledge

In spite of the fact that the Kwakiutl population was decreasing and young people as well as old were being struck down by infectious diseases, there were very few changes in traditional curing practices. The people did accept smallpox vaccinations and a few Western patent medicines, which they obtained from the Hudson's Bay Company, but for the most part they continued to use their traditional plant medicines. As no really effective Western medicines existed at this time for the endemic diseases except a gradual natural immunization, the Kwakiutl probably didn't lose much by this attitude.

Western practices and knowledge increased gradually, but it is very difficult to assess what they meant to the culture. The importance of Western technology undoubtedly varied from village to village and individual to individual. Literacy aided potlatch accounting, but was little used for its own sake. The people learned the art of home brewing, but this was not a positive contribution to their lives.

Art

The art of the potlatch period was exuberant and almost entirely devoted to crest representation. Typical examples were the painted housefronts, totem poles, masks, rattles, speakers' staves, and other dance and potlatch items. After 1860 housefronts were made of sawn boards painted with extravagant designs and often decorated with wings, beaks, and other protuberances made from lumber and glued on. Much gadgetry was used in the making of masks. Beaks could open and close, fish fins could flop, and secret compartments opened to reveal faces within faces.

Codere (1961: 479–480) quoted two authorities who differed as to the intrinsic artistic merit of this art. Drucker considered it vigorous, imaginative, and freed from formal limitations. Wingert believed it lacked necessary restraint. This became more true in the twentieth century, when the crest idea seemed to stultify the quality of artistic production. Perhaps as life became more secularized, art also lost its esthetic purpose and became routine.

THE POSTPOTLATCH PERIOD: 1930 to 1955

The 1920s were a time of rapid change and economic adversity for the Kwakiutl. They needed motorboats to replace the old and obsolete boats and equipment that they had previously rented from the canneries. The Kwakiutl, however, were not granted credit with which to buy new boats. The Japanese competition in fishing became more severe. The number of canneries was reduced, so that the men not only had fewer outlets for selling fish, but also their wives could no longer work for wages. The Great Depression simply continued a bad situation. Although there were a few potlatches given into the thirties, potlatching virtually ceased because recipients could no longer afford to return the gifts given to them or to maintain interest payments. Younger people began to see potlatching as a source of trouble and worry and wanted nothing to do with it when prosperity returned during World War II.

The following account of the modern Kwakiutl owes much to the works of Codere done in the fifties, to Ronald and Evelyn Rohner, and

Mask representing earthquake dancer. n.d.   Photograph courtesy of Museum of the American Indian, Heye Foundation.

to Harry Wolcott, who all worked there in the sixties, and to the autobiography of the modern Kwakiutl James Sewid, recounted by Spradley (1969) in *Guests Never Leave Hungry*.

Community Organization and External Relations

About 1921, Kwakiutl population stopped diminishing and began to grow. Codere recorded a total of 1,482 Southern Kwakiutl, omitting the Lekwiltok, in 1956 (1961: 484). Rohner gave the census of the Kwaw-

The village of Gilford Island, 1933.   Courtesy of Ronald P. Rohner.

kewlth Agency, which included the Lekwiltok and the Comox Band of
Coast Salish, as 2,500 in 1962 (1967: 20). Seventy-five percent of this
population was under 32, with a median age between 15 and 16.

The most important Southern Kwakiutl village was Alert Bay,
where approximately one-third of the Indian people lived. Other villages obtained supplies and services from Alert Bay and commonly
measured their distance from it in terms of how long it took to get there
by boat. Alert Bay, which had a population of 1,200 in 1962, was
divided into White and Indian sections. The Indian section included
homes, the agency, an Anglican church, several stores, some fishing
wharves, and schools, among which was the Indian residential school.
In the White section were most of the White residences plus the main
community services: hospital, fire and police stations, bank, post office,
high school, stores, restaurants, movie theaters, and fishing wharves.
The White population of Alert Bay included lumbermen, fishermen,
and workers in schools, agencies, and services. Most probably did not
intend to stay there for the rest of their lives.

There were 16 bands and 16 occupied reserves in the Kwawkewlth
Agency, although four of these bands amalgamated in the late sixties
(Rohner, 1967: 11). The Rohners did their research on Gilford Island, a
relatively small community having only 24 houses, of which 19 to 21
were occupied during their stay. The houses in one part of the village
were prefabricated units that had been shipped to the area from an air
force base. All homes stood on posts to elevate them about two feet off
the ground for protection against rising water. The focus of the com-

munity was the sea, and front housedoors commonly faced it. Gilford Island had one big house, which served as the Community Hall, and the house posts remained from another that had been a communal dwelling. Although the band membership was recorded as 188 with 174 people living on the reserve, Rohner found a total resident population of only 107 with 92 people living away. This figure fluctuated depending on the season and the number of children away at residential school. The population was young, 75 percent being age 30 or under. The old pattern of sharing one household among several nuclear families had broken down, and most families occupied their own homes, although it was still common for people, especially relatives and those in transit, to share one house.

Gilford Island was an isolated spot, two hours away from Alert Bay by boat. Two small Canadian communities, Simoom Sound and Echo Bay, were only 45 minutes away, and each had a small store, but most people preferred to shop at Alert Bay. The small islands were, on the whole, more depressed, conservative, and "tough" than Alert Bay.

Harry Wolcott was the teacher at "Blackfish Village" on tiny "Blackfish Island" (a pseudonym). This small community had only 13 occupied houses, with five standing empty. Outbuildings such as smoke houses and privies were scattered among the frame dwellings, which stood on posts. The only signs of previous traditional dwellings were house poles from two big houses and a couple of totem poles lying on the ground. About 125 people were in and out of the community during the year Wolcott was there; median age was 16.

Blackfish Village was also about two hours from Alert Bay by boat, and many people had left the village to move there permanently. A

Gilford Island village from the water looking into the forest behind, 1971.   Courtesy of Ronald P. Rohner.

Gilford Island village from behind the school and Big House, 1962.   Courtesy
of Ronald P. Rohner.

number of Blackfish people had also migrated to Vancouver. Most people residing away still maintained significant social ties with their
home community. Those who had moved away were often the best prepared to deal effectively with the White world.

All Kwakiutl people, including those in the small villages, now had
much contact with Canadian-American society and had taken on many
of its characteristics. They were exposed to this society in many ways:
in visits to Alert Bay, through the mass media, at school, in visits to
Vancouver and other southern cities, and in a few cases through working as migrant laborers picking hops and berries in Washington State.
The Indians were accepting of White power and technical superiority,
and many wanted their children to identify with the larger society
although they could not do so themselves. Most, however, still believed
that their culture was superior, especially in social organization. There
was a widespread distrust of the availability of justice, fair dealing, and
friendliness to Indians. The Canadians and Americans, in their turn,
saw the Indians as a people who were not going to vanish after all and
who probably would remain distinctively Indian within the larger society. They believed that Indians should have more to say about their
own futures and should be less restricted by the powers of church and
government (Hawthorn, Belshaw, Jamieson, et al., 1958: 60; quoted in
Codere, 1961: 486).

One Kwakiutl, James Sewid, created an exciting success story as judged by both White and Indian cultures. Living as an adult in Alert Bay, he held membership and leadership in organizations as diverse as the Nimpkish Band Council, Intertribal Council, Kwakwala Arts and Crafts Organization, Native Brotherhood Executive Board, Anglican Church, Kwakwala Prayer Group, Youth Guidance Committee, Alert Bay Board of Trade, Hospital Board, P.T.A., and Masonic Lodge. Coming from a noble Kwakiutl family, Sewid inherited many ceremonial positions of importance. In the economic sphere, he made an equally important name for himself as owner of several fishing boats with consistent record catches, sawmill and boat shop operator, and, at one

Wolf carvings on Big House front door, Gilford Island, 1962.   Courtesy of Ronald P. Rohner.

Chief Councillor at Gilford Island, 1962–63. A man noted for his good judgment and great strength.   Courtesy of Ronald P. Rohner.

time, operator of a small store in Alert Bay. Sewid, through his many activities, acted as a cultural broker and was able to interpret one culture to the other. His life story, *Guests Never Leave Hungry* (Spradley, 1969), makes fascinating reading.

Economic Organization

The big change in the economic functioning of the Kwakiutl during modern times was that they could no longer rely on their own resources for survival. Instead they were totally dependent on the overall Canadian-American economy and had to adjust to all its fluctuations. Since the 1920s most Kwakiutl men have been commercial fishermen, but this vital industry changed as it grew. In order to compete with the other fishermen who had outnumbered them since 1913, the Kwakiutl had to acquire power boats, power-driven nets and winches, radio telephones, echo sounders, and radar. To get them, the Indians bought shares with other men or mortgaged property to the fish company as collateral for loans. Some Indians did not seem to understand how this worked. One lost not only a $1,000 net, upon which he had failed to make payments, but also his boat, which had been collateral for the loan.

Along with its enormous growth, the fishing industry became centralized. Kwakiutl men no longer fished in their own neighborhoods but traveled long distances to fishing grounds. The fish, collected by refrigerated packers, were sold in southern cities. The local canneries, which used to employ women and children, had been abandoned, and the women were no longer able to find jobs outside their homes. The fishing season was heavily regulated for conservation purposes. In 1963 it was four days per week; in 1964, it was reduced to two. Strikes called by the fishermen's association cut further into fishing time. In 1963 a long strike during the summer meant not only that the men lost the

Village fisherman disentangling a salmon. The net in the water is supported by the cork-line behind the gill-netter. 1963.   Courtesy of Ronald P. Rohner.

income from fish they were not allowed to catch, but also that they were ineligible for unemployment benefits the following winter because they had not met the 15-week minimum working time (Rohner, 1967: 47–48).

Although most men worked in the fishing industry, a few were loggers, some were artists or worked as consultants to museums or anthropologists, and a handful were proprietors of their own small businesses. Many dug clams during the November to May season, but the money earned was enough only to supplement other sources. About half the people on Gilford Island were forced to rely on outside sources such as the Unemployment Insurance Commission, Family Allowance, and relief to get them through the winter. In 1962–1963, the mean income for the 24 adult men on Gilford was $2,800 (Rohner, 1967: 41).

The degree to which the Kwakiutl relied on their old subsistence sources varied depending on where they lived. In Alert Bay the people were no longer self-sufficient in food, although some canned salmon, deer, and berries and froze fish (Codere, 1961: 491). In Kingcome, a few people started planting vegetables, a real departure from traditional practice. On Gilford, many subsistence activities were still being practiced. People cut their own firewood, fished and dug clams for home consumption, hunted, and collected crabs, berries, seaweed, and barnacles to eat. They rendered euchalon oil, which was worth five dollars per gallon on the market. The basic diet for the people consisted of fish, potatoes, bread, and tea. Lack of items such as fruit, fresh vegetables, and milk meant that the people were often deficient in iron and calcium.

Almost all craft production had vanished except for a few people who carved masks and other objects for sale to tourists. Some canoes and fishing hooks were still made, and the women knitted heavy sweaters to sell to outsiders or crocheted objects with a vague Indian theme such as door curtains with eagle or thunderbird designs. Clothing conformed to local standards—high rubber boots, heavy wool shirts, and pants for the men while working, and suits for special occasions; dresses and sometimes bright shawls for the women. Teenagers enjoyed keeping up with modern fashions. Houses, too, conformed to standard Canadian-American styles, and appliances were purchased although the village lacked electricity. The few Kwakiutl objects that a family still possessed were stored in attics or closets and not displayed.

The practices of the Indian agency have, on the whole, been destructive for the Kwakiutl. The agency offered help, but only on its own terms. The Indians were assisted but given no chance to assume responsibility for their own lives and problems. The Kwakiutl themselves said that their old business sense had vanished. James Sewid was a notable exception to this generalization. He took pride in building his own house with no outside help and in managing his various enterprises.

Social Organization

Very little of the old social order with its rank and class structure remained. The nuclear family was the basic unit of social organization, although people were willing to help relatives with gifts or hospitality on a temporary basis. People who married almost always set up their own home rather than living with parents or relatives. Marriage to a resident of the same village was much more common than going outside for a spouse.

Young people were no longer given Indian names that had to be validated by a potlatch, nor did they know what their rank would have been under the old system. Potlatching itself was still carried on by a few elderly people, but they gave away money rather than goods because it was too much trouble to decide what each recipient wanted and could use. Some people, however, still used their wealth to enhance their social status. A prominent Kwakiutl leader spent an unusually large amount of money in financing a Native Brotherhood banquet. In Alert Bay, all housewives invited to the Wearever parties given to sell pots and pans felt that they had to buy the $250 set to uphold their social status. Drinking was often motivated by the desire to prove social equality with outsiders and to spend conspicuously among friends, although aggression also played a part in drinking behavior (Codere, 1961: 496–497).

Canadian-American standards in housing and household goods were the norm, and people tried to conform to them as well as they could. Although the Indians were extravagant in buying consumer goods, they were also careless in their use so that new watches, clothing, and appliances did not last as long as they should have. Although this might have been a survival of the conspicuous consumption of the old potlatch economy, it might also have been an emulation of the bad habits of Whites in the area (Codere, 1961: 498). On the whole, the more prosperous and assimilated a person was, the more he was looked upon as a leader. This ideal was so well established that Kwakiutl parents felt it was socially desirable for their daughters to marry White men because this would give them higher status.

Small island communities such as Gilford and Blackfish could not measure up to White standards very well because of low income and no electricity or indoor plumbing, but they made the attempt. On Gilford, Rohner found worn commercially made furniture, bare floors, and gas lamps in use, but most people made the substantial effort it took to keep their homes clean. Almost all homes contained transistor radios. Households were often large because very few people used contraception on a consistent basis, and children were wanted. On Gilford the mean age of marriage was 21, and no marriages had been arranged by parents since the forties. People often lived together before legally marrying, but this was considered acceptable behavior. Illegitimate children were easily taken into the society with no stigma.

CHILD CARE.   Children were reared very permissively and given much handling and attention by parents, relatives, and older siblings. About the age of six, more discipline was imposed, but this often took the form of yelling or commands, which the children easily ignored. Aggressiveness in children was encouraged. One parent on Gilford Island supported an older child who was hitting a younger one, trying to take his tricycle. As they grew older, children received a great deal of independence, sometimes bordering on neglect if the parents were involved with a drinking party. These traits of aggressiveness and independence, though in line with traditional Kwakiutl culture, led to a lot of trouble in the schoolrooms. Both Wolcott and Mrs. Rohner found keeping order their biggest problem. Children commonly arrived at school late or not at all, slept during class, fought with those around them, and ignored what the teacher was saying. School problems were compounded by the fact that a new teacher appeared almost every year, the old ones being driven away by isolation, loneliness, low pay, and the difficulties of teaching disruptive students. Some teachers were afraid of the Indians, and many made no attempt to consult with parents regarding their children's progress. With all the difficulties of the school situation, it was no wonder the Kwakiutl children scored well below the national averages on standardized tests. Some children attended boarding school at Alert Bay after graduating from the island schools, but there was not sufficient room for all who wanted to go. Another problem was the lack of good jobs in the area. Additional schooling brought no advantages to those Kwakiutl who were not planning to move to a city.

HEALTH CARE.   For health problems, all the Indians relied mainly on White medicine. Nurses from the Indian Health Services visited the islands about once a month to run child care clinics, give immunizations, and provide pre- and postnatal care. There was a hospital in Alert Bay. Some Indian folk medicines such as devil's club and balsam tea for tuberculosis and other ailments, or rubbing with eulachon grease to reduce fever, were still employed when White medicines were ineffective or the people did not want to bother seeking treatment. There were few signs that the people blamed sickness on evil sorcery as they once had. Accidents were a primary source of death and disability. Drowning was the leading cause of death, followed by motor vehicle accidents and burns suffered in house fires. Motor vehicle accidents, however, did not occur on the small islands such as Gilford because there were no cars there. After accidents, death came most often from pneumonia, diseases of early infancy, and cardiovascular problems. Some local sanitary practices were health hazards because people routinely emptied chamber pots and threw trash into the sea at their doorsteps.

SOCIAL CONTROL.   Small communities such as the one on Gilford Island were still tightly knit social organizations where the people supported each other in various ways. People cooperated in fishing, clamming, and working together. They also shared the care of children. Marriages normally endured for a lifetime even though one or both partners might be unfaithful on occasion. All relationships, including marriage, tended to be less demonstrative than those between Whites. Gilford Island was, on the whole, a law-abiding community, and villagers seldom needed to rely on outside forces such as the Royal Canadian Mounted Police. Deviant individuals were controlled through gossip and other forms of social pressure. Because their identity was anchored in the village, individuals were dependent on what others thought about them. This dependency usually resulted in a satisfactory degree of social control.

THE ROLE OF DRINKING AMONG THE KWAKIUTL.   Alcohol abuse, however, remained a serious problem. Since 1962 the Kwakiutl have shared the right of all Canadian citizens to buy liquor. Before 1951 drinking was illegal for them, and between 1951 and 1962 they were allowed to drink only on licensed premises. Thanks to White and Chinese friends in the area who acted as bootleggers, however, the Kwakiutl have been drinking for some time. Social drinking, in the sense of having a cocktail or two and then stopping, was rare. Most Indians who drank did not stop until they became intoxicated, and if the liquor was available, parties went on for several days with different people coming and going. On Gilford Island, the preferred drink was beer or red wine.

Rohner found that drinking behavior varied according to status. People who strove to get ahead and become prosperous either did not attend drinking parties at all or dropped in for only one or two drinks. Those who made no effort to leave the area or to improve their financial standing drank heavily. Children were often present at the drinking parties and sampled the supplies, even though many of them saw the damage it did to adults and vowed they would not drink. Some children also sniffed gasoline-soaked rags to produce a form of intoxication.

Drinking had one positive effect in that it promoted the release of normal inhibitions and allowed expression of aggressive feelings. The Kwakiutl, like many other Indian groups, normally hesitated to express their feelings and practiced avoidance rather than confrontation when they were angry. A classic example of this type of behavior will be seen in the discussion of the Hare in the next chapter. All too often, though, the feelings expressed when a person was drunk went too far. Rohner described a party he attended during which a large mirror was smashed, a new radio ruined, and a woman kicked in the stomach and back, an act that damaged a kidney (1967: 124). The release of aggression to this extent is obviously not a social asset.

Political Organization

The political organization of the Kwakiutl has changed completely since the potlatch period. No longer are political power and social status bound up in the potlatch system, for serious potlatching has ceased to exist. In the 1950s only two bands among the 12 still had chiefs. One of the chiefs, although he had inherited high rank and was the president of the Native Brotherhood, did not potlatch and was resented by the older men because of this. The other chief was being criticized by band

Carved house posts in the interior of the Big House at Gilford Island, 1962 (east end).   Courtesy of Ronald P. Rohner.

members for lack of literacy, failure to operate in modern ways, and the fact that his former status was now irrelevant (Codere, 1961).

The remaining ten bands operated with a system of elected councilors. By law, a chief councilor plus one council member for every 100 band members was elected every two years. Council size was not to be less than 2 or more than 12. Elected members had to be 21 years of age and be permanent residents on the reserve. Other desirable qualifications were a keen sense of social responsibility, the ability to deal with Whites, and interest in the job.

On Gilford Island, Rohner found the workings of the local council ineffective. Councilors were reluctant to tell the people what to do, for they felt no one would listen. This was especially evident when the council attempted to impose a nine o'clock curfew on the children of the village, and no councilor was able to enforce it, although a number of them tried. Councilors were responsible for keeping the village clean, clear of trash and in good repair; seeing to it that the water dam was cleared out; and running the sports club, the women's auxiliary, and the movie committee. They were able to oversee the last three activities because the community agreed on their importance, but they often complained bitterly that villagers were more interested in spending time and money on beer parties than on house repairs or cleaning up

Carved house posts in the interior of the Big House at Gilford Island, 1962 (west end).   Courtesy of Ronald P. Rohner.

the shoreline. Although the councilors supposedly had official power, people did not recognize it. Wolcott found a similar situation on Black-fish Island.

Ceremonialism and Religion

Although the Kwakiutl still performed dances, these had changed radically in character and meaning. Everyone who knew the steps was welcome to join in, a change from the past when only the person who had inherited the right to the dance could perform it. Elaborate winter ceremonials had vanished. Dances now celebrated weddings or the visits of dignitaries or simply entertained tourists. Although many younger people were eager to dance with the group, they often had problems getting anyone to teach them the steps and had to learn by observation, trial, and error. Elaborate tricks and illusions had disappeared from the

Charlie George dancing in his "Thunderbird" mask. Gilford Island, 1963. Courtesy of National Defense, Canada.

Potlatch ceremony held at Christmas, 1958. Alert Bay.   Photograph courtesy of Museum of the American Indian, Heye Foundation.

dances, and once lengthy dramas were compressed to a few minutes. Still surviving, though, were the songs and body movements, the masks, button blankets, and red cedar bark head and neck rings. The growing, non-Indian, public support was helping to revitalize this part of the old culture.

The importance of the church varied greatly depending on location. Alert Bay and Kingcome had resident priests and churches that served vital social functions. Their Women's Auxiliaries were active in holding bazaars and other gatherings involving everyone. Gilford and Blackfish Islands, on the other hand, had no resident priests and depended on traveling missionaries, who came rarely. Pentecostal services were also held in these villages, and people often attended whatever service was being given because there was nothing else to do. Although Rohner found beliefs ranging from piety to skepticism, institutionalized Christianity remained in, but not of, the community. Religion was always something imposed from outside, and the people did not normally initiate religious activities. In Alert Bay, James Sewid was an exception to this as he was to so much else. Not only did he lead Indian language prayer services for years, but he also was an Anglican lay reader, the only Indian to be given this honor. His belief in religion was strong and sure, and he did his best to live by the teachings of Christianity.

Art

Because the Kwakiutl no longer made ceremonial items to be used in winter dances, their art stagnated. Even the few totem poles and house-fronts that remained were allowed to rot away or be attacked by mischievous children. There was evidence, however, that latent abilities still existed. Wolcott found children in the classroom drawing traditional crest designs. An elderly and highly skilled carver, Mungo Martin, was able to make an excellent living by carving for the Museum of Anthropology at the University of British Columbia (Hawthorne, 1961). Indeed, anthropologists have assumed much of the responsibility for keeping art forms alive. The Indians, however, might now be realizing the importance of their artistic heritage. James Sewid certainly demonstrated this when he organized the building of a traditional big house in Alert Bay to house the Kwakwaleth Arts and Crafts Society and to provide a location for dances and sale items to attract tourists from boat cruises.

By and large, Kwakiutl art being produced today follows traditional designs and themes. One innovative artist, however, when the superintendent of the Indian Agency required him to fill out still more forms to receive needed help, went home and carved two figures, one emaciated and gasping and the other upright and grim with pursed mouth and an outstretched hand holding an official form (Hawthorne, 1961: 61).

CONCLUSION

Kwakiutl life today and yesterday cannot be appreciated without a sense of history. The Kwakiutl have been and are many things. In the early nineteenth century during the Prepotlatch Period, they were proud and independent inhabitants of the sea and beach who were comfortable within themselves as they lived out a pattern of existence of great depth, breadth, and flexibility. They were hunters, gatherers, and fishermen who understood and enjoyed the world they had made. During the Potlatch Period, the Kwakiutl were engulfed by the presence of Whites, who brought with them a radically different economy, religion, and political system and a number of virulent European diseases. Equally abrasive to the tenor of traditional Kwakiutl existence was the White attitude of righteous superiority to all other ethnic groups, coupled with a compelling determination to mold Indians into a White frame of reference. These and other related influences produced a rapid reduction in population numbers but changes of less magnitude in the areas of social and economic organization. The social and economic elements of traditional Kwakiutl life were far more congruent with their

White counterparts than was the case for other groups considered in this book. During the later part of this period, the Kwakiutl were haltingly integrated into Canadian life. This process continues in Postpotlatch times. In a qualified sense, the Kwakiutl are now an ethnically distinct element of the rural Canadian underclass. As such, they are politically impotent and for the most part socially and culturally separate from the larger Canadian population. Kwakiutl life is still arranged along traditional lines to the extent to which federal paternalism will allow. This condition will probably not alter within the next few generations.

REFERENCES

Adams, John W. *The Gitksan Potlatch: Population Flux, Resource Ownership and Reciprocity*. Toronto: Holt, Rinehart and Winston of Canada, 1973.

Benedict, Ruth. *Patterns of Culture*. New York: Mentor Books, 1934.

Boas, Franz. The Social Organization and the Secret Societies of the Kwakiutl Indians. *Report of the U.S. National Museum for 1895*. 1897.

———. Tsimshian Mythology. *Thirty-first Annual Report, Bureau of American Ethnology*. Washington, D.C.: Government Printing Office, 1916.

———. Ethnology of the Kwakiutl. *Thirty-fifth Annual Report of the Bureau of American Ethnology*. Parts 1 and 2. Washington, D.C.: Government Printing Office, 1921.

———. Contributions to the Ethnology of the Kwakiutl. *Columbia University Contributions to Anthropology*. Vol. 3. New York: Columbia University Press, 1925.

———. *Kwakiutl Ethnography*. Ed. and abr. Helen Codere. Chicago: University of Chicago Press, 1966.

Codere, Helen. Fighting with Property. *Monographs of the American Ethnological Society 18*. Seattle: University of Washington Press, 1950.

———. The Amiable Side of Kwakiutl Life. *American Anthropologist 58*, 334–351, April 1956.

———. The Understanding of the Kwakiutl. In Walter Goldschmidt, ed., *The Anthropology of Franz Boas*. American Anthropological Association Memoir No. 89, 1959, pp. 61–75.

———. Kwakiutl. In Edward H. Spicer, ed., *Perspectives in American Indian Culture Change*. Chicago: University of Chicago Press, 1961, pp. 431–516.

Curtis, E. S. *The Kwakiutl: The North American Indian, Vol. 10*. Cambridge, Mass., 1915.

De Laguna, Frederica. Under Mount Saint Elias: The History and Culture of the Yakutat Tlingit. *Smithsonian Contributions to Anthropology*. Vol. 7. Parts 1–3. Washington, D.C.: Smithsonian Institution Press, 1972.

Donald, LeLand, and Donald H. Mitchell. Some Correlates of Local Group Rank among the Southern Kwakiutl. *Ethnology 14*, 325–346, October 1975.

Drucker, Philip. The Native Brotherhoods: Modern Intertribal Organizations on the Northwest Coast. *Bulletin 168, Bureau of American Ethnology*. Washington, D.C.: Government Printing Office, 1958.

Ford, Clennan S. *Smoke from Their Fires. The Life of a Kwakiutl Chief.* New Haven: Yale University Press, 1941.

Hawthorn, Harry B. The Artist in Tribal Society: The Northwest Coast. In Marian W. Smith, ed., *The Artist in Tribal Society.* New York: The Free Press, 1961, pp. 59–70.

Kwakiutl. *British Columbia Heritage Series, Series 1, Our Native Peoples.* Vol. 7. Victoria, British Columbia: Provincial Archives, Provincial Museum, 1953.

LaViolette, F. E. *The Struggle for Survival: Indian Cultures and the Protestant Ethic in British Columbia.* Toronto: University of Toronto Press, 1973.

Piddocke, Stuart. The Potlatch System of the Southern Kwakiutl: A New Perspective. *Southwestern Journal of Anthropology 21,* 244–264, Autumn 1965.

Rohner, Ronald P. The People of Gilford: A Contemporary Kwakiutl Village. *Bulletin 225. National Museum of Canada.* Ottawa, 1967.

———, and Evelyn C. Rohner. *The Kwakiutl: Indians of British Columbia.* New York: Holt, Rinehart and Winston, 1970.

Rosman, Abraham, and Paula G. Rubel. The Potlatch: A Structural Analysis. *American Anthropologist 74,* 658–671, June 1972.

Spradley, James P., ed. *Guests Never Leave Hungry: The Autobiography of James Sewid, a Kwakiutl Indian.* New Haven: Yale University Press, 1969.

Suttles, Wayne. Review of *Kwakiutl Ethnography* by Franz Boas. Helen Codere, ed. *American Anthropologist 72,* 629–633, June 1970.

White, Leslie A. The Ethnography and Ethnology of Franz Boas. *Texas Memorial Museum Bulletin 6.* Austin: University of Texas, 1963.

Willey, Gordon R. *An Introduction to American Archaeology.* Vol. 1. *North and Middle America.* Englewood Cliffs, N.J.: Prentice-Hall, 1966.

Wolcott, Harry F. *A Kwakiutl Village and School.* New York: Holt, Rinehart and Winston, 1967.

CHAPTER 13

THE HARE
Those of the Hard, Cold Places

The Subarctic regions are frontiers of settlement. The harsh climate, which is marginal for plant growth and unfavorable to easy living, together with the great distances to major centers of development, produce an environment that is unattractive to man.

Heintzelmen and Highsmith in *World Regional Geography* (2d ed.)

These people here are all stupid just like old Indians.

From the graffiti on the wall of a modern Hare dwelling. In Savishinsky, *The Trail of the Hare*

The Subarctic is a vast, harsh area within which to live, yet it is populated by a number of small groups. The Hare are one of these Northern Athapaskan bands who occupy northwestern Canada. The term *Athapaskan* is an Algonquian word meaning "strangers," and it was used by the Cree to refer to the people who lived to the north. The Athapaskans, one of the largest indigenous linguistic groups in North America, include the Navajo and Apache tribes of southwestern United States and smaller groups in California and Oregon as well as the northern tribes.

Northern Athapaskan territory is classified as a subarctic forest zone. The topography and vegetation are varied and include mountains, taiga (swampy, coniferous forests), boreal forests, high plateaus, prairies, and many swamps, lakes, and rivers. Two major river systems, the Yukon and the Mackenzie, drain the area, flowing northward into the Bering Sea and the Arctic Ocean. The varied growth in the boreal forests includes black and white spruce, birch, cottonwood, and aspen and, in some regions, pine, larch, willows, juniper, and bush-sized alder. Edible vegetation is very sparse, but some Indian groups are able to find blueberries, low- and highbush cranberries, rose hips, crowberries, gooseberries, serviceberries, raspberries, and currants. Also available are wild onions, rhubarb, licorice plants, and the leaves and sap of willow and birch.

The climate of this region is characterized by short, warm, bright summers and long, cold winters. Temperature ranges from a possible high of 96° F. in summer to −70° F. in winter. Spring and fall are short, transitional periods.

THE ABORIGINAL BASELINE

There are indications that at least 15,000 years ago people were living in this area and using hunting traditions as old or older than any found to the south (Willey, 1966: 71–72). These traditions may have come from the Siberian Paleolithic and included tool inventories that began about 6000 B.C. and lasted from two to four thousand years. These were followed by the cultural tradition of the Athapaskan Indians of the western Subarctic and by the Eskimo cultural tradition of the whole of the Arctic. In the eastern Subarctic, the Archaic cultural tradition of the Eastern Woodlands can be traced from 2000 B.C. to historic times. Many people have been living in the Subarctic for a very long time, and the Hare may well have a cultural heritage more than two thousand years old.

Service (1966: 89–93) and Helm and Leacock (1971: 345–347) have described the outlines of the way of life in the mid-nineteenth century of the Algonquian and Athapaskan hunters of Canada. Their characterizations provide the necessary baseline with which Hare life in the 1960s and 1970s, as described by Savishinsky (1974), can be contrasted.

Population density in the Subarctic was less than that of the harsh tundra and coast region to the north. This condition can be explained by looking at the food resources in each area. As noted in the next chapter, the Eskimos had a fairly reliable food supply on the Arctic coasts. Many forest peoples, on the other hand, remained together in a single community only in the summer when fish were plentiful and easily caught. In the winter they were forced to divide into small groups in order to forage for scarce game.

FOOD SUPPLY.   In aboriginal times, the Athapaskan and Algonquian hunters were much alike. Cultural and social dissimilarities existed along a north–south rather than an east–west axis because of the geographical variations as the tundra gave way to heavier forests with more game. Game was the primary subsistence source and included caribou, moose, musk oxen, deer, bear, and, in the west, small buffalo. Many smaller animals, such as beaver, porcupine, rabbit, muskrat, and ground squirrel, were hunted or trapped. Fish were a vital food resource in the summer. Migratory waterfowl—ducks, geese, and swans—were a welcome addition to the diet in spring and fall. Other birds such as swallows and great snowy owls were eaten along with bird eggs. As very few plant foods were available in the summer, a secondary source of vegetable nutrients was the semidigested contents of caribou stomachs because these animals were able to browse on the ubiquitous lichen *Cladonia* and a number of small shrubs.

Similar methods of obtaining food were used throughout the subarctic forest. Hunters armed themselves with bow and arrows or spears. Many types of snares and deadfalls trapped the smaller animals. Moose calls lured these big animals during their mating season. Caribou could be easily speared if they were found swimming across lakes or streams. They were also herded into brush fences, which forced them into defiles where they could be killed en masse or kept running in a circle until exhaustion made the entire group easy prey. Fish were caught with either hooks or gillnets woven from rawhide or *bast*, the tough inner bark of the willow. In some areas fishweirs or traps were used. Nets could be set in the winter through holes chopped in the ice with horn chisels.

Food was prepared and preserved by similar methods throughout the region. Meat was roasted or stone boiled in bark or leather containers. It was preserved either through drying and storing on platforms or in trees or by being pounded into a flour and mixed with fat to become pemmican. Fish were sliced into thin slabs, which were dried in the sun or over a smoky fire or easily quick-frozen in the winter air.

TECHNOLOGY AND THE ARTS.   Animals provided more than food. Using sinew for thread, the women sewed caribou and moose hides into tunics, leggings, moccasins, mittens, and teepee coverings. Rawhide was cut into strips called *babiche* and used for snowshoes and sled and toboggan lacings. These sleds were pulled by women and children and pushed from the rear by the men. Dogs, so important today, were apparently not widely used in precontact times, except by people who lived close to the Eskimos and traded with them. The small number of aboriginal dogs was probably due to the fact that few people could afford to maintain many animals. Fur tunics were made from strips of rabbit hide with the fur left on. It was the wide use of these tunics that gave the "Hareskin" or Hare Indians their name during the initial contact period. Needles, chisels, awls, ladles, and skin scrapers were manufactured from caribou, moose, and deer bones and antlers.

The wood in the extensive forests was also used abundantly for such things as snowshoe frames, bows, arrow shafts, spear shafts, the framework for bark-covered canoes, and toboggans. Teepees in the Subarctic could be bark-covered as well as hide-covered, and double brush-covered lean-tos were sometimes used in the west. Baskets were made from birchbark and sewn together with spruce root. Women made gillnets for fishing from long strips of willow-bast rolled into twine.

Physical survival was an accomplishment because life was hard and the food quest never ending in this northern country. No one had the luxury of becoming a full-time specialist in the arts. The Athapaskans, however, did decorate their clothing and utensils with objects such as dyed porcupine quills sewn in geometric patterns, dried seeds, or sometimes pieces of amber or dentalium. In the west, ornaments such as nose pins and earrings of copper or dentalium were worn.

CONTACT WITH EUROPEANS.   Little is known about aboriginal social organization because the society was quickly influenced and altered by the fur traders during early native–European contact times. The traders and the explorers brought European diseases with them, and these took a terrible toll among Indian populations. In the 1780s, one smallpox epidemic greatly reduced much of the aboriginal population of Canada. Those Indians who survived became dependents of the large fur companies through their practice of credit for desired trade goods. Because of this, the Indians were always in debt and forced to trap fur-bearing animals to pay their bills. European goods—rifles, steel traps, canvas tents, stoves, clothing, food, tobacco, and alcohol—became desirable, and these goods, too, changed the style of life because the hunters could not travel as far or as fast when they were burdened with heavy equipment to drag along to their winter camps.

LIFE-STYLE. In this region people have probably always lived in small bands because the country cannot support large concentrations of population. Even these small bands came together only during the summer when fish were plentiful and at stated holiday times during the rest of the year. At other times, several family groups went off into the wilderness together to hunt and trap. Positions of leadership were poorly developed and applied only to specific and temporary situations, because independence has always been highly valued for adults. Hostilities with other Indian groups were uncommon, for the practice of sporadically occupying fixed areas within vast regions permitted each group to avoid others, and people were free to hunt outside their usual environs in times of shortage. What fighting that did occur was often with an alien language group, such as the Eskimos, when people trespassed on the others' hunting grounds or tried to capture their women. The Hare have always had a reputation for being reluctant and afraid to fight.

RELIGION. Belief in the supernatural and the spirit world was an essential part of daily life among the Athapaskans. Spirits lived in the land and water and in the animals that were hunted, and they were associated with states such as cold and death. All spirits had taboos, which had to be treated with caution, for some were evil and brought disease or death. Shamans were important members of the society, deriving their powers through either inheritance or dreaming. They were able to coax animal spirits to help them and could travel through the world with the aid of such beings. They cured the sick, predicted the weather, directed the hunters to game, ensured success in war, and made love potions. People feared them, and both men and women shamans exercised sexual license among their people.

Group ceremonialism was also important in holding the bands together. Games and dances were much enjoyed during the summer when people were together and had leisure time. Celebrations held for the first animal killed by a young man took the place of any formal puberty ceremony. There were more elaborate initiation ceremonies for girls than for boys. Shamans put on shows for the entire group, using such accoutrements as amulets representing various spirits, skins of animal helpers, and special cups, spoons, and tubes for curing. Much of what we know about the Athapaskan religion comes from myths and legends still remembered by older people in tribes that had later European contact. Unfortunately, much has been lost forever, for it has died with those of past generations.

With this general background in mind, we will examine a modern band of Hare Indians who live at Colville Lake, a village 50 miles north of the Arctic Circle. It is one of the few communities left in the Northwest Territories where the people live by hunting, trapping, and fishing for the most part. All material about Colville is taken from the publications of Savishinsky, who worked there from August 1967 to August 1968 and returned for a shorter period in the summer of 1971.

SETTING AND BACKGROUND

Colville Lake in the northeastern part of traditional Hare country was an old native camping ground. As far back as the early 1800s, it was a satellite of Fort Good Hope, a fur trading post 120 miles away by dogsled. (The airplane distance is 88 miles.) For 150 years, Fort Good Hope has served the Hare and other Indian groups, including the Kutchin and the Eskimo as a center for trade, socialization, medical help, and religion. A Catholic mission was established there in 1859, and its celebrations of Christmas, Easter, and the Feast of the Assumption in mid-August have continued through the years to draw the Indians to this community. In 1921 the Canadian government made treaties with the Mackenzie area groups, joining all Hare Indians together administratively as Band Number 5. The present-day community of Colville Lake includes people from various groups, but all use Fort Good Hope as a trading center.

The Hare have always consisted of small aggregates of people scattered over large areas of land. Mooney placed the aboriginal population at 750, and Kroeber estimated the population density for all boreal forest groups at 1.35 persons per 100 square kilometers (Savishinsky, 1974: 66). Population was small because of the incredibly harsh conditions of survival. In years when the caribou did not come or the rabbit population had reached the low point of its cycle, whole families could and did starve to death. All northern peoples have traditionally used infanticide and the desertion of sick or old members of their groups as necessary methods of keeping down numbers. When times improved, the survivors drew upon all their remaining relatives in order to establish new bonds to replace the old.

In 1967, Colville Lake had 75 people divided among 14 households, twice as many as its low point of only seven households in 1957. A number of factors contributed to this rise in population. Fort Good Hope had drawn many of the people away, but it began having problems of its own. Its population of 350 was outstripping the natural resources available to it, and opportunities for wage work were not sufficient to support everyone. People who had been educated were reluctant to leave the town and return to living off the land, so when they lost a job or could not find employment, they relied upon welfare payments to live. Neither these Hare nor others regarded such an existence as satisfactory. In the fall of 1959, a winter road was cut through the woods between Fort Good Hope and Colville Lake, and this made it much easier for people who wished to support themselves by fur trapping to get back and forth and not lose entirely their access to the services that Fort Good Hope provided. These included a Hudson's Bay Company store, a nursing station, the church, a school, an Indian agent, a game officer, an airstrip, and an electric power station. The journey had to be made on foot in the summer and by either dogsled or snowmobile in the winter. Even more important to the revival of Colville Lake than the road was the establishment of a mission and trading post within the community itself. These institutions meant that the Indians never had to travel from the village at all except to attend school or in case of a medical emergency. The priest was able to handle minor medical matters. Today, although the White personnel have changed, the situation remains much the same. The trader died in 1968, but his store was taken over by a young, capable native couple from Fort Good Hope. The priest left the church to marry, but he and his wife remained in the community (although his wife has now left the community and apparently divorced him) (Savishinsky, 1979). The ex-priest has been running a fishing camp catering to wealthy White tourists and also operating an airplane, which makes travel even easier for the Indians. Besides Fort Good Hope, towns within reach by air are Norman Wells, 124 miles away, and Inuvik, the site of the residential boarding school 220 miles away.

Seen from the air in summer, the land around Colville Lake appears deserted, its vast stretches of green and brown terrain lit by almost constant sunlight. A lucky visitor might notice an occasional moose or bear or see trout breaking the surface water of the lakes, but he or she would not observe the abundant small game and the mosquitoes, gnats, and insects thriving on the wet muskeg and many bodies of water. The prevalence of lakes and wet areas in the north is due not to excessive rainfall but to the permafrost only a few inches or feet below the surface. This prevents drainage of moisture from rain and melting snow. In the summer of 1971, Savishinsky noticed scars left by geologists who had been exploring the land for oil and minerals the previous winter and in the process were bringing civilization much closer to Colville Lake than it had ever been before. A traveler flying over the area in winter might see herds of caribou. He would certainly notice many tracks leading away from the village in all directions, the traces of families with their dogs and possessions moving to their bush camps within a hundred-mile radius of town.

Near an early winter fishing camp. Gill netting whitefish and trout from beneath the frozen lake surface.   Photograph by J. S. Savishinsky.

During the summer at the village, a man repairs his family's gill nets.   Photograph by J. S. Savishinsky.

MATERIAL CULTURE

Food and the need to hunt and fish for it remain, as they have always been, dominant factors in Hare existence. Although modern life has been enhanced by the trading post and the availability of some Western foods, these account for only about 30 percent of the Hare diet and include items such as canned goods, flour, sugar, packaged fruit for making alcoholic home brew, lard, and tea.

Fish are vital to feed not only the people but also the dogs upon which the Indians depend for winter travel. Trout, pike, whitefish, loche, grayling, and crooked-back are taken from Colville Lake and neighboring bodies of water. Nylon and rope gillnets, which have replaced the old willow-bark nets, are used through the ice in winter in the same places where tradition states that fish have always been plentiful. Fish not needed immediately are smoked after being gutted and

At a spring encampment a Hare Indian man ties wooden floats and rock sinkers to a gill net.   Photograph by J. S. Savishinsky.

A woman scrapes a caribou hide to soften it. The hair has already been removed. The hide will eventually be tanned over a smoky fire of rotten spruce wood; the moccasins worn by the woman have soles of tanned caribou hide. Moose hide is treated and used in the same way as caribou hide, but is thicker and more protective as footwear. Untanned caribou hides with the hair left on are used as sleeping blankets, jackets, and slippers.   Photograph by J. S. Savishinsky.

split open. Stickfish, used for dog food, are simply put up on poles in a complete condition and left to freeze, partially putrefying in the process.

The main source of meat in the people's diet continues to be caribou. The animals are in the area only for about seven months during the winter, so their meat is preserved for summer use either by freezing in underground icehouses or by drying or smoking. Old-fashioned methods of hunting caribou have been replaced by the use of high-powered rifles. Caribou herd together only in late spring, and it is their winter dispersal over a wide area that forces the band members to scatter also. In addition to the flesh, the back fat is especially valued because the people need it to generate heat to fight the winter cold. The only other large animals hunted are bear, which are feared and killed usually because the animals get in somebody's way, and moose, which are highly valued for their tough, thick hides, perfect for making mittens and mukluks. Moose are often obtained from relatives and friends in the Fort Good Hope area, where they like to feed on willow, poplar, and birch forest, nonexistent to the north at Colville. Caribou, which prefer the spruce-lichen forest of the Colville area, are traded in return.

Hares are snared by the women and, as in the past, constitute an important food source, which can sustain the population when larger animals are scarce. As some of Savishinsky's friends put it, when the hunt had failed, they were back to choking rabbits again. Other small mammals are also eaten as are waterfowl, which breed in the north during the spring, summer, and autumn. The only wild plant foods available to the people of Colville Lake are berries, some boiled mosses, and rose hips, and these are very limited in season.

Animals are hunted for fur as well as food, and fur trapping remains the major source of income. Marten, fox, squirrel, ermine, mink, wolverine, wolf, and lynx are taken in steel traps in the winter; beaver and muskrat are usually shot with small gauge rifles after they have emerged from their winter lodges. The income from the fur trade provides many Western goods the Indians have come to desire, including tents, stoves, most clothing, ropes, pots, axes, and ammunition.

At the village trading post a Hare Indian man (on the left with the cap) brings in part of his catch of marten pelts to be sold. The trader examines each pelt before deciding on the price he will offer for the furs.   Photograph by J. S. Savishinsky.

They can find, however, no substitute for boots and mukluks made of moose or caribou hide. Woolen, store-bought footwear is inadequate to keep feet warm in very cold weather.

SOCIAL ORGANIZATION

The 14 families of Colville Lake make up an unusual community, alternately coming together and then out of necessity dispersing again to small hunting and fishing camps. Most people live in this remote place by choice, and follow, as much as possible, the old way of life. A number of the Hare have tried living at Fort Good Hope and retreated from it when the opening of the road in 1959 and the trading post in 1960 made existence at Colville Lake not quite so difficult as it had been. The people of the settlement must be independent to survive, but along with independence also comes dependence upon each other and upon the two White residents, the missionary and the trader. The annual cycle of the Hare reflects the alternation between independence and dependence.

Beginning in mid-October, when the lakes freeze up, the band members disperse to their hunting and fishing grounds. They gather in Colville Lake again from mid-December to mid-January to celebrate the

Two children stand outside the tent at their family's winter bush camp. The tent is of canvas, and the end of a smoke pipe (stove pipe) can be seen projecting out of the tent above the entrance flap on the right side.   Photograph by J. S. Savishinsky.

An elderly man is bundled up in his grandson's sled for a trip from the village to the family's hunting camp. Elderly people and young children are transported between village and bush in this way. This photograph was taken in the early spring, and the young man standing behind the sled is wearing sunglasses to protect his eyes from the danger of snowblindness; snowblindness is a threat at this time of the year because of the glare of reflected sunlight off the snow and ice.   Photograph by J. S. Savishinsky.

Christmas season. Once again they scatter until mid-March, when all return for about a month at Easter time. Between the end of April and mid-June, when the lake ice breaks up, they disperse again. The summer, from mid-June to when the lakes freeze up again in October, is spent together in the village. The cycle contains a range of features, from traditional to Western, which affect the life-style of the Hare. It is governed by church holidays, trapping regulations, and school terms for children, but most importantly by the environment itself, for its dangers are the ultimate cause of movement. Although the Hare have taken on some Western timekeeping methods such as watches and calendars, in the most fundamental sense they operate on an ecological model of scheduling. They still contend with dangers such as freezing,

A Hare Indian boy holding a dead muskrat which has been caught in one of his family's traps. The photograph was taken during the spring (mid-May) at his family's trapping camp.   Photograph by J. S. Savishinsky.

starvation, wild animals, possible accidents when deep in the bush, and the difficulties involved in keeping up with the caribou. Caribou are notoriously erratic in their migration habits, and their total number are decreasing as well. Any population decrease or the imposition of hunting regulations for so major a food source can result in serious hardship for the Hare.

The uncertain level of supply is, unfortunately, characteristic of other food sources as well. Fish change their habits, so that nets have to be reset or moved to another lake. If the fishing fails when lake ice is heavy, it is sometimes impossible to set nets elsewhere. Waterfowl are migratory; moose are scarce at the best of times. Even small animals like hare, mice, and lemmings go through population cycles every few years. This affects income as well as the larder because these small mammals are the main food source of the fur-bearing animals that the Hare trap to sell. All the modern traps and rifles in the world cannot help the Hare if the animals are not there to catch in the first place. Staying at Colville Lake to buy Western food is no solution to this dilemma, for the money to buy the food has to be earned by trapping, and trapping successfully means spending long periods out in the bush.

A Hare Indian woman sits outside her village cabin with two young children. The photograph was taken during the summer when all families had returned from their trapping camps.   Photograph by J. S. Savishinsky.

IMPORTANCE OF SHARING.   One way the Hare get around these difficulties is through the practice of sharing. If someone kills a moose, he is expected to present the carcass to a close friend or relative, who then summons the entire village to the site of the kill. All are given a share of the meat to take home, although the major share of the meat and the valuable hide become the property of the successful hunter and the friend to whom he has given the moose. Caribou are not usually shared to this extent because they are much more plentiful, but if a man has poor luck hunting on occasion, he can expect his luckier friends to come to his aid. Favors like this are normally not paid for in cash but paid back in kind at a later date when fortunes have changed. Fish, which are vital for feeding the dogs every day, are likewise shared with those whose nets have been empty or with travelers passing through.

DIVISION OF LABOR.   The people at Colville Lake have many responsibilities and tasks, but these differ depending on age, sex, and the season of the year. Summer is the easiest time for all. The men continue to fish, as they do year around, but they have more free time to gossip; produce home brew; make or repair their canoes, outboards, sleds, and snowshoes; and perhaps earn some extra money through wage labor. Women, too, are freer to socialize after their cooking, sewing, and cleaning chores are done. Care of the children is mostly in the hands of the women, although fathers train their sons in the hunting, fishing, and construction skills that they need. Men are responsible for all building of the village homes, usually one-room dwellings made of spruce logs, as well as the bush camps, caches, dog compounds, and sleds. During the winter, life in the small bush camps is at once simpler and more hectic. The men hunt and trap and can be gone for days at a time following longer traplines and sleeping in small tents set up and down the line. They cut and haul firewood with the help of their wives and make journeys back to Colville Lake to sell furs and replenish supplies. The more successful trappers avoid frequent trips to town because this takes them away from their lines. A number of younger women own and drive their own dog teams, but women are at all times less mobile than the men because they are normally expected to be home tending to their chores. They snare small animals in the winter and help check fishnets, process all caribou and moose hides, make dried and smoked meat and fish, and sew all clothes, canvas canoe covers, and sled wrappers. Children join the work force early and from the age of five or six have their own tasks. Boys are treated somewhat more indulgently than girls and are allowed to be children a bit longer. In times of scarcity, boys are apt to receive more food and warmer clothing than their sisters.

SCHOOLING.   Schooling is often brief and intermittent for the children because the Hare fear, with good reason, that excessive schooling and not enough practical training would make the children unfit for life at Colville Lake. The children themselves resent the harsh discipline employed at the residential school in Inuvik and often resist going when the plane comes to pick them up in the fall.

BEHAVIOR PATTERNS.   Responding to the pressures of their harsh environment, the people of Colville Lake, in common with many North American hunting groups and hunting groups elsewhere, have developed a number of stylized patterns of behavior. They value highly the trait we call flexibility, by which they mean the ability to get along with different people, to be resourceful in any type of situation, and to meet and cope with emergencies. They practice restraint in all social relationships. People living in close proximity in a tent out in the bush find jobs to do outside such as chopping wood or checking traplines rather than quarreling with each other when disagreements arise. Rather than fight with his wife or brother, a man turns away and simply does not speak to them if he is angry. This restraint works on affectionate relationships as well. Open affection is shown only to young children and puppies. Adult relationships, although often deep and lasting, especially among siblings, are not openly demonstrative. Another highly valued trait is generosity. A visitor to a bush camp expects food to be offered to him and his dogs. People are generous with their time. If one man heads out to check fishnets in his frail canoe, others join him because in numbers there is safety. Finally, freedom is important to the Hare—freedom from time schedules, from overbearing strangers telling them what to do, from drunkenness and idleness, from discrimination, gossip, overcrowding—from all the things, in short, that they associate with living at Fort Good Hope or any other Arctic town.

STRESS AND MOBILITY

Stress and mobility and the relationship between them are very obvious factors in Hare life. Savishinsky (1974: xxii) defined *stress* as a perceived environmental situation that threatens the gratification of needs or an organism's well-being or integrity. He constructed a model that could also apply to other societies, provided that the general be separated from the particular. To test his model, he proposed three hypotheses:

1. If high mobility is necessary to a people because of their ecology, they will use this mobility also to relieve social stresses. This may be true even when they do not admit they are doing so.

2. If their ecology dictates to a group that there must be both extreme dispersal and extreme concentration, then both conditions will create stress. The tensions caused by each condition will, in part, be alleviated by movement either into large groups for purposes of socializing at a given time or away from people and the problems they are causing in other instances. Smaller groups will also create tensions that can be eased by temporary absence from the group on the part of individuals.

3. If the people in a group can be differentiated by such variables as age, sex, degree of acculturation, or status, this difference will be reflected in both their exposure and reaction to stress and their degree of the use of mobility to reduce this stress. [Savishinsky, 1974: 136 ff.]

How do these hypotheses work in practice? During holiday times and in the summer, the people are at first delighted to return to Colville Lake in order to meet their friends and be free of the isolation and tensions of the bush. All sorts of problems, however, soon arise. Drinking parties provide license for people to speak their minds, and some may say things that lead to fights and hard feelings. Gossip and sexual jealousies create tensions. There is limited privacy in the single-room houses, and people can sometimes be alone only when they visit the outhouse in the back. Recently, the people of Colville Lake have begun building room partitions in their homes to alleviate the problem of privacy. Young adults quarrel with their parents who insist they may not marry because they are needed to help out at home. Too many children in a family might create economic difficulties and make too much work for their mother. To resolve these problems created by too much proximity to others, a family group might move out to a fishing camp away from town or pay a visit to friends at Fort Good Hope. Young adults may pay visits to friends elsewhere in hopes of finding a desirable mate. Children can be informally adopted by other families who can use their help. If a person cannot leave, he or she can have vicarious contact with others through listening to the radio or sending and receiving letters and parcels. Drinking and gossip, although they may be destructive, also have the positive values of providing release from tensions, relaxation, and the chance to show indirect hostility toward other people.

Once the people have moved back to the bush, the kinds of tensions that they experience change. No one can ever forget the dangers of the climate and working conditions. People have frozen to death within living memory, and the perils of traveling through the wilderness to check traplines or pursue caribou are very real. Loneliness is prevalent, for a man may have no companions other than his immediate family, and with them he must share a small, crowded tent or hut. Older people who are having difficulty in performing their usual work fear that they may be rejected by the younger people, who see them now as a liability. If sickness or injury strikes someone deep in the bush, he or she may not be able to get help soon enough. Food can run short if hunting and fishing are unsuccessful. The Hare attempt to resolve problems like these first by being extremely careful of how they move about in the woods and exercising their extensive knowledge of the country and climate so they are not caught out in a storm. Loneliness may be relieved by a trip to town to get supplies, and more educated men often resort to this, but the really successful hunters realize they must stay on the job to succeed. People can change their location to be nearer some other group, or one individual may leave a group and work for a while with others. In cases of extreme tension, the entire family can leave the band at Colville Lake and join another group where either the husband or wife has relatives. Moves away from a community are almost never made to places where no relatives live. The problems of older people have been partially alleviated in modern times by the family allowances and old-age pensions they receive, making them an asset rather than a liability to a family. Finally, no season lasts forever, and there is always the return to the village to look forward to.

Dogs are a special source of both tension and pleasure in Hare life. Along with babies, puppies are cosseted and indulged. As they grow older, they provide a superb training vehicle for young children, who at age five or six take charge of a dog, train it, and teach it to pull a small sled. Men are proud of their dogs and take great pride in showing off their team and traveling with it under all conditions. People in the village pay close attention to the number of dogs a man has and whether or not they are in good condition. In spite of their concern for the animals, however, men, especially when drunk, will often use their dogs to express displaced hostility, whipping the team unmercifully or shouting curses at it.

One source of stress unique to Colville Lake was the feud that existed between the trader and the missionary. About a year after the missionary had arrived, he asked the trader in front of a visiting pilot why he had not attended morning mass. The trader was so incensed at what he regarded as an invasion of his privacy in front of an outsider that he never again spoke to the priest. The feud made life very difficult for the Indians, for both men kept close watch over who visited the other, and the people had to make special efforts to stay on the good side of both because they needed both for the services they provided. The Hare also hated the subordinate positions they were forced to assume in order to plead for credit at the trading post. This particular feud, of course, was resolved when the trader died, but the Hare still resent the White hunters and fishermen who come to the town in search of sport and treat the Indians as second-class citizens.

These various techniques to cope with stress apparently worked quite well, for Savishinsky noted that only one individual in the entire band had displayed any signs of mental unbalance during his stay and that she required hospitalization only periodically (1974: 218). In part, the techniques worked because they did not have to be used in constant and repetitive fashion by any particular individual or group. In addition, the Hare have learned to accept some stress as an inevitable part of existence. For the most part, stress and rewards are kept in balance much of the time so that the Hare can live in their harsh environment, reaping both the benefits and penalties of their heritage.

THE HARE AS HUNTERS AND GATHERERS

The Hare are one of the few living examples of the hunting and gathering way of life, which has been so important throughout human history. People have been on earth for about two million years, and for over 99 percent of this time they have lived as hunter-gatherers. For only the last 10,000 years have people used domesticated plants and animals, metals, or energy sources other than their own bodies. Only very recently have we had such things as states, cities, empires, nations, and the Industrial Revolution. As far as we know now, the hunting and gathering way of life has been the most successful that people have ever achieved. No one can predict whether or not our present nuclear and technological society will end by destroying itself and wasting the resources of the planet (Lee & Devore, 1968: 3).

Because of these facts, it is important to study the Hare and the few groups like them who are still hunters and gatherers. Remember, too, that their way of life and constant search for food were not necessarily as important to former groups of hunters and gatherers who lived in more gentle climates. As these peoples were replaced by agriculturalists, the only people who remained hunters and gatherers for the most part were those who lived in places where it was impossible to survive any other way. The Micmac, too, were hunters and gatherers originally, but they shifted to wage labor to support themselves in modern times. The Hare, unless they leave their territory, have no such option.

REFERENCES

Clark, A. M. The Athapaskans: Strangers of the North. In *The Athapaskans: Strangers of the North*. Ottawa: National Museum of Man, National Museums of Canada, 1974, pp. 17–42.

————., ed. *Proceedings: Northern Athapaskan Conference, 1971. Volumes 1 and 2.*

Canadian Ethnology Service Paper No. 27. Ottawa: National Museum of Man Mercury Series, 1975.

Helm, June. *The Indians of the Subarctic: A Critical Bibliography*. Bloomington: Indiana University Press, 1976.

———, and Eleanor B. Leacock. The Tribes of Subarctic Canada. In E. B. Leacock and N. O. Lurie, eds., *North American Indians in Historical Perspective*. New York: Random House, 1971, pp. 343–374.

Henriksen, Georg. Hunters in the Barrens: The Naskapi on the Edge of the White Man's World. *Newfoundland Social and Economic Studies No. 12*. St. John's: Memorial University of Newfoundland (printed by the University of Toronto Press), 1973.

Honigmann, John. Psychological Traits in Northern Athapaskan Culture. In A. M. Clark, ed., *Canadian Ethnology Service Paper No. 27. Proceedings: Northern Athapaskan Conference, 1971. Vol. Two*. Ottawa: National Museum of Man Mercury Series, 1975, pp. 545–576.

Lee, Richard B., and Irven Devore. Problems in the Study of Hunters and Gatherers. In Lee, Richard B., and Devore, Irven eds., *Man the Hunter*. Chicago: Aldine Publishing, 1968, p. 3.

McClellan, Catharine. My Old People Say: An Ethnographic Survey of Southern Yukon Territory. Parts 1 and 2. *Publications in Ethnology*, No. 6 (1). Ottawa: National Museum of Man, 1975.

Nelson, Richard K. *Hunters of the Northern Ice*. Chicago: University of Chicago Press, 1969.

Savishinsky, Joel S. Kinship and the Expression of Values in an Athabascan Bush Community. *Western Canadian Journal of Anthropology 2:1*, 31–59, 1970.

———. Mobility as an Aspect of Stress in an Arctic Community. *American Anthropologist 73*, 604–618, June 1971.

———. Coping with Feuding: The Missionary, the Fur Trader, and the Ethnographer. *Human Organization 31*, 281–290, Fall 1972.

———. *The Trail of the Hare: Life and Stress in an Arctic Community*. New York: Gordon and Breach Science Publishers, 1974.

———. The Dog and the Hare: Canine Culture in an Athapaskan Band. In A. M. Clark, ed., *Canadian Ethnology Service Paper No. 27. Proceedings: Northern Athapaskan Conference, 1971, Vol. Two*. Ottawa: National Museum of Man Mercury Series, 1975, pp. 463–515.

———. Trapping, Survival Strategies, and Environmental Involvement: A Case Study from the Canadian Sub-Arctic. *Human Ecology 6*, 1–25, March 1978.

———. Personal communication, 1979.

———, and Susan B. Frimmer. The Middle Ground: Social Change in an Arctic Community, 1967–1971. *Ethnology Division Paper No. 7, Mercury Series*. Ottawa: National Museum of Man, 1973.

Service, Elman. *The Hunters*. Englewood Cliffs, N.J.: Prentice-Hall, 1966.

Speck, Frank G. *Naskapi: The Savage Hunters of the Labrador Peninsula*. (New ed.) Norman: University of Oklahoma Press, 1977.

VanStone, James W. *Athapaskan Adaptations: Hunters and Fishermen of the Subarctic Forests*. Chicago: Aldine Publishing, 1974.

Willey, Gordon. *An Introduction to American Archaeology*. Vol. 1, *North and Middle America*. Englewood Cliffs, N.J.: Prentice-Hall, 1966.

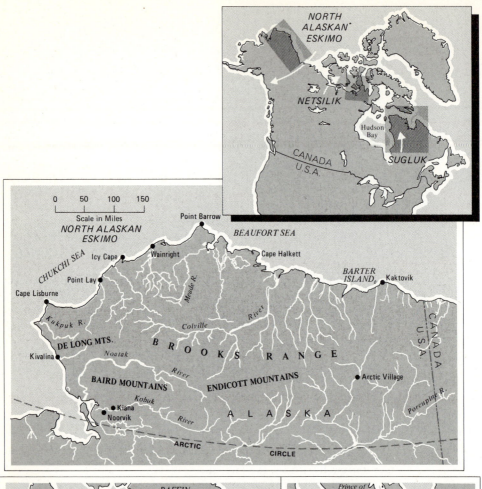

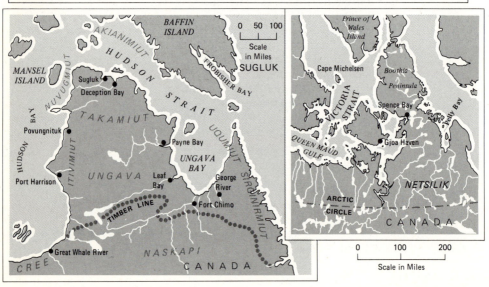

CHAPTER 14

THE ESKIMOS
The People of the Ice

When I was a child, they taught me how to hunt, how to survive, and how to support people. It was the only game: we had to have meat so it was something that we had to know. It's not the same now. Today it's more important to be able to work, carve, make money—that's what there is now. I shall teach my children the ways I know to earn a living which they will need to know. In those days they only hunted because they needed food. Today they work and carve because they need money.

Taqtu, an Eskimo man, in *We Don't Live in Snow Houses Now*, ed. S. Cowan

The Eskimos are not a tribe or grouping of tribes but a highly mixed ethnic category having a varied, complex history that also reflects a wide variety of adaptations to a diverse polar environment. The term *Eskimo* itself is an unfortunate one because many of the peoples so labeled by outsiders resent the term and instead refer to themselves as *Inuit,* usually translated as "the people" or "the human ones." The name *Eskimo* (in the form *Excomminquois*) is said to have come from the Abnaki *Esquimantsic,* or from *Ashkimeq,* the Chippewa equivalent, signifying "eaters of raw flesh" (Henshaw & Swanton, 1907. 434). Because the term *Eskimo,* however, has an almost universal acceptance among anthropologists and the general public, it will be used here.

The Eskimos cannot be understood without considering the nature of their geography, which, in general, is a vast area within the earth's circumpolar zone, referred to as the Arctic and Subarctic. The Arctic zone, consisting of the Arctic Ocean and the surrounding tundra, has little or no vegetation. Permafrost, or ground below 0° C., reaches a

Man harpooning a seal. n.d.   Photograph courtesy of Museum of the American Indian, Heye Foundation.

Ivory carver and friend. Alaska, 1905–1907.   Photograph courtesy of Museum of the American Indian, Heye Foundation.

depth of 1,000 feet in places and inhibits the growth of trees completely. Constant cold is maintained by the latitude and the Arctic Ocean, which freezes for most of the year. The subarctic zone, or taiga, where the Hare live, is distinguished from the Arctic by the growth of trees. Permafrost in the Subarctic is sporadic and not so deep as the Arctic.

The climate of the Arctic is extremely harsh. Winters are very long, and temperatures away from the coasts can range between 60 and 90 degrees below zero Fahrenheit. Snowfall is relatively light, but none of it melts during the winter, so that the snow cover is present for six or seven months of the year. When the snow does melt in spring, the ground becomes swampy and difficult to travel upon because the permafrost does not allow the water to drain. Summers are short and can be made miserable for humans by an abundance of insect life. There are more insects in ten miles of Arctic tundra than there are mammals in all of North America. Above the Arctic Circle, daylight lasts for 24 hours for part of the summer with corresponding 24-hour darkness in the winter.

The human population of the Arctic is very low because the land is unable to support many people. Both long winters and the permafrost inhibit the growth of vegetation, so that little plant life is available for either man or animals. Land animals such as caribou must thus migrate to the south to survive the winter. Sea creatures do better because the Arctic Ocean is rich in plankton, and oceanwide currents continually bring new food into the area, but whales, salmon, and waterfowl also migrate in winter.

Many people have a stereotyped idea of the Eskimo: a lone seal hunter standing poised over a hole in the ice, harpoon in hand, for hours on end; a crew of Eskimos setting out in their frail umiak after a whale; an Eskimo family snug in their igloo feasting on raw frozen fish; a party of hunters trapped on an ice floe in an Arctic blizzard—this is the very stuff of the drama of the North. Modern urban dwellers have always been fascinated by these people, who must survive under such extreme and demanding conditions. Today these pictures are blurring, and the old way of life is changing, yet the difficulties of survival for the Eskimos have not decreased. This chapter will describe Eskimo life the way it used to be and then show how some Eskimos have been influenced by the larger modern society.

An Eskimo, A. A. Thrasher (1976: 153–154) tells of the creation and what he believes is coming now to his people:

> The first of my people came on the ice, blown by the wind, brought by the magic of the Northern Lights and the North Wind. These used to hunt the cave bear that was as big as a whaleboat. The bear's tracks were so big a man could kneel in them. In those days the sea otter and the sea mink were bigger than man. The mink would chase boats and wait for men to fall overboard. They were man-eaters. In those days, in the Smoky Mountains were small people, about one foot tall. The children of these people used one caribou ear for a parka. They lived in trees and in houses built in the ground.
>
> And every time the half moon tipped, game was plenty.
>
> Then something called the new life came. The white man came from the outside world. My people were good hunters. My people were good trappers. My people were good fishermen. Now they are dying. The Inuit are dying. I can hear the story in the wind, which has come to take us away. . . .
>
> The land that was great has little game. The land of the caribou cannot feed my family. The musk ox, our pride has almost gone. The white fox is nearly gone from the ice. The Great Nanook is nearly gone from the ice. The seal for my kayak has nearly gone from the sea. The walrus for my meal is nearly gone from the sea. The white whale that brought my muktuk is going away. The black whale is going too. The fast-flying Atput duck is leaving. The King Loon is going away, and the King Eider Duck. The salmon is leaving the river, and the Arctic char is going away, with the white fish and the herring.
>
> I can see all these things going away forever from the land. The beautiful narwhal is going too. I can see the Northern Lights. In the cold nights the full moon still shines, the night owl still calls. My family is awake and

cannot sleep. The wolf calls to the full moon, but my dogs, the huskies, don't answer the wolf call. Listen to the North Wind. It has come to take us away. The name Inuvialuit will only be heard in the wind. The land will still be there, the moon will still shine, the Northern Lights will still be bright, and the Midnight Sun will still be seen. But we will be gone forever.

BACKGROUND

Over the years there have been many theories concerning the origins of Eskimos and how long they have occupied their present locations. Archaeologists have speculated about origins in Asia or from inland Indian groups who occupied the area west or south of Hudson Bay. Most authorities now accept the idea that the Eskimos were originally an Asiatic people whose distinctive culture existed before 3500 B.C. (Taylor, 1968: 9).

Crossing the Bering Strait, the Eskimos were able to establish themselves throughout the north, so that today they occupy parts of Siberia, Alaska, Canada, and Greenland. They did this by creating an ingenious way of life that was able to make use of every food source in the area. Eskimos are best known for their adaptation to a marine economy, their ability to harvest available seal, whale, walrus, and fish.

Although regional variations exist, all Eskimos have Mongoloid physical characteristics. They have broad faces, short, straight noses, and, in many instances, the epicanthic eye fold is present. The people are short to medium in stature with small hands and feet. Although their bulky clothing makes them look fat, they are in reality lean, heavily boned, and muscular. Hair is normally black, eyes are brown, and men have little or no facial hair. Alaskan Eskimos tend to be taller than their eastern Canadian counterparts.

The Eskimos possess a distinctive language stock, which can be divided into two major dialects, approximating the difference between English and German. Inupik is spoken by the Eskimos of northern Alaska and those in Canada and Greenland. Yupik is the dialect of the western Eskimos of Alaska and the Asiatic Eskimos (Oswalt, 1967: 28–29). Minor dialectic differences exist within these two major groups, but Peter Freuchen (1961) stated that his friend Knud Rasmussen was able to travel all over Canada and still be able to understand what his varied Eskimo hosts were saying.

The total Eskimo population at the time of historical contact was probably about 48,000 or less (Oswalt, 1967: 24–25). Of these, 26,000 were in Alaska, 2,000 in Siberia and the St. Lawrence Island, and 20,000 in Canada, Greenland, and Labrador. By 1966 the total population was estimated to be 73,000, 28,600 of whom were in Alaska (Chance, 1966: 6). As is usual with groups who had not been exposed to modern diseases, these figures conceal a decline after White contact, followed by a recovery when immunity levels built up and medical services improved.

All Eskimo culture shared similar characteristics, but it was far from uniform. Many variations were imposed by the climate, the food sources available, and the general difficulty of living. For instance, although almost everyone thinks of the Eskimos living in their snowhouses, in actuality, only those people in the central Arctic used the igloo. Elsewhere houses were constructed of wood, turf, or stone. The kayak and the umiak, or large skin boat, for fishing and whaling were used in some places and not in others. Some groups hunted caribou and salmon; others did not. The Caribou Eskimos of the Barren Grounds in Canada did almost no hunting of sea creatures. In Alaska resources were more abundant, so that the people were able to develop a more elaborate social organization, to build *karigi* or men's dance houses, and to settle in relatively permanent locations. To enhance their ceremonial life, they made elaborate masks, coiled baskets, and pottery. Trade and warfare were present. Elsewhere, in the harsher regions of Canada, life was a perpetual wandering of small groups from one food source to the next, and little formal social organization was possible. Because these variations exist and because the literature on the Eskimo is so extensive, I have chosen to describe three Eskimo groups, one as they lived in the past and two as they are living now. Facts given about the three groups may or may not conform to other Eskimo situations. Some additional materials pertaining to other Eskimo groups have been added to supplement the description of Eskimo life.

HOW ESKIMOS LIVED IN THE PAST—THE NETSILIK

The Netsilik were typical of the pan-Eskimo culture of precontact Canada, although their habitat was not so rich as that of some other groups. Their principal winter game animal was the seal, from which they took their name, which means "People of the Seal." The Netsilik inhabited a vast area of almost 9,000 square miles in central Canada along the Arctic coast. Small bands wandered periodically through this extensive territory. In 1923, when Knud Rasmussen studied them, there were only 259 Netsilik people.

Their varied terrain, characteristic of the Arctic Circle, included rocky Precambrian hills; wet, swampy tundra; no trees; and many lakes, ponds, and rivers as well as numerous bays, inlets, and islands adjoining the Arctic Ocean. Surprisingly, the Arctic is classified as a desert as very little precipitation falls there. The ground is continually wet in the summer, though, because of the permafrost, which begins only one foot below the surface. The climate in Netsilik territory is harsh. The sea begins to freeze in late September and does not become

Pitiak, Eskimo man, near kayak. Mackenzie Delta, Northwest Territory, Canada, ca. 1917. Photograph courtesy of Museum of the American Indian, Heye Foundation.

free of ice again until the end of July. January temperatures average −20° F. and can easily fall to −40° F. Summer temperatures rarely reach above 50° F. In this difficult land and under the most stringent climatic conditions, the Netsilik were able to survive as a people by dividing into small groups and hunting seal, caribou, and musk ox, with fishing in season for salmon trout in the sea and freshwater fish in the deep lakes.

The information about the Netsilik is taken from Asen Balikci's book, *The Netsilik Eskimo* (1970). Balikci has reconstructed the lives of the people as they were about 1923, when Knud Rasmussen studied many of the bands.

Technology and Subsistence

Life in the Arctic must be lived on its own terms. Raw materials with which to build the necessities of life are scarce, but the Netsilik were highly resourceful at using what there was. All men had to be proficient in hunting, protecting themselves against the elements, and in improvising tools should one of theirs be defective. All women had to be skilled seamstresses, not because they valued the appearance of the clothing they made, but because any gaps in the seams would quickly expose the wearer to frostbite or even death. Both sexes had to know enough about constructing shelters to survive if they were caught out on the winter ice in a storm. From very few, simple raw materials, the Eskimos constructed all they needed to sustain themselves. Snow, ice, animal bones, skins, sinews, stones, and some imported wood were all they had, and they made the most of them.

THE SNOW COMPLEX.   The Netsilik followed what most people consider the traditional Eskimo custom of building igloos from snow blocks to house themselves during the winter. A man would begin construction by drawing a circle in the snow. Standing inside this circle, with his *pana*, or snow knife, he would cut blocks of snow about 20 by 25 by 4 inches and place them on the perimeter. Each row overlapped slightly toward the inside so that the final shape of the igloo was that of a beehive. On the outside of the circle stood the man's wife, who plastered the outside of the igloo with loose snow using her *poabrit* or snow shovel to ensure that all the chinks were filled in. After the roof was carefully finished with smaller blocks of snow, snow was shoveled into the interior through a hole left for that purpose and used to make the sleeping platform and a kitchen table. Later this hole was closed up, and a porch and doorway were added to act as a windbreak. A hole for ventilation was made in the ceiling to ensure a constant supply of fresh air, and often a window made of freshwater ice was placed above the porch so that approaching visitors could be seen.

Eskimo dwellings, by middle-class standards, were unwholesome. Turner (1894: 187), writing during the latter part of the nineteenth century, spoke of the "Koksoagmyut" living near Fort Chimo, Ungava District. He recorded that the principal diseases that these people suffered were pulmonary troubles, caused from living in crowded huts too poorly ventilated to allow the escape of odors from their own bodies and from slowly decomposing animal food. Because all entrances had to be closed as quickly as possible to prevent the escape of heat, the people were forced to breathe and rebreathe the air filled with poisonous gases so that fully half of them died of upper respiratory problems.

Outside the igloo, snow was used to construct meat stands above the reach of the always hungry dogs, a shelter for the sled, and a small shelter to be used as a toilet. Animal figures for children to play with and snowmen for archery practice were made as well. Windbreaks from blocks of snow could hastily be constructed to protect a hunter out on the ice.

Blocks of ice could also be used to construct an igloo in the fall before sufficient snow had fallen. An icy coating protected sled runners, so that they would move smoothly. Fish caches could be made of ice if stones were not available. Finally, it was vital for the Eskimos to set up their winter camps near some ice at least a year old, for this would ensure the loss of its salinity, so that it could be melted for drinking water.

THE SKIN COMPLEX.   Caribou and sealskins were the most desirable, although both bear and musk ox pelts could be used for winter clothing if enough caribou had not been killed. These skins were much heavier than caribou hides and thus not as desirable. Caribou skin made excellent winter clothes because it was both light and very warm. It also provided mattresses and bedding, drums, and strong thongs used for many purposes. Sealskin was even stronger than caribou and was completely waterproof, making it ideal for summer boots needed when walking on wet marshy tundra. It was also used for kayak covers, for summer tents or roof sheets over igloos melting in the spring, for sled runners, and for coats and trousers. Clothes were sewn with bone needles and caribou sinew.

THE BONE COMPLEX.   Although bear bone was the hardest, caribou antler was the basic source material for most tools. From antler came spears, bows, double-pronged leisters, or spears for catching fish, ice picks, snow shovels, snow beaters, meat forks, blubber pounders, ladles, snow knives, tool handles, needle cases, toys, and ceremonial objects. Before iron was available through trade, flint provided weapon points and blades. Wood had to be imported or collected as driftwood for tent poles, kayak frames, and sled parts. These items were ingeniously glued together with dried blood warmed in the mouth.

THE STONE COMPLEX.   Soapstone quarried southwest of Pelly Bay was used for lamps and cooking pots. Small, shallow soapstone lamps were filled with melted blubber surrounded with a wick. They warmed the igloo, supplied heat for cooking, and were an essential source of heat below the drying rack for outdoor clothing.

SUBSISTENCE AND CAMP LIFE.   Because their game supply was both mobile and irregular, the Netsilik were forced to establish an annual migration cycle to take the best possible advantage of it. Caribou migrated north in the spring and returned to the tree line with cold weather. Salmon trout swam up the rivers to the sea in spring and returned to the lakes in fall. Seal, on the other hand, could be hunted only in winter and spring as the Netsilik had no techniques for open water sealing.

Summer for the Netsilik began in July, because the sea ice did not break up completely until the end of that month. The people moved inland off the melting ice, laden heavily, if they had been lucky, with many new sealskins with which to make summer tents and new kayaks. Storage rooms were built for winter supplies they would not be needing for a while, such as the sled, dog harnesses, drying racks, winter clothing, and seal oil kept in reserve for the next winter. In small groups, the people drifted off to streams where they knew from experience the fishing would be good. "Drifted" is perhaps a misnomer, for an Eskimo move was not an easy matter. All supplies, including kayaks and tents, had to be carried either by the people or by dogs in precariously balanced packs. Netsilik families could own only one or two dogs each, for the food was not abundant enough to share with dogs all year round. Young children rode in their mother's parkas or on their father's shoulders, and the old had to struggle along behind as best as they could, often not catching up with the group until evening had fallen and camp had been set up. Bearskins were used to pull heavy supplies because sleds, of course, were useless at this time of year.

At the chosen stream, stone weirs were built or repaired, and the people camped close to shore so that they could observe a school of fish making its way to the sea to spawn. This was a signal for the men to leap into the icy water and spear the trapped fish with their double-pronged leisters. Fish were often eaten raw, with great gusto after a winter diet of seal. They could also be cooked, and many were dried and cached securely in stone for winter. Fox and polar bears could and did rob fish caches, and this could lead to tragedy in a bad hunting year.

By the end of August, the fishing season was over, and the people broke up their camps in order to move inland after the caribou, who were coming together in big herds in preparation for their migration to the south. Caribou could be hunted in various ways. Pitfalls, their bottoms lined with sharp knives, were occasionally employed but were seldom successful. Single hunters sometimes were able to get close enough to kill one animal. The Netsilik were not expert archers, and a hunter would consider himself lucky to get a fatal shot. More often beaters were employed to drive the herd toward many archers in ambush. The kayak was invaluable in caribou hunting, for the animals often crossed the streams at known fording places. Hunters could wait at these with some confidence of success. Often a group of women and children were placed on the far shore, where they could frighten the crossing caribou back into the water toward the hunters in their kayaks. A family of four needed about 30 caribou skins to make its new winter clothing, and as caribou numbers varied and the animals were not always obliging enough to keep to known trails, fall hunting was an uncertain business.

Late fall, October and most of November, was a time of transition when little hunting could be done. The caribou were gone; the ice was not yet firm enough for seal hunting. Some river and lake fishing took place at this time, and a few eastern groups hunted musk ox, but a great deal of work had to be done to prepare for winter. The women were busy sewing clothing, a practice forbidden to them while any hunting was going on. The men brought their stored fish and caribou to the edge of the sea and repaired their sledges and dog harnesses. Life could not have been comfortable in this season as the tents were poor protection against the growing cold and winds, but the snow was insufficient for building igloos. The people, however, were able to enjoy songfests, meetings with friends, and community meals as they gathered together in larger groups in preparation for winter sealing. The winter was the time for the greatest concentration of people in one place, for sealing was an activity benefiting from many hands.

Seal hunting began some time between late November and early March, depending upon how much food each group had stored. The Arctic at this time was a desolate, lifeless place. Darkness reigned for most of the time; sea ice was seven feet thick; harsh winds and blizzards dominated the landscape. Camp was established on the sea ice near the observed breathing holes of seals. As a winter camp contained 50 to 100 people, a dance house of snow blocks incorporating four regular igloos as cornerstones was sometimes built so that the community had a central meeting place. Women and children were able to spend much time visiting and playing during the winter while the men stood for long hours over the breathing holes, waiting to harpoon the seal as it came up. The location of the winter camp had to be moved every month or so as the seal population in one area was thinned by the hunters. One man, usually the best hunter, acted as leader for the others in deciding where to hunt and when to move on, but this was a very informal arrangement, and that man was not considered the chief of the band in the usual sense.

In spring, several things happened to make sealing easier and more profitable. Seals bore their young out on the ice and often remained there for long periods basking in the new sun. Hunters were able to creep up on them and kill several before they could return to the water. White foxes were trapped at this time of the year, especially after traders had entered the area. Sea gull eggs and the birds themselves were harvested. Winter camps began to break up as the people moved off the melting ice in small groups to begin summer fishing and start the cycle again.

This annual cycle followed by the Netsilik did not result in abundant harvests of food. The people always had to struggle against the difficult weather and erratic movement of game. Without special social adaptations, they might not have been able to survive at all as a group. It is these social patterns that will be discussed in the next section.

Social Collaboration

Because they lived in such a harsh environment, the Netsilik and all Eskimos were dependent on making and keeping good social relationships. This section will show how such relationships were supposed to work. The next section describes social tensions and departures from the ideal caused by the stresses and strains of Arctic life.

Three basic types of relationships existed: those based on blood kinship, those based on collaboration in group activities, and those based on formalized partnerships. The most important and closest of the three was kinship. The basic units of Eskimo society were both the nuclear and the extended families. Although the nuclear family, consisting of husband, wife, and minor children, might travel alone from one hunting camp to another, it almost never lived alone for any extended period. Cooperation in hunting and food sharing was essential for survival and so, in another sense, was companionship with others in the midst of that unforgiving land. Residence in most cases was patrilocal; that is, a son would bring his new wife to his father's camp to live with his brothers and their families. There was a very practical reason for this. Whereas girls married at 14 or 15, boys were usually about 20, because they needed this much time to become proficient hunters and learn all the landmarks and habits of game in their area. Much of this information would have to be learned anew somewhere else. If a man had only daughters, he attempted to get a husband for his daughter who would live with him and help, but often the only young men who would agree to this were orphans or perhaps poor younger sons.

Although marriage among the Netsilik was very casual—the girl simply moved her things to the boy's igloo—the marriage bond itself was strong. All adults were expected to marry and indeed found life exceedingly difficult if they were not married because work was assigned according to sex, and each sex had a vital collaborative role to play. Men were the hunters and fishermen, the makers of tools and igloos, the ones who butchered the caribou and perhaps helped with the scraping of its heavy skin. Women butchered and skinned seals; made all the clothing, tents, and kapak covers from skins; cooked; supplied fresh drinking water; saw to the drying of clothes; helped to build the igloo; broke the trail for the dogs; and even helped to pull the sled in winter. In addition to the work bond, the sex bond was a strong one within marriage in spite of occasional wife swapping. The only taboo upon intercourse was a short one following childbirth, and sex between a man and his wife was considered a good and normal thing.

Children (especially male children, as we shall see in the next section) were welcomed eagerly into the family and treated with love and great permissiveness. Babies spent their first two years of life in almost constant proximity to their mothers, being carried in her parka by day and sleeping by her side at night. Mothers normally breast-fed their infants for several years, although mouth-to-mouth feeding of caribou or seal soup could also be used if the mother had no milk or the child was adopted. Eskimo mothers attempted to toilet-train their children very early, seating them on a pot on the mother's lap and blowing softly on their heads until the desired results had been achieved. Mistakes and bed-wetting, however, were not punished. Fathers played with and loved children of both sexes when they were infants, but about age four or five, a son's relationship with his father grew stronger. Sons were encouraged to imitate what their fathers did and were given toys that duplicated adult tools such as miniature sleds or weapons. Direct orders were seldom used in Eskimo education. Children learned what to do through the example of their elders and through teasing and joking directed toward their undesirable behavior. Girls followed a similar pattern of imitating their mothers. Between the ages of about 6 and 12, children divided their time between assisting their parents with tasks and playing with a group of children of the same sex as themselves. These play groups were very important because the older children were able to teach skills to the younger, and the group also established the basis for future partnerships and collaboration with those who were not blood relatives. They also set the pattern for the relationship of adults, for among the Eskimos the women associated primarily with women and the men with other men. Even sisters and brothers, as they grew older, established a relatively formal relationship, although two sisters or two brothers were often very close and intimate as adults.

An extended family could and did camp alone during the summer fishing season, but they joined other families at the larger winter sealing camps. One man, normally the eldest and most respected, acted as headman to make hunting and moving decisions. His wife was in charge of food distribution. An extended family normally ate together and shared all food resources. In times of scarcity, food was shared among all inhabitants of a camp, but normally each family was expected to provide for itself. Children were trained very early never to help themselves to food but always ask for what they wanted to eat.

Each Eskimo individual had a sense of his own personal kin relationships that extended beyond the group he happened to be living with at the time. All relatives, whether or not he knew them well, could be relied upon for support when he was traveling. Female relatives were also important as potential sources for wives as the Netsilik, contrary to most other Eskimo groups, often married cousins.

The second important type of relationship was collaboration, which meant simply that all people were expected to assume their fair share of the work. Men had to hunt unless they were injured or ill—there were no free dinners at an Eskimo camp. Although some types of hunting, such as seal stalking in the spring or fishing, were done by individuals acting alone, many things demanded the active cooperation of all able-bodied men. Stone weirs were built by the group, and all fished together to capture most of the fish run; caribou hunting demanded a division of labor; and breathing-hole sealing was accomplished most efficiently by having as many holes as possible covered by hunters.

The third type of important relationship was the partnership, a formalized sharing arrangement with a nonrelative or a very distant relative. Partnerships were often established very early, sometimes by the parents of a child, and they could be passed down through the generations. The butchering of a seal was regulated by meat-sharing partnerships. A hunter's wife cut the seal into 14 separate parts, and 12 of these parts were given to the 12 meat-sharing partners of the hunter, each receiving the same portion of the seal each time. Men with identical names often formed a partnership and gave each other gifts of equal worth. There were joking and wrestling partners and even avoidance partners, who were two men who had always acted diffidently to each other and were teased about it. Two men might have a formalized wife-swapping partnership and at the same time a song duel partnership. Wife-swapping partnerships had the potential for disintegrating into hostility if jealous feelings got out of hand. Cooperation with everyone was the key to success in the Arctic, and by and large these three systems of kinship, collaboration, and partnership worked well. In the next section, however, we will see the social tensions that were generated in routine daily life.

Social Tensions

Social tensions among the Netsilik were caused by a number of factors. Royal Mounted Police posts were few in number and scattered far apart. Hence, the control of disruptive behavior was largely the responsibility of the Eskimos themselves. The lack of females, created by the Netsilik practice of female infanticide, meant that there were not enough adult women to provide mates for everyone, a situation that could lead to wife stealing and even murder. The high mortality and mobility rates within the population meant that families were disrupted, promises were broken, and sometimes people were left without necessary support. Finally, derision and mockery, which were used for social control, sometimes got out of hand and became disruptive instead of helpful.

The practice of infanticide, usually female infanticide, was undertaken to reduce the number of useless mouths to feed. Sons were desired more than daughters because they would grow up to become hunters. The decision to let the baby die could be made by any member of the family, usually the strongest personality, immediately after birth. The baby could be smothered, left to freeze to death in the passageway of the igloo, or in the summer placed in a shallow grave to cry itself to death. The infant could be saved in a number of ways. Once a name had been given to it, it was not killed because the spirit associated with the name would be offended. If anyone asked that the infant be promised as a future bride, she would be allowed to live. A request for adoption by another family was also honored. Some infants were adopted literally out of their graves and saved in this manner.

It is difficult to understand why the Netsilik killed so many female children when they could foresee the problems it created in getting and keeping a wife. The high ratio of boys to girls was adjusted to some extent by the higher rate of male deaths caused by the risks they had to take as hunters, but many males ready for marriage still had problems. There were several ways to secure a mate. The easiest was to have one who had been promised at birth by the child's parents. The preferred way to make this arrangement was within the extended family, first cousins being the most desirable of all. First cousins were preferred because relatives could be trusted more than strangers to keep the promise made at birth when the time came for marriage. In addition, a girl marrying her cousin could often remain in the same camp with her parents and continue to help them. The Netsilik were extremely suspicious of strangers and disliked sending daughters far away from the household. If a Netsilik male had no promised bride, he or his parents were forced to take action to find one. He could travel to new communities or seek more distant relatives with daughters of the right age. If this tactic failed, he could resort to stealing the wife of another man or, in extreme cases, to murdering a husband in order to steal his wife. These practices, though not regarded as desirable, were usually accepted as faits accomplis. In spite of the scarcity of women, some of the best hunters were able to take two wives, often getting a younger one to help the older with the work. Polyandry was also practiced, with one woman having two husbands, but this custom seldom worked smoothly because the husbands were apt to be very jealous of each other. Sex created many problems for the Netsilik. Premarital sex, sometimes consisting of rape of young girls by older men, and adultery were common.

Another indicator of social tensions among the Netsilik was suicide. The suicide rate was unusually high, averaging one suicide every year and a half for a tribe of fewer than 300 people. In contrast to the pattern found among other Eskimo groups, the most frequent suicides were not those of aged people who considered themselves a burden upon their families. Netsilik males committed suicide more often than females, and most often the male was married, with children of his own. Netsiliks usually committed suicide either because someone personally important to them had died or because they were involved in a personal disaster such as illness or injury. Balikci speculated that they were willing to take their lives because of a lack of ties with other Eskimo groups and the world at large. This group was so small and so suspicious of all who were not relatives that individuals suffering a personal loss had little to fall back upon to support themselves. It was easier to give up than to forge new relationships. Disruptions have been increasing in modern times because some people have chosen to migrate to the newly formed Arctic communities and are lost to the band. The use of the rifle for hunting instead of traditional bow and arrow or harpoon has also lessened the need for cooperation among the people, for each hunter can now strike out for himself with some chance of success. Traditionally, the Netsilik valued aggressiveness, and perhaps men who did not measure up to the standard of good hunters felt that they had no recourse but to leave the battle by taking their own lives.

Additional conflicts were caused by the Netsilik's habit of using mockery and derision to effect social control. These could get out of hand and create resentments so that very trivial events could result in conflict. Mockery, gossip, and fear of sorcery were all indirect ways of social control. There were also more direct methods. Fistfights were entered into enthusiastically and often cleared the air, so that the participants could be friends when it was over. Drum duels and song competitions in which insults were traded served the same purpose. In extreme cases, when a person was so hostile or crazed that he was dangerous to those around him, execution by a member of the family was sanctioned. Finally, there was always the option of withdrawal by an individual or family to another side of camp or another location altogether to escape someone who was causing problems. The Netsilik were not a friendly people; they were suspicious, hostile, and untrustworthy toward all they deemed strangers, and strangers included even members of their own small tribe who were unknown to them. The difficulties of living in the Arctic must have been compounded by the difficulties in getting along with each other.

Religion

Their relationship with the supernatural was very important to the Netsilik and encompassed every aspect of their lives. Ideas about religion formed the intellectual basis of their culture and explained to them the past, present, and future. Religious beliefs helped to control fears, were relied upon in crises, and influenced the relationships of people to each other. Along with its positive facets, however, belief in the supernatural brought fear with it. Evil spirits could cause illness, powerful shamans and ordinary people both had powers to invoke these spirits, and strict taboos had to be meticulously observed lest the angered spirits of the animals would retaliate. To explain how these spirits worked, one must look first at what the Netsilik believed.

Spirits of all kinds inhabited the Arctic with the Netsilik. Human souls were possessed by all people, by names, and by ghosts. A man's soul gave him physical strength and courage, contributing to his success as a hunter. Women, too, had souls, but the Netsilik didn't say much about them. The soul of a name was transferred to a baby when that name was bestowed upon him or her, so named babies could not be deliberately allowed to die. The souls of good hunters and women who could withstand the pain of tattooing went to one of two heavens, where they enjoyed perpetual good hunting and fine weather. The souls of poor hunters and cowardly women, however, remained just below the surface of the earth in a land of misery, and these souls could cause trouble for those still living. Animals as well as humans possessed souls, and elaborate rituals were required to propitiate the soul of the caribou, seal, or bear who had been killed so that it would regenerate and the hunter could kill it again. Amulets such as animal teeth or skins were worn to bring luck with specific sorts of hunting. Strange creatures—monsters, giants, and dwarfs—inhabited the land and, disguised as ordinary Eskimos, could follow people. Shamans possessed personal spirits, which they could call upon at will, but which could sometimes refuse the call and turn upon the people.

Among this myriad of spirits, three stood out as most important. Nuliajuk, the spirit of the sea, had once been an Eskimo girl who had been thrown off a raft into the water by the other people. When she tried to clutch the side of the raft to come aboard, her fingers were cut off. These fingers were transformed into seals as she sank to the bottom of the sea, where she became the all-powerful protector of both land and sea animals. Nuliajuk did not like men very much and had to be propitiated constantly by correct observance of all hunting taboos. The second spirit was Narseuk, a giant baby born of a double-toothed monster. When his father was killed by a giant and his mother died, Narseuk was taken up into the sky to rule the weather. Because he hated men, he was wrapped tightly in caribou skins tied with thongs. If the Eskimo women neglected to report that they were menstruating and to observe the proper taboos for this time, the thongs were loosened, and Narseuk was able to unleash terrible storms upon the earth. Shamans had to make the dangerous journey up into the sky to tighten his bonds again. The third spirit, Tatqeq, the moon goddess, had a passive kind of benevolence. She was the daughter of an evil mother who had attempted to kill her and her brother. Killing the mother in turn, the two siblings formed an incestuous relationship and then escaped into the sky, where they became the sun and the moon. Tatqeq was good luck for hunting and was given credit for impregnating a woman sleeping in the moonlight. It is interesting to note that of these three major dieties, two were terrible creatures who had to be propitiated constantly, and the other was a rather bland, vaguely helpful goddess who offered no particular protection against evil. The spirit world was seldom regarded as a source of aid and comfort.

As we have seen, the Netsilik inhabited a world where physical existence was dangerous and difficult and where most spirits were potentially lethal and always unreliable. How did they cope with this double peril? They did so in two ways: the use of minor rituals such as taboos, special words, or observances, plus some malevolent magic; and the activities of very powerful shamans who were in direct contact with the supernatural.

Balikci (1970) gives four major examples of the use of taboos. First of all, they differentiated between land and sea animals. Seal and caribou had to be kept separate at all times. Women could not sew caribou skins while seal hunting was taking place; no one ate seal in a caribou camp. These taboos enforced the seasonal migration cycle. Second, taboos acted as defenses against uncontrollable dangers inherent in birth, death, and the pursuit of game. Mothers giving birth were isolated in small igloos, where they labored alone. Some activities were restricted for an entire year after the birth. Taboos involving death attempted to ensure that the spirit would not bother the living. When things went wrong, shamans could be consulted, but the observance of the taboo gave the people some assurance that they were in control. Third, taboos explained tribal misfortunes. There were so many taboos to keep track of that they were invariably broken by someone, and this could explain why trouble had come. Last of all, taboos strengthened and reinforced religious beliefs. The spirit world was always present to people, who had to remember the proper taboos to observe in every activity.

When the observances of taboos and other related customs failed, the people could turn to the shamans. Shamans were given formal training, usually beginning quite early when a young boy became an apprentice. Although each shaman controlled his own spirits called *tunraqs* and could call upon his *tunraqs* to heal people, the *tunraq* could sometimes disobey and turn upon him. Shamans were positive influences in that they controlled environmental threats, individual or group crises, and interpersonal relationships. Their influence, however, could become negative if they were too much concerned with their own prestige or if they used their powers to gain sexual satisfactions from beleaguered women or to work evil spells on members of the community. Ordinary people, too, could work evil spells, and Balikci presented the rather terrifying vision of a community where everyone was pleasant and friendly on the surface, but many were busily invoking evil spirits behind their victim's back. Life as a Netsilik could never have been easy.

CHANGES AND THE CAUSES OF CHANGE

Hughes (1965: 54) has reviewed widespread changes that have occurred in Eskimo societies since the close of World War II with respect to Greenland, Canada, Alaska, and Siberia. Some general trends that he has noted that apply to all four regions are greater population concentration into stable, year-round communities, increased use of Western technology, a greater demand for wage work and the appreciation of the worth of money, more government interference with tribal autonomy, the development of schooling and health and sanitation programs, and a decline in the practice of aboriginal religion. As individual Eskimos come more into contact with outsiders, some have begun to feel they are inferior because of their race or their socioeconomic standing. Like the Hare, however, the Eskimos have had much practice in coping with stress, and many are gradually adjusting to all the changes.

Against this general backdrop, two villages, Sugluk in Canada (Graburn, 1969) and Kaktovik in Alaska (Chance, 1966), and a general area, Eastern Canada (Brody, 1975), are considered as specific examples, reflecting to a degree the trends referred to above. These locations are considered together, but are divided by topic.

At various times in various places in the Arctic, three forms of White contact: the trader, the missionary, and the Royal Canadian Mounted Police, moved into the area to begin changing the lives of its people. The first of these, the trader, often belonged to the powerful Hudson's Bay Company of Canada. Traders came, of course, to make money, and the way they wanted to do it was to buy furs, primarily the fur of the white Arctic fox. Their problem was how to make the Eskimo stop spending all his time hunting for food and encourage him instead to trap for cash or credit. The way traders accomplished their aim was through the manipulation of credit. Eskimos were introduced to objects such as guns, nets, needles, tobacco, canvas tents, clothing, and processed foods. Once a desire for these items had been established, they were given credit for trapping equipment so that they could go out and obtain valuable fox furs to exchange at the trading post. As long as the price for furs remained high, this system worked quite well, at least for the good hunters who were willing to spend much of their time trapping. During the Great Depression and World War II, however, several bad things happened at once. The price for furs fell, and the war effort drained away supplies of ammunition and fuel. None was available to arm guns for hunting or to power new motorboats for fishing. In many places, the caribou numbers decreased, and marine life became scarcer. Much hunger and, in some places, actual starvation was the result. Traders during these hard times did not regard themselves as welfare agents. They were apt to extend credit and help only to those hunters who had been willing to trap for them in the past. Others were allowed to go hungry.

The second White representative, the missionary, came with the idea of changing Eskimo life. Missionaries saw Eskimo customs such as wife exchange, sexual freedom for the young, and some games as morally wicked. Other customs such as eating raw food and the disorder in homes were considered filthy. Through moral exhortation, offers of medical benefits, and threats of damnation, the missionaries attempted to move the Eskimos out of their traditional, ever-shifting camps into permanent settlements, where they would have access to a church, medical benefits, schools, and White-dictated social services. In the end they succeeded, and most Eskimos today are located in permanent, year-round settlements.

The third White influence, the Royal Canadian Mounted Police, brought with them southern Canadian ideas of justice, which often conflicted with what the Eskimos believed and practiced. The police tried for murder men who had strangled an aging relative upon that relative's request or who had taken a revenge sanctioned by Eskimo beliefs. Men living happily with two wives could be prosecuted for bigamy and their second wife removed. White judges and juries often sat on these cases and made little effort to ensure that the Eskimos understood the new rules under which they were living. One result of these practices was the establishment of small remote camps to which criminals fled until they felt it safe to return to society.

At the beginning of this period, the Whites came into the area to build trading posts, missions, and police posts, but the Eskimos continued to live in their camps and visit these agencies when necessary. As Whites grew more numerous, however, and their influence grew stronger, they began to urge all Eskimos to live in settlements where they could receive subsidized housing, regular schooling for their children, medical facilities, and various administrative services. Another influence toward sedentary life was the growing social concern for underdeveloped peoples as evidenced by the United Nations. Using the same topical format that was applied to the Netsilik, we will look now at the settlements of Sugluk and Kaktovik plus Brody's picture of various places in Eastern Canada.

HOW THE ESKIMOS LIVE TODAY

Technology and Subsistence

SUGLUK.   The settlement of Sugluk is located on the south side of Hudson Strait, which connects the Atlantic Ocean with Hudson Bay. It was established as a trading post about 1915. By 1920 approximately 120 Eskimos were trading there, and the first camp group moved permanently near the post in 1927. When Graburn did his fieldwork there in the 1960s, there were over 300 people living at Sugluk. They called

Sugluk in summer, 1959, looking northwest over the Inlet. Note the small Eskimo tents and the few "new style" scrap lumber houses; also the much larger white establishments, left to right: the Catholic mission, the Anglican mission, federal government buildings, and the Hudson's Bay Company. 1957.   Photograph courtesy of N. H. H. Graburn.

Mary Atchii outside her summer tent. Note guy ropes tied to boulders, her summer woman's parka and sealskin boots. 1959.   Photograph courtesy of N. H. H. Graburn.

Mark Kajjulik and his son lean against sleds stored up on barrels for the summer. Note on the left the leister (fishing spear) and sealskin drying on a frame, the tents in the background, and the Catholic Mission on the right. 1959.   Photograph courtesy of N. H. H. Graburn.

themselves Sallumiut, meaning "the people of Sugluk," although they had previously been part of a group called Takamiut, "the people of the shadow," because they were located in a northerly position on the Ungava Peninsula.

The people of Sugluk followed an annual cycle that involved some movement from the settlement. In spring, about April to June, many people moved to Sugluk Island, where they set up a tent camp to serve as a base for seal hunting. After the breakup of sea ice in late June, they continued seal hunting from the island with the use of boats. At some time during the summer, all people had to return to Sugluk for required medical inspection, and a number of men were able to get temporary jobs in construction work. The others continued hunting and fishing either from small boats in local waters or with Peterhead boats, ten-ton craft powered with a small engine and equipped with sails. Snow began falling in September, and fall was a poor time for the Sallumiut. Little wage labor was available, and the men could not set up traplines for white fox until November, when their pelts were in good winter condition. During this time, all families moved back to the settlement.

Whale hunting at Tirnirkjuak: the men of the Taiara band cut up six white whales to be loaded onto their Peterhead boat for transport back to Sugluk. 1959.   Photograph courtesy of N. H. H. Graburn.

Johnny Piluktu and his sled partner prepare to leave the igloo village at Qikirk-taluk island in winter 1964.   Photograph courtesy of N. H. H. Graburn.

Those fortunate enough to own shares in a Peterhead boat were able to take part in the annual hunt for walrus in October, but the necessary 250-mile journey was impossible for smaller boats. In 1957 a school was built in Sugluk, and this ensured that all families with children had to return to the settlement in fall. Winter was a time for trapping, some seal hunting, chores around the home, visiting, and some soapstone carving. Soapstone carving of traditional Eskimo scenes and figures is a fairly new development in the north. It was begun and encouraged by traders and missionaries, who saw it as a source of outside income for the people. Both have been willing to buy the work of the Eskimos for resale in the south. Unfortunately, not every Eskimo carver is an artist, and the quality of the work has varied greatly.

At Sugluk, the annual cycle has been insufficient to supply all the needs of the people, especially because the seal and fox population has been declining. This has been somewhat offset by growing numbers of caribou in the area, where the caribou population has been very poor for some time. By 1950 the people were dependent on government sup-port in the form of family allowances and welfare for about half their income. They were able to supply themselves with much of their food in the form of seal, ducks, geese, ptarmigan, fish, berries, mussels, and seaweed. Wage labor is the hope of many for the north, but in 1964 only ten men in Sugluk were employed full time. A number of others were able to find intermittent employment at such occupations as construc-tion at Frobisher Bay, mining exploration and development, cleaning up the settlement in spring, digging drainage ditches, and unloading ships and transporting the goods. Soapstone carving accounted for 15 to 20 percent of the income in the 1950s, but most people disliked doing it.

From this intermittent and variable income, the people had to buy a number of essential items. Much food and clothing were purchased, although sealskin boots were still made. Unfortunately, many women were losing the technique of sewing watertight seams. Tobacco has been essential to almost everyone since White contact. Furniture had to be purchased, and, if income permitted, luxury items such as phonographs and radios were popular. Hunters bought guns and ammunition, gasoline to run their boats, and tools and parts to maintain them. Recently, snowmobiles have become popular for winter hunting and trapping. Judged as a replacement for a dog team, they had the advantage of speed, immediate availability without the need for harnessing, prestige, and a cost for fuel that compared favorably to feeding a dog team all year around. They were, however, expensive to buy and maintain and were subject to breakdown, which could lead to tragedy if the hunter were alone and far from home. Dogs had two other important advantages: they could smell their way home in a storm, and they could be eaten in an emergency.

The Sallumiut no longer lived in their traditional igloos. Houses made of scrap wood or government-issued prefabricated units replaced these in the late 1950s. Furniture needs were minimal, for most families still retained the Eskimo custom of eating while squatting around a communal pot placed on the floor. Beds made of wood or cast-off cots were covered with the traditional mixture of skins, sleeping bags, and unused clothing. Because family size was increasing and houses were

Houses of the Kaitak family; these are a new style of winter houses made from scrap lumber and tent duck, replacing the former igloos. 1959.   Photograph courtesy of N. H. H. Graburn.

Qumak skins two harp seals *(qaigulik)* to be cut up for a community feast held in the Papigatuk tent. 1959.   Photograph courtesy of N. H. H. Graburn.

small, most family members found themselves sharing a bed. Electric lighting was available in Sugluk, but most people still used Coleman lanterns or wick lamps for light and oil-burning stoves for cooking and heating. During the summer, the style of living became somewhat more traditional. Canvas tents replaced those of sealskin, but the island hunting encampment showed the traditional cramped interiors with food scraps strewn around. Only younger couples valued neatness and cleanliness to any great extent.

KAKTOVIK.   Kaktovik is located in northern Alaska on Barter Island, 300 miles east of Point Barrow. The Eskimos here called themselves Innupiat, "the genuine people." When Norman Chance (1966) visited Kaktovik in the 1960s, it had just over 100 inhabitants. Kaktovik was a relatively new community, having been formed in the late 1940s and early 1950s when the military and the United States Coast and Geodetic Survey moved into the area and employed Eskimo labor. In 1953 the government began building a radar station attached to the DEW line system. DEW, or "Distant Early Warning," completed in 1957, consists of a series of central radar stations with support facilities ranging from western Alaska east to Baffin Island along the 68th parallel. For its construction, the government recruited every healthy Eskimo man in the area and paid them all high wages. The radar station was completed in 1957, but 75 percent of the men in Kaktovik were still employed full time at good salaries to provide maintenance. In this respect, Kaktovik was an extremely fortunate village.

Alaska has always been a good place to live for Eskimos because the marine life is much more abundant than in Canada. Traditionally, the people of Kaktovik lived in small, scattered, shifting settlements and hunted whales and walrus as well as seal, ducks, geese, caribou, and many species of fish. Houses were usually made of driftwood, and these Eskimos never lived in igloos. For many years slow changes have been occurring in their traditional life-style as powerboats replaced skin boats and rifles replaced harpoons. Increased needs for cash after World War II were supplied by short-term employment and welfare. These changes, however, were greatly accelerated when the radar station was installed and contacts with Whites working there increased.

Change permeated all areas of life. Houses were built from scrap lumber found on military dumps rather than driftwood. Food was more often purchased than killed, although weekend hunting and fishing have remained popular. After a post office was constructed in the 1950s, clothing and other supplies could be ordered directly from the south through mail-order catalogs. Regular medical care was available through military doctors, and transportation was there for hospitalization if necessary. In 1951 a full-time native teacher began classes, which were attended by adults as well as children. Villagers, supplied with electric generators, could enjoy washing machines, radios, phonographs, and tape recorders. Movies brought vivid descriptions of life outside the area. Throughout all these changing conditions, the people of Kaktovik were extremely fortunate in that they maintained traditional ties of sharing, cooperation, and interaction with each other and, in many cases, established mutual relations of friendship and respect with the Whites in the area.

Social Relationships

SUGLUK.   The people in Sugluk retained much of their traditional band organization, although Graburn saw signs of coming change in that the younger men were no longer willing to share the meat of successful hunting trips with the community at large. Four extended family bands have moved to Sugluk in the 40 years of its existence, each band consisting of between 45 and 65 members. A fifth group of people, whom Graburn refers to as the "Others," moved there independently as single families. These people normally attempted to affiliate with one of the existing bands. If they succeeded, they dropped their past family ties; if they failed, they became outcasts who were sometimes considered "crazy" by the community at large. Three of the bands were independent groups who moved to Sugluk as a unit. The fourth was a group of related families from different camps who moved from the Ivujivik area at various times. Because of their ties of kinship, they saw themselves as a separate entity, but they had no leader, they were ceasing to cooperate economically, and they were beginning to split into smaller groups. The major reason that the three cohesive bands stayed together was the perceived necessity for economic cooperation. Together a band could purchase, maintain, and operate a Peterhead boat during the summer fishing and sealing season. A Peterhead boat required a crew of eight to ten men to run it properly, so bands had to be large enough to supply this number. During the winter, not as much cooperation was required, and members of a band often split into small groups to trap.

Most households in Sugluk consisted of nuclear families. Fewer than 10 percent of households in the summer tent encampment contained two families. This figure, however, was greater in the winter because government-built housing was scarce, and people might be forced to share one house while waiting for others to be built.

The traditional practice of very early marriage for girls, at the age of 14 or 15, has been giving way to preference for marriage in the early twenties, and most young people now choose their own partners. It was quite usual for the couple to sleep together before the ceremony, which always took place in church. Children were still welcome and reared permissively.

Because of better health measures and less physical stress, families were larger than they used to be. Some of the problems in raising children today will be explored in the next section, social tensions.

KAKTOVIK.   In Kaktovik, the economic dependency of band membership was less than in Sugluk because wage labor was more plentiful. Melting snow, however, revealed that family ties were still important because, with the absence of snow cover, wires connecting the homes of extended family members to one generator, which they all shared, were evident. Single family units supplied their own generators. The easy availability of wage labor usually led to less sharing within the group, thus weakening extended family ties. Another influential factor was migration outside the area to seek jobs. This migration skewed the sex ratio and made it difficult for girls to find marriage partners. At Kaktovik in the past, first cousin marriage was common, but it has now declined, perhaps because the Eskimos are becoming more sophisticated about possible genetic effects of such unions upon the children. Choice of a mate was free from parental interference.

Visiting was an important village entertainment, and the traditional pattern of separation of the sexes continued. Men visited with men; women with women. Short trips away from the village for hunting, fishing, or collecting snow for drinking water were regarded as good recreation. Longer trips to camp or an extended boat trip were vacations. Although the *karigi,* or village dance houses, have vanished, recreation in the form of volleyball, baseball, playing pool, attending dances and movies, and celebrating national holidays was popular. The people of Kaktovik were fortunate in having a good relationship with the Whites living at the nearby radar station, and the two groups often mingled for recreational activities. At the same time, the Eskimos were able to prohibit those people whom they regarded as undesirable from entering the village.

Another much less optimistic picture of relationships with Whites was presented for Eastern Canada by Hugh Brody in *The People's Land* (1975). Brody described why the resident Whites were there and how they lived. Whites entered the north in large numbers following World War II, encouraged by a new northern policy on the part of the Canadian government. This policy was a mixture of altruism, national interest, and greed. The collapse of the trade in fox furs had left the Eskimos in an intolerable position, short of traditional food sources, of cash, and of the means to earn money. Recognizing their responsibility, the federal Canadian government attempted to improve the Eskimos' lot. Their approach was to supply better health services, educational facilities comparable to those in the south, and, when necessary, welfare and assistance payments. The government hoped that better education would make it easier for the Eskimos to get jobs, but no plans were made to change the economy. Little thought and almost no financial support was given to the idea of subsidizing hunters so that they could buy the equipment necessary to continue their traditional life of hunting and fishing.

The other concerns with the north, centering around the motives of national interest and greed, developed because the Cold War made the defense of this huge area imperative and because the industrialized world was increasingly concerned with finding new sources of fuel and minerals. As we have seen in Kaktovik, the installation of the DEW radar line probably did more for the Eskimo economy than anything else. Mining, however, has not proved as lucrative. For a mining company to make money, it must locate huge resources of a mineral or fuel to avoid having all the profits eaten up in large costs of transportation and building mining camps in the north. Eskimos represented a potential labor force already on the scene, but they had to be trained first. At the present, not many Eskimos have found employment in mining.

Once government policy had been set, the decision was made to try to attract Whites to the north by providing them with the amenities to which they were accustomed. To this end, pleasant homes were built, southern foods were made available, and good wages (including a bonus for living in the Arctic) were offered. These inducements, plus a genuine desire to help, attracted many young people to the area. Unfortunately, once they got there, the Whites tended to form their own middle-class enclaves, where they associated with each other but avoided, when possible, the Eskimos they had come to serve. Perhaps as a reaction to the difficulties of living in the Arctic, there has also been a large turnover in people, so that significant ties with the Eskimos did not have time to get established. Further problems have been created by the language barrier. Although younger Eskimos were becoming competent English speakers, the older ones often did not know the language well, and few Whites attempted to learn Eskimo.

According to Brody, most Whites saw Eskimos on two levels: first as the romantic idealized figure of the hunter and second as people living there in the settlement who did not quite measure up to what they had expected. Brody found that the Whites were prone to regard the Eskimos with suspicion no matter what the natives did or did not do. If girls were friendly, they were regarded as "loose." If they were shy and withdrawn to White males, they were "stupid." Families who followed the traditional pattern of living were thought to be dirty and lazy. Yet young men who were trying to learn modern ways were considered "delinquent." Any Eskimo seen drinking by Whites was regarded as an alcoholic. The only Eskimos who were generally approved by Whites were those who were quiet, cooperative, and good employees. In short, although most Whites in the north probably considered themselves liberals, in their dealings with the Eskimos they assumed a paternalistic stance, saying, in effect, "Take what I give you and do what I say and like it!"

This situation may change for the better as an aggregate of Whites who consider themselves permanent residents of the north is being slowly established. These are often men who have married Eskimo women and whose wives desire to stay in the north. The Canadian government has also recognized the need for a knowledgeable body of men who understand the problems and will remain in the area. There also needs to be more effort to get Eskimos involved in the administration of their own affairs. Until this happens, the Eskimos will often find themselves in the unfortunate position of living on the fringes of their own settlements as second-class citizens.

Social Tensions

All over the Arctic, the problems caused by rapid changes in style of living could be seen in the relations of children with others. Children, characterized traditionally as well-adjusted, cooperative, enthusiastic, reliant, and happy, have suddenly become antisocial, secretive, and

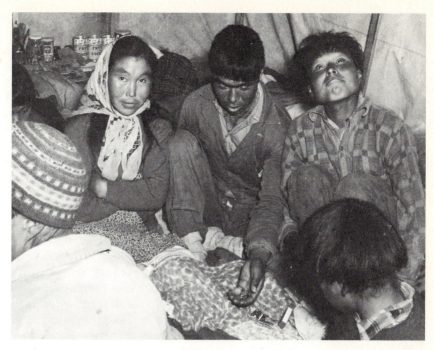

Sugluk. The young people pass the long summer night in Tunu's tent, playing and gambling. The stakes are ammunition (.22 shells).   Photograph courtesy of N. H. H. Graburn.

sometimes destructive. Thanks to better health care and easier living, there were more children than ever before, but there was less for them to do. As a result, the traditional peer group has become supremely important. Within it and given little supervision, children often got into trouble. In Sugluk, Graburn found that the girls were worse in this respect than the boys. Whereas boys were able to occupy themselves with the traditional fighting among themselves and active play, girls were pointlessly destructive. For example, three girls, ages 9 to 12, deliberately tipped over a can of molasses belonging to an old woman and then ate half of it while they were supposedly cleaning up the mess. Some girls, as they grew older, dressed elaborately, used excessive makeup, and then loitered around places where White men lived. All sources mentioned that while the old pattern of sexual freedom in adolescence continued, today it caused trouble. In the past, if a girl became pregnant, marriage followed and everybody was satisfied. Now both men and women often hesitated to assume the responsibilities of formal marriage. Such alliances have been delayed for women until they reach their twenties and for many, later than that. Those women who did not marry usually became promiscuous and often had illegitimate children. Such behavior did not contribute to the stability of the community. In Kaktovik a further problem was the outmigration of many young men, so that the girls had no one suitable to marry. Parental prohibitions against marriage added to this problem. Often parents or widowed fathers wished to keep daughters at home to help with younger children and refused to allow them to marry at the proper age. If this happened, the girl was likely to become promiscuous and not marry at all.

When marriage had been achieved and a family life established, further problems could arise. With the change to sedentary life, there has been a shift in the balance of authority between the sexes. Eskimo men traditionally dominated their wives and children. Now they were no longer resourceful hunters and suppliers of food, but wage earners or, even worse, unemployed household members who contributed little or nothing to family welfare. Women's influence increased as the home became more permanent and important. This, in turn, made the husbands suspicious of their wives and ultimately hostile to them. They were apt to display these tensions in unpleasant ways during a drinking bout. Eskimo men often had good reason to be suspicious because many women found the Whites around them desirable. The Whites, in turn, took advantage of the traditionally free sexual morality, but rarely allowed the relationship to become serious. This generalization was more apt to be true of casual laborers and construction men, as the society of permanent residents frowned upon any relationship with Eskimo women.

Social problems such as gambling, drinking to excess, and fighting were on the increase throughout the Arctic. Brody speculated that they were caused by equal parts of boredom and uncertainty. Young people too often faced an indeterminate, menacing future and sought immediate sensual gratification regardless of the ultimate cost. *Thrasher* (1976) is the horrifying story of an Eskimo from Aklavik, Anthony Apakark Thrasher, who was sent to the south for job training, discovered alcohol and the dregs of White society when he was thrown among them, and ended up serving time in both jail and an institution for the criminally insane. The book is a memorable treatise concerning the difficulties of preparing young adult Eskimo men for modern life. With the editorial assistance of Deagle and Mettrick, Thrasher tells of the problems, conflicts, and frustrations associated with urban migration when he was 19 years old.

> So the Canadian government flew Thrasher and a number of other young Eskimos from Tuktoyaktuk and Aklavik and Paulatuk to Edmonton, Alberta. The first flush toilet any of them ever used was on that plane. In

Edmonton they saw their first traffic lights and picked up jaywalking tickets in clumps before they learned to understand when they could cross the street and where. They had no idea how to use sidewalks, and a bunch of them would walk in formation, like mad soldiers, taking up the whole of the space so that there was no room for anyone else to pass. They bought Hudson's Bay suits and wore them over the pyjamas they had also bought for the first time.

Thrasher watched white men and tried to imitate their habits. So he slicked his hair down with Noxsema, brushed his teeth with shaving lather, and washed his face with mouthwash. He couldn't read labels and he chewed laxatives one after another, believing them to be candy.

Somewhere the baggage was lost so that the Eskimos arrived in Edmonton, to be billeted in a Skid Row hotel, with no money at all. Even before he had his first meal in a city restaurant, Thrasher was thrown in with bums and prostitutes and had got drunk and slept with a woman. While the Eskimos smiled for newspaper photographs, because they were told to smile, many of them were already deathly ill from the conditions and the heat they had been flown into. (Thrasher, 1976: ix).

Another modern problem was that suicide was increasing, especially among the young. Traditionally, older Eskimos who were a burden to their families had ended their lives, but now with pensions and old age assistance, they were more likely to be economic assets no matter how feeble. Exposure to formal education, far from leading to a satisfactory life as a wage earner, usually contributed to frustration and disillusion. The schools, which had assumed responsibility for many aspects of child rearing, too often labeled their graduates as failures. Although English was used throughout the curriculum, Graburn (1969) found that in Sugluk graduates still did not have an adequate grasp of the language. Part of the reason for this was that English was seldom used in Eskimo homes, and parents made little effort to see that their children learned it. Students regarded White-designed schooling as impractical. They were caught in a limbo with no incentive to follow the past and few skills to enable them to meet future demands in a White-dominated world. Vocational education, where it has been tried, has been more successful in fulfilling some student needs.

The nature of authority and of its direction was also an area of social tension. In Sugluk, a community council was formed in 1958, but its members found that in any meaningful decision about their lives, they were still at the mercy of the interests of White administrators. Direct control of Eskimo affairs was taken for granted by Whites, and they were very reluctant to cede their authority. Eskimo men found themselves politically powerless and had only limited access to intermittent opportunities for low-paying jobs as migrant workers or casual laborers. When these alternatives failed, they sometimes resorted to petty theft and begging for survival.

Funeral on the Niukluk River, Alaska; n.d. but probably late nineteenth century. Photograph courtesy of Museum of the American Indian, Heye Foundation.

Eskimos who stubbornly persisted in trying to lead a traditional life faced a different set of problems. Little welfare support was given to them for buying necessary supplies. The very land over which they have always hunted was imperiled because Eskimos made no treaties with the government. Often when the government found a site it wanted to mine, it paid the people a large sum for it, but no amount of money could ever adequately compensate an Eskimo community for the loss of such land.

Religion

Traditional Eskimo religion with its shamans has either radically decreased or disappeared entirely. Missionaries have been active among the Eskimos for a long time, and the people have eagerly embraced Christianity. The Anglican church in Sugluk claimed to have converted Eskimos as early as 1902, well before the settlement was established.

In Alaska, the Presbyterians and Episcopalians established missions long ago. Recently, an Assembly of God Church has joined the Presbyterians in Kaktovik. Chance (1966) found many aboriginal beliefs to be mingled with Christian ones. The Eskimos believed in a world of the supernatural consisting of God, Satan, and numerous vaguely defined devils who acted much like the evil creatures they once accepted. Although shamans no longer practiced actively, they still had powers over the spirits and could act covertly. The Evangelical emphasis upon the physical existence of devils and faith healing blended easily with older beliefs. Church attendance was usual among all Eskimos except hunters or people who had to work on Sunday.

Alaska, ca. 1900. Girls in cloth summer dresses. Photograph courtesy of Museum of the American Indian, Heye Foundation.

CONCLUSION

Eskimo life is and has always been difficult. Perhaps the most important and obvious persisting theme of Eskimo life centers on the difficulties and challenges associated with the necessity of depending upon uncertain resources that are limited in both time and space. Two centuries ago, all Eskimos lived out brief, hazardous lives as hunters and gatherers in a hostile, limited environment. Today all Eskimos are in the process of attempting to adjust to a hybridized White life-style developed in a temperate climate and then transported to the Arctic. The difficulties and dangers of such a process have not changed. Those few Eskimos who have migrated to urban places in the south on a temporary or permanent basis have also found their share of problems.

In contrast to most native groups in the south in Canada and the United States, the Eskimos have experienced change on a scale and at a rate that has seldom, if ever, been exceeded. There have been little time and few effective means at the disposal of Eskimo people to make a satisfactory adjustment to the results of such changes. As most, if not all, Eskimo communities are spatially isolated from many of the positive features that urban, nonnative life can offer and as they have only limited opportunities to take advantage of them through migration, their present and future lot would seem to be a hard one.

It seems reasonable to assume that the quality of Eskimo life will improve only to the extent and at the rate to which White-derived technology can suitably transform selected regions of the north into practical ecological variants of a southern, temperate round of existence. The possibilities of such an occurrence are difficult to assess at this time. However, all the ingredients for a distinct ethnic persistence for Eskimos are present. The exigencies of survival and the structure of opportunity ensure this result. The north will remain as Eskimo country hallowed by history, tradition, and immediate experience. The central currents of White life will continue to have, at best, a limited appeal for a small number of the Inuit. Contrary to the dire predictions of Thrasher cited at the beginning of the chapter, for the indefinite future the moon, the Northern Lights, and the Midnight Sun will continue to share the Arctic with the Eskimos, the survivors and beneficiaries of more than 4,000 years of successful adaptation to challenge and change.

REFERENCES

American Ethnological Society. *Proceedings Supplement, 1971: Alliance in Eskimo Society*. Ed. Lee Guemple. Seattle: University of Washington Press, 1972.

Balikci, Asen. *The Netsilik Eskimo*. Garden City, N.Y.: The Natural History Press, 1970.

Boas, Franz. The Central Eskimo. In *Sixth Annual Report, Bureau of American Ethnology*. Washington, D.C.: Government Printing Office, 1888, pp. 399–669.

Bogoras, Waldemar. The Eskimo of Siberia. *Memoirs of the American Museum of Natural History, Vol. 12*. 1913.

Briggs, Jean L. *Never in Anger: Portrait of an Eskimo Family*. Cambridge, Mass.: Harvard University Press, 1970.

Brody, Hugh. *The People's Land: Eskimos and Whites in the Eastern Arctic*. Harmondsworth, England: Penguin Books, 1975.

Chance, Norman A. *The Eskimo of North Alaska*. New York: Holt, Rinehart and Winston, 1966.

Cowan, Susan, ed. *We Don't Live in Snow Houses Now: Reflections of Arctic Bay*. Ottawa: Canadian Arctic Producers Limited, 1976.

Damas, David. Inguligmiut Kinship and Local Groupings: A Structural Approach. *Bulletin No. 196, Anthropological Series No. 64*. Ottawa: National Museum of Man, 1963.

Foulks, Edward F. The Arctic Hysterias of the North Alaskan Eskimo. *Anthropological Studies No. 10*. Ed. D. H. Maybury-Lewis. Washington, D.C.: American Anthropological Association, 1972.

Freuchen, Peter. *Book of the Eskimos*. New York: Fawcett World Library, 1961.

Gallagher, H. G. *Etok: A Story of Eskimo Power.* New York: G. P. Putnam's Sons, 1974.

Graburn, Nelson H. H. *Eskimos Without Igloos: Social and Economic Development in Sugluk.* Boston: Little Brown & Co., 1969.

————, and B. Stephen Strong. *Circumpolar Peoples: An Anthropological Perspective.* Pacific Palisades, California: Goodyear Publishing Co., Inc., 1973.

Henshaw, H. W., and J. R. Swanton. Eskimo. In F. W. Hodge, ed., *Handbook of American Indians North of Mexico. Bulletin 30, Part 1, Bureau of American Ethnology.* Washington, D.C.: Government Printing Office, 1907, pp. 433–437.

Hippler, A. E. *Eskimo Acculturation: A Selected Annotated Bibliography of Alaskan and Other Eskimo Acculturation Studies.* Institute of Social, Economic and Government Research. College, Alaska: University of Alaska, 1970.

Hughes, Charles. Under Four Flags: Recent Culture Change Among the Eskimos. *Current Anthropology 6,* 3–69, February 1965.

Jenness, Diamond. Eskimo Administration: IV, Greenland. *Technical Paper No. 19.* Montreal: Arctic Institute of North America, 1967.

————. *The People of the Twilight.* Chicago: University of Chicago Press, 1959.

Metayer, Maurice, ed. *I, Nuligak: The Autobiography of a Canadian Eskimo.* Richmond Hill, Ontario: Pocket Books, Simon & Schuster of Canada Ltd., 1971.

Mikkelsen, Ejnar, and E. Suiestrup. The Past Greenlander's Possibilities for Existence. *Meddelelser om Grønland.* Vol. 134. 1944.

Nelson, Edward N. The Eskimo about Bering Strait. *Eighteenth Annual Report, Part 1, Bureau of American Ethnology.* Washington, D.C.: Government Printing Office, 1899.

Oswalt, Wendell H. *Alaskan Eskimos.* San Francisco: Chandler Publishing Co., 1967.

————. *Napaskiak: An Alaskan Eskimo Community.* Tucson: University of Arizona Press, 1963.

Spencer, Robert F. The North Alaskan Eskimo: A Study in Ecology and Society. *Bulletin 171, Bureau of American Ethnology.* Washington, D.C.: Government Printing Office, 1959.

Swinton, George. *Eskimo Fantastic Art.* Calgary: University of Manitoba, 1972.

Taylor, William E., Jr. An Archaeological Overview of Eskimo Economy. In Y. F. Valentine and F. G. Vallee, eds., *Eskimo of the Canadian Arctic.* Toronto: McClelland & Stewart Limited, 1968, pp. 3–17.

Thalbitzer, William. The Ammassalik Eskimos. In *Meddelelser om Grønland.* Vol. 40. 1941, pp. 113–564.

Thrasher, Anthony Apakark. *Thrasher: Skid Row Eskimo.* In collaboration with Gerard Deagle and Alan Mettrick. Toronto: Griffin House, 1976.

Turner, Lucien M. Ethnology of the Ungava District, Hudson Bay Territory. In *Eleventh Annual Report, Bureau of American Ethnology.* Washington, D.C.: Government Printing Office, 1894, pp. 159–350.

CHAPTER *15*

THE FIRST AMERICANS IN THE LARGER CONTEMPORARY SOCIETY
The Parts and the Whole

It is a pity that so many Americans today think of the Indian as a romantic or comic figure in American history without contemporary significance. . . . Like the miner's canary, the Indian marks the shifts from fresh air to poison gas in our political atmosphere: and our treatment of Indians, even more than our treatment of other minorities, reflects the rise and fall of our democratic faith.

Felix S. Cohen in "The Erosion of Indian Rights, 1950–1953: A Case Study in Bureaucracy." *Yale Law Journal 2*, 390, 1953

This final chapter will show, as have many of the previous ones, that American Indians are vital, integral parts of American society and indeed are important currents in the American mainstream. Indians cannot be understood apart from that larger society because Indian behavior is and has been for more than a century closely interwoven in an economic, political, and social sense with its white counterpart. As Malcolm McFee (1972: 25) says of the Blackfeet reservation in Montana:

> . . . its population participates in the life of county, state, and nation in much the same way as its surrounding neighbors. The people share in the United States economy; they work for wages, farm, ranch, and engage in the businesses, services and government familiar to that economy. They send their children to the public schools, attend similar churches, and have in their midst the usual church, social and civic organizations. With few exceptions they wear the same kind of clothing, live in houses, drive automobiles, and enjoy the same radio and television programs . . . the expected rural American class structure appears to be present.

With very few qualifications, most of the Indian population of the United States is accurately characterized by McFee's statement. It is important to keep in mind, however, that although Indians today share many things with non-Indians, they are and will remain distinct for an indefinite future because of the influence of cultural tradition, history and its handmaiden chance, and the complex relationships that Indian people as individuals, communities, and tribes have with the American experience. It is these complex relationships and their results to which the bulk of this chapter is devoted. For those interested, other scholars studying this subject are R. D. Green (1973), R. F. Berkhofer, Jr. (1978), and K. H. Basso (1979).

X, Y, AND *Z* PEOPLE

The most important differences between Indians and non-Indians are the distinctive ways in which native Americans relate to the larger White-dominated society. Contemporary American Indian life can be described as a series of interrelated activities and individuals clustering around two centers and a kind of middle ground, which is the product of both poles, yet distinct from either. These three areas are defined in terms of their relationship to the larger society and to each other, and they are referred to as *X, Y,* and *Z,* largely because such terms as "left," "center," and "right," or "conservative," "moderate," and "radical" are value-laden and deceptive. In discussing this concept, I gratefully acknowledge the influence of R. J. Miller (1978) (1979), B. D. Miller (1978), and M. Rodin et al. (1978) with respect to using a systems approach. I, of course, am responsible for any distortions.

   X, Y, and *Z* are ideal types that fix the ever-changing dimensions of a complex variety of social, cultural, political, historical, and psychological forces or processes that make up the reality that is Indian life. Ideal types are hypothetical but convenient constructs used to outline or describe an area of interest. No particular Indian would fit exactly the descriptions provided below of X, Y, and Z, but all native peoples of North America are oriented along the lines of one of these three categories. Category content is not the prime factor of distinction but rather the pattern, direction, or form of orientation with respect to the larger society, which sets each of the three apart from the other. Both pattern and content have been determined by the fact that Indians are parts of a larger human organization generally referred to as a society consisting of a variety of ethnic elements conditioned by a distinctive way of life or culture. Culture, in turn, has been strongly influenced by the distribution and functioning of political power and also by the way that people think about themselves and others. Society, culture, politics, and psychology, in addition, have a history or occur through time and are influenced by this process as well.

In essence, X, Y, and Z consist of individuals who cluster around three points or centers that mark distinctive, discernible areas of orientation. The behavior of those in each of the three centers reflects distinct ethnic ideologies, the integrated assertions, theories, and aims that constitute a sociopolitical program. The coordinated but changing nature of such programs should be kept in mind.

What is not being referred to here is the synthetic or layered form of social organization prominent in many parts of Africa a generation ago, where a ruling European managerial class of people presided over a mass of powerless natives whose direct routine control was administered by European-led native civil servants, soldiers, and policemen. American Indians, in this sense, do not have a layered relationship to the remainder of.the society, but closely resemble distinctive threads continuously employed in a rich, multicolored tapestry. Indians may have been close to an African kind of model about 200 years ago along parts of the east coast and in the southwest, but this is by no means the case in contemporary times.

The theoretical position used here regards, explicitly and implicitly, a number of other orientations used in the past to characterize the position and significance of Indians in the larger society, such as acculturation–assimilation or "movements of social transformation," as being oversimplified and even wrong. This, however, is not to deny their validity elsewhere and at other times.

The X Indians

Those individuals clustering around pole X have a long and, by their own definition, a successful history of relations with Whites. They admire and emulate most aspects of White life, such as wealth, power, prestige, and the reflections of these in the material world, which include extensive formal education and good housing, health care, diet, clothing, transportation, and recreation. Taking a White spouse is common and accepted by others in this category. The sociopolitical program of *X* people is based on their earnest desire to obtain these material benefits as quickly as possible. They acquire wealth, power, and prestige by using such expedients as hard work, ability, and the manipulation of local, state, national, and even international political and industrial institutions to gain their ends. The political and social realities of the larger society are appreciated and sometimes even enjoyed. Lawyers, lobbyists, courts, and propaganda via newspapers and other media are used to manipulate local and state politics, the federal government, and their closely allied industrial counterparts so that all of them will function to serve the interests of *X* people. *X* Indians seek to use their Indianness to compete with Whites for White goals. *X* Indians, though being content with a White world, still seek to improve their positions in it. There is a strong "social climber" element in the orientation of those in this category. Typical Indian organizations associated with *X* people are the National Congress of American Indians, the Council for Energy Resource Tribes, and the National Tribal Chairmen's Association. Prominent Indian lawyers, a few artists, some tribal chairmen, a number of higher-ranking federal employees, and Indian scholars holding positions in various universities are highly visible advocates of this position.

In terms of characteristics of a different order are the facts that most *X* people are middle-aged or older and have lived or been away from their home communities much of the time. Some have been born and reared away from the home communities of their parents and have come to regard them as interesting and useful places to visit, but they have no desire to live there on a permanent basis. They regard many socially and politically prominent Whites as friends or working partners with many common interests. Some *X* people have a profound knowledge of traditional Indian ways whereas others do not. Allegiance to tribe, reservation, home community, family, or other social unit is highly variable, depending upon a situational and temporal definition often tinged with a perception of immediate and long-term personal advantage. Hence, *X* Indians reflect the individualism of Western European traditions rather than a native communalism.

X people can be found in virtually all Indian tribes, communities, and regions of the country. They see Whites as people with the opportunity to acquire the good things in life. *X* Indians attempt to present themselves to Whites as natives who understand and can successfully compete in the economic, social, and political spheres of the larger American society. Yet they also make it a point to distinguish themselves as Indians who draw on carefully selected aspects of their heritage—those Indian things that Whites most appreciate—to gain an advantage over their non-Indian competitors. These aspects include a special civil status in the eyes of the federal government, which has potentially favorable economic implications; spectacular Indian artistic and literary achievements, which are applauded internationally as well as in this country; and the prestige gained from the fact that "they were here first" and that those having roots elsewhere are not of the same quality. They are the "true Americans," or so their argument goes.

The *Y* Indians

Y Indians, in general, have considerable difficulty in getting along with Whites as compared to their *X* counterparts. They believe that most of the time Whites are to be regarded with distrust, even though *Y* individuals realize all too well that these same Whites possess the power and wealth that they must have or use if they are to achieve their goals. A very few *Y* Indians marry Whites. Such marriages are not approved by other *Y* people. *Y* individuals are usually not comfortable with Whites because of a past history of conflict and the marked differences in wealth, formal education, and political influence between them and the dominant elements of American society. Dramatic exceptions to this generalization are a number of prominent non-Indian entertainers and clergymen as well as some anthropologists and historians who have uncritically adopted *Y* ideology.

Y Indians as a rule lack the relatively high levels of formal education and wealth that *X* people possess. Some individuals within this category have been convicted of felonies and served time in state or federal prisons. They now regard themselves as former political prisoners who have been oppressed by a domineering White system.

In contrast to their *X* counterparts, *Y* Indians attempt to use their Indianness to avoid Whites and a White-dominated style of life. Although *Y* Indians desire improved levels of housing, personal and public health, and other attributes of affluent American existence, these things are not seen as virtues in themselves but as means toward a partial and carefully prescribed social and geographical separation from the larger non-Indian society with its standards of living, which are perceived as demanding, flawed, and abrasive because they are the essence of the industrial, urban-dominated world. Such a world, according to *Y* Indians, has developed at their expense and denial and that of their ancestors. It may well be that many of the more realistic *Y* Indians regard a geographical isolation from Whites as impossible and would willingly settle for a strengthening of emotional, cultural, and economic supports.

Although *Y* Indians seek the wealth, power, and prestige of the larger society, they desire them only in sufficient degree and kind to maintain and ensure a permanent escape from the evils of White domination such as arrest and imprisonment, poverty, and federal paternalism, so that they may live a kind of life consisting of a blend of traditional, tribal, and pan-tribal customs. The specifics of such a life often vary from community to community and from individual to individual and are, in fact, defined by opposition to, or contradiction of, White values. The heroes (or at least the symbolic representations of ideal Indians) of *Y* people are not the outstanding members of the *X* category or even their own colleagues but the political and military leaders of the nineteenth century such as Gall, Red Cloud, Geronimo, Sitting Bull, and Chief Joseph. Such heroes are politically convenient because their deeds, aspirations, and selves are safely in the past. In effect, they now can become whatever their current public wants them to be, usually benign personalities who opposed White domination a century ago.

To gain their ends, *Y* Indians use lawyers, lobbyists, courts, and the communications media in a restricted, qualified way. In one sense, *Y* Indians think in defensive terms whereas their *X* opposite numbers assume an aggressive stance. *Y* Indians, however, have a number of other ploys to cope with the perceived threats of the White majority not used by *X* people. Personal appeals to prominent White leaders such as the President of the United States have been tried, usually without success. Dramatic public conduct, often involving violence or the threat of violence—such as the takeover of the Bureau of Indian Affairs offices in Washington, D.C., the occupation of Alcatraz Island, Wounded Knee II, and the Longest Walk—can be used by *Y* Indians to attempt to make their own world in their own time.

Y Indians support and underwrite these activities with a number of magical and religious forms that are usually derived from traditional cultural roots and that use in particular elements of Plains ceremonial doctrine and ritual. They assert the inherent validity of their conduct with the statement "Spiritualism is the highest form of political consciousness." *Y* Indians condemn the political and social forms of the larger society, for they are convinced that these, out of necessity, must work against their own interests. The American Indian Movement and a number of related but less prominent organizations exemplify *Y* Indian ideology, which has been formally expressed in a number of public statements issued since 1968 and in a political tract: *A Basic Call to Consciousness: The Hau de no sau nee Address to the Western World*, Geneva, Switzerland, Autumn 1977 (*Akwesasne Notes*, 1978). All these pronouncements embody in a lofty but comfortably vague fashion a plan of action amounting to a close adherence to the ways of native

Americans prior to European conquest. Such ways were supposedly without travail or blemish, but they can no longer be emulated because of the corrosive results of White domination. The first step in an effort to regain these Indian ways is to remove the yoke of White oppression. The ideology of Y Indians is also reflected in a literature or contemporary mythology, some of which is produced by Y Indians and some of which is written by their White supporters. The newspapers *Wassaja* and *Akwesasne Notes* and, to a lesser and sporadic extent, the large number of tribal newspapers (cf. Hodge, 1976: 275–284) are good examples of the former, whereas Johanna Brand's *The Life and Death of Anna Mae Aquash* exemplifies the latter.

Y Indians vigorously suppress the actual cultural heterogeneity of precontact North America and either ignore or deny the conflicts, famines, diseases, and all the uncertainties and terrors that these and other factors engendered. Some Y Indians have a thorough knowledge of a number of traditional cultures or their early nineteenth-century variants, but others know little or nothing about such behavior. The allegiance of Y Indians to their tribes, reservations, communities, and families closely resembles that of the X people. Prominent Y Indians travel extensively. They appear to be equally at home in a city or on a reservation. Those who are less prominent are more likely to be reservation-based and unemployed.

The Z Indians

The characteristics of X and Y Indians shade into a central area referred to as Z. Z people embody variants of the attributes of X and Y, and yet they are clearly distinct from either. The most prominent distinguishing criterion is that of social and political consciousness. Z Indians do not consciously seek to compete with Whites in the same way that X Indians do. They regard adequate food, clothing, shelter, and formal education as the basic requirements they must have to maintain a position in an involved exchange system based upon goods, rights, obligations, and emotional support. This exchange system includes people living in the home community or reservation and those in cities. Cities are regarded as places to camp in while wages are earned. Ideally, Z Indians use these wages directly and indirectly to create a comfortable niche on the reservation for their late middle-aged and declining years. They seldom see Whites as either friends or enemies, but regard them as a part of the landscape in the same sense as they regard expressways, stadiums, traffic laws, taverns, and a host of other elements that make up modern urban living.

Z Indians prefer other Indians as spouses, particularly those who come from their own tribes or home communities. Having an Indian spouse strengthens and extends alliances. A non-Indian spouse usually has the reverse effect and hence is to be avoided. Z Indians not only avoid the frequent militant posture in word and sometimes deed of the Y Indians, but regard it as foolish or wrong. Z Indians find and hold unskilled, semiskilled, and occasionally skilled jobs so that they may successfully rear children who will grow up to support their aged parents and repeat the pattern. They usually accept without rancor the reality of a White-dominated society because they can do nothing to change this established order. Many urban Whites are often unaware that they have Z Indian neighbors, but rather believe that such people always live *out west* or *up north* or *died off a long time ago.*

Basically Z Indians have an opportunistic orientation to White society. They see it as a place where they can obtain some of the necessary elements of survival, but they feel no special committment to it. They express their Indian identity most frequently by helping to organize and attending urban-based Indian centers and by participating in powwows held in city parks, school gyms, or back home on the reservation. Many of them make frequent trips to their rural homes to visit or to help Indian friends and acquaintances. Occasionally, they will publicly discuss the Indian life of the past, but on such occasions they usually gloss over or ignore the negative aspects of modern Indian life such as alcoholism, suicide, hunger, disease, and poor housing. Z Indians believe that they must live in a White world to obtain wages and eventually pensions and social security. They receive immediate rewards in a far better standard of living than they would have had if they had remained in their rural home communities. They most often long for a way of life free of the hazards of the competitiveness and personal isolation of American existence, but they do not seek it if its realization includes the harsh actuality of a rural slum.

Many Z individuals would prefer full-time reservation residence, especially if permanent wage labor could be obtained in the form of a tribal government job or a job in a nearby reservation border town. Relatively few Indians, however, obtain such positions, largely because only a small number of such jobs are available. Those who do get these jobs seldom hold them for very long. People who hold tribal offices are often subjected to intense pressures by those who want their positions or who continually make unreasonable and arbitrary demands on them. Those Indians who find employment in reservation border towns are often subjected to the unpleasant effects of race prejudice to a far greater extent than they would have been in an urban center away from Indian settlements. In response to these pressures, people holding reservation jobs often leave and move to a city, delighted to be free of the problems of reservation life but all too aware of the fact that they will experience other difficulties inherent in urban residence.

Z Indians have the same variations in their participation in, and knowledge of, traditional native life and in their tribal, reservation, and personal allegiances that X and Y Indians do. Although their position in the larger society lacks both the rewards and penalties of X and Y Indians, they occupy more psychologically and socially comfortable niches. The attitudes of X and Y toward Z people reflect a kind of disciplined indifference. They neither seek nor avoid contact; they bestow neither high praise nor condemnation. Z people are Indians, "but not like us." The attitudes of X toward Y and the reverse are highly charged. Y views X as *apples* or *radishes* or *Uncle Tomahawks;* that is, red only on the outside but white inside. Those in X consider most of those in Y as troublemakers who lack their intelligence and ambition to compete effectively with Whites on their own terms. Z Indians have a kind of ambivalent attitude toward those in categories X and Y. Many Z people believe that the militancy of Y Indians on occasion can be justified, but yet Z Indians have no desire to participate in such behavior. X Indians are regarded with respect and admiration because their achievements reflect well on all other Indians. Yet at the same time, they are also occasionally viewed as selfish or arrogant because they keep themselves removed from so much that is routine, mundane, and necessary in the lives of most Indians today.

X, Y, and Z Indians Compared and Contrasted

Objectively, I believe that the categories X, Y, and Z all contain equal numbers of the wise and the foolish, the greedy and the generous, the well adjusted and the neurotic. In terms of actual proportions today, X Indians are numbered in the hundreds, Y Indians limited to a few thousand, and the bulk of the population would fall into the Z category. Further, by the definition used in this book, X, Y, and Z are all equally Indian in that they fulfill the legal requirements of being Indian, they regard themselves as Indian and are generally regarded as being so by others, and they occupy distinctive parts of the larger social network that may be validly labeled Indian. X and Z Indians live in a world that, for all its imperfections, *is*. The world of Y Indians does not now exist, but can be only desired. The present reality of Y people is heavily seasoned by fear, suspicion, frustration, and hate. All three ideologies have an uncoordinated, awkward, or unfinished posture about them. Each is still being defined in the vortex that is contemporary American life. All participate, however, in different ways in the larger system of American society. In short, X, Y, and Z construct three different systems, using elements from the various worlds.

X, Y, and Z Indians can be found in the same tribes, reservations, communities, and sometimes even the same families. Much of the turbulent, uneven, and amorphous quality of American Indian life stems from this fact. Most of the difficulties associated with Indian versus non-Indian, particularly federal relations, are due to this simultaneous and close coexistence of X, Y, and Z people in time and space and to the external nonperception of the systemic distinctions.

The X, Y, Z typology conforms reasonably well to the various Indian groups described earlier in this book. Specific historical, geographical, cultural, and social influences, however, distort the goodness of fit in many places. In other words, X, Y, and Z are subject to local and specific definitions depending upon time, location, tribe, reservation community, and reservation-urban area patterns of migration plus a possible additional number of factors. It must be emphasized here that such qualification does not render the general X, Y, and Z typology invalid. Further, it must be remembered that given the wide range in the specificity and the uneven quality of data, tribal and local community qualifications are more evident in some cases than in others.

In general, it is likely that in order of historical appearance, a Y orientation first crystallized following White contact and usually took the form of military resistance. This changed to a pervasive but largely passive kind of hostility manifested by contemporary Y Indians. The majority of Y Indians at the end of open conflict assumed an earlier form of the modern Z orientation. The reasons for such a partial differentiation of Y to Z varied from situation to situation. X Indians may well not have appeared until after the first quarter of the nineteenth century. Ely S. Parker, the Seneca (Tooker, 1978); Sarah Winnemucca, the Northern Paiute (Fowler, 1978); and Francis La Flesche, the Omaha (Liberty, 1978) may well have been some of the earliest examples of X type Indians. The presence of X, Y, and Z types simultaneously throughout the whole of modern North American society was not well established until after 1875.

Indians assume an X, Y, or Z orientation in the fullest sense when they reach adulthood. The chronological age of becoming an adult varies with individuals and their situations, but it usually happens before 40. Once an orientation is assumed, it is, as a rule, not changed. The middle years are the time of greatest activity, with the possible exception of the Y people, who usually manifest Y characteristics during early adolescence. Children tend to take the orientation of their parents.

THE MICMAC. Most of the Micmac who migrate to urban centers in eastern Canada and the United States to work are Z Indians. A very few Micmac might fall into the Y category, but this is uncertain. Probably few Micmac belong to the X category.

THE ONEIDA.   The Oneida, with their three communities, pose an interesting problem in that a common cultural heritage has been modified by the exigencies of migration, differential historical influence, and conformance to different forms of local and national government. Most of the Canadian and American Oneida are Z people. About 10 percent of the Wisconsin Oneida are Y. The proportions of Y's among New York State and Ontario Oneida are unknown to me. A few of the nonreservation-based Oneida may be close to, or are in fact, X's. Such people have little influence in their home communities and, in fact, may have never visited there.

THE CHEROKEE.   The Eastern Cherokee differ interestingly from their Western or Oklahoma counterparts. Again, the bulk of those in both places would fall into the Z category, but it is likely that more X's are present in Oklahoma than in North Carolina for some of the same reasons that have produced differential Oneida behavior. Y Cherokees are found in both eastern and western areas, but in relatively small numbers.

THE MENOMINEE.   The Menominees have few individuals in the X category. The bulk of their members fall into Z, and they may have as many Y people as the Micmac, Oneida, and Cherokee combined. Their involvement with reservation termination followed by subsequent restoration has possibly made a higher proportion of the Menominee people politically active than would have been the case otherwise. More Y's are found on the reservation than in urban areas, although some Menominee Y's can certainly be found in cities, particularly as students at universities and vocational schools. In the Menominee case, however, full-time wage labor on the reservation or in the city does appear to discourage a Y orientation. A politically militant orientation seems to require the bulk of one's time. The life story of Gabriel Brunette is a detailed and vivid example of the emergence of Z type Indians among the Menominee.

THE CHEYENNE.   As far as I know, X types are absent among contemporary Northern Cheyenne. Few of the residents of the Tongue River reservation have taken part in public protests against Whites and White institutions, yet hostility, often culminating in violence, occurs between Cheyenne and White individuals, with greater frequency than is the case between Whites and Eastern Cherokees, Menominees, Oneidas, and Micmacs. Perhaps the greater emphasis on open physical violence among all residents of the High Plains as contrasted with these other regions can account for this difference. Whereas some Northern

Cheyenne would come close to having a Y orientation as defined here, most maintain a variant of the basic Z pattern leavened with a keen distrust of most people who are not of the community.

THE NAVAJO.   Despite the fact that the Navajos have the largest tribe and reservation in the country, they are represented by relatively few X people, and these have appeared since 1965. Perhaps the nature of Navajo culture and their historical experience also predisposes them to have few Y-oriented members, and these few are not prominent among Y's from other tribes. As one Z Navajo friend put it, "These AIM guys come out here and all the time talk about 'uprise!, uprise!, uprise!' Now that is just crazy. You don't kill Whites off. You don't scare them. You keep them around and see how much you can squeeze out of them!" John Powell, Joe Sandoval, and Joseph Barnes all reflect different dimensions of the Navajo Z orientation. They would also heartily agree with my Navajo Z friend.

THE HOPI.   There are few Hopis in the X category. By the same token, the assumption of a Y orientation would go against the central canons of traditional Hopi life. The Hopis, instead, have given a special, localized definition to the Z posture. Although the vast majority of Hopis agree that they must understand and follow certain, selected aspects of the dominant White life, they have tacitly decided that they will be in, but not of, it. Almost 1,000 years of successful experience in dealing with harsh challenges from without assure them of the spiritual and tactical worth of such a position. Within this context, a Z orientation takes on a meaning shared with no other group of native American peoples.

THE PAPAGO.   The Papago data are of such a nature as to make it extremely difficult to determine how these people are represented in a contemporary X, Y, Z format. Unfortunately, far too little attention has been given to the Papago as individuals now or in the past. Perhaps some of this neglect is due to the nature of Papago life itself, which places little or no emphasis on indvidual distinctiveness and achievement but rather stresses the integrity or advantages of sound, functioning family and community groupings. Byrd Baylor's novel on the Papago, *Yes Is Better Than No* (1977), views modern Papago city residents as spending their time in reasonably quiet resentment and frustration over the restrictions imposed upon them directly and indirectly by the dominant White society and having a variant of the Z orientation.

THE POMO.   The Pomo, at least those of the Manchester Band, lack X category representatives. The Pomo situation poses a number of interesting questions concerning the expression of the X, Y, Z typology that available data cannot answer. For example, the Pomo show a kind of discontent and resentment over their lot in life, but few if any can be placed in the Y category. Perhaps some of the reasons for this may center around the remarkable degree of self-imposed social and spatial isolation from Whites. It appears that Whites or White domination are not viewed as the primary cause of their unfortunate position and that they feel the source of their misfortunes lies elsewhere. Perhaps another reason for their lack of assertiveness is due to the fact that an acceptable, if drab, compromise has been reached between their ambitions or aspirations and the narrow rigid constraints of social reality. Band and land size appear to be well balanced. Although the possibility of life's becoming better is slight or nonexistent, the chances of life's becoming worse is equally unlikely. Such a perception lends itself to a bland, passive Z stability, which will probably exist for a long time.

THE KLAMATH.   The Klamath, like the Pomo, lack X type representatives. They also have few, if any, Y individuals. Resentment or hostility stemming from the problems of living seems to be almost exclusively directed toward others in the group or at times even kept within the self. The fact that Klamath hostility does not take the form of sporadic, open rebellion in tandem with Y's from other groups may well be associated with the Klamath inability in the past to reach an effective consensus among themselves. The world of the Klamath is an individual world, or, at best, limited to a number of small, shifting alliances of temporary duration. Such a posture does not lend itself to the concerted, long-term resistance that is a Y orientation. Most Klamaths are Z Indians, but they have a kind of Z orientation markedly different from the other Z people discussed above.

THE KWAKIUTL.   The Kwakiutl may have a few X representatives, but not many. Correspondingly, they have few Y members. James Sewid seems to be a good example of a person who achieved the best that a Kwakiutl Z orientation could provide. Many who fall short of his achievements are also of the Z category but exemplify their failure through alcoholism, violence, and other forms of unsatisfactory interpersonal relations. Most Kwakiutl appear to want the good things of life according to White standards, but do not seek and seldom find White acceptance as social equals. Hence, they are Z people by default rather than by design, which is clearly not the case with the Menominee, Micmac, Navajo, or Northern Cheyenne. Z Kwakiutl appear to be closer in the content and structuring of their behavior to the Eastern Cherokee than to the others considered here.

THE HARE.   Given the isolation and other limiting factors of their environment, the Hare of the western Subarctic lack X and Y orientations. The band members of Colville Lake neither yearn for the excellence in White terms of X category Indians nor long to rebel along Y lines. Given their stability in population numbers, which is well balanced with food resource levels, a kind of stable Z posture has resulted. With all their physical hardships and the constant danger of death from an implacable environment, the Hare seem to have achieved a peace with reality not gained by other Indians mentioned in this book, with the possible exception of the Papago. Apparently for both, to have survived in the past, to be able to live in the present, and to anticipate a similar future are rewards enough.

THE ESKIMO.   The orientation of the Eskimo people varies among the different groups. The small Netsilik band must have resembled the Hare Z orientation in most respects. The Sallumiut of Sugluk are more closely a part of national Canadian life, but still remote enough to have a passive Z orientation. Among the people of the Alaskan village of Kaktovik, isolation, the demands of a stark Arctic environment, plus a reasonably good economic adjustment to the modern world, make the appearance of a Y orientation now unlikely. The potential for discontent is real, but such potential will probably not be realized for decades.

Those interested in learning more about the development of native political consciousness in Alaska and other parts of the Arctic are urged to consult A. M. Ervin's *Civic Capacities and Transculturation: The Rise and Role of the Alaskan Federation of Natives* (1974) and John Dyson's *The Hot Arctic* (1979) Both books describe a political elite who have been active in fighting the land claims issue before Congress and who have been very successful in doing so. The culmination of this and other trends should give the Arctic and subarctic peoples of North America a better definition within the X, Y, Z typology used here.

OTHER ASPECTS OF THE INDIAN EXPERIENCE

The purpose of these final pages is to indicate a number of topics that the interested student may want to consider, which go well beyond the scope of this book. Discussion is necessarily brief, as a number of crucial topics such as urban life, urban-reservation migration, demography, modern reservation living, government-Indian relations, the formation and functioning of tribal governments, reservation termination and its effects, and technological and economic development have already been discussed in considerable detail within the preceding chapters.

The Canadian Situation

As the previous chapters on the Kwakiutl, Micmac, Oneida, Hare, and Eskimo imply, the relations between Indians and Canadians differ in certain crucial respects from those of their counterparts to the south. The very definition of Indianness has a different legal context and significant behavioral implications.

A personal communication from John L. Taylor of the Canadian Indian Rights Commission (1978) states in part:

> Further to your question regarding the official meaning of "Indian," "Inuk" (plural Inuit), "Metis," and "non-status Indian," I offer the following. The Government of Canada considers an Indian to be a person entitled to be registered as an Indian under the provisions of the Indian Act. Hence the term is often qualified by the words "registered," "status," or "treaty" usually in the prairie region only.
>
> Other persons of Indian ancestry are colloquially termed "non-status Indians" or "Metis." Sometimes these words are used interchangeably. When used with more precision "non-status Indian" refers to a person who is of Indian ancestry but for some reason does not qualify for registration as an Indian or have been enfranchised. A large number in this category are Indian women who have lost status by marrying men who are not registered Indians. "Metis," strictly speaking, refers to persons of mixed Indian and non-Indian ancestry. Neither non-status Indians or Metis have any legal standing different from other Canadian citizens.
>
> "Inuit," by virtue of a 1939 Supreme Court of Canada decision, *Re Eskimos,* are "Indians" within the meaning of the British North America Act of 1867 section 91 (24) which gave jurisdiction to the Parliament of Canada over "Indians, and Lands reserved for the Indians." They are not, however, considered Indians under the Indian Act and are not subject to its provisions.
>
> There are no treaties with the Inuit, although some are parties to the James Bay Agreement (1977) which technically is not a treaty. Only about half the registered Indian population have treaties and, with one puzzling exception, there are no treaties with non-status Indians or Metis. Special provision was, however, made for Metis land grants in the prairies and the north-west under the Manitoba Act of 1870 and various Dominion Lands Acts.

Those wishing a fuller description of the legal situation for Indians in Canada may consult the *Official Consolidation of the Indian Act* (Canada, 1963). A fuller understanding of the history and current status of Metis people in Canada may be gained by consulting four works: Taylor

(1973, revised, 1975), Howard (1974), Slobodin (1966), and Pelletier (1973). Available Metis newspapers also provide much information on specific topics of local and contemporary interest. Examples are *Mal-I-Mic News* (New Brunswick); *The Forgotten People* (Ontario); *Le Metis* (Manitoba); and *New Breed* (Saskatchewan). Correspondence with Metis organizations such as the Federation of Metis Settlements (Alberta) and the Ontario Metis and Non-Status Indian Association will provide additional information. The addresses of these newspapers and organizations are given in the Reference section at the end of this chapter under the entry "Organization". Native status in Canada is closely linked with Indian, Metis, and Inuit claims. A good starting point for research here is the Research Resource Centre publication *Indian Claims in Canada* (1975).

Canadian Native urbanization is similar to that of the United States. There are, however, some important differences. The Office of Indian Affairs and Northern Development (Canada, 1976) has maintained a Placement and Relocation Program for Natives since 1957. The Canadian program, however, has never been so financially generous as its American counterpart. In addition, there has been an increasing tendency to encourage Natives to rely upon the types of employment assistance available through a variety of national and provincial agencies to all citizens of the country. Because of extremely limited financial resources, the Departments of Indian Affairs and Northern Development and Manpower and Immigration have a very restricted role in the movement of Canadian Natives from reserves to cities. Accordingly, such migration that does occur is dependent upon the means of individuals and families. Employment opportunities that appear to have a special appeal to Indians are those available near the reserve.

Rudy Platiel of the *Toronto Daily Star* (February 22, 1971) summarized his view of Native–government relations within an urban situation as follows:

> While the department of Indian Affairs and Northern Development assumes responsibility for Indians on the reserve, the department relinquishes this responsibility when he (the Indian) migrates to the city.
>
> In the city, the new arrival is shuttled between agencies by workers who know nothing of Indian history and can offer little understanding and kindness. Often they are referred to friendship centers which are understaffed, under-financed and ill-equipped to deal with the range of problems referred to them.
>
> The real tragedy of this situation lies in the inability of all our leading and social institutions to aid the migrating Indian in his adjustment to the city.

Those interested in the question of reserve–urban migration in Canada should refer to the germinal work of Linda M. Gerber of the Center for

Population Studies, Harvard University, particularly those listed in the Reference section.

There are a number of important coordinated research efforts concerning native peoples in Canada. Among the more useful of these is the Cree Developmental Change Project, which seeks to increase the understanding of the processes of economic, social, and political change and development among the Cree so that some of the problems posed by contemporary living may be resolved. One report emerging from this study is that of Chance (1968). Two additional studies deserve careful attention since they concern both rural and urban resident people: Hlady et al. (1967) and Lagasse et al. (1959). Canadian Indian communities as well as individuals are faced with a number of serious problems not of their own making. Hutchison and Wallace (1977) discuss a mercury poison crisis that has occurred in the small Ojibway community of Grassy Narrows in northwestern Ontario.

One of the largest and most controversial developments in Canada is the James Bay Project in northern Quebec. Five large rivers are to be dammed and their flow diverted into two of them. The watershed area to be affected amounts to a quarter of the total area of Quebec. The cost could exceed $10 billion. The short-range and ultimate benefits of such a project to the native peoples involved are questionable. Walter Pitman of the *Toronto Star* (October 2, 1973) has said, in part: " . . . the James Bay hydro-electric project has been put forward by politically threatened Premier Robert Bourassa. It may or may not create 125,000 jobs; it may or may not produce power at a competitive price, but it will certainly destroy the way of life of 6,000 Cree and Eskimo people in the basin to be flooded." This position is echoed in print by a number of others, including Richardson (1976); Gardner (1976); *Akwesasne Notes* (1973); and Weinstein (1976). Two other sources argue the opposite: Editeur officiel du Quebec (Canada, Quebec, 1976); and Bourassa (1973). In spite of the conflict, the James Bay project was approved on November 11, 1975, when the Cree and Inuit peoples in Northern Quebec signed away their aboriginal rights to 410,000 square miles of land (Gardner, 1976: 17).

Surprisingly, a recent issue of the *Yukon Indian News* of Whitehorse (September 12, 1978) reported in two articles, "The Dam(n)ing of James Bay" and "James Bay Settlement Viewed Favourably by Crees," that the Crees now approve of the project. The latter article states in part:

> The Cree of James Bay did not stop the huge hydro project from going ahead, but they did negotiate an agreement which, although highly criticized by Indians outside of Quebec is generally viewed favourably by the Cree themselves. And the agreement is not as bad as the amount of criticism it has generated would suggest.
> The strengths of the agreement, as the Cree point out, lie in the rein-

forcement of the traditional economy and the strengthened government controls over their lives.

The Cree have signed away their aboriginal rights, but in their place they have a number of pieces of legislation which spell out clearly what their rights are. And they're considerable.

To the entire region of James Bay they retain the right to hunt, fish and trap year round. In addition, they have exclusive harvesting rights to all furbearers, porcupine, black bear, Whitefish, sturgeon, burbot and other species.

These opinions were voiced after the chiefs of the Yukon visited the James Bay Cree in Quebec for over a week in late August. The Yukon Chiefs had the chance to meet with many Cree leaders, lawyers, and advisers and to travel to many Cree communities to get firsthand impressions from a good number of the 6,000 Indians who are affected by the settlement.

Despite these notes of optimism, the amount of personal and social adjustment for the Indians to make will be immense. Elsewhere the *Yukon Indian News* stated:

> The Indian community [Fort George] of 2,000 is located on an island at the mouth of La Grande Riviere. After La Grande is dammed four times, and the waters of the Caniapiscau, Opinaca and Eastmain Rivers are diverted into it, the flow is expected to almost double. As a consequence, there are fears the island may erode away, so the entire community is going to be moved five miles inland. The cost of the move is estimated at close to $50 million of which the James Bay Energy Corporation will pay $40 million and the federal government the other $10 million. While many of the residents are skeptical that many of the old Indian Affairs houses can be moved without falling apart, most are looking forward to the move. In addition to many new houses, the new community will have a sewer system, new schools, a new hospital and many other services not currently available, including an indoor area. . . .

The developments associated with the James Bay Project will be of considerable interest to all serious students of Indian affairs for some time to come.

H. B. Hawthorne et al. (1966–1967) have produced a general survey of the contemporary Indians of Canada. Though of considerable interest, this work raises far more questions than it answers. The Cree Harold Cardinal (1969, 1977) provides in his two books valuable but controversial statements with respect to the welfare of contemporary Indians in Canada, as does James Burke (1976), who concentrates on the situation in Manitoba. Patterson (1972) offers a more phlegmatic treatment. Additional references regarding the natives of Canada past and present can be obtained from bibliographies produced by Abler, Sanders, and Weaver (1974) and Hodge (1976).

Contemporary Indian Life in the United States

In this book I have concentrated mainly on the description of 13 specific Indian groups. In this section I make some suggestions to enable the reader to go beyond the specifics and look at the whole picture of American Indian life today. Contemporary American Indians in the United States cannot be understood without a sense of history. A comprehensive, albeit conventional and even chauvinistic, description of the conquest of the frontier is offered by Billington (1974). Using the somewhat different focus of Indian–White interaction, particularly in the area of government, another historian, Paul Prucha (1970, 1975, 1977), provides a helpful understanding of the roots of much of today's Indian life. Smith and Kvasnicka (1976) include a series of excellent papers written by experts on five crucial topics: major resources of the National Archives and Records Service for Indian historical research, Indian assimilation in the nineteenth century, Indian collections outside the National Archives and Records Service, the role of the military, and recent research on Indian reservation policy. Another essential source is the famous "Meriam Report" (L. Meriam et al., 1928). The general tone of this work is set by a statement on page 3: "An overwhelming majority of the Indians are poor, even extremely poor, and they are not adjusted to the economic and social system of the dominant white civilization." The report then goes on to consider such topics as health, education, general economic conditions, family and community life and the general activities of women, the migrated Indians, legal aspects of the Indian problem, and missionaries. Detailed systematic suggestions are offered regarding the governing of Indians by federal authorities. A careful study of this book will be richly repaid.

Two issues of the journal *The Annals of the American Academy of Political and Social Science* (Simpson & Yinger, 1957; Yinger & Simpson, 1978) present a broad spectrum of issues and the facts that support or refute various political and social stances prominent within the last 50 years. Issues of special interest in the earlier number are reservation termination, economic development, land claims, and political participation. With respect to reservation termination, Oliver LaFarge and others argued that if the federal supervision of Indian lands were ended, the fortunes of resident Indians would severely worsen. Senator A. V. Watkins of Utah and those of similar persuasion within and without the federal government assumed the position that reservations prevented Indians from realizing their full potential as human beings because they allegedly encouraged bureaucratic interference in Indian affairs, indolence, irresponsibility, and dependence on welfare. They also prevented a variety of White interests from benefiting from the sale of Indian lands and natural resources. As described in the chapters on the Klamath and Menominee, during the 1950s and 1960s some reservations were terminated, but their fortunes and those of other terminated peoples did not improve.

The Indian Land Claims situation concerns a number of involved questions centering around the fact that many Indians in the past have lost lands to White interests and not received adequate compensation for such losses. The Indian Claims Commission Act of 1942 was an attempt to establish a legal means to settle such claims made by Indians against the federal government. Such a means has been costly and time consuming for all concerned, partly because of the issues involved and partly because of the cumbersome judicial process itself. N. O. Lurie (Simpson & Yinger, 1957: 56–70) discusses the Indian Claims Commission Act and some of its implications.

Indian economic development in the 1950s and for the following decade took two main directions: the off-reservation movement, or relocation of individuals and families on either an independent or government-sponsored basis, and the industrial development of rural or reservation communities through the use of local natural resources and the establishment of reservation businesses and industries. Ideally, both processes were to complement each other. However, they seldom did. The emphasis on economic development underlined the fact that Indian communities could not financially support their residents. Such support directly and indirectly had to come from government subsidies and off-reservation wage work by Indians.

The nature of Indian political participation during this same time was unsatisfactory. Indians were not allowed to govern themselves. Federal interference via the Bureau of Indian Affairs and other agencies was rampant. At the same time Indians seldom participated in national, state, and local politics for a number of reasons. The literacy requirement for voting in Arizona kept thousands of Navajos and others away from the polls. The net result of their inability to develop effective tribal governments and significantly to influence White politics around them was their failure to protect their own interests adequately. This time, however, was a period of increasing political consciousness on the part of all Indians. It was to culminate in a political renaissance in the 1970s within many groups.

In the 1978 issue of *The Annals of the American Academy of Political and Social Science* (Yinger & Simpson, 1978) the papers by Butler, an Officer on the Bureau of Indian Affairs, are of particular interest, especially the conclusion that the effective administration of Indian affairs is becoming an increasingly difficult task despite the trend toward Indian self-government and the tendency for other federal agencies, such as the various segments of Health, Education, and Welfare, to assume responsibilities in this direction. A large and highly varied number of federal and state agencies attempt to work in harmony with local Indian community governments to resolve current problems and to promote future welfare. Because of a number of complex reasons, such results cannot always be achieved. The sheer number, highly varied composition, and the multiplicity of functions of such agencies make effective coordination of effort difficult. It is the typical case of "damned if you do and damned if you don't." Broadly based attempts to deal with complicated problems in a massive and general way produce disappointing results and lead to charges of governmental inefficiency. On the other hand, overly specific approaches to individual situations that, on the surface at least, are all part of the same pervasive poverty often exacerbate the feeling of bureaucratic frustration. One example is the governmental vacillation between program aids and general grants. Program aids, designed to achieve specific goals, are often resented by the client they are meant to serve because they tend to meddle in his affairs. General grants, designed to afford the client an opportunity to seek his own best answers, are conversely resented because government is perceived as abdicating its responsibilities. The national policy toward Indians, often characterized as imperfect, indecisive, and inconsistent, to a large degree reflects the attitude of society to the Indian minority. To a lesser degree, it may also reflect some of the changing demands made by Indians upon their government.

SOME POLICIES OF THE U.S. GOVERNMENT.   The federal government has attempted to discharge its responsibilities toward Indians via the Bureau of Indian Affairs, an agency within the Department of Interior; the Public Health Service, which functions within the Department of Health, Education, and Welfare; the Office of Economic Opportunity; and the Department of Housing and Urban Development. There is often no clear practical agreement within or between these offices as to a satisfactory definition of just what their responsibilities are operationally at any specific moment or over a period of time. General directives can be and are issued regarding various policies and programs, but their implementation is normally left to the discretion and resourcefulness of the area or subarea offices on the assumption that specific solutions are best developed at the local level. As one moves up or down various bureaucratic levels, delegation and scope of authority are frequently nebulous and uncertain. The net result of this situation is that officials, no matter how well motivated they might be, often find it difficult to carry out their duties effectively in the best interests of the Indians concerned.

The origin and development of federal Indian policy is involved and difficult to justify in the light of the national public interest. The problem of effective Indian administration centers in the fact that counter to government expectations American Indians continue to maintain their cultural and social identity (Castile, 1974: 220–221). Not only do they fail to join the mainstream of national life—or join it only in a highly qualified fashion—but also by all valid measures their standard of living ranks well below that of all other ethnic groups.

Many attempts have been made to treat or remove the superficial symptoms of gross Indian poverty without removing or even clearly identifying the basic causes of such a condition. The federal approach to the social and cultural nature of Indian life constitutes a hopeless paradox. For almost a century, the official attitude has taken two approaches. Indians are viewed at times as an aggregate of isolated individuals stripped of distinctive culture and tradition who for their own good should be helped to participate fully in the larger, non-Indian society. Whether Indians realize it or not, according to this view, they really *want* to be Whites, albeit Whites with an Indian genetic background. This notion is consistent with the basic approach (in theory) that the United States "system" is based on the individual. On other occasions, the reverse or reciprocal approach has been adopted. This policy argues that Indians have at least the fundamentals of a distinct, viable way of life that should be protected and extended whenever and wherever possible. Yet "pluralism" requires this version whenever a group can argue that as a group it can articulate with the larger society and maintain its own individuality (Miller, personal communication, 1979).

In short, Indians have been regarded by the federal government at times as existing and at other times as not existing. Efforts promoting one position are effectively negated by efforts supporting the opposite viewpoint. The general results of such a vacillation have been negative for all concerned. The majority of Indians, even when in the most charitable frame of mind, regard any federal effort on their behalf with suspicion. Competent, hardworking federal officials at all levels of government frequently believe that Indians will not cooperate effectively with them no matter how apt their efforts might be. The safest and most practical stance for both sides to assume all too often is one of wary and weary inertia. Frequent and sometimes arbitrary changes of personnel within federal and tribal governments can aggravate the situation. Today the Indians and the government at its various levels of operation both face challenges far more difficult than either perhaps consciously realizes.

SOME POLICIES OF STATE GOVERNMENTS.   On the state level, ideally the same agencies and offices that serve other state citizens also function on behalf of Indians. In addition, now or in the recent past, a number of departments have special responsibilities toward Indian citizens. In Wisconsin, for example, these are the Department of Agriculture, the Department of Justice, the Department of Natural Resources, the State Highway Commission, the Equal Rights Division, the Employment Service, the Department of Public Instruction, and the Department of Health and Social Services. The difficulties associated with Indian administration at the federal level are also reflected in the state situation. In a real sense the delivery of state government services is structured along some of the same lines as they are in the national government, because the state frequently works concurrently with its federal counterpart to meet or administer its obligations. A recent example of this is Judicare, a program designed to provide legal services in civil matters free of charge to people regardless of ethnic background when those people cannot afford to pay for the services themselves. Clients are allowed to choose their own private attorneys. The responsibility for eligibility determination under Judicare is ordinarily relegated to nonlegal state agencies and officials authorized to issue Judicare cards that prospective clients then present to the lawyers. Attorneys who serve under this program are paid with federal funds.

LACK OF UNDERSTANDING BY WHITES.   An additional impediment to the effective support of Indian interests by federal, state, and local governments is the assumption that the nature of Indian life is adequately understood by all those who have contact with Indians, but especially by government officials. Common but essentially false assumptions are that Indians closely resemble poor Whites who live for the most part in rural areas or that all Indians are alike in aspirations, aptitudes, and community and personal problems. If these assumptions were true, uniform policies of administration for Indians should have uniformly satisfactory results. The current status of most Indians throughout the country eloquently testifies to the error inherent in these misconceptions.

Also essential reading in the 1978 *Annals* (Yinger & Simpson) is the statement on contemporary Indian religion by Wax and Wax. The remarks on the use of the cactus peyote in its institutionalized setting, the Native American Church of North America, are of special interest, particularly the conclusion that the cult had a special appeal for those Indians who had lost much of their traditional religion during the latter half of the nineteenth and early part of the twentieth centuries. This view is complementary to that taken by David F. Aberle when he said about the Navajos: " . . . the initial spread of peyotism was promoted by the profound dislocation that resulted from livestock reduction and control" (Aberle, 1966: 353). Other dislocations and disruptions have occurred elsewhere for other Indian groups that have produced a variety of results beyond the realm of the religious. In short, religious change and stability appear to be associated with a wide variety of other factors. The Waxes' remarks on current religious practices of the Oklahoma Cherokee are exciting, as is their conclusion that further pan-Indian, neotraditional, revivalistic, and millenarian movements may be anticipated. An instructive case in point is James H. Howard's discussion of the Plains Gourd Dance (1976: 243–259).

LEGISLATION AND LITIGATION.   N. O. Lurie's analysis of the Indian Claims situation (Yinger & Simpson, 1978) is essential reading for all those who seek a comprehensive understanding of this vital aspect of current Indian life in the United States. Her remarks evaluate the Indian Claims Commission since its inception in 1946. Despite the fact that some procedural reforms in operation have been made in the 1960s, the commission has been a disappointment to Indian claimants because it has favored narrow construals and parsimonious settlements. Indians have generally favored per capita distributions rather than programmed use supported by the government, such as investment in securities or tribal enterprises.

Also in the 1978 *Annals,* Vine Deloria, Jr.'s paper on legislation and litigation concerning American Indians during the period between 1957 and 1977 is a good starting point for those interested in the relationship between Congress and contemporary American Indians. His other writings, particularly those listed in the Reference section, also warrant careful consideration. Although readers may not agree with everything that Mr. Deloria says, they will have no difficulty understanding what he means. The extent to which Deloria's opinions coincide with those of other Indians is open to question. Vine Deloria, Jr., is a Sioux enrolled at the Standing Rock Reservation, North Dakota. He holds a B.S. degree from Iowa State University, a Bachelor of Divinity degree from the Lutheran School of Theology, and a LL.B. diploma from the University of Colorado Law School. His advocacy on behalf of Indian interests in the form of writing and public speaking has made him well known to a large sector of the general public.

ECONOMIC DEVELOPMENT.   The area of economic development represents one of the crucial dimensions of modern Indian life. In practice, economic development seems to mean that public and private agencies—mostly the federal government—will attempt to cure the ills of Indian people by spending money on a wide variety of projects. Happiness and even social salvation is a large, well-funded program that means many things to many different people. Disappointment is often the lot of those who trust these programs. In an article in the *Wall Street*

Journal entitled "Indian Tribes Find Great White Father Is Big Loss Leader," Bruce Koon (1978: 1) states in part:

> The Commerce Department and many Indian tribes are finding that the tourist business can throw you faster than a mustang. In a program designed to help the tribes, the department's Economic Development Administration since 1967 has poured about $61 million into development of 63 tourist facilities on reservations in 19 states. The EDA reasoned that resorts blossoming in the hinterlands would generate cash and jobs for hard-pressed tribesmen.
>
> Instead, the Indians have been left holding a sackful of operating losses. In a study sponsored by the Ford Foundation and the Bureau of Indian Affairs, Harry Clement, a tourism consultant, estimates that the tourist projects already have rolled up operating deficits exceeding $20 million and are still losing; he believes the operating losses of the 12 largest projects total $10,000 a day. Tribal investments of $15 million also are in jeopardy.
>
> Following Murphy's law, almost everything that could go wrong did go wrong. Hotels and motels were built in the wrong places, thanks in part to Alice-in-Wonderland feasibility studies. Underfinancing by the EDA, with the money doled out in fits and starts fiscal year by fiscal year, left the project exposed to vicious inflation in construction costs. Management has been chaotic or nonexistent; the Indians hadn't any experience running resorts. No funds were granted for training or advertising, and promotion was lacking.
>
> The White Mountain Apache, who live on a reservation here in eastern Arizona, are struggling with one of the more ambitious EDA-backed projects. It is the Sunrise hotel and ski resort, built with $5.1 million of federal funds and $1.5 million from the tribe. According to a feasibility study commissioned by the Apache, the hotel's average occupancy would run at 58% and the overall facility would show a cumulative profit of $300,000 after five years of operation. Neither projection has proved accurate. . . .

Not all such projects fail, of course. Many of them do succeed, but when they do, it is because a host of factors are taken into consideration other than projected profit and loss. For example, the social and cultural background of the Indian community in question, its relationship to non-Indians in the area, the needs, desires, and expectations of the Indians most concerned are all important variables for both developers and hosting Indians to ponder. The literature on the economic development of American Indians and Eskimos is extensive, but a good starting point is Snodgrass (1968).

The development of the tourist industry on a reservation is but one form of economic development for contemporary American Indians. In general, such development usually concerns the advantageous use of local timber, mineral, and food resources. There has also been a regular but largely ineffectual attempt to attract outside industry to a reservation setting where it would, ideally, employ resident Indians. An Economic Development Administration report (U.S. Department of Commerce, 1972) briefly chronicles some of the current efforts that they hope will lead to economic self-sufficiency of Indian communities. Three examples follow below.

The Metlakatla Indian Community on Annette Island in the Alaskan panhandle about 700 miles north of Seattle had an economy traditionally based on salmon fishing and processing. Such an economy is limited by factors of competition, equipment, and modern fishing regulations, as we have seen among the Kwakiutl. The EDA is investigating the possibility of fish hatcheries, the economic feasibility of a shingle and shake mill, and the value of minerals on the island for extractive operations.

The Blackfeet Reservation is located in north-central Montana. The mainstay of the economy to date is land used for a variety of ranching and agricultural purposes. The EDA in conjunction with the Blackfeet people is attempting to realize a fuller agricultural potential by organizing a variety of cooperative agricultural programs such as feedlots and a livestock sales center on the reservation. Other efforts are being made to improve the economic prospects of the tribe through planning an industrial park, providing for street improvements in the town of Browning, and developing a tourism and recreational complex.

Finally, at Zuni Pueblo, 40 miles south of Gallup, New Mexico, the EDA has since 1967 approved ten projects on the reservation. Five of them were concerned with a 20-acre industrial park with air facilities. Others financed a training center and some business loans. Although not all these projects have been successful, they have had a positive influence on the Zunis, increasing the capabilities of their tribal leaders, bettering their financial position, enhancing the skill levels of the people, and increasing tribal awareness of its resource limitations and economic expectations.

Attempts at economic development sometimes rely upon non-Indian private funds or proceed strictly on an independent self-help basis. No matter what the sources of funding are, the essential intent of such efforts remains the same. Indians and Indian communities are eager to become economically independent of outside White assistance, particularly federal support. At the same time, they want such economic independence to mesh well with a traditional or distinctive Indian way of life that incorporates modern standards of public health, housing, transportation, and other selected elements of modern life. Some exceptions to this general intention may be found such as at the Hopi settlements of Hotevilla and Bacabi, but these occurrences are rare.

It is significant and depressing to note that at this time few, if any,

Indian communities have achieved such independence largely because in the conventional sense it cannot be gained only through short-term, sparsely funded projects. True economic independence coupled with a desired social and cultural autonomy such as has been achieved by the Hutterites has eluded Indian people. The Hutterites, an Anabaptist, European-derived group living in the Great Plains area of the United States, have been described by Hostetler and Huntington (1967). A combination of factors such as racial prejudice, special federal status, deeply engrained poverty, atomistic forms of social organization, and other variables all prevent the Indians from making a Hutterite-like adjustment. In short, it is unlikely that the economic development programs of the near future in themselves will provide the desired economic independence. A viable political and social climate must accompany or even precede this economic development.

LAW AND EDUCATION.   Indian law as both a practice and process is gaining increasing prominence in recent decades. One of the most important initial references is M. E. Price (1973). Those with a keen interest in the subject should carefully read all numbers of the *American Indian Law Review* produced by the University of Oklahoma College of Law. Many other law journals also publish important material in this area.

Formal education has been doing many things for and to the American Indian for a very long time. The literature on this subject is immense and uneven, with much of it of dubious value. One good survey is that of Margaret Szasz (1974). A particularly apt description of what formal education can do to an Indian is contained in D'Arcy McNickle's novel *The Surrounded* (1936).

POLITICAL DEVELOPMENTS.   One important fact of contemporary Indian life that is too often overlooked is the varying unity and diversity that exists at the different levels of Indian life. Frequently, there are abrasive factions or divisions within tribes that persist over generations. Robert Burnette (1971) has provided an absorbing account of political factionalism within and without the Rosebud Sioux community in South Dakota. An interesting description of the Quinault tribal leader Joe De La Cruz operating under conditions of little or no factionalism is contained in Wilcox (1978).

There may also be great, long-term antagonism existing between tribes who have lived closely together for many years. The reservation boundary dispute between the Navajo and Hopi tribes has been discussed earlier in this text. As an example of intertribal antagonism, a teacher on the staff of a Northern Plains mission school that had pupils from several different tribes, once remarked to me, "The Whites have in the past and now done many wrong things to the Indians, but all that is nothing compared to what the Indians often do to each other."

Yet in spite of these and other differences, Indians frequently work and live together. Pan-Indianism is an important part of Indian life as a study of a number of works will suggest: Howard (1955), Kurath (1957), Schusky (1957), Corrigan (1970), Northrop (1970), Hertzberg (1971), Sanford (1971), and Hirabayashi et al. (1972). These references are largely concerned with powwows and a number of other nonpolitical activities both in and away from an urban situation. Pan-Indianism can be generally defined as joint activities performed by Indians outside of an overtly tribal context. A social and psychological identity as Indian is emphasized as contrasted with a specific tribal identity. Pan-Indianism can imply acculturation or assimilation, but most often should be seen as an expression of common interests. The existence of Pan-Indian activity does not necessarily imply the weakening of tribal ties. Political Pan-Indianism is evident in the affairs of organizations such as the National Congress of American Indians and the Council of Energy Resource Tribes (CERT), who work together to obtain the maximum possible benefits from tribally held energy resources.

THE MASS MEDIA.   Indian journalism is an area that has been neglected far too long by students of the Indian experience. The Yakima Richard LaCourse is writing a germinal account that should be of considerable interest to a wide audience. What follows is taken from an outline supplied to me by LaCourse, who has given me generous permission for its use. He begins his analysis by considering Cherokee efforts to produce the first weekly Indian newspaper, *The Cherokee Phoenix*, in 1828. He then discusses later nineteenth-century efforts made in conjunction with Christian missions and federal Indian schools. By the end of the nineteenth century, over 90 publications had been originated by and for Indian communities and tribes over most of the United States and Alaska. In 1911 the Society of American Indians was formed representing "a literate Indian middle class not altogether reservation-oriented." This group eventually produced two publications. In 1916 an Apache, Carlos Montezuma, published the important *Wassaja,* and a number of related papers followed. In 1932 the "New Deal" press of John Collier, commissioner of Indian Affairs, emerged, to be followed in the 1950s by a small number of urban Indian newspapers and newsletters often associated with urban Indian Centers. The National Indian Youth Council formed in 1961 and began the publication of the activist paper *Indian Voices*, which ended in 1968, to be followed by the militant *Americans Before Columbus*. In 1968, *Akwesasne Notes* was born on the St. Regis reservation in New York. These and lesser known papers marked the *Alcatraz Generation*, a time of symbolic and paramilitary

Indian protests that occurred throughout the country. In 1970 a number of Indian editors joined to form the American Indian Press Association.

Indian radio appeared in the early 1950s in Oklahoma and the Southwest. Participation in television began in the 1970s, and in May 1973 the "Navajo Nation Report," the first daily Indian news and affairs show, began broadcasting over KOAI-TV in Flagstaff, Arizona. A number of other tribes throughout the country, including Alaska, intend to follow the Navajo example.

Indian journalism will play an increasingly prominent role in American life in the years to come. Those with a genuine interest in Indian activities should read the many excellent Indian newspapers now being published.

MAJOR CONCERNS IN THE 1970s.   Approximately 50 years after the appearance of the Meriam Report the Indian Policy Review Commission began to issue its findings based upon two years, 1975 to 1977, of coordinated, intensive research concerning eleven task force study areas: (1) trust responsibility and federal Indian relationship; (2) tribal government; (3) federal administration and structure of Indian affairs; (4) federal, state, and tribal jurisdiction; (5) Indian education; (6) Indian health; (7) reservation development; (8) urban and rural nonreservation Indians; (9) Indian law revision, consolidation, and codification; (10) terminated and nonfederally recognized Indians; (11) Indian alcohol and drug abuse. These areas represent the major concerns of the contemporary Indians of the United States in the 1970s. Thus far, thousands of pages showing the results of this research have been published by the United States Government Printing Office, and thousands more await printing. These materials warrant careful attention.

A WHITE BACKLASH.   One of the most significant events of the past few years is the emergence of a White backlash. One Indian publication, *The Coalition News,* reprinted a statement by Charles C. Trimble (1977: 1), which summarized the situation well.

> Federal policy toward Indians can be likened to a pendulum with decade-long swings from pro-Indian to anti-Indian policy and back again. The past decade has witnessed the swing from termination policy to self-determination policy. The 95th Congress appears to be on the verge of beginning a downward swing of the pendulum back to an era of anti-Indian policy. That downward swing is being referred to in national Indian circles as the "White Backlash."
>
> The backlash phenomenon is being attributed to several factors among which are: (1) the dramatic occupations and disruptions by paramilitant Indian groups demanding that the United States live up to its treaty obligations to Indian tribes; [e.g. the BIA "take-over" in Washington

Common grave with marker for those Whites killed with Custer. Custer himself is buried at the U.S. Military Academy, West Point. Photograph by Ken Kania, 1979.

(McNickle, 1975); Alcatraz (Indians of All Tribes, 1972); and Wounded Knee II (Burnette and Koster, 1974)]; (2) greater assertions of sovereign rights and powers by increasingly sophisticated tribal governments; and (3) major Indian victories in the courts regarding land claims, taxing powers and exemptions, and hunting and fishing rights. In addition, resentment by non-Indian people on and near reservations to what they feel is unlimited federal funds going to Indian reservations for "womb to tomb" services.

The backlash is manifesting itself in two forms. First, growing anti-tribal state organizations on the state-level that comprise the Interstate Congress for Equal Rights and Responsibilities (ICERR). Second, the backlash is having its effects on Congress. . . .

INDIAN PROTESTS. One of the most dramatic Indian protest events began at Alcatraz in February 1978. Nonviolent in nature, this was called "The Longest Walk." A relatively small number of militant Indians wanted to give notice to the general public and to federal non-Indian leaders in Washington, D.C., that they objected strongly to a number of bills before Congress that would unfairly limit their use of Indian lands, hunting and fishing rights, and water. The bills would also unduly restrict a number of land claims under consideration and would relieve the federal government of the responsibilities encompassed by treaties made some time ago. The Cunningham-Meeds Omnibus Indian Jurisdiction Bill, now amended and reintroduced as the Native American Equal Opportunity Act, H.R. 13329, proposes to do not only this but abolish the Bureau of Indian Affairs as well. Other issues are also at stake. The Indians protested by walking across the country from Alcatraz to the nation's capital, where they hoped to meet with President Carter and other high government officials. Along the way the initial group was periodically joined by other Indians. The non-Indian response to the Walk varied from enthusiastic approval

532

through indifference to scorn. Law enforcement officials monitored all activities associated with the event closely. The Indians arrived in Washington in July. They were unsuccessful in their attempts to confer with the President. Some congressional leaders spoke with them briefly. The net results of this effort cannot be determined now, but if nothing else, the sincere commitment of the marchers was clearly demonstrated for all to see. There will be other walks and protests.

A trenchant statement by F. C. Miller (1971: xvi) puts into perspective all the problems of American Indians today:

> Perhaps the crucial question is, why are the American Indians a high priority as a topic for reports, but a low priority for action?
>
> There are, of course, the obvious answers. Some would answer the question in political terms. Although Indians are symbolically important in American politics, they are a relatively small group and rather widely scattered in small communities, so they do not represent an important voting bloc. Others would say that Indians are culturally disadvantaged, or that they are not effectively organized or that they lack leadership.
>
> My own inclination is to search for the answer in the realization that the "Indian problem" is a system problem; that is, it is a result of the way the American economic and social system operates. It may be exacerbated by misguided policies, inefficient administration, inferior education, paternalism, and lack of local participation. But all these phenomena are symptoms of the problem, not causes. The implication of this view is that no piecemeal solution can cure the ills; it can simply relieve the symptoms. The ills will not be cured until the system is reconstructed so that it no longer operates to the severe disadvantage of groups such as the First Americans.

Photo by Ken Kania, 1979.

INDIANS AS AMERICANS.   Finally, while Indians clearly do have an ethnic distinctiveness, they are also most emphatically Americans. What
does this statement mean? It means that the First Americans are a part
of the same society, subject to most of the same laws, and conditioned
by the same economic, political, and historical currents as more than
220 million other people are. Yet this obvious fact is ignored or denied
by most non-Indians. The close integration of American Indians into
American society and its irrational denial can be quickly and vividly
demonstrated by a tour of the Custer Battlefield National Monument in
southeastern Montana. The battlefield lies on a separate tract within the
Crow reservation. A small but well-organized museum plus a series of
maps and markers make it possible for any visitors to acquire a good
understanding of "Custer's Last Stand." The non-Indian tourists come,
see, think, shudder, and leave. Few if any notice another carefully
appointed site immediately to the west, which contains the well-
marked graves of White and Indian soldiers who fought and died
together in two world wars, Korea, and Vietnam. The immediate and
latent effects of this reality, its implications, and its denial have been
discussed throughout this book.

REFERENCES

Aberle, David F. The Peyote Religion among the Navaho. *Viking Fund Publica-
cations in Anthopology No. 42.* New York: Wenner-Gren Foundation for
Anthropological Research, Inc., 1966.

Abler, Thomas S., Douglas E. Sanders, and Sally M. Weaver. *A Canadian Indian
Bibliography 1960–1970.* Toronto: University of Toronto Press, 1974.

Akwesasne Notes. James Bay Project: Manifest Destiny in the North. Vol. 5: 6,
22–23, Early Winter 1973.

A Basic Call to Consciousness: The Hau de no sau nee Address to the Western
World. Geneva, Switzerland, 1977. (*Akwesasne Notes*, 1978.)

Basso, Keith H. *Portraits of "The Whiteman": Linguistic Play and Cultural Symbols
among the Western Apache.* New York: Cambridge University Press, 1979.

Baylor, Byrd. *Yes Is Better Than No.* New York: Charles Scribner's Sons, 1977.

Berkhofer, Robert F., Jr. *The White Man's Indian: Images of the American from
Columbus to the Present.* New York: A. A. Knopf, 1978.

Billington, Ray A. *Westward Expansion: A History of the American Frontier.* 4th
ed. New York: Macmillan Publishing Co., 1974.

Bourassa, Robert. *James Bay.* Montreal, Quebec: Harvest House Ltd., 1973.

Brand, Joanna. *The Life and Death of Anna Mae Aquash.* Toronto: James Lorimer
and Co., 1978.

Burke, James. *Paper Tomahawks: From Red Tape to Red Power.* Winnipeg:
Queenston House Publishing, Inc., 1976.

Burnette, Robert, *"Good Leader" of the Rosebud Sioux: The Tortured Americans.*
Englewood Cliffs, N.J.: Prentice-Hall, 1971.

——, and John Koster. *The Road to Wounded Knee*. New York: Bantam Books Inc., 1974.

Canada. Office of Indian Affairs and Northern Development. Personal Communication, June, 1976.

——. *Official Consolidation of the Indian Act. R.S.C. 1952, c. 149 as Amended by 1952–53, c. 41; 1956, c. 40; 1958, c. 19; 1960, c. 8; and 1960–61, c. 9.* Ottawa: The Queen's Printer, 1963.

Canada, Quebec. Editeur officiel du Quebec. *The James Bay and Northern Quebec Agreement.* 1976.

Cardinal, Harold. *The Unjust Society: The Tragedy of Canada's Indians.* Edmonton, Alberta: Hurtig Publishers, 1969.

——. *The Rebirth of Canada's Indians.* Edmonton, Alberta: Hurtig Publishers, 1977.

Castile, George F. Federal Indian Policy and the Sustained Enclave: An Anthropological Perspective. *Human Organization 33,* 219–228, Fall 1974.

Chance, Norman A., ed. *Conflict in Culture: Problems of Developmental Change among the Cree.* Ottawa: Canadian Research Centre for Anthropology, St. Paul University, 1968.

Corrigan, Samuel M. The Plains Indian Powwow: Cultural Integration in Manitoba and Saskatchewan. *Anthropologica* N.S., 253–277, 1970.

Deloria, Vine, Jr. *Custer Died for Your Sins: An Indian Manifesto.* New York: The Macmillan Company, 1969.

——. *We Talk, You Listen: New Tribes New Turf.* New York: The Macmillan Company, 1970.

——, ed. *Of Utmost Good Faith.* New York: Bantam Books, 1972.

——. *God Is Red.* New York: Grosset & Dunlap, 1973.

——. *Behind the Trail of Broken Treaties: An Indian Declaration of Independence.* New York: Dell Publishing Co., 1974.

——. *The Indian Affair.* New York: Friendship Press, 1974.

Dyson, John. *The Hot Arctic.* Boston: Little Brown and Co., 1979.

Ervin, Alexander M. Civic Capacities and Transculturation: The Rise and Role of the Alaskan Federation of Natives. Ph.D. dissertation, University of Illinois-Urbana, 1974.

——. Civic Capacities and Transculturation: The Rise and Role of the Alaskan Federation of Natives. Ph.D. dissertation, University of Illinois-Urbana, 1974.

Fowler, Catherine S. Sarah Winnemucca, Northern Paiute ca. 1844–1891. In Margot Liberty, ed., American Indian Intellectuals. *1976 Proceedings of the American Ethnological Society.* St. Paul: West Publishing Co., 1978, pp. 33–34.

Gardner, Eddie. James Bay One Year After. *Canadian Association in Support of the Native Peoples 17:3,* 16–20, December 1976.

Gerber, Linda M. Community Characteristics and Out-Migration from Indian Communities: Regional Trends. Center for Population Studies, Harvard University, November 1977.

——. The Development of Canadian Indian Communities: A Two-Dimensional Typology Reflecting Strategies of Adaptation to the Modern World. Center for Population Studies, Harvard University, September 1977.

————. Trends in Out-Migration from Indian Communities Across Canada: A Report for the Task Force on Migrating Native Peoples, Canada Department of the Secretary of State. Center for Population Studies, Harvard University, March 1977.

————. Strategies of Adaptation and Out-Migration from Canadian Indian Communities: Resources, Opportunities, Boundary Permeability and Minority Survival. Center for Population Studies, Harvard University, January 1978.

Green, Rayna D. The Only Good Indian: The Image of the Indian in American Vernacular Culture. Ph.D. dissertation, Indiana University, 1973.

Hawthorne, H. B., et al. *A Survey of the Contemporary Indians of Canada: Economic, Political, Education Needs and Policies.* (2 vols.) Ottawa: Indian Affairs Branch, 1966–1967.

Hertzberg, Hazel W. *The Search for an American Indian Identity: Modern Pan-Indian Movements.* Syracuse: Syracuse University Press, 1971.

Hirabayashi, James, et al. Chapter 7. Pan-Indianism in the Urban Setting. In T. Weaver and D. White, eds., *The Anthropology of Urban Environments, Number 11.* The Society for Applied Anthropology Monograph Series, 1972, pp. 77–88.

Hlady, Walter, et al. *Resolving Conflicts—A Cross-Cultural Approach February 10 to May 14, 1967, Kenora, Ontario.* Winnipeg: Department of University Extension and Adult Education, The University of Manitoba, 1967.

Hodge, William H. *A Bibliography of Contemporary North American Indians: Selected and Partially Annotated with Study Guide.* New York: Interland Publishing Co., 1976.

Hostetler, John A., and G. E. Huntington. *The Hutterites in North America.* New York: Holt, Rinehart and Winston, 1967.

Howard, James. The Pan-Indian Culture of Oklahoma. *The Scientific Monthly 18,* 215–220, November 1955.

————. The Plains Gourd Dance As a Revitalization Movement. *American Ethnologist 3,* 243–259, May 1976.

Howard, Joseph. *Strange Empire: Louis Riel and the Metis People.* Toronto: James Lewis and Samuel, 1974.

Hutchison, George, and Dick Wallace. *Grassy Narrows.* Toronto: Van Nostrand Reinhold Ltd., 1977.

Indians of All Tribes. *Alcatraz Is Not an Island.* Ed. Peter Blue Cloud. Berkeley: Wingbow Press, 1972.

Koon, Bruce. Indian Tribes Find Great White Father Is Big Loss Leader. *Wall Street Journal,* April 21, 1978.

Kurath, Gertrude P. Pan-Indianism in Great Lakes Tribal Festivals. *American Journal of Folklore 70,* 179–182, 1957.

Lagasse, Jean H., et al. *A Study of the Population of Indian Ancestry Living in Manitoba* (3 vols.). Winnipeg, Manitoba: The Department of Agriculture and Immigration, 1959.

Le Metis. 300–275 Portage Avenue, Winnipeg, Manitoba, R3B 2B3.

Liberty, Margot. Francis La Flesche Omaha, 1857–1932. In Margot Liberty, ed., *American Indian Intellectuals: 1976 Proceedings of the American Ethnological Society.* St. Paul: West Publishing Co., 1978, pp. 45–60.

McFee, Malcolm. Modern Blackfeet Montanans on a Reservation. New York: Holt, Rinehart and Winston, 1972.

McNickle, D'Arcy. Chapter 28. The Indian War That Never Ends. In *They Came Here First: The Epic of the American Indian.* (Rev. ed.) New York: Perennial Library, Harper & Row, 1975, pp. 261–278.

———. *The Surrounded.* New York: Dodd, Mead and Co., 1936.

Mal-I-Mic News. New Brunswick Association of Metis and Non-Status Indians. Suite 4, 390 King Street, Fredericton, New Brunswick, E3B 1E3.

Meriam, Lewis, et al. *The Problem of Indian Administration.* Baltimore, Maryland: Johns Hopkins Press, 1928.

Miller, B. D. General Systems Theory: An Approach to the Study of Complex Societies. *The Eastern Anthropologist 31:1*, 15–30, 1978.

Miller, Frank C. Introduction. In *The Problem of Indian Administration.* New York: Johnson Reprint Corp., 1971, p. xviii.

Miller, R. J. Culture, Civilization, System: Anthropological Approaches to Complexity. *The Eastern Anthropologist 31:1*, 1–13, 1978.

———. Personal Communication, 1979.

New Breed. Association of Metis and Non-Status Indians of Saskatchewan. No. 2, 1846 Scarth Street, Regina, Saskatchewan, S4P 2G3.

Northrop, Gordon D. Pan-Indianism in the Metropolis: A Case Study of an Emergent Ethno-Syncretic Revitalization Movement. Ph.D. dissertation, Michigan State University, 1970.

(Organization). Federation of Metis Settlements. #1108 Markum Place, 10235–124 Street, Edmonton, Alberta, T5N 3W6.

———. Ontario Metis and Non-Status Indian Association. 5300 Yonge Street, Suite 208, Willowdale, Ontario, M2N 5R2.

Patterson, E. Palmer, II. *The Canadian Indian: A History since 1500.* Don Mills, Ontario: Collier-Macmillan Canada Ltd., 1972.

Pelletier, Emile. *Aboriginal Rights: Volume Two of a Study of the Statutory and Aboriginal Rights of Metis People in Manitoba.* Winnepeg: Manitoba Metis Federation Press, 1973.

Pitman, Walter. James Bay Blunders Full Speed Ahead. *Toronto Star,* October 2, 1973.

Platiel, Rudy. *Toronto Daily Star,* February 22, 1971.

Price, Monroe E. *Law and the American Indian: Readings, Notes and Cases.* Indianapolis: Bobbs-Merrill Co., 1973.

Prucha, Francis Paul. *American Indian Policy in the Formative Years: The Indian Trade and Intercourse Acts, 1790–1834.* Lincoln: University of Nebraska Press, 1970.

———, ed. *Documents of United States Indian Policy.* Lincoln: University of Nebraska Press, 1975.

———. *A Bibliographical Guide to the History of Indian-White Relations in the United States.* Chicago: University of Chicago Press, 1977.

Research Resource Centre. *Indian Claims in Canada: An Introductory Essay and Selected List of Library Holdings.* Ottawa: Indian Claims Commission, 1975.

Richardson, Boyce. *Strangers Devour the Land: The Cree Hunters of the James Bay Area versus Premier Bourassa and the James Bay Development Corporation.* New York: A. A. Knopf, 1976.

Rodin, Miriam, Karen Michaelson, and Gerald M. Britan. Systems Theory in Anthropology with CA Comment. *Current Anthropology 19*, 747–762, December 1978.

Sanford, Margaret. Pan-Indianism, Acculturation, and the American Ideal. *Plains Anthropologist 16–53*, 222–227, 1971.

Schusky, Ernest L. Pan-Indianism in the Eastern United States. *Anthropology Tomorrow*, 116–123, December 1957.

Simpson, G. E., and J. M. Yinger, eds. *American Indians and American Life: The Annals of the American Academy of Political and Social Science*. Vol. 311. May 1957.

Slobodin, Richard. *Metis of the Mackenzie District*. Ottawa: Canadian Research Centre for Anthropology, St. Paul University, 1966.

Smith, Jane F., and R. M. Kvasnicka, eds. *Indian-White Relations: A Persistent Paradox*. Washington, D.C.: Howard University Press, 1976.

Snodgrass, Marjorie P. *Economic Development of American Indians and Eskimos, 1930 through 1967*. U.S. Department of the Interior, July 1968.

Szasz, Margaret. *Education and the American Indian: The Road to Self-Determination, 1928–1973*. Albuquerque: University of New Mexico Press, 1974.

Taylor, John Leonard. Historical Introduction to Metis Claims in Canada. December 1973 (rev. June 1975). Mimeographed.

———. Personal Communication, February 22, 1978.

The Forgotten People. 77 Metcalfe Street, Suite 200, Ottawa, Ontario K1P 5L6.

Tooker, Elisabeth. Ely S. Parker, Seneca, 1828–1895. In Margot Liberty, ed., *American Indian Intellectuals: 1976 Proceedings of the American Ethnological Society*. St. Paul: West Publishing Co., 1978, pp. 15–32.

Trimble, Charles E. The 95th Congress and Indian Affairs: A Report on Indian Legislation. *The Coalition News*, December 1977, p. 1.

U.S. Department of Commerce. *Indian Economic Development: An Evaluation of EDA's Selected Indian Reservation Programs*. Vol. 2. Boise Cascade Center for Community Development, Economic Development Administration, 1972.

Weinstein, Martin S. *What the Land Provides: An Examination of the Fort George Subsistence Economy and the Possible Consequences on It of the James Bay Hydroelectric Project*. Montreal: Grand Council of the Crees (of Quebec), 1976.

Wilcox, Desmond. The Indian Chief Joe De La Cruz. In *Americans*. New York: Delacorte Press, 1978, pp. 145–171.

Yinger, J. Milton, and George E. Simpson, special eds. *American Indians Today: The Annals of the American Academy of Political and Social Science*. Vol. 436. March 1978.

INDEX

INDEX